VOICES OF ISLAM IN SOUTHEAST ASIA

The **Institute of Southeast Asian Studies (ISEAS)** was established as an autonomous organization in 1968. It is a regional centre dedicated to the study of socio-political, security and economic trends and developments in Southeast Asia and its wider geostrategic and economic environment.

The Institute's research programmes are the Regional Economic Studies (RES, including ASEAN and APEC), Regional Strategic and Political Studies (RSPS), and Regional Social and Cultural Studies (RSCS).

ISEAS Publications, an established academic press, has issued more than 1,000 books and journals. It is the largest scholarly publisher of research about Southeast Asia from within the region. ISEAS Publications works with many other academic and trade publishers and distributors to disseminate important research and analyses from and about Southeast Asia to the rest of the world.

VOICES OF ISLAM IN SOUTHEAST ASIA

A Contemporary Sourcebook

Compiled and edited by
Greg Fealy and Virginia Hooker

INSTITUTE OF SOUTHEAST ASIAN STUDIES
Singapore

First published in Singapore in 2006 by
ISEAS Publications
Institute of Southeast Asian Studies
30 Heng Mui Keng Terrace
Pasir Panjang
Singapore 119614

E-mail: publish@iseas.edu.sg
http://bookshop.iseas.edu.sg

The responsibility for facts and opinions in this publication rests exclusively with the authors and their interpretations do not necessarily reflect the views or the policy of the Institute or its supporters.

ISEAS Library Cataloguing-in-Publication Data

Voices of Islam in Southeast Asia : a contemporary sourcebook / edited by Greg Fealy and Virginia Hooker.
  1. Islam — Southeast Asia.
  2. Islam — Doctrines.
  I. Fealy, Greg, 1957–
  II. Hooker, Virginia Matheson, 1946–
  III. Series
BP63 A9V88   2006

ISBN 981-230-367-7 (soft cover)
ISBN 981-230-368-5 (hard cover)

The cover image is a medallion motif from *Al Qur'an Mushaf Istiqlal* [The Istiqlal Illuminated Qur'an], Section 1-10, frontispiece (Jakarta: Yayasan Festival Istiqlal, 1995). The Arabic calligraphy reads: *Bi al rasm al 'Uthmani* [in the Uthmani style] (referring to the style of calligraphy).

The originals of the illuminations are displayed at Bayt al-Qur'an & Museum Istiqlal [House of the Qur'an and Istiqlal Museum], Jalan Raya Taman Mini Indonesia Indah, No. 1, Jakarta Timur. Reproduced by kind permission of the Board of the Bayt al-Qur'an & Museum Istiqlal Taman Mini Indonesia Indah.

Copy editing: Beth Thomson and Sue Mathews
Typesetting and book design: Beth Thomson
Graphic design: Miranda Ball

Printed in Singapore by Seng Lee Press Pte Ltd

Contents

PART II   EXTRACTS FROM PRIMARY SOURCES

11   Sharia   137

M.B. Hooker and Virginia Hooker

Tables, Figures, Maps and Boxes

TABLES

FIGURES

MAPS

BOXES

Colour Plates

Acknowledgements

This sourcebook is the result of an extensive consultative and collaborative process between Australian and Southeast Asian academics and Muslim leaders as part of the 'Islam in Southeast Asia: State, Society and Governance' project based at the Australian National University (ANU), Canberra. It has been made possible by the generous funding provided by the Australian Department of Foreign Affairs and Trade (DFAT) through the Australian Committee for Security Cooperation in the Asia-Pacific (Aus-CSCAP) at the ANU. We are grateful to the Minister for Foreign Affairs, the Hon. Alexander Downer, MP, and DFAT staff for their continuing support and interest in the project. We also express our thanks to Professors Anthony Milner and Desmond Ball, the co-chairs of Aus-CSCAP, Mr John Buckley, its executive director, and Ms Andrea Haese, the project administrator, who managed a large and complex program of activities with remarkable efficiency and good humour.

Particular thanks are due to Dr Sally White, who served as project coordinator from August 2004 to June 2005. She also wrote one of the book's chapters and played a significant intellectual and editorial role in shaping the final text. Her critical eye, sound judgement, knowledge of Islamic issues and warm collegiality proved invaluable for the editors.

A team of expert regional advisors provided advice on selecting and locating appropriate documents and other materials, and also contributed contextual information on some of the extracts. The advisors and their fields of specialized advice were:

Dr John Funston (ANU, Canberra): Thailand, Malaysia, Singapore and Brunei
Professor M.B. Hooker (ANU, Canberra): Islamic law and history
Dr Kit Collier (ANU, Canberra): the Philippines
Mr Curt Lambrecht (ANU, Canberra, and Yale University, New Haven): Burma (Myanmar)
Associate Professor Greg Barton (Deakin University, Geelong, and Asia-Pacific Center of Security Studies, Honolulu): liberal Islam in Indonesia and Malaysia
Dr Jacob Ramsay (Asian Research Institute, Singapore): Cambodia and Vietnam

We are grateful to each of these scholars for their valuable assistance. We would also like to thank Ms Sidney Jones from the International Crisis Group, Jakarta, for passing on and helping us to interpret various documents on radical Islam, and Dr Ahmad Fauzi for assisting us to locate documents on Malaysian Islam. Mr Mohd Mohiyudin Mohd Sulaiman provided numerous useful texts on Burmese Islam.

The sourcebook project was formally launched in August 2004 with a conference in Canberra featuring scholars of Southeast Asian Islam from across Australia and the region. The papers presented at the conference and ensuing discussion of key issues relating to Islam in the region provided the foundation of the sourcebook project. We are indebted to the following participants for their contributions:

Professor Masykuri Abdillah (Syarif Hidayatullah State Islamic University, Jakarta)
Dr Tgk H. Muslim Ibrahim (Aceh Ulama Consultative Council, Banda Aceh)
Mr Mohd. Mohiyuddin Mohd Sulaiman Al Hafiz (International Islamic University Malaysia, Kuala Lumpur)
Dr Sumit Mandal (Universiti Kebangsaan Malaysia, Kuala Lumpur)
Mr Muhammad Ismail Yusanto (Hizbut Tahrir Indonesia, Jakarta)
Associate Professor Ahmad Shboul (University of Sydney, Sydney)
Datu Professor Michael Mastura (Sultan Kudarat Islamic Academy Foundation Inc., Sultan Kudarat, Maguindanao)
Professor Julkipli M. Wadi (University of the Philippines, Quezon City)
Dr Zulkieflimansyah (Prosperity and Justice Party; University of Indonesia, Jakarta)
Mr Amrih Widodo (ANU, Canberra)
Mr Shanon Shah bin Mohd Sidik (Sisters in Islam, Kuala Lumpur)
Associate Professor Thanet Aphorvasan (Thammasat University, Bangkok)
Mr Solahudin (Southeast Asian Press Alliance, Jakarta)
Ms Farha 'Ciciek' Abdul Assegaf (Rahima, Jakarta)
Mr Syafiq Hasyim (International Center for Islam and Pluralism, Jakarta)
Emeritus Professor Clive Kessler (University of New South Wales, Sydney)
Associate Professor Julie Day-Howell (Griffith University, Brisbane)
Professor M.B. Hooker (ANU, Canberra)

The second stage of the project entailed identifying appropriate documents for inclusion in the sourcebook and translating them. Apart from advice from our expert consultants, we also had a team of research assistants locating material. Our research assistants were:

Mr Bernhard Platzdasch
Mr Yon Machmudi
Mr Akh Muzakki
Mr Hamdan Juhannis
Mr Chin Tong Liew

Given the centrality of the primary source materials to this sourcebook, accurate translations were critical to the success of the project. We were fortunate to have highly competent translators. They were:

Mr Dave McRae (Indonesian)
Dr Elisabeth Jackson (Indonesian)
Ms Justine FitzGerald (Indonesian)

Ms Amelia Fyfield (Indonesian)
Ms Petra Mahy (Indonesian)
Ms Ulla Keech-Marx (Indonesian)
Mr Mohammad Taufiq Prabowo (Arabic and Indonesian)
Dr Khasnor Johan (Malay)
Mr Ghassan al-Shatter (Arabic terms and transliterations)
Mr Jason Hall (Thai)
Mr Jarrod Weir (Thai)

We would also like to thank Mrs Chintana Sandilands for assisting with the translation of some Thai-language materials.

In addition to this, we were fortunate to have a number of other staff assisting with various aspects of the project. Ms Jill Wolf, Mrs Claire Smith and Ms Debbie Phillips typed in English-language texts and Ms Helen Glazebrook and Ms Allison Ley undertook the onerous task of obtaining permission to reprint extracts from the many authors and publishers whose material appears in this book.

The Centre for Strategic and International Studies (CSIS) and the Centre for the Study of Islam and Society (PPIM) at Syarif Hidayatullah State Islamic University Jakarta co-hosted a workshop in the Indonesian city of Bogor in February–March 2005. We are grateful to Dr Jusuf Wanandi and Mr Philips Vermonte from CSIS and to Dr Jamhari Makruf and Dr Jajang Jahroni for their assistance in staging this workshop. A draft manuscript of the sourcebook was presented to participants and each chapter was discussed in detail. The corrections and suggestions received during this workshop were of great assistance in revising the text. Workshop participants were:

Mr Adian Husaini (International Institute of Islamic Thought and Civilization, Kuala Lumpur)
Professor Azyumardi Azra (State Islamic University Syarif Hidayatullah, Jakarta)
Dr Iik Arifin Mansurnoor (Universiti Brunei Darussalam, Bandar Seri Begawan)
Dr Jajang Jahroni (State Islamic University Syarif Hidayatullah, Jakarta)
Dr Jamhari Makruf (State Islamic University Syarif Hidayatullah, Jakarta)
Ms Jasmin Jamsari (Save the Children Federation, Jolo, Sulu)
Professor Thoha Hamim (State Islamic Institute Sunan Ampel, Surabaya)
Mr Nasharudin Mat Isa (The Islamic Party of Malaysia (PAS), Kuala Lumpur)
Professor Merle Ricklefs (National University of Singapore, Singapore)
Dr Siti Ruhaini Dzuhayatin (Sunan Kalijaga State Islamic University, Yogyakarta)
Dr Yudi Latif (Paramadina University, Jakarta)
Mr Ulil Abshar-Abdalla (Liberal Islam Network, Jakarta)

Other colleagues who provided valuable advice include Emeritus Professor Anthony Johns, Mr Ismail Yahya, Mr Arif Zamhari, Professor Tim Lindsey, Professor Bambang Pranowo, Mr Ahmad Zainul Hamdi, Dr Philip Taylor and Mr Philip Knight. Professor Anthony Milner read the entire draft manuscript and provided helpful comments. Various Aus-CSCAP members, in particular Dr Sandy Gordon and

Associate Professor Sameena Yasmin, also offered useful suggestions. The staff of the Menzies Library at the ANU and the National Library of Australia provided wonderful support and helped us to locate numerous obscure documents and images.

The task of editing, designing and typesetting a book as complex as this is daunting. We were most fortunate to have had the services of an exceptional copy editor, Ms Beth Thomson. Assisted by Ms Sue Mathews, Beth had a remarkable capacity to spot errors and inconsistencies as well as propose ways of improving the intelligibility of extracts and commentaries. Their intelligent suggestions have added greatly to the quality of the book and we are indebted to them for their patience and rigorous editing. Mr Alan Walker compiled the index with meticulous care and Mr Anthony Bright in the Cartography Department of the Research School of Pacific and Asian Studies at the ANU prepared the maps. Ms Miranda Ball prepared the colour section of the book. Mrs Triena Ong and her staff at the Institute of Southeast Asian Studies, Singapore, have been a constant source of encouragement and advice.

Finally, we would like to thank all the authors, artists and publishers who kindly granted us permission to use their material in this sourcebook.

Timeline

Year (Common Era)	Region	Event
c. 570	Mecca	Birth of Prophet Muhammad.
610	Outside Mecca	First of the revelations of the Qur'an given to Muhammad.
622	Mecca to Yathrib (renamed Medina)	With a group of followers, Muhammad leaves the hostility he faced in Mecca and establishes Islam in Yathrib, renamed Medina (the [Prophet's] city). The move is known as the Hijrah (the Migration/ Withdrawal) and the year of the migration becomes the first in the lunar-based Muslim calendar.
630	Mecca	Muhammad occupies Mecca.
632	Medina	Muhammad receives the last revelation of the Qur'an and dies in this year.
632–34	Medina	Abu Bakr replaces Muhammad as leader of the Muslim community, becoming the first of the four 'Rightly Guided Caliphs'.
634–44	Medina, Iraq, Syria, Egypt	'Umar ibn al-Khattab replaces Abu Bakr, and Muslims conquer Jerusalem.
644–56	Medina, North Africa, Iran, Afghanistan, Sind (northwest India)	'Uthman succeeds 'Umar as caliph.
656–61	Medina	'Ali ibn Talib, the last of the Rightly Guided Caliphs, succeeds 'Uthman. He has two sons by Muhammad's daughter Fatimah, the second of whom, Husayn, becomes the founder of the Shi'i Imams.
661	Damascus	'Ali ibn Talib assassinated; leadership of Muslims shifts to Muawiyyah I, who founds the Umayyad caliphate.
Early 8th century	Spain	Muslim conquests in Spain.

762	Baghdad	Baghdad established as the capital of the Abbasids. Until the 9th century it is the centre for Islamic sciences, law and arts.
767–820	Mecca, Yemen, Baghdad, Egypt	Life of Abu Abdullah Muhammad ibn Idris al-Shafi'i, founder of Shafi'i school of law, which is widely followed in Southeast Asia.
1035	Vietnam	Kufic inscriptions in the Bình Thuận region (north of Ho Chi Minh City).
1099	Jerusalem	Christian Crusaders conquer Jerusalem.
1187	Jerusalem	Salah al-Din (Saladin) defeats the Crusaders and Jerusalem returns to Muslim rule.
11th century	Champa (southern Vietnam)	Muslim inscription indicates Islamic presence.
Late 13th century	North Sumatra	Muslim gravestones indicate Islamic presence in north Sumatra.
1310	Philippines	Muslim gravestone in Jolo, Sulu archipelago, attests to presence of Islam.
Late 14th century	East Java, southern Philippines, Terengganu (north-east Malaysia), Patani (southern Thailand)	Gravestones and inscriptions indicate presence of Muslim communities with Muslim rulers.
Early 15th century	Malacca	Malay rulers convert to Islam and the religion spreads through the Malay-speaking world of coastal Southeast Asia.
c. 1450	Philippines	Tausug sultanate established in Sulu archipelago.
Late 15th century	Brunei	Muslim gravestones attest to the presence of Islam.
Mid-16th to mid-17th centuries	Aceh	Muslim rulers of Aceh support Muslim scholars and promote serious study of Islam and Sufism.
Early 17th century	South Sulawesi	Sultan converts to Islam and supports Muslim scholars.
Mid-18th century	Central Java	Javanese style of Islam and Sufism developed at royal courts.
Late 18th century	Palembang (south Sumatra)	Sultan of Palembang fosters Islamic scholarship and encourages Arab scholars to settle and intermarry with local elite women. 'Abd al Samad al-Palimbani, the offspring of such a union, becomes an influential writer and teacher in Mecca and Medina, where he teaches Muslims from Southeast Asia.

1787	Central Arabia	Death of Muhammad ibn 'Abd al-Wahhab, founder of the Wahhabi reform movement.
Late 18th to early 19th centuries	West Sumatra	Pilgrims return from Mecca impressed with Wahhabi reforms. They begin to implement them, thus initiating the Padri War, which ends in 1838.
Late 18th to early 19th centuries	Mecca to Southeast Asia	Patani-born scholar Dawud al-Fatani lives and teaches in Mecca–Medina and writes prolifically in Malay for the guidance of Southeast Asian Muslims.
Late 18th century	Banjarmasin (south Kalimantan)	Muhammad Arshad al-Banjari (1710–1812) studies in Mecca and returns to revitalize Islam and Islamic education in south Kalimantan.
Mid-19th century	Singapore	Singapore attracts Hadrami and Indian scholars, who teach and establish publishing houses. Lively Malay Islamic culture at Riau–Lingga royal courts south of Singapore.
Late 19th to early 20th centuries	East coast Malay Peninsula	Growth of local religious schools; local production and writing of religious texts with support of local ruler. Widespread influence of Tok Kenali (1868–1933).
Late 19th to early 20th centuries	Cairo to Southeast Asia	Influence of Salafiyya reform movement, led by Jamal al-Din al Afghani (1839–97) and Muhammad Abduh (1849–1905).
1901	Philippines	The Philippines becomes a US colony after Spain's defeat in the Spanish-American War (1898–1901).
1902	Thailand	Patani sultanate brought under Thai (Siamese) administrative rule.
1906	Brunei	Brunei becomes a British protectorate
1906	Singapore	Islamic reformist journal *al-Imam* begins publication; becomes leading organ of the Salafiyya-inspired Kaum Muda (Young Group).
1909	Thailand, Malaysia	Under Anglo-Siamese Treaty, Thailand cedes Perlis, Kedah, Kelantan and Terengganu to the British and Britain acknowledges Thai sovereignty over Pattani, Yala and Narathiwat.
1912	Indonesia	Muhammadiyah established in Yogyakarta by Ahmad Dahlan.
1926	Indonesia	Nahdlatul Ulama formed to protect the interests of traditionalist Islam.
1938	Thailand	Ultra-nationalist Phibun Songkram regime in power (1938–44), leading to assimilationist policies that trigger violence from aggrieved Muslims in the south.

1942	Burma (Myanmar)	Muslim–Buddhist conflict breaks out in Arakan.
1943	Indonesia	Japanese administration establishes Masyumi with Nahdlatul Ulama and Muhammadiyah as its two main components.
1945	Indonesia	Independence declared but clause requiring Muslims to uphold sharia omitted from the constitution.
1945	Indonesia	A conference of Islamic organizations decides Masyumi will be the sole political vehicle for Indonesian Muslims (November). Most Muslim groups are supportive.
1946	Malaysia	United Malays National Organisation (UMNO) formed.
1946	Indonesia	Ministry of Religious Affairs established.
1946	Burma (Myanmar)	Northern Arakan Muslim League founded.
1946	Philippines	The United States grants independence to the Republic of the Philippines.
1946–54	Vitenam	Warfare against French colonial forces (First Indochina War).
1947	Thailand	Haji Sulong issues seven demands for devolution of authority to the southern Muslim states; he is arrested by the central government in the following year.
1947	Malaysia	Reformist Hizbul Muslimin party formed.
1948	Thailand	Dusun Nyor uprising in Narathiwat province results in the deaths of 400 Thai-Malay Muslims and 30 police (28 April).
1948	Burma (Myanmar)	Rohingya insurgency in Arakan state (April).
1949	Indonesia	Kartosoewirjo's Darul Islam proclaims Indonesian Islamic State (7 August).
1950	Singapore	Eighteen people killed in sectarian rioting.
1951	Malaysia	Persatuan Islam Sa-Tanah Melayu, later renamed Parti Islam Se Malaysia (PAS, The Islamic Party of Malaysia) formed.
1952	Indonesia	Nahdlatul Ulama splits from Masyumi and creates party under its own name.
1954	Thailand	Haji Sulong disappears while in police custody (August).
1955	Indonesia	First democratic elections; Islamic parties win almost 44 per cent of the vote.
1957	Thailand	Renewed assimilationist stance by government of General Sarit Thanarat sparks further conflict in the Malay-dominated southern states.

1957	Malaysia	Malaya (excluding Singapore, Sabah and Sarawak) gains independence from Britain.
1959	Indonesia	Muslim parties fail to win the necessary two-thirds majority in the Constituent Assembly to have the 'sharia clause' inserted into the constitution; President Sukarno dissolves the assembly and with army support establishes the 'Guided Democracy' regime (June–July).
1959	Thailand	Barisan Nasional Pembebasan Patani (BNPP, National Liberation Front of Patani) formed.
1959	Malaysia	PAS performs strongly in elections, gaining about half the Malay vote and winning government in the states of Kelantan and Terengganu.
1962	Indonesia	Kartosoewirjo is captured and executed for treason (September); Darul Islam rebellion collapses.
1962	Burma (Myanmar)	Military rule begins; range of discriminatory measures implemented against Muslims.
1963	Thailand	Barisan Revolusi Nasional (BRN, National Revolutionary Front) established.
1963	Malaysia	Federation of Malaysia formed (including Singapore, Sabah and Sarawak).
1964	Singapore	Thirteen lives lost in religious clashes (July and September).
1965	Singapore	Singapore leaves Malaysia and becomes an independent state.
1965	Indonesia	Coup attempt in Jakarta; army led by Soeharto quickly regains control.
1966	Indonesia	Soeharto takes effective control of government and begins his military-based 'New Order' regime; Sukarno marginalized (March).
1966	Singapore	Administration of Muslim Law Act (AMLA) creates government-supervised framework for managing Muslim affairs.
1968	Singapore	Majlis Ugama Islam Singapura (MUIS, Islamic Religious Council of Singapore) established.
1968	Thailand	Pertubuhan Pembebasan Patani Bersatu (PULO, Patani United Liberation Organization) formed.
1968	Philippines	'Corregidor Incident' in which group of Christian soldiers murder between 28 and 68 Muslim soldiers (18 March); outcry from Muslim groups.
1969	Philippines	Nur Misuari forms Moro National Liberation Front (MNLF).

1969	Malaysia	Racial riots follow general election in which UMNO's vote drops; more than 200 killed (May).
1971	Malaysia	Influential Muslim reform group Angkatan Belia Islam Malaysia (ABIM, Malaysian Islamic Youth Movement) established.
1972	Philippines	Outbreak of MNLF rebellion in Mindanao.
1972	Philippines	President Marcos declares martial law; there is brutal military repression of Muslim rebels but political and economic concessions are also given to Muslims.
1973	Indonesia	Regime forms Partai Persatuan Pembangunan (PPP, United Development Party), an amalgamation of four existing Islamic parties.
1974	Malaysia	Government establishes Yayasan Dakwah Islamiah Malaysia (YADIM, Islamic Preaching Foundation of Malaysia).
1975-9	Cambodia	Cham Muslims persecuted under Khmer Rouge, resulting in an estimated 90,000 deaths.
1977	Philippines	Code of Muslim Personal Laws introduced.
1978	Burma (Myanmar)	200,000 Rohingyas flee across the border into Bangladesh to escape persecution in Arakan under regime's Naga Min Operation.
1978	Philippines	Split in MNLF sees Salamat Hashim form the Moro Islamic Liberation Front (MILF) (February).
1981	Malaysia	Prime Minister Mahathir recruits ABIM leader, Anwar Ibrahim, to UMNO; Anwar enters cabinet in the following year.
1982	Burma (Myanmar)	Rohingya Solidarity Organisation (RSO) formed.
1984	Brunei Darussalam	Independence declared (1 January).
1984	Thailand	Government establishes Southern Border Provinces Administrative Centre (SBPAC) and Civilian–Police–Military (CPM) Task Force 43 to address security problems and the grievances of Malay Muslims.
1984	Indonesia	Troops shoot more than 100 Muslim protesters in Tanjung Priok port district of Jakarta (12 September).
1984–85	Indonesia	Regime forces all social and religious organizations to adopt the religiously neutral Pancasila state ideology as their sole ideological basis.
1986	Thailand	Muslims in south form Wadah (Unity) faction, initially within the Democrat Party but later joined by the National Aspiration Party (NAP) (1992).

1987	Burma (Myanmar)	Arakan Rohingya Islamic Front (ARIF) established as a breakaway from RSO.
1989	Indonesia	Clashes between army and militant Muslim villagers in Lampung lead to deaths of dozens of civilians (early February)
1989	Philippines	Central government agrees to established an Autonomous Region in Muslim Mindanao (ARMM) (August); referendum held in November.
1991	Philippines	Abu Sayyaf Group established.
1991	Thailand	Bersatu (United) formed from loose coalition of BNPP, BRN and PULO.
1992	Malaysia	Government forms high-level Islamic thinktank known as Institut Kefahaman Islam Malaysia (IKIM, Malaysian Institute for Islamic Understanding).
1992	Burma (Myanmar)	Exodus of 300,000 Rohingyas into Bangladesh after regime crackdown.
1993	Malaysia, Indonesia	Abdullah Sungkar establishes Jemaah Islamiyah in Malaysia after falling out with Darul Islam leadership (January); most members are Indonesians.
1994	Malaysia	Government bans Darul Arqam.
1995	Thailand	Wadah faction politician Wan Muhammad Nor Watha becomes interior minister, the first Malay Muslim to hold full ministerial office.
1996	Philippines	Government agrees to Nur Misuari becoming governor of ARMM (June); peace treaty with MNLF signed in September.
1997	Southeast Asia	Asian financial crisis hits Southeast Asia (August).
1997	Malaysia	Jabatan Kemajuan Islam Malaysia (Jakim, Malaysian Department of Islamic Development) formed.
1998	Indonesia	Soeharto steps down and is replaced by Vice-President Habibie (May).
1998	Cambodia	Tol Lah, a Cham Muslim, becomes co-deputy prime minister to Hun Sen.
1998	Malaysia	Mahathir sacks Anwar Ibrahim as deputy prime minister; shortly afterwards Anwar is charged with sexual offences and corruption.
1998	Burma (Myanmar)	Arakan Rohingya National Organisation (ARNO) formed.
1998	Philippines	Abu Sayyaf founder, Abubakar Abdulrazak Janjalani, killed (December).

1999	Indonesia	Muslim–Christian violence breaks out in Ambon, Maluku (February); later spreads to other parts of Maluku and Central Sulawesi; thousands die over next four years.
1999	Malaysia	UMNO returned in general election but its vote drops sharply; PAS vote rises to its highest level ever.
1999	Indonesia	First free and fair elections in 44 years; Islamic parties gain less than 40 per cent of the vote; the chair of Nahdlatul Ulama, Abdurrahman Wahid, is elected president (October).
2000	Singapore	Muslim protests force government to drop plans to close *madrasah* (Islamic schools).
2000	Malaysia	Al-Ma'unah group seizes weapons from army depots; three killed in subsequent shoot-out (July).
2001	Malaysia	Security agencies begin series of arrests of members of Kumpulan Mujahidin (or Militan) Malaysia (KMM, Malaysia Mujahidin/Militant Organization); about 70 arrested in all.
2001	Malaysia	Mahathir declares that Malaysia should be seen as an Islamic state (29 September).
2001	Indonesia	Majelis Permusyawaratan Rakyat (MPR, People's Consultative Assembly) dismisses Abdurrahman Wahid and replaces him with his vice-president, Megawati Sukarnoputri (23 July).
2001	Singapore	Security services begin arresting members of Jemaah Islamiyah cell said to be plotting attacks in the city (December); 30 arrested over next six months.
2002	Indonesia	Terrorist attack by Jemaah Islamiyah in Bali kills 202 people (12 October).
2002	Thailand	Thaksin government abolishes SBPAC and CPM Task Force 43 (May).
2003	Cambodia	Government closes two Islamic schools and expels tens of foreign teachers and preachers accused of having terrorist links (May–June).
2003	Malaysia	Mahathir retires as prime minister and is replaced by Abdullah Badawi (October).
2004	Thailand	More than 100 Malay insurgents attack an army depot in Narathiwat, killing four Buddhists and seizing weapons and ammunition; government declares martial law in the south (4 January).
2004	Thailand	More than 200 insurgents attack police and military posts in Yala, Pattani and Songkla; 107 rebels killed, including 32 at the historic Krue Se Mosque (28 April).

2004	Thailand	Seven Muslim protesters shot by security officials in Tak Bai, Narathiwat; another 78 die, many through suffocation, while being transported by truck to an army base (25 October).
2004	Malaysia	Anwar Ibrahim released from jail after successful legal appeal (September).
2004	Malaysia	UMNO recovers in general elections; PAS loses 20 of its 26 parliamentary seats.
2005	Indonesia	Second Bali bombing kills 21 people (1 October).

Arabic Transliteration System and Key Phonetic Symbols[a]

Arabic	Transcription System Used in This Book	Conventional/IPA Transcription	Comparison Transcription	Phonetic Description	Approximate in English
ا	Not provided	Not provided	ʔ	Glottal plosive	
ب	b	b	b	Voiced labial stop	b
د	d	d	d	Voiced alveolar stop	d
ض	ḍ	ḍ	ḍ	Emphatic voiced alveolar stop	Does not exist (similar to Don)
ف	f	f	f	Voiceless labio-dental fricative	f
ه	h	h	h	Voiceless glottal fricative	h
ح	ḥ	ḥ	ḥ	Voiceless pharyngeal fricative	Does not exist
ج	j	ʒ	j	Voiced palato-alveolar fricative	j (as in jelly)
ك	k	k	k	Voiceless velar stop	k
ل	l	l	Not provided	Aveolar lateral	l
م	m	m	Not provided	Bilabial nasal	m
ن	n	n	n	Alveolar nasal	n
ق	q	q	q	Uvular stop	Does not exist
ر	r	r	r	Alveolar trill	r
س	s	s	s	Voiceless alveolar fricative	s
ص	ṣ	ṣ	Ṣ	Emphatic voiceless alveolar fricative	Does not exist (similar to Sahara)
ت	t	t	t	Voiceless dental fricative	t
ط	ṭ	ṭ	ṭ	Emphatic voiceless alveolar stop	Does not exist (similar to Tokyo)

	a	IPA	Phonetic description	English equivalent
ز	z	z	Voiced alveolar fricative	z
ظ	ẓ	ḍ	Emphatic voiced alveolar fricative	dh or z (depends on region)
ء	'	Not provided	Glottal stop	Vocalic stop
ع	ʿ	ʕ	Voiced pharyngeal fricative	Does not exist
ش	sh	ʃ	Voiceless palato-alveolar fricative	sh (as in shoes)
ث	th	θ	Voiceless dental fricative	th (as in three)
ذ	dh	ð	Voiced dental fricative	th (as in there)
خ	kh	χ	Voiceless velar fricative	kh (does not exist)
غ	gh	ɣ	Voiced velar fricative	gh (does not exist)
ي	y	y	Palatal glide	y (as in yellow)
و	w	w	Bilabial approximant	w (as in wall)

Vowels: there are three basic short vowels in Arabic and three long ones. These are:

Vowel	a	IPA	Phonetic description	English equivalent
´	a	a	Short low back vowel	as in 'Amsterdam'
ا	aa	a:	Long low back vowel	as in 'far'
ِ	i	i	Short high front vowel	as in 'inside'
ي	ii	i:	Long high front vowel	as in 'clean'
ُ	u	u	Short high back vowel	as in 'to go'
و	uu	u:	Long high back vowel	as in 'noon'

IPA = International Phonetic Alphabet.

a Combined and modified by Ghassan Al Shatter, The Australian National University, Canberra.

Source: Transcription adopted in this project: Mansouri (2004); conventional/IPA transcription: modification of Mansouri (2005); comparison transcription: Fassi Fehri (1993).

Glossary

Key: Ar.: = Arabic; BR = Brunei Darussalam; BU = Burma (Myanmar); DU = Dutch; IN = Indonesia; ML = Malaysia; PH = Philippines; SEA = Southeast Asia; SG = Singapore; S. PH = southern Philippines; S. TH = southern Thailand; TH = Thailand; VN = Vietnam

Term	Explanation
abangan Muslims (JV, IN)	nominal or less strict Muslims, usually in reference to Javanese Muslims
ABIM (ML)	Angkatan Belia Islam Malaysia (Malaysian Islamic Youth Movement); founded 1971
Abu Sayyaf Group (S. PH)	Father of the Swordbearer; a Moro nationalist movement formed in 1991 by the Libyan-trained Abubakar Janjalani, a former middle-ranking MNLF leader
adat (SEA)	customary or traditional law (as distinct from Islamic law)
ahad (Ar.: *'aahaadun*)	term used to describe Hadith whose veracity is regarded as good but not beyond doubt
Ahl al-Kitab (Ar.: *ahlul-kitaabi*)	'People of the Book'; term used in the Qur'an to refer to Jews and Christians, who, like Muslims, have scriptures recognized as having been revealed by God
Ahli Sunnah Wal-Jammah (IN; Ar: *'ahlus-sunnati wal-jamaa`ati*)	'those who follow the tradition of the Prophet and the [consensus of the] community'; long-hand term for the majority Sunni branch within Islam, though some self-ascribed Sunni groups use the term in a narrow and exclusivist way
ahli sunnah waljammah (ML)	see Ahli Sunnah Wal-Jammah
Ahlus Sunnah wal Jamaah (IN)	see Ahli Sunnah Wal-Jammah
ahlusunnah wal-jamaah (IN)	see Ahli Sunnah Wal-Jammah
ahluts-tsughur (Ar.: *'ahluth-thughuuri*)	'people of the frontier'; common term in Salafi jihadist literature to describe those who fight to defend Islam from its enemies
'Aisyiyah (IN)	the women's wing of Muhammadiyah, formed in 1917 and named after the youngest wife of the Prophet Muhammad
akbar	see *jihaad akbar*
akhlak (IN, ML; Ar.: *'akhlaaqun*)	morals, morality, ethics (the motivation behind an act)
akhlaq	see *akhlak*

akidah (IN, ML; Ar.: `aqiidah*)	articles of faith, belief
al-Fatihah (Ar.: *al-Faati<u>h</u>ah*)	the title of the first chapter of the Qur'an, meaning 'the opening', 'the beginning'; its verses are an essential part of daily prayers and are regarded as having talismanic powers
al-hikmah/alhikmah	see *<u>h</u>ikmah*
Al-Jama'atul-Islamiyatu	see Jemaah Islamiyah
Allahu Akbar (Ar.: *allaahu akbaru*)	God is the greatest
al-Qaeda (Ar.: *al-qaa`idah*)	The Base; jihadist organization formed by Osama bin Laden in the 1980s to gather fighters and funds for the war against Soviet Union occupation of Afghanistan; from the mid-1990s the leading transnational terrorist movement
amali (Ar.: *'a`maalun*)	work, service, deeds
amar ma'ruf nahi munkar (Ar.: *'al-'amru bil ma`ruufi wan-nahyu `anil munkari*)	to do good and avoid evil
amir (Ar.: *'amiirun*)	commander, leader
amir al-hajj (SEA; Ar.: *'amiirul-jihaadi*)	leader of the haj
AMLA (SG)	Administration of Muslim Law Act
APEC	Asia-Pacific Economic Cooperation
aqidah (IN)	see *akidah*
aqiida	see *akidah*
Ar.	Arabic
Arafat (Ar.: `arafaat*)	the name of a plain 27 kilometres southwest of Mecca where all pilgrims must assemble on the 9th day of the pilgrimage month to pray and reflect on their lives between midday and sunset; this is one of the obligatory rites of the haj (see also *wukuf*)
ARIF (BU)	Arakan Rohingya Islamic Front; founded in 1987 as a breakaway movement of the RSO
arkaan addiin (Ar.: *'arkaanud-diini*)	the pillars of the religion (Islam) which are compulsory obligations for every Muslim – refers to the declaration of faith; the five daily prayers; the wealth tax or *zakat*; observing the fast during the fasting month; and undertaking the pilgrimage to Mecca if able
ARMM (PH)	Autonomous Region in Muslim Mindanao formed in 1990 and comprising 5 provinces in the Sulu archipelago and western Mindanao
ARNO (BU)	Arakan Rohingya National Organisation, founded in 1998 through an alliance between the ARIF and the RSO
asbab nuzul (Ar.: *asbaabun-nuzuuli*)	circumstances and context for the revelation (of the chapters of the Qu'ran)
asgar	see *jihaad asgar*
ashgar	see *jihaad asgar*
as-Salaf as-Saalih (SEA; Ar.: *'as-salafus-saalihu*)	the 'Pious Ancestors'; the first few generations of the Muslim community, who are seen as providing an exemplary model of proper Islamic thinking and behaviour

aswatuhâ (Ar.: *'awsaṯuhaa*)	'middle path', avoiding extremes
aurat (Ar.: `awrah*)	those parts of the body that must be kept covered in public
`awrah* (Ar.)	see *aurat*
azan (Ar.: *'adhaanun*)	call to prayer
`azl* (Ar.: `azlun*)	coitus interruptus
b.	born
baatil (Ar.: *baaṯilun*)	false, untrue, harmful (often placed in contrast to *haqq* or truth)
Bangsamoro (S. PH)	Moro People; generic name for the 13 ethno-linguistic groups of Muslims in the Philippines
BBMP (S.TH)	Barisan Bersatu Mujahideen Patani (United Mujahideen Front of Patani)
BCE	Before Common Era
Bersatu (S.TH)	United; a loose coalition of BNPP, BRN and PULO formed in 1991
bilal (Ar.: *bilaal*)	Muslim male whose duty is to summon worshippers to the mosque for each of the five daily prayers by calling from the mosque minaret
BIN (IN)	Badan Intelijen Negara (National Intelligence Agency)
BNPP (S. TH)	Barisan Nasional Pembebasan Patani (National Liberation Front of Patani)
bomoh (ML, BR, SG)	spiritual medium, traditional healer
BRN (S. TH)	Barisan Revolusi Nasional (National Revolutionary Front); socialist-inclined Malay Muslim organization founded in 1960 by Narathiwat religious teacher, Abdul Karim Hassan
bupati (IN)	head of a *kabupaten* (regency, district)
cay (VN)	kingship spirits
CE	Common Era
Chat Thai (TH)	Thai Nation
Chularajamontri (TH)	literally, Supreme Royal Counsellor, but more colloquially, head of Islamic affairs; he also carries the title of Syaikh al-Islam
CLD KHI (IN)	Counter Legal Draft Kompilasi Hukum Islam (Counter Legal Draft to the Compilation of Islamic Law)
CPM Task Force 43 (TH)	Civilian–Police–Military Task Force 43; founded by the Thai government in 1980 to coordinate security in the Muslim 'south', and particularly to stop extra-judicial killings and kidnappings of suspected Muslim insurgents; dismantled by the Thaksin government in May 2002
d.	died
da'i/dai (IN; Ar.: *daa`iyah*)	the person performing Islamic outreach (see *dakwah*)
dakwah (IN, ML, SG, BR; Ar.: *da`wah*)	'call'; preaching, predication, Islamic outreach
dalil `aqli (Ar.: *daliilun naqliyyun*)	argument based on reasoning rather than scriptural quotation
dalil naqli (Ar.: *daliilun `aqliyyun*)	an argument of principle based on quotations from the Qur'an or Hadith
DAP (ML)	Democratic Action Party

Darul-Ifta (S. PH)	House of Opinion; the group of Islamic scholars responsible for issuing fatwa in the southern Philippines
Darul Arqam (ML, SG, IN; Ar.: *darul 'arqami*)	House of Arqam; refers to one of the early converts to Islam who opened his home to the Prophet Muhammad as a place from which to spread Islam; the name was used by a group founded in Malaysia in 1968 but banned by former Prime Minister Mahathir in 1994 as 'deviant'; in Singapore the name refers to the Muslim Converts' Association established in 1980
Darul Islam (SEA)	Abode of Islam; place where Islamic law and teachings are upheld; in Indonesia it is also the name of an Islamic-state movement that rose up in rebellion against the central government (1948–62) – it remains active in a largely non-violent form
Dato' (ML)	title bestowed by Malaysian sultans for service to their state
Dato' Seri (ML)	title one grade higher than Dato' bestowed for service to the state or nation
dato' yutitham (S. TH)	Muslim judge in the four southern provinces who hears cases involving Muslim family law and inheritance issues
datu (S. PH)	headman; honorific term for respected person
dawah (PH, BU)	see *dakwah*
DDII (IN)	Dewan Dakwah Islamiyah Indonesia (Indonesian Islamic Propagation Council)
deen (Ar.: *diinun*)	religion or faith; more specifically, it means living in obedience to God (for which one will be held accountable on the Day of Judgement)
dhikrun	see *dzikir*
dhul hijjati	see Dzulhijjah
din	see *deen*
DPR (IN)	Dewan Perwakilan Rakyat, the national parliament
dukun (IN)	traditional healer
dzanniy	see *zanni*
dzanny	see *zanni*
dzikir (Ar.: *dhikrun*)	'remembrance'; repetitions of phrases containing the name of God that are chanted repeatedly and rhythmically in order to 'remember' or be mindful of God
Dzulhijjah (Ar.: *dhul hijjati*)	the last month in the Muslim calendar; the haj rituals are performed between the eighth and thirteenth days of this month
Eid al-Fitr	see Idul Fitri
faddala (Ar.: *fadlul-lahi*)	to give preference to someone or set someone before or above someone else
fadhalallah	see *faddala*
fardhu a'yn (Ar. *fardu 'aynin*)	a category of religious duty which must be performed by every Muslim (see *arkaan addiin*)
fardhu kifaya (Ar.: *fardu kifaayatin*)	a category of religious duty which must be performed by at least one member of the Islamic community on behalf of all – ensuring that bodies are buried with the appropriate rituals, for example; because it is a communal obligation, if it is not carried out, the entire community bears the responsibility for its neglect
fardu 'ain	see *fardhu a'yn*

fardu kifayah	see *fardhu kifaya*
fasakh (IN, ML; Ar.: *faskhun*)	annulment of marriage by formal application to religious court by the wife, based on husband's disability or failure to provide maintenance
faskh	see *fasakh*
Fatayat NU (IN)	the young women's wing of NU
fatwa (SEA; Ar.: *fatwaa*)	religious opinion given by a scholar who has the authority to do so
fi sabilillah	see *jihad fi sabilillah*
fikh (IN, ML, SG, BR; Ar.: *fiqhun*)	jurisprudence; legal prescriptions
fikih	see *fikh*
fiqih	see *fikh*
fiqh	see *fikh*
fitrah (SEA; Ar.: *fitratun*)	natural tendency; original characteristic
fitri	see *fitrah*
fitroh	see *fitrah*
FK3 (IN)	Forum Kajian Kitab Kuning (Forum for the Study of Kitab Kuning)
FKIT (IN)	Forum Kajian Islam Tradisional (Forum for the Study of Traditional Islam)
FPI (IN)	Front Pembela Islam (Islamic Defenders' Front); Islamic vigilante group formed in 1999 to combat immoral behaviour in Indonesian society
FULRO (VN)	Front Unifié de Lutte des Races Opprimées (United Struggle Front of the Oppressed Races)
fuqaha (Ar.: *faqiihun*)	experts in Islamic jurisprudence (*fiqh*)
furu' (Ar.: *furuu'un*)	analyses of differences in legal opinion; new and original legal problems
Gama'a Islamiyah	Islamic Community; the name of a militant Egyptian organization
Gerakan Tarbiyah (IN)	Education Movement; the name of a Muslim Brotherhood-inspired campus Islam movement that arose in Indonesia in the 1980s
ghazwul fikri (Ar.: *'al-ghazwul-fikriyyu*)	the war of ideas
GMIP (S. TH)	Gerakan Mujahideen Islam Pattani (Pattani Islamic Mujahideen Movement); established in 1995 by Libyan-trained Narathiwat activist, Nasoree Saesang, to fight for independent Pattani state
GRC (SG)	Group Representation Constituency
Guided Democracy (IN)	semi-authoritarian regime led by President Sukarno, 1959–66; the ideology of that period
hadd (Ar.: *haddun*)	see *hudud*
Hadiith	see Hadith
Hadith (SEA; Ar.: *hadiithun*)	report or account of the words and deeds of the Prophet Muhammad transmitted through a chain of narrators; Hadith are a basic source for Islamic law
haj (Ar.: *hajjun*)	annual pilgrimage to Mecca between the eighth and thirteenth days of the month of *dhul hijjati* to perform specific rites
Haji (SEA; Ar.: *haajjun*)	title used by a male who has performed the haj

Hajjah (SEA; Ar.: *haajjah*)	title used by a female who has performed the haj
Hakikat	see Haqiqah
halal (SEA; Ar.: *halaalun*)	'released' (from prohibition); term denoting what is permitted or lawful in Islam
Haqiqah (Ar.: *haqiiqah*)	(Divine) Truth
haqq (Ar.: *haqqun*)	truth; that which is right
haram (SEA; Ar.: *haraamun*)	'forbidden'; term for actions or things prohibited by Islamic law
harb (Ar.: *harbun*)	'warfare'
hazar (Ar.: *hadharun*)	'be cautious' (especially of possible hostilities)
hibah (Ar.: *hibah*)	gift given without expectation of return while the donor is alive, in contrast to an inheritance received after the donor's death
hijab (SEA; Ar.: *hijaabun*)	'shelter', 'protection'; curtain, veil or covering
hijrah/Hijrah (Ar.: *hijrah*)	migration, flight, withdrawal (particularly from a threatening environment); in Islam refers specifically to the move from Mecca to Medina in the year 622 CE by the Prophet Muhammad and his closest followers so that Islam could flourish in a more welcoming environment; the year marks the first in the Muslim (lunar) calendar, which is referred to as 1H
hikmah (Ar.: *hikmah*)	knowledge, wisdom; occult sciences
hisbullah/*hizbullah* (Ar.: *hizbul-lahi*)	party of God
Hizb-e-Islami Mujahideen (Ar.: *hizbul-mujaahidiinal islamiyyi*)	Party of Islamic Holy War Fighters; active in Kashmir and Afghanistan
Hizbul Muslimin (ML)	Islamic Party; the first Islamic political party in Malaya, established in 1948 and banned by the British later in the same year.
Hizbut Tahrir (Ar.: *hizbut-tahriiri*)	Liberation Party; founded in Jerusalem in 1953 with central aim of reviving the caliphate; the Indonesian branch was active from 1982
Hj	see Haji
HMI (IN)	Himpunan Mahasiswa Islam (Muslim Tertiary Students Association)
HT	see Hizbut Tahrir
HTI (IN)	Hizbut Tahrir Indonesia (Liberation Party of Indonesia); the Indonesian chapter of Hizbut Tahrir
hudud (SEA; Ar.: *huduudun*)	plural of Arabic *hadd* ('limit', 'prohibition'); a legal term for the offences and punishments set out in the Qur'an and Hadith, with the prescribed penalties ranging from various forms of corporal punishment to death; the offences are theft, illicit sexual relations, false accusations of illicit sexual relations, consumption of intoxicating substances, apostasy and highway robbery
hujjah (Ar.: *hujjah*)	supporting evidence, proof (for an argument)
IAIN (IN)	Institut Agama Islam Negeri (State Islamic Institute); provides degrees at tertiary level
ibadah (SEA; Ar.: *`ibaadah*)	worship, religious rituals and duties (see *arkaan addiin*)

ICM (BU)	Islamic Council of Myanmar
ICMI (IN)	Ikatan Cendekiawan Muslim Indonesia (Association of Indonesian Muslim Intellectuals); established in 1990 under the leadership of B.J. Habibie and with the sponsorship of President Soeharto
Id al-Adha (SEA; Ar.: `iidul-ad-haa)	'the feast of the sacrifice'; held on the tenth day of *dhul hijjati* after the conclusion of the haj rituals to remember Abraham's willingness to sacrifice his son when tested by God; unblemished animals are slaughtered and their meat is distributed to the poor
Id al-Fitr (TH)	see Idul Fitri
'iddah (Ar.: `iddah)	waiting period a woman must observe after the death of her spouse or divorce, during which she cannot remarry
Idul Fitri (SEA; Ar.: `iidul-fitri)	the 'small feast'; celebrations to mark the end of the fasting month (Ramadan)
ihdad (Ar.: *hidaadun*)	prescribed mourning period (four months and ten days) for a widow (see *'iddah*)
ihram (SEA; Ar.: *ihraamun*)	a state of ritual purity for pilgrims before beginning the haj and *umrah*, signified by special dress and behaviour (hair and nails must not be cut, sexual abstinence)
ijma' (Ar.: *'ijmaa`un*)	agreement or consensus of expert legal opinions
ijtihad (Ar.: *'ijtihaadun*)	independent judgement, based on recognized sources of Islam, on a legal or theological question (in contrast to *taqliid*, judgment based on tradition or convention)
IKIM (ML)	Institut Kefahaman Islam Malaysia (Malaysian Institute for Islamic Understanding)
ilmu (IN, ML)	knowledge
imaan	see *iman*
imam (SEA; Ar.: *'imaamun*)	'model', 'exemplar'; spiritual leader of Muslim community or group, leader of congregational prayers
imamatul uzma (Ar.: *'al-'imaamatul-`uzmaa*)	supreme leader or caliph
iman (SEA; Ar.: *'iimaanun*)	faith
IRAC (BU)	Islamic Religious Affairs Council
Islam Hadhari (ML; Ar.: *'islaamun hadaariyyun*)	Civilizational Islam; title of Malaysian government ideology developed under Prime Minister Abdullah Badawi, regarding the 'essential features' of Malaysian Islam and directions for strengthening these
Islam kaffah (IN)	'perfect' or 'complete' Islam, particularly in reference to Islam being a complete system governing human life
Israk-Mikraj (Ar.: *'al-'israa'u wal-mi`raaju*)	'Night Journey' undertaken by the Prophet Muhammad from the Grand Mosque in Mecca to al-Aqsa Mosque in Jerusalem followed by his ascension to heaven; it is celebrated annually on the 27th day of the month of Rajab
istighfar (Ar.: *'istighfaarun*)	asking (God's) forgiveness
istimata (Ar.: *'istimaatah*)	'prepared to die', martyr
istislah (Ar.: *'istislaahun*)	juristic reasoning based on consideration of the public good

Jabatan Agama Islam (ML)	State Islamic Department
jahiliah	see *jahiliyah*
jahiliyah (Ar.: *jaahiliyyah*)	'ignorance of Islam'; historically it refers to the period in Arabia before the revelation of Islam and its spread by the Prophet Muhammad
jahilliyah	see *jahiliyah*
Jakim (ML)	Jabatan Kemajuan Islam Malaysia (Malaysian Department of Islamic Development)
Jamiyah (SG)	Muslim Missionary Society
jampi (IN, ML)	spells
jemaah (Ar.: *jamaa`ah*)	congregation, community, group
Jemaah Islamiyah (SEA; Ar.: *jamaa`atun 'islaamiyyatun*)	Islamic Community; covert jihadist Islamic organization founded in Malaysia in 1993 and based in Indonesia since 1998
JI (SEA)	see Jemaah Islamiyah
jihaad akbar (Ar.: *jihaadun 'akbarun*)	'greater jihad'; the Prophet Muhammad is reported to have referred to the struggle against one's desires as the 'greater jihad' and war against Islam's enemies as the 'lesser jihad' (see also *jihaad asgar*)
jihaad asgar (Ar.: *jihaadun 'asgharun*)	lesser jihad, in particular the physical battle against the enemies of Islam (see also *jihaad akbar*)
jihad (SEA; Ar.: *jihaadun*)	'to strive', 'to exert', 'to fight'; meaning can range from personal struggle against sinful tendencies to assisting the community in holy war
jihad al-nafs (Ar.: *jihaadun-nafsi*)	'personal jihad', particularly with the sense of self-restraint and self-discipline
jihad asghar	see *jihaad asgar*
jihad fisabilillah (Ar.: *jihaadun fii sabiilil-laahi*)	jihad in the path of God with death leading to martyrdom (*shahid*)
jihad pishabillilloh (S. TH)	see *jihad fisabilillah*
jihadan kabiran (Ar.: *jihaadun kabiirun*)	'great jihad' or 'total jihad' (see also *jihaad akbar*)
jihadun nafs (Ar.: *jihaadun-nafsi*)	see *jihad al-nafs*
JIL (IN)	Jaringan Islam Liberal (Liberal Islam Network); founded in 2001
jilbab (IN, Ar.: *jilbaabun*)	women's head covering that leaves only the face exposed
JIM (ML)	Jamaah Islah Malaysia (Malaysian Reform Community)
jin (Ar: *jinnun*)	supernatural, invisible beings; jinn
Jong Islamieten Bond (DU)	Young Muslims League; a pro-Indonesian nationalism organization formed in 1925
Ka'bah (Ar.: *ka`bah*)	the 'House of God'; a cube-like building about 14 metres long, 12 metres wide and 17 metres high, situated in the Grand Mosque of Mecca; it is the orientation point (*kiblat*) for all Muslims when they pray; circumambulation (*tawaf*) of the Ka'bah is one of the rites of the haj
kaaffah	see *Islam kaffah*
kadi (Ar.: *qaadiyun*)	'judge'; judge in a sharia court

kafir (Ar.: *kaafirun*)	'non-believer' (in Islam)
Kaum Muda (IN, ML, SG, BR)	'Young Group' of religious reformists, referring especially to the early decades of the twentieth century
Kaum Tua (IN, ML, SG, BR)	'Old Group' of religious conservatives, referring especially to the early decades of the twentieth century
Keluarga Maslahah (IN)	'Family Welfare'; NU concept regarding the family
keluarga sakinah (IN)	'happy family'; program adopted by 'Aisyiyah, the women's wing of Muhammadiyah, to inculcate family values
K.H. (JV)	Kiai Haji (see *kiai*, Haji)
khalifah (Ar.: *khaliifatun*)	caliph; 'deputy of God' in the sense that each individual should strive to implement the will of God; term used to describe the 'successors' of the Prophet Muhammad as religio-political leaders of the Muslim community
Khana Kau (TH)	see Kaum Muda
Khana Mai (TH)	see Kaum Tua
KHI (IN)	Kompilasi Hukum Islam (Compilation of Islamic Law) promulgated in 1991
khilafah (Ar.: *khilaafatun*)	caliphate – the office as well as the dominion of the caliph (see *khalifah*)
khilafiah (Ar.: *khilaafiyyah*)	contentious legal matter on which the opinion of ulema is divided
khutbah (Ar.: *khutbah*)	'introduction', 'preface'; sermon especially delivered during Friday communal prayers
kiai (JV)	'noble', 'lofty'; title of religious scholar or leader
kiblat (Ar.: *qiblah*)	the direction Muslims face when praying (toward Mecca)
KIKJ (IN)	Kajian Islam dan Keadilan Jender (Studies in Islam and Gender Justice)
KISDI (IN)	Komite Indonesia untuk Solidaritas Dunia Islam (Indonesian Committee for World Islamic Solidarity); formed in 1986 to promote the cause of overseas Muslims in conflict zones
kitab kuning (IN)	'yellow books' (a reference to the colour of the pages); commentaries on the Qur'an and Islamic law used as teaching texts in *pesantren*
KMM (ML)	Kumpulan Militan/Mujahidin Malaysia (Malaysian Militant/Mujahidin Organization); according to the Malaysian government, a terrorist organization linked to Jemaah Islamiyah, though details of its operations are at present sketchy
kodrat (Ar.: *qudrah*)	power; the ability or capacity to do a particular thing; aptitude
Koran	see Qur'an
kortep (S.TH, Ar.: *khatiibun*)	'preacher' (of the mosque sermon)
KPPSI (IN)	Komite Persiapan Penegakan Syari'at Islam (Committee for the Preparation of Enforcement of Islamic Sharia); formed in 2000 to campaign for comprehensive implementation of Islamic law in South Sulawesi
kudrat	see *kodrat*

kuffar (Ar.: *kuffaarun*)	infidels, unbelievers (plural of *kafir*)
Kufic	an early style of Arabic calligraphy whose square, angular qualities lend it to decorative use
kufr (Ar.: *kufrun*)	'unbelief'; rejection of the message of Islam
KUHP (IN)	Kitab Undang-Undang Hukum Pidana (Criminal Code of Indonesia)
Lakas (PH)	Lakas ng Bayan (People Power)
Laskar Jihad (IN)	Holy War Fighters; paramilitary force formed in 2000 by Ja'far Umar Thalib and disbanded in 2002
Laskar-i-Tayyiba	military wing of Pakistan-based militant group Markaz-ud-Dawa-wal-Irshad
LKiS (IN)	Lembaga Kajian Islam dan Sosial (Institute for the Study of Islam and Society); a Yogyakarta-based non-government organization
LS-ADI (IN)	Lingkar Studi-Aksi untuk Demokrasi Indonesia (Study-Action Circle for Indonesian Democracy)
LSI (IN)	Lembaga Survei Indonesia (Indonesian Survey Institute)
M (IN)	'Masehi' (Christian); used with dates, indicates *anno Domini* (AD)
madani (IN, ML; Ar.: *madaniyyun*)	civilized; with reference to civil society
madhhab	see *mazhab*
madrasah (SEA; Ar.: *madrasah*)	'place of study'; Islamic school or college
madzhab	see *mazhab*
mahar (Ar.: *mahrun*)	marriage payment from groom to bride
mahfudhah (Ar.: *mahfuuzaatun*)	memorization: learning the Qur'an by heart
mahram (Ar.: *muharramun*)	'forbidden'; in Islamic law it describes close male relatives (father, brother etc.) whom a woman may not marry; it is therefore permissible for a woman to be alone in their company
Majlis Agama (ML)	Majlis Agama Islam dan Isti'adat Melayu (Council of Islamic Religion and Malay Customs)
Majlis Tarjih (IN)	Majlis Tarjih dan Pengembangan Pemikiran Islam (Council on Law-making and Development of Islamic Thought); founded by Muhammadiyah in 1927
Makkah (Ar.: *makkah*)	Mecca, the holiest city of Islam
maksiat (IN, ML, SG, BR)	immoral act, immorality
Malay Islamic Monarchy	see *Melayu Islam Beraja*
maqashid al-syari'ah (or *syari'at*)	see *maqasid al-syariah*
maqasid al-shari'ah	see *maqasid al-syariah*
maqasid al-syariah (Ar.: *maqaasidush-sharii'ati*)	the five noble purposes of sharia, the primary goals of sharia; they are protection of religion; protection of life (self); protection of generations (family); protection of property; and protection of intellect
maqasid as-syari'ah	see *maqasid al-syariah*
m'arifah	see *ma'rifah*

ma'rifah (Ar.: *ma`rifah*)	knowledge; direct experience of the divine; in Sufi practices, gnosis
masajid (Ar.: *masjidun*)	mosque
Masjidil Haram (Ar.: *'al-masjidul-ḥaraamu*)	Grand Mosque (in Mecca); the focus of the haj
maslahah	see *maslahat*
maslahat (Ar.: *maslaḥah*)	benefit, the common good; a juristic approach that prioritizes the welfare of the community
Masyumi (IN)	Majelis Syuro Muslimin Indonesia (Indonesian Muslim Consultative Council); Japanese-sponsored Islamic organization formed in 1943; it transformed itself into an Islamic party in 1945 and was banned by Sukarno in 1960
MATA (ML)	Majlis Agama Tertinggi Sa-Malaya (Pan Malayan Supreme Religious Council)
Mawlid (Ar.: *mawlidun*)	birthday (of the Prophet Muhammad) believed to be on the twelfth day of the month Rabi al-Awwal
mazhab (IN, ML; Ar.: *madhhabun*)	'direction'; school of legal thought; the four main schools in Sunni Islam are Shafi'i, Maliki, Hanafi and Hanbali (sometimes spelled 'Hambali'), distinguished from each other by their different methods of jurisprudential reasoning
Melayu Islam Beraja (BR)	Malay Islamic Monarchy; the official state ideology of Brunei Darussalam
Mendaki (SG)	Council for the Development of the Muslim Community
MIB	see *Melayu Islam Beraja*
MILF (S. PH)	Moro Islamic Liberation Front; formed by Salamat Hashim in 1978 as a more Islamically inclined breakaway from the MNLF
MMI (IN)	Majelis Mujahidin Indonesia (Council of Indonesian Mujahideen); established in 2000 in Yogyakarta
MNLF (S. PH)	Moro National Liberation Front; formed by Nur Misuari in 1969 to struggle for an independent Muslim state in Mindanao
MNP (ML)	Malay Nationalist Party
moulvi (BU)	regional variant of the Persian *mullah* (religious scholar)
MPR (IN)	Majelis Permusyawaratan Rakyat (People's Consultative Assembly); Indonesia's supreme decision-making body
MPU (IN)	Majlis Permusyawaratan Ulama (Ulama Consultative Council (of Aceh))
MQ (IN)	Manajemen Qolbu (Heart Management) a contemporary self-help movement founded by Indonesian preacher, Abdullah Gymnastiar
muamalah (Ar.: *mu`aamalaatun*)	'business dealings and transactions'; refers to human interactions in society governed by Islamic law as distinct from human obligations to God, such as worship (see *ibadah*)
mu'amalat (ML)	see *muamalah*
mudlarabah (Ar.: *mudaarabah*)	contracts based on profit and loss sharing
mufassir (Ar.: *mufassirun*)	scholar who specializes in Qur'anic commentary
mufti/Mufti (SEA, Ar.: *muftiyun*)	jurist capable of giving authoritative legal opinion (fatwa)
Muhammadiyah (IN)	modernist Islamic organization founded in 1912 by Ahmad Dahlan

muharabah (Ar.: *mu<u>h</u>aarabah*)	armed robbery
muhasabah (IN, ML; Ar.: *mu<u>h</u>aasabah*)	examination of conscience
MUI (IN)	Majelis Ulama Indonesia (Indonesian Council of Ulama)
MUIS (SG)	Majlis Ugama Islam Singapura (Islamic Religious Council of Singapore)
mujahid (Ar.: *mujaahidun*)	'holy warrior'; someone who engages in jihad
Mujahideen	see *mujahid*
mujahidin (Ar.: *mujaahiduuna*)	plural form of *mujahid*
mullah (Ar.: *muwallaa*)	'master'; title of religious scholar or functionary
munafik (Ar.: *munaafiqun*)	'hypocrite'; term used for Muslims of weak faith, apostates, and Muslims who convert to other faiths
Muslim Brotherhood (Ar.: *al-'i<u>kh</u>waanul muslimuuna*)	Muslim reform movement founded in Egypt by Hasan al-Banna in 1928; Muslim Brotherhood-inspired groups are now found in many parts of the Muslim world, including Indonesia and Malaysia
Muslimat NU (IN)	the women's wing of NU
nafakah (Ar.: *nafaqah*)	financial support, child support, maintenance
nafaqa (S. PH)	see *nafakah*
nafkah (IN, ML)	see *nafakah*
NAP (TH)	National Aspiration Party; formed 1992
nash (Ar.: *na<u>ss</u>un*)	text from which law is derived; legal principle or argumentation
Nasyiatul 'Aisyiyah (IN)	the young women's section of Muhammadiyah
nasyid (IN, ML; Ar.: *na<u>sh</u>iidun*)	a style of popular music using Islam-based lyrics and *a capella* singing
NCIA (TH)	National Council of Islamic Affairs
NEP (ML)	New Economic Policy; policy launched by the Malaysian government in 1971 after the race riots of 13 May 1969
New Order (IN)	self-ascribed title of the Soeharto regime (1966–98)
New PULO (S TH)	a breakaway group from PULO in the mid-1980s led by Arong Mooreng and Abdul Rohman Bazo
NII (IN)	Negara Islam Indonesia (Indonesian Islamic State); title of state proclaimed by Darul Islam movement on 7 August 1949
NU (IN)	Nahdlatul Ulama (Revival of the Religious Scholars); Indonesia's largest Islamic organization, established in 1926 by Hasyim Asy'ari and Wahab Chasbullah to promote traditionalist Islam
nusyuz (Ar.: *nu<u>sh</u>uuzun*)	marital disobedience; for women, it often entails leaving home without their husband's approval; for men, it is taken to mean harsh abuse or failure to provide a livelihood
nyai (IN)	wife of a *kiai*; female ulema and teacher in Indonesia (particularly Java)
OIC	Organization of Islamic Conference; established in 1969 as a peak international forum for Muslim political leaders
OMA (PH)	Office of Muslim Affairs
P3M (IN)	Perhimpunan Pengembangan Pesantren dan Masyarakat (Association for the Development of Pesantren and Society)

PAN (IN)	Partai Amanat Nasional (National Mandate Party); founded in August 1998 with Amien Rais (former general chair of Muhammadiyah) as leader
Pancasila (IN)	the 'Five Principles' constituting the national ideology of the Indonesian state; they are: belief in the one supreme God; just and civilized humanity; national unity; democracy led by wisdom and prudence through consultation and representation; and social justice
PAP (SG)	People's Action Party
PAS (ML)	Parti Islam Se Malaysia (The Islamic Party of Malaysia); broke away from UMNO in 1951 under the leadership of Islamic scholars and has become the main source of opposition to UMNO governments
PBB (IN)	Partai Bulan Bintang (Crescent Moon and Star Party); founded in July 1998
PBUH/pbuh	peace be upon him, used after the name of the Prophet Muhammad
PCIA (TH)	Provincial Council for Islamic Affairs
PDI-P (IN)	Partai Demokrasi Indonesia-Perjuangan (Indonesian Democratic Party of Struggle); established by Megawati Sukarnoputri in 1998 and, since the 1999 general election, the country's largest party
penghulu (IN, ML)	head of village; Muslim official whose tasks have traditionally included giving fatwa, presiding at weddings, managing mosque activities and serving as sharia judges
People of the Book	see Ahl al-Kitab
Persis (IN)	Persatuan Islam (Islamic Association); reformist Islamic organization founded in 1923
Perti (IN)	Persatuan Tarbiyah Islamiyah (Islamic Education Association); Sumatra-based traditionalist organization founded in 1930
pesantren (JV, IN)	'place of the *santri*'; traditional Islamic boarding school
pesantren kilat (IN)	an intensive, condensed brief course of religious instruction
Pious Ancestors	see *as-salaf as-saalih*
PK (IN)	Partai Keadilan (Justice Party); formed 1998 with its core membership drawn primarily from Gerakan Tarbiyah, renamed Partai Keadilan Sejahtera (PKS) in 2003
PKB (IN)	Partai Kebangkitan Bangsa (National Awakening Party); formed in 1998 and based largely on an NU constituency
PKS (IN)	Partai Keadilan Sejahtera (Prosperity and Justice Party) formerly Partai Keadilan (PK, Justice Party)
PNI (IN)	Partai Nasionalis Indonesia (Indonesian Nationalist Party)
pondok (ML, S.TH)	traditional Islamic boarding school
ponoh (S. TH)	see *pondok*
PPIM (IN)	Pusat Pengkajian Islam dan Masyarakat (Centre for the Study of Islam and Society)
PPP (IN)	Partai Persatuan Pembangunan (United Development Party); established under regime pressure in 1973 by amalgamating four Islamic parties: NU, Parmusi (the successor to Masyumi), Perti and Sarekat Islam
PPTI (IN)	Partai Politik Tarikat Islam (Muslim Tarekat Political Party)
PSII (IN)	Partai Sarekat Islam Indonesia (PSII; Indonesian Islamic Union Party); an offshoot of Sarekat Islam

PULO (S. TH)	Pertubuhan Pembebasan Patani Bersatu (Patani United Liberation Organization); formed in 1968 by Tengku Bira Kotanila to wage armed struggle for an independent Muslim state in southern Thailand
Q	Qur'an
QS	Qur'an Surah (Chapter of the Qur'an); used when quoting from the Qur'an
qadi	see *kadi*
Qanun (IN)	as used in contemporary Aceh, refers to laws and regulations inspired by Islam and enacted by the government
qath'iy	see *qat'i*
qati	see *qat'i*
qat'i (Ar.: *qaṭ'iyyun*)	a definitive or categorical principle in the Qur'an or Hadith whose meaning cannot be negotiated or reinterpreted
qawwamuna (IN, ML; Ar.: *qawwaamuuna*)	leaders, maintainers
qiradl (IN; Ar.: *qarḍun*)	a contract under which capital is lent for use (e.g. trade) and the resulting profits are divided on the basis of agreed shares; the arrangement is considered to benefit both the lender and the borrower
qisas (Ar.: *qiṣaaṣun*)	retribution through compensation as punishment for capital crimes and assault, the extreme form of compensation being 'a life for a life'
Qishas	see *qisas*
qitaal	see *qital*
qital (Ar.: *qitaalun*)	battle, war
qiwaamah (Ar.: *qiwaamah*)	leadership; see also *qawwamuna*
qiyas (Ar.: *qiyaas*)	in Islamic law, reasoning by analogy to solve a new issue not directly provided for already
qodrati	see *kodrat*
Qur'an (Ar.: *'al-qur'aanu*)	God's word revealed to the Prophet Muhammad and the supreme source and absolute authority for Islam
r.	ruled
rajam (Ar.: *rajmun*)	death by stoning, the *hudud* punishment for a married man who has unlawful sexual intercourse
Ramadan (Ar.: *ramaḍaanu*)	ninth month of the Islamic calendar during which fasting is required
Ramuwan (VN)	regional variant of Ramadan
reformasi (IN, ML)	political, social and economic reform
RIF (BU)	Rohingya Independence Force, founded 1964
Rightly Guided Caliphs	the first four caliphs (Abu Bakr, Umar, Uthman and Ali, covering the period 632–661 CE), who are venerated as close Companions of the Prophet and whose rule is considered by Sunnis to be a golden age of Islam
RIHS	Revival of Islamic Heritage Society or Jamiat Ihya al-Turath al-Islamiyyah (often called just 'at-Turots' in Indonesia); a Kuwait-based salafist educational and outreach organization

riyadhah (IN, ML; Ar.: *riyaadah*)	spiritual exercises
RPF (BU)	Rohingya Patriotic Front, founded 1973
RSO (BU)	Rohingya Solidarity Organisation; founded 1982
S	see Surah
sa'adah (Ar.: *sa`aadah*)	happiness, good fortune
sabab nuzul (Ar.: *sababun-nuzuuli*)	reasons for and context of the revelation of the verses of the Qur'an; these are studied to better understand and interpret the Qur'an
sabr (Ar.: *sabrun*)	fortitude, patience, forbearance
sahiih (Ar.: *sahiihun*)	genuine, truthful, valid
sa'i (Ar.: *sa`yun*)	one of the rites of the haj and *umrah*, performed by walking or running briskly seven times between the two mounds of Safa and Marwa (just outside the walls of the Grand Mosque), a distance of 374 metres
sakinah (IN, ML; Ar.: *sakiinah*)	used specifically in the context of a *sakinah* family, that is, a family that is based on a valid marriage, that has the blessing of God and that is able to foster feelings of love among its members so they are happy, calm, peaceful and able to lead devout lives
salaf (Ar.: *salafun*)	'to precede'; widely used to denote *as-salaf as-saalih* or the Pious Ancestors
salafi (Ar.: *salafiyyun*)	term for those who seek to emulate the practice of the Pious Ancestors; see Salafism
Salafi jihadist	term that has gained popularity in recent years for describing that small and most militant subgroup of *salafis* who regard the use of extreme violence against perceived enemies of Islam as a religious obligation
Salafism	term used to describe movements that seek to return to the teachings and example of the early generations of Muslims; in recent decades it has been used to denote the most strictly puritanical of these movements
Salafiyya (Ar.: *salafiyyah*)	'*salaf*-like', 'those who follow the Pious Ancestors'; the term is often used to describe the early twentieth-century Islamic reform movement led by Jamal al-Din al-Afghani and Muhammad Abduh
salat (IN, ML; Ar.: *salaah*)	the prescribed ritual prayer to be performed five times a day
salawaat	plural of *salaah*
santri Muslims (IN)	pious Muslims who seek to adhere strictly to the ritual and legal requirements of Islam
Sarekat Islam (IN)	Islamic Association; established 1912 as successor to Sarekat Dagang Islamiyah (Islamic Commercial Union, 1909); in 1923 renamed as a political party, Partai Sarekat Islam Indonesia, which had little political success
saw/s.a.w. (Ar.: *sallal-laahu `alayhi wa sallama*)	blessings and peace be upon him; used after the name of the Prophet Muhammad
sawm (Ar.: *sawmun*)	fasting; performed during the month of Ramadan, it is one of the five pillars of Islam
sa`y	see *sa'i*

Sayid	see Sayyid
Sayyid	title of descendants of the Prophet Muhammad
SBPAC (TH)	Southern Border Provinces Administration Centre; established in 1980 by the Thai government to improve security in southern provinces; abolished in 2002
Shafi'i (Ar.: *shaafi'yyun*)	one of the four main Sunni law schools and the dominant school in Southeast Asia
shahaadah	see *shahada*
shahada (SEA; Ar.: *shahaadah*)	bearing witness; declaration of faith that there is no god but God and Muhammad is the messenger of God
shahid (PH)	see *syahid*
shalat (IN, ML)	see *salat*
sharia (Ar.: *sharii'ah*)	Islamic law
sheikh (Ar.: *shaykhun*)	'leader', 'elder', 'chief"; title of a Muslim political or religious leader; in Sufism, it refers to the spiritual master of a brotherhood
Shi'a, Shi'ism (Ar.: *shii'ah*)	'faction', 'party'; second largest branch after Sunni within Islam
Shi'ite	adherents of Shi'a Islam
sholat (IN)	see *salat*
SI	see Sarekat Islam
silsilah (Ar.: *silsilah*)	'name-chain'; genealogy
Sisters in Islam (ML)	Non-government organization founded in 1987 to protect and promote the rights of Muslim women
solah (SG)	see *salat*
solat (IN, ML)	see *salat*
SPDC (BU)	State Peace and Development Council; the ruling junta
Suara Bangsamoro (S. PH)	Voice of the Moro People
Sufi (Ar.: *suufiyyun*)	one who practises Islamic mysticism
Sufism	see Tasawuf
Sunnah (Ar.: *sunnah*)	'custom', 'usage'; established custom and normative precedent in Islam based on the example of the Prophet Muhammad
Sunni (Ar.: *sunniyyun*)	majority branch of Islam (see Ahli Sunnah Wal-Jamaah)
Sura	see Surah
Surah	Chapter (of the Qur'an)
Surat	see Surah
SWT/s.w.t./swt (Ar.: *subhaanahu wa ta'aalaa*)	*Subhanahu wa Ta'ala* (Almighty God)
syahadat	see *shahada*
syahid (Ar.: *shahiidun*)	'witness'; a martyr who dies fighting for and bearing 'witness' to the truth of Islam
Syaikh al-Islam (TH; Ar.: *shaykhul 'islaami*)	chief theologian and highest ranked ulema
syi'ar Islam (IN; Ar. *sha'aa'irul-islaami*)	any activities that glorify and celebrate Islam (for example the congregational Friday prayers)
tafsir (Ar.: *tafsiirun*)	exegesis, particularly of the Qur'an

tahlil (Ar.: *tahliilun*)	praising God by repeating the Arabic words meaning 'there is no god but God'
tajwid (Ar.: *tajwiidun*)	Qur'anic recitation in accordance with the rules for correct pronunciation and intonation
takwa (IN; ML; Ar.: *taqwaa*)	God-fearing; observing God's commands; piety
talak (Ar.: *ṭalaaqun*)	'cutting', 'freeing'; word spoken by husband to divorce his wife
talaq (PH)	see *talak*
taqwa	see *takwa*
tarbiyah, Tarbiyah (IN, ML; Ar.: *tarbiyah*)	'education', encompassing moral and intellectual elements (see also Gerakan Tarbiyah)
tarekat (IN, ML; Ar.: *ṭariiqah*)	'road', 'way', 'method'; in mysticism refers to methods used to come into the presence of God; a Sufi group or order
tarikah	see *tarekat*
tarikat	see *tarekat*
tariqa	see *tarekat*
tariqah (S. TH)	in southern Thailand the term has specific connotations of Sufi practices that promote invulnerability and increase personal power (see also *tarekat*)
tarsila (PH)	see *silsilah*
tasauf (SG)	see Tasawuf
Tasawuf (IN, ML; Ar.: *taṣawwufun*)	Sufism, Islamic mysticism
tasbih (IN, ML; Ar.: *tasbiiḥun*)	praising God; the memory beads used when saying prayers in praise of God
tauhid	see *tawhid*
tawaf (Ar.: *ṭawaafun*)	'to walk around'; refers specifically to one of the rites of the haj and *umrah*, namely to circumambulate the Ka'bah seven times
tawhid (Ar.: *tawḥiidun*)	the doctrine of the unity of God; monotheism; in Sufism refers to merging with the unity of the universe
ta'zir (Ar.: *ta'ziirun*)	penalties imposed at the discretion of a sharia court judge
telekung (ML)	white head and upper body covering worn by women
ṭib (Ar.: *ṭibbun*)	tradition of medicine practised by Muslim doctors
TII (IN)	Tentara Islam Indonesia (Indonesian Muslim Army); military wing of Darul Islam
TRT (TH)	Thai Rak Thai (Thais Love Thais); a political party founded in July 1998 by Thaksin Shinawatra; it won the 2001 and 2005 elections
tudung (ML)	women's headcovering
UIN (IN)	Universitas Islam Negeri (State Islamic University)
ukhuwah Islamiyah (Ar.: *'ukhuwwatun 'islaamiyyatun*)	Islamic brotherhood/solidarity
ulama (IN, ML; Ar.: *'ulamaa'un*)	plural of *alim*, 'learned'; Islamic scholar(s)
ulema	see *ulama*
Uli al-Amri	see Ulil Amri

ulil amri/Ulil Amri (Ar.: *ulwl 'amri*)	those with authority, in the sense of power to implement Islamic governance in the widest sense
umat	see *ummah*
ummah (Ar.: *'ummah*)	the Islamic community in the broadest sense of 'all Muslims'
ummat	see *ummah*
UMNO (ML)	United Malays National Organisation
umrah (Ar.: `*umrah*)	pilgrimage to Mecca which may be performed at any time other than the time specified for the haj; the rites for the *umrah* are fewer than for the haj and include: being in a state of *ihram*; *tawaf*; and *sa'i* (qv)
umroh (IN)	see *umrah*
ushul fiqh (Ar.: *'usuulul fiqhi*)	'the roots of jurisprudence'; the principles and methods enabling development of practical legal rules
usrah (Ar.: *'usrah*)	'family'; small group or cell used in Egypt by the Muslim Brotherhood as the basic organizational and training unit and adopted in Indonesia and Malaysia
usroh	see *usrah*
ustad (Ar.: *'ustaadhun*)	religious teacher
Wadah (TH)	Unity; political faction formed in 1986
Wahhabi (Ar.: *wahhaabiyyun*)	Saudi-based religious purification and social reform movement founded in the late eighteenth century by scholar Muhammad ibn 'Abd al-Wahhab (1703–87)
wakaf (Ar.: *waqfun*)	'confinement', 'prohibition'; perpetual charitable trust for religious purposes; endowment or property donated for a religious purpose
wali (Ar.: *waliyyun*)	from the Arabic meaning 'close to'; in Indonesia and Malaysia it can refer to a person close to God and therefore a 'saint'; it may also refer to someone who can act as a legal guardian to fellow Muslims (for example, to brides or orphans)
Wanita JIM (ML)	Wanita Pertubuhan Jamaah Islah Malaysia (Women of the Malaysian Reform Community); small but influential Malaysian Muslim women's organization
waqf	see *wakaf*
waqfun	see *wakaf*
WTC	World Trade Center
wukuf (SEA; Ar.: *wuquufun*)	'stopping/staying'; specifically staying on the Plain of Arafat 25 km east of Mecca on the ninth day of Zulhijjah between midday and sunset for prayer and reflection
wuquf	see *wukuf*
YADIM	Yayasan Dakwah Islamiah Malaysia (Islamic Preaching Foundation of Malaysia)
Yang di-Pertuan (BR)	Head of State [of Brunei]
Yang di-Pertuan Agong (ML)	King [of Malaysia]
zahid (Ar.: *zaahidun*)	'ascetic'; one who renounces worldly pursuits for a spiritual purpose
zakat (Ar.: *zakaah*)	'purification'; wealth tax, the payment of which is one of the five pillars of Islam

zakat al-mal (Ar.: *zakaatul-maali*)	'alms tax'; obligatory payments on behalf of the poor; the rate is 2.5 per cent of disposable income; this tax is commonly avoided but in Malaysia is compulsory; in Indonesia the government is attempting regulation
zakat fitrah (Ar.: *zakaatul-fitri*)	payment (often in the form of food) to mark the end of the fasting month by those who have to those who are in need, always paid/given
zanni (IN; Ar.: *zanniyyun*)	directives or principles taken from the Qur'an and Hadith which have been reached on the basis of expert argumentation; it therefore implies the use of human powers of deduction to interpret divine meaning
zhanny	see *zanni*
zhulm (Ar.: *zulmun*)	tyranny
zikir (IN, ML)	see *dzikir*
Zulhijjah (IN; ML)	see Dzulhijjah

1 Introduction to the Sourcebook

Virginia Hooker and Greg Fealy

'Various forms of Islam are logical consequences of the
process of the cultural synthesis that occurs when
Islam enters into a certain cultural setting.'
(Jamhari 2002: 33)

Islam is believed by its followers to be God's final revelation to human beings. Its sources are the Qur'an – God's words to His Messenger, the Prophet Muhammad – and the Sunnah, the body of knowledge that has been collected about the Prophet's life to serve as an example for all Muslims. The interpretation of these two sources began in the Middle East and centred especially on the Prophet's two cities of Mecca and Medina, still the revered sites of Islam that are visited by millions of Muslim pilgrims each year. Muslim scholarship derives its inspiration from exerting every effort to understand God's messages for humankind. The efforts of the scholars who wrote during the ninth to fourteenth centuries CE, the period of the greatest flowering of Islamic civilization, are still taught and consulted widely by contemporary Muslim scholars.

This book approaches Islam from the perspective of its more than 200 million followers in Southeast Asia. Their interpretations of Islam, their efforts to be 'better' Muslims, the issues that they struggle to resolve and their visions for the future of Islam in its local contexts are presented in their own words and images. In editing this book, the guiding principle has been to present material that reflects the diversity of thinking of Southeast Asian Muslims on issues that they see as critical in the late twentieth and early twenty-first centuries.

Islam is not the original or the sole religion of any Southeast Asian nation. The history of its transfer to the region is described briefly in the country overviews in this book (Part I). The diversity of peoples and cultures in Southeast Asia is a characteristic feature of the region and has influenced the expression of Islam more than any other factor. Just one example, the vernacular languages of Islam in Southeast Asia, illustrates the point clearly. The language of the Qur'an is seventh-century 'classical' Arabic. All Muslims strive to read and recite the Qur'an in its holy language, and many study Arabic formally to better understand and interpret God's words. Very few Christians make a comparable effort to study New Testament Greek or ecclesiastical Latin to better understand the Bible. Most read the Bible through

translations into their own language. By contrast, it is 'normal' for Muslims, wherever they live, to be taught at least small sections of the Qur'an so that they can
recite them in Arabic. Southeast Asian Muslims have developed strong networks of
Islamic schools and colleges so that their children can be educated about Islam. A
small percentage of students become specialist scholars with full fluency in Arabic
but the majority learn about Islam through their own vernaculars. The vernacular
thus becomes a bridge between the original source and the contemporary faithful.
The Arabic terms are transferred from their forms in Arabic script to the vernacular,
and usually written using romanized script. The languages of Islam in Southeast Asia
are therefore numerous and diverse.

The classical Arabic of the Qur'an and medieval Islamic scholarship, recorded
in Arabic script, is taught and used by Muslim scholars in all Muslim communities,
wherever they are physically located. Mastery of this language, its script and its
scholarly literature has created a universal world of Muslim scholarship open to all
Muslims who master its demanding texts. These scholars are the intellectual elite of
Islam; their number is small, and they are venerated and highly respected. Their writings are quoted throughout the Muslim world and are translated into Southeast Asian
languages, especially Indonesian and Malay.[1] The borderless world of the internet
makes this scholarship accessible to anyone who can log on to a computer.

Although Arabic is the key to the classical learning of Islam, English is growing
rapidly as the medium for contemporary scholarship and internet discussions. English will never replace Arabic (the language of the divine revelation of the Qur'an)
as the premier language of Islam, but as increasing numbers of Muslims are educated
at Western universities and others include Western social sciences and humanities
in their tertiary education courses, more seminal works by Muslim intellectuals are
being published in English.[2]

In the local communities where ordinary Muslims go about their daily affairs,
however, the richness of Southeast Asian Islam is expressed in local languages. In
southern Thailand, for example, Muslims speak dialects of Malay flavoured with
words used only in that area and mixed with forms borrowed from Thai, English and
Arabic as well as Indian languages brought by Muslim preachers who have settled
there. In the southern Philippines, Tagalog is one of the main vernaculars but, as in
southern Thailand, dialects with restricted currency are commonly used. Muslims in
Brunei Darussalam and Singapore use Malay as their vernacular, but again it is not
identical to the 'standard' language of the Malay peninsula. In Indonesia, the Islamic
vernaculars are as varied as the ethnic groups who use them, but it is Javanese, the

---

1   The works of the Egyptian scholar Yusuf al-Qaradawi (now living in Qatar) are an excellent
example. A prolific writer on a range of topics, his books are often cited by Southeast Asian Muslims,
including Anwar Ibrahim, Malaysia's former deputy prime minister (see extract 11-8). References to
al-Qaradawi's thinking appear in a number of primary sources quoted in this sourcebook.
2   Muslim intellectuals whose works are influential in Southeast Asia and who publish in English
include Fazlur Rahman, Edward Said, Farish A. Noor, Seyyed Hossein Nasr and Muhammad Khalid
Masud. Their publications are read in the region both in English and in the form of local translations.

language of the largest and most politically dominant ethnic group, that exerts most influence on scholarship and pronunciation.[3]

One of the main purposes of this sourcebook is to reflect accurately the diversity and richness of the vernacular 'Islams' in Southeast Asia. The editors have therefore retained the local words used by Southeast Asian Muslims themselves for Islamic terms derived from the Arabic. This has resulted in variations in the spellings of some terms within the sourcebook. However, where confusion could occur, an explanation is provided as well as a transliteration of the Arabic (Ar.) equivalent in brackets. It is important, the editors believe, that the terminology of Southeast Asian Muslims themselves is made available to readers beyond the region itself, so that the context, content and 'personality' of Southeast Asian Islam is recognized and better understood.

It is impossible to discuss subjects as broad as Islam and the Muslim community in Southeast Asia without seeking to categorize and describe major groupings and trends. Defining these categories and their labels is nearly always contentious, both among scholars and also within the Muslim community itself. Terms such as 'radical', 'extremist', 'fundamentalist', 'terrorist', 'moderate', 'liberal' and 'progressive' are widely used in the scholarly and general literature, though often with diverse meanings. Although key terms are described in the commentaries and, briefly, in the glossary, the editors have included here a discussion of the main categories referred to in the text and definitions of frequently used terms (Box 1.1).

THE STRUCTURE OF THE SOURCEBOOK

Preliminary Material

The preliminary pages contain a map showing concentrations of Muslim populations throughout Southeast Asia (see the inside cover map), a glossary, a timeline of events important to Islam in Southeast Asia, and a table of transliteration systems for Arabic script, including the system used for transliterating Arabic terms in this sourcebook.

Glossary

The glossary has been compiled to be used as a key source of information about Islam in Southeast Asia. It is a reference of first resort for terms, abbreviations and acronyms that appear more than once in the sourcebook. (Terms or names which appear only once are explained where they occur.)

A guiding principle for the glossary, as for the book as a whole, has been to give preference to the vernacular languages of Islam in Southeast Asia. Where a word has

---

3   Javanese is the language used by most members of Nahdlatul Ulama (NU, Revival of the Religious Scholars), probably the largest Muslim organization in the world. Its current membership is estimated to be in excess of 35 million. Indonesia's second-largest Islamic organization, Muhammadiyah, also has a strong Javanese element in its membership.

BOX 1.1   TERMINOLOGY

Characterizations and typologies of Islamic movements and streams of thought are bedevilled by disputes over the meanings of key terms. Labels such as 'fundamentalist', 'moderate', 'Islamist', 'terrorist', 'jihadist', 'liberal', 'progressive', 'Wahhabist', 'salafist', 'traditionalist' and 'modernist' are frequently used in different ways by different scholars and, in many cases, there is limited consensus as to their precise definition. In this sourcebook, the editors have sought to limit the use of contentious terms, but it is impossible to discuss contemporary Islam without recourse to some of this nomenclature. When these terms occur in this book's commentaries, they are used in a value-neutral and non-judgemental way.

Radical Islam refers to those Islamic movements that seek dramatic change in society and the state. The comprehensive implementation of Islamic law and the upholding of 'Islamic norms', however defined, are central elements in the thinking of most radical groups. Radical Muslims tend to have a literal interpretation of the Qur'an, especially those sections relating to social relations, religious behaviour and the punishment of crimes, and they also seek to adhere closely to the perceived normative model based on the example of the Prophet Muhammad (the Sunnah). In this sense, many radical Muslims might also be described as *fundamentalists* because of their self-ascribed commitment to what they see as the fundamental teachings of their faith. Unlike texts that use 'radical' to denote groups that use violence to achieve their goals, this sourcebook employs the term in referring to both peaceful and violent forms of Islamic struggle.

Islamism is another term that has acquired a wide variety of meanings in general and scholarly usage. For the purposes of this book, Islamists are those who seek formally to make Islam the basis for public life, particularly politics, but also economics, culture and society. Islamists view the world primarily, if not exclusively, through an Islamic prism and commonly see implementation of sharia as central to their agenda. There is considerable, but not total, overlap between Islamism and radicalism as categories. While many Islamists aspire to bring about an Islamic transformation of society, other Islamists are committed to gradual change and work within the existing political structures to achieve this.

Terrorism is the most problematic of terms to define. Scholars, governments, lawyers and international bodies have produced a plethora of definitions for terrorism, and the points of disagreement remain considerable. Indeed, some writers have argued that definitions of 'terrorism' are inherently subjective and politically driven. The editors, mindful of the contentious nature of the term, use it sparingly. The term is employed in two ways:

first, to refer to acts that aim to instil terror within a community, particularly through the use of unexpected and shocking violence against non-combatants by clandestine groups or agents; and second, to describe those who have been convicted of terrorism.

Salafism is another term that has been used in different ways at different times, and its contemporary application is open to considerable dispute. Salafism is drawn from the Arabic word *salaf*, meaning 'to precede' or 'to go before'. It is commonly used as shorthand for as-Salaf as-Saalih, the Pious Ancestors, a reference to the first three generations of the Muslim community, who are seen as providing an exemplary model of Islamic thinking and behaviour. In one sense, most Muslims would see themselves as being in some way salafist as they seek to emulate some, if not all, aspects of the behaviour of the as-Salaf as-Saalih. Historically, the term Salafiyya (literally, '*salaf*-like') has been applied to the early twentieth-century reform movement within Islam led by Jamal al-Din al-Afghani and Muhammad Abduh. But in recent decades the term has been used in a very specific way to describe those who regard themselves as the strictest adherents to the model set out by the early generations of Muslims.

Salafism is often seen as synonymous with *Wahhabism*, the strict Islamic reform movement named after the eighteenth-century scholar Muhammad ibn Abd al-Wahhab. Wahhabism is the predominant creed of Saudi Arabia. However, the followers of this movement do not refer to themselves as Wahhabis, and it is best to regard the Wahhabi movement as falling within the broader category of Salafism. Salafist groups in Southeast Asia look to prominent Saudi scholars for authoritative judgements on Islamic law.

Salafi jihadism is a distinct substream within Salafism comprising those who believe that violent jihad is the only way to achieve their goals. This group, often referred to as *salafi jihadiyah*, has risen to prominence since the *mujahidin* war against Soviet forces in Afghanistan in the late 1970s and 1980s. (For a more detailed discussion of Salafism and Salafi jihadism, see section 14.2.)

Moderate Islam is another term that has been used widely in recent times, particularly as a binary opposite to radical or terrorist Islam. In this book, we take moderate Muslims to be those who are disposed to be temperate and restrained, who are generally ready to compromise, and who reject violent or severe behaviour. Numerous Muslim groups regard this as an apt descriptor for their outlook on both Islam and their place in the world.

Liberal Muslims are those who favour change and reform. Often they are critical of traditional practices and institutions and they bring forward new ideas to challenge established thinking.

a multiplicity of spellings across the region, a dominant spelling has been chosen as the main entry in the glossary, with variants cross-referenced to it. For example, the Arabic word *dhikr* (used in Southeast Asia to describe the repeated chanting of phrases used to 'remember' God) is spelled *dzikir* and *zikir* in Indonesia, and *zikir* in Malaysia. In the glossary, the Indonesian form *dzikir* is given as the main entry, with the country where that spelling is used (Indonesia) and the Arabic transliteration provided as additional information. The other forms are also listed in the glossary, cross-referenced to *dzikir*. Where the meaning of words differs according to region of usage, this is also noted.

The glossary draws on a range of sources of information but has used three dictionaries as the main references for definitions. They are *A Comprehensive Indonesian–English Dictionary* (Stevens and Schmidgall-Tellings 2004) for Indonesian; *Kamus Perwira: Bahasa Melayu/Bahasa Inggeris* (Kelana and Lai Choy 1998) for Malay; and *A Dictionary of Modern Written Arabic* (Wehr 1966).

Timeline

The Prophet Muhammad lived in the seventh century CE. Events during his lifetime and in the succeeding centuries were crucial for the growth and spread of Islam. The major events of Islamic history are well known to Southeast Asian Muslims and shape their understanding of Islam. They are less well known to non-Muslims, and so have been presented in this sourcebook as a chronological list, a timeline. For the nineteenth and twentieth centuries, the period of greatest change for Southeast Asian Muslims, major political events of national and international significance are also included. The timeline can be consulted to establish dates for significant moments in the history of Islam. It also serves to provide comparative information on events with internal significance for Southeast Asian Muslims. The timeline shows, for example, that the Darul Islam rebellion was at its height in Indonesia at the same time as the communist insurgency in Malaya and the wars against the French in Indochina were taking place.

Part I: The Context of Southeast Asian Islam

The country overviews that comprise Part I of the sourcebook describe the development and current state of Islam in Brunei Darussalam, Burma (Myanmar), Cambodia and Vietnam, Indonesia, Malaysia, the Philippines, Singapore and Thailand. Communities of Muslims are found in each of the nations of Southeast Asia, and represent almost 40 per cent of the region's population.[4] In Indonesia, Malaysia and Brunei Darussalam, Islam is the religion of the majority of the population. In Singapore, Thailand, the Philippines, Burma (Myanmar), Vietnam, Cambodia and Laos, Muslims are a religious minority.

---

4   Southeast Asia's 214 million Muslims are the region's largest religious community, followed by Buddhists (196 million or 36 per cent) and Christians (114 million or 21 per cent).

Table 1.1 shows the current number of Muslims in the countries covered by this sourcebook. The figures cited in the table are the most recent available. Often these population statistics are slightly higher than those cited in the country overviews because many of the latter quote the most recent census data rather than estimates of current population. The *percentage* of the Muslim population in each country is, however, the same as that in the overviews.

Table 1.1   Populations of Southeast Asian Muslims

Country	Total Population	Muslim Population		% of Total Southeast Asian Islamic Community
		(no.)	(%)	
Brunei Darussalam	365,000	245,000	67.12	0.11
Burma (Myanmar)	42,909,000	1,716,000	4.00	0.80
Cambodia	13,607,000	700,000	5.14	0.33
Indonesia	214,995,000	189,195,000	88.00	88.26
Laos	6,217,000	400	0.01	0.0002
Malaysia	23,953,000	14,371,000	60.00	6.70
Philippines	87,857,000	4,393,000	5.00	2.05
Singapore	4,426,000	663,900	15.00	0.31
Thailand	65,444,000	3,010,000	4.60	1.40
Vietnam	83,536,000	65,000	0.08	0.03
Southeast Asia	543,309,000	214,359,300	39.45	100.00

Source: Most of the total population figures for individual countries are drawn from CIA (2005). The population figures for Indonesia are from Indonesia's central statistics agency, Biro Pusat Statistik (reported in the *Jakarta Post*, 4 July 2003), compiled in preparation for the 2004 general elections.

The demographic status of Muslims in modern nation-states has implications for the way Islam is administered and viewed by the relevant state authorities. To establish the context for the position of Islam in each country, the authors of the overviews have written concise descriptions of the demographic profiles of Muslims, given brief historical accounts of the transfer of Islam to each country, and provided some information about the status of Islam before the modern era.[5]

For the modern and contemporary periods, the overviews describe how Islam is administered through the organs of the state as well as at the local level by religious officials. They give considerable attention to analyses of 'political' Islam and incidents of violence perpetrated in the name of Islam. Each overview describes the

---

5   In most Southeast Asian countries this refers to the status of Islam under colonial rule.

character of Islam in the individual nation as well as issues of specific concern to local Muslim communities.

The country overviews may be read for the discrete, specific and up-to-date information they provide on Islam in a particular Southeast Asian nation. Within the context of the sourcebook as a whole, they provide the background for the material presented in Part II.

Part II: Extracts from Primary Sources and Commentaries

Each of the six chapters in Part II describes a different facet of Islam in Southeast Asia through extracts from primary sources. The chapters are self-contained in the sense that each may be read without reference to the others, although cross-referencing is given where appropriate. The chapters begin with a brief introduction to the theme and content of the chapter. The extracts then follow. Each extract is preceded by a commentary, usually prepared by the editor(s) of the chapter.

The extracts from primary sources are the heart of the sourcebook. They represent the opinions and reflections of Southeast Asian Muslims, expressed in their own words. One of the greatest challenges facing the editors was that of selection. The amount of material written, published, and available on the internet is impressively vast. A project team supported the editors in the task of selecting the primary sources and extracting material from them for inclusion in the sourcebook. Muslim leaders and academics from across Southeast Asia also offered advice and opinions at two workshops held during the course of the project.[6] The choice of the themes under which the extracts were grouped, however, was made by the editors themselves.

The rationale for the choice of themes was based on identifying topics that are creating debate both within Southeast Asia and beyond. Initially five themes were selected: 'Sharia', 'Islam, State and Governance', 'Gender and the Family', 'Jihad' and 'Interactions: Global and Local; Muslims and Non-Muslims'. While participants at the first conference agreed that these five themes reflected contentious issues, they felt that the sourcebook as planned would not convey the personal and more private views of Muslims on what being a Muslim actually means at an individual level. This led to the inclusion of a sixth theme, 'Personal Expressions of Faith', to introduce the essential principles of Islam and present more intimate and reflective views on the place of Islam in people's daily lives.

The members of the project team used five criteria to identify key documents that influence (or have influenced) the thinking of Muslims on the six themes. These criteria were that the material had to:

- be from a primary (not a secondary) source;
- be written or spoken by Muslims or apply directly to Muslims (such as law texts and legal codes);

---

6 Details of the workshops and a full list of contributors to the project are given in the acknowledgements.

- be from the recent past, or be material that elucidated the origins of a contemporary issue or movement;
- articulate a particular perspective on an issue; and
- be representative of the views of groups of Muslims and illustrate the points of argumentation being made to defend publicly held positions.

The extracts presented in the sourcebook reflect these criteria and provide examples of the range of thinking on each major issue presented in the book.

One of the features of the sourcebook is its presentation of material that is difficult to obtain or that has not previously been published. The editors believe that some of this material is so important to a better understanding of Islam in Southeast Asia that they have included lengthy extracts. The length of extracts should not, however, be taken as an indicator of the popularity of a particular view within the wider Muslim community. For example, in the 'Jihad' chapter, long extracts from the writings of two convicted terrorists, Imam Samudra and Mukhlas, are given, even though such views are anathema to the overwhelming majority of Southeast Asian Muslims.

There are several reasons for citing these writings extensively. First, they give a very rare insight into the motivations and rationale of the region's terrorists – none of these writings have appeared in English before and only a small number of Southeast Asian Muslims have read the Mukhlas document. Second, although terrorists and those who sympathize with them make up only a tiny portion of the Muslim community, terrorist attacks in Southeast Asia over the past five years have had a deep impact on the security and economic environment, the internal dynamics and discourse of the Islamic community, and international perceptions of the nature of Islam in the region. So, in the case of terrorism, the significance of the thinking and the acts that follow from it is far greater than the numbers who subscribe to such views.

Opinion on jihadist and other radical extracts among Southeast Asian participants at the two sourcebook workshops was divided: some of the academics and Muslim leaders regarded them as valuable texts that deserved to be quoted at length; others felt that disproportionate space was being devoted to 'fringe' material that might distort impressions of the nature of Southeast Asian Islam. The editors understand this concern but believe that the inclusion of the extracts is essential because of what they reveal about regional thinking on terrorism. Furthermore, it is often necessary to present radical materials in order to understand important aspects of the mainstream or liberal discourses, which are themselves often responding to radical viewpoints.

Another special feature of the sourcebook is the large number of extracts that are published here for the first time in English. The sourcebook thus makes a wide range of primary source material in Southeast Asian languages accessible to English-speaking readers. The extracts have been translated by a team of expert translators and the editor(s) of each of the thematic chapters. Great care has been taken to achieve final translations that accurately reflect their originals. Wherever possible, two translators have worked on the material, the second cross-checking the work of the first. The editors have tried to achieve a balance between a literal translation that is true to the original even if it may be difficult to follow, and a translation that helps the reader to understand the intention and flavour of the original text. Editorial amendments are enclosed in square brackets.

Trying to transfer the intention and meaning of complex documents into intelligible English is a challenge in any context. For material that describes and analyses intricate argumentation based on doctrinal evidence, that task is particularly difficult. The editors believe it is crucial that the 'difficult' documents of contemporary Islam be made more accessible to interested readers in order to increase appreciation of the nature of contemporary debates. Much of the material in the chapters on 'Sharia', 'Jihad' and 'Gender and the Family' exemplifies these challenges. The complexity of the argumentation in the original material reflects the often sophisticated level of discourse among the region's Muslims. The argumentation in the extracts provides the meat for the debates that are now shaping the positions of liberal, mainstream, conservative and literalist groups.

A further word should be added about the spread of material in the thematic chapters. Obtaining appropriate primary-source material from the Muslim communities in Cambodia and Vietnam has been almost impossible, and the quantity of literature available from Burma (Myanmar), Brunei Darussalam, Singapore and southern Thailand is limited.[7] Although we have been able to obtain interesting material from the southern Philippines, Singapore, Brunei Darussalam, and the Muslim areas of southern Thailand, the majority of extracts in the sourcebook are from Indonesia and Malaysia. The Muslims in these nations not only make up the overwhelming majority of Southeast Asia's Islamic community (about 95 per cent) but also have well-developed systems of Islamic education and media that specialize in disseminating material on Islam. The weighting of extracts in the sourcebook reflects the heavier concentration of Islamic material and the richness of public debate on Islamic issues in Indonesia and Malaysia.

As mentioned above, each extract is preceded by a commentary, clearly designated as such and usually written by the editor(s) of the chapter. Presented in an objective and non-judgemental style, the commentaries provide contextual information about the extracts. They give some background about the life and influence of the author of each extract, the significance of the material and its special features. The commentaries are intended not to support or criticize the positions and argumentation of the writers but rather to help the reader identify what those positions and arguments are.

EDITORIAL CONVENTIONS

The presentation of the material in Part II of the sourcebook follows a uniform set of conventions so that readers can differentiate between information that is from a primary source and information provided by the editors and other contributors to the book. Here, we provide information about the conventions used, the transcription

---

7   In some of these countries, a good deal of the literature taught in Islamic schools and study groups comes from non-Southeast Asian sources. For example, in western Burma, Rohingya Muslims make extensive use of texts from South Asia, which either are in Arabic or have been translated into the vernacular.

system for Arabic words and the approach to English translation of passages from the Qur'an.

Primary Sources

Preserving the authenticity of the primary sources has been a basic principle in preparing the sourcebook. The editors and translators have taken care to present the material in the extracts in a form that reflects the original as accurately as possible. As much as possible, spellings, inconsistencies, quotations, punctuation and the use of capitalization, italics, underlining and bold within the extract are reproduced as they appear in the original. Typography also follows the original as much as possible, to preserve the 'flavour' of the document. In cases where the material is difficult to understand, editorial amendments or explanations are given in square brackets.

If the original language of the primary source is English, this is noted in the citation at the head of the extract. As with the translations, the stylistic and typographical characteristics of extracts written in English have been preserved without editorial intervention, although clarification or additional explanation has been provided in footnotes or square brackets where necessary.

If an extract is not quoted in full, omissions made by the editors are indicated by an ellipsis within square brackets – [...] – at the place of the omission. For lengthy extracts, the page number of the original text is given next to the ellipses to indicate with greater accuracy where the cuts have been made. Where ellipses in extracts are not shown in square brackets, readers should assume that they also occur in the original documents.

Arabic Transliterations

Arabic is the language of the Qur'an and of the great works of Islamic scholarship, as described at the beginning of this chapter. All the terminology of Islam (exegesis, doctrine, law, mysticism) is from Arabic. Arabic grammar is complex and very exact, and Muslims all over the world consider mastery of Arabic grammar to be essential before higher study of Islam can be undertaken. Great care is taken to ensure that the exact meaning of God's words can be grasped, and this can only be achieved if each word is analysed fully and any ambiguities explained. Grammatical analysis forms a large part of Qur'anic exegesis (interpretation). In many modern Arabic texts written using Arabic script, not all vowel signs are included in the script; readers have to fill them in as they read, based on familiarity and context. In the Qur'an, however, every vowel sound is represented in the script so that there can be no misunderstanding about each of the sacred words in the scripture.

There is no standardized system for representing in romanized form Arabic terms that have been borrowed by, or are used in, Southeast Asian languages. Also, the local pronunciations of Arabic words, or words derived from Arabic, may vary considerably from 'standard classical' Arabic. Because this sourcebook presents the views of Southeast Asian Muslims in their own words, words derived or borrowed from Arabic are reproduced here in their Southeast Asian forms. If the word in its Southeast Asian vernacular form is difficult to follow or identify (for a reader famil-iar with Arabic, for example), a transcription of the standard Arabic equivalent is given in brackets immediately after the word or phrase.

The system used in the sourcebook for transliterating Arabic words and phrases is set out in the preliminary pages (see pages xxx–xxxi). Two other transliteration systems are also listed to assist those more familiar with other systems.[8] The system used in the sourcebook was chosen for its restrained use of unusual symbols (so that the non-specialist is not intimidated), its closeness to the word as pronounced and its general acceptability to scholars of Arabic. The transliterations provide suf-ficient information for specialists to find the words in Arabic dictionaries. Specialists should also note that Arabic phrases and sentences are transliterated as they are read in Arabic: all singular words appearing out of context and ending with *taa'marbuuta* [*tun*] are transliterated as they are read in Arabic, not as they are written (thus, for example, *madrasatun* is transliterated as *madrasah*); and all words not ending in *tun* are transliterated as they are written in Arabic with nominative case endings.

Arabic transliterations are used mainly in Chapter 10 (the 'explanatory' chapter about Islam) and in the introductory or 'commentary' sections of chapters when basic principles of Islam are being described. Arabic words used in the primary sources (the extracts) have been preserved in their original form, with the trans-literation immediately following in square brackets where necessary. Arabic terms that are now in common usage in English are given in their Anglicized form, using the spellings given in the *Oxford English Dictionary*.[9] These words include fatwa, Hadith, imam, haj, jihad, Ramadan, sharia, sheikh, Shi'a, Sufi, Sunni and ulema. As these terms have now been incorporated into English, they are not given in italics. The word 'God' has been used to translate 'Allah' in all vernacular texts, but the word 'Allah' has been retained where it occurs in English-language texts. All Arabic words in the glossary have been transliterated.

Spelling of Names

The names of Middle Eastern and Southeast Asian Muslims can be spelled in many different ways. The names of most Middle Eastern Muslims referred to in the source-book have been spelled according to common Western usage. Thus the name of the Messenger of God is given as Muhammad rather than Muhammadun, and the name of the classical scholar al-Ghazali is presented in this form rather than as al-Ghazaalii. The guide for spelling the names of Southeast Asian Muslims who lived

---

8   The editors are grateful to Ghassan Al Shatter of the Centre for Arab and Islamic Studies (Middle East and Central Asia) at the Australian National University, who has prepared the Arabic translitera-tions for the sourcebook.

9   Terms have been obtained from 'Oxford English Dictionary Online' (OUP 2006) and, in some instances, from the *Australian Oxford English Dictionary* (OUP 1999).

before the time of standardized spelling systems (that is, before the mid-twentieth century) has been *Ensiklopedi Islam Indonesia* (Nasution et al. 1992), compiled by a team of leading Southeast Asian scholars. In the case of contemporary Southeast Asian Muslims, we have followed their own preferred spelling or the spelling used in the primary source, providing clarification where necessary.

Quotations from the Qur'an and Hadith

The Qur'an is the Word of God, the basis of Islam and the primary source *par excellence* for all Muslims.[10] Scholars, intellectuals, preachers, teachers and ordinary women and men turn to their scripture for guidance throughout their lives. References to Qur'anic chapters and verses are frequent.

Muslims often quote the Qur'an in Arabic, its original form. Where this occurs in extracts used in the sourcebook, the English translation recently published by M.A.S. Abdel Haleem has been used (Haleem 2004).[11] Where Qur'anic quotations appear in an extract and have been translated by its author into a Southeast Asian language, we have translated them into English based on their vernacular form. To assist readers to compare the Southeast Asian interpretation with the original Arabic, Haleem's translation is also given as a footnote.

Each of the Qur'an's 114 chapters has its own name and number, and within each chapter (*surah*) the verses (*ayah*) are numbered sequentially. Because the citation style for Qur'anic references is not uniform, the convention adopted in the sourcebook is to preserve the original form of the citation as given in the primary source (the extract) but to standardize the reference to Haleem's translation given in the associated footnote. Thus 'Q14: 12, Haleem' refers to the Qur'an, chapter 14, verse 12, as translated by Haleem (2004).

Many of the extracts presented in the sourcebook also refer to Hadith as authoritative sources for their argumentation. The Hadith are accounts of the actions and sayings of the Prophet Muhammad and his Companions, and are used as a source of guidance for right actions and attitudes. The Hadith give details of the Prophet's life and, very importantly, provide contextual information concerning the circumstances of revelation and of the Prophet's understanding of it. The body of Hadith is generally accepted as representing the Sunnah of the Prophet Muhammad. The authenticity of Hadith is therefore a subject of scholarly scrutiny. Authentic Hadith should consist of two parts: the first lists the names of those who have transmitted the account (the chain of authority that leads back to someone close to the Prophet); the second is the actual account (the substance of the Hadith). Scholars of Hadith

---

10 A brief introduction to the Qur'an and its compilation is given in Haleem (2004: ix–xxix).

11 Selecting an English version of the Qur'an from the many that exist is difficult. We have chosen to use Haleem's translation because of its lucid, contemporary language. For readers interested in comparing English translations of the Qur'an, three versions are available online at the Noble Qur'an website of the University of Southern California's Muslim Students Association (<http://www.usc.edu/dept/MSA/quran/>).

have developed a complex system of categories based on the reliability of the chain of transmission for the Hadith. There are three broad categories of Hadith – those that are considered reliable and true, those that are considered unreliable because of 'weak' chains of transmission, and those that are considered false – with various grades of acceptability in between.

The Hadith were assembled into major collections more than 200 years after the death of the Prophet Muhammad, namely during the ninth century CE. The compilations of the scholars al-Bukhari (d. 870 CE), Muslim ibn al-Hajjaj (d. 875 CE) and al-Tirmidhi (or Tirmidzi) (d. 892 CE) are all respected as authoritative versions of Hadith. They are cited regularly by Southeast Asian Muslims, as indicated by their listings in many of the extracts in the sourcebook.

When references to Hadith appear in an extract, a note in square brackets is added to assist the reader to identify the reference as being to a collection of Hadith.

COPYRIGHT

Every effort has been made to seek permission to reprint from the copyright holder of each of the extracts and images used in the sourcebook. A full list of permissions is given at the end of the book. The editors would welcome correspondence from any publisher or author not listed and will amend the list of copyright permissions in any subsequent printing of the book.

IN CONCLUSION

The Qur'an emphasizes the contrast between the perfection, omnipotence and compassion of God and the limited nature of humankind. This contrast has been recognized and expressed by Muslims through the centuries since the Prophet Muhammad. It is the theme of Sufism, scholarship, architecture, poetry and decorative arts. It draws on the contrasting but balancing concepts of the limitless essence of the divine and the limited capacity of humankind; the infinite nature of God and the finite form of humankind; the eternal nature of God and the transitory nature of this world; and the eternal life of reward that awaits those who obey the commands of God and the eternal life of suffering that awaits those who do not. In Islam, the mortal world is ephemeral and is merely preparation for the eternal period that will follow death. These are the concepts – powerful and awe inspiring – that Southeast Asian Muslims consider and reflect on in all aspects of their lives.

The extracts, commentaries, country overviews and supporting explanatory material assembled in this sourcebook are presented in the spirit of contributing to a deeper understanding of Islam as it is being practised now throughout Southeast Asia. For non-Muslims, and Muslims also, the material selected for inclusion in the book provides examples of the debates taking place among Muslims in the region. Through the extracts, readers are able to trace the contestation and thrust of contemporary debates, the arguments and counterarguments on issues of importance for Southeast Asian Islam. It may also be that the range and diversity of material in the sourcebook contributes to a re-examination of, and further dialogue about, the challenges currently facing Muslims and non-Muslims alike in the early twenty-first century.

PART I

Country Overviews

2 Brunei Darussalam

*John Funston**

Among the countries of Southeast Asia, Brunei is unique in styling itself an Islamic monarchy. Its Islamic identity is expressed in the country's full name – Brunei Darussalam (Abode of Peace) – and an official ideology entitled *Melayu Islam Beraja* (MIB, Malay Islamic Monarchy). The development of Islam in Brunei shares many common experiences with neighbouring countries, but there has been no comparable growth of political Islam, much less the militancy that has sometimes been apparent elsewhere.

DEMOGRAPHY

Statistics on religious affiliation are difficult to obtain, but there are some data indicating that over 80 per cent of Brunei's citizens are Muslim. In Brunei's complex social mix, seven ethnic groups are entitled to citizenship by law: Brunei, Kedayan, Tutong, Dusun, Bisaya, Belait and Murut. A small number of others, mostly Chinese, have also been granted citizenship. Statistics collected in the 1980s showed that around 7 per cent of the indigenous groups – mostly Dusun, Bisaya and Murut – were not Muslim; neither were most Chinese (Kershaw 2001: 9–10).

The picture is different, however, if residents rather than citizens are the focus. Around a quarter of Brunei's 365,000 inhabitants are temporary residents, foreigners who supplement the labour force by supplying professional and skilled labour; only a minority of these are Muslims. A census in 1991 found that just over two-thirds of all Brunei residents were Muslim, followed by 13 per cent Buddhist, 10 per cent Christian and 10 per cent other religions (Md Zain 1998: 64).

HISTORY

Brunei's ruler adopted the title of Sultan in the fourteenth century, and since then Islam has been an integral part of Brunei identity. This was followed by a golden

---

* I am grateful for the comments of Dr Iik Arifin Mansurnoor.

age around the end of the fifteenth century when Bruneian influence covered most of Borneo and several surrounding islands. By the late nineteenth century Brunei had lost most of its territory to European encroachments, and in 1906 the remainder came under British rule as a protectorate (headed by a British 'resident').

Under a system similar to that in Malaysia, Islamic affairs remained, theoretically, in the hands of the royal family and Muslim officials. In practice, however, British intervention was extensive, and most apparent in the area of Muslim family law. First introduced in 1906, these laws went through various manifestations and amendments until ratified by the State Council as the Mohammedan Marriage and Divorce Registration Enactment No. 3 1913 (Iik Arifin 1996: 52–3).

Islam adapted gradually to regional change during the colonial era, but without the divisions and clashes found elsewhere between reformists (the Kaum Muda, or Young Group) and conservatives (the Kaum Tua, or Old Group). The absence of conflict within Bruneian Islam has puzzled historians. Among the likely reasons are the slow development of urbanization (Islamic reformism has usually been strongest in urban areas), remoteness from centres of Islamic reform in the Middle East, South Asia and even Southeast Asia, and royal support for religious harmony (Iik Arifin 1996: 51–2).

As Brunei moved towards self-rule it began to give Islam a major focus in national affairs. The 1959 Constitution affirms that the sultan is the head of Islamic affairs and decrees that:

> The religion of Brunei Darussalam shall be the Muslim religion according to the Shafe-ite [Shafi'i] sect of that religion: Provided that all other religions may be practised in peace and harmony by the person professing them in any part of Brunei Darussalam.

The Proclamation of Independence on the attainment of full independence on 1 January 1984 included the following:

> ... Brunei Darussalam is and with the blessing of Allah (to whom be praise and whose name be exalted) shall be for ever a sovereign, democratic and independent Malay Muslim Monarchy [founded] upon the teachings of Islam according to Ahlis Sunnah Waljamaah ...[1]

ADMINISTRATION OF ISLAM

Islamic affairs in Brunei are closely controlled by the Ministry of Religious Affairs, headed by a minister and deputy minister since 1986. In earlier manifestations under the British, it was the Office of Traditions, Religion and Welfare (Pejabat Adat Istiadat, Ugama dan Kebajikan) in 1954 and the Department of Islamic Affairs (Jabatan Hal Ewhal Ugama) in 1960. At independence Islamic affairs came under the Office of the Prime Minister before becoming a full ministry. The ministry is divided

---

1 'Proclamation of Independence Brunei Darussalam', <http://www.brunei.gov.bn/government/mjty_ speech.htm>, accessed 29 March 2005. Ahli Sunnah Wal-Jammah is the majority Sunni branch within Islam (see glossary).

into several departments responsible for Islamic law (sharia), sharia courts, mosque affairs and a missionary centre (Pusat Dakwah Islamiah) among other matters.[2]

The ministry has a wide range of responsibilities. It advises the government on all matters related to Islamic affairs. It also organizes all major Islamic functions, including various Islamic festivities and annual Qur'an-reading competitions, and supervises mosques. It organizes the annual pilgrimage to Mecca (the haj) at subsidized rates. The office of the Mufti occupies a prominent position and his religious rulings (fatwa) have great influence. The sharia courts, in charge of personal and property law and offences against Islam, were given expanded authority in 2001, part of a process of 'transforming the administration of courts and the legal system into an Islamic system' (Mohamad Yusop 2002: 89). The sermons read in mosques every Friday are provided by the ministry. It previously supervised Brunei's many Islamic schools, until the Education Ministry assumed this responsibility in 2001.

The ministry also conducts an active Islamic outreach (*dakwah*) program. While this is mainly focused on making Muslims better Muslims, outreach to non-Muslims is also important. Between January and July 2000, 300 conversions were reported, making a total of around 10,000 over 30 years (Horton 2001: 105).

THE NATURE OF BRUNEIAN ISLAM

Islam provides a unifying experience for its Brunei followers. As Kershaw (2001: 11) notes, 'Much time is taken up with activities centred on the mosque, or State-sponsored Koran-reading competitions and celebrations of religious feast-days'. As in neighbouring countries, Bruneian Islam is mostly moderate, allowing women to occupy senior positions in public life, for instance. It remains extremely liberal in some areas. For example, a range of international television programs is available on relay to virtually all Bruneians, and a London rock-music radio station is transmitted locally.

Nevertheless, there has been a gradual strengthening of Islamic influence since independence. The influence of the *dakwah* movement has led to women adopting more Islamic dress in the workplace – covering all but the face and hands. (At social events, however, women often will not dress so conservatively.) Sharia has been strengthened in an attempt to address a range of social problems among youth, particularly drug usage. The availability of alcohol was restricted at independence, but it could still be purchased in bottle shops or private clubs, and at various times was available on the state-run Royal Brunei Airlines. By the 1990s such exemptions had been removed.

The government has also increasingly promoted the official MIB ideology – upholding the Malay and Islamic identity of the country (*Melayu, Islam*) and the importance of monarchy (*Beraja*). This started slowly after independence, but the ideology is now taught in schools and is a subject of instruction and research at Brunei Darussalam University. Following many articles and speeches, a book-length

---

2   See details at <http://www.religious-affairs.gov.bn/jabatan/jabatan.htm>, accessed 29 March 2005.

account finally appeared in 1998 (Md Zain 1998). Kershaw (2001: 26) notes that 'its predominant content is theological, as befits the author who is Minister for Religious Affairs, and its overall coherence derives more from theology, and Middle Eastern history, than from insights into Brunei's own past'.

Islam has arguably become the most prominent component of the tripartite ideology, although there has been no shortage of accounts stressing its compatibility with monarchy and Malay identity (Braighlinn 1992). The current sultan and head of state, Haji Hassanal Bolkiah Mu'izzaddin Waddaulah, takes his role as Islamic leader seriously. While often portrayed in colourful terms by the Western media, in Brunei he is widely perceived as embodying the virtues of a caring ruler (see plate 3 in the colour section of this book). (The lifestyles of other members of the royal family are sometimes quietly faulted.) Since making the haj for the first time in 1987 – returning to rapturous public applause – he has undertaken the pilgrimage almost annually.

As stipulated in the constitution, non-Muslims are allowed to practise their own religions. They are not permitted to proselytize among Muslims, however. Bruneians take this prohibition seriously; in 2000 and 2001 at least seven Christians were detained on such grounds under the Internal Security Act, which permits detention without trial (Kershaw 2003: 50; US State Department 2001). Religious leaders often perceive a potential Christian threat to the sultanate, and are also strongly 'anti-West', notwithstanding the government's pro-Western stance on most foreign policy issues (Kershaw 2003: 50).

Islam in Brunei is as much influenced by the supernatural as elsewhere in the region, reflected, for example, in a belief in ghosts (*hantu*) and the powers of spirit mediums (*bomoh*).[3] In other respects, the Ministry of Religious Affairs closely guards against what it sees as 'deviationism' from the Shafi'i school (Ahli Sunnah Wal-Jammah) of jurisprudence and theology. It banned the Malaysian organization Darul Arqam in 1991 (Iik Arifin 2002: 82) and detained six people under the Internal Security Act in September 2003 after an alleged attempt to revive it (Mohamad Yusop 2004: 8).

Islam has assumed a different political form in Brunei to that in neighbouring countries. It has, of course, been used to help legitimize the government, in particular through the MIB ideology. Individual cabinet members stand out for their enthusiastic support of Islamic causes, most notably the former minister of education, Pehin Dato Haji Abdul Aziz Umar. Unlike in other Southeast Asian countries, however, the mobilization of Islam for oppositional politics has made no headway in Brunei. Although the government did take some steps towards reducing royal absolutism in 2004 (including reinstating an appointed Legislative Council), the MIB ideology has not encouraged the emergence of an Islamic movement in potential conflict with the monarchy. Perhaps as a consequence, there has also been no sign of extremist Muslim organizations establishing a foothold in Brunei.

---

3   Details about the introduction of Sufi orders to Brunei are given in Iik Arifin (2005: 52, 56–8).

3   Burma (Myanmar)

Curtis Lambrecht*

Muslims in Burma are dispersed geographically and are highly diverse in ethnicity, religious practice, socio-economic background, and social and political integration. Historically, Muslims have often been the targets of communal violence, and many live a tenuous existence, especially under the military government that has ruled since 1962. With the exception of the Rohingya, Burma's Muslim communities have not generally mobilized politically along religious or ethnic lines.

THE ISLAMIC PEOPLES OF BURMA

Estimates suggest that Muslims constitute approximately 4 per cent of Burma's 50 million people.[1] These Muslim communities can broadly be categorized into four groups: the Rohingya, the Panthay, the Malay (Pashu) and the ethnically diverse immigrant communities from Bangladesh, India and Pakistan (Figure 3.1). A fifth group, often of mixed religious and ethnic heritage, designate themselves Burmese-Muslims or Zerbadee.[2]

Islam reached Burma through Muslim seamen as early as the eighth century. In subsequent centuries, Arab, Persian and Indian Muslim traders settled in coastal trading towns (Arasaratnam 1989). Muslims also served as mercenaries and administrators to Burmese kings. Beginning in the sixteenth century, Burmese kings settled Muslim prisoners, refugees and soldiers in central Burma, dispersing them to prevent a united rebellion against the kingdom. The descendants of these people retain their Islamic faith but are otherwise largely assimilated into their Burmese surroundings.

Chinese Muslims, referred to as the Panthay, arrived in Burma as early as the thirteenth century, and in greatest numbers in the late nineteenth century following the Ch'ing government's crushing of an Islamic sultanate in Yunnan. Intermarriage

*   I am heavily indebted to Mohd Mohiyuddin Mohd Sulaiman for his advice and assistance in gathering information. I also wish to thank Project Maje and Andrew Selth for providing important primary source materials. Errors and omissions are mine alone.

1   This figure is based on the 1983 census. Although the military government's census is notoriously inaccurate and politicized, this figure appears to be consistent with earlier sources (Yegar 1972, 2002).
2   The Kaman, a small Muslim population residing in Arakan, Bangladesh and India, could arguably be categorized as a sixth group.

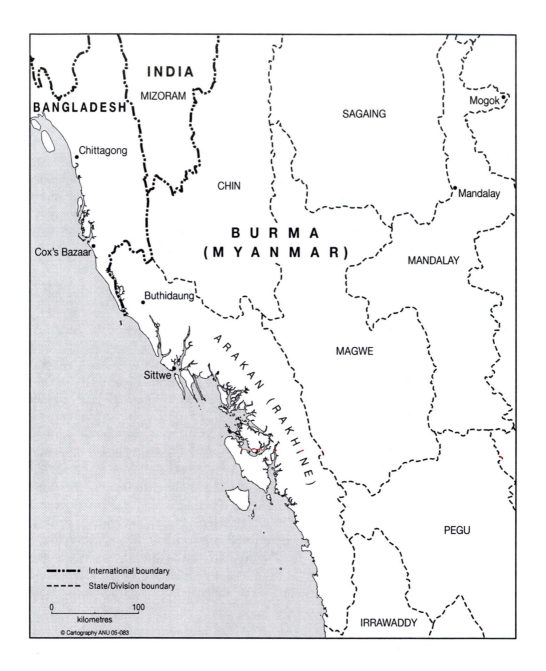

Figure 3.1   The Major Muslim Communities of Burma

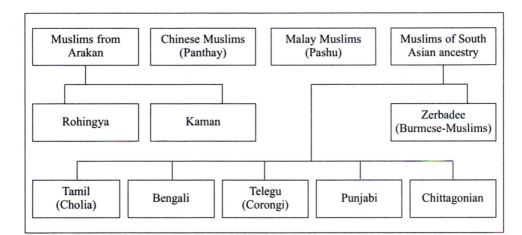

between Panthay and Burmese is reportedly common. The Panthay live predominantly in northeast Burma, although small communities also exist in Mandalay, Rangoon and Mogok (Yegar 1966).

The Rohingya probably first migrated eastward to Burma in the fifteenth century when a nominally Muslim kingdom ruled an empire that at its ascendancy stretched from Dacca and the Sundarbans to Moulmein. Today the Rohingya reside predominantly in southwest Burma in Arakan (Rakhine) state, and are most heavily concentrated in that state's three northernmost districts. Sizeable numbers of Rohingya also reside in Rangoon and other urban areas. The 1983 census recorded the presence of almost 500,000 'Bangladeshi' in Arakan; many of those so identified probably consider themselves to be Rohingya. The Rohingya language is similar to the Bengali dialect Chittagonian; it does not have a written form. Frequent army-conducted 'immigration verification' campaigns have made the Rohingya a diaspora community. Rohingya dissident groups claim a population of 2 million in Burma and 1.5 million in other countries, including Thailand, Bangladesh, Malaysia, Pakistan, Saudi Arabia, Jordan, the United Arab Emirates and Qatar (Yegar 2002).

Approximately two-thirds of Muslims in Burma are descendants of South Asians of various ethnicities who migrated to Burma under British colonial rule. They comprise a diversity of ethno-linguistic groups; many retain their ethnic identities (Chakravarti 1971).

A fifth group, who designate themselves Burmese-Muslims, have sought to assimilate themselves culturally and linguistically. Such persons are often of mixed South Asian and Burmese (Burman, Shan, Kachin) ancestry.[3] Muslims of mixed ancestry are generally regarded as 'half-breeds' (*kabya*) and ostracized by both South Asian and Burmese communities.

---

3   The Burman are Burma's largest ethnic group, said to comprise 50 per cent or more of the population.

ISLAM AND THE STATE

The Burmese government has progressively marginalized Burma's Muslims. Although some of Burma's most prominent early nationalists were Muslim, anti-Muslim sentiment within Burmese nationalism coalesced in opposition to the economic prominence enjoyed by South Asians under colonial administration, their massive and rapid immigration, and their intermarriage with Buddhists. These tensions were rooted in Burmese conceptions of ethnic and racial difference (and thus were felt also towards Hindu immigrants) as well as religious differences, particularly between Muslim and Buddhist marriage laws. Popular resentment towards immigrant communities was captured in a line from a popular Burmese song: 'Exploiting our economic resources and seizing our women, we are in danger of racial extinction' (cited in Khin Yi 1988: 97).

Since 1962, the military government has attempted to rally the populace around narrow racist and Buddhist conceptions of the nation and to evoke and manipulate fears of foreign domination and the impending dissolution of the state. Of all Burma's diverse ethnic and religious minorities to suffer as a result of this process, Muslims have probably been the most affected. Between 1963 and 1967 some 300,000 Indians, most of them Muslim, fled Burma after the military nationalized private business (Yegar 2002). Many Muslims are now denied any form of citizenship by a 1982 law that accords full citizenship only to the 'national races' (that is, those the government regards as indigenous) and others who can document their direct descent from ancestors resident in Burma before the first Anglo-Burmese war in 1823.[4] Only full citizens are permitted to work in the civil service and run for political office.

Anti-Muslim sentiment is widespread and often vitriolic. This is reflected in and instigated by xenophobic government propaganda, which has proliferated. In 1989, for example, *New Light of Myanmar*, a government-run newspaper, ran a series of 15 articles entitled 'In Fear Our Race May Become Extinct', authored under the pseudonym Myo Chit Thu (literally, 'patriot' or 'one who loves his race'). These articles recount the various ways in which the 'foreign' Indian, Pakistani and Chinese races have historically exploited the Burmese. Chief among their crimes has been marriage to 'Burmese girls', creating 'mixed blood in our country'. One article concludes with the exhortation 'to love our race … and keep the spirit of nationalism alive to prevent our race from being swallowed up by others' (20 February 1989). Although Islam is never specifically mentioned, Buddhism has long been synonymous with Burmese nationalism, and government propaganda elsewhere presents other religions as alien. Nominally illegal literature that is circulated discreetly is explicitly anti-Muslim, presenting stories about Muslim men exploiting and sexually abusing young Burmese girls. In light of strict censorship laws and the relatively wide circulation of such material, many believe that the government condones or even publishes this literature (Human Rights Watch 2002).

4　Although the U Nu administration (1949–58, 1960–62) recognized the Rohingya as one of the national races in 1961, this status was revoked under military rule (Jilani 1999).

In the past two decades, violence between Muslim and Buddhist communities has erupted regularly in isolated incidents across the country. In many instances it appears that the government instigates or condones this violence in order to divert attention from the nation's economic and political problems. The military authorities have also attempted to mobilize support domestically and abroad by claiming that Muslim terrorists and separatists are active in Burma. For example, in one publication the junta justified its refusal to honour the 1990 elections on the grounds that Muslims living in Rangoon were plotting to declare independence for northern Arakan (Nawrahta 1995).

Rohingya groups have long accused the government and Buddhist Rakhine of ethnic cleansing and even genocide (Yunus 1995; RPF 1976).[5] Periodic military operations in northern Arakan have led to the repeated flight of Rohingya into Bangladesh, most dramatically in 1978 when 200,000 fled Burma, and in 1992 when 300,000 fled (Yunus 1994). There are frequent and credible reports of Burmese authorities continuing to persecute Muslim communities, particularly in the border regions, and of government authorities or their Rakhine proxies demolishing mosques and Muslim cemeteries and confiscating the religious lands (Ar.: *waqfun*) on which they stand, in some cases to build pagodas (Amnesty International 1992; Human Rights Watch 2002). The construction of new mosques is strictly prohibited.

ISLAM AND INSURGENCY

Of Burma's various Islamic-based insurgencies, those of the Rohingya have been the most significant.[6] Like many Burmese insurgencies, the Rohingya uprisings have been distinctly ethnic in character. The Rohingya have long demanded ethnic rights and territorial autonomy in addition to Islamic rights. They have recruited exclusively among Rohingya populations in Arakan. They have made no effort to represent or advocate on behalf of other Burmese Muslim communities.[7] Like many other Burmese insurgency groups, Rohingya insurgent movements have been fissiparous. Rohingya factionalism is probably due to the military's highly repressive counter-insurgency strategies, the poverty of northern Arakan, the lack of domestic financial support for the insurgents and personality differences among leaders.

Rohingya insurgency began in April 1948, when Muslim scholars (*moulvi*)[8] in Buthidaung called for struggle (jihad) against Arakan 'infidels'. The army quelled the movement in 1954 (Yegar 1972, 2002). In 1964 students at Rangoon University formed the Rohingya Independence Force (RIF), which subsequently formed an

---

5 The Rakhine are an ethnic minority predominant in the state of Arakan (Rakhine).

6 For a brief description of other Muslim insurgencies, see Selth (2003).

7 However, Rohingya insurgents have been coalition members in broader democratic fronts (Smith 1991).

8 *Moulvi* is derived from the Arabic term *mullah*, or 'knowledgeable one', and refers to a religious leader who has completed eight or more years of tertiary study on Islamic doctrine.

alliance with the Mujahid Muslim National Liberation Party.[9] In 1973 the RIF was amalgamated with disparate armed Muslim groups and re-formed as the Rohingya Patriotic Front (RPF) under the leadership of Mohammad Jafar Habib (also known as A.B. Jafar).

In 1978 discontent with the RPF leadership prompted the departure of many senior members. These included Nurul Islam and Mohammad Yunus, who formed the Rohingya Solidarity Organisation (RSO) in 1982 (Jilani 1999). The two leaders have split and reunited several times, forming the Arakan Rohingya Islamic Front (ARIF) in 1987, the Rohingya National Alliance in 1995 and the Arakan Rohingya National Organisation (ARNO) in 1998. In 2000, ARNO split into ARIF under Nurul Islam and two RSO factions led respectively by Mohammad Yunus and Mohammad Zakaria (Selth 2003). In the past decade, Rohingya military operations have been limited.[10]

Rohingya insurgencies have received varying degrees of financial support from the diaspora community. The insurgents have been based almost exclusively in Bangladesh. RSO factions are alleged to have links with radical Islamic groups such as the Bangladesh-based Jamaat-e-Islami, Harakat-ul-Jihad-ul-Islami and Islami Chhatra Shibir, and Kashmir/Pakistan organizations such as Harakut-ul-Mujahideen.[11] On at least one occasion an RSO representative attended a meeting organized by Abu Bakar Ba'asyir, the head of Jemaah Islamiyah, to establish an international *mujahidin* association; Nurul Islam, also present at this meeting, reportedly expressed opposition to the use of violence (ICG 2002a). In 2001 Osama bin Laden claimed to have operatives in Burma, and there are reports that approximately 100 Rohingya were trained in Afghanistan by that country's radical Hizb-e-Islami (Islamic Party) *mujahidin* group (Lintner 2002a, 2002b). However, many of these operatives were drawn from exiled Rohingya in Pakistan who may never have been to Burma.

ISLAMIC FAITH AND PRACTICE

Although restricted in various ways by the military government, Islamic religious practice is active and diverse.[12] According to one source, there are 2,620 mosques in Burma.[13] Islamic schools (*madrasah*) throughout the country serve as the primary source of Islamic education, which is apolitical and limited to matters of faith (see colour plate 8). The government has made no effort to integrate the *madrasah* into the national education system. Over 400 Islamic organizations operate throughout the country, the majority of them not registered. The government limits official per-

---

9   By the early 1970s, supplied with abundant arms from Bangladesh's war of liberation, the *mujahid* movement was second in strength only to the Arakan branch of the Communist Party of Burma (Smith 1991; Jilani 1999).

10   But see an appraisal by Leider (2005: 125–38).

11   These connections are summarized in Selth (2004).

12   This section draws heavily on Sulaiman (2003).

13   See Min Naing (2003: 23), who cites 'Tha Thana Yaung Htun Pyoung Se Hpoe' [Shine the Bright Light of Religion] by the Ministry of Defense (n.d.: 73).

mission for Muslims to make the haj holy pilgrimage (Human Rights Watch 2002). However, exit visas are often arranged on false pretences, and pilgrims must in any event apply for a Saudi visa in a third country as the Kingdom of Saudi Arabia does not maintain an embassy in Burma.

A Burmese translation of the Qur'an is published by the Dawah Academy of the International Islamic University in Islamabad and distributed in Burma through the Pakistan embassy. The scope of Islamic literature is otherwise focused on explicating the basic tenets of the faith and the life of the Prophet Muhammad. Few if any books are available inside Burma on more sensitive issues such as the application of Islamic law (sharia), the founding of an Islamic state or militant jihad. The only openly active Islamic missionary group is the India-centred Tablighi Jama'at, which attempts to instil greater piety in Muslims; it does not proselytize to non-Muslims. There does not appear to be any sustained movement to implement sharia in Burma.

Many of Burma's mosques and Islamic organizations reflect the South Asian ethnicities of the communities they serve. For example, Islamic teachers (ulema) of South Asian descent often teach in Urdu and dress in an Indian manner. Similarly, community names such as Soorti and Cholia are adopted as mosque names. Such organizations do not, however, seek to exclude Muslims of other ethnic origins.

In contrast, the Islamic Religious Affairs Council (IRAC), Islamic Council of Myanmar (ICM) and Myanmar Muslim Organization have advocated a 'modern Myanmar Islam' and sought to extricate Indian cultural influences from their practice of Islam. For example, IRAC downplays the role of the *moulvi* and the *madrasah*. An IRAC-founded *jam'iyyat* (congress of religious elders) conducts annual religious examinations for aspiring religious officials. The ICM advocates that Burmese be used as the medium of communication in all religious matters, including the delivery of sermons, and publishes Islamic materials in Burmese only.

Sunni Islam is predominant, although there are small numbers of Shi'ites in Burma. Within the Sunni majority, there is significant variation in the interpretation of Islamic doctrine. Many urban-educated Muslims, for example, follow a liberal interpretation of Islam on contemporary matters such as jihad, women's rights and religious customs and practice (Sandar Chit 2003).

In contrast to many other Burmese minorities, Burma's diverse Muslim populations are inadequately researched and poorly understood. Little is known about the culture, religious practices and social and economic integration of contemporary Burmese Muslims. Of the existent contemporary research, most is focused on documenting human rights atrocities committed against the Rohingya or investigating Rohingya links with broader Islamic terrorist networks.[14] Little is known about the welfare of other Muslim groups in Burma, and despite much conjecture about Rohingya insurgents' links with terrorist organizations, we still know little about the insurgencies' organization, social bases or ideological orientation. It is clear, however, that Burma's Muslims are only tenuously integrated into Burmese society and that they have often been the targets of hostility and violence. Unfortunately these problems are likely to persist.

---

14   Moshe Yegar's work is the notable exception (see Yegar 1966, 1972, 2002).

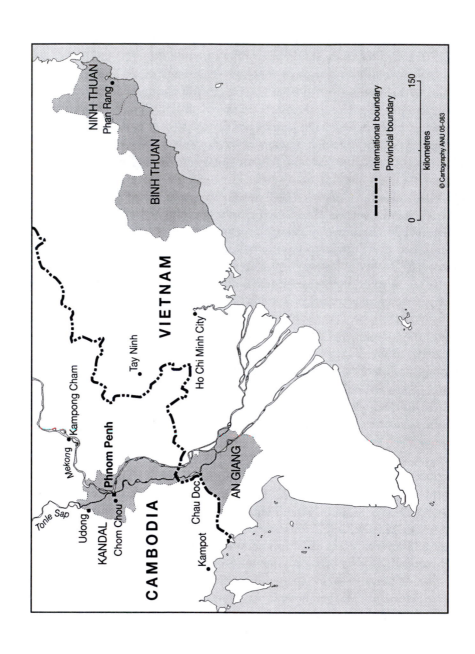

4   Cambodia and Vietnam

Jacob Ramsay

INTRODUCTION

Islam in southern Vietnam and Cambodia has possibly the oldest textual history of all Muslim communities in Southeast Asia. Originating from the now defunct kingdom known collectively as Champa, which stretched from present-day Quảng Bình province in central Vietnam south to Bình Thuận province just north of Ho Chi Minh City, this region's Muslim communities claim one of Southeast Asia's oldest Kufic inscriptions, dated 1035 CE (Ravaisse 1922: 247–89). While some have viewed the quality of this text as a reflection of the 'dismal level of literacy' of the author and audience of early Cham Muslims (Ali 1991: 127), and despite the pressures exerted by ethnic Viet settlement throughout this region from the fifteenth century, Islamic culture has flourished here in a variety of communities and forms ever since.

Islam is officially recognized by both the Socialist Republic of Vietnam and the Kingdom of Cambodia, although as a religion associated with the Cham ethnic minority. In Vietnam as in Cambodia the great majority of Muslims are ethnic Cham, although there are small communities of ethnic Khmer and Malay Muslims as well. Population figures are difficult to come by but recent estimates suggest that the total Muslim community is less than 65,000 in Vietnam and around 700,000 for Cambodia. There is also a small community of approximately 400 Muslims in the Lao People's Democratic Republic, a small number of whom are Cham but most of whom are foreign residents.[1] In Vietnam Muslims represent less than 1 per cent of the population, which is predominantly Buddhist (about 52 per cent) and Catholic (about 8–10 per cent). In Cambodia, by contrast, Muslims represent over 5 per cent of a population widely renowned for the prominence of Theravada Buddhism. While Cambodia's Muslims have increased their political profile over the last decade and achieved some representation in the national parliament, the Muslim minority in Vietnam is still very much treated as a marginalized community subject to national policies of ethnic integration.

---

1   These estimates are from the US State Department (2004). Other recent estimates for Cambodia place the community at around half a million (Dovert and Madinier 2003: 69). The Muslim community in Vietnam is also dispersed in small pockets throughout Phan Rang and the Mekong delta.

Apart from the political issues faced by religious groups under Communist Party rule in Vietnam, the lack of statistical data stems from the fact that Islam is represented by several quite distinct communities – both indigenous ethnic Cham and migrant communities from the Malay world – that have dispersed due to conflict, migration and sectarian differences.

COMMUNITIES

The Muslim Cham in the southern coastal areas of Bình Thuận and Ninh Thuận provinces are the oldest continuous Islamic group in the region and one of the socio-cultural sources of other Muslim communities in the Mekong delta and Cambodia. They are known as the Bani Cham and practise a localized – and somewhat unorthodox – form of Islam focused on the observance of local kingship and indigenous spirit cults shared by the Hindu Cham Balômon community also living in this region.[2] The Bani are led by an ordained priestly group, the Halau Tamumay Awar, which is composed of six ranks and has a rotating leadership decided each year after Ramuwan (Ramadan) (Nakamura 2000: 56). The priests are also responsible for fasting for three days at the beginning of the Ramadan month on behalf of the wider community, and stay at the mosque, or *thang muki*, for the entire 30 days of Ramadan. Only the priests fast during Ramadan, and only for three days. Bani society, as with the wider Cham community around Phan Rang, is organized matrilineally and women are responsible for key religious observances. The Bani do not pray five times daily; rather, they pray communally once a week. On Fridays, after prayers, a young girl from each household brings a food offering to the mosque. At prayers, men recite only after the women; during certain ceremonies, such as funerals, secular female leaders, known as *muh poh*, assist the priests (Nakamura 2000: 56). The 'unorthodox' nature of Bani Islam is believed to be the result of the interaction between indigenous cultural practice and exposure to Shi'a influence in early times, perhaps coinciding with the arrival of the eleventh-century Kufic inscriptions brought by Persian or Indian merchants travelling to the region (Ner 1941; Collins 1996: 52; Nakamura 2000: 57–9).

The Cham Muslim community further south, from Ho Chi Minh City west to Tay Ninh and the Mekong province of An Giang, adheres to Sunni Islam and follows the Shafi'i school. This community migrated from the Bình Thuận area following the political strife and conflict accompanying the Vietnamese expansion from the fifteenth century. It currently numbers around 20,000 people, concentrated around the river city of Châu Đốc on the Cambodian border (Nakamura 2000: 55). It is believed the Cham here converted to Sunni Islam following intense contact with traders and teachers from the Malay archipelago. Today they maintain strong networks within this milieu. (See colour plate 2 for an example of local mosque architecture.)

As a result of migration and the cumulative effects of conflict, trade and travel, the Cham Muslim community has spread across the Mekong delta and into Cambo-

---

2   See Nakamura (1999) for a detailed ethnographic discussion of the Phan Rang Cham.

dia where several branches have formed. In his discussion of Cambodia's Muslims, Collins (1996) identifies three main categories, the Jahed, the Cham and the Chvea, reflecting both ethnic and sectarian differences.[3]

The Jahed represent the oldest link with Muslims from the Phan Rang area. 'Jahed', from the Arabic word *zaahidun* (meaning pious, devout) is a reference to this community's devotion to traditional Cham-Islamic practices informed by mystical Sufi teachings. The group defines its identity according to its historical roots in Champa and its adherence to Cham religious texts (in Cham script). It is understood that this community fled south and west from the defunct kingdom of Panduranga – now modern-day Bình Thuận and Ninh Thuận provinces in Vietnam – after the Nguyễn lords subjugated the region in 1692, and settled around Udong, Phnom Penh and Kampong Cham; today it numbers around 23,000 people and constitutes only about 10 per cent of Cambodia's Muslims (Trankell 2003: 33). The Jahed adhere to the Shi'a-influenced Islam of their Bani relatives in Phan Rang, which in its localized form was inspired by the nineteenth-century leader Prah Meng Sen (or Imam San) whose grave on Chetrya mountain in Udong is the focal point of the cult of the *cay* or kingship spirits originating from Panduranga (Trankell 2003: 33–4; Dovert and Madinier 2003: 75).

The largest group, which constitutes over 80 per cent of Muslims in Cambodia, identifies itself simply as 'Cham', in reference to its ethnic ties with Champa. The Cham share the same refugee past as the Jahed but – like the smaller Chvea community composed of Muslims of Malay and Javanese descent – follow Sunni practices (Collins 1996: 44). This community might be described as reformist in terms of its turning away from more traditional Bani practices in order to embrace the more orthodox Sunni Islam introduced in recent decades by missionaries from Malaysia and the Middle East. Its members use both Malay and Arabic texts for religious instruction and speak both Cham and Khmer.

The distinction between the Cham and the Chvea (from the Khmer word for 'Java') is blurred on account of their shared religious practices, but the Chvea speak only Khmer. In fact, the Chvea refer to themselves as 'Khmer Islam' in reference to their assimilation into Cambodian society. The Chvea constitute a minority but are still an important community. Focused around the coastal town of Kampot, the community originated in Java and the Malay archipelago. Like Cham communities in the neighbouring Mekong delta provinces, the Chvea practise the Shafi'i school of Sunni Islam. They maintain strong ties with its religious texts and with Malay Muslims.

Apart from the 'indigenous' Cham and Khmer Muslims spread across the region, the major cities of Hanoi, Ho Chi Minh City and Phnom Penh have long supported vibrant migrant communities from Indonesia, Malaysia and India. According to a website on 'Vietnamese Muslims' (Le 2002), there are around 50 mosques in Ho Chi Minh City alone, many of which support migrant groups from Indonesia, India and the Middle East. While these communities burgeoned during the French colonial era (1862–1954), regime change in north Vietnam and subsequent conflict in the south and in Cambodia under the Khmer Rouge all but led to their disappearance.

---

3   The following discussion draws predominantly on Collins (1996: 44–60).

RECENT HISTORY

From the 1960s to the 1980s, Cambodia was the location of the most tumultuous changes to the region's Islamic community. Communist hostility to the Cham arose at first in response to agitation for the re-establishment of a Cham kingdom – on Vietnamese territory – by Cham leaders, including Muslims.[4] This was a particularly active period for secessionist groups, composed predominantly of ethnic minorities from Vietnam's central highlands. Although the Cham organized in 1962 under the banner of the Front for the Liberation of Champa, several years later, under the direction of Les Kosem, a Cambodian Cham, it merged with the umbrella group Front Unifié de Lutte des Races Opprimées (FULRO, United Struggle Front of the Oppressed Races).[5] Active throughout the 1960s, such groups gained considerable support under the Lon Nol regime in Cambodia (1970–75), and as a consequence suffered the full force of political persecution under the Khmer Rouge (1975–79). Estimates of the number of Cham (both Muslim and non-Muslim) killed in the genocide vary greatly, but the most widely accepted figure is that of Ben Kiernan – around 90,000 victims, or just under one-tenth of the more than 1 million who perished under the regime (Kiernan 1985: 30).[6] While FULRO agitated with its allied groups within the broader context of political secessionism, Cham and Khmer Muslims responded with particular hostility to the atheistic ideology of communism.

This combination of Cham secessionism based on historical grievance and resistance to the religious threat posed by the communist movement in Vietnam, Cambodia and Laos is captured in a tract, *The Martyrdom of Khmers [sic] Muslims*. According to Collins (1996), this was published on the occasion of Cambodian participation in the First Congress of the Afro-Asian Islamic Organization, held in Bandung, Indonesia, in October 1970. The tract states:

> [T]he previous regime [of Norodom Sihanouk (1953–70)] in order to realize its objectives of eradicating the practice of all religions, had collaborated with the anti-religious invading groups, namely the Vietcong/North Vietnamese and Pathet Lao, and having noted that with the collaboration and connivance of the former regime with the Vietcong/North Vietnamese and Pathet Lao, the Cambodian Muslims and their mosques were not protected but allowed and exposed to be destroyed and oppressed by the enemies of Islam ... (Khmer Republic 1974: 7, quoted in Collins 1996: 33).

The threat is expressed in the following passage on Vietnamese expansion, which demonstrates the potent mix of ethno-nationalism and religious identity that defined Cham activism in the prelude to the Pol Pot era.

> CHAMPA was annexed by the conquering Vietnamese. The Chams that remained became Muslims in a massive, historic conversion. The present-day Chams are in

---

4 Sadly, Cham and Muslim history in Vietnam for this period is not well documented.
5 For a detailed discussion of FULRO's history and political connections in Cambodia and Vietnam, see Hickey (1982). See also Scupin (1995: 315–20) for further analysis of Cham ethno-nationalism.
6 Kiernan also provides one of the most detailed discussions of the Cham during the political turmoil of the 1970s under the Lon Nol and Pol Pot regimes.

physical danger of extinction. The Vietcong policy is to exterminate as many of them as possible and to 'Vietnamize' the few who remain. The Vietcong's plan has three stages: genocide, de-Islamization and intensive conversion to communism (Khmer Republic 1974: 15, quoted in Collins 1996: 34).

As Collins highlights, there are widely varying interpretations as to whether the Muslim Cham were targeted specifically on account of their ethnicity and religious beliefs during the genocide perpetrated under Pol Pot in the Democratic Kampuchea era (Collins 1996: 34). Available research documents the massacre of whole villages in some provinces; Chanda, for example, claims that 'over sixty thousand Cham minority people – mostly in the Kampong Cham area – were massacred for their Islamic faith' (Chanda 1986: 250, quoted in Collins 1996: 37). However, Vickery (1986: 2) argues compellingly that no specific policy led to this devastation and that the suffering of the Muslims and the Cham was similar in severity to that of the rest of Khmer society.

CONTEMPORARY DEVELOPMENTS

Over the last decade, the United Nations-supervised resolution of conflict in Cambodia and socio-economic reforms in Vietnam have seen a dramatic improvement in the fortunes of the region's Muslim communities. While little has changed for the Bani community in Phan Rang in terms of economic development, new contacts with Islamic charitable and religious organizations from Malaysia and the Middle East have led to an Islamic revival in Sunni communities in Ho Chi Minh City in Vietnam and the Mekong delta in Cambodia. Similar developments have seen the reconstitution of political representation in Cambodia.

In 1994, Ahmad Yahya helped found the Khmer Islamic Association, which has since acted as a political voice for both Islamic issues and human rights in Cambodia. The association was established to fund scholarships for Muslim students to attend Norton University, the largest private university in Phnom Penh (Dovert and Madinier 2003: 72). Yahya, who fled to the United States in the 1970s, has consistently been involved in national politics since 1993 and is currently serving as a member of parliament under the opposition leader Sam Rainsy. In March 2004, he successfully negotiated the first weekly Cham-language radio broadcast on Radio Free Asia. This represented a coup for the Cham community considering the tight controls over media broadcasting under the Hun Sen government and the Cham population's position in general as an economically deprived community. Another Cham Muslim, Tol Lah, served as minister of education and co-deputy prime minister from November 1998 until his death in April 2004.

The Kuwait-based Revival of Islamic Heritage Society (RIHS) has had a particularly active role in funding the construction of mosques and schools in Cambodia, and in sponsoring a number of students to undertake the haj each year. Spearheading the renovation of the Cambodian Islamic community, this organization vigorously promotes the strengthening of 'orthodox' values through its outreach activities across the country. The main centre of the RIHS is in Chom Chou, near Phnom

Penh, and is directed by a Cham, Mohammed Youssef Sosbohamath (or Sos Moha-mat) (Dovert and Madinier 2003: 74). The school employs teachers from across the Muslim world, from Yemen to Thailand, and each year sends a number of students abroad to study in other centres.

The recent proliferation in Cambodia of religious and educational programs sup-ported by foreign Islamic organizations has been the source of some tension between communities and has caused concern for the government. According to Dovert and Madinier (2003), since the early 1990s a number of communities around Phnom Penh have received the sustained attention of missionaries promoting a return to orthodox Sunni values and practices through the concept of *dakwah*, which is char-acterized by peaceful proselytization of orthodox values. Some communities, such as Phum Trear village in Kampong Cham province north of Phnom Penh, have bene-fited greatly from the inflow of funds from overseas donors. However, the practice of two quite different interpretations of the faith, often within the same or neighbouring communities – not to mention suspicion and the attribution of terrorist links among the mission ranks by local leaders – has seen a rise in community tensions and also increased government surveillance. For example, Hunt (2004) reports that villagers in Phum Trear have expressed concern at rumours that missionaries seek out orphans to send overseas to Islamic schools (*madrasah*). But more substantial is the concern that increased mission activity has raised the Cham Muslim profile with the state and led to increased police visits to communities (Hunt 2004). Notwithstanding the pressures of reconciling traditional and orthodox views, community leaders and dig-nitaries adhere to a middle ground by expressing a preference for the implementation of Islamic law (sharia) while accepting and emphasizing the need to submit to the kingdom's legal system (Dovert and Madinier 2003: 76).

Since 11 September 2001, suspicions of terrorist links have led to the closure of two schools and the arrest of several foreign missionaries on suspicion of links with Jemaah Islamiyah (JI). The obvious source of state suspicion was intelligence that the mastermind behind the October 2002 Bali bombing, Riduan Isamuddin (better known as Hambali), spent six months in Cambodia from around the end of 2002 to early 2003. This led to the closure in May 2003 of the Um al Quran school 30 kilo-metres north of Phnom Penh and a school in Kandal province south of the capital, and the arrest in May and June 2003 of an Egyptian, two Thai men and a Cambodian accused of having links with JI.[7] Another 28 foreign missionaries were also expelled from the country at this time.

However tenuous the links between the Muslim Cham community in Cambodia and JI or other terrorist organizations, Phnom Penh has been careful to act in line with its Association of Southeast Asian Nations (ASEAN) neighbours, particularly Thailand, in monitoring closely the activities of foreign Islamic organizations. In fact, the May 2003 crackdown on Um al Quran school and on foreign missions oper-ating in the country preceded by several weeks the visit of then US Secretary of State

---

7   See Dovert and Madinier (2003: 74), Crispin (2003), Hunt (2004), Osborne (2004) and de Féo (2005). According to Amnesty International (2004), as of September 2004 the four men were still awaiting trial.

Colin Powell for an ASEAN meeting in Phnom Penh. Given the broader historical marginalization of the Cham in Vietnam and Cambodia as a people without a state, and the recent upheavals of the Pol Pot regime, the Cham in general and especially Cham Muslims face further uncertainty as potential suspects in the 'war on terror'.

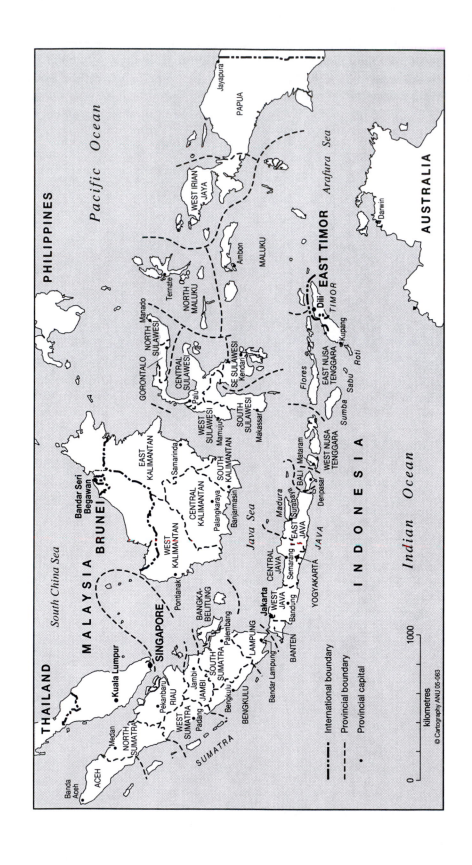

5   Indonesia

Greg Fealy, Virginia Hooker and Sally White

Indonesia has the largest Muslim population of any nation. According to the 2000 census, there are 177.5 million Muslims in Indonesia; they make up 88.2 per cent of the total population and about 13 per cent of the world's 1.3 billion Muslims (Surya-dinata, Arifin and Ananta 2003: 103–12).[1] The highest concentration of Muslims is in the central and western islands of the archipelago. The most densely populated island, Java, is 94.1 per cent Muslim, Sumatra 91.2 per cent and Sulawesi 78.1 per cent. Some care is needed when interpreting this information as Indonesian citizens are required, for official purposes such as census data and citizen identity cards, to select one of five formally recognized religions. In addition to Islam, these are Catholicism, Protestantism, Hinduism and Buddhism. This leads to some inflation in the number of Muslims, because citizens who follow an 'unrecognized' faith or who are only nominally Muslim often find it expedient to list themselves as Muslim. Nearly all of Indonesia's Muslims are Sunni although a very small but growing number are interested in Shi'ism.

Indonesia's Islamic community (*ummah*) is remarkably diverse, spanning a wide array of ethnic groups, socio-economic classes, political and doctrinal orientations, and cultural dispositions. Not surprisingly, the task of categorizing this vast *ummah* has sparked strong debate among scholars. During the past century, the typology of Indonesian Islam has been dominated by four categories: *abangan, santri,* tradition-alist and modernist, the last two being subcategories of *santri. Santri* and *abangan* are terms used to denote relative Islamic piety. The American anthropologist Clif-ford Geertz popularized their usage in academic circles in the 1960s, although, as Ricklefs has shown, their provenance can be traced back to the eighteenth century (Ricklefs 2006). *Santri* Muslims are those who seek to adhere strictly to the ritual and legal requirements of Islam. They are likely to pray five times a day, fast during the holy month of Ramadan, pay the wealth tax (*zakat*) and, if able, undertake the pilgrimage to Mecca. For these Muslims, Islam is a central if not defining part of their lives. *Abangan* Muslims are nominal or less orthopractic Muslims. This category ranges widely, from those who seldom if ever attend to Islamic devotions to

---

1   According to the *Encyclopaedia Britannica Book of the Year*, 2003, Pakistan has the next largest number of Muslims after Indonesia (140 million), followed by India (123 million), Bangladesh (112 million) and Turkey (65 million).

those who lead rich but highly syncretic religious lives in which Islam is blended with other religious or spiritual observances. These non-Islamic elements may be drawn from folk beliefs or from Hinduism and Buddhism, both of which had a strong presence in the archipelago before the arrival of Islam. Although the term *abangan* is only correctly applied to Muslims in Indonesia's largest ethnic group, the Javanese, it is often used to refer to less observant Muslims in other ethnic groups (Geertz 1976; Ricklefs 2006).

The terms 'traditionalist' and 'modernist' apply only to *santri* Muslims. They denote primarily a doctrinal divide, but one that is often overlaid with socioeconomic, political and cultural content. Traditionalists have two defining characteristics: they seek to preserve the authority of medieval Islamic scholarship, and they tend to be more tolerant of local customs. In practice this entails, first, a strict adherence to one of the four classical Sunni law schools (almost invariably the Shafi'i school, founded on the precepts of the ninth-century jurist and theologian Muhammad ibn Idris ibn al-Abbas ibn Uthman ibn Shafii), and second, a willingness to combine local mystical and spiritual practices with the more orthodox elements of Islam. Often the 'local' aspect includes the veneration of 'saints' (*wali*) and famous Islamic scholars (*kiai*) as intermediaries between God and humans; belief in the magical or supernatural powers of blessed individuals; and engagement with cultural or spiritual rituals designed to ensure communal and individual well-being. The orientation to classical jurisprudence and legal schools reflects a view that the scholars of that period possessed an erudition unrivalled in subsequent centuries and that their teachings offer the most authoritative interpretation of how Islam should be practised. Thus a sense of 'tradition', both classical Islamic and local, is at the heart of this stream within Islam. The largest traditionalist organization in Indonesia is Nahdlatul Ulama (NU, Revival of the Religious Scholars). Established in Surabaya in 1926 by K.H. Hasyim Asy'ari and K.H. Wahab Chasbullah, it claims to have 35–40 million members, most of them on Java. As its name suggests, NU is dominated by Islamic scholars, whose authority is usually based on demonstrated knowledge of classical Islam. Other, smaller, traditionalist organizations include Mathlaul Anwar, Jamiyatul Washliyah and Persatuan Tarbiyah Islamiyah (Perti, Islamic Education Association) (van Bruinessen 1996a).

Modernists (also often referred to as reformists) regard the theology and ritual practices of the traditionalists as impure and a deviation from the original teachings of Islam. Modernism as a movement began in the Middle East in the late nineteenth century and spread in Indonesia during the early decades of the twentieth century. The modernist critique of traditionalism had two main elements. The first is that 'un-Islamic' accretions and innovations during the medieval and early modern periods had corrupted the faith and led Muslims into error. The second is that 'blind adherence' to medieval dogma had led to stagnation and atrophy, the consequences of which were apparent in the fact that, by the nineteenth century, much of the Muslim world had been subjugated by European colonial powers and Islam had lost the intellectual and scientific efflorescence of earlier centuries. Modernists argued that the way to revive Islam and make it relevant to the contemporary world was to cleanse the faith of its later impurities and return to the pristine teachings found in the Qur'an and the example of the Prophet Muhammad. As well as returning to unimpeachable sources of guidance, they said, Muslims needed to learn from Western advances in education, science and politics and adopt those elements that were not prohibited by Islam but that would help to strengthen and modernize the Muslim community. The main modernist institution in Indonesia is Muhammadiyah, which now boasts a membership of 25–30 million. Other modernist organizations include Jami'yyat al-Islah wal-Irsyad (Union for Reformation and Guidance, commonly known as just al-Irsyad) and Persatuan Islam (Persis, Islamic Association) (Noer 1973).

In recent decades the Islamic community has become more complex and variegated, due in large part to rapid social and economic change. A far higher percentage of Muslims are now well educated, urban dwelling, professionally employed and middle class than in the 1950s and 1960s. They are also consumers of ever more rapid flows of information resulting from globalization. External influences, especially from the Middle East, now have a greater impact on Indonesian Muslims, and the interactions between endogenous and exogenous Islamic variants are more intricate. This has led some scholars to query the relevance of the *santri–abangan* dichotomy and the traditionalist–modernist typology. Certainly, the number of self-ascribed *abangan* Muslims in today's Indonesia is very small compared with the 1950s, although in rural areas of Java the term would still seem to have analytical usefulness. By contrast, the number of *santri* Muslims has grown considerably since the 1970s, a consequence of accelerating Islamization, particularly in urban areas. Many more Muslims now pray and fast regularly and seek to live their lives strictly according to Islamic law.[2] Meanwhile, the pre-1970s divide between traditionalism and modernism has narrowed considerably and the ritual and doctrinal differences that once set the two groups apart are now widely regarded as inconsequential. The convergence of traditionalism and modernism has led some scholars to argue for the existence of a new category, 'neo-modernism', which combines the knowledge and respect for classical learning with a receptivity to modern, including Western, influences (Barton 1995).

HISTORICAL BACKGROUND: PRE-MODERN AND COLONIAL

The peoples of the islands that now constitute Indonesia have, by necessity, always been in contact with the merchants, sailors and travellers who participated in the networks of trade and exchange characterizing the lands south of China and east of India. Where it has been to their advantage, most groups of Indonesian peoples have accepted and adapted elements of the belief and faith systems of the travellers. Although contact with Muslim merchants must have occurred earlier, the earliest known evidence of Islam in Indonesia comes from several thirteenth-century gravestones in north Sumatra and east Java (Andaya and Ishii 1999: 169). From that period onward, evidence for increasing acceptance of Islam comes from the adop-

---

2 It should be noted that the proportion of Muslims has remained relatively stable for three decades. The 1971 census, which offers the earliest reliable data on religion in Indonesia, put the proportion of Muslims at 87.5 per cent.

tion of Arabic names and titles by local rulers (Milner 1983: 34–45), the construction of mosques, the appointment of religious officials, and royal patronage for Muslim scholars to teach and write religious handbooks.[3]

It has become clear that by the early seventeenth century acceptance of Islam had moved beyond the elite sphere, with communities throughout the archipelago embracing the religion but not observing all aspects of Islamic law. Eighteenth- and nineteenth-century records in the Middle East (see Azra 2004) refer to the long periods of time spent there by Muslims from Sumatra, South Sulawesi, Kalimantan (Borneo) and Java who came to study not just with one of the famous religious teachers of the day but with several.[4] When they returned to their homeland they attracted their own students and followers, to whom they passed on the 'mainstream' Islam they had been taught abroad. In this way, Islamic scholarship from Mecca, Medina, the Yemen, Syria and India flowed in vernacular form to Indonesian Muslims, keeping them in close contact with the leading thinkers of the time (see examples in Azra 2004). Alongside this pattern of direct communication with the Holy Land, other, more locally based, networks also developed. In early eighteenth-century central Java, for example, texts under royal aegis creatively linked Islamic and Javanese thought-worlds, producing esoteric works of local genius (Ricklefs 1998).[5]

Any Muslim from the archipelago who was able to undertake the pilgrimage to Mecca (haj) could observe at first hand Islam in an Arab milieu. Some were inspired to introduce what they learned there in their home regions, often triggering socio-political foment when established figures of authority battled to retain their influence against the new ideas. A prime example is provided by the case of three Minang-kabau pilgrims who returned to west Sumatra from the Holy Land in 1803. There they had observed the purification of Islam (of all innovations in the faith later than its first 300 years) as a result of the capture of Mecca by Wahhabis, followers of Muhammad ibn 'Abd al-Wahhab (1703–87). The pilgrims' attempts to transfer Wahhabi ideals to their own communities led to a 30-year civil war in west Sumatra and challenged the established formulation of relations between the 'great tradition' of Islam in the centres and an Islamic 'little tradition' that mixed with *adat* (customary law) at the local level (Azra 2004: 147).

Almost a century later, from the early 1900s, social foment again resulted from the active transmission of the teachings of Muhammad Abduh (1849–1905) and Rashid Rida (1865–1935) from Cairo to the archipelago through regular publications in Malay. Aimed at the younger generation of Muslims who were concerned that Islamic societies seemed to be lagging behind the technological advances of the West, the followers of Abduh urged their fellow Muslims to follow more carefully

3   Under the patronage of the Queen of Aceh, the north Sumatran scholar Abdu'r-Ra'uf (c. 1615–93) prepared the first Qur'anic commentary in Malay, carefully editing an Arabic text so that it could be used to teach students. It has remained in use throughout the Malay–Indonesian world.

4   In their search for specialized knowledge, some stayed away from their homeland for as long as 20–30 years; several, for example al-Nawawi of Banten (1813–97) and Ahmad Khatib of west Sumatra (1852–1916), remained permanently in the Holy Land to write and teach. They maintained strong links with their fellow countrymen and their writings remain influential (Azra 2004).

5   For further examples from Java, especially from the seventeenth century, see Day (1983: 154).

the precepts of Islam and to use their God-given sense of reason to forge their own path in an increasingly modern world (Eliraz 2004).

The wave of Islamic reformism inspired by the ideas of Abduh and Rida arrived in what was then the Dutch East Indies in the early decades of the twentieth century. This was a time when the colonial government had finally succeeded in establishing some control over the entire archipelago after quelling the Acehnese rebellion in 1912. The policies of the colonial authorities toward Islam during this period were dictated largely by a Dutch scholar of Islam, C. Snouck Hurgronje, the mastermind of the campaign against the Acehnese. The opening of the Suez Canal in 1869 and the introduction of the steamship saw a rapid increase in the number of pilgrims making the journey to Mecca in the latter decades of the nineteenth century. This led to Dutch fears of Islamic 'fanaticism' undermining their authority in the colony. Snouck's two-pronged approach to this issue was, first, to suppress any overtly political expression of Islam, and second, not to interfere with other aspects of the Islamic faith, including the haj (Benda 1958: 20–30). Muslims would be free to implement the five pillars of their faith (*arkaan addiin*), marry and be buried according to Islamic law.

Nevertheless, the autonomy of Muslims was to some extent illusory. In 1882, the Dutch colonial government established the so-called Raad Agama (religious court) to hear cases of divorce requiring the involvement of a religious judge, and to make rulings in disputes involving inheritance (Hisyam 2001: 59–62). Although these courts were not subordinate to secular courts, native religious officials, such as the *penghulu* who generally served as judges, were made civil servants, and the Dutch were able to exercise influence through their appointment and dismissal. In 1895, the Dutch introduced a marriage ordinance that regulated certain aspects of Islamic marriage law, most controversially by requiring the presence of designated officials at marriage ceremonies. A new ordinance in 1929 introduced fines for those who conducted marriages without the presence of officials, including the groom and the guardian (*wali*) of the bride (White 2004).

Other areas of concern for Muslim groups included the Guru (Teacher) Ordinance of 1925, which restricted the provision of religious education by requiring all classes to be registered with local Dutch-appointed officials, and regulations that mosques be under the supervision of the *bupati*, the highest grade of native civil servants, again Dutch-appointed. Issues such as these led to increasing tensions between Muslim groups and the colonial government. Opposition to what was seen as Dutch interference in Muslim life peaked in 1937 with the introduction of an ordinance that removed the authority of religious courts to deal with matters of inheritance, giving that authority to secular courts. In the same year, a marriage ordinance was proposed that would have allowed Muslims to undergo a civil marriage, required marriage to be monogamous and ensured that all divorce take place before a judge of the secular court. The draft ordinance was quickly withdrawn in the face of opposition from Islamic organizations.

The introduction of Islamic reformism or modernism into the Dutch East Indies led to an increasingly self-confident Islamic community, as the above discussion indicates. It also inspired the formation of a number of Islamic organizations, the largest of which was Muhammadiyah. Founded in Yogyakarta in 1912 by K.H. Ahmad Dahlan, its earliest members were mainly religious officials, religious teachers and merchant traders. It established modern Islamic schools teaching a wide range of general as well as religious subjects. By 1938 it had spread throughout the archipelago and had a total of around 250,000 members. A number of smaller Islamic organizations were also formed during this period. Jong Islamieten Bond (Young Muslims League) was important not for its size, but because it was the launching pad for a number of Muslim intellectuals who in the 1920s and 1930s, and into the post-independence period, engaged in spirited public debate with nationalists of a more secular orientation about the form an independent Indonesian state might take. Such figures included Mohamad Roem and Mohammad Natsir.

Most reformist organizations established women's wings, the largest and most influential of these being 'Aisyiyah, the women's wing of Muhammadiyah. It was established in 1917 as a way of bringing women into the reformist movement. It provided women with religious education, with general education through a system of girls' schools, and with new opportunities to engage in social and community life (White 2004).

The growth of reformist organizations also provoked a reaction from traditionalist Muslims seeking to preserve their religious authority, and NU's formation was, in part, a response to this. As mentioned previously, traditionalist Muslims rejected the reformist emphasis on the Qur'an and Sunnah of the Prophet as the only authentic sources of Islam. Over time the doctrinal differences between traditionalists and reformists declined. However, divisions between the two different strands of Islamic thought hindered the development of a unified Islamic movement that could challenge either the colonial state or the secular nationalist movement that developed under the leadership of Indonesia's first post-independence president, Sukarno. Despite a number of attempts to bring the two groups together, traditionalists and reformists were only able to unite on specific issues, such as in opposition to the proposed marriage ordinance in 1937. It took the arrival of the Japanese in 1942 to finally unite (by decree) the Islamic community into one organization representing Islamic interests: Majelis Syuro Muslimin Indonesia (Masyumi, Indonesian Muslim Consultative Council).

SINCE INDEPENDENCE

Political Islam

Islam's impact upon politics and the state in Indonesia has been far less than its statistical dominance might suggest. Despite the country's large Muslim majority, Islamic parties have never gained more than 44 per cent of the vote in a general election; nor have they succeeded in their efforts to 'Islamize' the Indonesian constitution. The reasons for this are complex, but three key factors have been: (1) the rejection by a significant minority of Muslim voters of Islamist agendas, especially those entailing comprehensive implementation of sharia; (2) the lack of political unity among Islamic parties; and (3) the presence of authoritarian, overtly secular regimes for much of Indonesia's post-independence history.

In the early years of independence, Islamic groups sought to realize in politics the ideal of *ukhuwah Islamiyah* or Islamic brotherhood. In 1945, nearly all Islamic organizations supported the transformation of the formerly apolitical Masyumi into a party representing all Islamic groups. During its early years, the division of power between modernists and traditionalists was relatively even, but in 1952 NU split from Masyumi citing frustration with its perceived marginalization. From this time on, tension and acrimony between modernists and traditionalists became a hallmark of political Islam. Although both sides continued to speak of Muslim solidarity, on most issues they saw themselves as rivals who were competing for legitimacy within, and leadership of, the Islamic community.

Indonesia's first election in 1955 proved disappointing for Islamic parties, the start of many setbacks at the ballot box. Masyumi gained 20.9 per cent of the vote, just ahead of NU's 18.4 per cent. The total Islamic party vote was 43.9 per cent, well below the majority that most Muslim politicians were expecting. The result showed that many Muslims were not attracted to Islamic party policies that sought to formalize the role of Islam within the state and politics. Many of these Muslims preferred to vote for secular nationalist or leftist parties (Boland 1971; Fealy 2003).

The political tide swung more dramatically against Islam in the following decades. Declining public confidence in parliamentary democracy and mounting regional and economic problems provided the impetus for an authoritarian shift in the late 1950s, led by President Sukarno and the army. Both Sukarno and the military saw Islam as a threat to their 'Guided Democracy' regime and set about undermining it. Masyumi was banned in 1960 and the remaining Islamic parties were forced to subscribe to the largely secular ideological tenets of the regime. The coming to power of Soeharto's army-based 'New Order' regime in 1966 brought with it even tighter restrictions on political Islam. The regime refused to allow the re-emergence of Masyumi, although it did eventually agree to a new modernist party with a compliant leadership. NU was similarly marginalized from power, though it maintained its electoral popularity. In 1973, the regime forced the merger of all four Islamic parties to create Partai Persatuan Pembangunan (PPP, United Development Party). It then progressively stripped the party of its Islamic symbols and content and manipulated traditionalist–modernist rivalries within the party leadership to ensure constant instability and electoral damage. PPP's highest vote during the New Order was 29 per cent; its lowest was 15 per cent. The nadir for Islamic politics came in 1984–85, when the regime required all social and political organizations to adopt the religiously neutral state ideology of Pancasila as their basis. This meant that Islamic groups could no longer be formally based on Islam. On threat of being banned, all but one major Islamic organization reluctantly agreed. At the same time as it was suppressing Islamic parties, the regime also sought to co-opt Islamic leaders and groups for its own electoral cause. It dispensed generous patronage (but minimal power) to those willing to ally themselves with it or, at the very least, remain politically neutral (Fealy 2003).

Relations between Islam and the regime improved from the late 1980s, as Soeharto began cultivating support among Islamic organizations, primarily to offset

declining allegiance from the military. The regime began making legislative conces-
sions to Islamic sentiment by agreeing to such things as an expanded jurisdiction
for religious courts, the lifting of a ban on the wearing of head coverings in state
schools, and support for the introduction of sharia banking. It also allowed devout
Muslims greater access to government largesse and strategic positions in the bureaucracy (Effendy 2004).

The downfall of the Soeharto regime in mid-1998 saw the start of Indonesia's
democratic transition. As in the 1950s, Muslim leaders anticipated strong electoral
support for Islamic parties. They believed that the Islamization of Indonesian society
would inevitably result in more Muslims voting for Islamic parties. More than 40
Islamic parties of both Islamist and non-Islamist persuasion were formed during the
next year, 21 of which would eventually contest the 1999 general election.[6] Once
again, however, political Islam failed to realize its ambitions. The vote for Islamist
parties was 16 per cent, but the non-Islamist Islamic parties won another 22.2 per
cent. The total vote for 'Islamic' parties was thus 38.2 per cent. In the 2004 election,
Islamist parties gained 21.3 per cent of the vote and the non-Islamist parties 17 per
cent, giving the 'Islamic' parties a total vote of 38.3 per cent. Thus, at a time when
the observance of Islam in public and private life was at an unprecedented level,
political Islam remained weaker than in the 1950s (Fealy 2001; Baswedan 2004).
Many Muslims appeared to differentiate Islam as a religion from its political manifestations. Another aspect of post-Soeharto Islamic politics also warrants special
mention: its fragmentation. Whereas in the 1950s most modernists had supported
Masyumi and most traditionalists NU, at the turn of the new millennium the former
were spread across at least six parties and the latter dominated five parties.

Islam and the State

Islam–state relations have been one of the most contentious issues in Indonesia's
post-independence history. This issue has divided the Muslim community and
caused hostility between Muslims and non-Muslim religious minorities. The broad
parameters of the debate have remained remarkably constant for more than 60 years.
On one side are the Islamists who want Islam to be given special acknowledgement
and authority in the state and society. They seek constitutional recognition of sharia
and the comprehensive implementation of Islamic laws. They have also often sought
stipulations that the president be a Muslim and proposed the adoption of Arabic
terms in the constitution and statutes in order to render a more Islamic flavour to
national life. In short, they seek a 'confessionalized' state and political system in
which religious identity suffuses and defines Indonesia's character. The Islamists
put forward several arguments to justify basing the state on Islam: first, the constitution and laws should reflect the fact that most Indonesians are Muslim; and second,

---

6   Islamist parties were those formally based on Islam and including in their programs, to varying
degrees, a commitment to greater sharia implementation. Non-Islamist Islamic parties were based on
Pancasila and had more pluralist political agendas.

Islamic laws and values are based on God's final revelation and therefore offer a superior code for moral and legal behaviour than do man-made laws. On the other side of the debate is a broad group of non-Muslims and 'secular' Muslims (including *santri* Muslims as well as those who are less observant or syncretistic). They argue that the state should be religiously neutral or secular as a matter of principle and that Islamizing the state would lead to discrimination against minorities and might cause predominantly non-Muslim regions of Indonesia to secede. For them, religious life is a private matter and the state should be 'deconfessionalized'.

The first major confrontation between groups in favour of and opposing an Islamized state took place in the months leading up to Indonesia's independence in August 1945. The committee charged with drafting a constitution quickly became deadlocked on the 'Islamic issue' and a subcommittee was formed to hammer out a compromise. This was achieved on 22 June when the subcommittee agreed to a constitutional preamble known as the Jakarta Charter containing a seven-word clause that obliged Muslims to implement Islamic law. It also agreed to Islamize some of the language of the constitution and require the president to be Muslim. This compromise was accepted soon afterwards by the full committee but was eventually rejected by a new committee that met on 18 August, the day after independence was declared. Muslim committee members reluctantly agreed to drop the 'Islamic' elements of the draft constitution after warnings that Christian regions would leave the fledgling republic. Islamic groups again tried to Islamize the constitution in the late 1950s and late 1960s, but failed on both occasions. The New Order regime effectively outlawed debate on Islamizing the state, and it was not until after Soeharto's resignation that the issue re-emerged. Several Islamic parties proposed the reinsertion of the 'seven words' into the constitution, but they were soundly defeated (Boland 1971: 54–75; van Bruinessen 1996b: 19–34; Fealy 2003).

While Islamic groups failed to gain formal constitutional recognition of sharia, they did succeed in gaining state involvement in religious affairs. In 1946 the government established a Ministry of Religious Affairs, the main purpose of which was to service the needs of the Islamic community. Specifically, the ministry oversaw Islamic courts, administered marriage, divorce and inheritance issues, controlled pilgrimage matters, channelled funds to Islamic schools, colleges and tertiary institutions, and monitored the quality of religious texts. The ministry is still one of the largest in the government even though it is losing some of its functions to other departments; the religious courts, for example, now come under the Supreme Court.

Cultural Islam

In the 1970s and 1980s, when political Islam was under the greatest pressure from the New Order regime, another movement emerged within Indonesia that was to have a major impact on Muslim attitudes towards Islam and the state, that of 'cultural Islam'. This was not so much a single, coherent movement as a number of different streams that had in common a desire to reform and revitalize Indonesian Islam and move the Muslim community away from what was seen as damaging confrontation with the regime. The movement was 'cultural' in that it eschewed formal political activity and sought to advance the interests of Muslims through intellectual, educational, social and artistic means. Rather than imposing 'Islamic values' via the state, exponents of cultural Islam wanted to make people better Muslims by appealing to their minds and sensibilities. Leading figures came from both modernist and traditionalist backgrounds, with the most prominent being Nurcholish Madjid (an intellectual); the later NU chair and president of Indonesia Abdurrahman Wahid; the later Ministry of Religious Affairs senior researcher and state secretary Djohan Effendi; and economist and social commentator Dawam Rahardjo.

Cultural Islam intellectuals were critical of Islamic parties and their agendas. They argued that the parties had achieved neither electoral nor legislative success and had pursued policies that were divisive and harmful to the image of the Muslim community. They were especially dismissive of the 'Islamic state' issue, arguing that the Qur'an did not prescribe a state structure and that efforts to 'sharia-ize' the constitution had alienated religious minorities and less observant Muslims, thereby playing into the hands of regimes that sought to marginalize Islam from national life. Thus, Muslims needed to find new approaches to revitalizing and empowering their communities. For many in the cultural movement, this involved rethinking 'Islamic knowledge' and developing innovative ways of interpreting and applying the faith to make it more relevant to contemporary life. Young intellectuals produced new Islamic-based theories on such wide-ranging issues as gender equality, environmental protection, human rights, religious tolerance and democratization. These ideas were then popularized during the late 1980s and 1990s by elite and middle-class-focused NGOs such as Nurcholish's own Paramadina Foundation, and also through grassroots activity conducted by community groups and mass socio-religious organizations such as Abdurrahman's NU (Barton 1995; Hefner 2000).

The impact of cultural Islam has been significant. It has sparked an intellectual vitality in Indonesian Islam and has given renewed religious legitimacy to the values of pluralism and tolerance. The lack of contemporary political support for Islamic state proposals also probably owes much to this movement. Furthermore, many key figures in cultural Islam, especially Nurcholish Madjid, played an important role in Soeharto's downfall and the subsequent transition to democracy.

One other significant consequence of the New Order's repressive policies – one that also has some parallels with cultural Islam – was the rise of 'campus Islam'. The term refers to a number of university-based movements, including Gerakan Tarbiyah (Education Movement), Hizbut Tahrir (Liberation Party) and Jemaah Tabligh (Preaching Community). The largest of them, Gerakan Tarbiyah, emerged in the early 1980s after the regime banned political activity on campuses. Much of the inspiration for the Tarbiyah movement came from Middle Eastern sources, especially Egypt's Muslim Brotherhood. Tarbiyah groups adopted the Muslim Brotherhood's model of forming small, tight-knit cells (commonly referred to as *usrah*, literally 'family') as incubators of pious, professionally successful young Muslims, and also borrowed Brotherhood concepts of Islam as an all-embracing and self-sufficient system. The movement was overtly apolitical in its early years and expanded rapidly across state university campuses, controlling many of the student senates of large universities by the early 1990s. As the New Order teetered in early 1998, Tarbiyah activists began to conduct direct political activity, firstly forming an anti-regime student organization that was to play a pivotal role in the demonstrations that brought down Soeharto, and in August of that year forming Partai Keadilan (PK, Justice Party). At the 1999 election, PK gained 1.4 per cent of the vote. This jumped to 7.3 per cent in the 2004 elections, which the party contested under the new name of Partai Keadilan Sejahtera (PKS, Prosperity and Justice Party). It is confident of further growth in electoral support in coming elections.

Radical Islam

Throughout Indonesian history, a small minority of the Islamic community has been inclined towards violent jihadism. The most important radical movement has been Darul Islam, whose primary aim was to found an Islamic state in Indonesia. Darul Islam first emerged in the mid-1940s in west Java under the charismatic leadership of S.M. Kartosoewirjo. In 1949 he declared the formation of an Indonesian Islamic State (Negara Islam Indonesia, NII) based on sharia, and Darul Islam forces began insurgency operations against the republic. By 1954, rebel forces in four other provinces (Central Java, Aceh, South Sulawesi and South Kalimantan) had joined Darul Islam, leading to the most serious internal security challenge faced by the central government during the first two decades of independence. At its height in the mid-1950s, Darul Islam had tens of thousands of fighters across Indonesia and controlled significant tracts of the mountainous and jungle hinterlands in West Java, Aceh and South Sulawesi. The rebellion took a heavy human and economic toll. Estimates of the number killed range from 15,000 to 40,000, and some half a million people were displaced. The movement began to collapse in the late 1950s, due to a combination of military campaigns by the republic and amnesty offers to local Darul Islam groups. Kartosoewirjo was captured and executed in 1962 and the last of the other major rebel leaders was killed in 1965 (van Dijk 1981; Horikoshi 1975).

Darul Islam was moribund during the late 1960s but several of its former commanders began to revive the movement in a covert form from the early 1970s. It grew steadily in size during the 1980s, recruiting younger-generation members from old Darul Islam families and attracting new cadres on university campuses. It also experienced serious and sometimes bloody internal schisms.

In 1993, a new and more lethal radical movement known as al-Jama'ah al-Islamiyyah – commonly referred to as Jemaah Islamiyah, or JI – was founded by two former Darul Islam leaders, Abdullah Sungkar and Abu Bakar Ba'asyir. JI saw itself as the heir of Darul Islam, although it sought to achieve the goal of an Islamic state through more militant means. Many prominent members of JI were veterans of the *mujahidin* war against the Soviet Union in Afghanistan during the 1980s and early 1990s who had been recruited through Darul Islam channels. Beginning in mid-2000, JI members began a series of attacks on churches, culminating in the Christmas Eve bombings in Jakarta and five other Indonesian cities and towns that left 19 dead. Following this, JI began targeting Westerners, launching a massive bomb attack on two

Bali nightclubs on 12 October 2002 that killed 202 people. Though sometimes cast as the Southeast Asian wing of al-Qaeda, JI in fact has a high measure of autonomy. Many of JI's senior leaders have been arrested and tried since the Bali bombing in October 2002 or have become fugitives. The organization and its offshoots remain active, however, and continue to pose a serious threat for the foreseeable future. This was made evident by the second Bali bombing on 1 October 2005, which killed 21 people (ICG 2002a, 2002b, 2005a).

JI represents the most extreme manifestation of post-Soeharto Islamic radicalism, but it is by no means the only one. Also prominent have been a range of paramilitary and vigilante groups. The largest of these was Laskar Jihad (Holy War Fighters). Formed in January 2000, Laskar Jihad's avowed aim was to defend Muslims who it believed were victims of Christian aggression in Maluku and Central Sulawesi from 1999 to 2002. Another high-profile group was Front Pembela Islam (FPI, Islamic Defenders Front), founded in 1998, which aimed to combat perceived immorality and iniquity in Indonesian society. It regularly attacked nightclubs, brothels and gambling dens and opposed what it termed 'deviant' Islamic sects. Some radical groups have pursued their aims peacefully. In Indonesia, Hizbut Tahrir, which advocates the restoration of a global caliphate, eschews violence and gains most of its members through intellectual and preaching activities. Since 2002, most radical organizations have experienced a reversal in fortunes. FPI, for example, has largely ceased its vigilante attacks and Laskar Jihad disbanded in October 2002.

In recent years, radical groups in Indonesia have become the focus of much media and scholarly attention. Viewed from one perspective, this is warranted given the security threat posed by the more violent radical groups. From another perspective, however, the focus on radicalism has been disproportionate. In terms of membership, radical groups are only a fraction the size of mainstream organizations: the largest of them has at most several tens of thousands of members, compared with tens of millions of members for NU or Muhammadiyah. Furthermore, the pattern of Islamic history in Indonesia is that radicalism can expand quickly due to unusual political or socio-economic conditions only for short periods. Then, invariably, the moderate mainstream within the Islamic community rejects and marginalizes radical groups and reasserts the irenic and tolerant values found within the faith. Such a process appears to have been under way since 2002.

6 Malaysia

John Funston

When Malaya achieved independence in 1957, analysts generally expected that Islam would play a declining role in national affairs. Popular theories of post-colonial political development posited the decline of religion and the triumph of Western-style secularism. The governing Alliance coalition, led by the United Malays National Organisation (UMNO), had a Western-educated leadership with a strong focus on economic development. In addition, the Chinese and Indian minorities that together made up half the population were overwhelmingly non-Muslim. Despite analysts' predictions, however, Islam has become progressively more important in the daily lives of Malaysian Muslims, and in the country's politics.

DEMOGRAPHY

The Muslim proportion of the population contracted when Malaya expanded to become Malaysia in 1963 – the new states of Sabah, Sarawak and Singapore were all predominantly non-Muslim. Singapore left the federation just two years later, and with their higher birth rates the proportion of Muslims gradually increased. Growth rates were particularly high in Sabah, where Muslims increased from 40 per cent of the population in 1970 to 51 per cent a decade later, assisted by active conversion efforts and the extension of citizenship to Muslim refugees from the southern Philippines. The population of neighbouring Sarawak, however, is still less than 30 per cent Muslim. On the peninsula the highest Muslim concentration (over 80 per cent) is in the 'Malay heartland' states in the northeast and north: Kelantan, Terengganu, Kedah and Perlis.

In the 2000 census the total Muslim population was 60.4 per cent, up from 58.6 per cent in 1991. All Malays and a small number of Indians are Muslim. Malaysian Chinese are mainly Buddhist (19.2 per cent) or Christian (9.2 per cent). Most Malaysian Indians are Hindu (6.3 per cent).[1]

---

1   Data are from the 1991 and 2000 censuses as reported in Department of Statistics Malaysia (2000).

HISTORICAL BACKGROUND

Islam, of the Shafi'i school, was brought to Malaysia by Arab and Indian traders and scholars around the beginning of the fourteenth century (Hooker 1983). Its subsequent spread was due to both political factors and proselytizing. The Malacca sultanate adopted Islam as the court religion a few years after it was founded in the early fifteenth century. Islam then spread as the sultanate established its influence throughout the peninsula.

Until the late nineteenth century the administration of Islam was village based. Then, in an attempt to strengthen Malay society against the expansion of British control, some of the sultans began to enact Islamic law (sharia) as the primary law for their Muslim subjects, and to unify Islamic organizations under the state bureaucracy. These efforts continued under British rule. When the major British expansion began in the late nineteenth century, the British worked through the prevailing system of Malay sultanates (states), taking control in most areas but leaving Islam and Malay customs in Malay hands.

From the perception of the sultans, however, expanding sharia was intended to enhance royal more than divine power. This brought them into conflict with 'sharia-minded' members of the society, who were becoming increasingly influential throughout the Islamic world during the eighteenth and nineteenth centuries (Milner 2002: 147, 151–2). Islamic reformists influenced by the Egyptian Salafiyya[2] movement led by Muhammad Abduh established a foothold through the Singapore-based journal *al-Imam* [The Leader] in 1906, and were outspoken in criticizing royal shortcomings on Islamic matters.

In 1915, a Majlis Agama Islam dan Isti'adat Melayu (Council of Islamic Religion and Malay Customs, often known as the Majlis Agama) was established in Kelantan. It has been described as 'a central council of religion with sweeping administrative and coercive powers limited only by the final authority of the Sultan in State Council', without precedent in the Islamic world (Roff 1974: 103). The Kelantan Majlis Agama advanced the enactment of sharia, established control over village religious officials, assumed full authority to define 'correct' Islamic doctrines and became involved in a wide range of other activities, such as the provision of both religious and secular education and the publication of Islamic and other literary works. A similar model was subsequently adopted by the other Malay states. Through this process a close relationship between the state sultan and Islam was established from the early twentieth century.

Islam also played an important role in bringing social change at the beginning of the twentieth century – often in competition with those urging royal (*kerajaan*) or race or nationalist (*bangsa*) based alternative visions for the Malay community (Milner 2002). Islamic reformists, known locally as the Kaum Muda (Young Group), spread their views initially through *al-Imam*, then through other publications and Muslim school teachers. They attacked the inadequacies of the sultanates and their religious bureaucracies and called for a return to the purity of early Islam, together with the development of Malays through a combination of modern (Western-style) education and religious studies, including Arabic language study. Some of their writings were openly political, espousing anti-colonialism or pan-Malayism (union between the Dutch East Indies and Malaya). Though widely opposed by members of the religious establishment (the Kaum Tua, or Old Group) – as well as the *kerajaan* and *bangsa* alternatives – they established a strong sympathy for reformist Islam throughout the country.

After World War II Islamic reformism established its own organizations, first Majlis Agama Tertinggi Sa-Malaya (MATA, Pan Malayan Supreme Religious Council) in March 1947, then Hizbul Muslimin (Islamic Party) one year later. MATA

---

2 Literally, 'those who follow the Pious Ancestors' (see glossary).

and Hizbul Muslimin were in effect the religious wing of the Malay Nationalist Party (MNP), an organization representing the socialist-inclined left wing of Malay nationalism, in opposition to more conservative groups aligned to UMNO. Hizbul Muslimin campaigned for independence and an Islamic State (*Darul Islam*). According to one party leader, however, while Hizbul Muslimin pursued the aims of both Malay nationalism and Islam, the former took precedence over the latter. The party's activities were cut short in August 1948 when seven leaders, including the president and most of the executive committee, were arrested by colonial authorities for activities said to have hindered British actions against the Malayan Communist Party (Funston 1981: 168).

Persatuan Islam Sa-Tanah Melayu (Pan Malayan Islamic Organization), later called Parti Islam Se Malaysia (PAS, The Islamic Party of Malaysia), was established in 1951. PAS was formed by the defection of UMNO's religious department but during its early years underwent a metamorphosis from which it emerged as a composite of a number of different interests. It attracted former members of Hizbul Muslimin, the MNP and a variety of intensely Malay nationalist parties that rose briefly in futile opposition to UMNO during the first half of the 1950s, as well as conservative members of the religious elite. Leadership, however, fell largely to those with a Hizbul Muslimin-type background. After an inauspicious start, PAS won a seat in the 1955 home rule election, the only party outside the Alliance coalition to do so. This provided it with the foundation for a more substantial challenge to UMNO after independence.

It was UMNO, however, in concert with non-Malay partners in the Alliance, that determined the constitutional position of Islam in independent Malaya. In an influential memorandum submitted in 1955 to the Reid Constitutional Commission (established to draw up a constitution for an independent Malaya), the Alliance argued that Islam should be the 'official' religion, but that religious freedom should be guaranteed and Malaya should be considered a 'secular' state. Ultimately the wording adopted was that Islam would be 'the' religion of the country, a wording believed sufficient to convey the intended notion of a secular state. UMNO also ensured that under Malaya's federal system Islam remained a state rather than a national responsibility, making it one of the few areas of power left in the hands of the states. Both these provisions had implications for the future development of Islam: the designation of Islam as 'the' religion of the country created ambiguity as to whether Malaya was to be an 'Islamic state'; and the decision to leave Islam in state hands made the coordination of Islamic affairs far more complex.

ADMINISTRATION OF ISLAM

With Islamic affairs remaining a state responsibility, the major administrative responsibility has fallen to the state Islamic departments (Jabatan Agama Islam), which after independence took over the tasks of the former Majlis Agama. These departments supervise mosques (in most cases providing a standardized weekly sermon) and Islamic schools; maintain Islamic law with their own moral police (to enforce regulations such as those relating to observance of fasting, decent attire and prohibitions against close proximity between unmarried couples); collect *zakat* (wealth tax); and certify those authorized to preach. They have become vast bureaucratic organizations with powers that have increased greatly since the resurgence of Islam from around the 1970s brought about by the *dakwah* (proselytization) movement (see below).

The Sultan is the head of Islamic affairs in all states that have a sultan; in the territories (Kuala Lumpur and Labuan) and in Penang, Malacca, Sarawak and Sabah, the Yang di-Pertuan Agong (King) performs this role. But much power lies in the hands of the Mufti, an official appointed by the state administration, and the Islamic departments. The Mufti generally sits as an ex officio member of the state executive council. His powers include issuing authoritative rulings (fatwa) on aspects of Islamic law or practice that have the force of law.

In the initial years of independence the federal government had very limited involvement in Islamic affairs. This changed only in 1968 when the Council of Rulers (the state sultans) formed the Majlis Kebangsaan Bagi Hal Ehwal Ugama Islam Malaysia (Malaysian National Council for Islamic Affairs) with a secretariat in the Office of the Prime Minister. This council, chaired by the prime minister, remains one of the major institutions for formulating policy on Islamic affairs.[3] Its secretariat was conceived initially as an organization with limited powers to coordinate the various state Islamic bureaucracies. However, the secretariat's activities expanded rapidly during the early 1970s to include the supervision of federal-government Islamic schools and the publication of Islamic materials. It also established an Islamic research centre and (in January 1974) an Islamic missionary foundation, Yayasan Dakwah Islamiah Malaysia (YADIM, Islamic Preaching Foundation of Malaysia). In 1974 the secretariat was upgraded to a Division of Religious Affairs (Bahagian Ugama). It underwent further expansion as the Division of Islamic Affairs (Bahagian Hal Ehwal Islam) in 1984 and finally became the Malaysian Department of Islamic Development (Jabatan Kemajuan Islam Malaysia, or Jakim) in 1997 (Jakim 2003: 20–9, 37). Its importance was also emphasized by the appointment of a deputy minister in 1973 to oversee its activities, and of a full minister from 1997.[4]

A major concern of government leaders at the federal level has been to ensure that Islamic laws are consistent across the states. Besides the work of Jakim and its antecedents, a National Fatwa Committee (Jawatankuasa Fatwa Kebangsaan Bagi Hal Ehwal Ugama Islam) was established in 1970. However, it has a somewhat modest status – its members serve on a voluntary basis – and to gain the force of law its recommendations must be taken back to the states for approval.[5] In another move towards centralization, the sharia courts were taken over from the states and

3 Besides the prime minister as chair, it includes a deputy chair appointed by the Council of Rulers, state representatives (normally the *mentri besar* or chief minister) and five others appointed by the Council of Rulers. However, the states of Kedah and Pahang have never joined, and Johor left in 1983 (Jakim 2003: 20, 37).

4 I am grateful to Kikue Hamayotsu for her insights into the administration of Islam in Malaysia.

5 Approval is not assured: not all of the committee's recommendations have been accepted by the states.

reorganized on a federal basis in 1998, under the Department of Shariah Law (Jaba-tan Kehakiman Syariah Malaysia) in the Office of the Prime Minister.

A further important step in enhancing Islamic understanding was the formation in 1992 of Institut Kefahaman Islam Malaysia (IKIM, Malaysian Institute for Islamic Understanding) under the Office of the Prime Minister. IKIM is a prestigious think-tank that hosts high-level conferences on Islam, authors regular columns in both English- and Malay-language newspapers, runs television programs and is generally responsible for articulating government policy on Islamic affairs.

THE NATURE OF MALAYSIAN ISLAM

Islam in Malaysia is widely seen as both moderate and enlightened, rejecting extrem-ism in any form. It accords a high social status to women, who have achieved top positions in the bureaucracy and academia and have participated actively in politics through the women's sections of the major parties (though women are still under-represented in parliament and cabinet). Malaysian Islam has also generally coexisted peacefully with the 40 per cent of the population who are non-Muslim.

Moderation was very evident around the time of independence (1957). Few women wore head coverings, and Western-style clothing such as short skirts was common. Men were clean-shaven. Muslims did not eat pork or (generally) consume alcohol, but otherwise felt free to eat in non-Muslim restaurants and houses. Adher-ence to such requirements as praying five times a day and weekly mosque attendance was not rigorous. Islamic programs made up only a small part of radio and television fare, and Malay films and other forms of entertainment were very Westernized. Alco-hol was often served at government functions, which seldom opened with prayers.

This situation changed with the advent of the *dakwah* movement in the late 1960s. The movement was started by university students led by Anwar Ibrahim, who later became deputy prime minister. It was inspired by the writings of authors such as Sayyid Qutub, Hasan al-Banna and Abu al-Ala Mawdudi, and gained further impe-tus with the establishment of Angkatan Belia Islam Malaysia (ABIM, Malaysian Islamic Youth Movement) in 1971. What began as a tolerant and liberal movement was taken up more stridently by others. The Islamic Republic group, advocating a full Islamic state with sharia, began to dominate university politics in the 1980s; it was loosely allied with Malaysian students in the Islamic Republican Council in Britain, which in 1990 formed the NGO Jamaah Islah Malaysia (JIM, Malaysian Reform Community). Darul Arqam, which combined a large commercial operation (selling approved Islamic products) with Sufist beliefs and a simple lifestyle emulat-ing Islam at the time of its origins, attracted a large following. And federal and state government departments set up their own conservative *dakwah* groups.[6]

The *dakwah* movement had implications in a range of areas. By the mid-1980s most Malay women were wearing a mini-*telekung*, 'a triangular head-dress that comes down to the chest or a round one that comes down even further to the waist'

---

6   See Zainah (1987), Chandra (1987), Jomo and Ahmad Shabery (1992) and Saliha (2003).

(Zainah 1987: 33). Many wore this together with the *hijab*, 'an ankle-length one piece long sleeve robe … Only the face and hands are visible, the robe hiding completely the shape of the body' (Zainah 1987: 33). Many Muslim men now grow beards. It is no longer sufficient for food to be pork-free; it must be strictly *halal* (prepared in accordance with Islamic prescriptions). Attendance at mosques and attention to prayer times are much more rigorously adhered to. Islamic programs take up a large part of radio and television time. And alcohol is no longer served at government functions, which now invariably start with prayers.

The forces of globalization and Westernization have nonetheless exerted pressures in a different direction. Western music and television programs are widely available and attract Muslim as well as non-Muslim interest. Federal and state Islamic departments often seek to provide protection against such evils, regularly raiding night-clubs and other centres of vice and arresting Muslims for consumption of alcohol or (in the case of women) immodest attire. The heated controversy these raids cause in the media reveals that Muslim society is deeply divided over whether such activities should be actively policed or left to the conscience of the individual.

Malaysian Islam prides itself on its orthodoxy, and Islamic leaders react strongly against any movement regarded as 'deviationist'. Muslims are frequently reminded that they are Sunni (Ahli Sunnah Wal-Jammah), and Shi'a Muslims are not allowed to practise their religion openly (Saliha 2003: 111–12); some have even been detained under the Internal Security Act, which permits indefinite detention without trial. Islamic leaders have a great fear of followers becoming apostates, and although there is no evidence that significant numbers have ever been attracted to this, there is regular panic when rumours of mass desertions spread. Conservative members of the Malaysian Ulama Association have been quick to accuse liberal Islamic thinkers of 'insulting Islam' (Farish 2002: 319–25).

Notwithstanding this focus on orthodoxy, traditional beliefs maintain a strong hold on many Muslims. Reports of 'ghost' sightings appear regularly in the media. The *bomoh* (spiritual medium) remains a powerful figure consulted by, among others, leading Malay political figures. And martial arts linked with invincibility cults continue to have a strong appeal. In July 2000 a group found practising such beliefs, Al-Ma'unah, seized arms from army depots and staged a shoot-out in which three people were killed.

MILITANT ISLAM

While Malaysian Muslims have generally eschewed extremism, the Al-Ma'unah incident is not the only case of religious violence. During the colonial era, Islam was often a rallying cry in sporadic uprisings against colonial rule. More recently, in August 1978, extremists desecrated some 28 Hindu temples throughout the penin-sula, until temple guards intercepted one attack and killed four intruders. In October 1980, eight assailants were killed when they attacked a police station in Johor. In November 1985, 14 villagers and four police were killed during a conflict in Memali in the state of Kedah. In both the Memali and Al-Ma'unah cases the circumstances remain controversial, with many Malays believing that security forces mishandled these incidents or were implicated in them.

The popular Darul Arqam organization was also accused of militancy. In 1994 the National Fatwa Committee declared it a deviant Islamic sect; the government then banned it and detained its leaders under the Internal Security Act. Among major accusations levelled against it was a claim that it had organized a military wing in Thailand, trained to wage war on the Malaysian government. The government did not provide proof of such militancy, however, and many analysts have concluded that other factors were behind the ban.[7]

Since June 2001, under the Internal Security Act, the government has arrested over 70 alleged extremists said to belong to Kumpulan Militan/Mujahidin Malaysia (KMM, Malaysian Militant/Mujahidin Organization) or Jemaah Islamiyah (JI). The nature of KMM remains shrouded in mystery, but investigations into the Bali bombing of 12 October 2002 have shown that Malaysia was a centre for JI activities. Nearly all detainees or suspects linked to Bali had permanent resident status in Malaysia and had spent years there, encouraged by government willingness to provide sanctuary for regional Islamic dissidents.

Nonetheless the Malaysian JI has a regional focus, not a national one. Most of its leaders have been Indonesians. The small number of Malaysians who joined – some of whom obtained senior leadership positions – were drawn in after participating in Islamic study groups led by Indonesians, or after fighting with the *mujahidin* in Afghanistan in the 1980s. The activities of the Malaysian JI have focused on terrorist plans in Indonesia, Singapore and the Philippines rather than in Malaysia.

THE RISE AND RISE OF POLITICAL ISLAM

While extremism has been the exception, political Islam has grown steadily in importance – building on the role of Islam in the nationalist movement, its ambiguous constitutional definition, the *dakwah* movement and the government's Islamization program. A series of highlights marked its progress until the 2004 election, which many analysts regard as a watershed in entrenching a commitment to 'moderate' Islam.

The first post-independence election in 1959 brought an unexpected setback to UMNO when PAS won power in two states (Kelantan and Terengganu) and gained around half the Malay vote. Islam played only a minor part – issues of Malay nationalism and education, state parochialism and class were important as well – but became more important later. Although PAS soon lost power in Terengganu, this marked the beginning of a split in the Malay vote; since 1959, 30–50 per cent of the Malay vote has always gone to PAS. Another high point came in 1969, when PAS secured

---

7   Doctrinal differences may also have been a factor, although one scholar has argued that the government did not make a convincing case of deviationism (Ahmad Fauzi 2004). Perhaps more important, however, was Darul Arqam's political challenge to the government, in the form of a claim by its leader that he was more popular than Prime Minister Mahathir and would one day lead the country.

around half the Malay vote. It then went into decline, losing office in Kelantan in 1978 and only regaining it in 1990. Its best result ever was in 1999, when it swept both Kelantan and Terengganu and won 27 seats in the federal parliament.

The 1969 election was quickly followed by racial riots beginning on 13 May in which some 200 lives were lost. Parliamentary democracy was suspended for 21 months before being reconstituted in a form that restricted political liberties, entrenched Malay political dominance and ensured stronger affirmative action for Malays under the country's New Economic Policy (NEP). To regain political ground UMNO sought to embellish its Islamic credentials. It did this by establishing a coalition with PAS, formalized in the National Front (successor to the Alliance) in 1974 and maintained until December 1977; by strengthening the prominence given to Islam in national affairs (for example by announcing a new cultural policy that put Islam at the centre); and by expanding the religious bureaucracy under the Office of the Prime Minister.[8] At the same time the NEP increased the number of Malays in tertiary institutions and strengthened student organizations, which, under the leadership of Anwar Ibrahim, had begun to campaign strongly on Islam and related issues.

At the beginning of the 1980s both UMNO and PAS became more strongly Islamic. Dr Mahathir became prime minister in 1981 and brought Anwar Ibrahim into the party in 1982. Together they introduced policies such as 'inculcating Islamic values' into the administration, and 'balancing spiritual and material development'; they also established major institutions such as the International Islamic University and the Islamic Bank. Anwar rose through the ranks and became deputy prime minister after being elected deputy leader of UMNO in 1993.

In the same period PAS ousted its long-serving head, Dato' Asri Muda (effectively its leader since 1965); promoted younger members such as Ustaz Fadzil Noor and Ustaz Hj Hadi Awang (both former leaders of ABIM and future leaders of PAS); made strident demands for the establishment of a full Islamic state; and established an indirectly elected Majlis Syura Ulama (Ulama Consultative Body) as its top policy-making institution.

The beginning of the Asian economic crisis in 1997 led to a questioning of UMNO's rule, with a focus on the issues of corruption, injustice and lack of democracy. Many Malaysians were deeply disturbed by Mahathir's sacking of his deputy in September 1998, Anwar's subsequent bashing at the hands of the police chief, and the multiple humiliations heaped on Anwar by the media and in the courts. All of these issues gave rise to calls for *reformasi* (reform). PAS aligned itself with the *reformasi* movement, and tens of thousands of Malays left UMNO to join it. Malays voted strongly for the party in the 1999 election.

After a disastrous election result, UMNO sought to regain lost ground by outbidding PAS on Islamic issues. In April 2000 the UMNO-controlled Perlis state legislature passed draconian laws for the rehabilitation of Muslims deemed to have strayed from the true path; a similar bill to go before parliament in September was

---

8 The National Front initially included Alliance members – particularly UMNO, the Malaysian Chinese Association and the Malaysian Indian Congress – and four former opposition parties, the most important being PAS and Gerakan. Total membership has since fluctuated, but currently stands at 14.

withdrawn at the last moment. In October UMNO agreed at a special meeting in Johor to introduce full Islamic law (including controversial *hudud* provisions from Islamic criminal law) at an appropriate time. On 29 September 2001 Mahathir declared Malaysia an 'Islamic state' – the timing no doubt influenced by his desire to outflank PAS after he had declared all-out support for the United States in the 'war on terror' following September 11. Mahathir had frequently made such a claim in the past, but went further on this occasion by announcing it at a meeting of UMNO's coalition partner, Gerakan, then convening a meeting of all members in the ruling National Front to endorse this. Later he told UMNO and parliament that Malaysia was a 'fundamentalist Islamic state'. Mahathir's rhetoric encouraged stronger action by others. In October the Information Department distributed a booklet – *Malaysia Is an Islamic State* – that clearly relegated non-Muslims to a secondary position. It was withdrawn after a time, but similar articles remained on Jakim's website.[9]

Despite such rhetoric, non-Malays rallied behind Mahathir after September 11, preferring his track record to the uncertain promises of PAS. Although not replicated to anything like the same extent among Malays, this arrested the slide in his popularity and enabled him to retire in October 2003 while apparently still in firm control.

PAS initially responded to these developments with an attempt to draw up a moderate 'Islamic state' document of its own. It had moved down this path while Fadzil Noor remained leader but the process was derailed after his unexpected death in June 2002. The eventual Islamic state document, released in November 2003, was far less conciliatory, though PAS did release additional supplementary assurances that addressed some non-Muslim concerns (Liew 2004). A PAS initiative to declare jihad against America after its invasion of Afghanistan – widely misinterpreted as a call for military assistance for the Taliban – attracted widespread adverse international attention, even though the government position was little different in substance.

THE 2004 ELECTION – THE END OF AN ERA?

Most accounts of the 2004 election present it as a disaster for PAS and a triumph for the moderate Islamic policy known as Islam Hadhari (Civilizational Islam) under the new prime minister, Abdullah Badawi. There is some evidence for this in the dramatic decline in the number of parliamentary and state seats won by PAS. Its parliamentary representation fell from 26 seats to six. It was trounced in the Terengganu assembly, where it was defeated 28 to four; and it barely held on to power in Kelantan, where it won 24 seats compared to UMNO's 21 seats. On 24 March 2004, the *Christian Science Monitor* declared:

> The sweeping victory of Malaysia's secular rulers … emphasises the narrow appeal of Muslim hard-liners in Southeast Asia, where strict religion-based politics run up against multiethnic realities. Muslim voters dealt a potentially knock-out blow to the conservative PAS.

---

9 'Remove "Offensive" Articles from Website, Jakim Told', *Malaysiakini*, 5 December 2001.

However, a closer look at the results – focusing on the proportion of the popular vote rather than seats gained – yields a different interpretation. The percentage of those voting for PAS hardly changed at all, even though PAS campaigned on something considerably less than an even electoral playing field (Funston 2005). Islam Hadhari may eventually prove to be a progressive form of Islam, but its details were not explained during the electoral campaign and have not been explained subsequently despite several promises of a book to elaborate its meaning. In addition, the campaign represented very much a familiar attempt by UMNO to outbid PAS: Abdullah was represented in advertising as an Islamic scholar; the party manifesto promised that the Qur'an would be taught to Muslims in all public schools; and several well-known Islamic scholars stood as UMNO candidates.

The 2004 election thus seems to have been a continuation of the traditional UMNO–PAS rivalry that has pushed Malaysia in a more conservative Islamic direction. So far there is only limited evidence that this has aided extremists. Incidents of violence have been relatively few, and their circumstances have been a matter of conflicting interpretations – though the emergence of JI may have been assisted by Malaysia providing sanctuary and support to Islamic dissidents from across the region, particularly from the 1980s. These included Abdullah Sungkar, Abu Bakar Ba'asyir and Acehnese separatists from Indonesia, as well as Moro leaders from the southern Philippines and Thai Malays. However, for the most part, the move towards conservatism has taken place in an environment where the government has acted to reduce democratic space, particularly after the 'Anwar crisis' in the late 1990s. Given the persuasiveness of the case that democracy strengthens the forces of Islamic moderation (Ahmad 2000: 76–80), this may be a cause for long-term concern.

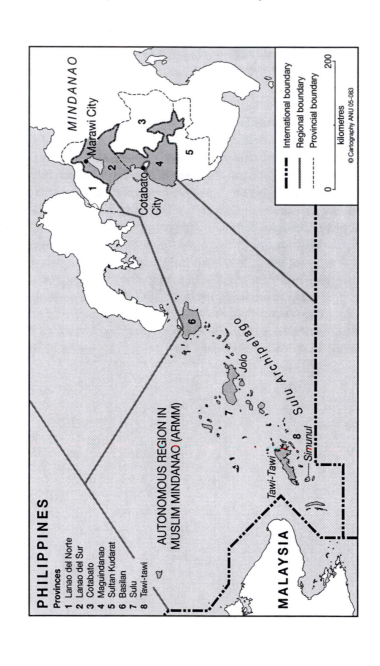

PHILIPPINES

Provinces
1 Lanao del Norte
2 Lanao del Sur
3 Cotabato
4 Maguindanao
5 Sultan Kudarat
6 Basilan
7 Sulu
8 Tawi-tawi

AUTONOMOUS REGION IN
MUSLIM MINDANAO (ARMM)

MALAYSIA

MINDANAO

Marawi City

Cotabato
City

Jolo

Sulu Archipelago

Tawi-Tawi

Simunul

International boundary
Regional boundary
Provincial boundary

0   200
kilometres

© Cartography ANU 05-083

7   The Philippines

Kit Collier

MUSLIMS IN THE PHILIPPINES

Professed by between 4 and 5 per cent of a national population numbering 87 million, Islam in the Philippines possesses more the quality of an ethnic marker than a singular religious tradition. Efforts by Muslims and non-Muslims alike to impose an imagined unity on this peripheral outpost of the global Islamic community (*ummah*) have repeatedly been defeated by the tyrannies of distance and cultural diversity. Yet attenuated orthopraxy has not precluded a sense of shared Muslim difference in the face of dominant Philippine institutions. The country's approximately 4 million Muslims are heavily concentrated in the southwestern provinces of the large southern island of Mindanao and the adjacent Sulu archipelago, which stretches to nearby Malaysian Sabah. There, a diaspora of several hundred thousand more Philippine Muslims (Moros)[1] have taken up residence since the outbreak of separatist civil war in the early 1970s, many permanently.

Comprising about one-fifth of the population in the Mindanao–Sulu region as a whole, Muslims are a majority in only five of the region's 26 provinces: Maguindanao, Lanao del Sur, Sulu, Tawi-tawi and Basilan.[2] There are significant Muslim minorities (ranging from 15 to 30 per cent) in Cotabato, Sultan Kudarat and Lanao del Norte provinces. The Muslim-majority provinces had the five lowest human development indices in the Philippines in 2000, with poverty rates ranging from 36 per cent (Maguindanao) to 92 per cent (Sulu), against a national average of 27.5 per cent (World Bank 2003: 11). The five provinces, together with the Islamic city of Marawi, make up a still evolving Autonomous Region in Muslim Mindanao (ARMM), first established in 1990.

---

1   The collective term 'Moro' was first applied to Southeast Asian Muslims by sixteenth-century Portuguese and Spanish adventurers, for whom the struggle with Iberian Moors was a recent memory. It was taken up by American colonial officials in the Philippines at the turn of the twentieth century and appropriated by Philippine Muslim nationalists in the 1960s.
2   The Philippines as a whole is made up of 79 provinces.

Tribal loyalties based on ethno-linguistic distinctions preceded, and are often in tension with, Philippine Muslims' collective Islamic identity. There are conventionally 13 Muslim tribes,[3] the largest of which are the Maguindanaon, Tausug, Maranao, Sama, Iranon and Yakan. The most fundamental socio-political distinction is between the mainland Maguindanaon, Maranao and Iranon on the one hand, whose languages are closely related, and the archipelagic Tausug, Sama and Yakan on the other, whose languages are more diverse but who historically shared a common orientation towards the Sulu sultanate rather than its mainland Maguindanao rival.

ORIGINS OF ISLAM AND EARLY STATE FORMATION

As in much of Southeast Asia, the origins of Philippine Islam lie in a blend of trade, missionary activity and conquest. Some of the region's earliest archaeological testaments to Islamic influence are found on Jolo, Sulu's central island, where a gravestone belonging to a foreign Muslim named Tuan Maqbalu has been dated to 1310, and on Simunul island, Tawi-tawi, where a mosque is believed to have stood in the village of Tubig Indangan since around 1380. The Tausug people of Sulu[4] take pride in being the first of the tribes of the present-day Philippines to embrace Islam, having instituted some time after 1450 a sultanate that became a significant force in the region. Trading ties with Cham kingdoms in what is now southern and central Vietnam are documented as far back as the beginning of the eleventh century (Scott 1989: 3–4, 27) when, linguistic evidence suggests, ancestors of today's Tausug migrated to Sulu from an established polity in the Butuan area of northeastern Mindanao. These longstanding ties to the north with Champa, and with China, to which Butuan and later Sulu sent regular tribute missions, may have contributed as much to Sulu's early acceptance of Islam as did Indian and Arab influences mediated through the Malay archipelago to the west.

The Maguindanaon[5] trace their own Islamization to the arrival of a nobleman and descendant of the Prophet, Sharif Kabungsuan, who fled the Portuguese conquest of Malacca in the early sixteenth century. Islam's consolidation on mainland Mindanao was similarly spurred by Spanish intervention in the highland country of Lanao in 1639–40, when Maguindanao's revered Sultan Kudarat made common cause against the invader with the then still barely Islamized Maranao–Iranon[6] peoples. The Maranao have never looked to a unified sultanate, but rather to a confederal system of aristocratic hierarchy, while the Iranon were traditionally seafaring privateers, raiding across the Malay archipelago to take slaves for sale on the Sulu mar-

---

3   The term 'tribe' is avoided by many scholars, but we have used it in this context because it is the term that the various Moro enthno-linguistic groups use to describe themselves.

4   In Tausug, Sulu is called 'Lupah Sug', meaning 'land of the sea currents'. Similarly, 'Tausug' connotes 'people of the current'.

5   Maguindanaon: 'people of the flood plain'.

6   Maranao: 'people of the lake'; Iranon: 'people of the (Illana) bay'. Linguistic evidence suggests that the Maranao and Iranon diverged only in recent historical times; the distinction may not have been so clear in Sultan Kudarat's time, although the Maguindanaon were already distinct.

ket, which prospered with the growth of the eighteenth-century China trade (Warren 2002).

LAW, THE STATE AND THE INSTITUTIONALIZATION OF ISLAM

As in the rest of Southeast Asia, most Philippine Muslims follow the Shafi'i school of law, formally manifested in the mid-eighteenth-century Maguindanaon code called the *Luwaran* [Selections] and a national Code of Muslim Personal Laws introduced in 1977. The *Luwaran* is based on both local customary law (*adat*) and classical Shafi'i sources, including the seventeenth-century *fiqh* text *Mir'aah al-Tullaab* [Mirror for Seekers] prepared by Abdu'r-Ra'uf of Singkel for the ruler of Aceh in the mid-seventeenth century, which circulated widely throughout island Southeast Asia (Hooker 1984: 41). Further references in the *Luwaran* are made to classical Arabic texts such as the *Minhaaj al-Taalibiin* [Method for Seekers] of Muhyi ud-Din Abu Zakariya Yahya an-Nawawi[7] and other classical Arabic texts widely used throughout Southeast Asia (Buat 1976: 119; Tan 2003a: 39). Although the epitome of historical Islamic scholarship in the southern Philippines, the *Luwaran* 'lacks the direct treatment of religion' characteristic of comparable Malay and Indonesian texts (Hooker 1984: 23) and, dwelling principally on slavery, property relations and punishment, is more revealing of traditional hierarchy than of Islam as such.[8]

The 1977 Code of Personal Laws 'consists largely of an abstract of Shafi'i law relating to marriage, divorce and maintenance, and succession ... [m]ore Islamic in content than anything known in the pre-Code period' (Hooker 1984: 232). In this respect it perfectly mirrors the role of the colonial and post-colonial state in systematizing, institutionalizing and rationalizing an otherwise inchoate Philippine Islam, in an ongoing effort to integrate it into the wider body politic.

Two individuals – both of Middle Eastern and Christian extraction – have been especially prominent in this effort to impose a symbolic unity on Islam in the Philippines. The first, Najeeb M. Saleeby, as Agent for Moro Affairs from 1903, led attempts by the US colonial regime (1898–1946) to consolidate the Muslim community around a common sense of identity. In that year, Philippine Commission Act No. 787 creating the Moro province brought Muslims together under a unified politico-military administration for the first time in history, and mandated the collection and codification of customary Muslim law. Saleeby accordingly translated and published the *Luwaran*, the Sulu codes of 1877 and 1902, and the *tarsila* (Ar.: *silsilah*; 'name-chain') – legitimizing genealogies by which local sultanates claim descent from the Prophet (Saleeby 1905, 1908). Although Governor Leonard Wood felt that nothing in the Muslim legal codes was 'worthy of codification' (Gowing 1979: 37), Saleeby's influence was strongly felt in colonial education policy, and a new generation of

---

7 Al-Nawawi (1233–78 CE) was a famous scholar of Islamic jurisprudence and Hadith from Damascus. His writings on law and Prophetic tradition are widely used by Southeast Asian Muslims.

8 This is even more true of the equivalent Sulu codes of 1877 and 1902, which for Hooker (1984: 25) typify the 'dragging in of Islam at the last moment' into Philippine Muslim texts.

Muslim leadership arose under US auspices possessing 'a shared and self-conscious ethnoreligious identity ... transcend[ing] ethnolinguistic and geographical boundaries' (McKenna 1998: 109).[9]

The second seminal state intellectual, who drew heavily on Saleeby's work, was Cesar Adib Majul (1923–2003). Majul acquired an early knowledge of Islam from his Greek Orthodox father, a former functionary at the Ottoman Court, but his first interest (pursued at Cornell University in the United States) lay in the constitutional ideas of the (northern) Philippine Revolution against Spain (1896–98). Majul transposed this modern anti-colonial framework to the south in his enormously influential *Muslims in the Philippines* (1973), arguing that four centuries of armed clashes between Moros and Spaniards in the archipelago amounted to a coherent proto-nationalist struggle (Majul 1999). The publication of Majul's magnum opus coincided with the emergence of a revolutionary new Bangsamoro (Moro People) national project led by Nurullaji ('Nur') Misuari's Moro National Liberation Front (MNLF). Misuari, a left-leaning student activist at the University of the Philippines and an ethnic Sama from Sulu, was Majul's research assistant during the writing of the book in the 1960s, but re-imagined Muslim nationalist historiography as the basis for secession rather than assimilation into a multi-ethnic Philippines.

Misuari was just one of about 8,300 Muslim students to receive scholarships from the government's Commission on National Integration between 1958 and 1967 (Gowing 1979: 184). This scholarship program, together with the Mindanao State University system, was the product of a Special Committee on Moro Affairs convened by the Philippine Congress in 1954. These measures, modest as they were, represented Manila's boldest initiatives to improve Muslims' socio-economic position between independence in 1946 and the outbreak of the MNLF rebellion in 1972; however, like similar colonial policies, they fed the Muslim sense of difference rather than stemming it. State policy towards Islam became more proactive following President Ferdinand Marcos's declaration of martial law in September 1972, combining brutal military repression in Mindanao with a 'policy of attraction' towards the Muslim elite. Here Majul played an important role. Marcos created an Institute of Islamic Studies at the University of the Philippines, with Majul appointed as its first dean (1974–80). He also served as chair of the Philippine Amanah Bank (now renamed the Al-Amanah Islamic Investment Bank) and as chair of the Presidential Commission, which drafted the 1977 Code of Muslim Personal Laws (enacted by Marcos as Presidential Decree 1083).

The implementation of Presidential Decree 1083 has been slow and uneven. It took eight years to establish its five sharia district courts, which have jurisdiction over Muslims in 10 provinces and six cities of Mindanao. Three of the five district courts, and 31 of the mandated 51 circuit courts, still had no judges as of 2003; only 24 circuit courts had actually been established. Difficulties appear greatest in far-flung Tawi-tawi, where there were no circuit judges at all, and only one court. The Maranao region of Lanao, by contrast, boasted its own district court judge, with nine

---

9   Saleeby's role in this respect stands in contrast to that of his Dutch East Indies contemporary, C. Snouck Hurgronje, who emphasized the centrifugal force of local *adat*.

of 11 circuit judgeships filled and only one circuit court yet to be created (Solamo-Antonio 2003: 14–16, 48).[10] Most cases actually filed in court are women's petitions for divorce by anulment (*faskh*) and for child support (*nafaqa*), and men's petitions for divorce by repudiation (*talaq*), but far more cases are resolved informally. The main obstacles to wider resort to sharia courts seem to be lack of qualified judges, lack of financial support from the government, and lack of community interest in the system as presently constituted. Discussions were under way in early 2005 between Islamic scholars and NGOs on possible amendments to the 1977 code.

State involvement in other areas of Muslim life also grew during the martial law era (1972–81; martial law remained in effect in Muslim Mindanao until 1986). Marcos created the Philippine Pilgrimage Authority in 1979 to coordinate and facilitate performance of the haj, which grew from an average of 807 pilgrims in the five previous years to 1,880 during the ensuing decade, and about 3,000 today.[11] In 1987 this function was taken over by the Bureau of Pilgrimage and Endowment in the Office of Muslim Affairs (OMA), the lead government agency dealing with Philippine Muslims, under the Office of the President, who also appoints the *amir al-hajj* (leader of the haj). Maharlika Village, a project initiated by Marcos in 1973 to provide homes in Manila for better-off Muslims, has become a staging point for the haj and a refuge for squatters displaced from Manila's other area of major Muslim concentration, Quiapo.

CONTESTING STATE INSTITUTIONS

Control over key aspects of Muslim life is sometimes contested between state and civil society, often reflecting internecine community struggles. Maharlika's Blue Mosque was long administered by the National Housing Authority, which oversaw the entire project. Control was later transferred to the city of Taguig, then to the OMA; following the assassination of the OMA's local administrator in late 2004, temporary authority was vested in Sultan Kiram of Sulu, who resides nearby. Control over such major mosques is an important source of political prestige and charitable funding from domestic and overseas sponsors, as well as the ordinary faithful.[12] In another controversy, in 2001 the OMA took authority to issue *halal* food certifications away from the private-sector Islamic Dawah Council, depriving it of significant export-related income. The Philippine Supreme Court overturned the measure, deciding in the council's favour in July 2003.[13]

---

10   The *Philippine Star* reported in December 2003 that 35 of the 56 mandated district and circuit courts had judges, only one of whom was female (*Philippine Star*, 13 December 2003: 16).

11   See Panda (1993: 76), and interview with Abdurahman U. Amin, Permanent Chief Liaison Officer and MNLF Special Envoy to the Organization of the Islamic Conference, Cotabato City, 23 November 2004.

12   Interview with Sultan Jamalul Kiram III, Maharlika Village, Bicutan, Taguig, Manila, 19 November 2004.

13   Interview with Haji Abdul Rahman Linzag, president of the Islamic Dawah Council of the Philippines, Manila, 16 April 2005.

The state has also sought to integrate Islamic school (*madrasah*) education into the national system, especially after President Marcos issued an order to that effect in March 1982. But uncertainty remains over such fundamental questions as the number of *madrasah* in the country, which also vary widely in status (informal, independent, affiliated to a wider network, accredited by the Department of Education, accredited by foreign bodies). One recent survey counted 673 *madrasah* with 4,187 teachers and another counted 440 *madrasah* with 3,433 teachers, but both appear far from complete (Asia Foundation and ARMM 2004; BEAM 2004). As is the case with the sharia court system, commitment to *madrasah* education is strongest in the Lanao region, which accounts for between 46 and 66 per cent of the schools surveyed. The OMA reportedly tallies 1,890 *madrasah* nationwide, more than 800 of these in ARMM (*Manila Times*, 18 November 2003).

But the most contentious issue of all has been territorial, arising from the mass migration of Christians from the central and northern islands south to Mindanao. This movement peaked in the 1950s and 1960s, shifting electoral control away from Muslim elites, particularly in Cotabato in 1967–71. Muslim traditional leaders (*datu*), including local rulers like Udtog Matalam of Pagalungan, Cotabato, responded by ethnicizing their appeals to consolidate core voting blocs: Matalam declared the formation of a Muslim Independence Movement in 1968. As *datu* in Cotabato and Lanao began sponsoring overseas military training for groups of militant youths, some Christian politicians supported militia atrocities against Muslim civilians. Led by Nur Misuari, the MNLF then launched an armed campaign for Bangsamoro independence in reaction to Marcos's seizure of dictatorial powers.

Although Muslim politics has been dominated by the question of secession since 1972, the MNLF is overwhelmingly a secular movement; sweeping territorial demands have accompanied a loose definition of Moro nationhood that even encompasses Christians.[14] A peace pact signed in Tripoli in December 1976 envisaged an autonomous region encompassing as many as 13 provinces – a proposal that soon collided with demographic reality when rejected in a plebiscite. Today's truncated ARMM has grown out of a further 1987 accord reached in Jeddah, and a 'Final Agreement' on the implementation of the Tripoli framework concluded in Jakarta in September 1996. Largely an executive effort under President Fidel Ramos (1992–98), the process leading to the Jakarta agreement failed to build consensus in the Philippine Congress or with key Christian stakeholders. Implementing legislation has thus restricted funding from the financially strapped central government, and the anticipated flood of foreign aid and investment in ARMM has not materialized. Corruption and capacity issues and the continuing presence of what many Muslims experience as an alien occupying force – the Philippine army – compound disappointment with autonomy. This has contributed to the fracturing of the MNLF and a concomitant rise of more self-consciously Islamic alternatives.

The Moro Islamic Liberation Front (MILF), a splinter group that has taken up the separatist mantle since the MNLF accepted autonomy in 1996, defines its

---

14   The MNLF slogan, *Bangsa, Hulah, Agama* (Nation, Homeland, Religion), captures the movement's rank ordering of sources of identity, with religion a clear third.

goals in religious terms and no longer seeks control of Christian-majority areas.[15] With 10,000–15,000 full-time combatants under arms, and many more reservists, the MILF is Southeast Asia's most formidable separatist movement. Its founding chairperson, Salamat Hashim (1942–2003), was one of a generation of Philippine Muslims who won scholarships not from the Commission on National Integration, but from Cairo's al-Azhar University. Other influential graduates with Middle Eastern training include Abdulbaki Abubakar, Omar Pasigan and Mahid Mutilan. Each might be considered the supreme Islamic scholar of his respective ethno-linguistic group: Tausug, Maguindanaon and Maranao. Abdulbaki Abubakar is closely associated with Misuari and the MNLF. Sheikh Pasigan is styled Grand Mufti of Cotabato, heads the Philippine Darul-Ifta (House of Opinion)[16] and sits in the upper echelons of the MILF. And Mutilan, who has served as the provincial governor of Lanao del Sur and as ARMM vice-governor, leads the Ulama League of the Philippines and one of only two explicitly Islamic political parties of any significance, the Ompia (Reform) party. Ompia, established in the wake of the 1986 'People Power' uprising that overthrew Marcos, has won local posts in the Lanao region, while the electoral ambitions of the pro-Misuari Musawara (Consultation) party, which first ran in 2001, have likewise been limited to municipal positions in Sulu.

Muslims have received roughly proportional representation in the lower chamber of the thirteenth Philippine Congress (2004–07), with 12 out of 237 representatives, two of them women, professing Islam as their religion. All belong to secular parties: seven to the ruling Lakas (People Power) party of President Gloria Macapagal-Arroyo (2001–), three to national opposition parties and two to 'party-list' groups. The party-list system, introduced in 1998, allows voters to select a second candidate, in addition to their district member, to represent a 'marginalized sector' of society. Despite this provision, no explicitly Islamic party has emerged to contest politics in the national arena. A left-wing Muslim party, Suara Bangsamoro (Voice of the Moro People), has failed to win any seats, while the two incumbent Muslim party-list representatives also emphasize ethnicity and progressive reformism over Islam.[17] The upper chamber, constituted as a single national electorate, is now without a Muslim among its 23 senators, although Muslims have served with distinction in the past. Elsewhere in national government, there were two Muslim cabinet secretaries and one Court of Appeals associate justice in early 2004; seven senior officers in the armed forces, including one brigadier general; and 169 senior officers in the national police, four with the rank of one-star general (Republic of the Philippines 2004).

---

15 Its founding chairman, Salamat Hashim, broke with the Misuari-led MNLF in December 1977, only naming his faction 'MILF' in 1984 following the Iranian revolution and the Soviet invasion of Afghanistan.

16 This is a body of Islamic scholars that is responsible for issuing religious rulings (fatwa).

17 At present 24 of 237 seats in the House of Representatives are allocated to sectoral parties. One of the two Muslim party-list members belongs to a regional left-wing party, Anak Mindanao (Children of Mindanao), and the other to a local Lanao indigenous rights group, Ang Laban ng Indiginong Filipino (ALIF, Struggle of the Indigenous Filipino). Notwithstanding its Arabic acronym (*alif* is the first letter of the Arabic alphabet) and indigenous appeal, this second party's nomenclature is unabashedly national – and Tagalog.

The rise of transnational jihad groups such as Jemaah Islamiyah, determined to insert themselves into the Philippines' endemic ethno-religious conflicts – and the equal determination of the United States to combat them – represents a new variation on a familiar historical theme. Despite a century of external impositions – the colonial administrative grid, grand intellectual re-imaginings of history, Marcos's centralizing despotism and the polarized battlelines of the war on terror – Islam in the Philippines remains irremediably tribal and pluralistic. Its panoply ranges from the folk beliefs of subsistence peasants and the quietly expanding ranks of the Tablighi Jamaat[18] to cyber-savvy 'Yuplims' and Christian 'reverts' (*balik-Islam*),[19] aristocratic *datu* and wistful sultans, radical, levelling Wahhabi[20] ulema and the ruthless depredations of the Abu Sayyaf Group. To the extent that any sense of identity does bind the Muslim peoples of the Philippines, it is a sense of shared difference more than an internal singularity – which, in the absence of an outside catalyst, melts away into fractiousness.

---

18   Tablighi Jamaat is an Indian Islamic reform movement founded in 1927 by Mawlana Muhammad Ilyas. It focuses on preaching and other kinds of religious activity rather than politics. It has a strong presence in many Southeast Asian countries, including Indonesia, Burma and Malaysia.

19   Yuplims are 'young, upwardly mobile Muslims'. The *balik-Islam* – those who have 'returned to Islam' (on the assumption that all Filipinos were Muslim prior to Spanish rule) – are sometimes called the '14th tribe' of Philippine Islam, and are estimated to number between 100,000 and 200,000. Many are former overseas workers in the Middle East, where about 1.5 million Filipinos are employed, and provide a significant channel for Saudi-funded *dakwah*, free of indigenous Muslim cultural 'accretions'.

20   Wahhabism is a reform movement founded by Muhammad ibn 'Abd al-Wahhab in the late eighteenth century. Now the dominant sect in Saudi Arabia, it is notable for its strictly puritanical interpretation of Islam.

8   Singapore

John Funston

Singapore's Muslim population is small in absolute terms compared to those in countries such as the Philippines and Thailand, but in percentage terms it is the largest Muslim minority in Southeast Asia. Government policies designed to integrate Muslims into the Singapore mainstream have, to a large extent, been successful. Though not as well off as a community as the majority Chinese, Muslims (mostly ethnic Malays) have benefited from the spectacular economic growth Singapore has experienced since becoming a separate and independent country in 1965. Still, a small number of individuals have rejected integration and opted for militant opposition. That was dramatically illustrated between December 2001 and September 2002 when Singapore authorities arrested over 30 members of Jemaah Islamiyah (JI) for planning to bomb various foreign embassies and public sites.

DEMOGRAPHY

Singapore is a multi-ethnic and multi-religious state. According to the 2000 census[1] Muslims in Singapore number around 15 per cent of residents aged 15 years and over. Chinese are the dominant ethnic group (79 per cent). Most Chinese are adherents of Buddhism or Taoism, or hold other traditional Chinese beliefs. The Indian community, 7 per cent of the population, is mainly Hindu, although nearly one-third is Muslim. Christians, mainly Chinese and Indian, make up 14.6 per cent of the population.

Some 85 per cent of Muslims (313,780) are Malays, with the other 15 per cent made up of 45,927 Indians, 2,687 Chinese and 6,891 others (most probably of Arab descent). Muslims are not concentrated in particular areas in the city-state. Prior to independence most Malays lived in semi-rural villages (*kampong*) in more remote areas, but this separateness was eroded after independence by the government's housing estate policy, which required accommodation for all ethnic groups to be mixed.

---

1   Statistics are taken or calculated from the 2000 census. See <http://www.singstat.gov.sg/keystats/c2000/topline2.pdf>, accessed 14 March 2005.

HISTORY

Until selected by Sir Thomas Stamford Raffles as a British maritime base in 1819, Singapore was a Malay outpost under the influence of sultanates in Sumatra and Johor. Under the British, Singapore thrived as an entrepôt port, and an influx of Chinese soon led to the Malays and local sea-peoples becoming a minority.

Britain ruled Singapore directly as a colony. In some respects this gave Malays less autonomy over Islamic affairs than they had in Malaya and Brunei. However, Britain allowed Muslims more freedom to express opinions than was available in the Malay sultanates, and the removal of royalty enhanced the social prominence of Islamic leaders (Milner 2002: 153–63). Singapore's role as a major international port also facilitated travel for Muslims in Southeast Asia and visits by Islamic scholars from the Indian subcontinent and the Middle East. Singapore quickly became a centre for Islamic studies and publishing, and a regional focus for the reformist movement in the early twentieth century. The British also sought to gain Muslim support by allowing Islamic law (sharia) for personal and property affairs, and promoting social welfare through a Muslim and Hindu Endowment Board established in 1906.

Singapore was the centre of British administration for peninsular Malaya until the establishment of the Malayan Federation in 1948, and many Singaporeans could envisage no future other than in association with the peninsula. Malay Muslims in particular looked forward to membership in Malaya as part of the dominant political group in the country. Singapore obtained independence in 1963 as part of an expanded federation renamed Malaysia, but Singapore's Chinese-led People's Action Party (PAP) clashed with the Malay-led Alliance over the issue of Malay political pre-eminence and Singapore was ordered out of the federation two years later.

The PAP, first elected to office in the days of internal self-rule in 1959, obtained separate independence under circumstances that made it acutely aware of the need to integrate the city-state's Malay-Muslim minority. Religion-based riots had occurred in 1950, when 18 people were killed during protests against a court decision to return 13-year-old Maria Hertogh, a Dutch girl raised by Muslims, to her Catholic parents. Two further riots occurred in July 1964 (on Prophet Muhammad's birthday) and September 1964 while Singapore was part of Malaysia, mainly reflecting local Malay opposition to PAP attempts to oppose Malay federal dominance; 36 lives were lost in these two clashes. The Singapore constitution therefore provided for religious freedom, but with the explicit proviso that this not be allowed to create animosity between different religious groups. One of the first laws passed was the Administration of Muslim Law Act (AMLA) in 1966, creating a government-supervised framework for the administration of Muslim affairs.

In subsequent years several further initiatives addressed the issue of protecting intercommunal relations, nearly all with a view to integrating the Malay-Muslim community. A high-level Presidential Council was established in 1970. Renamed the Presidential Council for Minority Rights in 1973, it was responsible for vetting all parliamentary legislation to ensure it did not disadvantage minorities. In 1987 the government introduced the Group Representation Constituency (GRC) scheme for parliamentary elections, establishing multiple-member constituencies in which at least one member had to represent an ethnic minority. These were first used in the 1988 election, when around half the candidates contested single-member constituencies and half GRCs. In the latest election (2001) only nine seats were allocated to single constituencies. The remaining 75 seats were distributed between 14 GRCs, from which 12 Muslims were returned.[2] Finally, a Maintenance of Religious Harmony Act in 1990 reinforced existing provisions against inciting religious unrest.

ADMINISTRATION OF ISLAM

The centrepiece of the AMLA when it came into effect in 1968 was Majlis Ugama Islam Singapura (MUIS, Islamic Religious Council of Singapore), located under the Ministry of Community Development. In the 1990s the responsible minister was also designated minister-in-charge of Muslim affairs. However, Dr Yaacob Ibrahim, who was appointed minister for community development and sports in 2001, has retained responsibility for Muslim affairs since being appointed minister for the environment and water resources in August 2004.

The MUIS website cites its principal functions as:[3]

- administration of *zakat* (wealth tax), *wakaf* (property endowment), haj (pilgrimage) affairs, *halal* certification and *dakwah* (Islamic outreach) activities;
- administration of Islamic schools (*madrasah*) and Islamic education;
- issuance of fatwa (religious edicts);
- provision of financial relief to poor and needy Muslims; and
- provision of developmental grants to (Muslim) organizations.

MUIS is, in addition, responsible for supervising sharia law relating to marriage, divorce and the division of property. Decisions in the sharia courts may be referred to an appeal board under MUIS.

The main decision-making body in MUIS is its council. Headed by a president, it comprises the Mufti of Singapore together with persons nominated by the responsible minister and others nominated by Muslim organizations. All are appointed by Singapore's president. Under the council is a directorate made up of three clusters: Islamic development (education, mosque development, public outreach); assets management (*halal* certification, haj services, *zakat*, *wakaf*); and corporate services (finance, human resources, information systems). After being established with government assistance MUIS now raises most of its own funds, but still receives annual budgetary assistance. In 2005 it received S$17 million (about US$10.2 million), and another S$3.5 million (US$2.1 million) for the special purpose of enhancing racial and religious harmony through partnership with other ethnic and religious organizations.[4]

---

2   Details are available at <http://www.singapore-elections.com/ge2001/>, accessed 15 April 2005.
3   See <http://www.muis.gov.sg>, accessed 29 March 2005.
4   See <http://www.mof.gov.sg/budget_2005/expenditure_estimates/attachment/MCYS_EE2005.pdf> and <http://www.mof.gov.sg/budget_2005/expenditure_overview/mcys.html>, accessed 12 April 2005.

Two major responsibilities assumed by MUIS are the supervision of mosques and of *madrasah*. Since the 1970s MUIS has embarked on a major mosque-building enterprise at newly established government housing estates. These large modern structures serve as centres for a wide range of Muslim religious and social activities. Over S$100 million (US$60 million) has been spent on this, most raised from contributions by Singaporean Muslims.

Singapore has six full-time and 27 part-time *madrasah*. The former combine secular topics with Islamic education and Arabic language teaching; the latter, based at mosques, are intended to supplement state schools and provide basic religious education only. In the recent past the *madrasah* suffered acutely from funding problems: they were unable to provide facilities comparable to those of state schools or offer teachers reasonable salaries (Che Man 1991: 16–19). However, growing Islamic consciousness in recent decades has increased the demand for *madrasah* education, and MUIS has given attention to upgrading the schools.

Muslims in Singapore have generally accepted MUIS as the major institution managing Islamic affairs. Some hold reservations about it because of its government links (Che Man 1991: 4), but it has established close working relations with all other major Muslim groups, including Jamiyah (Muslim Missionary Society), Pergas (Singapore Islamic Scholars and Religious Teachers Association), Mendaki (Council for the Development of the Muslim Community) and the Association of Muslim Professionals.

THE NATURE OF SINGAPOREAN ISLAM

Singapore has been outspoken on the international stage in support of 'moderate' Islam. This has been articulated most forcefully by non-Muslim leaders, particularly Singapore's founding prime minister (currently minister mentor), Lee Kuan Yew. Muslims have generally supported the government position, while qualifying their support on a number of specific issues. At a major convention organized by Pergas in 2003 on the theme 'Moderation in Islam in the Context of the Singapore Muslim Society', speakers pointedly rejected the religio-cultural model of Indonesia's nominal (*abangan*) Muslims and the secular ideology of Turkey – examples Singaporean leaders have extolled in the past – as appropriate models for a moderate form of Islam. They also upheld the right of Muslims to pursue the realization of an Islamic political system, complete with *hudud* punishments,[5] while recognizing that existing realities in Singapore necessitate working within the framework of a secular state (Pergas 2004: 96–159, 318–23). Singapore Muslims opposed government attempts around 2000 to abolish the *madrasah* and educate all children in state schools, eventually forcing the government to back down; they also campaigned against a government ban on schoolgirls wearing Muslim headscarves (*tudung*) and against the establishment of a casino, but without success. Finally, Muslims have

---

5   Punishments set out in the Qur'an for six categories of offences.

distanced themselves from their government's pro-American foreign policy, criticizing the United States on issues such as the invasion of Afghanistan and Iraq.

In a post-colonial world, where modern communications link Muslims across the globe more directly than ever, Singapore's role as a regional centre of Islamic activism has declined. Nonetheless important regional links remain. As in neighbouring countries, most Singapore Muslims follow Sunni teachings of the Shafi'i school. The *dakwah* movement has increased religiosity and created greater interest in following Islamic requirements in such areas as dress and diet. Still, most Muslims have accepted their position as a minority in a multi-religious, cosmopolitan and predominantly Chinese Singapore – circumstances that virtually require adherence to moderate Islam. That message is strongly emphasized in the many lectures and publications put out by all major Muslim organizations.

Why, then, did the extremist doctrines of JI and al-Qaeda appeal to a significant minority? Some of the explanations used to explain this phenomenon in other contexts clearly do not apply. Poverty was not a major factor; the JI members arrested in 2001–02 were generally financially secure. Neither were any of those arrested *madrasah*-educated. Did members of this group feel alienated from a government dominated by non-Muslims? Notwithstanding the various PAP measures to integrate Muslims into the mainstream, there can be no doubt that pockets of Malay Muslims do feel this way, so this may be a background factor. Still, the concerns of Singapore's JI members seem to have had little to do with Singapore but more with anti-American and global Islamic issues. Evidence given in the Singapore government's white paper on the JI arrests shows members' particular fascination with the Taliban in Afghanistan (Ministry of Home Affairs 2003). JI leader Ibrahim Maidin wrote naively to the Taliban leader asking whether he was the caliph of all Muslims, and if Muslims in non-Muslim states should all migrate to Afghanistan. The JI members were also preoccupied with promoting regional Islamic causes. The skilful recruitment and indoctrination procedures followed by JI's Malaysia-based Indonesian leaders, who were frequent visitors to Singapore, also played a part (Ministry of Home Affairs 2003: 15–17).

Since the government crackdown in 2001–02, a handful of additional JI members have been detained, but there has been no evidence of ongoing activity by this organization. The threat of detention under the Internal Security Act (permitting indefinite detention without trial) and the government's documentation of JI activities have probably done a great deal to dissuade potential supporters. The support of all major Muslim organizations for the government's actions, together with their involvement in the rehabilitation of JI supporters, has been no less important.

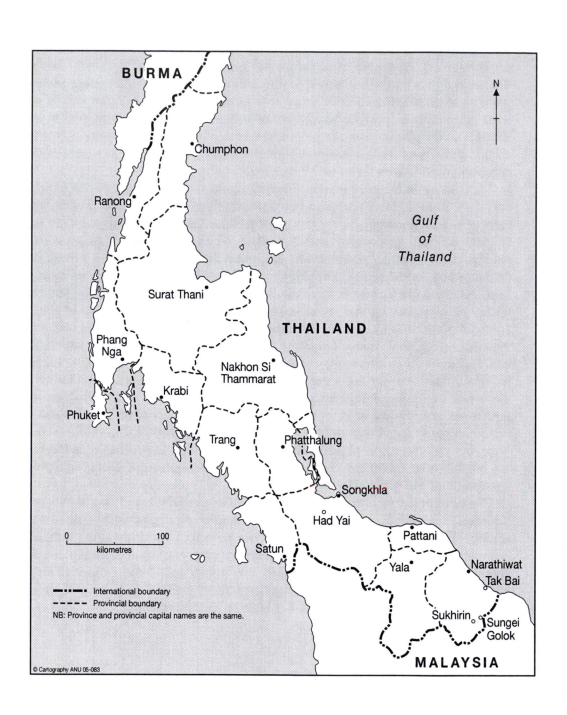

9   Thailand

John Funston

Thai Muslims are a minority in a country where over 90 per cent of the population is Buddhist. There are Muslims throughout the country, but most reside in what Bangkok Thais refer to as the 'deep south', the tri-province area of Narathiwat, Pattani and Yala, together with neighbouring Satun and Songkhla. These ethnically Malay Muslims are divided from other Thais not only by religion, but also by broader cultural differences. With the exception of many Thai speakers in Satun and Songkhla, most share the culture and language of their neighbours in Malaysia.

The deep south has a centuries' old tradition of conflict with the central government based in Bangkok (Surin 1985; Che Man 1990b). In the 1980s and 1990s, however, democracy expanded throughout Thailand, and Muslims began to play a key role in both national and local administration. This was arguably one of the most successful examples of political integration of any Muslim minority. That changed with the emergence of a more complicated international environment associated with September 11 and the war on terror, and new domestic policies. Violence resumed in December 2001, and escalated dramatically in 2004 when over 500 people were killed.

DEMOGRAPHY

The number of Muslims in Thailand has long been contested, with academic and media accounts often twice as high as official estimates (Omar Farouk 1988: 1–2). Many contemporary media reports put their number at 10 per cent or more of the population. Chaiwat (2004: 157) argues that:

> if the number of Muslims is calculated from the 3,113 mosques in Thailand, with an estimate of 183 households per mosque, each with eight members, then there are some 4.5 million Muslims or 7.3 per cent of the total population.

The 2000 census, however, puts the number of Muslims at 2,815,900, or 4.6 per cent of the total population of 60,617,200, up from 4.1 per cent in 1990.[1] In the four

---

1   Census details have been taken directly or calculated from <http://www.nso.go.th/pop2000/final rep_e.htm>, accessed December 2004.

southernmost provinces around 70 per cent of the population is Malay-Muslim; Songkhla also has a significant Malay-Muslim component, although it is less than 25 per cent of the provincial population. The census puts total Malay Muslims in the five southern provinces at 1,769,818, and at 2,345,800 for the 14 southern provinces as a whole. There are smaller numbers of Muslims in Bangkok (274,100) and the central region (156,400, most of them living in or around the former capital of Ayutthaya), drawn from diverse countries in Central Asia, South Asia and the Middle East, or forcibly resettled from the south after warfare (Omar Farouk 1988: 5). Since the late 1970s many Muslims have migrated to Bangkok from the Middle East, to the extent that one area 'has become known as the Arab quarter, and is sometimes referred to as mini-Beirut of the East' (Scupin 1998: 246). The census also reports isolated pockets throughout the central plains, and around 26,000 Muslims in the north – mostly ethnic Chinese living around Chiang Mai – though media reports suggest much higher figures.[2]

HISTORICAL BACKGROUND

The tri-province area was known as Patani from around the fifteenth century. (This name is still used by Malays supporting autonomy for the region, with Satun and Songkhla sometimes added; it is distinct from the province of Pattani, spelt with a double 't'.)[3] Shortly after, it became one of the leading centres of Islam in Southeast Asia and a major player in the politics of the Malay peninsula. However, its main relationship was with its powerful northern Thai neighbour, which allowed varying degrees of independence under a loose suzerainty. This ended with administrative reforms that brought the area under direct Thai rule in 1902, an arrangement confirmed by the Anglo-Siamese Treaty of 1909 when Thailand ceded neighbouring Kedah, Perlis, Kelantan and Terengganu to the British.

Conflict with governments in Bangkok continued and sometimes intensified after 1902. In the early years opposition was led by the ousted royal families and charis-

---

2   It is possible that there are more than 250,000 Muslims in the north. The *Bangkok Post* (13 March 2005) refers to 100,000 Muslims mainly around Chiang Rai and Tak provinces. Professor Desmond Ball has had years of research experience in this region and believes there are around 100,000 in Chiang Mai and Chiang Rai. He also believes there are more than 100,000 Indo-Burmese Muslims along the border in Mae Hong Son, Tak and Kanchanaburi provinces, including around 15,000 in the official refugee camps, though few of these would be Thai citizens.

3   According to McVey (1989: 35):

> The Thai provinces that were once part of old Patani are Narathiwat, Yala and the present Pattani. Satun, which has played little active part in the rebel movement, never belonged to it; nor did Songkhla, whose one-third Muslim population has also not engaged significantly in the revolt. The Muslims of those states have not the same sense of historical pride and unwillingness to adapt to alien rule nor are the same lineages recognised as legitimate sources of leadership. Coupled with this, particularly in Satun, is the more relaxed Islam of the Malayan west coast. There are only a very few religious schools in that province, and its people have been relatively willing to send their children to such Thai government schools as were established. Moreover, the Muslims of Satun have moved almost wholly, and those of Songkhla considerably, to the use of Thai rather than Malay.

matic Islamic leaders – leadership increasingly falling to the latter as royalists lost their positions and Islam was strengthened in response to increasing 'Thaicization' (Matheson and Hooker 1988). The frequency and intensity of conflicts varied with the extent to which governments in Bangkok sought to impose Thai cultural norms on the region. The ultra-nationalistic policies of the first Phibun Songkram government (1938–44) caused bitter clashes, and thousands fled to neighbouring Malaya. In April 1947 charismatic religious leader Haji Sulong issued his famous seven demands, urging devolution of power to Muslims in the four southern provinces.[4] Haji Sulong was arrested, and this, together with the return of Phibun for a second term after a coup on 8 April 1948, led to the Dusun Nyor uprising in Narathiwat around 28 April. Some 400 Malays and 30 police were killed in this incident. Haji Sulong was released in 1952 but disappeared in August 1954 while in police custody.

Conflict intensified after the coup led by General Sarit Thanarat in 1957, giving birth to new forms of resistance. Sarit strengthened assimilationist policies, trying in particular to assert control over Islamic schools (*pondok* – sometimes spelt *ponoh*).[5] In response Malays formed several unstable, covert organizations, all broadly committed to independence for the south. Three major groups were Barisan Nasional Pembebasan Patani (BNPP, National Liberation Front of Patani), formed in 1959, Barisan Revolusi Nasional (BRN, National Revolutionary Front), formed in 1963, and Pertubuhan Pembebasan Patani Bersatu (PULO, Patani United Liberation Organization), formed in 1968.[6] All split and were reorganized in the 1980s (Che Man 1990b: 98–114). One section of the BNPP formed Barisan Bersatu Mujahideen Patani (BBMP, United Mujahideen Front of Patani) in 1985, and perhaps became or merged with Gerakan Mujahideen Islam Pattani (GMIP, Pattani Islamic Mujahideen Move-

---

4   The seven demands, as listed by Surin, were:

    '1   The appointment of a high commissioner to govern the Greater Patani Region with full authority to dismiss, suspend, or replace all government officials working in the area, the individual must be a native of the region and be elected by the people in general election held for that specific purpose;

    2   Eighty percent of government officials serving in the region must be Malay-Muslims (so as to reflect the population ratio);

    3   Malay and Siamese shall be accepted as official languages;

    4   Malay shall be taught in primary schools;

    5   Muslim law shall be applied in the region with separate Islamic courts independent from the government's judicial system;

    6   All revenue collected in the region shall only be expended for the welfare of the people in the region;

    7   The Provincial Islamic Council shall be given full authority over Islamic legislation on all Muslim affairs and Malay culture under the supreme authority of the high commissioner referred to in No. 1' (Surin 1985: 152)

5   Sarit forced the *pondok* to come under the direct supervision of the education ministry. In return for financial assistance they were converted into 'private Islamic schools', using Thai as the medium of instruction and teaching normal secular subjects alongside Islamic ones. In practice a number of *pondok* schools continued to exist, teaching only Islamic subjects in Malay and Arabic. Over 200 such schools registered in May 2004 when the government insisted they must.

6   In broad terms the BNPP represented a coalition of the aristocracy and conservative Islamic class. The BRN had a more radical Islamic 'republican' orientation, with its base in the *pondok*. PULO focused more on secular nationalism, although from time to time it too emphasized Islam.

ment) 10 years later. In 1991 the BNPP, the BRN and PULO formed a loose coalition as Bersatu (United), which a PULO breakaway (New PULO) and the GMIP may have joined at some stage (ICG 2005b: 6–16; Anwar and Supalak 2004: 93–104).

The separatist groups benefited from foreign assistance. Their main operational centres until the 1980s were in Malaysia. Middle Eastern Islamic charities provided financial support, while countries such as Libya, Syria and, in the 1980s, Afghanistan provided military training (Che Man 1990b).

At their peak, the separatist organizations had around 1,500 fighters under arms. They were implicated in such incidents as the bombing of Bangkok's international airport (4 June 1977), a bombing attempt during a royal visit to the south (22 September 1977) and the bombing of Had Yai train station (8 February 1980). Government buildings, particularly schools and police stations, were often key targets, as were state school teachers and government officials (Surin 1985: 240–3; ICG 2005b: 6–16).

Separatist opposition to the government was not, however, simply a royalist–Islamic response to Thaicization. Writing in the late 1980s, McVey (1989: 47–8) argued that more inchoate forms of peasant resistance were also a factor:

> [C]hiefly leadership has been disrupted and partially transformed; religious leaders have been divided and inclined to compromise with an encroaching modernity; ... [T]he real energy of the violence has lain elsewhere, with peasant unrest. ... [T]he Muslim insurgency calls on much the same forces as have fuelled the broader rural unrest in Thailand, those engendered by rapid economic development unaccompanied by a real increase in administrative capability or in political and social integration.

THE PEACEFUL DECADES

Security problems did, however, ease considerably in the 1980s and 1990s, in parallel with the expansion of democracy throughout Thailand and the election of governments that showed greater sensitivity to Muslim cultural needs. Muslims had been elected or appointed to parliament in the past, but in small numbers and at a time when parliament had little influence over the executive (Surin 1985: 82–3). In 1986 Muslims established a Wadah (Unity) faction, initially within the Democrat Party. Wadah left the Democrat Party two years later and in 1992 joined the National Aspiration Party (NAP) of former army head and later prime minister General Chavalit Yongchaiyudh (Daungyewa 2005). Acting through the Wadah faction, Den Tohmeena (the son of Haji Sulong) became a deputy minister in the powerful Ministry of the Interior (1992–95). In 1995 another member of Wadah, Wan Muhamad Nor Matha, became the first Malay to hold a full ministerial portfolio (transport and communications). He subsequently held several ministerial portfolios until the 2005 elections, apart from a period as parliamentary speaker (1996–97). Highly regarded former Foreign Minister Surin Pitsuwan (1997–2001) is also a Muslim from the south, although he does not speak Malay and comes from the province of Nakhon Si Thammarat rather than the 'deep south'. The 1997 Constitution provided for the first ever elected upper house (senate). Based on representation at the provincial level, it allowed more opportunities for Muslim representation.

In addition, and perhaps more surprisingly, two military-dominated administrative structures known as Civilian–Police–Military (CPM) Task Force 43 and the Southern Border Provinces Administration Centre (SBPAC),[7] both established at the beginning of the 1980s, changed the situation in the deep south. The CPM task force effectively coordinated activities by the security agencies, while the SBPAC provided a focus for listening to Muslim concerns and representing their interests. As *The Nation* (6 May 2002) observed:

> The centre has been praised for its fine job of promoting national reconciliation between the Muslim South and the rest of the Buddhist-dominated country. Besides serving as a forum where community leaders can voice their grievances, the centre has been instrumental in promoting Islamic banking, permission for female Muslims in public institutions and schools to wear headscarves, and preparations for the annual Hajj pilgrimage.

By the late 1980s the secessionist movements had largely subsided, although violence still flared occasionally. In August 1993, 34 schools were torched; according to statistics provided by former Prime Minister Chuan, there were 70 violent incidents in 1997, 37 in 1998, 14 in 1999, eight in 2000 and 28 in 2001 (*Bangkok Post*, 11 November 2002).[8]

VIOLENCE RESUMES

In December 2001 five police and a village defence volunteer were killed on Christmas Eve, marking the beginning of an escalation in violence. What caused this new round of violence remains controversial, but conflict over many months between the police and the army (the paramilitary 'Rangers') – traditional rivals for influence in the region – seems to have been a major factor; official army and police reports in 2002 argued that this was the case (Funston 2006). Violence took a new, apparently ethnic, form on 29 October 2002 when arsonists attacked five public schools, a Buddhist temple and a Buddhist shrine. Violence continued throughout 2002 and 2003. Directed particularly against police and security forces, it left at least 50 dead.

A further dramatic escalation occurred on 4 January 2004 when a group of more than 100 insurgents raided an arms depot of the 4th Army Engineers in Narathiwat. The insurgents killed four Buddhist Thais and seized a cache of 413 light infantry weapons and 2,000 rounds of ammunition. As a diversionary move, they also torched 20 public schools, burned rubber tyres and planted fake explosives in neighbouring Yala.

Martial law was then declared over wide areas of Narathiwat, Yala and Pattani, and extended to the entire area in February. Nonetheless violence continued on an almost daily basis, targeting state schools and offices, the security forces, government officials and also the general public, including many Muslims (see Box 9.1).

---

7 CPM Task Force 43 and the SBPAC were initially headed by the commander of the southern Fourth Army; in 1996 a deputy permanent secretary in the Ministry of the Interior took over this role for the SBPAC.

8 Ball (2004: 105–11) provides further details of violent incidents during this period.

BOX 9.1   RECENT SECURITY DEVELOPMENTS

4 January 2004: Insurgents raid an arms depot in Narathiwat, killing four Buddhist Thais and seizing a cache of arms. They also torch 20 public schools, burn rubber tyres and plant fake explosives in neighbouring Yala.

22 and 24 January 2004: Three Buddhist monks are killed (one each in Narathiwat, Yala and Pattani) and two others injured, the first time monks have been targeted.

12 March 2004: High-profile Muslim lawyer Somchai Neelaphaijit, acting on behalf of several southerners, 'disappears' near Bangkok while apparently in police hands.

27 March 2004: A motorcycle bomb explodes in front of a hotel nightclub in the border village of Sungei Golok, Narathiwat – widely seen as the first time militants have targeted civilians and an imitation of the Bali bombings albeit on a smaller scale.

28–29 March 2004: A coordinated torching of 39 government buildings takes place in Pattani, Songkhla and Yala.

30 March 2004: A huge volume of explosives is stolen from a quarry in Yala: 1.4 tons of ammonium nitrate, 56 sticks of dynamite and 176 detonators.

28 April 2004: Around 200 Muslims attack 11 police and military posts in Pattani, Yala and Songkhla. In what is one of the bloodiest days in modern Thai history, 107 rebels and five security officials are killed. A government-appointed Independent Fact-finding Commission later describes the killing of 32 Muslims in Pattani's historic Krue Se Mosque as involving a 'disproportionate' use of force. Most victims were young and had attacked security posts armed only with knives and *parang* (swords usually used to slash grass or trees).

16 May 2004: Three separate explosions occur almost simultaneously in three Buddhist temples in Narathiwat.

29 May 2004: Suspected separatists behead an elderly Thai villager in Narathiwat and leave a note threatening to kill more 'innocent Buddhists'.

26 August 2004: A bomb explodes in an outdoor market in Sukhirin, Narathiwat, killing one person and wounding at least 31, including eight children.

17 September 2004: A Pattani judge becomes the first high-ranking official to be killed by suspected insurgents.

25 October 2004: Police fire on a large crowd protesting at the detention of six village defence volunteers whose shotguns had been stolen by insurgents, killing seven. The police then detain 1,300 protestors, 78 of whom suffocate while being transported in crowded trucks from the protest site in Narathiwat's Tak Bai district to an army camp in Pattani.

17 February 2005: A powerful car bomb leaves at least six people dead and about 50 injured in Sungei Golok, Narathiwat (outside the same hotel targeted on 27 March), the first car-bomb attack on Thai soil.

3 April 2005: Three bombing attacks take place in Songkhla, including at Had Yai international airport and the entrance to a Carrefour supermarket, killing two.

14 July 2005: Up to 60 militants take part in synchronized attacks in Yala. Five explosions, four arson attacks and several other incidents cause power blackouts and chaos. One soldier is killed and 19 others injured.

15 July 2005: Cabinet approves an executive decree giving the prime minister wide-ranging powers to handle states of emergency, including detention without charge, censorship of news and the interception of telephone calls.

19 July 2005: The government imposes emergency rule in the three southernmost provinces, but after strong public criticism opts to begin with only seven of the 16 measures allowed under the executive decree.

ADMINISTRATION

Thailand has a highly centralized official Islamic administration. While the king is patron of all religions, the head of Islamic affairs is the Chularajamontri, or Syaikh al-Islam, based on an institution established in the tenth century to distinguish the religious/moral leadership from the holders of political and temporal power. The first appointee, in the early seventeenth century, was a Persian from the Shi'a branch of Islam. Subsequent appointments were all Shi'a, until royal decrees in 1945 and 1948 and the Patronage of Islam Act in 1947 paved the way for leadership by members of the Sunni majority (Imtiyaz 1998: 284).

Until these legislative changes, the appointment of the Chularajamontri was largely a royal prerogative. Subsequently he was elected by members of the National Council of Islamic Affairs (NCIA) and the heads of the Provincial Councils for Islamic Affairs (PCIAs). Since the passage of a new Administration of Islamic Organizations Act in 1997, election has been by members of PCIAs.[9] The Chularajamontri is then formally nominated by the prime minister and appointed by the king.

The Chularajamontri is appointed for life, advises the government on all Muslim matters, issues authoritative religious rulings (fatwa) and has extensive powers to regulate Islamic affairs.[10] There have been a total of 14 Chularajamontri so far, and only four since the changes in the 1940s. All have come from Bangkok or Ayutthaya – election arrangements have allowed other provinces to outvote southern Muslims, even though a southerner played a major role in drafting the 1997 law. The Chularajamontri has often been ignored by southern Muslims, although the current leader is working hard to establish a rapport.

The Chularajamontri is assisted by the 48-member NCIA – 36 are elected every six years by PCIAs and 12 are nominated by the Chularajamontri, then appointed by the king on the advice of the Ministry of the Interior. The Chularajamontri is ex officio president. According to Che Man (1991: 6), he has dominated the activities of the NCIA: 'Most fatwa, for instance, were issued in the capacity of the Chularajamontri rather than of the NCIA'. Both the Chularajamontri and the NCIA are part of the Thai bureaucratic system, belonging to the Islamic Centre of Thailand, which is administered jointly by the Ministry of the Interior and the Ministry of Culture (the latter replaced the Ministry of Education after an administrative reorganization in 2002).

PCIAs can be established in any province with at least three mosques, and have 9–30 members. Members are elected by provincial imam (mosque council heads) and then appointed by the provincial governor, a member of the Ministry of the

---

9   In 1997 there were 29 PCIAs with a total of 384 members; by 2005 the number of PCIAs had increased to 36 (*Bangkok Post*, 24 November 2005).

10   The administrative responsibilities of the Chularajamontri include regulating the administration of registered mosques; distributing subsidies and grants to mosques; maintaining a register of all registered mosques; publishing religious literature; declaring the celebration of Islamic festivals such as Id al-Fitr and Id al-Adha; organizing the annual Mawlid (birthday of the Prophet) celebrations; coordinating travel arrangements for the haj; appointing the *amir al-hajj* (leader of the haj) for Thai pilgrims; granting *halal* certification for food produced by Thai industries; and providing notarial services (Imtiyaz 1998: 285).

Interior. Their functions include providing advice on Islamic affairs to provincial governors, supervising mosques, resolving disputes about family and inheritance issues in accordance with Islamic law, and issuing fatwa (Che Man 1991: 6; Chaiwat 2004: 163).

Mosques in Thailand are required to register with the government and establish a managing council of 7–15 members elected by adult Muslims in the community. Unlike officials at higher levels, council members do not receive any government salaries or allowances (Che Man 1991: 14–15; Omar Farouk 1988: 15–20).

One final institution existing only in the four Muslim-majority provinces is that of *dato' yutitham* (Muslim judge), selected by competitive examination and appointed by the minister of justice.[11] Each of the four provinces has two *dato' yutitham*, whose main duty is:

> to formulate and deliver judgments on family and inheritance cases involving Muslims. Though the actual judgment must be delivered by a Thai judge, *Dato' Yutithams* countersign it (Che Man 1991: 10–11).

Muslims can elect, however, to have family and inheritance cases heard by the civil courts, or – as is more frequently the case – to refer such cases to local religious functionaries.

A form of Islamic law has been recognized in the four southernmost provinces since 1902 (except for a brief period under Phibun in the late 1940s). In the face of Muslim opposition, Thai authorities began to compile and translate Islamic family and inheritance law as early as 1929, a process that was completed in 1941. This law was formally adopted in 1946 with the Application of Islamic Law Act, 'proclaimed amidst uproar and protest among the Malay-Muslims' (Surin 1985: 141).

THE NATURE OF ISLAM IN THAILAND

Analysts generally agree that Muslims have been integrated successfully into the Buddhist-dominated state. In Scupin's words:

> [T]he Muslim community in Thailand has acknowledged the need to move away from rigid ethnic and religious exclusive tendencies in favor of cooperation and political integration. Though there are still tensions and conflicts between Muslims and Buddhists in Thai society, the prospect for more ethnic and religious harmony in a pluralistic civil society seems to be a predominant trend (Scupin 1998: 258).

Islam arrived from different sources. In the south, after the Patani court converted to Islam in the sixteenth century, itinerant Sufi preachers spread the faith to villagers. Southern Muslims are mainly Sunni of the Shafi'i school, though, as with their counterparts in Malaysia, older influences remain important. Anthropologists have

---

11   Until recently the *dato' yutitham* were elected by imam in the respective provinces after sitting an examination (Che Man 1991: 10). Now they are selected on the basis of competitive examination (correspondence from Dr Ibrahem Narongraksakhet, head of the Department of Islamic Studies, College of Islamic Studies, Prince of Songkla University, Pattani).

noted a division of jurisdictions between the village imam (responsible for Islamic affairs) and the *bomoh* (responsible for spirits and magic) (Fraser 1960). Millenarian and invincibility cults, sometimes associated with Sufism (*tariqah*), also continue to attract support. As Surin (1985: 252–3) notes:

> In the context of Southern Thailand the word *tariqah* connotes involvement in the study and practice of sorcery, witchcraft and black magic. Members usually believe that they have supernatural power to defend themselves against enemy attack.

Such groups were particularly prominent during the rebellions in 1948 (Surin 1985: 274). They were also involved in the attacks of 28 April 2004; those captured told of participating in prayer sessions and drinking 'holy water' before the attack so that they would be invulnerable to bullets (*Bangkok Post*, 13 May 2004; Nidhi 2004).

In the sixteenth- and seventeenth-century capital of Ayutthaya, Persians from a Shi'a background were the most important group of Muslims, taking over the new office of Chularajamontri. Although soon outnumbered by Sunni Muslims, the Shi'a have remain a significant minority.

From the outset, Malay Muslims in the tri-province region have tended to move in different directions to other groups of Muslims. Beyond this region a common language helped Muslims merge culturally with the wider Thai community. Even in Muslim-majority Satun, for example, a remarkably high 20 per cent of marriages are between Muslims and Buddhists (Nishii 2003: 2). Politically, 'Thai-speaking Muslims are more similar to Buddhists in political orientations than they are to their Malay-speaking Muslim counterparts' (Albritton 2000: 378).

Nonetheless the diverse Muslim groups have experienced a number of developments in common. All were exposed to the process of Islamic reform that began early in the twentieth century, to the Islamic outreach (*dakwah*) movement commencing in the 1970s, to the radicalization associated with the post-September 11 international environment, and to concern over the recent escalation of violence in the south.

Muslims throughout Thailand have long been influenced by international developments. Southern Muslims have traditionally gone to Malaysia and Indonesia to study, and preachers from these countries have taught in the south. Muslims from all regions go to the Middle East in large numbers, on pilgrimages and for advanced Islamic education. In the 1960s as many as 30,000 southern Thailand Muslims lived in Saudi Arabia (Che Man 1990b: 110). And as pressures on *pondok* education increased from the 1960s, more pursued Islamic education in neighbouring countries as well as in Pakistan and the Middle East.

Islamic reform in Thailand dates from the arrival in Bangkok of an Indonesian political refugee, Ahmad Wahad, in 1926. The religious reformists were known among Malay-speaking Muslims as the Young Group (Kaum Muda, the term used in Malaysia) or, in Thai, as the New Group (Khana Mai); the religious conservatives were called the Old Group (Kaum Tua in Malay or Khana Kau in Thai). Ahmad Wahad's influence soon came to be felt in other areas, including the south, through his network of students and followers (Scupin 1980: 1,225). Haji Sulong promoted similar doctrines after coming under reformist influence while studying in Mecca in the late 1920s (Surin 1985: 147–8; McVey 1989: 41, fn 14). Another Indonesian,

Haji Abdullah, established a southern *pondok* in the 1960s 'where he began to teach Islamic modernism and criticized the widespread popular forms of Islam, *bomohs*, and other animistic beliefs and practices' (Scupin 1998: 252).

The *dakwah* phenomenon reached Thailand in the 1970s, brought by Muslims influenced while studying abroad by the writings of modern Islamic thinkers such as 'Sayyid Qutb,[12] Muhammad Iqbal,[13] Abdul Ala Maududi,[14] Ali Shariati,[15] Muhammad Asad,[16] and Hasan al-Turabi[17] as well as other Southeast Asian Muslim leaders such as Anwar Ibrahim of Malaysia' (Scupin 1998: 254). Government attempts to close *pondok* schools may have been another motivating factor (Surin 1985: 248–50). *Dakwah* was further strengthened by international developments such as the Iranian revolution, and by the money from Middle Eastern and Iranian charities that poured into local schools and missionary activities. Centres for learning and propagating Shi'a teachings were established in Bangkok and the south during this time. And while it is difficult to be precise about numbers, some Sunni Muslims converted to Shi'a beliefs, one of the few cases in the Muslim world where this has happened (Scupin 1998: 256–7).

September 11 heightened tensions between Muslims and non-Muslims throughout the world. While there was initial Muslim sympathy for America, this quickly evaporated when the United States responded in a manner widely interpreted as not a war against terror, but a war against Islam. The subsequent US invasions of Afghanistan and Iraq united Muslims throughout the country. They organized demonstrations up to 50,000-strong in the south, boycotted Coca-Cola and other products produced by the United States and Britain, and sold Osama T-shirts to raise funds for humanitarian assistance to Afghanistan. The Thai government's support for the United States, and its dispatch of troops to the two war zones, exacerbated Muslim concerns (Chaiwat 2004: 158–67).

Finally, escalation of the conflict in the south, particularly since January 2004, has seen Muslims in all areas unite. Muslim academics in Bangkok and the south, the office of the Chularajamontri and the national and provincial Islamic councils, Muslim parliamentarians and NGO leaders (often together with non-Muslim NGO leaders) have worked cooperatively to argue for a more conciliatory government approach to southern problems.

---

12   Sayyid Qutb (1906–66) was an Egyptian Islamic thinker and activist who emphasized Islam as a comprehensive way of life and called for greater social activism by Muslims.

13   Muhammad Iqbal (1877–1938) was an Indo-Pakistani political writer, lawyer and activist.

14   Abu al-Ala Mawdudi (1903–79) was an Indo-Pakistani reformist thinker and politician who founded Pakistan's Jamaat-i Islami.

15   Ali Shariati (1933–77) was one of the most influential Iranian Shi'ite intellectuals and political activists.

16   Muhammad Asad (born Leopold Weiss) (1900–92) was a journalist and scholar of German Jewish background who converted to Islam as a young man and wrote extensively on Islamic issues.

17   Hassan al-Turabi (1932–) is a Sudanese Islamist intellectual and political leader. Educated at the University of London and the Sorbonne, he has held important positions in the Sudanese government since the late 1970s and is seen as the architect of Sudan's move to become an Islamic state.

POLITICAL ISLAM

The reformist movement brought political Islam to Thailand. A close associate of 1932 coup leader Pridi Phanomyon was Chaem Promyap, a Cairo-educated Khana Mai Muslim. He changed the role of the Chularajamontri in the 1940s to one more directly involved in Islamic advancement, and acted in this office for two years before being forced into exile after the 1947 military coup. Haji Sulong led southern political opposition in the 1940s and early 1950s. Other reformist-influenced organizations included the political pressure group Young Muslim Association of Thailand, established in 1964, and the Peace Front political party which (unsuccessfully) stood 11 candidates in the 1975 elections (Scupin 1980: 1,231–3).

Muslims also have a long history of representation through the Democrat Party, established in 1946, and the Wadah faction. As noted, Wadah left the Democrats in 1988, two years after its founding, and joined the NAP in 1992; it then joined the ruling Thai Rak Thai (TRT, Thais Love Thais) when the TRT absorbed the NAP in 2002. On the eve of elections in February 2005, 10 of the 11 members of the House of Representatives in the four southern provinces were TRT members, four of them late crossovers from the Democrats. In a notable electoral reversal – and a clear signal of Muslim opposition to government policies towards the south – the Democrats won 10 seats while one went to the small opposition party Chat Thai (Thai Nation).

A majority of southern Muslims have pursued power through established institutions, as a high voter turnout at the 2005 polls (despite security concerns) demonstrated. However, a minority have sought to secure power through clandestine means. Such groups virtually disappeared in the 1980s and 1990s. Although they have made a comeback since then, they remain a small minority.

CONTINUING CRISIS IN THE SOUTH

The escalation of violence in the Muslim south in 2004 perplexed the government and analysts alike. No group has come forward to claim responsibility for anti-government attacks. No specific demands have been made. Militant international Islam, separatism, mishandling by security forces, criminality and economic backwardness have at various times been held responsible.

All these factors may have played a part, although evidence available so far in relation to international Islam indicates that while organizations such as Jemaah Islamiyah have had a presence in Thailand, they have not succeeded in attracting many Thais to their point of view. It nonetheless remains puzzling as to why the remaining factors, which are all longstanding, should cause a sudden escalation of violence. The answer seems to lie in a combination of changed international circumstances and shifts in domestic policy (Funston 2006; ICG 2005b).

As noted, post-September 11 international changes have politicized Thai Muslims, making them more conscious of their Muslim identity and drawing them into conflict with the government's pro-US policies. At the same time the opportunities for Muslims to air their views have contracted. A critical development in this respect was the dissolution of the SBPAC – an institution that had listened to and represented Muslims – on 1 May 2002, after the police argued that it was no longer needed because separatism and ethnic conflict had ended and only criminal problems remained. On the economic front, government emphasis on large development projects advanced the interests of others at the expense of Malay Muslims concentrated in small primary industries such as fishing and agriculture. One Thai academic, arguing in similar terms to McVey for an earlier period, dismisses the importance of Islamic leaders and separatists, and sees the violence as a millenarian peasant revolt against increasingly difficult times for the south's primary-industry-driven economy (Nidhi 2004). Muslims also opposed legalization of the underground lottery in early 2003, the provision of scholarships from the proceeds of this lottery, and the mooted legalization of casinos and prostitution, on the grounds that such policies conflict sharply with Islamic teachings.

But in the eyes of most Muslims, the key factor in exacerbating security problems has been the government's resort to harsh security measures to end the violence. The attack on 4 January 2004 was followed by the introduction of martial law and widespread reports of Muslim leaders disappearing, the most prominent being a Muslim lawyer who disappeared on 12 March while apparently in police hands. A government commission found that killings at the historic Krue Se Mosque on 28 April had involved a disproportionate use of force, and 85 died at Tak Bai on 25 October while engaged in peaceful protest. Such incidents, which conflict with more conciliatory military doctrines used successfully against communists in the 1970s and 1980s, have shaken Muslim trust in government, strengthened sympathy for militants and entrenched a vicious circle of violence (ICG 2005b). The challenge for the government and Muslims alike is to break this circle. The establishment in March 2005 of a 48-member National Reconciliation Commission, headed by Anand Panyarachun, a former prime minister, provides some hope that the government may seek to move in this direction.

PART II

Extracts from Primary Sources

10   Personal Expressions of Faith

Virginia Hooker

> 'Religion is not knowledge but the daily wherewithal to turn the
> wheel of life because, if we do not have faith, do not carry out the
> prescribed religious duties, we are like walking corpses.'
> (Hajjah Trie Utami Sari binti Sujono Atmotenoyo)[1]

INTRODUCTION

This chapter focuses on the ways individual Southeast Asian Muslims choose
to express piety in their everyday lives. How, for example, do they translate the
Qur'an's directives for a pious life from the original seventh-century Middle Eastern
context and apply them to their own vastly different circumstances? Why do they
feel that observance of God's rules is so important to them as individuals? If they
feel that adaptations or compromises have to be made, how do they know they are
still fulfilling God's commands? What are the 'Islamic' values that Muslims seek to
uphold and express in their own lives? The answers vary greatly. To reflect the spectrum of responses, this chapter draws on a wide range of source material – from the
popular media to more serious and considered reflections. It is notable that many of
the individual views make direct links between implementing Islam's teachings and
improving society. Contemporary Muslims want to put Islam into action.

The chapter describes the rise in religiosity over the past century; the five ritual
obligations of Islam; expressions of Islamic mysticism (Sufism); and manifestations
of piety (through choices made about religious education and religious teachers,
style of dress, and health and healing practices). It concludes by describing a range
of attitudes to Islamic culture and the arts. Extracts from interviews with a range of
Indonesian Muslims add personal and revealing snapshots of the views of ordinary
Muslims. The interviews were conducted in Jakarta between December 1999 and
January 2000 as part of Virginia Hooker's long-term research project, 'Living with
Devotion: Islamic Doctrine and Practice in Indonesia'. They are referred to in this
chapter as the 'Living with Devotion' project (see, for example, footnote 1).

---

1   Interviewed in Jakarta, 17 January 2000 (then 32 years old, artist, singer, dancer, media announcer).
['Living with Devotion' project.]

EXTRACTS AND COMMENTARY

10.1   THE RISE IN RELIGIOSITY

Commentary   For many Muslims in Southeast Asia, especially those who have benefited from rapid development and are now members of the new, self-conscious middle
classes, increased prosperity has enabled participation in global communications technology and conspicuous consumerism. Greater opportunities to enter higher education,
both secular and religious, have allowed them to access the thinking and writing of
Muslim intellectuals and activists whose material is now appearing in an explosion of
internet sites and books. These opportunities have also enabled them to read an eclectic
array of contemporary social science writings and deepen their knowledge of Western
ideology and theories (especially on topics such as democratization, marketing and
management, and human rights). A new pride in being Muslim has emerged. But the
sense of Muslim identity is often accompanied by the dilemma of how to express that
identity in a modern world. Increased prosperity, consumerism and global technology
provide contemporary Muslims with more choices about how to express their piety
than at any time since the beginning of Islam.

A sentiment expressed in many of the extracts in this chapter, and one that was
expressed in the early years of the twentieth century by the 'modernist' or 'reformist'
Muslims, is the desire to experience the deeper meaning behind the prescribed forms
of worship in Islam. For example, Dr Chandra Muzaffar, a Malaysian Muslim who is
president of the International Movement for a Just World (JUST, a non-government
organization), is critical of the purely formal observance of Islam. He urges Muslims to
consider the 'values' approach to their religion. His views appeal to many younger-generation Muslims who seek to remain true to Islam while also addressing the pressing
issues of human need in contemporary societies. He writes:

> It is well nigh impossible to expect the rituals and symbols approach to address the myriad
> of problems facing Muslims. What is needed is a new, creative and dynamic approach
> which, inspired by spiritual and moral values – the most significant of which would be
> justice and compassion – attempts to formulate specific policies directed towards the
> elimination of poverty or the eradication of corruption or the enhancement of human
> rights. It is important to link policies and programmes to values not only to ensure that
> the moral dimension of the goal at hand is sustained but also to emphasise that the task
> itself is an act of virtue (Chandra 2005: 5).

The results of an Indonesian survey show that increasing numbers of Indonesian
Muslims are following recommended devotional practices, and decreasing numbers are
engaging in non-Islamic practices (*Tempo*, 30 December 2001: 48). The 2001 survey
was conducted by Pusat Pengkajian Islam dan Masyarakat (PPIM, Centre for the Study
of Islam and Society) at the Universitas Islam Negeri (UIN, State Islamic University)
in Jakarta, in order to establish the profile of the Islamic community in Indonesia. The
majority of respondents declared that they regularly observed Islamic devotional practices. Less than 4 per cent said they rarely or never fasted during the month of Ramadan
and only 9 per cent rarely or never prayed five times a day.

One explanation for the apparent rise in Islamic religiosity is given in the following
extract from an interview with Zainah Anwar, executive director of Sisters in Islam, a
Malaysian activist group.

Extract 10-1: Zainah Anwar

'Feminist Islam', excerpt from the transcript of an interview with Zainah Anwar conducted by Terry Lane [in English], 'In the National Interest', Radio National, Australian Broadcasting Corporation, <http://www.abc.net.au/rn/talks/natint/stories/ s915192.htm>, dated 3 August 2003, accessed 6 September 2005.

Zainah Anwar: What is very interesting in the Muslim world, unlike in the West and in the Christian world, [is that] there is a theory that as you modernise, as you develop, religion becomes less important, but in the Muslim world that's no[t] so, and in fact what you have seen in the past 20 or 30 years, was the phenomenon of Islamic revivalism, where middle-class Muslims, upwardly mobile middle-class Muslims, [were] going back to their faith and becoming more rooted in their faith. And so of course there is that small group of Muslims who don't practice the religion and all the rituals of the religion. But I would say, certainly in Malaysia, that the majority of Muslims, no matter how Westernised they are in their lifestyle, actually do practise the basic tenets of the faith, of praying, of fasting, and doing the Hajj (going to the pilgrimage). So in fact in much of the Muslim world, the reverse is happening, of people, more secular people, more Westernised people, actually getting more in touch with their faith.

Terry Lane: Is that a reaction? It's often interpreted in the West as being a reaction against American cultural domination, and that in order to prove that we are, if anything, not controlled culturally by America, the reaction will be to become more traditional in some way.

Zainah Anwar: Well I wouldn't reduce it to just one reason. I mean there are many, many reasons. I think for many Muslim countries, you know we're part of a developing world, a less developed world, so the whole challenge of transition from traditional to modern societies, from rural to urban areas, the dislocation that is happening in the lives of so many Muslims, given the challenges of today, the challenge of modernity, the challenge of change, the loss of your support systems, you move from rural areas to urban areas, all these challenges of competing in a globalised world, and of course the dominance of Western culture, and trying to find your roots and your identity again, I think for many, many reasons, all these reasons, that going back to religion gives you a sense of belonging, a sense of something that's familiar, that you grow up with. It gives you security and confidence and a sense of identity in what is a very confusing, challenging transitional period in your life.

10.2 THE PILLARS OF THE RELIGION

Commentary   There are five principal obligations required of a Muslim, referred to as the five 'pillars' of the religion or *arkaan addiin* (Ar.: *'arkaanud-diini*). They are the declaration of faith (Ar.: *shahaadah*), the five daily prayers (Ar.: *salawaat*), the obligation to pay the wealth tax (Ar.: *zakaah*), fasting during the month of Ramadan (Ar.: *sawmun*) and undertaking the pilgrimage to Mecca (Ar.: *hajjun*). The pillars are set out in the Qur'an. For further guidance on how to observe them, Muslims refer to the example of the Prophet Muhammad's life (Sunnah). The Sunnah is based on carefully sourced reports or accounts (Hadith) of the Prophet's utterances and behaviour as witnessed by his contemporaries and handed down through a chain of reliable people.[2] A 41-year-old Indonesian Muslim interviewed in 2000 speaks for many when he explains:

> God sent Muhammad to show people how to behave and His words came to Muhammad through the angel Gabriel. The behaviour of the Prophet was not dictated by his own desires but rather followed God's way (M. Fathiqul Islam, Jakarta, 5 January 2000).

The five pillars of Islam are discussed in turn below.

10.2.1 The Declaration of Faith

Commentary A Muslim declares his or her faith by reciting in Arabic: 'There is no god but God and Muhammad is the messenger of God'. This profession is at the heart of belief. To become a Muslim, the following six conditions, based on the profession, must be met: it must be repeated aloud; it must be perfectly understood; it must be believed in the heart; it must be professed until death; it must be recited correctly; and it must be uttered without hesitation (Adamec 2001: 98).

The Arabic word *shahaadah* means 'to attest' or 'to bear witness'. The public affirmation of belief in only one God whose messenger was Muhammad is the strongest statement of belief a Muslim can make. The Arabic root also has a derivative which means 'martyrdom' – to die bearing witness to Islam. The following extract, by a young Indonesian born in a rural area of Java in 1958, gives a personal view of the significance of the concept 'bearing witness'.

Extract 10-2: Anharudin

Anharudin (1999), 'Kesaksian Seorang Anak Petani Muslim' [Testimony of a Farmer's Son], pp. 191–218 in Ihsan Ali-Fauzi and Haidar Bagir (eds), *Mencari Islam: Kumpulan Otobiografi Intelektual Kaum Muda Muslim Indonesia Angkatan 80-an* [Seeking Islam: Intellectual Autobiographies of Young Indonesian Muslims of the Generation of the 80s], Penerbit Mizan, Bandung. Extract: p. 209.

[…] In the first instance, Islam is bearing witness (*syahadah*), that is, accepting and at the same time totally surrendering to the Creator, the One God. *Syahadah* is something which is also 'human', because acceptance and belief in the process of the creation of the natural world will provide meaning for people in every action in this life. Nevertheless, because the [manifestation of the] Oneness of God in the secular context is social justice, then bearing witness or *syahadah* to God signifies 'love' of justice and a commitment to establish justice in real life. *Syahadah* also means accepting or intellectually acknowledging Muhammad as God's Messenger, or as a 'model' for humankind in establishing social justice. He is the social thinker who provided the intellectual basis to comprehend social structure and injustice in society.

---

2   The orally transmitted Hadith were collected by scholars in the late tenth century CE, with the compilations of al-Bukhari and Muslim ibn al-Hajjaj being accepted as the most authentic (Ar. *sahiihun*).

10.2.2 The Five Daily Prayers

Commentary The Qur'an commands believers to perform *salaah* – prescribed physical movements with accompanying prayers – five times each day. For many Muslims this is an essential part of daily life, as expressed in the following extracts.

Extract 10-3: Susilowati SP

Excerpt from the transcript of an interview with Susilowati SP (then 29 years old and involved in agribusiness), Jakarta, 11 December 1999. ['Living with Devotion' project.]

For Muslims the most important thing is to pray five times a day; there is no religious duty more central than prayer because it is totally obligatory. We have been charged to uphold the prayers; the word used is 'uphold', so not just carry out prayer [...] [T]he direct benefit is to teach us to live in a disciplined, organized and clean way.

Extract 10-4: Teguh Hidayat

Excerpt from the transcript of an interview with Teguh Hidayat (then 34 years old, accountant), Jakarta, 20 January 2000. ['Living with Devotion' project.]

There is nothing more important than the obligatory prayers; wherever you ask, that will be the answer. If you ask why, well, because they're obligatory; if you neglect them it's a sin, but if you do them then you'll be rewarded by God. We were created by God, so it's right that we should worship God as a sign of our gratitude.

* * * * *

Commentary A more formal explanation of the five daily prayers is given by Jamal Mohamed U Soe Thein, a Burmese Muslim who studied at al-Azhar University, Cairo, before studying philosophy at Yangon University in Burma. He is currently vice-principal of the Education Division at Darul Arqam, Singapore. He urges parents to teach their children that each of the five pillars of Islam is more than a ritual and that each pillar encompasses spiritual and social values as well as being a form of worship. The Darul Arqam group in Singapore is an association for Muslim converts.[3] It publishes the *Muslim Reader* magazine, one of whose functions is to educate its readers about Islam, as seen in the following extract.

Extract 10-5: Jamal Mohamed U Soe Thein

Jamal Mohamed U Soe Thein (2005), 'Transcending Rituals: Gearing to Develop Values' [in English], *Muslim Reader*, 23(1): 9–10. Extract: pp. 9–10.

To fully realise spiritual contact with God, a Muslim performs the prescribed formal prayers daily. [...]

---

3 Further information about the group is given on its website, <www.darul-arqam.org.sg>.

The *solah* [Ar.: *ṣalaah*] is a reminder of God's presence because it requires a Muslim to recite verses from the Qur'an, thereby prompting an individual to understand its meanings. The five timings correspond to five periods of the day – dawn, afternoon, late afternoon, after the sunset, and night – when Man stops to reflect on the day's activities, thereby making room for him to muse about God. [...]

The postures in *solah* comprise standing, bowing, prostrating and sitting repeatedly. These actions internalise in the Muslim mind expressions of submission, humility and adoration of the higher power that is God.

When a Muslim stand[s] up to pray, he is the embodiment of humility and devotion – hands joined in a supplicating posture, eyes downcast and neck bent low, feet parallel to each other oblivious of the happenings around him. To an acute observer, this brings to mind a picture of gravity and quietness, etiquette and dignity. A Muslim bows to his Creator by placing his nose and forehead on the ground, and at other points supplicating to Him with hands outstretched. In a congregational prayer, these postures physically demonstrate the equality of all mankind.

* * * * *

Commentary   It is obligatory for Muslims to perform ritual ablutions before beginning the prayers, to wear clothing that covers the `*awrah*[4] and to face in the direction of Mecca. Prayers may be performed at times other than the five prescribed times. On Fridays, at the time of the midday prayer, congregational prayers are held in mosques. The congregation is arranged in neat rows behind a leader, with women separated from men. An exhortatory sermon (Ar.: *khuṭbah*) is delivered to the congregation.

The following extract is by Imam Samudra (alias Abdul Aziz), a senior Jemaah Islamiyah (JI) figure and the field leader of the Bali bombing team. Born in Serang, Banten, in 1970, Samudra was drawn into Darul Islam circles through his contact with local religious scholars. Darul Islam is a movement for an Islamic state that notably rebelled against Indonesia's central government from 1948 to 1962. The extract shows how essential Samudra believes it is to perform the daily prayers and how critical he is of his fellow Muslims who do not fulfil their religious obligations. In his view they are headed for destruction while, heeding the advice of a teacher, he and his own special group of friends uphold the commands of Islam.

Extract 10-6: Imam Samudra

Imam Samudra (2004), *Aku Melawan Teroris* [I Fight Terrorists], Jazera, Solo. Extract: p. 31.

One or two of the things my elementary school teacher taught me helped me not to be too drawn into the current of destruction of young teenagers. At least, it planted in my still immature mind a feeling or an 'intuition' that class '1A' was heading towards destruction. How could it not be so? A large number of the students had demolished the pillars of religion. They neglected their prayers. We started studying at 1 pm and

---

4   The Arabic word `*awrah* in the singular means 'imperfection' or 'weakness' and in the plural can also mean 'genitals'. Different schools of Islamic law differ concerning the precise legal meaning, but in general terms the word refers to those parts of the body that should be covered to preserve modesty.

finished at 5:30 pm. The time for the sunset prayer was 5:45 pm. When did we have time to do the Mid-afternoon Prayer? Praise be to God, three classmates and I used the short rest time to leave the school and do the Afternoon Prayer across the road in the Den-Bek mosque. [...]

10.2.3 Obligation to Pay the Wealth Tax

Commentary The payment of *zakaah* (*zakat* in Southeast Asia) is an obligation for every Muslim with the means to pay the tax. In theory, it offers the means to redistribute wealth and protect the needy. It has two elements: *zakaatul-maali* (wealth tax) and *zakaatul-fiṭri* (food given to those in need to mark the end of the fasting month, by those who have the means to do so) (Ariff 1991: 2). Failure to contribute *zakaatul-fiṭri* is believed to undermine the performance of the Ramadan fast and so is rarely avoided. By contrast, the payment of *zakaatul-maali* is often avoided, despite the fact that state legislation and state institutions stipulate the amounts to be paid and provide agencies for their collection. Some avoidance is based on the belief, often justified, that the state agencies are corrupt. More seriously, there are sound theological arguments that the duty to pay to the designated classes of recipients is a personal one and that the state cannot transfer this duty to itself. The duty remains personal.

In a personal response, a young Indonesian woman links the avoidance of wealth tax with the decline of Islamic civilization. In her view, it represents a failure by Muslims to put their religion into practice.

Extract 10-7: Susilowati SP

Excerpt from the transcript of an interview with Susilowati SP (then 29 years old and involved in agribusiness), Jakarta, 11 December 1999. ['Living with Devotion' project.]

There is one thing that seems trivial but which has a significant influence on the rise or not of Islam in this country, and that is that not all of the Muslim community are aware of their obligation to pay *zakat* to those entitled to receive it. At most the *zakat* they remember to pay is the *zakat fitrah* given every year in the lead-up to Idul Fitri.[5] In fact, the concept of *zakat* has long been a strategy to empower the community, [so] why has Muslim civilization experienced a decline? The answer is perhaps because [members of] the Muslim community itself are increasingly inconsistent in carrying out the teachings of their religion and prefer exotic, outside civilizations which glorify life in this world.

10.2.4 Fasting during the Fasting Month

Commentary The month of Ramadan, the ninth in the Muslim calendar, is considered especially sacred because it was during this month that the Qur'an was first sent down to the world. The sanctity of the period is marked by fasting (Ar.: *ṣawmun*) and religious

---

5 Idul Fitri (Ar.: `*iidul-fiṭri*; the small feast) is the celebration marking the end of Ramadan.

activities. The beginning and end of the month are calculated according to strict rules by astronomers and mathematicians and announced publicly on radio and television, in the press and through local mosques. During the period from just before sunrise to just after sunset, all adults who are in good health must abstain from consciously taking into the body any material substances (including smoke) and abstain from sexual intercourse. Exceptions are made for menstruating, pregnant, nursing or birthing women; those of unsound mind; those who have to perform heavy labour or travel; and the sick and frail. The ending of the fasting month is celebrated with several days of feasting known as Idul Fitri and exchanges of greetings of goodwill and forgiveness for offences given and received during the previous year. If it is not possible to fast every day during Ramadan, those days can be made up during the following months.

The end of the fasting month provides an opportunity to celebrate new beginnings. Religious leaders and politicians alike mark the occasion with stirring addresses. The following extract is taken from one such speech by the late Salamat Hashim (1942–2003), chair of the Moro Islamic Liberation Front (MILF), addressing his followers in December 2001. In reminding them of the many benefits of fasting and the historic victories the Prophet Muhammad achieved against his enemies during the fasting month, he notes that 'this significance of Ramadan in our lives should give hope to the oppressed Muslims in the Bangsamoro homeland and the whole world'. In this way he links the benefits obtained from individual fasting with the well-being of local Muslim communities in the southern Philippines and others who may be oppressed elsewhere.

Extract 10-8: Salamat Hashim

Salamat Hashim (2002), 'Second Message: "*Id el Fitr* Message to the Bangsamoro Nation"' [in English], pp. 16–18 in *Referendum: Peaceful, Civilized, Diplomatic and Democratic Means of Solving the Mindanao Conflict*, Agency for Youth Affairs–MILF, Camp Abubakre As-Siddique, Mindanao. Extract: pp. 16–17.

Sawm, as one of the pillars of Islam, is the basic [basis] of jihad [effort, striving] which all Muslims, as part of their physical, spiritual, ideological, moral[,] intellectual, psychological and mental development, have to go through annually. It is a 'training ground' to where believers momentarily retreat and withdraw to recharge and prepare so that they are better equipped with the strength of *imaan* (faith) and the faculty of understanding to confront all the challenges that the material world can throw at them.

> [Hashim then lists the 'diabolical forces arrayed against Islam' and the wars in Palestine, Afghanistan, Chechnya, Jammu–Kashmir and his own Bangsamoro homeland, which have inflicted massive devastation and dislocation.]

Yet, in the face of all these large-scale oppression, persecution and consuming hatred against Islam that we are now going through, we, Muslims, who have been trained in Ramadan to bear the hunger and thirst of *sawm*, to practice *sabr* [fortitude] in the most trying of times, to show mercy where there is cruelty, to enshrine charity for and solidarity with weak and deprived where there is indifferences and selfishness, to seek solace and communion with the Creator through *salat* [prayer] where there is godlessness all around us, to shield ourselves with *taqwaa* [piety] where there is corruption and arrogance, should be confident that no obstacle, no power on earth no matter how seemingly formidable and invincible, can ultimately withstand the power of faith that Ramadan has instilled in us. [...]

10.2.5 The Haj

Commentary It is obligatory for every adult Muslim who has the means to do so to perform a pilgrimage (haj; Ar.: *hajjun*) to Mecca once in his or her lifetime (Q3: 96–7).[6] The individual must be present in Mecca by the first week of the month of *dhul hijjati* (the last month in the Muslim calendar) and there fulfil the prescribed rituals dressed in simple, prescribed garments and in a state of ritual purity (Ar.: *ihraamun*). To be acceptable to God, the activities must be performed as stipulated; to ensure that this is achieved, special guides assist pilgrims.

There are in fact two forms of pilgrimage to Mecca. The first, as described above, is known as the haj and is undertaken between the eighth and tenth days of *dhul hijjati*. The climax of the haj is the assembly of all pilgrims (numbering several millions) on the Plain of Arafat (Ar.: `arafaat`), the place where it is believed Adam and Eve met after being expelled from paradise and where the Prophet Muhammad gave his final message to his followers. From midday to sunset the pilgrims engage in meditation and prayer before travelling by night to arrive the following day at Mina, where animals are sacrificed and the ritual of stoning two pillars (thought to represent Satan) occurs. To be present in the Prophet's cities of Mecca and Medina and to join the several million other Muslims assembled from across the world to perform the same rituals is an overwhelming experience for most pilgrims (see also Roff 2003).

The other form of pilgrimage, the `umrah`, is not obligatory and may be performed at any other time of the year. It is therefore less crowded than the haj and allows pilgrims greater opportunities to approach sacred objects such as the Black Stone set into one side of the Ka'bah (House of God). Pilgrims do not perform the period of reflection on the Plain of Arafat or the stoning and sacrifice ceremonies.

Southeast Asian Muslims have been participating in the haj since at least the seventeenth century. A small number stayed for many years in the Middle East, studying with famous scholars before returning to Southeast Asia to teach (Azra 2004). After their return from the haj, pilgrims receive an enthusiastic welcome from family and community members and are entitled to use the title 'Haji' for a man and 'Hajjah' for a woman.

The following extract is from the Indonesian women's magazine *Noor*, designed for an urban middle-class readership. This first-person account by a pilgrim stands for many others, especially in its description of the impact of actually seeing places intimately associated with the life of the Prophet Muhammad. Hajjah Margaretha was raised as a Christian but converted to Islam to marry. Having been told that requests sincerely made during prayers performed at the Mosque of the Prophet in Medina would be granted, she asked God for several things, including that He give her a sign that she had been accepted as a Muslim. All her requests were granted.

---

6 'The first House [of worship] to be established for mankind was the one at Mecca. It is a blessed place; a source of guidance for all people; there are clear signs in it; it is the place where Abraham stood; whoever enters it is safe. Pilgrimage to the House is a duty owed to God by people who are able to undertake it. Those who reject this [should know that] God has no need of anyone' (Q3: 96–7, Haleem).

Extract 10-9: Margaretha Andi Agus

Margaretha Andi Agus (2004), 'Hijrah Usai Umroh' [Change after the *Umroh*], *Noor*, 7 December: 60–2. Extract: p. 62.

We went to see the Grand Mosque in Mecca. I was awestruck. The mosque was so splendid and full of power. I could not take my eyes from the most holy place on the face of the earth. Slowly tears rolled down my cheeks. It was as if someone whispered, as if something awoke my consciousness, arousing a strong desire to perform the rituals of the *umroh* to the utmost of my ability – with total devotion and with full commitment. Against all odds my steps were light as I performed the sevenfold circumambulation of the Ka'bah, and I was even able to perform the *sa'i*[7] at a run. I recited my prayers fluently. Was this God's answer to my prayer? I was even given the opportunity to kiss the Black Stone and pray at Hijir Ismail.[8] How amazing!

After completing all the main rituals of the *umroh* I felt reborn. Without further questioning or difficulties I was absolutely convinced that Islam was the absolute true path. I had discovered my identity as a Muslim. God gave me what I had asked for. […]

* * * * *

> **Commentary**   In the following extract Dr K.H. Didin Hafidhuddin, an academic associated with Partai Keadilan Sejahtera (PKS, Prosperity and Justice Party) in Indonesia, explains the significance of the pilgrims' gathering on the Plain of Arafat in the month of *dhul hijjati*. He emphasizes the importance of applying the wisdom gained from the haj experience to real-life problems, particularly in the pilgrim's homeland. Further information about Hafidhuddin appears in section 14.1.1 (see also colour plate 17).

Extract 10-10: Didin Hafidhuddin

Didin Hafidhuddin (2004), 'Kearifan dan Kebijakan' [Understanding and Wisdom], pp. 149–53 in Hasyim Muzadi, Didin Hafidhuddin and Ahmad Syafii Maarif (eds), *Refleksi Tiga Kiai* [Reflections of Three *Kiai*], Penerbit Republika, Jakarta. Extract: pp. 149–51.

As we know, in the month of Dzulhijjah, Muslims from all corners of the earth with diverse cultural and language backgrounds and possibly different social status, prepare themselves for the peak of the haj rituals, namely conducting the *wukuf* [period of reflection] on the Plain of Arafah on 9 Dzulhijjah. *Wukuf* is the main pillar of the haj; even if in ill-health, an individual must conduct the *wukuf* themselves, as it cannot be delegated to any representative. In an authenticated Hadith (the account of Imam Ahmad and Imam Tirmidzi) the Prophet of God, blessings and peace be upon him, said: 'The haj is the *wukuf* on the Plain of Arafah'.

---

7   *Sa'i* [Ar.: *sa'yun*] is one of the rites of the haj and *'umrah*. See the glossary for a full description.
8   A space near the Ka'bah said to be the site of the graves of Abraham's wife Hagar and of their son, Ismail.

Even though pilgrims have only a very limited, brief period on the Plain of Arafah, beginning from the time the sun begins to decline from its midday point until it sets, this time is very important, perhaps the most important time in the pilgrims' lives. During this time all pilgrims, wearing the same *ihram* [pure] clothing and with pure and calm hearts and thoughts, devoutly recite the *tasbih* [verses sanctifying God], the *tahmid* [verses praising God], the *takbir* [verses exalting God], the *tahlil* [verses acknowledging that there is only one God], the *istighfar* [verses asking for God's forgiveness] and the *dzikir* [verses remembering God][9] individually and together, and pray to Almighty God to request [fulfilment of] all their desires and needs.

The atmosphere becomes all the more solemn and full of devotion as each member of the congregation individually reflects upon and performs *muhasabah* (self-introspection and self-evaluation) of all their behaviour throughout their lives. Perhaps for each member of the congregation, a depiction will flash by in their minds of how dull and lacklustre their daily behaviour is, towards Almighty God, towards their family, towards their friends and towards other people. They may not even realize how strongly their tears are flowing as they remember these sins. The record of the past is so clear and vivid in their minds.

Such is the configuration of the *wukuf* on the Plain of Arafah, steeped in an atmosphere of spirituality and heavenly power. The physical body is present on the Plain of Arafah, but the heart and mind drifts far and high to the throne of God, in dialogue with the Creator, Almighty God, the All Merciful, All Loving and All Forgiving.

Arafah, in etymological terms, has the same root word as *ma'rifat* [Ar.: *ma'rifah*], which means an increasingly deep familiarity with the presence of Almighty God and with oneself. A person who correctly and sincerely performs the *wukuf* on the Plain of Arafah will possess increasingly deep *ma'rifat* and an increasingly high level of understanding and wisdom. The more aware one is that one is a weak creature in great need of the guidance and help of Almighty God, the higher one's social responsibility and empathy. A person who possesses understanding and wisdom will try to distance themselves from materialistic, egotistical, hedonistic and arrogant traits. As such, a person who possesses wisdom will obtain and possess much goodness, as expounded in QS 2:269: '... And upon whomsoever is bestowed *alhikmah* (understanding and wisdom), truly upon him will be bestowed many rewards ...'.[10]

It is this learning and wisdom that pilgrims must take back with them to their homeland to face various tasks and responsibilities, and solve various complex problems that our society and nation presently face.

10.3 SUFISM

Commentary Sufism (Ar.: *tasawwufun*) is the direct experience of God through meditation, the repetition of phrases containing the name of God and the recitation of Qur'anic verses. It is the spiritual aspect of Islam and is regarded as a balance for the

---

9 In Indonesian this word is spelled *dzikir* and *zikir*, in Malaysian it is *zikir* and in Arabic *dhikrun*.

10 'and He gives wisdom to whoever He will. Whoever is given wisdom has truly been given much good, but only those with insight bear this in mind' (Q2: 269, Haleem).

formalism of the sharia (Islamic law).[11] Sufistic practices assist in direct experience of the divine (Ar.: *ma'rifah*), also described in extract 10-10, and fulfil the spiritual yearning of human beings. Both sharia and Sufism guide individuals in expressing their relationship to God and experiencing His qualities.

In the writings of Southeast Asian Muslim scholars dating back to the early seventeenth century, there is evidence that tensions developed between scholars who had studied Sufism under specialist teachers and those who had not. One result of incomplete understanding was an overemphasis on mystical practices at the expense of fulfilling the basic duties of Islam as expressed in the sharia. Complete adherence to the sharia is the path to spiritual purification, but this will have no meaning for believers if they do not also practise the spiritual exercises of Sufism that will lead, eventually, to full understanding of the Truth (Ar.: *haqiiqah*). Conversely, practising Sufism without the discipline of sharia will not lead to understanding. The path to the Truth has defined stages, with special forms of recitations[12] appropriate for each stage.

In the contemporary world, belonging to a Sufi group can provide great spiritual comfort, not only in the uncertainty and alienation of rapid social change or economic downturn, but also as an individual contemplates the significance of life in this world. In the following extract, a member of the Khalwatiyah order describes what he gains from membership of his Sufi group.

Extract 10-11: *Syukron*

Excerpt from the transcript of an interview with Syukron (then 31 years old, with no permanent work), Jakarta, 28 January 2000. ['Living with Devotion' project.]

Khalwatiyah emphasizes *dzikir* [Ar.: *dhikrun*] as a means of remembering God Most Holy and Most High. With *dzikir* we are urged to reflect on how little time we have in this life in which to do good. But even so, we also have to consider the importance of life in this world. Balance, that's what Islam is about; think of your death as though you will die tomorrow and think of your life as though you will live for another 1,000 years.

* * * * *

Commentary   One of the most widely read books on Sufism, written for a general audience by a modern Southeast Asian Muslim, is *Tasauf Moderen* [Modern Sufism]. Its

---

11   Howell (2001: 702, note 2) explains that Sufism as understood by Muslims is more broad than the common Western equation of Sufism with an exotic form of mysticism. Rather, she suggests that a definition which encompasses 'the interiorization and intensification of Islamic faith and practice [...] allows us to recognize that devotional practices and religious concepts associated with Sufi traditions are often employed by Muslims as spiritual enhancements of their everyday lives, even when they are not undertaking a mystical path of dramatic personal transformation in hopes of direct experience of the divine ...'.

12   Howell (2001: 704, note 7) provides further details and defines the two main forms of recitation as follows. *Dhikrun* is the repetition of phrases containing the name of God. These are chanted repeatedly and rhythmically so that they can 'stimulate altered states of consciousness under certain conditions'. *Wird* are brief Qur'anic passages chosen to meet specific spiritual needs and recited a number of times. These recitations may also be used for the purpose of spiritual protection or healing.

author was Dr Haji Abdul Malik Karim Amrullah, better known as Hamka (1908–81). He was jailed during the Guided Democracy period for alleged anti-government activities. He used his time in jail to complete a monumental exegesis of the Qur'an, *Tafsir al-Azhar* [The al-Azhar Exegesis]. Later, he established a school and college in Jakarta modelled on al-Azhar University in Cairo. In the late 1970s Hamka was appointed chair of Majelis Ulama Indonesia (MUI, Indonesian Council of Ulama), the government-backed body that formulates 'official' fatwa (religious rulings) for Indonesian Muslims.

Hamka's *Tasauf Moderen* has undergone numerous reprintings; evidence of its continued relevance is that in 2004 an extract was published in a journal for young Muslim professionals in Singapore. Hamka's views on the nature of Sufism reflect his insistence that Muslims have a responsibility to engage actively with the problems of the real world.

Extract 10-12: Hamka

Hamka (2004), 'Introducing Tasawwuf' [in English], *Muslim Reader* 22(2): 7–9. [Excerpt from Hamka's *Tasauf Moderen* (Modern Sufism), originally published 1939; English translation by Nazri Lim Abdullah.] Extract: p. 9.

Then the progress of the Muslims, wrought through the auspices of labouring in the cause of Allah, gradually gave rise to groups of men known as the *Sufis*. Their lives which had earlier been ones of renunciation and a disciplined abstention from the worldly achievements of others later devolved into excesses. The true *Sufis* found contentment in their own hearts, day by day delving deeper and deeper until there arose within them the vision of gnosis (*m'arifah*), and of the meaning of bliss (*sa'adah*), and of knowledge of the ways (*tariqa*) for the spiritual traveller to obtain a close and unremitting relationship with his or her God. [...]

[Hamka then criticizes those Muslims who believe that Islam should encourage retreat from worldly affairs because material wealth is not important. He counters this with the following quotation from Rashid Rida (1865–1935):[13]]

'[...] The excessive inculcation of aversion for worldly wealth in the hearts of Muslims has contributed to their becoming disadvantaged and forms one of the reasons why they are taken advantage of by their adversaries. On the other hand, ease and comfort does give rise to pride and conceit, negligence of one's obligatory duties, and a habituation to things prohibited.'

So said Rashid Rida. Hopefully, the foregoing explanation has clarified the purpose of our book [*Tasauf Moderen*]. We named it *Tasawwuf* in the sense Al-Junaid[14] understood it – 'To leave off offensive behaviours and to take on praiseworthy manners' – and to explicate this idea in a 'modern' interpretation. We recall the original meanings of *Tasawwuf*, which are to purify the self, to train and uplift the stature

---

13   Rashid Rida was a follower of the great nineteenth-century Egyptian reformer Muhammad Abduh and an influential figure in the modernizing and energizing of Muslim thought.

14   Abu al-Qasim Junaid of Baghdad was a famous ninth-century CE Sufi who insisted on the close connection between sharia and Sufism.

of the human personality, to renounce greed and caprice, and to control the sexual appetite from exceeding what is normal for the sound individual.

* * * * *

Commentary   The following extract is from a brief autobiographical memoir by Dr Yudi Latif (1964–), written in 1990. During the 1980s, as Islamic outreach (*dakwah*) activities strengthened on university campuses, he believed that predication must be accompanied by what he termed 'the fire of love'. The extract describes why he believes this is so important. A student activist in Bandung in the late 1980s, Latif became a member of Ikatan Cendekiawan Muslim Indonesia (ICMI, Association of Indonesian Muslim Intellectuals) in the early 1990s. A prolific writer and commentator, he is currently a deputy rector of Paramadina University in Jakarta.

Extract 10-13: Yudi Latif

Yudi Latif (1990), 'Dari Islam Sejarah, Memburu Islam Ideal (Mi'raj Tangisan Seorang Kurban Sejarah)' [From Historical Islam, Chasing Ideal Islam (The Tearful Journey of a Victim of History)], pp. 221–40 in Ihsan Ali-Fauzi and Haidar Bagir (eds), *Mencari Islam: Kumpulan Otobiografi Intelektual Kaum Muda Muslim Indonesia Angkatan 80-an* [Seeking Islam: Intellectual Autobiographies of Young Indonesian Muslims of the Generation of the 80s], Penerbit Mizan, Bandung. Extract: pp. 239–40.

It is not always easy to nurture 'the fire of love' except through doing serious and continuous forms of spiritual exercises (*riyadhah*). The best form of *riyadhah* to fan 'the fire of love' is worship (*'ibadah*). We have to change our usual form of worship from the worship of a slave to that of a lover. As Iqbal[15] said, in worship when man meets his God it is not like the meeting of a slave with his master, but rather the meeting of a lover with his beloved. Worship with the consciousness and from the position of a slave inhibits man's communication with God. Worship like that is sterile and devoid of morality and will culminate in the death of love. Whereas worship with the mentality of 'lovers' is not viewed merely as submission or compliance to the will of God, but rather [is viewed as] actively trying to comprehend, perceive and spread God's attributes (of love) in historical reality. Thus, by worshipping from the perspective of 'love', people are in a continual dialogue, between the effort to make subjective (to make transcendent) all objects in the presence of the Great Creator, and the effort to objectify all subjective experiences (meeting the Great Creator) in real life.

The ultimate perception of the love of God is to reach the point of experiencing gnosis (*ma'rifah*), where man is able to integrate all reality into the presence of God the Great Creator. The ultimate in spreading the love of God is manifest in the experience of Divine Truth (*hakikat* [Ar.: *haqiiqah*]), in which man observes the love of God on earth, to later actively see and greet life around him with a feeling of love.

---

15   Muhammad Iqbal (1876–1938), Punjabi intellectual, nation builder, poet and mystic who urged dynamism and renewal in Islamic thinking.

It is only people with an awareness of *ma'rifah* and *hakikat* who can truly love God and truly love mankind. And it is only people like this who are really prepared to step into the heart of society, to play the role of social prophets, who can help unloosen the chains of polytheism, ignorance, poverty and oppression that shackle their lives. Who in the end will transform the long weeping into the soft smile of victory in the next millennium, 2000. If it pleases God. Amen!

* * * * *

Commentary   Magazines for the Muslim middle classes in Malaysia, Singapore and Indonesia regularly carry articles discussing aspects of Sufism. While rarely covering the deeper and esoteric aspects of Sufism, the articles usually explain the calming and uplifting qualities that believers experience through mystical practices, qualities that assist Muslims who face pressures in their professional and personal lives. The following extract is taken from a magazine interview with Sulaiman Ibrahim, lecturer in the Faculty of Islamic Studies at the National University of Malaysia.

Extract 10-14: Sulaiman Ibrahim

Excerpt from an interview with Sulaiman Ibrahim conducted by Wan Mohd Hafiz Wan Hamzah, 'Kepentingan Tasawuf dalam Kehidupan' [The Importance of Mysticism in Life], *al Islam*, March 2005, pp. 64–5. Extract: pp. 64–5.

'[...] Mysticism in Islam is knowledge about the personal experience of religion through the heart and feeling. A person with the spirit of a mystic will give greater priority to compassion and love, good moral behaviour, regardless of where the person happens to be.

'Mysticism has various stages. This definition of mysticism is leaving behind bad moral behaviour and moving towards more uplifting morality. Being honest and trustworthy, guarding against disloyalty and jealousy and liking peace, that too is included in the category of mysticism', he [Sulaiman Ibrahim] explained.

He went on to say that mysticism is like a vitamin for the spirit and is much needed by the believer regardless of level, rank, wealth or poverty.

In the modern world of today, we can see that mental illnesses such as stress have become widespread among urban dwellers [...]

'But if we observe believers who have practised mysticism, stress does not overwhelm them. They are more calm and able to accept the chaos of life in a metropolitan city. Mysticism teaches us to be always in contact with God. It will train body and spirit to be more patient and accepting', he said.

In brief, mysticism is knowledge that teaches us how to cleanse the heart of wickedness and to be disciplined to raise the level of yearning through various practices, such as saying *zikir*.

'In mysticism, the most important thing is to train oneself to always say *zikir* and remember Almighty God every day in the course of daily life. When driving, eating, working and so on. Saying *zikir* is not reserved for particular times.'

* * * * *

Commentary   The recitation or chanting of the names of God has been popularized through special audio recordings and public performances as if it were an art form. Celebrity religious teachers such as Abdullah Gymnastiar (better known as Aa Gym; see extracts 10-24 and 10-38) and Arifin Ilham use the practice during mass meetings of followers, and they record cassettes and CDs that are in great demand. The cover notes on the audiocassette 'Tausiyah Dzikir & Nasyid' [Ar.: *tawshiihun dhikrun & nashiidun*] provide Arifin Ilham's views on the importance of *dhikrun*. See also colour plate 17.

Extract 10-15: Muhammad Arifin Ilham

Muhammad Arifin Ilham (2004), *Tausiyah Dzikir & Nasyid* [Advice through *Dzikir* & *Nasyid* Songs], audiocassette cover notes, Nadahijrah Forte Entertainment, Jakarta.

Personal *Dzikir*

Dzikir are the most nutritious spiritual food for humankind, because *dzikir* can calm the heart of the reciter. Ibnu Taymiyyah [a medieval scholar] said: 'I never stop reciting *dzikir* for God except to rest my soul, so that I can prepare another form of *dzikir*'. Almighty God has even promised in the Qur'an that *dzikir* will bring us peace. 'Namely, those who believe their hearts will be at peace by remembering God. Remember, it is only by remembering God that your hearts will be at peace ...' (Ar-Ra'ad: 28).[16] On the other hand, numerous cases prove that many sick people cannot be cured by medicine. When they surrender themselves by praying, saying *dzikir* and surrendering to God, they are healed. ... May this album, Advice through *Dzikir* and *Nasyid* Songs, become a part of our *dzikir* activities. Attend *dzikir* meetings, practise personal *dzikir* and enjoy God's most delicious guidance ... the *dzikir* of God.

10.4   MANIFESTATIONS OF PIETY

10.4.1   Education of Children

> 'Our children are gifts from God, aren't they, so we should not only look
> after them but also equip them with understanding about their religion
> because, as their parents, for sure we'll be held to account later.'
> (Teguh Hidayat)[17]

Commentary   Some Muslims believe that secular education has failed to develop the full human potential of individuals – that is, to be 'pious and righteous servants [of God]' (Ismail 2003). Secular education, in their view, produces people who are materialistic and individualistic. According to Ismail Yusanto, a leading member of Indonesia's Hizbut Tahrir (Liberation Party)[18] movement, what is needed is a holistic approach

---

16   'those who have faith and whose hearts find peace in the remembrance of God – truly it is in the remembrance of God that hearts find peace' (Q13: 28, Haleem).

17   Interviewed in Jakarta, 20 January 2000 (then 34 years old, accountant). ['Living with Devotion' project.]

18   Hizbut Tahrir is an international movement calling for the restoration of a universal caliphate.

based on an Islamic paradigm. In this approach, there would be a balance between the following three elements: the formation of an Islamic identity (Ar.: *shakhsiyyatun 'islaamiyyatun*); mastery of Islamic culture (Ar.: *thaqaafah*); and life skills (technology and vocational skills). Education should involve collaboration between three groups – family, school or campus, and society – and each of these groups must support the implementation of doctrine (Ar.: `*aqiidah*) (Ismail 2003).

The three elements of education essential for the full development of Muslim identity, as outlined by Ismail Yusanto, are difficult to combine within the education system provided by modern nation-states, whose primary purpose is to develop national unity and state citizens. The following extract, by leading educationist Professor Azyumardi Azra, analyses the impact of the growth of private Islamic schools, some of which do exemplify the characteristics described as ideal by Ismail Yusanto. Professor Azra believes that the religious education offered in such schools extends beyond the pupils to their parents, and thus has a wider social impact. Besides being rector of Indonesia's leading state Islamic university, State Islamic University Syarif Hidayatullah Jakarta, Professor Azra is one of Indonesia's foremost historians of Islam.

Extract 10-16: Azyumardi Azra

Azyumardi Azra (1999), 'Kebangkitan Sekolah Elite Muslim: Pola Baru "Santri-nisasi"' [The Rise of Elite Muslim Schools: A New Pattern of '*Santri*-ization'], pp. 69–82 in *Pendidikan Islam: Tradisi dan Modernisasi menuju Milenium Baru* [Islamic Education: Tradition and Modernization Approaching the New Millennium], Logos Wacana Ilmu, Jakarta. Extract: pp. 69, 79–80.

For at least the past two decades, a trend towards Islamization or re-Islamization has been evident among Indonesian Muslims. The term that has become popular to describe this tendency is '*santri*-ization' – an English form based on the Javanese term *santri* meaning 'those from *pesantren*', or more generally meaning 'those who devoutly follow Islamic teachings' in contrast to *abangan*, those who are nominal Muslims. [p. 69] [...]

Santri-ization of the Muslim Middle Class

The emergence and mushrooming of 'elite Muslim schools' and good Islamic schools (*madrasah*) clearly will have a far-reaching impact on the future of Indonesian Muslim society. Elite schools and *madrasah* that offer a quality education make a contribution not only to the improvement of Islamic education in Indonesia, but also to the process of *santri*-ization of Muslim society.

The process of *santri*-ization can be described in two ways. First, the students from those schools have already undergone 're-Islamization' [...]. [B]esides studying general subjects, they study the Islamic sciences, beginning with how to recite the Qur'an and how to perform the prayer rituals correctly through to basic Islamic teachings. However, the process of developing the teachings and practices of Islam would certainly be more intense if done in *madrasah* and schools that use the live-in system.

The Indonesian branch, Hizbut Tahrir Indonesia (HTI, Liberation Party of Indonesia), has focused on spreading its message through non-violent means. See chapter 12 for further details.

Second, students then bring the Islam they have learned at school back home. In many cases they even teach their parents, who often know only a little about Islam, how to perform the prayers, for example, and how to perform other Islamic rituals. In general, the parents feel embarrassed because of their lack of knowledge about particular Islamic teachings and practices. As a result, so that they do not disappoint their children, they begin to study Islam, either by themselves or through private teachers employed to teach them about Islam.

Thus, a new pattern of re-Islamization or *santri*-ization is emerging in middle-class Muslim circles, not only among the children, but also among their parents. [pp. 79–80]

* * * * *

Commentary In Southeast Asia the forms of Islamic schooling are diverse and the terminology for different kinds of religious schools is quite complex. In the rural areas of southern Thailand and Malaysia, an Islamic school where pupils live in small buildings near their teachers and study mainly religious subjects is called a *pondok* (hut) (see further Che Man 1990a). In Java, the same kind of live-in school is called a *pesantren* (the place of *santri*, that is, devout Muslims), and in Aceh the term *dayah* is used. The cost of attending these rural schools is based on what the parents can afford to give the teachers and the small amounts needed to pay for the children's simple meals. In poor or remote areas, *pesantren* may offer the only means to education for many girls and therefore their existence is essential if girls are to gain any literacy and numeracy skills. The term *madrasah*, used in most parts of Southeast Asia, also refers to Islamic schools. In contrast to *pondok* and *pesantren*, students in *madrasah* are taught in classes graded according to educational level (rather than in subject-based groups). The range of subjects offered by small religious schools is very limited, as described in the following extract. The author, Tubagus Furqon Sofhani (1966–), studied planography (printing processes) at Bandung's famous Institute of Technology. During the 1980s he was active in the Salman Mosque Islamic revival movement.

Extract 10-17: Tubagus Furqon Sofhani

Tubagus Furqon Sofhani (1990), 'Antara Serang dan Bandung: Sebuah Pencarian Gagasan' [Between Serang and Bandung: A Search for Ideas], pp. 133–54 in Ihsan Ali-Fauzi and Haidar Bagir (eds), *Mencari Islam: Kumpulan Otobiografi Intelektual Kaum Muda Muslim Indonesia Angkatan 80-an* [Seeking Islam: Intellectual Autobiographies of Young Indonesian Muslims of the Generation of the 80s], Penerbit Mizan, Bandung. Extract: pp. 135–6.

My first religious education was from my parents, who taught me much about reciting the Qur'an and who instilled basic religious attitudes. Not long afterwards, when I was six, I was sent to a *madrasah* for seven years. There I was introduced to a range of knowledge: Arabic syntax and grammar, the traditions of the Prophet's life (Hadith), jurisprudence (*fiqh*), Qur'anic recitation (*tajwid*), the doctrine of the unity of God (*tawhid*), mathematics, learning [the Qur'an] by heart (*mahfudhah*) and so on. The teaching method resembled that used in *pesantren*, with more emphasis on rote learning than on understanding the particular principles. Each lesson had to be memorized by the following week. Personally I could memorize the lesson, but I didn't learn much from it. A large proportion of the students left halfway through before completing their studies.

The changes that were occurring in society were not acknowledged by institutions for religious education, which clung to traditional methods and materials. Their biggest weakness lay in their teaching methodology, which failed to inspire students to continue on with their studies. [...]

The teaching given at the *madrasah* reflects my understanding of Islam at that time. Islamic education went only as far as the rituals of worship, supplemented by some basic knowledge of Asharite theology[19] and acquaintance with tools of knowledge such as [Arabic] grammar and syntax and so on. In the mornings I attended ordinary [state] school and in the afternoons went to the *madrasah*. I did this for seven years until I completed *madrasah* and primary school. Either consciously or unconsciously I felt there were two separate camps of knowledge: what I was taught at the *madrasah* and what I was taught at school. In other words, I was not able to see knowledge holistically, but rather as bits and pieces that didn't seem to connect into one system. The knowledge I was taught in the *madrasah* seemed to be closely linked with transcendent matters, and did not make a practical contribution to my daily life. The knowledge I was taught in state school seemed to have no links with transcendent matters but did make a practical contribution to my daily life. Acknowledged or not, the dual worlds of education tended to make me think in a divided way, leaning towards the secular side, because it was no longer possible to see knowledge holistically and linked with transcendent matters. Nevertheless, beneath the deficiencies in the *madrasah* system of education, I was aware and convinced that that kind of education made a great and much needed contribution, especially in one's early years, to forming a sense of morality and providing basic religious knowledge.

* * * * *

Commentary   It is important to know something about the early religious education of individuals who later in their lives use violence in the name of Islam. In the case of the Indonesian Imam Samudra, it is clear that the teaching he received at a *pesantren kilat* (an intensive, condensed course of religious instruction for senior high school students held during the normal school holidays of the fasting month) came at an impressionable period of his life and fuelled a religiosity that he went on to develop along very literalist lines.

Extract 10-18: Imam Samudra

Imam Samudra (2004), *Aku Melawan Teroris* [I Fight Terrorists], Jazera, Solo. Extract: pp. 32–3.

---

19   Abu al-Hasan al-Ash'ari was a tenth-century CE scholar who taught in Baghdad. He founded a branch of theology that taught that revelation is superior to mankind's ability to reason. His thinking was followed by al-Ghazali (twelfth century CE) and by Muslims associated with the Shafi'i and Maliki schools of law.

God Most Compassionate. Most Loving. Most Knowing. He and only He, the One who gives us Guidance. He did not allow my adolescence simply to be 'set ablaze' by the wave of secularism and materialism spawned by Pancasila [the five principles of the Indonesian state ideology]. Once, at the end of second-semester examinations, the entire school was on holiday for two weeks. It was during Ramadan. Several Muslim organizations, including Muhammadiyah and Persis,[20] had joined together to run a Ramadan school. With the encouragement of my parents, my older sister and my older brother, God moved my heart to take part in the school for a week.

I was fascinated by the scientific, fair and simple explanations and teaching, and with the sincerity of the teachers and the committee. There I learnt about [the dangers of] innovation not based on doctrine, about the example of the Prophet, about polytheism and about Islam. The explanations of issues concerning social interaction between the sexes stabbed my heart.

It was still fresh in my mind, the explanation that my religious teacher at junior high school gave, that when walking, female students must be on the left-hand side and male students on the right. This is because it is the custom in Indonesia for women to walk on the left. Now, when the lady religious teacher at the Ramadan school asked the participants how men and women should walk when they are together, instinctively and very confidently I answered exactly as my religious teacher at junior high school had explained. Other participants answered the opposite, but most people agreed with my answer.

After the atmosphere had calmed down, the lady religious teacher explained that it was forbidden in Islam for a man to walk beside a woman who was not a close relative, whether the man was on the right or on the left, whether there was one couple or several couples. She then gave the argumentation from the Qur'an and the sayings and traditions of the Prophet as the legal basis for her explanation.

Her explanation made me surprised, sad, and a million other feelings. I felt it was the first inner conflict I had experienced. How could it not? Ever since I had been to school, I was used to interacting and playing with female students who did not cover those parts of the body that Islam requires to be covered. Speaking to them freely without feeling as though I was sinning. And every time it was my turn to recite the prayers at the flag-raising ceremony, there were several female students who would willingly put their school ties round my neck; others dressed me in their hats; then we would laugh happily in the way of teenagers, without feeling we were sinning in even the smallest way. If there were those who didn't like what we did, we just thought they were jealous, or jumping to conclusions, or behind the times. So we kept it up; we didn't care one bit, even in front of other people. What a disaster!

For me, the week of Ramadan that year was full of guidance and blessings. That was the starting point that made me understand how beautiful Islam is, how great it is, how perfect it is. It was there that I understood that Islam is the one and only path to a noble life in this world and the next. In fact, before that I had only thought of Islam as mere rituals. From that time I began to understand what the meaning of life

---

20   Muhammadiyah is Indonesia's largest modernist Islamic organization, founded in 1912. Persis is a reformist Islamic organization founded in 1923.

was, what the meaning of religious devotion was. I began to comprehend and feel devotion before God. I understood that my past was wrong. *God forgive me!!!*

* * * * *

Commentary In Southeast Asia, the term *madrasah* is used for Islamic schools that have graded classes. They may be partially state funded or wholly privately funded. In Indonesia, 80 per cent are privately owned and funded, and about 30 per cent of *madrasah* graduates continue on to tertiary education. In the southern Philippines, organized Islamic education is available only in urban centres, where many of the *madrasah* teachers are from Saudi Arabia. In rural and more remote areas of the southern Philippines, and in Burma, there is no system of graded formal Islamic education. Instead, children are taught the basic rituals and some Qur'anic recitation. In Thailand's northern Tak province, refugee Burmese Muslims attend a local school but receive instruction in Islam from the local mosque. This seems to be the norm for the thousands of Burmese Muslims living in towns and camps on the Thai–Burma border.[21] In stark contrast to the lack of formal Islamically-based education in Burma and the southern Philippines is the plethora of Islamic kindergartens and private colleges springing up in Jakarta and Kuala Lumpur. In Indonesia, the mass social organizations Nahdlatul Ulama (NU, Revival of the Religious Scholars) and Muhammadiyah have long-established kindergartens and offer a full range of Islamic education to tertiary level.

In both Malaysia and Indonesia, the government has increasingly been concerned that students educated mainly in Islamic studies (at private or state institutions, at the secondary and tertiary levels) lack the professional and vocational skills to find employment other than through becoming religious teachers themselves. The curricula of the Institut Agama Islam Negeri (IAIN, State Islamic Institutes) and Universitas Islam Negeri (UIN, State Islamic Universities), as well as those of the private Islamic universities in Indonesia, include professional subjects as part of degree courses in some faculties (Hooker and Lindsey, forthcoming). In Malaysia, there are calls to expand the employment opportunities available to graduates of Islamic studies by ensuring that they take non-religious subjects when obtaining their qualifications. This approach supports the framework outlined by Ismail Yusanto (see above), whose Islamic paradigm for education includes professional and vocational skills.

The issue is a topical one in Malaysia. The following extract from the middle-class magazine *Majalah i* describes how institutions are adding professional courses to their Islamic studies programs.

Extract 10-19: Saharom Abd Aziz

Saharom Abd Aziz (2005), 'Pengangguran Pelajar Lulusan Agama: Apa Penyelesaiannya?' [Unemployed Religious Studies Students: Is There a Solution?], *Majalah i*, March: 20–5. Extract: p. 21.

In our nation several universities offer courses in Islamic Studies. These include the University of Malaya, the National University of Malaysia, the International Islamic

---

21 See <www.childsdream.org/ed/howwehelp.asp?current>, accessed 31 March 2005; and *Bangkok Post*, 13 March 2005, <www.bangkokpost.net/130305>, accessed 31 March 2005.

University, the Malaysian Islamic University College (KUIM) and the Selangor Darul Ehsan Islamic College (KISDAR).[22] How far do the courses they offer meet today's needs? Are students exposed to subjects like information and communications technology, commercial management, accountancy, mathematics and so on which are necessary for finding work?

Looking at students who take Islamic Studies, only sharia offers specialization in several areas, including law, administration and economics. Whereas other subjects, such as Revelation Studies, Doctrine, Islamic Outreach, Arabic, and Qur'anic and Hadith Studies, are limited to religious studies only.

Therefore, to ensure that Islamic education departments meet the needs and requirements of today, a comprehensive study needs to be done. Thus, the Cabinet decision to make it compulsory for all students in higher education taking Islamic Studies to also take one extra subject in another field is very welcome, to broaden their knowledge so they can find employment more easily.

The Faculty of Islamic Studies, National University of Malaysia, has been pro-active in establishing a strategy and implementing a raft of new courses for the past two years to ensure its graduates have the skills and are competitive in meeting the needs of industry and society.

* * * * *

Commentary   The issue of opportunities for access to education for Muslim girls and women is one of concern for Southeast Asian Muslims. In Malaysia, Singapore and Indonesia, members of the Muslim middle classes seem motivated to ensure that their daughters have access to an education that will enable them to develop careers. While in the past the teaching profession has been regarded as the domain of women, there are numerous advertisements in middle-class magazines offering special courses designed for women who are planning careers in management and business. The theological arguments for supporting the education of women are outlined in the following extract from an article in *Noor*.

Extract 10-20: Leli Nurrohmah

Leli Nurrohmah (2005), 'Menilik Pendidikan bagi Perempuan' [Looking at Education for Women], *Noor*, March: 102–3. Extract: p. 103.

Islam emphasizes that the right to education is a pillar of empowerment. When Islam came to Arab society it provided the opportunity for women to have the same access to knowledge as men.

Islam regards education as a right for each person, man or woman, as pointed out in a Hadith: '*To seek knowledge is the responsibility of every Muslim*' (the account of Ibn Majah, al-Baihaqi and Ibn Abd al-Barr). Every Muslim means Muslims whether male or female, without gender differentiation, having the same responsibility to seek various forms of knowledge. When seeking knowledge becomes the responsi-

---

22   KUIM: Kolej Universiti Islam Malaysia; KISDAR: Kolej Islam Selangor Darul Ehsan.

bility of every Muslim, then the whole socio-political structure of society must be conditioned so that the responsibility can be taken up fully by everyone.

In another Hadith the Messenger of God urged that in providing education there should be no differentiation between males and females: '*Teach your children riding, swimming and archery*' (H.R. At-Turmudzi).

Imam Bukhari notes that Aisyah, daughter of Abi [Abu] Bakr and wife of the Prophet Muhammad, blessings and peace be upon him, had praised the Anshar women[23] for always studying, when she said: 'The best women are those from among the Anshar; they are never diffident about studying religion' (the account of Bukhari, Muslim, Abu Dawud and an-Nasa'i). They were even bold enough to raise it with the Prophet, blessings and peace be upon him, when they felt that their right to study was not being met compared with the opportunities given to the male companions.

It is even related in another Hadith that once several women came to the Prophet Muhammad, blessings and peace be upon him, to complain that their knowledge was insufficient and to request the Prophet of God to make special time for them, to which the Prophet agreed. This later gave rise to many women becoming well-known transmitters of Hadith.

★ ★ ★ ★ ★

Commentary The following extract is another from the writings of the great Indonesian scholar Hamka. From 1967 to 1981, Hamka wrote a regular column, 'Heart to Heart', for a popular Islamic publication, *Panji Masyarakat* [Banner of Society]. Here, he reminds parents that it is their responsibility to ensure that their children know and understand the heritage of Muslim civilization.

Extract 10-21: Hamka

Hamka (2002), 'Pokok Pegangan Hidup Kita' [Our Basic Principles for Living], pp. 146–50 in Yousran Rusydi (ed.), *Dari Hati ke Hati tentang Agama, Sosial-Budaya, Politik* [Heart to Heart on Religion, Society, Politics], Penerbit Pustaka Panjimas, Jakarta. Extract: pp. 146–7.

Having explained how heavy the responsibilities of Muslim youths are in the preceding writings, the question now arises: *What is it that we are going to defend?* Our ancestors set up one Culture in this country, that of Islam! That is what we shall defend.

When Islam began to penetrate this country and our ancestors accepted it peacefully, or when our ancestors themselves went venturing overseas to Muslim countries, Mecca, Medina, Egypt and Istanbul, then later Baghdad and Damascus, they returned home bringing a system of living based on and drawn from Faith (*Iman*).

They established a state; they set up a system of justice which – *praise be to God* – was in harmony with the peace within our people's spirit. Magnificent and

---

23   Anshar or Ansar, meaning 'helpers': those people of Medina who supported the migration of the Prophet Muhammad and his followers from Mecca to Medina in 622 CE and ensured that Muslims were protected and their religion allowed to flourish.

famous Islamic kingdoms prevailed, *their fame extending to the lands above the winds* [lands north of the equator].

And even though Western colonialism subsequently came to this country, we were able to stand firm in our steadfast individuality. Because of the heritage left by our ancestors.

Those Islamic kingdoms of old, from Malacca to Aceh, from Demak to Pajang and Mataram, from Banten to Cirebon and Sunda Kelapa (Batavia), from Kampar to Johor, to Makassar, to Maluku, have all left behind a name for themselves. It is true what Said Jamaluddin Al-Afghani[24] once said: '*Kingdoms and their kings may crumble, but the people and their mosques will never fall*'.

Human beings cannot live forever; when their time comes, they must die. But Muslims, or groups whose lives are informed by these Islamic ideas or aspirations, can be eternal and withstand desert after desert, century after century. That is, [they can do this] on the condition that the strength of past generations continues to endure to be passed on to the generations that follow. What ancestors leave to their descendants is not gold and silver but doctrine (*akidah*).

But ruptures may occur between fathers and their children, or between grandmothers and their grandchildren, if the spirit and essence of Islam are no longer passed on. That is, [ruptures may occur] when a father is still joining in communal prayer in the mosque, while his children are continually spending every afternoon at the cinema. We see the nature of the symptoms in grandmothers and grandchildren going their separate ways or fathers and children being at odds. Or the daughter and her mother both walking in the main street; the grandmother, the father and the mother still think within an Islamic milieu, dress according to Islamic law, while the daughter or grandchild is already far removed in her thinking from those who have nurtured and raised her. If care is not taken to preserve the ties that bind, namely an Islamic milieu, an Islamic outlook and a love of the Qur'an and the Prophet, it may be that their opposition will become increasingly polarized, such that they can never be reconciled. There are hundreds of cases of devout parents who have never neglected to pray five times daily, whose children have suddenly become Catholics! It all starts because the parents are drawn in and want their child to join the ranks of the educated. They hear reports that in Christian schools classes are orderly and teachers are able. All of a sudden, while the father and mother are starting their prayers with *Allahu Akbar* [God is the Greatest], the child brings her hand to her chest and forehead, making the sign of the cross!

There are many who have converted, but still more who have dropped their ties with Islam, the vision and love of Islam wiped clean from their hearts. They detest all that smacks of Islam. They hate to hear the call to prayer before dawn. They hate to see pilgrims wearing turbans, and they detest all that has an Arab flavour. So that in their derision they cannot distinguish between the Qur'an, the Prophet Muhammad,

---

24 Said Jamaluddin al-Afghani (or Jamal al-Din al-Afghani) (1838–97 CE) was a famous scholar. He claimed to be Afghani but was born and raised in Iran. With Muhammad Abduh he advocated the reform of Islam and supported greater emphasis on science and technology in Islamic education. He was a strong critic of Western colonialism and actively used Islam for political ends.

Arabia, and dates and camels! They are in awe of Karl Marx or Abraham Lincoln; and they are sick of hearing the name Umar bin Khatab[25] or Ali bin Abi Thalib.[26] It may well be that while the father still thinks within Islam, his offspring are already thinking in the American way!

The Islamic characteristics have disappeared from their hearts and disappeared from the palette of their lives.

* * * * *

Commentary   The following brief comments by Indonesian parents show how seriously they view the religious education of their children.

Extract 10-22: Teguh Hidayat

Excerpt from the transcript of an interview with Teguh Hidayat (then 34 years old, accountant), Jakarta, 20 January 2000. ['Living with Devotion' project.]

Because of my background where I didn't get much religious learning at home, I've tried to give my own children more religious education at home; I even got a religious teacher for them even though they recite the Qur'an with their parents. For me, there doesn't need to be any difference in education for boys and for girls.

Extract 10-23: Sri Tugiyem

Excerpt from the transcript of an interview with Sri Tugiyem (then 30 years old, pharmacist), Jakarta, 7 January 2000. ['Living with Devotion' project.]

Teenagers are starting to act up, because they have fewer basic principles. Religious education should be given from the age of three years so that they're strong, starting from kindergarten. Teach them about what Islam is, what Islam's morals are, [about] Islamic education, and tell them that God exists. If their religious education is strong, God willing, they won't go off the rails, in terms of morals and so on.

10.4.2   Charismatic Teachers and Self-education

Commentary   K.H. Abdullah Gymnastiar (1962–), known to his followers as Aa Gym, has become an iconic figure during the *reformasi* or post-New Order period (after 1998) in Indonesia. His dashing style and smooth rhetoric as a preacher have gained him immense popularity. Although he does not have a *pesantren* background, in 1987 he founded his own *pesantren* in Bandung, called Pesantren Daarut Tauhid. He teaches a

---

25   'Umar ibn al-Khattab was one of the Companions of the Prophet Muhammad and the second of the Rightly Guided Caliphs.

26   Cousin and son-in law of the Prophet Muhammad, 'Ali ibn Talib was the fourth and last of the Rightly Guided Caliphs and also became the first imam of the Shi'a Muslims. He was murdered in 661 CE.

modern form of Sufism, in the tradition of Hamka (see extracts 10-12 and 10-21), based on self-discipline, meditation and the practical application of Islamic teachings through a system known as 'Manajemen Qolbu' or MQ (Heart Management). His program has become famous throughout Indonesia and internationally.

As outlined above (see section 10.3), Islamic mysticism encourages believers to cleanse and purify their hearts and souls in preparation for closeness to God. Aa Gym has developed this as his 'trademark' training practice. He expresses it as: 'First the heart must be cleansed. Second the heart must be cleansed. And third, the heart must be cleansed so that an individual's full potential can work effectively and productively' (Hernowo and Ridwan 2002: 7). A unique feature of the mass meetings Aa Gym holds for his followers is the 'ritual weeping' that accompanies his prayers (Howell 2001: 719). The weeping expresses repentance for misdeeds and is also a feature of the meetings of another Indonesian 'celebrity' religious teacher, Arifin Ilham (see extract 10-15).

Aa Gym's MQ program has been developed through massive commercialization and marketed through television, newspapers, books, cassettes, CDs and short text messages for mobile phones, all syndicated throughout Indonesia. (An example is given in the colour section of this book; see plate 17.) He teaches positive attitudes and active engagement with the important issues of daily life. Like the Malaysian charismatic leader Nik Aziz (see extract 10-25), he is forthright in his condemnation of corruption among the higher echelons of society. The following extract is from one of his newspaper articles posted on his website <ManajemenQolbu.com> and written in the context of the devastation caused by the tsunami of 26 December 2004.

Extract 10-24: Aa Gym

Aa Gym, 'Membangun Semangat Baru' [Developing a New Spirit], <jkt.detik.com/kolom/aagym/mq/200502/20050218-230047.shtml>, dated 18 February 2005, accessed 4 April 2005.

Most Holy God, whose being embraces all things. Most Meticulous and Most Perfect so that He needs absolutely nothing from His servants. There is nothing of significance or worth we can give, because God is All Perfect sufficient unto Himself. My good brothers and sisters, we know that our country has been greatly afflicted by disaster but, God willing, a time will come when our country will rise and become respected. The conditions are as follows:

We must have spirit – if up to now our people have been severely bruised, it is not because of the poverty of nature but because of poverty of spirit – like what for instance? We are all slow to smile at others and begrudge forgiving others. So if my brothers and sisters agree let's try to make 2004 a year of harmony for all. No further discord – what's the point? It doesn't bring any benefits; indeed it's really sad to see a rich nation like this have internal wrangling. Therefore we need leaders who favour harmony, we need clever people who can bring harmony and we need people who want harmony. If God wills.

We must have self-confidence – in 2004 we must have people who believe in themselves. Look at sections of our brothers and sisters abroad who are ashamed to admit they are Muslims. Have confidence; if we have lost our self-confidence then who will respect us? Therefore, so our nation can be prosperous and progress, the secret is never to feel inferior and never to be ashamed to be Indonesian, because we are a great nation. Certainly we are now being tested with catastrophic conditions like the present ones, but if we can unite, God willing, this nation will rise again!

We must be obedient to God – always remember that we are a large nation with a rich environment. For others, harvesting trees takes 20 years, but in our land it only takes 10 years because the rays of the sun are bounteous [and] the rains flow copiously, sometimes even causing floods. But why are there so many calamities, landslides, narcotic drugs, corruption, all disasters heaped upon our country? Truly we belong to God and truly we return to Him.

My brothers and sisters, perhaps the cause of it is that until now we have been very arrogant and turned our backs on God who governs the heavens and the earth. We feel great, but who is great? It is not humans who are great; do not humans come from a drop of sperm and end up as corpses full of filth? Who is great in Indonesia? There is no-one who is great; what is great is if we can cause our society to be obedient to God who governs the heavens and the earth. So we can always improve ourselves and, God willing, God will provide what is best for His servants.

My brothers and sisters, the Messenger of God himself once said: '*The believers with the most perfect faith are those with the highest morals*' (H.R. Tirmidzi). Thus, noble morals undoubtedly provide the highest measure, so we can reflect on ourselves, whether we are fit to be His chosen beings. Let us reflect because, who knows, at this time we are on a path which can bring us within reach of the crown of glory or, the opposite, lead us into the abyss of humiliation. *And God knows the truth.*

* * * * *

Commentary   Malaysia also has charismatic teachers, one of the best known of whom is Dato' Haji Nik Abdul Aziz bin Nik Mat (1931–). He is spiritual leader (*murshid'ul am*) of Parti Islam Se Malaysia (PAS, The Islamic Party of Malaysia) and chief minister of the Malaysian state of Kelantan, but his role in the main opposition party in Malaysia has denied him a national audience.

In contrast to Aa Gym and Arifin Ilham, whose followers are largely from the Muslim middle class, Nik Aziz pays great attention to communicating with the 'ordinary', especially rural, constituents of his state. When he discusses leadership of the Muslim community and socio-political change, his political power in Kelantan gives him the means to effect many of the changes he suggests.

Nik Aziz was born in Kelantan to a family with both aristocratic origins and religious authority and was educated almost entirely within the Malay Islamic schooling system. In the 1950s he studied in India at the Deobandi College of Islam, which emphasized the responsibility of religious leaders to safeguard the purity of Islam. He studied *fiqh* at al-Azhar University in Cairo, where he was also exposed to the thinking of Hasan al-Banna, Sayyid Qutub and the Muslim Brotherhood (Ar.: *al-'ikhwaanul muslimuuna*). Returning to Malaysia, he joined PAS in 1967, believing religious leaders had the responsibility to care for the material as well as the spiritual needs of other Muslims (Farish 2003: 205–9). The extract presented below, taken from the Friday public lectures Nik Aziz delivers, is an example of his skill in expressing Qur'anic exegesis in a vernacular idiom that connects with the individual experiences of his audience. Like the speeches of Aa Gym, those of Nik Aziz call for a stronger commitment to applying

Islam to all aspects of daily life. Unlike Aa Gym's talks, however, those of Nik Aziz contain direct appeals for support for a particular political party.

Extract 10-25: Farish A. Noor on Nik Aziz

Farish A. Noor (2003), 'The Localization of Islamist Discourse in the *Tafsir* of Tuan Guru Nik Aziz Nik Mat, *Murshid'ul Am* of PAS' [in English], pp. 195–235 in Virginia Hooker and Norani Othman (eds), *Malaysia: Islam, Society and Politics*, Institute of Southeast Asian Studies, Singapore. [Translation of excerpt cited on p. 218.] Extract: p. 232: note 56.

While in our graves the angels Munkar [and] Nakir[27] will not ask us how much money we have brought with us, or how many weapons. They will ask: Who is your God? What is your religion? Who is your Prophet? In which direction do you pray? Answer with confidence. They will not ask: whose child are you? Are you a people's representative [politician]? Are you a King? Are you a *Tok Guru* [teacher]? On the field of Mashyar (on Judgement Day) it will be the same ... When you answer you have to answer as our Prophet has taught you, for there is nothing as strong as the argument of the Prophet. Then your soul will be as contented as that of Saidinna [our lord] Bilal, who, when convinced of the Prophet's teachings, was prepared to confront his boss, his leaders. Even though he was beaten he kept saying Ahad: God almighty. When exposed to the desert heat he kept saying Ahad. When they covered his chest with heavy rocks, he kept saying Ahad, Ahad, God almighty. If we were to use the political terminology of today, we can say PAS, PAS, PAS. Whether we want to say Ahad, Ahad, Ahad or PAS, PAS, PAS – the two are the same – because for us religion and politics must be made one.

* * * * *

Commentary   The mass audiences who follow charismatic teachers provide very public evidence of the thirst for greater religious knowledge and guidance on how to fulfil God's directions correctly. The public meetings (called 'religio-tainment' by some) are not to everyone's taste and there are many other ways to gain deeper knowledge of Islam. Radio and television programs are designed around question-and-answer sessions in which individuals can phone in a query to be answered by religious teachers of both sexes. Very popular in Indonesia are neighbourhood study groups that meet fortnightly and are led by local religious teachers. Mosques run youth programs and discussion groups, and in places with Muslim-minority populations (Burma, southern Thailand and the southern Philippines) these may provide the only source of religious education. Books, magazines, pamphlets and newspaper columns also provide guidance on the correct observance of Islam on a daily basis. The following extracts, from interviews with a range of Indonesian Muslims, indicate the rich variety of sources people use to increase their understanding of Islam.

---

27   The two angels who interrogate the dead in their graves about their belief in the Prophet Muhammad as the messenger of God. If they answer correctly they are left in peace until Judgement Day.

Extract 10-26: Bangun Sugito (Gito Rollies)

Excerpt from the transcript of an interview with Bangun Sugito (stage name: Gito Rollies) (then 53 years old, musician, singer), Jakarta, 17 January 2000. ['Living with Devotion' project.]

I get religious teaching from anyone; I've had so many teachers I can't name them all – even friends; all of it raised my awareness. I also often read books by Yusuf al-Qaradawi.[28] [I get it] from the TV sometimes, especially the early morning talks on Islam, but not the radio. I get religious knowledge from the benefits I get from doing good, and from outreach activities (*dakwah*); in the end I get results. So by putting knowledge into practice, even if it's only a little, God willing, God will give more. For me, all sources that can support religious knowledge and teaching are useful.

Extract 10-27: Trie Utami Sari binti Sujono Atmotenoyo

Excerpt from the transcript of an interview with Trie Utami Sari binti Sujono Atmotenoyo (then 32 years old, artist, singer, dancer, media announcer), Jakarta, 17 January 2000. ['Living with Devotion' project.]

I only learn from one teacher, the Prophet, and it's clearly noticeable. I have to be careful buying books. I buy lots of books about women's issues and the place of women in Islam. So I don't just randomly buy books written by people outside Islam; I don't want to read them [...] So I tend to read books about doing good deeds, the Bukhari–Muslim collection of Hadith and the Qur'an, which is what I mostly read. Now and then I also read *'Uquud al-Lujjayn*,[29] which sets out the relationship between husband and wife. I also read a lot of books on praying, and I find there are lots of things to be learnt there. I'm the kind of person who doesn't like watching television and I don't really like the radio either, because of an awareness that's increased over the last five years that I don't want to be enslaved by TV. I don't allow my eyes to see things I don't need to see. Praise be to God my husband will become a good leader (*amir*) [for me], in the sense that a good leader follows the Prophet, follows the regulations which are in the Qur'an.

Extract 10-28: Tumpal Daniel

Excerpt from the transcript of an interview with Tumpal Daniel (then 35 years old, printer), Jakarta, 28 January 2000. ['Living with Devotion' project.]

I also deepened my understanding of Islam by reading books, both the works of Indonesian Muslim figures and those from other countries. One [writer] who made an impression was Ali Shariati, a Muslim thinker from Iran. I also read the books and

---

28   An increasingly influential scholar, born in 1926 and now working from Qatar. He has a strong global media presence in the Muslim world and many of his books have been translated into Indonesian. See chapter 11 for further details.

29   The book *'Uquud al-Lujjayn* [The Joining of the Two Oceans] is described further in chapter 13.

works of the Indonesians Mohammad Natsir, Sili Gazalfa, Amien Rais, Nurcholish Madjid, Dawam Rahardjo and others.[30]

[...] [T]he obstacle I was most conscious of was language, because I was educated at a state high school; I never went to an Islamic school (*madrasah*). Not knowing Arabic was an impediment to understanding religious books, so I only read translations. Even so, the most basic work is the Qur'an and, God willing, I am able to read that.

10.4.3   Dress

> *Commentary*   There is currently a trend for Muslims to express Islamic identity through their style of dress. Both men and women should dress modestly and ensure that certain parts of the body are covered (see further chapter 13). The choice of dress available for both sexes and all ages is extremely diverse. A fashion industry based entirely on 'Muslim' garments has developed and provides lucrative returns for designers and retailers. An example from *Noor* magazine is shown in the colour section of this book; see plate 20. The following extracts have been chosen to show the reasons individuals give for their choice of dress.

Extract 10-29: Khairunisa

Excerpt from the transcript of an interview with Khairunisa (then 23 years old, tertiary student), Jakarta, 15 January 2000. ['Living with Devotion' project.]

A person must express their image or self-identity, for example, if they're a Muslim. The Qur'an specifies that a woman who identifies herself as a Muslim should wear a headscarf. So I think I really have to demonstrate my Islamic identity in the way that the Qur'an stipulates, that is, by wearing a headscarf. This also differentiates me from other people. When people see someone walking without a headscarf, they're unsure about their identity – whether they are Muslim or not – but if they see a woman wearing a headscarf they see straight away the Muslim identity of that person.

Extract 10-30: M. Fathiqul Islam

Excerpt from the transcript of an interview with M. Fathiqul Islam (then 41 years old, agricultural technologist), Jakarta, 5 January 2000. ['Living with Devotion' project.]

We should imitate how the Prophet dressed. For example, I wear a turban. Why? Because the Prophet wore a turban; look at the Wali Songo,[31] Diponegoro [and] Imam Bonjol,[32] because that's what people wore in the past. They didn't just wear it;

---

30   For more details on some of these Indonesian Muslim thinkers, see chapter 5.
31   The nine legendary 'saints' credited with spreading Islam in Java.
32   Nineteenth-century anti-colonial leaders.

they were imitating something. The teachers, they're the ones I emulate. Those who have passed away were imitating those before them, and so on from the Prophet. That's the symbol of Islam. Grow your beard; keep your beard neat. Moreover symbols for us are identity; symbolic identity is also a matter of moral character.

Extract 10-31: Endah Dwi Lestari

Excerpt from the transcript of an interview with Endah Dwi Lestari (then 27 years old and working in the computer business), Jakarta, 9 December 1999. ['Living with Devotion' project.]

This headscarf that I wear, for example, is not a symbol but an obligation for a Muslim woman to cover those parts of the body that Islam requires [to be covered], but the headscarf is also not a guarantee that a person is a good Muslim, because what is most important is to pay attention to your attitude and everyday interactions.

10.4.4 Health and Healing

Commentary   The foundations of modern Western medicine were built on the medical treatises of great Muslim scholars such as Ibn Sina of Avicenna (980–1037 CE), whose work *al-Qaanuun fit Tib* [The Canon of Medicine] shows his mastery of both Greek and Islamic sources. From such classical works has grown a respected tradition of medicine (Ar.: *tibbun*) practised by Muslim scholars who have specialized in that area and who incorporate the recitation of Qur'anic verses and meditation into their healing methods. Alongside the development of *tibbun* was a tradition of occult sciences (Ar.: *hikmah*) that drew on pre-Islamic elements and used pre-Islamic symbols such as magical squares, a tradition to which even the respected twelfth-century scholar al-Ghazali contributed (van Bruinessen 1990: 262).

Muslims in Southeast Asia can draw on the traditions of both *tibbun* and *hikmah* as well as local indigenous healing practices, often based on animism. In rural areas of the southern Philippines, for example, it is reported that the causes of illness are sometimes ascribed to bad spirits or wrongdoing by oneself or one's ancestors. Cures may be effected by religious teachers using indigenous practices and Qur'an-based prayers, while protection may be obtained through *kaja* rituals, that is, rituals that include the recitation of Qur'anic verses and prayers at the graves of one's ancestors (Jamasali 2005). The link between piety and illness is reflected in the belief that impious behaviour can cause illness and, consequently, that Islam-based knowledge and rituals can bring calm and thus restore health and well-being. This is particularly clear in the following extract taken from an explanation by a Muslim doctor in Indonesia.

Extract 10-32: Muhammad Hembing Wijayakusuma

Muhammad Hembing Wijayakusuma (2003), 'Akupunktur, Mengungkap Hikmah' [Acupuncture, Revealing Divine Wisdom], pp. 77–84 in *Pengalaman Religius Tokoh dan Selebritis* [Religious Experiences of Leading Figures and Celebrities], Book II, Yayasan Indonesia Maju, Jakarta. Extract: pp. 83–4.

I also instil in my patients [the thought] that God has caused a particular disease for a reason, and the lesson can only be grasped by those of God's servants who think. With this understanding, patients can be more informed in applying the treatment, because healing requires a process; it doesn't just happen. If we are wholehearted, God will certainly hear His servants, God the All Healing. In principle, we continue to spread the message of the truth which we believe in, as it is stated [in the Qur'an]: *spread [the word], if only one verse.*

The calm a patient gets through Islam in some cases leads to spiritual peace. He or she becomes optimistic, enjoys food and can sleep properly. This greatly assists the healing process and, if God wills, health will be restored.

Prayer can also be part of the method of healing. I see many people praying because of feelings of wrongdoing, sin, or [because] they feel they have left God. If the prayers are done earnestly, with belief in the justice of God, if God wills, their inner being will be filled with calm. Such feelings become a fresh breeze that can bring more hope for restored health.

Focused prayers and *zikir* [Ar.: *dhikrun*] directed to God will condition the mind to achieve calm and stability. I base this belief on Ar-Ra'ad: 28, which says: '*Know that by remembering God your hearts will be at peace*'.[33] From here, a positive influence flows through to the body's organs, gradually making them normal, including the nerves. Nerves can become calm because of better blood circulation. A calm and stable spirit leads to a state of relaxation. This means the mind of the patient is healthy, including the brain because the cerebral cortex functions more efficiently.

* * * * *

> *Commentary*   The following extract describes attitudes of villagers in West Java in the 1960s and shows clearly their respect for both Islamic and non-Islamic healing practices. Saiful Muzani[34] (1962–) had four years of Western-based medical training before studying at the State Islamic Institute – now State Islamic University (UIN) – in Jakarta and at Ohio State University where he wrote a doctoral dissertation on 'Islam, Democracy and Civil Culture'. He is currently with Lembaga Survei Indonesia (LSI, Indonesian Survey Institute) and the Freedom Institute as well as PPIM.

Extract 10-33: Saiful Muzani

Saiful Muzani (1990), 'Transformasi Ilmu dan Masyarakat: Obsesi Seorang Anak Desa' [The Transformation of Knowledge and Society: A Village Child's Obsession], pp. 157–87 in Ihsan Ali-Fauzi and Haidar Bagir (eds), *Mencari Islam: Kumpulan Otobiografi Intelektual Kaum Muda Muslim Indonesia Angkatan 80-an* [Seeking Islam: Intellectual Autobiographies of Young Indonesian Muslims of the Generation of the 80s], Penerbit Mizan, Bandung. Extract: pp. 158–9.

---

33   Q13: 28 is given in footnote 16.
34   In the book from which the extract comes his name is spelt Muzani, but in more recent publications he has used another spelling of his name, Mujani.

To solve practical problems, people in my village used supernatural 'knowledge'. But what they meant by this kind of 'knowledge' was prayers or incantations, and many of them were from verses in the Qur'an. If a villager was sick, he or she would be brought to a *kiai* [religious teacher] for incantations to cure the illness. If they wanted to start planting out the rice seedlings in the fields, they usually asked for guidance from a *kiai* about exactly when and where to plant; and when the rice was yellowing and ready to be harvested, it was usual to prepare an offering for the rice goddess *Dewi Sri* who was believed to protect agriculture. To do that they burned incense and sacrificed a chicken. To protect themselves from enemy attack, to give themselves magic powers, they would use supernatural knowledge obtained from *kiai*, leaders of certain Sufi orders and also often from traditional healers (*dukun*). The difference between a traditional healer and a *kiai* was that the traditional healer was skilled at solving practical problems through magic without being well versed in Islam, whereas the *kiai*, besides having that kind of knowledge, was also well versed in religion, able to read Islamic texts (*kitab kuning*) and had the authority to explain issues connected with Islam. Sometimes traditional healers and *kiai* were differentiated on the basis of the source of their knowledge (supernatural power). The *kiai*'s [knowledge] was based on Islam, particularly on the Qur'an and the deeds and sayings of the Prophet Muhammad as well as prayers passed down by sheikhs like Sheikh Abdul Qadir Jailani.[35] On the other hand, the traditional healers based their knowledge on animism and, according to the *kiai*, got their knowledge from the devil. This then was the relationship between knowledge and the practical needs of the villagers when I was a child.

* * * * *

Commentary The choice of treatment for an illness may be based on practical considerations of affordability (traditional practitioners being less expensive than Western-trained doctors) as well as the specialization of the practitioner. Some Muslims choose a mixture of treatments. Attitudes to issues such as birth control, organ transplants and blood transfusions are discussed in more detail in Hooker (2003). The choice of healing practice is not based purely on factors like rural or urban background or on whether or not an individual is well educated. Urban, tertiary-educated Muslims may choose to use 'Islamic' treatments in their search for better health and also accept supernatural practices which in other contexts they would find unacceptable.

Dato' Dr Haron Din (1940–), head of the Information Section of PAS, built his reputation as a religious scholar on his success as a practitioner of Islam-based treatments for illnesses. He has a PhD from Cairo University and in 1991 founded a highly successful practice based on Islamic healing called Darus Syifa', near the Malaysian National University, south of Kuala Lumpur. His patients include Malaysian Muslims from all walks of life. The following extract is from a work written jointly with Dr Amran Kasimin (1945–), lecturer in Malay studies, National University of Malaysia, who has a PhD from the Department of Religious Studies, University of Aberdeen. The extract refers in general terms to the power of prayer, and the book itself lists specific prayers for the treatment of particular illnesses. Muslims interested in this kind of therapy can also purchase cassette tapes and booklets of the appropriate prayers.

---

35 Abdul Qadir Jailani (1077–1168 CE) was the Iranian founder of the popular Qadiriyah Sufi order.

Extract 10-34: Amran Kasimin and Haron Din

Amran Kasimin and Haron Din (1997), 'Penutup' [Conclusion], pp. 218–21 in *Doa & Rawatan Penyakit* [Prayers & the Treatment of Diseases], Percetakan Watan Sdn. Bhd., Kuala Lumpur. Extract: pp. 219–20.

It is the nature of human beings to find it difficult to remember God, the more so if they are well off and have no problems. They are more inclined to think of God when afflicted by accidents, if they are poor, sick or facing death. [...] There is a clear link between prayer and those in despair, without hope and without support. It is only then that human beings realize and wake up to the need for prayer, and call upon God. How can prayers like that cure illness or overcome problems if those offering the prayers are despairing and without hope?

Almighty God made human beings and supernatural beings (*jin*) to worship Him. That was the purpose of their creation. Prayer is the brain of worship. For humans the brain controls everything. The brain (reason) is the factor which differentiates humans from animals. Without prayer and worship an individual is no different from someone who lives without a brain.

Almighty God commands each servant to pray always, even if it is in an effort to obtain something simple such as salt. God promises to grant someone's prayer, sooner or later, in this world or the next, depending on His will and decree, on certain mysteries not understood by humans and also on the quality of the person who is praying. The closer a servant is to God, the more easily the prayer will be answered.

It is not the sequence of prayers, the ceremonies carried out or the particular conditions which must be fulfilled that are factors in the cure. The primary factor is the power or approval of God to allow the illness to be cured, and the related issue of the quality of the person offering the prayer. For the prayer to be granted, the person must have those qualities praised by God, and not be a person who is immoral, who ignores God's laws, who is hypocritical or who creates dissension among their fellows. [...]

Prayers are not mantras or spells (*jampi*) or even incantations, although they are often confused by many people. In certain situations society expects people who perform healing to use prayers to diagnose the cause of the illness. To diagnose illness, modern equipment in hospitals and the skills of doctors trained in particular fields are the most appropriate. They are the professionals with authority [...] Their expertise should be used, not ignored.

10.5   ISLAMIC CULTURE AND CIVILIZATION

Commentary   The history of Islamic civilization is taught widely in Islamic educational institutions. As well as providing inspiration for contemporary Muslims, the achievements of Muslim intellectuals and scientists and their contribution to world civilization are being used as the basis for a 'civilizational dialogue' between Islam and the West. Although expressed in universal terms, the descriptions of Islamic culture and civilization in the 'dialogue' emphasize the personal pride individual Muslims take in the glorious past that was Islam. In the following extract it is clear that contemporary Muslims are drawing on the past to forge new roles for Islam in the current age.

Osman Bakar is one of Malaysia's foremost intellectuals and holds the Chair of Philosophy of Science at the University of Malaya. He has degrees in mathematics from London University and a doctorate in Islamic philosophy from Temple University in the United States.

Extract 10-35: Osman Bakar

Osman Bakar (1997), 'Islam's Destiny: A Civilizational Bridge between East and West' [in English], pp. 7–14 in Osman Bakar (ed.), *Islam and Civilizational Dialogue: The Quest for a Truly Universal Civilization,* University of Malaya Press, Kuala Lumpur. Extract: pp. 8, 9, 12–13.

> Thus have We made you a middle nation that you might be witnesses over the whole human family or the world community (2: 143).[36]

[…] The notion of the 'middle nation' is a key concept in the understanding of the civilizational nature and identity of Islam. In Islam, civilization-consciousness is deeply rooted in such Qur'anic ideas as a common human ancestry, a common humanity, universal goodness of man, universality of divine favours to the human race, the wisdom of ethnic and cultural pluralism, inter-cultural cooperation in the pursuit of the common good for all mankind, global social justice, a common responsibility for the protection of our planet Earth, and above all it is rooted in the idea of 'middleness' as conveyed by the above cited verse. [p. 8] […]

The contribution of Islam to universalism and the development of a common human civilization that is truly universal is not going to be limited to the realm of the past. Islam is a living civilization that is capable of displaying an even greater dynamism in the future than it has ever shown in the past. As such, it will continue to believe in and argue for, not only the possibility of a universal civilization but also its desirability. [p. 9] […]

Various expressions of extremism in many parts of the contemporary Muslim world are clearly not in accord with the true civilizational identity of Islam. But we believe these phenomena are mere episodes in Muslim history that are peripheral to Islamic life and civilization. Understandably, they have occurred mainly as hasty and uninformed responses to the evils and injustices of the contemporary world and out of sheer ignorance and frustration. Still, they are not to be condoned for Islam clearly teaches that ends do not justify means!

We may illustrate the idea of middleness as applied to human culture and civilization with the following examples. In politics, Islam strikes a middle position between the kind of theocracy that is so much hated and feared in the West and secular modern democracy founded on excessive individualism that also originated

---

36 'We have made you [believers] into a just community, so that you may bear witness [to the truth] before others and so that the Messenger may bear witness [to it] before you. We [previously] made the direction the one you used to face [Prophet] in order [now] to distinguish those who follow the Messenger from those who turn on their heels: that test was hard, except for those God has guided. God would never let your faith go to waste [believers], for God is most compassionate and most merciful towards people' (Q2: 143, Haleem).

in the West. Islamic 'democracy' seeks to harmonize the rights of God with the rights and duties of man. In economics, Islam strikes a balance between the secular capitalism of what used to be the 'Free West' and the atheistic socialism of the Communist Bloc. In theology, Islam seeks to synthesize the idea of a transcendent God and that of an immanent God. In the domain of social institutions, Islam's position on marriage, for example, is somewhere between the position adopted by some religions of not allowing divorce altogether and the contemporary position adopted by many in the West that no longer believes in marriage as a sacred institution. In philosophy, Islam has struck a balance between extreme forms of rationalism and empiricism, the kinds of which have featured prominently at various points of time in Western intellectual history. We can go on enumerating these 'middle positions' of Islam in many other areas of human life and thought.

It is in the light of this idea of middleness in cultural and civilizational terms that Islam has conversed and developed relations with other civilizations, learnt and incorporated ideas from them, synthesized and developed them, disseminated them in new and more developed forms to other civilizations, including those from which it has originally borrowed. [pp. 12–13]

* * * * *

> ***Commentary***   The following extract is from a reflection on the relationship between artistic expression, pluralism, local culture and Islam. The author, Omar Fathurrahman, also describes some of the varieties of Islamic art forms. The writer is a researcher at PPIM at the State Islamic University (UIN), Jakarta. His articles were featured in a pamphlet distributed during Friday services at over 300 mosques in and around Jakarta between 2001 and 2004. The pamphlet, *Buletin al-Tasamuh* [Bulletin of Tolerance], was published in Jakarta by Lingkar Studi-Aksi untuk Demokrasi Indonesia (LS-ADI, Study-Action Circle for Indonesian Democracy), which is part of Program Pendidikan Agama dan Demokrasi (Program for Education in Religion and Democracy). Because it is obligatory for Muslims to attend the Friday noon prayers held as congregational meetings, there is a potential audience of tens of thousands for such pamphlets.

Extract 10-36: Oman Fathurrahman

Oman Fathurrahman (2002), '"Menjadi Islam" melalui Seni' ['Becoming Islamic' through Art], *Buletin al-Tasamuh*, 23(27 September): 1–6. Extract: pp. 2–4.

They say *Indang*[37] is one of the local forms of art in the Pariaman region,[38] with verse forms taken from key teachings of the Shattariyyah order.[39] The performers

---

37   A traditional Minangkabau (West Sumatra) performance of sung verses and dancing accompanied by tambourines.

38   A town and district in the province of West Sumatra.

39   A Sufi order founded in the late fourteenth century CE in Gujerat (western India) and developed in Medina by the great Sufi scholars Ahmad al-Qushashi and Ibrahim Kurani. Among their pupils was Abdu'r-Ra'uf of Singkel (north Sumatra), who took the practices of the order back to north Sumatra (Aceh) in the mid-seventeenth century. It is thus one of the oldest Sufi orders in Southeast Asia (see

refer to themselves as the 'Satari' but probably some of them, especially the children, know nothing about the Shattariyyah, an order which provides knowledge about the transcendental qualities of God in its teachings and *dzikir* [Ar.: *dhikrun*].

According to several performers, the art of *Indang* is one form of modification of the teachings of mysticism that constitute the 'highest level' of Islamic teachings. These were later received, adopted and expressed 'in more simple terms' through art forms. Or we can reverse the logic: *Indang* is a local traditional art form that adopted elements of mysticism into its verse forms. Thus, whatever small degree of spirituality is in it, it is clear that the art of *Indang* constitutes one of the mediums, at the very least for those who perform it, through which they express their closeness to the Creator.

In this article I do not want to discuss in depth the art form of *Indang*, or the various other local art forms that are heavy with the qualities of God's greatness, and indeed there are many of them in our nation; *Indang* is just an illustration and an example. What I do want to say, through this example, is how diverse the artistic expression of an individual or a community is and how they [the individual and the community] want to say that the form of that expression is a form of 'Islamic art'.

Perhaps some Muslims think Islamic art is limited to particular forms and languages, such as the recitation of prayers and beautiful [Qur'anic] verses in the form of songs; the art of mosque architecture, which is filled with the qualities of light; and Arabic calligraphy and geometric lines in the form of decorations for walls, pottery, silver and bronze, many of which incorporate verses from the Qur'an or Hadith, or other Arabic phrases. However, in fact, Islamic art is not limited to particular forms, but rather to themes, values and norms based on the qualities of the godhead. Thus, what is called Islamic art may take very varied forms of expression. It may be expressed through words, as in novels, short stories, poetry, verse forms and so on. Or it can also be expressed through physical movement such as dance, as performed in the West Sumatran *Indang* mentioned above, or through other art forms, for example, *wayang*.[40] Moreover, in the context of Indonesian Islam, with its very diverse 'variants', artistic expression will also be very diverse, although, according to a recent survey by the Centre for the Study of Islam and Society at the Islamic University of Jakarta, in October 2001, the differences are no longer as striking. In Java, for example, we find that the symbols of *abangan* Islam[41] and orthodox *santri* Islam[42] blend several arts and cultures. In keeping with their differences in understanding, appreciation and knowledge of Islamic teachings, the symbols of each will certainly express its art in differing forms.

So is there some latitude in what is called Islamic art? Yes and no. Yes from the point of view of form, and no if we consider themes, values and norms, because

---

Azra 2004). It was taken to West Sumatra in the late seventeenth century by Burhan al-Din, one of Abdu'r-Ra'uf's pupils. For its later history, see Fathurahman (2003).

40   *Wayang* is the Indonesian shadow puppet performance.
41   Nominal Muslims.
42   Pious Muslims who adhere strictly to the ritual and legal requirements of Islam.

Islam has outlined the vision and humanitarian tasks that each Muslim must bear, whatever his or her lot. In the Qur'an, Ali Imran 3: 110,[43] for example, God calls on humans to do good and avoid evil (*amar ma'ruf nahi munkar*). With reference to His call, whatever the activities of individual Muslims, or groups of Muslims, including in the arts, he or she is not absolved from three main themes: 'to do good (humanization)'; 'to prevent evil (liberation)'; and 'to believe in God (transcendence)'. Now, as far as an art form is able to represent these three themes and values – humanizing and liberating human beings and bringing them to God – then it is appropriate to talk about Islamic art whatever its form. On the other hand, however hard someone tries to form a category called 'Islamic art', it will not be legitimate unless it expresses the three themes mentioned above. To quote Kuntowijoyo,[44] [the essence of] Islam is the relationship with God and the relationship with human beings (*hablun min allah dan hablun min al-nas*), and because of that, Islamic art must reflect humanization plus transcendence, liberation plus transcendence.

Finally, even in matters of art, it is time we studied [ways to] benefit from and understand the plurality of artistic expression as something that is positive, not something that is negative. It would seem wise to exploit the diversity of symbolic expression to enrich Islamic art, so that it is not the property of one group alone, and may even become ethnic art, national art, syncretic art, traditional art or modern art, uniting with society and not exclusive, with the result that even more people may 'become Islamic' through art. *And God alone knows the truth.*

* * * * *

Commentary   Islam forbids any representation of the sacred because this implies 'that the value of revelation is not an absolute but can be mediated through some other form' (Hooker 2003: 82). There is also concern that representations might be used for worship, and idolatry is strictly forbidden in Islam. If the purpose of the representations is instruction and education, as in medical drawings or for children's play (for example, dolls), the representations are generally permissible (Hooker 2003: 84). Views on the permissibility of music and dance are divided, based on the issue of whether the music and dance enhance feelings of morality and sobriety or, on the contrary, encourage immorality and distract believers from worshipful thought.

In Southeast Asia there has generally been more flexibility towards the acceptability of artistic expression in connection with religion. From the early period of Islam in the region, literature and court arts were used to teach about Islam as well as to entertain (for inspiring examples, see Kumar and McGlynn 1996). In the contemporary context, didacticism and entertainment continue to be linked and 'moral benefit' is used as a criterion for permissibility. Thus, pop groups who sing religious songs are accepted by many Muslims, whereas similar groups performing non-religious music may be branded as decadent, morally harmful and 'Western', not Islamic.

---

43   '[Believers], you are the best community singled out for people: you order what is right, forbid what is wrong, and you believe in God. If the People of the Book had also believed, it would have been better for them. For although some of them do believe, most of them are lawbreakers' (Q3: 110, Haleem).
44   The late Professor Kuntowijoyo (1943–2005) was one of Indonesia's leading social historians.

The following extract describes how, as a Muslim activist in Bandung, West Java, in the mid-1980s, Yudi Latif found himself deeply attracted to the atmosphere he found at Padjadjaran University among members of the Gelanggang Seni Sastra, Teater dan Film (GSSTF, Literature, Theatre and Film Forum). In his view, Islamic arts are central to any discussion about how the future of the Islamic world is to be configured.

Extract 10-37: Yudi Latif

Yudi Latif (1990), 'Dari Islam Sejarah, Memburu Islam Ideal (Mi'raj Tangisan Seorang Kurban Sejarah)' [From Historical Islam, Chasing Ideal Islam (The Tearful Journey of a Victim of History)], pp. 221–40 in Ihsan Ali-Fauzi and Haidar Bagir (eds), *Mencari Islam: Kumpulan Otobiografi Intelektual Kaum Muda Muslim Indonesia Angkatan 80-an* [Seeking Islam: Intellectual Autobiographies of Young Indonesian Muslims of the Generation of the 80s], Penerbit Mizan, Bandung. Extract: p. 233.

[...] The circumstances of my involvement in the GSSTF were certainly not just to find a cathartic outlet (release from tension) but were motivated by a deep awareness that development of the arts is an absolute condition when discussing issues concerning the construction of the future of Islamic civilization or when dreaming about the possibilities for rebuilding the Islamic world. This is not only because art is a manifestation of the human creative spirit that is mystical and inherently religious, and that throughout the history of human civilization has always been closely linked with religion. More than that, as a result of the dynamics of capitalist industrial society, art has been totally reduced to just a language of sexual passion, misguided pleasure and escapist entertainment that has been massively effective in spreading consumerism, hedonism and secularism. Each 'witness' [believer] has a moral responsibility to nurture alternatives to this, that is, art that is more constructive and more Islamic. Ironically, while the tentacles of negative art forms threaten religious values, activists and proponents of Islam themselves still view the world of art warily or do not consider its importance in supporting the renewal of the Islamic world. Because of that I felt called. [...]

* * * * *

Commentary   The call to prayer and the recitation of the Qur'an, two essential expressions of Islam, could be classified as 'music'. Both are, of course, permitted activities because in both instances they remind Muslims of their religious duties and obligations. But are all kinds of music permitted? The recording of Qur'anic recitation on cassette and CD, for example, is controversial and varying opinions exist about the permissibility of listening to such recordings. On the question of using Qur'anic quotations in popular songs, however, there are injunctions in the Qur'an that can be cited to indicate this is not permissible: '... recite the Qur'an in measured tones' (Q73: 4)[45] (see Hooker 2003: 86). Nevertheless, over the past two decades countless groups – male, female and mixed – have performed religious songs, the majority incorporating verses from

---

45   'or a little more; recite the Qur'an slowly and distinctly' (Q73: 4, Haleem).

the Qur'an. In Malaysia and Indonesia, particularly since the late 1990s, the style of music called *nasyid* has attracted fervent audiences of young Muslims. In Malaysia it was pioneered by the male group Raihan, singing in *a capella* style, the lyrics including Arabic phrases and Islamic sentiments (see Kahn 2003: 153, and plate 11 in the colour section of this book). The following extract presents Aa Gym's lyrics for a *nasyid* song entitled 'Istighfar' [Asking for Forgiveness] performed by the group known as BPM (Be Proud as Muslim). The song begins with repetition of the refrain *Astaghfirullah Rabbalbarooya*, accompanied by very strong syncopated rhythms played on drums and percussion. A solo male voice sings the first verse in Arabic. The rest of the song is in Indonesian, with the male voice backed by soft female singing.

Extract 10-38: Aa Gym

Aa Gym (2004), 'Istighfar' [Asking for Forgiveness], in Muhammad Arifin Ilham, *Tausiyah Dzikir & Nasyid* [Advice through *Dzikir & Nasyid* Songs], audiocassette cover notes, Nadahijrah Forte Entertainment, Jakarta.

[Verse 1, sung in Arabic]

Arabic	*English*
Astaghfirullah Rabbalbarooya	I ask Allah, the People's Lord, for forgiveness
Astaghfirullah minal khotooya	I ask Allah for forgiveness from grievous sins
Rabbi zidni 'ilman nafian	O Lord, increase my knowledge
Wawafiqli amalan maqbulan	And guide me towards acceptable deeds
Wawahabli rizqan wasian	And grant me bounteous wealth
Watub 'alaiyya taubatannasuha	And grant me true forgiveness
Watub 'alaiyya taubtaannasuha	And grant me true forgiveness

[Verses 2–4, sung in Indonesian]

Verse 2	*Verse 3*	*Verse 4*
God's love is all-captivating	God grants us pardon and	Allah my God, whom
Even though we betray Him	accepts our repentance	my heart adores
His grace knows no end	Even though our sins fill the	How I long to meet You
Always waiting for us to	universe	Oh Allah my God,
return to Him	Oh, my brother, repent at	whom my heart adores
Always waiting for us to ask	once	Allow me to meet You
His forgiveness	For your time draws near	Allow me to meet You
	For your time draws near	

* * * * *

Commentary   The increasing popularity of Islam-inspired forms of music has generated anxiety among very conservative Muslims about the permissibility of listening to such performances. Fatwa on the lawfulness of music usually focus on the types of instruments permitted and whether or not unlawful mixing of the sexes is being encouraged. These fatwa often refer to the account of the scholar Zakariya al-Ansari (d. 1520 CE), who describes how the Prophet Muhammad allowed his wife 'A'ishah to watch a performance of music and dance (Riza 2004: 75). This provides the basis for tolerance of music, but in classical Islam there were strict prescriptions about the types of instruments permitted and the effect of the music. Instruments that convey rhythm were allowed, but those that add emotion were not. Thus, small drums and tambourines were permitted but wind and stringed instruments were not, as they were associated with licentious behaviour. In the modern context, a minority of Muslims adhere to the classical prescriptions on music but the majority take a broader view, as described in the next extract.

Extract 10-39: *Tya Sulestyawati Subyakto*

Tya Sulestyawati Subyakto (2002), 'Salawat dan Harmoni Kehidupan' [Prayer and Harmony in Life], pp. 71–6 in *Pengalaman Religius Tokoh dan Selebritis* [Religious Experiences of Leading Figures and Celebrities], Book I, Yayasan Indonesia Maju, Jakarta. Extract: p. 75.

Sharia and its essential truth

As I understand it, our religious life must surely embrace sharia and its essential truth. I have to work hard to put into effect all the rules of religious conduct, such as prayers, fasting, paying *zakat*, doing good deeds, being obedient to both my parents and so on. But in addition, and no less importantly, I must understand the essential truth of all the religious rules I put into practice. At the level of sharia, the reason we pray is to obtain spiritual reward, isn't it? But sometimes we pray but can't feel that spiritual reward. What is spiritual reward anyway? Well, if we have been able to understand just a little, or have even been able to feel the pleasure of the rewards of prayer, then even if we do not pray we can actually feel it just by remembering it.

It is said music is forbidden to Muslims. But I say no, it is not, as long as we know how to use it. If it is used for the purpose of generating noise, encouraging sacrilege, then certainly, it is forbidden to Muslims. But if it is used to glorify Islam, unite the nation, make us feel close to God and His messenger, and encourages us to carry out our religious duties, then surely it brings spiritual reward.

There are still those who believe that Islamic music is merely the sort of thing that uses tambourines or Arabian stringed instruments. That is certainly not the extent of it. What we have to look at are the lyrics. Arabian ethnic music certainly has its own distinctive harmonic minor and scale. It is undoubtedly suited to use in religious songs. But its value is only in creating Arabian ethnic nuances or connotations that are certainly for the most part Islamic. Only the thing is that even without Arabian nuances a song may still be regarded as religious if the spirit of the song is truly worthy.

* * * * *

Commentary Muslims in Indonesia and Malaysia have hotly debated the issue of the power of performance and the possibility that audiences may be so inflamed by some forms of art that they will be stimulated to commit immoral acts. The focus of the discussions has been the sensuous and erotic dancing style of a young East Javanese woman known as Inul Daratista (real name, Ainur Rokhimah). Her 'drilling' hip and bottom movements have drawn condemnation from some Muslim scholars, support from others, and concern about freedom of expression issues from other social groups.

In Malaysia, Dewan Pemuda PAS Pusat (Central Council for PAS Youth) roundly criticized the Ministry for Heritage, Arts and Culture for allowing Inul to perform in Malaysia, on the grounds that she would stimulate immoral acts by young and old.[46]

An editorial in the daily *Jakarta Post* of 6 May 2003 recorded that an opinion poll by *Tempo* magazine:

> found that by far the majority of Indonesians defend Inul's right to gyrate onstage, even though almost 60 percent of respondents considered the movements 'erotic'. More than 78 per cent of respondents were against banning Inul from performing in public [...]'[47]

A painting of Inul entitled 'Berdzikir bersama Inul' [Reciting *Dzikir* with Inul] by the popular and revered Javanese religious scholar K.H. A. Mustofa Bisri is shown in the colour section of this book (see plate 9). In the painting, Inul dances inside a circle formed by seated ulema who seem captivated by her performance. Despite his impeccable credentials as a religious scholar, Mustofa Bisri received intense criticism for his apparent appreciation of Inul's skills, including a threat to set fire to the mosque in Surabaya in which the painting was being exhibited in March 2003.

The publicity surrounding the Inul phenomenon has prompted more serious evaluations of what the issues actually are. The following two extracts present the views of a 'liberal' Muslim thinker and an opponent of 'liberal' interpretations of Islam.

Ulil Abshar-Abdalla is a prominent member of the Indonesian organization Jaringan Islam Liberal (JIL, Liberal Islam Network). In the following extract, he argues that social stability should not rest on religious values alone but must also include other values, such as freedom of expression. In his view, the reaction against Inul demonstrates that religious norms dominate the public sphere to the exclusion of other norms. He urges greater public debate about the issue of what he terms 'overmoralization' by some religious leaders.

Extract 10-40: Ulil Abshar-Abdalla

Ulil Abshar-Abdalla (2003), '"Over-Moralisasi" dalam Soal Inul: Tentang Tempat Agama dalam Ruang Publik' ['Overmoralization' in the Inul Case: The Place of Religion in the Public Sphere], pp. 134–49 in FX Rudy Gunawan (ed.), *Mengebor Kemunafikan: Inul, Seks, dan Kekuasaan* [Drilling Hypocrisy: Inul, Sex and Power], Kawan Pustaka, Depok, and Galang Press, Yogyakarta. Extract: pp. 143–7.

There is a danger if religion is overly imposed as a norm regulating all aspects of life. 'Overmoralization' of social life through the revalidation of religious norms within society can produce somewhat unhealthy effects. The fading of Pancasila as a 'public norm' has certainly facilitated the return of religion to centre stage as a source of norms that very decisively shape society's views. Thus, symptoms of 'overmoralization' are merely a consequence of the absence of universal and generalized public norms. The case of Inul is just one example. Other symptoms are the proliferation of symbols and the articulation of religion in almost every sphere of life. An overly obsessive consciousness about what food/drink is permissible/not

---

46   See <http://harakahdaily.net/article.php?sid=1248>, accessed 4 April 2005.
47   See <http://www.thejakartapost.com/detailededitorial.asp?fileid+20030506.E01&irec=0>, accessed 6 May 2003.

permissible (*halal/haram*) for Muslims has developed very strongly within society. The issue of pornography has also begun to be widely discussed and we have to admit that religious views have been very prominent. The expression of religious piety through dress has also flourished in society. It is even the case that certain characteristically 'religious' expressions have begun to be bandied about. A number of Muslims no longer like to refer to God by the Malay word *Tuhan*, replacing it with the [Arabic] word *Rabb*. Fasting is no longer so called, being referred to instead as [the Arabic] *shaum*. Prayer is no longer called praying, but rather the Arabic *shalat*. The revalidation of Islamic law in various regions has been translated in a verbal and vulgar fashion with the installation of signs in Arabic script and language. All these signal widespread symptoms which may be called symptoms of 'the remoralization of public space'.

What's wrong with all this?

Certainly there are positive as well as negative aspects to these symptoms. What is positive is that society in ways such as this has succeeded, for some, in overcoming a kind of 'social alienation' or sense of isolation born of the processes of socio-political modernization, which have destroyed old bonds and identities. However, the negative aspects are also numerous: the flaunting of communal identities in this way can produce dangerous social polarization. In sociology, society is usually described as a 'social fabric', as a social interweaving made up of a number of given norms, institutions and patterns of relationship. Surely a society becomes a 'fabric' because there is something that can bind the different elements within it into something 'cohesive' and integrated. Social integration can occur only if there are common norms. If these norms disappear, a society will experience disorder and polarization. The flaunting of particularistic identities must always be weighed up against other considerations such as the importance of re-establishing general norms of a public and universal nature for all members of society.

Another aspect which cannot be ignored is that modern life is increasingly tending towards 'differentiation' between, and the autonomy of, different spheres of life. Religion no longer constitutes a 'super system' that it is hoped will regulate or explain everything. The art world, for example, is becoming more and more autonomous and separate from other fields. Artistic norms develop according to their own logic and cannot simply be made subordinate to norms external to the art field. And so it is with other fields. In a spirit of social development such as this, religion ultimately also occupies a 'small field' of an autonomous nature within society. There are those who would oppose this development by trying once again to turn religion into a 'total' system that seeks to subordinate other spheres of life. This would clearly be difficult to do, and even if it could be done it would create more than a few casualties. I was not surprised by the statement of my friend Dr Moeslim Abdurrahman[48] that if Islamic law were implemented just like that, the victims would be

---

48 A former journalist and author of the influential book *Islam Transformatif* [Transforming Islam] (Moeslim 1997), Moeslim Abdurrahman has been active in Muslim intellectual circles, including supporting the new generation of young Muhammadiyah intellectuals.

women and ordinary people. If Islamic norms on 'modesty' were applied literally, it is not inconceivable that they would produce many victims. Finally, religion and those who are religious must be conscious of the fact that in the development of modern life, religion has become an autonomous and separate subsystem, but not a super system. Religion has limits. Religion can become a public norm once more if it undergoes a process of publicizing its values. What Haji Oma Irama[49] did is an indication of two things: religion wants to re-enter public space without undergoing a process of 'publicizing'; yet this method clashes with a value already established within society, namely freedom of expression.

* * * * *

Commentary   In the following extract, Adian Husaini draws on points of Islamic scholarship as well as the thinking of the late Hamka to support his view that Inul and all those who promote her performances (entrepreneurs, mass media and so on) are a threat to Islamic authority. In fact, he describes the situation as a battle between the moral authority of Islam and the forces supporting secularism and mass commercialization. He believes the fate of the Islamic community as a whole depends on the outcome of this battle. Adian Husaini is a prominent Muslim intellectual, active in both Indonesia and Malaysia. A former journalist and a prolific commentator on Islamic issues in the Indonesian print media, he is also a popular speaker in Jakarta mosques. The extract below is taken from the transcript of one of his broadcasts for Jakarta Radio DAKTA 92.15 FM.

Extract 10-41: Adian Husaini

Adian Husaini (2004), 'Inul, Budaya Syahwat, dan Eksistensi Umat' [Inul, the Culture of Lust and the Existence of the Muslim Community], pp. 15–25 in *Hendak Kemana (Islam) Indonesia?* [Whither (Islam in) Indonesia?], Media Wacana, Jakarta. Extract: pp. 23–5.

Nowadays, moral boundaries are toppling one by one. TV entertainment programs in Indonesia reveal the phenomenon of a society that has lost hold of itself and forgotten to be mindful of its God, a hedonistic society gripped by a culture of lust, and too permissive in accepting destructive alien cultural values.

The main direction of the current of the culture of lust is to promote promiscuity, whereas in fact the Prophet, on whom be blessings and peace, warned, 'If promiscuity and usury engulf a country, the inhabitants of that country have acquiesced to the raining down of God's punishment upon themselves' (HR Thabrani and Al Hakim). [Hadith]

The phenomenon of the dominance of a hedonistic culture in society can be seen from how enthusiastically people worship celebrities. TV programs about celebrity news are lapped up greedily by advertisers because they attract high ratings. This phenomenon is what was referred to in the Qur'an:

---

49   Rhoma Irama, a well-known Indonesian singer, was vehemently critical of Inul's performances.

'So when they forget the warning (from God) given to them, We shall open all the doors of happiness for them; so that when they are rejoicing with what has been given to them, We shall torture them suddenly, so that then they will be struck dumb and without hope' (QS. Al-An'am: 44).[50]

In view of this, the phenomenon of Inul and the swelling of the current of the culture of lust within our society – which is broadcast every minute by the television media – requires serious attention, because it relates to the existence of a religious community. This is a critical battlefield involving forms of cultural warfare, warfare of opinions and economic warfare.

Indonesia's Muslim community should be aware that it is in a very critical condition. This community is truly on the verge of destruction. As far back as the 1970s, Hamka wrote:

What threatens our people and our nation now is total disintegration. On the outside we are still an independent nation, but the spirit of the people has been destroyed from within, fallen into subjugation more terrible than before. The people are being poisoned, or are taking poison to kill themselves, with the collapse of morals and the rampaging of immorality.

What this great religious leader warned against, almost 30 years ago, must be a reminder to us all. Are we able to play a role in staving off the massive wave of cultural destruction that is engulfing the world's largest Muslim nation?

The problem is certainly not whether we are able to or not, for rather it is a responsibility which it is compulsory to perform in a serious and professional manner. *And God knows the truth.*

---

50   'So, when they had forgotten the warning they had received, We opened the gates to everything for them. Then, as they revelled in what they had been given, We struck them suddenly and they were dumbfounded' (Q6: 44, Haleem).

11 Sharia

M.B. Hooker and Virginia Hooker

> 'This is My path, leading straight, so follow it, and do not follow
> other ways: they will lead you away from it – This is what He
> commands you to do, so that you may refrain from wrongdoing'
> (Q6: 153, Haleem)

INTRODUCTION

Islamic law (sharia) is at the heart of Islam, a religion which may be described as theology in legal form. Sharia means 'path' (to water), to life in the hereafter and proper conduct in the temporal world. It is God's guidance for human beings in all aspects of their lives – in their worship of God and in their relationships with each other. Its sources are in the Qur'an (God's guidance as revealed to the Prophet Muhammad), the Sunnah (the examples gathered from reports of the sayings and behaviour of the Prophet Muhammad during his lifetime) and, for practical purposes, the jurisprudence (*fiqh*) textbooks that were compiled during the early centuries of Islam. The *fiqh* textbooks contain prescriptions; each of the Sunni schools of law (*madhhab*) and the Shi'a has its own standard collections produced over the past 1,400 years of scholarship.[1]

The basic premise of sharia is that the fundamental duty of human beings is to obey God in all things, including social and personal relations. During the twelfth century, the great scholar al-Ghazali (1058–1111 CE) listed the five purposes of sharia (*maqasid al-shari'ah*) as protection of religion; protection of life; protection of intellect; protection of generations (of human beings); and protection of property. In the classic interpretation of sharia, there are defined offences (for example, adultery, theft, apostasy) with defined penalties (*hudud*). The penalties fall into three main classes: physical penalties; compensation (*qisas*); and other penalties imposed at

---

1 According to al-Ghazali, perhaps the most respected of the great classical scholars of Islam, studying *fiqh* gave a student exemption from fighting a holy war, and if a student died while still studying *fiqh*, he was regarded as a martyr (*shahid*) as if he had been killed in a holy war (Snouck Hurgronje 1931: 169).

the discretion of a judge (*ta'zir*) depending on the classification of the offence. This classic position still applies in Saudi Arabia and some other places. However, it is not the current definition of sharia in contemporary nation-states that have selected from and reformulated sharia for the purposes of the state. The classic position remains important, however, because it is the fundamental reference point for contemporary Muslim groups that advocate radical reform of existing laws or the drafting of new codes.

The emergence of modern nation-states in the Islamic world was accompanied by supporting constitutions, law codes and statute law which, in many cases, included the incorporation of selected sections of customary law and sharia. There are several approved intellectual methods for the adaptation of sharia to contemporary issues and conditions. One is *ijtihad*, defined as a method to 'exert all capacities to find a sharia ruling which can be used to reach a legal decision'.[2] It was the practice advocated by Ibn Taymiyyah (1263–1328) and refined by later scholars such as the nineteenth-century reformist scholar Muhammad Abduh and the influential contemporary scholar Yusuf al-Qaradawi. Other approved methods of reasoning followed by legal experts are *ijma'* (agreement or consensus of expert opinions); *qiyas* (reasoning by analogy); and *istislah* (reasoning based on the public good). In the modern era, these methods have also been used to find accommodations between laws of the nation-state and selected Islamic laws. It is the view of many classically trained scholars (ulema) that seeking accommodation between secular and sacred law results in a dangerous diminution of the jurisdiction and application of the classical concept of sharia, which should be the sole law for Muslims.

ISLAMIC LAW IN SOUTHEAST ASIA

History and Administration

Islamic law in Southeast Asia has its own expression but is, and always has been, in touch with trends in other parts of the Muslim world, particularly the Middle East and South Asia. In the heartlands of Southeast Asian Islam (Malaysia, Indonesia and the Philippines), the last 200 years have seen elements of sharia selected and reformulated in English and Dutch forms: cases, statutes and codes.[3] These colonial interventions have essentially secularized sharia, restricted its jurisdiction to matters of private law (largely family law) and removed it from its classical roots in *fiqh* textbooks.[4]

---

2   As-Syaukani's definition as cited in al-Qardlawy [*sic*] (1987: 2). Al-Qaradawi suggests that this definition is perhaps the most accepted by experts in Islamic law.
3   There is insufficient hard evidence to suggest what form of sharia is being used in Burma, Cambodia or Vietnam.
4   The same thing has happened in North Africa and the Middle East (see Layish 2004).

The post-colonial statutes and codes are elaborations of the colonial material. They are much more detailed in content and administration but the approach is essentially the same. Religious judges (*qadi*) can make competent rulings based solely on the state-sponsored compilations of Islamic law. State-appointed judges no longer require deep knowledge of Arabic, an understanding of the history of Islam or specialist knowledge of the classical texts.[5] Instead, they must know the laws of the nation-state and the various codes and precedents in which sharia is now expressed (Hooker 1999). The codes are not 'Islamic' in the classical sense; they are described more accurately as 'laws for Muslims' or 'sharia-inspired' laws. Many religious scholars in Malaysia and Indonesia – often effectively marginalized by the secular forms and administration of Islamic law – view this secular sharia as a travesty. They see it as a denial of Revelation, the Sunnah of the Prophet and the truths of Islam.

The first successful reaction against such an emasculation of sharia was the Iranian revolution in 1979. Other states such as Pakistan and Sudan attempted to impose sharia punishments drawn from seventh-century Arabia for breaches of the criminal law. The responses in Pakistan have particular relevance to Southeast Asia, because it can be argued that the so-called Hudood Ordinances, introduced during the time of President Zia al Haq (1977–88), have influenced the formulation of sharia codes in Malaysia and possibly Indonesia (see section 11.6).

The Southeast Asian reactions to the reduction of sharia to forms that are supervised by the nation-state have not been violent but they have been persistent and, with the strengthening of civil society, are able to be expressed more openly. In Indonesia in particular, the corruption of the Soeharto government and the longer-term effects of the economic crisis of 1997–98 led numbers of ulema and concerned Muslims to claim that since secular laws had failed the people, it was time to implement God's laws in a more rigorous fashion.[6] It is believed that this will not only accomplish God's purposes for human beings but also cure the many social ills in Islamic society today.

Table 11.1 shows clearly the disparate nature of 'official' forms of sharia as currently implemented in the nation-states of Southeast Asia. There are, however, important shared features: sharia is in a form determined by the state; it is restricted to family and personal law, administration of *waqf* (endowment of property for religious purposes), the haj and collection of *zakat* (wealth tax); and it is implemented through religious courts whose officers and judges now rarely have a strong education in classical *fiqh*. Punishments for offences against religion (for example, drinking alcohol or unlawful proximity) are taken from secular law, not classical sharia.

Indonesia's Kompilasi Hukum Islam (KHI, Compilation of Islamic Law), the sharia-inspired laws referred to in Table 11.1, was compiled in the knowledge that it was far from perfect. Yet its drafters believe that their primary aim of producing laws

---

5   For the Malaysian material see Hooker (1984: chapters 3 and 4); for the Philippines see Hooker (1984: chapter 6); for Indonesia see Hooker and Lindsey (2002).

6   See, for example, the arguments outlined in Ismail (2003: 137) and a more detailed analysis in Salim and Azra (2003: 1–16).

Table 11.1   The Current Position of Islamic Law in Southeast Asia

State	Relation to Constitution	Text of Law	Courts	Administration
Brunei Darus-salam	*Melayu Islam Beraja* (Malay Islamic Monarchy)	Administration of Islamic Law Enactment.	Religious courts. Appeals to sultan as head of religion.	Ministry of Religious Affairs administers courts, *zakat, waqf,* haj and Centre for Islamic Outreach (Pusat Dakwah Islamiah).
Burma (Myanmar)	None	The British Indian legislation is retained. Family law is found in: • Burma Laws Act 1898 (section 13); • Kazi Act 1880; • Mussalman Waqf Acts 1913 & 1923. In addition, acts of the Union of Burma are: • Muslim Divorce Act 1953; • Marriage & Inheritance of Buddhist Women Act 1954 (sections 4, 20, 25, 26). There are also special provisions in the (British) civil & criminal procedure codes. See further U Khin Maung Sein (1987: 42).	General courts.	Ministry of Religious Affairs works with Islamic Council of Myanmar.
Indonesia	None, other than the first principle of Pancasila (Belief in One Almighty God)	Compilation of Islamic Law (KHI) (1991). Qanun Aceh (2002) (for Aceh only). National banking system laws (7/92; 10/98; 23/99) allow sharia banking. *Zakat* provisions: • Zakat Management Law No. 38/99; • Ministerial Decision No. 581/99; • Directorate General Decision No. D/291/2000; • Technical Guidance on Zakat Management.	Religious courts. Appeals ultimately to Supreme Court.	Supreme Court administers courts. Ministry of Religious Affairs administers *zakat* through the Zakat Collection Agency (Badan Amil Zakat) and oversees *waqf* and haj.

Country	Constitutional reference	Legislation	Courts	Administration
Malaysia	Federal Constitution 1957 (article 3) Federal Constitution 1988 (article 121(1A) & schedule IX) Federal Constitution 1957 (list I, schedule IX: 'Islam Is a State Matter')	Each state in the federation has enactments of Muslim/Islamic laws. Federal Islamic banking laws. Haj provisions: • Hajj Law No. 17/99; • Ministerial Decision No. 371/02; • Directorate General Decision No. 125/02.	State religious courts. State appeal courts. Federal court is the authority on what is 'Islamic'.	Since 1998, Department of Sharia Law (Jabatan Kehakiman Syariah Malaysia) in the Prime Minister's Office administers courts. State Department of Religion administers *zakat, waqf.* Pilgrimage Fund Board (Lembaga Tabung Haji) administers haj.
Philip-pines	Constitution of the Republic of the Philippines (article XV(II))	Code of Muslim Personal Laws (1977) places Islamic law in this form as part of the national law and is applicable to all Muslims in the Philippines.	Religious courts. Appeals ultimately to Supreme Court of the Philippines.	Through the religious courts. Office of Muslim Affairs (in the Office of the President) administers haj, *waqf.*
Singapore	No constitutional reference	Administration of Muslim Law Act (Act 20 of 1999).	Religious courts. Shariah Appeal Board.	Islamic Religious Council of Singapore (Majlis Ugama Islam Singapura), constituted under the Administration of Muslim Law Act, administers haj, *halal* certification, *waqf, zakat,* mosques and religious schools.
Thailand	No constitutional reference Law enacted by Royal Decree 1997	Administration of Islamic Organizations Act BE 2540 (1997) repeals the earlier Patronage of Islam Act [Mosque Act] 1947 and royal decrees of 1945 and 1948.	Religious courts. Chularajamontri (Syaikh al-Islam) appointed by the King for life to advise him on all Islamic matters.	Ministry of Interior and Ministry of Education.

that meet the needs of contemporary society has, to a large extent, been achieved. In the words of one of the drafters, Professor Harahap (1992: 37), 'What we sought were provisions and rulings of needs which could systematize and improve the arrangement and order of Islamic social life'.

In Malaysia and Singapore there has been no similar debate about a compilation of Islamic laws because the sharia has always been recognized (within the limits of family law and trusts) as the law for Muslims. This was British colonial practice from the early nineteenth century. On independence, both Malaysia and Singapore took over existing colonial laws, later amending and elaborating them. Debate on these laws for Muslims (for example by local non-government organizations and human rights groups) is about various statutory provisions, not about whether the statutes should exist, which is taken as a given in the Malaysian Federal Court and in legal policy in Singapore.

The situation in Malaysia is complex. As part of a federation, each of the states and the Federal Territory has authority to draft and administer its own 'Islamic' (sometimes 'Muslim') law enactments under schedule IX of the Federal Constitution. The legislation in different states is broadly similar but there are also some quite important variations. At present the policy of the federal government is to promote standardization so far as possible, but this is constrained by list 1, schedule IX of the Federal Constitution.

Sharia in Contemporary Contexts

In Islam, Muslims must follow God's path (sharia) as set out in the Qur'an and exemplified by the life of the Prophet Muhammad (described in the Sunnah). Yet the steps between these two sources of law and their implementation in all aspects of a Muslim's daily life are complex. The attempts by nation-states to formulate codes of Islamic law or laws for Muslims (as outlined above) have not satisfied all Muslims. This has provided rich ground for debates about the nature of those laws, about the pros and cons of the full implementation of sharia, and about the relationship between socio-historical conditions and the eternal principles of divine law. As well, contemporary Muslim scholars who have developed theories and methodologies from Western social sciences to find new meanings in older sources have invigorated debates about the interpretation of Qur'anic injunctions and the classical *fiqh* texts that have been a feature of Islamic legal discourse over many centuries.

The remainder of this chapter will present some of the issues being debated by Southeast Asian Muslims, by quoting from their own words and writings. Sections 11.1–11.8 present a range of positions about whether or not full implementation of sharia is possible. The extracts reflect the varying motivations and aims of the parties concerned. Section 11.9 focuses on three issues of particular concern to contemporary Muslims: insurance, inheritance, and how sharia is interpreted in crisis or emergency situations.

EXTRACTS AND COMMENTARY

11.1   'ISLAMIC LAW YES, ISLAMIC LAW NO' [7]

Commentary   Currently no nation in Southeast Asia implements sharia as the sole national law. The 'sharia-inspired' laws listed in Table 11.1 apply only to Muslims and are restricted to issues of family law, collection of *zakat*, administration of *waqf* and administration of the pilgrimage to Mecca. To date, no political party that has succeeded in winning government at a national level has proposed extending sharia into other areas of law. In both Malaysia and Indonesia, however, some Muslim-based parties have campaigned for more comprehensive implementation of sharia, rarely elaborating on the details of what form the sharia would take or how it would be enforced. So far, these parties have not attracted the mass support necessary for gaining power at the national level.

The extracts in sections 11.2–11.9 begin with a consideration of the basic principles used for applying sharia in modern contexts and move on to more specific examples of attitudes to the implementation of sharia law, both for and against.

11.2   MAINSTREAM POSITIONS

Commentary   The following extract describes some of the issues inherent in formulating laws for contemporary Muslims using the Qur'an and Sunnah. It is taken from an article that appraises the contributions to sharia scholarship in Indonesia by the late Prof. Dr H. Satria Effendi Zein (1949–2000). He was a leading educator in sharia at major Indonesian universities, deputy chair of Majelis Ulama Indonesia (MUI, Indonesian Council of Ulama) and a member of several national sharia boards for banking and insurance. He also served as Indonesia's official representative to the Majma' al-Fiqh al-Islami (Association for the Study of Islamic Law) of the Organization of the Islamic Conference (OIC). He was particularly interested in seeking an intellectual basis for applying Islamic law in modern societies. The footnotes to the original article have been preserved but are shown as endnotes to the extract rather than at the bottom of the page as in the original. They are indicated in the text by superscript square brackets.

Extract 11-1: Fathurrahman Djamil on Satria Effendi M. Zein

Fathurrahman Djamil (2004), 'Karakteristik Pemikiran Fiqh Prof. Dr. H. Satria Effendi M. Zein, MA' [Features of Prof. H. Satria Effendi M. Zein's Thinking Concerning *Fiqh*], pp. 522–34 in Satria Effendi M. Zein, *Problematika Hukum Keluarga Islam Kontemporer: Analisis Yurisprudensi dengan Pendekatan Ushuliyah* [Problems in Contemporary Islamic Family Law: The Legal-Principle Approach to Jurisprudential Analysis], Prenada Media, Jakarta. Extract: pp. 523–8.

---

7   This is the English translation of the Indonesian title of a book written in response to the debates stimulated by groups supporting greater recognition of sharia law in Indonesia (Zein and Sarifuddin 2001).

B. The Discourse of Modernity in Islamic Law

Through the opening of this rational and dynamic Islamic legal discourse, Mr Satria became known as an Islamic legal expert who paid attention to the development of society and social change. He wrote [papers about] various ideas concerning Islamic law[8] and social change delivered at a number of seminars at various Islamic tertiary institutions, both state and private. The general impression from his various writings was that Islamic law is dynamic, adaptive and relevant to the changes and development of society [...] By virtue of his concepts and thoughts, ultimately many Islamic legal experts have been able to engage with the discourse of modernity.

When speaking about Islamic law and modernity, Mr Satria sought to bring to the fore two tendencies, akin to those that he drew from the *Mafhum Tajdid al-Din* of Bustahami [or Busthami] Muhammad Sa'id, namely a *salafi* or traditionalist tendency and an *ashrani* or modernist tendency.[1] These two tendencies are considered to be diametrically opposed to one another. The first group is of the opinion that normative Islamic laws are very limited in number, whilst legal and human dilemmas are never-ending and without limit (*al-nushus mutanahiyah wa al-waqa'i ghairu mutanahiyah*). Because of this, Islamic law as God's law must be safeguarded so that it remains in its divine position, by carrying out in a literal manner what is written in the holy scripture, whilst social developments can be resolved by way of understanding the holy scripture, in accordance with the development of the traditions of Muslim societies. In this context a distinction is drawn between Islamic law on the one hand and jurisprudence on the other.

The problem that emerges from this group's way of thinking is whether all verses of the Qur'an can be made into sources of normative Islamic law. Debate about this issue is never-ending. The existence of regulatory[9] verses and non-regulatory verses is a simplification of the solution to this problem. In this regard, Satria Effendi was of the opinion that the term 'regulatory verses' referred to those that explained laws of obligation in the form of commandments or prohibitions.[2] If this solution is considered correct, the next issue relates to the interpretation of the intended legal verses. Can the holy scripture associated with laws be interpretable? The discourse of *qath'iy* [Ar.: *qaṭ`iyyun*] and *dzanniy* [Ar.: *ẓanniyyun*][10] appears to constitute an interesting problem, although the most recent developments tend towards the conclusion that verses of the Qur'an are capable of multiple interpretations, and hence there are no longer any verses of a *qath'iy* nature.[3] The consequence has been that laws in Islam have been dominated not by Islamic law (sharia), but by jurisprudence (*fikih*) which is by nature relative. The relativity of jurisprudence is related to who interprets Islamic law, where it is interpreted and when. In this context, tradition, culture and evolution are certainly involved in understanding normative Islamic law.

---

8   The two key legal terms in this extract are *syariah* (occasionally *hukum Islam*) and *fikih*. They have been translated consistently throughout the extract as 'Islamic law' and 'jurisprudence' respectively.

9   'Regulatory' refers to those verses of the Qur'an that directly express prescription.

10   *Qath'iy* (or *qat'i*) refers to a definitive or categorical principle in the Qur'an or Hadith whose meaning may not be negotiated or reinterpreted; *dzanniy* (or *zanni*) refers to directives or principles based on the Qur'an or Hadith that have been reached on the basis of expert argumentation (that is, as a result of the use of human reasoning to interpret revelation).

At this level it is believed that Islamic law which derives from God's grace is capable of multiple translations. [...]

In actuality the normative legal group have acknowledged that contained within sources of normative Islamic law are socio-cultural elements that serve as a background to the revelation of legislative verses. It is assumed that every legislative verse has a background or a reason for why it was revealed (*sabab nuzul*). This means that verses of the Qur'an associated with Islamic law are not asocial or ahistorical.

The second group, who believe that normative Islamic law in and of itself can be used as a mould by all societies within a variety of traditions and cultures, seek to understand Islamic legal norms that existed during the Medina period[11] as basic norms, the spirit of which must be delved into and implemented in the lives of the Muslim community in accordance with their various conditions. In their search, they focus on two things: first, making Islamic legal norms into moral values and social ethics; and second, seeking the roots of [the concept of] the common good which was the foundation of the Islamic legal norms of Medina.

In connection with their research focus oriented towards substantive law, a number of Muslim thinkers believe that Islamic law is not merely a source of legislation but, more than that, is moreover a reflection of the sources of moral norms and social ethics. Fazlul [or Fazlur] Rahman, for example, is of the opinion that stipulations or norms found in Islamic law must be understood in the context of society's universal morals and ethics. Justice, freedom and equality are believed to be the aspirations of Islamic law that ought to provide the foundation in determining laws. Even if the Qur'an specifically sets out regulations concerning human social interaction, whether civil or criminal, those [regulations] cannot be understood as being confined to what is written in the text. Rather, the Islamic legal aspirations contained within it must be scrutinized intelligently. Because of this, when Muslim communities have changed and their situation differs from that of early Muslim societies, changes to legal stipulations are a certainty.[5] Meanwhile, the second research focus of substantive law is directed towards a search for the primary aim of making Islamic legal norms law. The bulk of these aims are directed towards the general good, which is made the primary aim. Khalid Masud,[12] for example, believes that the general good, reflected in the 'five principles' of Islamic law,[13] constitutes the basis for the norms of Islamic law, which of itself can be used as a mould by all Muslim societies with their diversity of traditions, cultures and civilizations.[6] It can be seen that the two research focuses above share a strategic similarity in their efforts to find the roots of

---

11   The Prophet Muhammad withdrew from the persecution he faced in Mecca and moved to Medina in 622 CE to establish a community there. It came to be regarded as the model for all Islamic communities.

12   Professor M. Khalid Masud is a leading contemporary Muslim scholar based in Lahore. Masud's analysis of al-Shatibi's concept of 'public good', his doctrine of *maqasid al-shari'ah* (the five principles of Islamic law) and the challenge of using these concepts to respond to social change appears in Masud (1977).

13   Defined by most scholars as protection of religion; protection of life (self); protection of generations (family); protection of property; and protection of intellect.

tradition and culture within Islamic law. Universal moral and ethical values and the universal five principles actually constitute the essence of their concepts.

Mr Satria, seen from the point of view of his persistence in popularizing al-Syathibi's[14] concepts, has tried to accommodate the concepts of the substantive law school as developed by the modernists. Certainly, he did not use modernist methodology entirely, but sought to present the general good as the objective of Islamic law. So strong was his commitment to implementing the theory of the basic aims of Islamic law (*maqashid al-syari'ah*) that he stressed that 'knowledge of the basic aims of Islamic law is the key to the success of [Muslim legal] experts in deriving rulings which are based on scholarly reasoning'.[7] In this context al-Syathibi sought to prove that the factors of tradition and social practice had an influence on understandings of Islamic legal norms. He deduced that Islamic law is based on the general good, which is differentiated into general good of a primary (*dlaruriyat*), secondary (*hajiyat*) and tertiary (*tahsiniyat*) nature.[8] For him, the general good of the primary type is universal and is recognized by all peoples and religions. The general good of the secondary type is constituted by laws and social practices assimilated into Islamic law, with regard for the general good of the public, such as matters of *qiradl*[15] or *mudlarabah*.[16] The tertiary type of the general good is laws informed by more refined elements of social practice, like proper behaviour, cleanliness and cultural norms along with other traditions. According to al-Syathibi, Islamic law adopts these elements because they are all considered to reflect the propriety and cultural choices of a society.[9] He gives the following illustration: leaving the house without covering one's head is regarded in the East as a violation of proper behaviour, whereas in the West this is not the case, and in fact the reverse may be true.[10]

[Footnotes]

[1]   Busthami Muhammad Sa'id, *Mafhum Tajdid al-Din* [The Concept of Religious Modernization] (Kuwait, Dar al-Da'wah, 1984), p. 91 onwards.

[2]   Satria Effendi M. Zein, *Problematika Hukum Keluarga Islam Kontemporer* [Problems of Contemporary Islamic Family Law], Faculty of Islamic Law (*Syariah*) and Law (*Hukum*), Syarif Hidayatullah State Islamic Universty Jakarta, 2003, p. 127.

[3]   M. Quraish Shihab, *Membumikan Al-Qur'an* [Bringing the Qur'an Down to Earth] (Bandung: Mizan, 1997), Printing XIV, p. 138.

[4]   Bassam Tibi, *Islam and the Cultural Accommodation of Social Change* (Oxford, Westview Press, 1991), p. 63. [The text to which this reference applies is not included in the extract.]

[5]   Fazlur Rahman, *Islam* (Chicago: University of Chicago Press, 1979), p. 115. See also Fazlur Rahman, *Islamic Methodology in History* (Islamabad: Islamic Research Institute, 1984), p. 1.

[6]   Khalid Masud, *Islamic Legal Philosophy: A Study of Abu Ishaq Al-Shathibi's Life and Thought* (Islamabad: Islamic Research Institute, 1977), p. 221. See also his work: 'Pencarian Landasan Normatif Syariah Para Ahli Hukum Muslim' [Muslim Legal Experts' Search for a Normative Foundation for Islamic Law], in Dick van der Meij (ed.), *Dinamika Kontemporer dalam Masyarakat Islam* [Contemporary Dynamics in Islamic Societies], INIS, Jakarta, p. 9.

---

14   The Andalusian jurist Abu Ishaq Ibrahim al-Shatibi (d. 1388 CE); see footnotes 12 and 13.

15   A contract under which capital is lent for use (for example, for trade) and the resulting profits are divided according to the contract. The arrangement is considered to benefit both the lender and the borrower.

16   Contracts based on profit and loss sharing.

[7]   Satria Effendi M. Zein, 'Maqashid al-Syari'at dan Perubahan Sosial' [The Aims of Sharia and Social Change], published in *Dialog* (Publications and Development Body of the Indonesian Ministry of Religious Affairs, No. 33, year XV, January 1991), p. 29.

[8]   Abu Ishaq al-Syathibi, *al-Muwafaqat fi Ushuul al-Syari'ah* [Conformance in the Fundamentals of Sharia] (Beirut: Dar al-Kutub at-Ilmiyyah, no date), Volume 2, p. 7.

[9]   *Ibid*, Volume 2, p. 216.

[10]   *Ibid*.

* * * * *

Commentary   The Compilation of Islamic Law (KHI), effective in Indonesia since 1991 as the 'official' law for regulating the personal (family) law of Indonesian Muslims, represents a 'middle of the road' approach to enacting sharia legislation that is acceptable to the state and many Indonesian Muslims (but see extract 11-3). The KHI consists of three volumes covering marriage, inheritance and gifts for pious purposes.

The drafters of the KHI claim that an effort was made to use *fiqh* opinions cautiously because overuse of *fiqh* texts and opinions runs the risk of overshadowing the sharia. Professor M. Yahya Harahap was one of the drafters of the KHI. In the following extract, he outlines the differences between sharia and *fiqh* and also sets out what he sees as the consequences of judges making decisions based on different schools of law (*mazhab*).

Extract 11-2: M. Yahya Harahap

M. Yahya Harahap (1992), 'Informasi Materi Kompilasi Hukum Islam: Mempositifkan Abstraksi Hukum Islam' [Background to the Compilation of Islamic Law: Positivizing Abstract Islamic Law], *Mimbar Hukum* 5(3): 21–63. Extract: pp. 21–2.

Introduction

It is probably not an overstatement to say that there has been confusion about the understanding and implementation [of Islamic law] in Indonesian Muslim society. This has not been limited to ordinary Muslims. It has extended to religious scholars, general education and higher Islamic education. All of them identify *fiqh* with sharia or 'Islamic law'.

The identification of *fiqh* with Islamic law has given rise to serious errors of implementation. In preparing their decisions for cases in the jurisdiction of the Religious Court (Pengadilan Agama), the judges turn to *fiqh* books of the schools of law, which are their first points of reference. This results in disparities between the decisions emanating from the religious courts depending on which school of law is followed and favoured by individual judges. [...]

[...] Surveys have shown that judges with strong backgrounds in a particular school of law are authoritarian, doctrinaire and descriptive [rather than analytical in their judgements]. They will not move one inch from the opinion of the authority they favour. If the presiding judge is from a Muhammadiyah background, or does not follow a particular school of law, he will always refer to the the Qur'an and Sunnah. His views are more flexible; he will use legal thinking based on the use of 'informed opinion' [Ar.: *ra'y*] and take the teachings of the schools of law as guidance.

This is the picture based on research into the history and decisions of the religious courts. There is disputation between the schools of law and the law becomes a secondary issue. Judgements are not based on law but are based on the doctrines of the schools of law as set out in the *fiqh* texts. The disputation is most striking when cases are taken to appeal [where appeal judges from different schools of law give different opinions]. [...]

[...] [I]t is erroneous to identify Islamic law with *fiqh*. *Fiqh* is not positive law that has been formulated systematically and in a unified way. It is the content of teachings or the science of Islamic law. For this reason *fiqh* is referred to as the doctrine of Islamic law. Or more accurately, *fiqh* is the opinions and teachings of the leaders of the schools of law. The books of *fiqh* are not 'law books'; they are books containing the opinions and independent judgements (*ijtihad*) of those leaders.

* * * * *

Commentary   As Professor Harahap admitted in his article on the drafting of the KHI, the Compilation has weaknesses. These were highlighted as part of the debate in Indonesia on the full implementation of sharia. Some groups proposed that the KHI be upgraded in status from a presidential decree to a draft law of state (Rancangan Undang-Undang) and its scope widened beyond family law and inheritance. In view of its significance for Indonesian Muslims and the fact that it was formulated in the context of the New Order ideologies of male-led households, the Ministry of Religious Affairs invited its Gender Mainstreaming Team to prepare a discussion paper to re-examine the KHI. The group commissioned to carry out the review produced a report entitled 'Counter Legal Draft Kompilasi Hukum Islam' (CLD KHI). It provoked its own controversy, especially among groups of conservative, older Muslim scholars. At the time of writing the status of the Counter Legal Draft was unclear. However, the document has succeeded in raising gender mainstreaming issues, as its authors intended (see chapter 13). The team sets out its aims in the following extract.

Extract 11-3: Gender Mainstreaming Team

Tim Pengarusutamaan Gender (2004), 'Pendahuluan' [Introduction], pp. 1–5 in *Pembaruan Hukum Islam: Counter Legal Draft Kompilasi Hukum Islam* [Reforming Islamic Law: The Counter Legal Draft to the Compilation of Islamic Law], Ministry of Religious Affairs, Jakarta. Extract: p. 4.

II. Agenda and Ideals

This program aims to offer a [new][17] formulation of sharia in keeping with democratic life and reflecting the genuine character of Indonesian culture as an alternative to the demands for the formalization of total sharia implementation on the one hand, and the need to establish democracy in the Indonesian nation-state on the other.

In the [new] formulation of sharia, all citizens have the same status and access to justice; minorities and women are protected and guaranteed equal rights. The formu-

---

17   The square brackets in this extract are in the original.

lations are based on the basic aims of Sharia Islam (*maqashid al-syari'at*), that is, to establish values and principles of social justice, the welfare of the community of human beings, universal compassion and local wisdom. It has been prepared in Indonesian with current idioms, not Arabisms, and can be understood by Indonesians.

This formulation will draw on the material points of the Compilation of Islamic Law [KHI], studies of legal history, the sociology of law, the politics of law and deconstruction of the teachings of Islam. Besides the writings and opinions of experts which have been sources for the study, empirical evidence and law as it is found in society have been important considerations. The three areas covered were: [1] the *content of Islamic law*, [2] the *structure of Islamic law* and [3] the *culture and implementation of Islamic law*.

* * * * *

Commentary Professor Ahmad Shafii Maarif was national chair of Indonesia's largest modernist organization, Muhammadiyah, between 2000 and 2004. Born in West Sumatra in 1935 and holding a doctorate from the University of Chicago, he was a leader of the important Muslim student association Himpunan Mahasiswa Islam (HMI, Muslim Tertiary Students Association) as well as Muhammadiyah, which he joined in 1955. He is also a professor at the State Islamic University of Yogyakarta (UIN Sunan Kalijaga). He has promoted and participated in interfaith dialogues and is recognized as a proponent of moderate interpretations of Islam, reminding radical groups in Indonesia that Muhammadiyah's motto is 'dare to live', not 'dare to die'. The next extract is taken from an interview originally published in the newspaper *Republika* on 4 September 2000, at a time when views for and against the restoration of the Jakarta Charter to the constitution were raging (see chapters 5 and 12). In response to the question, 'As a nation with the largest Muslim majority, do you think we have the right to demand the implementation of sharia as the basis for state law?', Professor Maarif replied, very succinctly, as follows.

Extract 11-4: Ahmad Shafii Maarif

Ahmad Shafii Maarif (2001), 'Pertimbangkan Dampak Yang Akan Timbul' [Assessing the Fallout], pp. 41–4 in Kurniawan Zein and Sarifuddin HA (eds), *Syariat Islam Yes, Syariat Islam No: Dilema Piagam Jakarta dalam Amandemen UUD 1945* [Sharia Yes, Sharia No: The Dilemma of the Jakarta Charter in the Amendment to the 1945 Constitution], Paramadina, Jakarta. [Originally published in *Republika*, 4 September 2000.] Extract: pp. 43–4.

Certainly we are the nation with the largest Muslim majority in the world. Yet it should be remembered that historically, Islam entered Indonesia mainly through a process of acculturation with local cultures. As a result of the spread of Islam in that way, we now see three groups of Muslim communities in Indonesia. *First*, the group of 'marginal' Muslims often called *abangan* [nominal] Muslims. *Second*, *santri* [practising] Muslims who are syncretic. And *third*, *santri* Muslims who are seriously trying to practise Islam in accordance with sharia.

If sharia were to become the basis for state law, the last group of *santri* Muslims would probably be able to adapt to it. But the other groups might reject it. As you know, the actual number of those who are syncretic and nominal Muslims is quite high. You can imagine what would happen if sharia were actually to be implemented as state law. Dissension would occur not only between Muslims and non-Muslims, but also within the Muslim community itself. This would clearly be dangerous.

* * * * *

Commentary Both Indonesia and Malaysia have majority Muslim populations and have recognized this in the provision of detailed, sharia-inspired personal laws administered by state-sponsored agencies. In Thailand, on the other hand, the Muslim population is a small minority of the total population but is largely grouped in a well-defined geographical area (the four southern provinces of Pattani, Yala, Narathiwat and Satun; see chapter 9). Ethnically, culturally and spatially, this Muslim population has many links with the Malay population of the northernmost Malaysian states on the Malay peninsula. On the southern side of the Thailand–Malaysia border, Muslims have access to a well-developed system of Islamic courts and support services. On the northern side, the Thai side, sharia law is available for personal matters, but is not as well supported.

For the Muslims living in areas within Thai national borders, sharia-based laws have been applied by local judges in religious courts since at least the eighteenth century and probably earlier. After 1902, however, as Bangkok's control over the southern Malay regions increased, national courts were established in parallel with Muslim courts. Unlike the case in 'British' Malaya, Bangkok removed juridical power from the local sultans and vested it in judges who were selected locally but had to be approved by Bangkok (Loos 2004–05: 8). That system still persists, and eight judges (two in each province) hear 200–300 cases each year, mostly concerning inheritance (Loos 2004–05: 6). Under current regulations, Islamic family law is applied only to Muslims residing in the four southern provinces. Those who live outside those provinces, or whose disputes arise elsewhere, cannot appeal to the Islamic courts. Moreover, Muslims in the four provinces do not have the right of appeal to non-Islamic (national) law for family law issues.[18]

In Thailand, the Thai Constitution (1997) states that the King is the patron of all religions. The Administration of Islamic Organizations Act, which currently regulates laws for Muslims in Thailand, was enacted by the Royal Decree of a Buddhist monarch. The act replaces three pieces of legislation from the late 1940s. It gives authority to the Minister of Interior and the Minister of Education to administer the act. Thus, responsibility for the implementation of the act's provisions falls to non-Muslim, secular authorities.

The highest Muslim official and leader of the Muslims of Thailand, the Chularaja-montri, is appointed by the King after the nominee has been approved by Islamic provincial committees throughout Thailand.

The extracts from the act presented here set out in considerable detail the duties of the Chularajamontri, the Central Islamic Committee of Thailand and the Islamic Provincial Committee. When compared with the state-sponsored sharia laws for Muslims

---

18   These details are taken from Loos (2004–05: 10); she points out that Islamic family law is 'territorial law rather than personal law'.

in majority populations, it is very clear that the Thai act is purely administrative in purpose and function and makes no mention of the form or content of the Islamic law that will be implemented.

Material of this kind is difficult to obtain in English, so a rather lengthy extract of the act is given here to indicate the hierarchical nature of the formal organization of Islam and its representative nature. The delineation of the functions and responsibilities of the provincial committees indicates how authority for the implementation of Islamic law is vested at local levels.

Extract 11-5: Thailand Administration of Islamic Organizations Act (1997)

Prarachabanyat Karn Boriharn Ongon Sasana Islam BE[19] 2540 [Administration of Islamic Organizations Act B.E. 2540 (1997)], 17 October 1997, promulgated by King Bhumibol Adulyadej.

Administration of Islamic Organizations Act B.E. 2540 (1997)
By the Signature of His Majesty King Bhumibol Adulyadej
17 October B.E. 2540 (1997)
Being the 52nd year of the Present Reign [...]

Chapter 1

General Provisions

Section 8 The Chularajamontri has the following authority and functions:
1   To give advice and offer his thoughts to the government service on Islamic religious activities.
2   To appoint a group of qualified people to give advice on Islamic law.
3   To issue declarations advising the result of moon watching in accordance with section 35(11), to enable the setting of important religious days.
4   To issue declarations about judgements of Islamic law.

Section 9 The Chularajamontri shall cease to hold the position upon:
1   Death
2   Resignation
3   Royal Command providing that the Chularajamontri shall cease to hold his position because he lacks a necessary qualification or possesses a prohibited characteristic as per section 7 [...]

Chapter 3

Central Islamic Committee of Thailand

Section 16 There will be a committee named the 'Central Islamic Committee of Thailand' which shall include the Chularajamontri, who has been royally appointed,

---

19   BE = Buddhist Era, in Thailand dating from 543 BCE.

to be the Chairman. The committee will also be comprised of members from Islamic Provincial Committees, and there shall be one representative from each Islamic Provincial Committee. The other members of the committee, who will comprise one-third of the committee, shall be chosen directly by the Chularajamontri.

The selection of the representatives from Islamic Provincial Committees and the selection of other committee members, as mentioned in paragraph one [the preceding paragraph in this extract], shall be in accordance with regulations and procedures as specified by Ministerial Order.

The committee members shall decide amongst themselves who shall be Vice President and who shall fill the other necessary positions of the committee. [...]

Section 18 The Central Islamic Committee of Thailand shall have the following authority and functions:

1   To give advice to the Minister of Interior and the Minister of Education in performance of this Act.
2   To give advice and recommendations about Islam to Islamic Provincial Committee(s) and Islamic Committee(s) of the Mosque.
3   To appoint a subcommittee to perform tasks that the Central Islamic Committee of Thailand will assign.
4   To issue regulations related to assets and management of profits/interests of the office of the Islamic Committee of the Mosque.
5   To issue procedural and administrative regulations and to control the administration of Islamic Provincial Committee(s) and Islamic Committee(s) of the Mosque.
6   To perform the duties of the Islamic Provincial Committee in provinces where there is no Islamic Provincial Committee. In this situation, the Central Islamic Committee of Thailand will appoint the nearest Islamic Provincial Committee to perform the duties on that province's behalf.
7   When there is disagreement, to make decisions in accordance with section 41.
8   To make an accurate register of assets, documents, income and expenditure of the office of the Central Islamic Committee of Thailand.
9   To issue declarations and certify activities related to Islam.
10 To support Islamic religious activities and education.
11 To coordinate with the government sector in relation to activities related to Islam.
12 To perform other duties as specified in this Act. [...]

Chapter 4

Islamic Provincial Committee

Section 23 In provinces where there are believers of Islam and at least three mosques, as per section 13, the Central Islamic Committee of Thailand shall declare that the said province shall have one Islamic Provincial Committee. The Islamic Provincial Committee shall consist of at least nine members, but no more than 30 members.

In the selection of the Islamic Provincial Committee, the Ministry of Interior shall appoint mosques in that province to nominate the persons to select the Islamic Provincial Committee. This shall be done in accordance with the regulations and procedures specified by Ministerial Order.

The president, vice-president, secretary and other necessary positions within the committee are to be chosen by the committee members themselves.

The Ministry of Interior shall announce the persons chosen to be president, vice-president, secretary and committee members in the Government Gazette. [...]

Section 26 The Islamic Provincial Committee shall have the following authority and functions:

1 To give advice and make recommendations about Islam to the Governor of the Province.
2 To oversee and inspect the work performance of the Islamic Provincial Committee in the province and in other provinces where the Central Islamic Committee of Thailand has assigned responsibility to that Committee.
3 To reconcile differences and make determinations on complaints from elders of the Mosque where they see that there has been an injustice from the Islamic Committee of the Mosque.
4 To oversee the selection of the Islamic Committee of the Mosque to make sure it is done properly.
5 To consider when to appoint and relieve the Islamic Committee of the Mosque.
6 To investigate whether the Islamic Committee of the Mosque members shall cease to hold their position as per section 40(4).
7 To order that Islamic Committee of the Mosque members are suspended during an investigation.
8 To consider when to establish, move, merge or dissolve a mosque.
9 To make caretaker appointments when there are vacancies in the positions of imam, *kortep* and *bilan*.[20]
10 To issue marriage or divorce certificates in accordance with Islamic Law.
11 When requested, to reconcile disputes about family and inheritance matters according to Islamic Law.
12 To make an accurate register of assets, documents, income and expenditure of the office of the Islamic Provincial Committee, and to report the financial status and asset management to the Central Islamic Committee of Thailand every year in March.
13 To issue declarations and certify Islamic religious activities in the province.

* * * * *

---

20 The imam leads mosque worship in a general sense and this is exemplified by his position during congregational prayers when he heads the body of worshippers. The *kortep* (Ar.: *khaṭiibun*), or 'preacher', delivers sermons in the mosque. The *bilan* (Ar.: *bilaal*) summons worshippers to the mosque for each of the five daily prayers through his ringing delivery of the call to prayer.

Commentary   Singapore, like Thailand, has a minority Muslim population. While the administration of Islam in the small island-nation differs markedly from that in Thailand, the realities of minority status are recognized in Singapore as they are in Thailand. The following extract is from the text of a sermon delivered by a representative of Majlis Ugama Islam Singapura (MUIS, Islamic Religious Council of Singapore) on Friday, 18 October 2002. The original title of the sermon was 'Hudud dalam Islam' [*Hudud* in Islam]. The text of the sermon was circulated in Malaysia in *Harakah Daily* – the newspaper that is the official voice of Parti Islam Se Malaysia (PAS, The Islamic Party of Malaysia) – on 27 April 2005. MUIS is responsible for the administration of Islam in Singapore and represents the official voice of Islam in the republic. The sermon begins by reminding the congregation about the meaning of sharia; it then goes on to explain the meaning of *hudud* and the obstacles to introducing *hudud* laws for Muslims when they are a minority group. Each of the points made in the sermon is supported by references to relevant verses in the Qur'an.

Extract 11-6: Islamic Religious Council of Singapore (MUIS)

Majlis Ugama Islam Singapura (2005), 'Hudud dalam Khutbah Jumaat Singapura' [*Hudud* Described in Singapore Friday Sermon], *Harakah Daily*, 27 April 2005.

There are various meanings of sharia according to the religious scholars. There are those who give a broad meaning to it and those who give a special meaning to it. However, what is demanded of the Islamic community is that they practise Islam as a way of life.

Almighty God decreed: 'And whoever seeks religion other than the religion of Islam, it (that religion) will never be accepted from him, and he in the after-life will be among the people who suffer loss' (Ali-Imran: 85).[21]

Further, the Islam that is to be upheld is a religion that must cover three aspects – *Aqidah*, that is, faith; *Amal Ibadah* or performance of devotions, and law which is also called *fiqh*; and *Akhlaq*, or good behaviour and morality.

Each of these three parts contains details and priorities that cannot be ignored.

On this basis, when we talk about upholding the sharia in a general and broad sense, that is, the upholding of Islam itself, then it means the entrenchment of genuine faith, true laws and praiseworthy morals.

And if we mean the implementation of sharia in a specific sense, on the other hand, that is, the aspect of jurisprudence or laws such as *hudud*, then truly, in Islam, the aspect of entrenching faith and the development of morals cannot be neglected.

In fact, faith has to form the basis of the implementation of law, and the implementation of law must be accompanied by practising the most praiseworthy morals.

It is not enough to merely confess the faith.

It is not enough for a Muslim just to have faith and to claim to be a Muslim without observing the law and morals, and the reverse is also the case.

---

21   'If anyone seeks a religion other than *islam*: complete devotion to God, it will not be accepted from him: he will be one of the losers in the Hereafter' (Q3: 85, Haleem).

There are some people who say: 'Why is it necessary to do this or that … the important thing is good intentions. What is the use of doing this and that if one's behaviour is still not correct? Isn't what is important the essence of the teachings of Islam rather than its form?'

These are words that are not accurate because if we accept the argument that 'the important thing is good intentions … the important thing is essence, not form', then human beings will have the excuse to neglect all religious duties.

People will say: 'Why pray, if one still does this and that … what is the use of going on the haj, but still not being aware, like someone who just calls himself a "Pak Haji"[22] … why fast, if it is only to the extent of experiencing hunger … what is important is that there must be good intentions'.

We should understand that a person who carries out the teachings of Islam is not a person who is without sin. So it is not impossible that a woman who wears the *hijab*,[23] for example, still performs sinful acts such as gossiping and being spiteful.

In this respect God will reward her for wearing the *hijab* and also punish her for the bad things she does and the despicable qualities in her heart.

Hudud law is one of the branches of Islamic criminal law. Its original meaning is limitations or whatever prohibitions are imposed by Almighty God, as He decreed:

'These are the limitations prohibited by God, so you are not to approach them' (Al-Baqarah: 187).[24] […]

Hudud, qisas and *ta'zir* constitute Islamic criminal law.

Offences considered as *hudud* offences are:

First, committing adultery, which is punishable by 100 lashes for a male or a female offender who is unmarried, as decreed by Almighty God in the chapter of An-Nur, verse 2,[25] and stoning to death if it is committed by a married offender, as is recounted in a Hadith told by Ibn Majah and described as a punishment meted out by the Prophet, blessings and peace be upon him, to Ma'iz and Al-Ghamidiyyah as recorded by Al-Bukhari and Muslim [collections of Hadith].

Second, accusing a person of adultery without evidence, which is punishable by 80 lashes, as decreed by Almighty God in the chapter of An-Nur: 4.[26]

---

22 The title that a male may use after completing the pilgrimage to Mecca.

23 Literally 'curtain' or 'veil'; here it refers to covering the head and body when in public.

24 'You [believers] are permitted to lie with your wives during the night of the fast: they are [close] as garments to you, as you are to them. God was aware that you were betraying yourselves, so He turned to you in mercy and pardoned you: now you can lie with them – seek what God has ordained for you – eat and drink until the white thread of dawn becomes distinct from the black. Then fast until nightfall. Do not lie with them during the nights of your devotional retreat in the mosques: these are the bounds set by God, so do not go near them. In this way God makes His messages clear to people, that they may guard themselves against doing wrong' (Q2: 187, Haleem).

25 'Strike the adulteress and adulterer one hundred times. Do not let compassion for them keep you from carrying out God's law – if you believe in God and the Last Day – and ensure that a group of believers witnesses the punishment' (Q24: 2, Haleem).

26 'As for those who accuse chaste women of fornication, and then fail to provide four witnesses, strike them eighty times, and reject their testimony ever afterwards: they are the lawbreakers' (Q24: 4, Haleem).

Third, drinking alcohol, which is punishable by 40 strokes. The Prophet, blessings and peace be upon him, said: 'Whoever drinks alcohol must be caned' (as recorded by At-Tirmuzi) [collection of Hadith].

Fourth, stealing, which is punishable by amputation of the hand as decreed by Almighty God in the chapter of Al-Maidah: 38.[27]

Fifth, robbing, which is punishable according to the degree of seriousness of the act as decreed by Almighty God in the chapter of Al-Maidah: 33.[28]

Some religious scholars also include rebellion against a country and apostasy as *hudud* crimes. [The Qur'anic reference given as footnote 28 seems to apply here.]

Complete Comprehension

To understand *hudud* crimes comprehensively, it is necessary to understand also the aspect of method of proof, method of implementation and the philosophy behind it, as well as its divine wisdom, so that misunderstanding of Almighty God's law will not arise.

Today many criticize the punishment of amputation of the hand for stealing, for example, as a punishment that is brutal, without understanding the intended meaning of stealing. When is stealing punishable by the amputation of the hand? What then is the philosophy of Islamic law? It is as if stealing a dollar or two only would mean amputating the thief's hand.

Members of the congregation, to explain all aspects of *hudud* surely cannot be done during this sermon.

Think before Speaking

What is important is that it is necessary to understand that *hudud* is a part of our religion that is incumbent upon us to understand as well as we can before we speak about its implementation or criticize it.

Because *hudud* punishments have been determined in the Qur'an and Sunnah, it is therefore obligatory on all Muslims, wherever they may be, to believe in the validity of *hudud* law.

Doubting and disputing the validity of *hudud* law may damage faith because the decree of Almighty God must be respected: 'And whoever does not decide according to what has been sent down by God, they are infidels' (Al-Maidah: 44).[29]

---

27   'Cut off the hands of thieves, whether they are male or female, as punishment for what they have done – a deterrent from God: God is almighty and wise' (Q5: 38, Haleem).

28   'Those who wage war against God and His Messenger and strive to spread corruption in the land should be punished by death, crucifixion, the amputation of an alternate hand and foot, or banishment from the land: a disgrace for them in this world, and then a terrible punishment in the Hereafter' (Q5: 33, Haleem).

29   'We revealed the Torah with guidance and light, and the prophets, who had submitted to God, [and] the rabbis and the scholars all judged according to it for the Jews in accordance with that part of God's Scripture which they were entrusted to preserve, and to which they were witnesses. So [Children of Israel] do not fear people, fear Me; do not barter away My messages for a small price; those who do not judge according to what God has sent down are rejecting [God's teachings]' (Q5: 44, Haleem).

Nevertheless the implementation of *hudud* must be carried out after all infra-structure has been prepared, such as having trained staff and a judicial system that is effective.

Other than that, the general community must be ready to accept *hudud* because the Islamic way of life is built not on the authority of the laws but on faith and the inner belief of humankind.

What is important also is that *hudud* law can only be implemented by an Ulil Amri [Islamic political authority]. *Hudud* cannot be implemented by an individual or an Islamic organization.

A father cannot apply *hudud* to his child who drinks alcohol, and an Islamic organization cannot attack a *hudud* offender or nightclubs in the streets.

To introduce *hudud* in a society that has long left Islam also requires observing the principle of *tadarruj* [gradualism]. *Hudud* does not have to be implemented in its entirety all at once, because even Almighty God imposed *hudud* law step by step.

Nevertheless, it must be understood that *hudud* law is only a part of the many religious obligations that must be carried out by the Muslim community.

Order of Priority

Due to this, it is necessary to observe an order of priority of obligations that must be fulfilled according to the circumstances of place and time.

It is in this context that the Muslim community in Singapore who live as a minority group look upon the issue of *hudud*; that is, while we believe in it, we nevertheless have a reality and priority that differ from those of other Muslim communities.

Although it is demanded that we uphold *hudud*, our inability to do so does not mean that our Islamic character or our status is lower than that of other Muslim communities in the eyes of Almighty God. This is because we are required to try and abide by the limitations that exist.

11.3 THE SPIRIT OF THE LAW

Commentary In Malaysia and Indonesia, where Muslim majority populations are supported by state-sponsored, 'sharia-inspired' laws, the laws for Muslims (especially the KHI described above) regulate family and personal laws. But the concept of sharia is all-encompassing and broader than the state-sponsored codes. Many Muslim scholars argue that more could be done to give sharia a central role in the daily affairs of Muslims. However, differences exist about how this can be accomplished. Some argue for contextual interpretations and expansion of *fiqh* methodology (the spirit of the law). Others argue against that approach in the sincere belief that the letter of the law must be followed through literal interpretations based on the classical medieval texts of Islam.

M.A. Sahal Mahfudh is president (*rais 'am*) of Nahdlatul Ulama (NU, Revival of the Religious Scholars), Indonesia's largest Muslim social organization, and general head of its Sharia Board. He has also been chair of MUI, the body that issues the 'official' guidance (fatwa) on religious issues in Indonesia. In 2003 he was awarded an honorary doctorate from the State Islamic University Syarif Hidayatullah Jakarta in recognition of his contribution to the development of the science of *fiqh*. In this extract from the journal of the International Center for Islam and Pluralism (ICIP), he describes what he terms 'social *fiqh*' and explains its significance for contemporary Muslims. The responsibility for implementing sharia, he argues, lies with individual Muslims in the course of their daily lives. He is also strongly of the opinion that the cultural context of Muslim communities must be taken into account when developing Islamic regulations (*fiqh*).

Extract 11-7: *M.A. Sahal Mahfudh*

M.A. Sahal Mahfudh (2004), 'Social *Fiqh*: An Attempt to Expand *Qawli* and *Manhaji* Paradigm' [in English], *ICIP Journal*, 1(1): 1–10. Extract: pp. 4–5, 9–10.

The Social *Fiqh* Paradigm

Islamic shari'ah is the application of *aqîdah* (Islamic theology). *Aqîdah* guarantees the life and the prosperity of all humankind. This guarantee relates specifically to the way in which one should manage life. In principle, the main goal of Islamic shari'ah, as explained in detail by '*ulama*' in the doctrine of *fiqh*, is to order the lives of mankind, in this world and the hereafter, in individual, community and state life.

Islamic shari'ah governs the relationship between humans and God, which in *fiqh* becomes the component of '*ibâdah* (act of religious devotion) both in social, individual, *muqayyada* (bound by conditions and principles) or *mutlaqah* (aspects of technical operations that are not bound by certain conditions and principles).[30] Shari'ah also regulates relationships among people in the form of *mu'asharah* (human relationships) and *mu'âmalah* (transaction relationships to fulfill life's needs). Beside that, shari'ah also regulates the relationships and arrangement within the family, which are formulated in *munâkahah* (marriage) principles. To organize relationships, in order to guarantee peace and justice, shari'ah also contains rules, which are elaborated on in the components of *jinâyah* (criminal law), *jihâd* (religious struggle) and *qada* (Islamic court).

Several of the components of *fiqh* mentioned above form a technical operation [derived] from [the] five shari'ah goals (*maqâsid al-shari'ah*). These include, the maintenance of religion, the mind, ones [one's] soul, legacy, and wealth. These components integrally and wholeheartedly govern the main elements of a person's life, in an effort to implement *taklîf* [the commandments of God] in order to achieve prosperity in this world and the hereafter, as a life goal for all human beings.

Elements of prosperity, within the present world and the hereafter[,] mutually influence each other. When this is connected with Islamic shari'ah, as is elaborated on within *fiqh*, with its starting point of the five principles of *maqâsid al-shari'ah*, then it will become clear that shari'ah has the basic goal of obtaining complete physical and psychological prosperity for all humans. This means that human beings become the target but also have a key position in achieving the above-mentioned happiness.

---

30   The author, an expert in Islamic jurisprudence, is contrasting the technical terms *muqayyada* and *mutlaqah*. The former describes guidance or rulings to which a range of conditions apply, whereas the latter does not limit the guidance to particular conditions or circumstances.

Above is an explanation for a paradigmatic framework to develop *fiqh*. In other words, *social fiqh* is derived from a view that the solution for complex social problems is the main purpose of Islamic shari'ah. The solution to these social problems is for Muslim people to fulfill their responsibilities, with their obligation as Muslims to realize the happiness and advantages for the public interest (*al-masâlih al-'âmmah*). In this case, advantages for the public mean the primary need of a certain group of people in a certain area for the sake of supporting the exterior prosperity of that area. The needs may include *darûriyah* (necessary) dimensions or basic needs, which may then become the principle [principal] tool to achieve religious salvation, a peaceful mind, and the happiness of ones [one's] soul, fete [fate], descendants and wealth. There may also be the presence of *hâjjiyah* (secondary dimensions) or *takmiliyah* (complementary dimensions).

The above classification of a human being's basic needs is indeed different to that formulated in 'secular' economic science. In secular economic science it is believed that ones [one's] primary needs are those concerning their biological needs. Religion is thus not considered a primary need. The inclusion of religion as a primary need shows us that from the beginning of the paradigmatic formulation, *fiqh* must accept the divine (*ilahiya*) package. Religion as a need thus has to be accepted. In this context, *fiqh* indeed has a paternalistic characteristic, because it sees humans as immature beings, thus needing religion to be enforced upon them from the outside, regardless of whether the person really feels they need it or not.

In short, it can be formulated that the social *fiqh* paradigm, is based on the notion that *fiqh* must be read in the context of the fulfillment of three human needs. These include primary needs (*darûriyah*), secondary needs (*hâjjiyah*) and supplementary needs (*tahsîniyah*). Social *fiqh* is not only a tool to see events in a clear cut black and white perspective as the *fiqh* perspective is obliged to do, but it also becomes a paradigm of social meaning.

Results that have already been formulated in a series of NU serial discussions, in corporation [cooperation] with RMI (Rabitah Ma`âhid al-Islamiyah: Association of Islamic Pesantrens) and P3M (Perhimpunan Pengembangan Pesantren dan Masyarakat: Association for the Development of Pesantren and Society), show that social *fiqh* possesses five principle [principal] features. They are: (1) the interpretation of *fiqh* texts contextually; (2) the shifting method of using *madhhab* from textual (*madhhab qawli*) to methodological (*madhhab manhaji*); (3) basic verification to show the difference between principle [principal] teachings (*usûl*) and branches (*furû'*); (4) *Fiqh* as a social ethic, not as state positive law; and (5) the introduction of methods of philosophical thinking, particularly within social and cultural problems.

If we look even further into this, the above five characteristic are indeed based on the notion that the construction of laws, written in various *fiqh* books, are applicable in certain situations to solve various contemporary social problems. The development of social *fiqh* does not at all erase the role of classical thinking. With this notion in mind, the development of *fiqh* is not expected to go too far or uproot *fiqh* from its orthodoxy tradition. The problem arises of how now to accept the classical paradigm. For this purpose, the principle of *al-muhâfazatu 'ala al-qadîm al-sâlih wa al-akhdhu bi al-jadîd al-aslah* (protecting the good older tradition, but obtaining the contemporary better one) will always be the guide. [pp. 4–5] [...]

Conclusion

The status of Islam as a universal teaching, in the sense that it is implemented to protect the life of the people, without being limited by regional barriers, can only be upheld if we understand the religion as possessing an element of openness. In the context of Indonesia, Islam should be able to show its tolerance in the wisest form, as a result of Indonesia's plural societies. This can only be achieved by using *sunna-tullah* [God's laws revealed to humankind through His Prophets]. At the same time, internally it must be able to adjust its teachings (with its practical ways represented in the forms of *fiqh*) to surrounding cultural and regional issues, without losing its real essence.

It is this kind of religious implementation, as can be understood from history, that will make people accept Islam as *aqîdah* [faith], without alienating people painfully from their cultural roots; which has assisted in developing one's character, personality and traditions.

To deny the implementation of this model, will only lead a society outside of religious protection. If there are still people, who consider being a true Muslim, they will surely need to separate/classify the different dimensions of their life. These dimensions will then need to be adjusted according to certain things, those things that need to refer to Islamic teachings and guidelines, and then there are those things that must be taken into consideration as purely world-life dimensions.

For this purpose, we need to make efforts of paradigmatic change within religious practical teachings, that being *fiqh*. The paradigmatic change in viewing *fiqh* is a must. *Fiqh* cannot be seen just as a tool to measure the truth of orthodox religion, but must also be considered as a tool that can read social reality and then be prepared to take the position of facing this social reality. In this case, *fiqh* has a dual function, firstly as a tool to measure social reality with shari'ah ideals, concluding with the decision of *halal* or *haram* laws, permitted or prohibited; and secondly at the same time it becomes a tool for social engineering. Within the science of law, there is always a dual function; the function of law as social control and as social engineering.

Both of the functions of *fiqh* mentioned above will only be made possible if the products and thinking of *fiqh* are developed contextually. Contextual *fiqh* approaches can be carried out, by putting the products of *fiqh* within classical texts and academic life in their present and respective contexts. The products of *fiqh* can become models to develop *madhhab qawli*. The contextual *fiqh* approach can also work by expanding the *manhaji* perspective, through the application of *usûl al-fiqh* and *fiqh* norms, as well as, through the integration of the *'illat* (reasoning) and the benefit (*hikmah*) of laws.

* * * * *

Commentary   Further factors in the contextual approach are the recognition that the Qur'an was revealed incrementally and in response to particular issues confronting the

Prophet. Some Muslims therefore believe that it is important to interpret the verses of the Qur'an in the context in which they were revealed.

The contextual approach is not the only approach that emphasizes the spirit rather than the letter of sharia sources. An influential Yemeni/Egyptian scholar, Yusuf al-Qaradawi, is often cited for his innovative views on the role of *fiqh*. Anwar Ibrahim, former deputy prime minister of Malaysia, places al-Qaradawi in the line of Abu Ishaq Ibrahim al-Shatibi (from Andalusia, d. 1388 CE). This great jurist formulated the theory of *maqasid al-shari'ah* six centuries ago but 'has been relegated to obscurity'.

Extract 11-8: Anwar Ibrahim

Anwar Ibrahim (1996), 'Islam in Southeast Asia' [in English], pp. 111–25 in *The Asian Renaissance*, Times Books International, Singapore. Extract: p. 119.

[…] In essence, his [al-Shatibi's] jurisprudence entails attaching priority to the promotion of the humanitarian and compassionate values of Islam which are of universal and perpetual significance, as opposed to the literalism and legalism of mainstream Islamic jurisprudence. The latter effectively portrays Islam as a static religion which has lost its relevance. Ulema such as Muhammad ibn Ashur, Sheikh Yusuf al-Qaradhawi and the late Sheikh Muhammad al-Ghazali, however, have taken the lead in expounding al-Shatibi's approach from a background of traditional Islamic scholarship. Sheikh al-Qaradhawi particularly is an advocate of the *fiqh al-awlawiyyat*, the understanding of priorities, as a juristic basis for social policies. Under this approach, which seems to be gaining acceptance among the mainstream ulema of Southeast Asia, the application of the *hudud*, fixed punishments prescribed by the Quran and the Traditions of the Prophet of Islam for certain offences, is not necessarily among the top priorities of contemporary Muslim societies.

* * * * *

Commentary The growth of literalist interpretations of the Qur'an and Sunnah motivated a group of Muslim NGOs to propose *maqasid al-shari'ah* as an alternative method to understand the teachings of Islam. The group works under the name Kajian Islam dan Keadilan Jender (KIKJ, Studies in Islam and Gender Justice). By using the principle of 'for the public benefit' or 'for the welfare of all' (*maslahat*), it aims to approach sharia holistically and create *fiqh* that will provide equality, justice and humanitarianism. Of interest is the fact that many individual members of KIKJ are active within NU, the Muslim organization often associated with rather traditional views and practices. The efforts of some of NU's younger generation to seek more liberal interpretations of traditional *fiqh* positions reveal the diversity of attitudes that exist within NU. The KIKJ found the approach of al-Qaradawi to be most helpful in achieving its aims.

Yusuf al-Qaradawi, mentioned in extract 11-8 and its commentary, is increasingly influential in Indonesian and Malaysian Islamic thinking. Born in Egypt in 1926, educated at al-Azhar University and a former member of the Muslim Brotherhood, he has lived and worked in Qatar since the 1960s. His approach has been summarized thus: 'al-Qaradawi argues for a balanced implementation of Islamic law, meaning both the balance between new and established views as well as between different doctrines' (Gräf 2005: 47). His popularity in Southeast Asia may be ascribed to his dedication to seeking 'the middle way' (*minhaj al-wasatiyya*), combined with the accessibility of his thought through his TV appearances on al-Jazeera, the many translations of his works available in Indonesian, and his own internet site <http://www.qaradawi.net> (Gräf 2005: 47). The following extract, an analysis by Zuhairi Miswari, provides an example of al-Qaradawi's view that jurisprudence must be re-invigorated to enable sharia to be applied in contemporary societies.

Extract 11-9: KIKJ on Yusuf al-Qaradawi

Zuhairi Miswari (ed.) (2003), *Dari Syariat menuju Maqashid Syariat: Fundamentalisme, Seksualitas dan Kesehatan Reproduksi* [From Sharia to the Principles of Sharia: Fundamentalism, Sexuality and Reproductive Health], Ford Foundation and Kajian Islam dan Keadilan Jender, Jakarta. Extract: pp. 56–7.

[…] Dr Yusuf al-Qaradhawi perceives the sterility of jurisprudence to be indicated by the systematization of jurisprudence, which starts with discussion of worship. He states that such characteristics of jurisprudence have sterilized jurisprudence's viewpoint on social, political and economic problems.

As such, al-Qaradhawi has proposed alternative thinking to reform jurisprudence into reality jurisprudence (*fiqh al-waqi'*) and priority jurisprudence (*fiqh al-awlawiyat*), namely jurisprudence that can become a new light for problems of humanity that emerge in the midst of society. In this context, it is hoped that sharia will no longer be solely of vertical character, only analysing problems of the relation between mortals and God, but will try to cut a path through problems of humanity. Jurisprudence is thus encouraged to touch upon issues of gender equality (*fiqh al-mar'ah*), state administration (*fiqh al-dawlah*), citizenship (*fiqh al-muwathanah*) and so forth. In this sense it is increasingly apparent that the dynamization of jurisprudence is an initial step to deconstruct sharia and its static, exclusive and discriminative face to become a dynamic, inclusive and egalitarian sharia.

11.4   THE LETTER OF THE LAW

Commentary   In late 2001, a survey of almost 2,000 Indonesian Muslims from 16 different provinces was carried out to establish their views on how Islam affected their lives and their views on the role of Islam in public life (*Tempo*, 30 December 2001: 44–51). The results suggested that there are more practising than non-practising Muslims in contemporary Indonesia. For example, only 4.4 per cent of those interviewed said they rarely or never fasted during Ramadan and only 9 per cent said they rarely or never prayed five times a day.

When asked whether the state should implement sharia, 61.4 per cent said they believed the state had a duty to do this for Muslims. However, only 42 per cent said they supported *hudud* punishments such as stoning for illicit sexual intercourse and only 29 per cent said they agreed with amputation for theft. Thus many respondents seemed to distinguish between sharia as an essential part of their understanding of Islam and the total implementation of all its provisions.

In contrast to the position of the majority of *Tempo* respondents, extract 11-10 argues for complete implementation of all aspects of sharia, which is referred to as *Islam kaffah* ('perfect' or 'complete' Islam). It is believed this can be achieved through following the letter of the law, referred to also as 'literalist' or 'scripturalist' Islam.

A number of activist Muslim organizations that appeared in Indonesia after the fall of the New Order regime include the full implementation of sharia as one of their primary goals. One of them is Hizbut Tahrir Indonesia (HTI, Liberation Party of Indonesia). In a major position paper entitled 'Save Indonesia with Sharia', Muhammad Ismail Yusanto,[31] a leading spokesperson for HTI, begins with the passionate statement that Indonesia is weeping because its rich natural resources have been squandered by greedy local entrepreneurs and plundered by foreign companies. This situation was exacerbated by the economic crisis of 1997–98, he argues, with the result that millions of Indonesians live in poverty, are unable to gain an education and have been driven to crime. The following extract from his paper (like extract 11-11 below) argues that only the full implementation of sharia can improve life for Indonesians.

Extract 11-10: Muhammad Ismail Yusanto

Muhammad Ismail Yusanto (2003), 'Selamatkan Indonesia dengan Syariat' [Save Indonesia with Sharia], pp. 137–71 in Burhanuddin (ed.), *Syariat Islam: Pandangan Muslim Liberal* [Sharia: Liberal Islam Views], Jaringan Islam Liberal and the Asia Foundation, Jakarta. Extract: pp. 168–71.

ATTITUDE TO ISLAMIC LAW

Facing calls for the implementation of Islamic law, it is recognized that not all Muslims in Indonesia are supportive. There are those who do not care, and there are also those who in fact oppose it. For various reasons, this antagonistic group essentially disagree with Islamic law being implemented in Indonesia. According to them, Islamic law is only for Muslims and even then it can only be applied in a homogeneous society in which all the people are Muslim. They also reason that if Islamic law were implemented, non-Muslims would be oppressed. And in addition, in their opinion the implementation of Islamic law would bring about regression in society. Modernization would cease and we would return to living as a backward society.

An apathetic, let alone hostile, attitude to calls for the implementation of Islamic law is surely not appropriate for a Muslim to display. All arguments put forward by people who are in opposition are thoroughly off the mark. Islamic law was conferred not only for Muslims but for all humankind. In actual fact, under Islamic law, freedom of religion and worship for non-Muslims will be guaranteed. Not only that: their lives, possessions and dignity will also be protected. In short, Islamic law will bring good to all human beings who live under its protection. Islamic law also poses no obstacle whatsoever to modernization. In actuality under Islamic law, a modern, civilized society will be created as explained above.

---

31   Section 12.1.10 provides further details concerning Muhammad Ismail Yusanto.

So, there is no reason whatsoever for opposing Islamic law. Let alone for this to be done by a Muslim. Someone who claims to be a Muslim must be a complete Muslim (*kaaffah*): *'O people of faith, enter into Islam fully and follow not in the footsteps of Satan, for truly Satan is a real enemy for you' (al-Baqarah: 208).*[32]

He must also be aware that his faith in Almighty God doesn't just mean believing in the existence of God, but must be accompanied by submission to all His decrees. Almighty God is All-Knowing and All-Just. God is the essence of that which is All-Knowing of right and wrong, what is good and what is not good, what reaps benefits and what brings harm. God's laws are eternal and always appropriate for application in every time and place. It was God who created all of humankind, so He is the one who is All-Knowing about human nature and how to bring order to the life of humankind as individuals and as a society. In other words, humankind's ties with Islamic law are a consequence of faith in Almighty God. So it is appropriate to question the 'Muslimness' of those who reject Islamic law. *'In the name of God, they in truth are without faith who make you a judge in a case they would argue, and then not feel burdened by the decision you issue, and accept it in its entirety' (An-Nisa': 65).*[33]

The attitude that ought be shown by a Muslim towards Islamic law is submission, as stated in the chapter of An-Nuur, verse 51: *'Verily the words of those who have faith, if they are called to God or His Prophet that the Prophet might pass judgement among them, are the words, "We hear and we obey". They are the lucky ones'.*[34]

So it is entirely inappropriate for Muslim men and women, when God and His Prophet have imposed Islamic law as the code [of law], to toss aside Islamic law and look for other regulations. *'And it is not appropriate for Muslim men and women, once God and His Prophet have imposed a stipulation, to make (other) choices about their affairs. And whomsoever betrays God and His Prophet has strayed and is completely lost' (al-Ahzab: 36).*[35]

With this submission, a good Muslim will implement all Islamic laws with utmost sincerity, as God commanded: *'Whatever the Prophet gives unto you, accept. Whatever is forbidden you, abandon. Put your faith in God. Verily God's judgement is very harsh' (al-Hasyr: 7).*[36]

---

32 'You who believe, enter wholeheartedly into submission to God and do not follow in Satan's footsteps, for he is your sworn enemy' (Q2: 208, Haleem).

33 'By your Lord, they will not be true believers until they let you decide between them in all matters of dispute, and find no resistance in their souls to your decisions, accepting them totally' (Q4: 65, Haleem).

34 'When the true believers are summoned to God and His Messenger in order for him to judge between them, they say, "We hear and we obey". These are the ones who will prosper' (Q24: 51, Haleem).

35 'When God and His Messenger have decided on a matter that concerns them, it is not fitting for any believing man or woman to claim freedom of choice in that matter: whoever disobeys God and His Messenger is far astray' (Q33: 36, Haleem).

36 'Whatever gains God has turned over to His Messenger from the inhabitants of the villages belong to God, the Messenger, kinsfolk, orphans, the needy, the traveller in need – this is so that they do not just circulate among those of you who are rich – so accept whatever the Messenger gives you, and abstain from whatever he forbids you. Be mindful of God: God is severe in punishment' (Q59: 7, Haleem).

As for those who reject Islamic law, are they still fit to breathe the oxygen created by God, consume God's blessings, live on God's earth, and live with the spark of life given to them by God? So there is absolutely no reason to reject Islamic law.

Meanwhile, without Islamic law can we hope for the emergence of a better structuring of life? Or can we hope to gain the benefits from Islam that [it is] believed will come and bring compassion? If not, why are we still happy to live for so long without Islamic law as we do now? On the one hand we complain that life is getting harder and more unsafe, the prices of everything are rising, immorality is rampant, pornography is easy to find, teenagers are becoming increasingly brutal, bureaucrats are increasingly not to be relied on, but on the other hand why do we just ignore Islamic law, which we believe must surely be able to solve all our problems and regulate the life of society properly? Why is it stored away like some old antique, and not applied in real life? It is the same as someone getting really cranky when they are ill, but then they just stare at the medicine in their hand. How will they ever be cured?

And God alone knows the truth.

* * * * *

Commentary The Malaysian political party PAS defines itself as 'an Islamic Political party based on the Holy *Qur'an* and *Hadith* of The Prophet Muhammad' (Nasharudin 2001: 2; see also colour plate 14). PAS is the main rival to the United Malays National Organisation (UMNO), the largest party in Malaysia's ruling Barisan Nasional (formerly Alliance) coalition. Despite its longstanding dominance in the polls, UMNO's share of the vote has been declining steadily since PAS's emergence onto the political scene in the 1990 general elections. The following extract is taken from an official PAS statement of its ideology. The author, Nasharudin Mat Isa (1962–), was secretary general of PAS when he compiled the document. In June 2005 he was elected deputy president of the party.

Extract 11-11: Parti Islam Se Malaysia (PAS)

Nasharudin Mat Isa (2001), *The Islamic Party of Malaysia (PAS): Ideology, Policy, Struggle and Vision towards the New Millennium* [in English], The Islamic Party of Malaysia, Kuala Lumpur. Extract: pp. 14–16.

The struggle to implement *Syari'ah* Law if PAS wins the [federal] Election has always been the main target ever since the formation of PAS. Due to that, PAS struggled to explain and elaborate the contents of the *Qur'an* and *Hadith* to the people towards the formation of the Islamic State. [p. 14] [...]

[The constituents of the state in Medina in the time of the Prophet Muhammad are then described.]

This clearly shows that the society that was united by the Prophet (PBUH)[37] in Madinah [Medina] during that time was **plural, multi-racial and heterogeneous in nature**. And as stated in history, all of them agreed to be ruled under the Prophet

---

37 PBUH: peace be upon him.

based on the *Syari'ah*, Law of the Muslims. Is it not identical in nature that Malaysia is also [a] plural, multi-racial and heterogeneous society just like it was in Madinah 1400 years ago? And why all the fuss that '*Syari'ah* Law could not be implemented in Malaysia!' Therefore PAS continues in its struggle to educate the people of Malaysia – Muslims as well as non Muslims – to understand the very basic teachings of Islam: the systems of '*Aqidah* (faith), '*Ibadah* (worship), *Munakahat* (family) and *Mu'amalat* (social, economic and political system). [...]

PAS did try to propose the *Hudud* Laws, as a first part of the *Syari'ah* Law to be implemented in Kelantan. After it was passed by the State Assembly, and after running through a lot of problems, it went to a deadlock and was opposed strongly by the Federal Government. Terengganu [a state on the east coast of peninsular Malaysia] now plans to institute parts of the Islamic Laws in its administration such as the principles of *al-Hisbah* (Ombudsman).

Due to the latest development in Malaysia considering that PAS managed to rule two of the 14 States, perhaps it is timely that PAS launch a widespread campaign to explain its Islamic policy to the people. The people has [*sic*] been confused by UMNO and its coalition. Inevitably, it is most important for PAS to explain to two of the States [Kelantan and Terengganu], that many aspects of the *Syari'ah* Laws will actually protect its citizens from various malpractice of its politicians as compared to the present Civil Laws.

PAS's struggle shall not cease here. We understood very well that the struggle to establish Allah's *Syari'ah* on Earth, as started by the early Prophets until Prophet Muhammad (PBUH)[,] is a very long and winding journey, as warned by God Himself:–

> '*If there had been immediate gain (in sight), and the journey is easy, they would (all) without doubt have followed you, but the distance was long (and weighed) on them. They would indeed swear by Allah: "If we only could, we should certainly have come out with you". They would destroy their own souls; for Allah does know that they are certainly lying*'.[38]

We will continue to pursue our aims and objectives within our reach to realize our ultimate goal – the Islamic State based on the *Qur'an* and *Hadith*. If we fail or could not be able to realize this goal now during our times, then our children, grandchildren, great grandchildren and so forth will proceed [with] this struggle. The struggle will definitely continue based on the same ideology, and perhaps with certain adjustments in the policy, but inevitably the very same struggle for the same objectives and goal as clarified clearly in the *Qur'an*:–

> '*And fight on them until there is no more tumult or oppression and there prevails justice and faith in Allah ...*'.[39] [pp. 15–16]

---

38   'They would certainly have followed you [Prophet] if the benefit was within sight and the journey short, but the distance seemed too great for them. They will swear by God, "If we could, we certainly would go out [to battle] with you", but they ruin themselves, for God knows that they are lying' (Q9: 42, Haleem).

39   '[Believers], fight them until there is no more persecution, and [your] worship is devoted to God alone: if they desist, then God sees all that they do' (Q8: 39, Haleem).

11.5 SECULAR LAWS HAVE FAILED

Commentary The rise in corruption, greater sexual freedom, 'immodest' forms of dress fostered by Western fashion trends, drug addiction and a perceived increase in serious crime have led some Muslim groups in Southeast Asian nations to claim that the state has failed to protect its citizens from physical and moral danger. In their view, only full implementation of sharia laws can restore order to society and well-being to its citizens.

A second extract[40] from the 'Save Indonesia with Sharia' paper of Ismail Yusanto presents the views of the Indonesian party HTI.

Extract 11-12: Muhammad Ismail Yusanto

Muhammad Ismail Yusanto (2003), 'Selamatkan Indonesia dengan Syariat' [Save Indonesia with Sharia], pp. 137–71 in Burhanuddin (ed.), *Syariat Islam: Pandangan Muslim Liberal* [Sharia: Liberal Islam Views], Jaringan Islam Liberal and the Asia Foundation, Jakarta. Extract: pp. 146, 167–8.

It is clear that following the failure of capitalist and socialist ideologies to fulfil expectations, it is sharia, and only sharia, that has the answer to the range of problems that ensnare this country, whether they be economic, political, socio-cultural or concerning education. The implementation of sharia will enable Indonesian society, the majority of which is Muslim, to be more in touch with the spirit of Islam as a manifestation of life's purpose, that is, the worship of God. [p. 146] [...]

Islam through sharia will definitely not halt modernization but rather place it firmly in a framework of service to God. If modernization is understood as the development of the civil sphere (*madaniah*), the material benefits of technology that can improve the quality, security, enjoyment and ease of human life, in the fields of communication, transportation, production, health, education, housing, food, clothing and so on, then Islam certainly has no objections. In other words, human beings may make use of all the results of developments in science and technology. However, all patterns of life, whether at the personal, family or social level, must stay firmly on the sharia path. This is not what we see with Western lifestyles, where modernization has degraded human beings by permitting what is forbidden by God and forbidding what He has permitted. The West has misinterpreted modernization. Is it modern for women, who should be respected, to be treated as sex objects, sashaying along half-naked, modelling designer clothes while being watched by countless eyes and media cameras, their bodies displayed in public just for the sake of money? Is it also modern for men and women to have sexual relations without marriage, or same-sex marriage? How is that different from animals? In fact animals are better, because so far there is no evidence that homosexuality or lesbianism is found in the animal world even among the most filthy. Is it modern to allow the economic system to develop uncontrolled, where capitalists are like leeches sucking human blood, or reaping profits without lifting a finger because of the practice of usury?

---

40 The first is extract 11-10.

Sharia offers a system for human life, totally fulfilling people's spiritual and physical needs. Through sharia, human beings are guided to make what is *halal* (permitted) and *haram* (forbidden) their yardstick for behaviour. As a result, in the midst of modernity, thanks to technological progress, human beings can live in an orderly way, respecting sacred values, safeguarding the dignity of man as ordained by God, established through complete service to Him. [pp. 167–8]

* * * * *

Commentary   The draft sharia code of Majelis Mujahidin Indonesia (MMI, Council of Indonesian Mujahideen), whose leader (*amir*) is Abu Bakar Ba'ashir, emphasizes that only sharia can restore order to the chaos reigning in Indonesian society. The drafters of the MMI code also offer it as a reform to the existing penal code of the Republic of Indonesia, which they see as having the two deficiencies of being (a) colonial[41] and (b) not within the spirit of *reformasi*. See extract 11-20 for a comparison of the MMI and Kelantan codes.

Extract 11-13: The MMI Code

Central Headquarters of the Majelis Mujahidin (2002), 'Proposal for a Criminal Code for the Republic of Indonesia Adjusted to Accord with the Sharia of Islam' [in English], Yogyakarta, 1 July. [Translation of 'Usulan Undang-Undang Hukum Pidana Republik Indonesia Disesuaikan dengan Syari'ah Islam'.]

INTRODUCTION

Bismillah … ['In the name of God', written in Arabic script]

In the effort to bring about the supremacy of law and bring order to the community social life of the people of Indonesia, there are many things that have been attempted by various groups that feel they have an interest in this matter; however, they have not shown any meaningful improvements thus far. What actually happened has in fact been the opposite of what was hoped for.

The secular system of laws and legislation that has been applied by the government has in fact caused there to be a multiplicative increase in criminality, disharmony of life, moral decadence and the decay of human values. A further consequence, which has gone hand in hand with the increasing weakness of the law enforcement authorities, is the occurrence of brutality and anarchy by the community in punishing those who commit criminal acts. This shows among other things that secular law is not capable of providing shelter and protection, peace, justice and a sense of security to the community, because the edifice of the secular legal system is based only on empirical rationality, which can never stretch to reach the psychic aspect of humanity that is so very wide and complex.

---

41   The Kitab Undang-Undang Hukum Pidana (KUHP, Criminal Code) is essentially the colonial penal code promulgated by the colonial government of the Netherlands East Indies.

Therefore, as long as the legislation that orders the life of the community is not based on law that is in harmony with the primordial essence of man and humanity, that legislation will damage the equilibrium of human life, because it will be unable to fulfil the basic demands of human life itself. And there is no law whatsoever in this world that is capable of fulfilling this matter, except if man submits to the law of Allah and His Prophet totally and comprehensively.

As a religion that is universal in nature and *rahmatan lil alamin* [a mercy for all the worlds],[42] the sharia of Islam does not only speak about matters of law and punishment; on the contrary, it also functions to guide, shelter and protect, and guarantee the safety, security and prosperity of mankind, as individuals, as a community, as a nation and as a state. The sharia of Islam guarantees and gives the protection of law, at the very least, to five fundamental needs of human life.

First, it guarantees the freedom of human beings to have religion (*hifdzud din*). Second, it protects the faculty of reason from influences that damage its function in life (*hifdzul 'aql*). Third, it guarantees purity of descent, so that there can be no doubts about the familial ties between a person and their parents (*hifdzun nasl*). Fourth, it shelters and guarantees the safety of human life, both as an individual and as a species (*hifdzun nafs*). And fifth, it guarantees and protects the property rights of human beings, both as personal rights and as communal rights (*hifdzul mal*).

The firm and clear guarantees of sharia such as those enumerated above can never be matched by secular laws. With sharia guarantees such as those, man has been given a basic reference to make regulations and laws that are necessary if there is no *nash* [clear stipulation] in the Qur'an and the Sunnah, with his own *ijtihad* [independent reasoning], as long as they continue to refer to the principles above. This means that Islam does not nullify man's initiative in making laws and regulations that are necessary on the basis of the situation and conditions of his times, as long as they are intended to guarantee the above five basic principles.

On the basis of the reasons above, the institution of Majelis Mujahidin, which has the objective of upholding the sharia of Islam in the lives of individuals, families, the community and the state, has prepared a Criminal Code adjusted to accord with the sharia of Islam, as a contribution to the reform of the Criminal Code [*KUHP*] that is the colonial legacy of the Dutch and has become outdated and no longer in line with the spirit of *reformasi*, yet strangely continues until now to have its applicability in Indonesia maintained.

May Allah send down His grace on the publishing of this Criminal Code adjusted to accord with the sharia of Islam, so that it may bring benefits and make a contribution to the effort to bring about justice and prosperity for all people. Amen, O Answerer of Those Who Ask.

Jogjakarta, 20 Rabi'ul Akhir 1423 H
1 July 2002 M[43]

* * * * *

---

42   This set of square brackets and all square brackets that follow in this extract are in the original.

43   'M' is the Indonesian equivalent of 'AD'.

Commentary   In the southern Philippines, the late Salamat Hashim (1942–2003), founder and chair of the Moro Islamic Liberation Front (MILF), described the success of Islamic courts in regions under MILF control. In his view they were necessary because state-sponsored laws were not effective. This is an extract from an interview he gave in December 1986.

Extract 11-14: Salamat Hashim

Salamat Hashim (2002), *Referendum: Peaceful, Civilized, Diplomatic and Democratic Means of Solving the Mindanao Conflict* [in English], Agency for Youth Affairs–MILF, Camp Abubakre As-Siddique, Mindanao. Extract: p. 36.

[…] Also, presently we have our own courts. Even Muslim employees working in government go to our courts. For example, someone loses a carabao [buffalo]. If he complains to the government, nothing will happen. But if he complains to the MILF authorities, they will try their best to find who took the carabao. As a matter of fact, our problem now is that we have many people in our prisons, and we do not have enough food to feed them. So you see, our Christian neighbors should not be apprehensive about Islamic courts. We already have Islamic courts, and we have not cut off the hands of the people until now.

* * * * *

Commentary   As seen in extract 11-14, Salamat Hashim specifically states that when Islamic courts pass sentence on local Muslims in Mindanao, judges use incarceration rather than physical punishments for crimes. A more recent case in Indonesia has created heated debate about the use of extreme forms of physical punishment following the literal interpretation of Islamic laws concerning rape and unlawful sexual intercourse.

In Ambon in May 2001, during the inter-religious violence occurring in Maluku, a member of the paramilitary group Laskar Jihad (Holy War Fighters) who had come to Ambon to 'protect' the local Muslim population was sentenced to death by stoning (*rajam*) for the rape of a 13-year-old Ambonese girl. The sentence was passed by the commander of Laskar Jihad, Ja'far Umar Thalib, after an investigation which he led and during which the accused (known as both Abdullah and Abdurrahim) repeatedly confessed to his crime. The offender embraced the penalty as a way of atoning for his sin. In his view, punishment in this world was preferable to eternal punishment in the next.

Before implementing the sentence, Ja'far Umar Thalib addressed his followers to explain his decision. In his speech he drew a link between obedience to God's law and God's help in winning the holy war in Maluku.

Extract 11-15: Rajam: Ja'far Umar Thalib's Position

Ja'far Umar Thalib (2001), 'Ceramah Panglima Laskar Jihad Ahlus Sunnah wal Jamaah[44] dalam Pelaksanaan Hukuman Rajam di Ambon Selasa, 27 Maret 2001'

---

44   Laskar Jihad Ahlus Sunnah wal Jamaah is the full official name of the organization, but it is more commonly referred to simply as 'Laskar Jihad'.

[The Address of the Commander of Laskar Jihad when Implementing the Sentence of Death by Stoning in Ambon, Tuesday 27 March 2001], Dewan Pimpinan Pusat Forum Komunikasi Ahlus Sunnah wal Jamaah [Central Leadership Council of the Communication Forum of Ahlus Sunnah wal Jamaah], <Laskarjihad.or.id>, dated 30 March 2001, accessed 13 September 2004.

Fellow Muslims whom I love and honour, today we will implement God's law, that is, *rajam*, for our brother Abdullah who is married with children and a member of Laskar Jihad Ahlus Sunnah wal Jamaah.

My fellow Muslim brothers, Almighty God has commanded us to uphold this law and, in truth, this law should be carried out by a Muslim government.

But regrettably the government of Indonesia is led by a head of state who is an apostate and infidel who belittles and humiliates Islamic law and even belittles and humiliates Muslims.

Similarly, the holy war in Maluku to defend the Muslims there should have been the responsibility of a Muslim government. But this holy war too was belittled and ignored by the Indonesian government, especially by its head of state, so the Muslims had to take responsibility for defending themselves from the attacks of infidels on them.

The issue of the *rajam* punishment has been discussed with religious elders, among others Sheikh Muqbil ibn Hadi al Waadi'iy. He explained that in Yemen, which is headed by a Muslim leader who fails to offer the protection of the law to his people, the tribal heads have implemented the law in their own territories. [...]

The Prophet of God, on whom be blessings and peace, stated that when even one Qur'anic law was upheld on God's earth, then all the territories which upheld that law would receive blessings from the heavens for 40 days and 40 nights [...].

[...] Thus we place our trust in Almighty God to carry out this law in the hope of blessings from Almighty God, and this is continuing proof that we are unwavering in our resolve to eliminate all forms of immorality on the face of God's earth.

And there is also the earnest desire by the Muslims to obey God's sharia; and may it be seen thereafter by God as our pure intention to follow his religion; and, on those grounds, may God bring us victory in our holy war.

* * * * *

Commentary The following extract relates to the case discussed in extract 11-15, of the sentencing of a rapist to death by stoning. It is taken from a media interview with Hardi, spokesperson for Laskar Jihad. The case received intense media attention and aroused strong feelings both for and against the literal interpretation of the physical penalties set out in the Qur'an. Some experts argued that these severe penalties were symbolic and intended to deter offenders. Hardi, on behalf of Laskar Jihad, argued that the letter of the law must be upheld. The extract was initially published in *Republika* but has since been reprinted in a book by Adian Husaini that includes many of the press reports on the stoning.

Extract 11-16: **Rajam:** *Laskar Jihad's Position as Recounted by Hardi*

Adian Husaini (2001), 'Rajam Digugat, Jihad Dihambat' [Stoning Challenged, Jihad Obstructed], pp. 3–41 in *Rajam dalam Arus Budaya Syahwat* [Rajam in the Current of the Culture of Lust], CV Pustaka al-Kautsar, Jakarta. [Transcript of an interview with Hardi first published in *Republika* on 10 May 2001.] Extract: pp. 6–7.

Once Laskar Jihad was convinced that *rajam* was the best sentence, they told this to Abdullah [also known as Abdurrahim]. 'We told him about all the virtues of people who undergo *rajam*. Among other things, we told him that all his sins would be forgiven by God and Heaven would be his reward', said Hardi. After this, Abdullah was asked to choose if he wanted this punishment or not.

'If he had refused, we wouldn't have been able to force him', said Hardi. It was left to him as to whether he wanted to be punished now and be free from the tortures of the grave and hell, or whether he would avoid the punishment of *rajam* and suffer torment in the hereafter. 'Praise be to God, he chose to undergo the punishment of *rajam*.'

Abdullah was also given the chance to contact his family and reconsider once more whether or not he would undergo the punishment. 'If he had declined, we would have let it go. The matter would remain between him and God.'

Abdullah chose to undergo *rajam*. He signed an admission of unlawful intercourse. [...] Laskar Jihad promised that it would guarantee the education of his three children (the eldest of whom was four) till they finished.

'We only want to uphold God's law', said Hardi. He [Hardi] believes that, God willing, enforcing this law will make this country blessed with peace by God, particularly Ambon where the sentence of *rajam* was carried out.

* * * * *

Commentary   The sentence described in extracts 11-15 and 11-16, and its execution, became a focus for widespread debate in Indonesia about *hudud* penalties and about who had the authority to implement them. A number of leading experts on Islamic law in Indonesia argued that the offender should have been tried according to state criminal law because Islamic law can only be applied fully in an Islamic state (which Indonesia is not). When Ja'far Umar Thalib, the commander of Laskar Jihad, appeared in court charged with assault and murder, the leader of the defence team, Hartono Mardjono, argued that whereas the police viewed *rajam* as a crime, under Islamic law it was a religious duty and the appropriate penalty for the crime. He further emphasized that the alleged rapist had admitted his crime, had requested the punishment and had submitted willingly; his wife had also agreed to the punishment. Mardjono likened the implementation of *rajam* to the act of circumcision, which can be viewed as assault but is accepted as traditional law and is therefore outside state law (*Gatra*, 8 May 2001).[45]

Ja'far Umar Thalib and his supporters also made the point that he had not decided on the sentence of *rajam* by himself. He had consulted several religious elders in the

---

45   Ja'far Umar Thalib's defence team was successful. He was released from detention and no further charges were laid.

Middle East by phone, most notably Sheikh Muqbil bin Hadi al Waadi'iy in Yemen, who had advised that there must be certainty that the implementation would not cause greater disaster than had already occurred.

The argumentation in support of the implementation of capital punishment by a group of Muslims (rather than by more formal authorities such as a Muslim ruler or judges and sharia experts) is provided in the following extract by Adian Husaini, a prominent advocate of the full implementation of sharia. He also suggests that the perpetrator of the offence could be called a 'sharia hero' for willingly accepting the punishment appropriate to his crime.

Extract 11-17: Rajam: *Adian Husaini's Position*

Adian Husaini (2001), 'Pengantar Penulis' and 'Hukum Rajam dalam Tinjauan Syariat Islam dan Konteks Indonesia' [Author's Introduction, and Sentence of Stoning from the Sharia Perspective in the Indonesian Context], pp. ix–xiv and 83–148 in *Rajam dalam Arus Budaya Syahwat* [Rajam in the Current Culture of Lust], CV Pustaka al-Kautsar, Jakarta. Extract: pp. x–xi, 133–4, 136, 142.

In his book, Ibnu Taimiyah[46] was of the opinion that *hudud* must be carried out by Muslims in whatever situation. [It should be carried out whether] there is a Muslim leader (*khalifah*) who effectively applies Islamic laws, or whether the leadership is fragmented – and there are many Muslim leaders – or the Muslim community is fragmented and spread across various countries and groups. [pp. x–xi] [...]

But, Ibnu Taimiyah added, 'If the ruler does not implement *hudud* or is incapable of implementing it, then the implementation of the *hudud* is no longer entrusted to him, with the note that it can be carried out without the ruler ... **And if the *hudud* can only be implemented by a group in society, and not by the ruler, then it is obligatory (*wajib*) for the *hudud* to be implemented, if in its implementation it does not occasion danger or have a negative impact that is worse than not implementing the aforementioned *hudud*. This issue is part of doing good and avoiding evil (*amar ma'ruf nahi munkar*).** [pp. 133–4] [...]

If Ibnu Taimiyah's opinion is used, then a Muslim community that wants to implement *hudud* in a state that does not apply – or even opposes – implementation of Islamic law, as in Indonesia, needs to be careful and to carry out a scrupulous evaluation. Never let the implementation of *hudud* create greater harm for the Muslim community. It is this 'harm' which must be carefully evaluated. [p. 136] [...]

Everyone, especially the government of the Repubic of Indonesia, would do well to learn from the case of Abdurrahim [Abdullah; see extracts 11-15 and 11-16], and bestow the honour of 'upholder of the law' on him. Unlike those in positions of power, he gave his life willingly, because he feared the torments of God on the Last Day. Compare him with those in power who pile up sins daily – because they let their

---

46   Famous jurist of the Hanbali school of law, 1263–1328 CE, who worked in Damascus and Cairo. His teachings, which incline to literal interpretation of texts, have been followed by groups such as the Wahhabis (a Saudi-based religious and social reform movement) and, more recently, some Islamist groups.

people die, of starvation and oppression – and continue to hold onto their positions of power, while each day trumpeting their sacrifice for the people and the nation. Because of that, very ironically and strangely, the Muslims who were just carrying out their religious duty were accused of committing the murder of Abdurrahim. [p. 142]

* * * * *

> ***Commentary*** Farish Noor, a Malaysian political scientist and Muslim intellectual, is also a human rights activist who monitors 'repressive' interpretations of Islam in Malaysia. He has published a major history of PAS, which supports the implementation of sharia in Malaysia and has formulated codes of sharia law for the states of Kelantan and Terengganu. In the following extract he explains why some Malaysians support the use of *hudud* laws.

Extract 11-18: Farish A. Noor

Farish A. Noor (2002), 'Why Hudud? (Why Not?)' [in English], pp. 313–18 in *The Other Malaysia*, Silverfishbooks, Kuala Lumpur. Extract: pp. 317–18.

To understand the appeal of PAS's *Hudud* proposals today, one would therefore have to look at the corresponding failure of its counterpart, the civil legal system. PAS has always called for the creation of an Islamic State and the introduction of *Shariah* law in the country. (Although the party's own understanding of what such an Islamic State would look like has changed over the years, from the time of Dr. Burhanuddin al-Helmy to Asri Muda to Yusof Rawa,[47] and then on to the present generation of *Ulama* leaders.) But for the first four decades of its history, PAS made little gains as far as the *Shariah* issue itself was concerned. It was only from the 1990s onwards that PAS has made *Shariah* its main weapon against the UMNO-led Government, and with some success.

That this shift took place at a time when Malaysians were exposed to a string of major corporate and political scandals could not be a simple coincidence: as the scandals grew in scale as well as number, the public's faith in the civil legal system was tested and pushed to the limit as more and more corporate misdemeanours were brushed under the carpet or kept under wraps. The Constitutional crisis of 1982–3, the UMNO legal battle of 1987, the second Constitutional crisis of 1991–93, the financial crisis of 1997 and the Anwar Ibrahim crisis of 1998[48] all contributed to the steady erosion of public confidence in not only the ruling coalition, but also the institutions of State such as the police, legislature and judiciary.

---

47   Three consecutive presidents of PAS: Burhanuddin al-Helmy (1956–69), Asri Muda (1969–82) and Yusof Rawa (1982–89).

48   Anwar Ibrahim was dismissed as deputy prime minister, then arrested in September 1998 on charges of sodomy and corruption. The conduct of his trials attracted international and some national criticism and resulted in concurrent sentences of 15 years. After Mahathir retired as prime minister, the Federal Court upheld an appeal by Anwar and reversed his conviction after he had served six years in jail. He was released in 2004.

Faced with such stark realities, it is hardly a surprise if so many among the younger generation of Malay-Muslims today have given up on the secular developmental model. Though this does not pretend to be an exhaustive analysis, one can tentatively conclude that one of the main reasons *Shariah* and *Hudud* have become so popular among many Malay-Muslims is the failure of the secular option itself. The solution to the 'problem' (if it merits being described as such) is to restore the integrity and credibility of the civil legal apparatus itself. Rather than demonising PAS's *Shariah* project and engaging in an endless debate about the religious credentials of 'PAS's *Hudud*' or 'UMNO's *Hudud*', it would be simpler to reform the civil legal system in the country so that it once again does what it is meant to do: handing out justice in an open, fair and consistent manner according to the fundamental principles of the Malaysian Constitution.

11.6   SHARIA AS A SYMBOL OF ISLAMIST IDEOLOGIES

Commentary   The restricted nature of state-sponsored Islamic laws and their bureaucratization by agencies of the modern nation-state is rejected by Muslims who believe that sharia must not be compromised by secular considerations, such as those outlined by the drafters of the KHI (see extract 11-2). In their view the nation-state is only acceptable to the extent that it promotes and implements the Divine Will and this can be achieved only through the full implementation of sharia. Alternatives to the state-sponsored forms of sharia have been formulated during the past several decades in Southeast Asia and their shared characteristic is the purpose of reasserting the primacy of Revelation as the basis for the public law (constitution, crime, punishment) in the nation-state. The 'truth', it is argued, is in the place and time of the Prophet Muhammad and his close associates who outlived him, and the Qu'ran and Sunnah must constitute the basic law for all aspects of life, including public life. From these fundamental sources are taken the rules and prescriptions for all aspects of human life because they are God-given and so *must* be true for all places and all times. Put like this, faith will triumph, must triumph. It is a huge act of belief but also a political act because religious authority is directly challenging the right of the nation-state to determine legislation.

We have chosen two texts from Malaysia and two from Indonesia as examples of contemporary attempts to draft sharia codes to stand as symbols of the primacy of Islam in all spheres of life. Of particular interest in the Malaysian cases (extracts 11-19 and 11-22) is the fact that they are derived from and supported by the political party PAS, which stands openly in opposition to Malaysia's ruling coalition, Barisan Nasional.

Extract 11-20 is taken from the draft criminal code of MMI; this code has clear links with the Syariah Criminal Code of Kelantan, Malaysia (extract 11-19). MMI was one of a number of Islamist groups to emerge following the downfall of the authoritarian Soeharto regime. The lifting of restrictions on freedom of speech and association allowed long-suppressed Islamist activists to form new organizations and promote their agendas, many of which emphasized the necessity of comprehensive implementation of sharia law. MMI was established as an umbrella organization for a wide range of these pro-sharia groups (Fealy 2004: 113–14).

Extract 11-23 is taken from a draft code from South Sulawesi. It was submitted to the provincial parliament of South Sulawesi for implementation in 2001 (Salim

Table 11.2　Kelantan Sharia Criminal Code 1993

Part	Subject	Punishment
Preliminary (clauses 1–3)	Definitions and categories of offences	
Part I: *Hudud* Offences (clauses 4–23)	Theft, robbery, unlawful sex, false accusations of unlawful sex, consumption of alcohol, apostasy	Caning, amputation, stoning, death, imprisonment
Part II: *Qisas* (clauses 24–38)	Forms of killing, assault and injury	Compensation to be paid as diya (calculated as one diya = 4.450 gm of gold)
Part III: Evidence (clauses 39–47)	Rules of evidence (largely concerning sexual misconduct) follow classical *fiqh* rules	Not applicable
Part IV: How Punishment Is Carried Out (clauses 48–55)	Descriptions of punishments with reference to caning and amputation	The schedule only describes canes and caning
Part V: General Provisions (clauses 56–62)	General provisions concerning establishment of sharia courts and appeal court	Not applicable
Part VI: Court (clauses 63–72)		

Source: Ismail (1995: 105–8).

2003: 224) but it has not yet been officially implemented. It is an interesting example of a 'local' code, but it is specifically focused on the whole province of South Sulawesi rather than the lower district level. Like the district codes (see section 11.8), however, it claims to be inspired by local culture as well as sharia.

Each code must answer two questions. First, in returning to the sources of Islam, what exactly is being selected?[49] Second, how are the selections supposed to make the Muslim populations 'more Islamic'?

11.6.1　The Malaysian Kelantan Code and the Indonesian MMI Code

Commentary　The government of Kelantan, a state on the northeast coast of peninsular Malaysia, drafted a code with the avowed aim of implementing Qur'anic imperatives. The contents of the code are wholly about punishment for offences 'against Islam'.

49　The Southeast Asian sharia literature is based on the idea of selection from the classical Arabic adapted to the perceived needs of Islam in its local manifestations. The indigenous texts of Southeast Asia are original in their adaptations. For further details see Hooker (1986) for pre-modern texts; Hooker (1984) for colonial laws; and Hooker (1984, 1999) for post-colonial Muslim laws.

Figure 11.1 Genealogy of Recent Sharia Codes

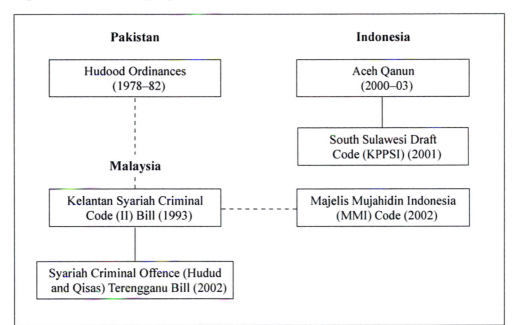

Note: A dashed line indicates a probable but not proven link.

Ismail (1995: 105–42) shows the full code, which is a minimalist document in which the whole of the *fiqh* on crime is condensed into 72 clauses. No criteria are given for this very limited selection. Table 11.2 shows the six parts of the code.[50]

The Kelantan code was among the first of the sharia codes to appear in Southeast Asia, so it stands as a point of reference for subsequent codes. The draft criminal code circulated in 2002 by MMI is particularly close to the Kelantan code and for that reason is presented here alongside the Kelantan material. Figure 11.1 illustrates the relationship between the recent sharia codes of Malaysia and Indonesia.

The phrasing and content of the Kelantan Code and the Pakistan Hudood Ordinances (1978–82)[51] show some similarities. There is little hard evidence that the Kelantan code bill drew directly from the Hudood Ordinances, but the Pakistan material (including judicial decisions) was circulating widely in Malaysia during the 1980s and was the subject of extensive commentary in the two leading Malaysian law journals.[52]

---

50 There are also five schedules that serve as appendices to the code. They provide a glossary and transliteration of Arabic terms, and three tables outlining compensation for injury and the regulations for whipping (such as the dimensions of the cane to be used).

51 Introduced by Zia al-Haq, President of Pakistan (1977–88), as part of his program of 'Islamization', the Hudood Ordinances included the punishments for unlawful sex, false accusations of unlawful sex and theft. Data on the implementation of the ordinances show an extremely high rate of appeals (60 per cent), over half of which were successful. Most appeals involved poor, rural, illiterate women (Kennedy 1988: 307–16) and indicate that the ordinances discriminated against women from the most vulnerable areas of society.

52 These were *Jernal Hukum* [Journal of Law] and *Journal of Malaysian and Comparative Law*; see

In analysing the code and its purpose, it is necessary to understand the socio-political context in which it is presented. The state government of Kelantan is dominated by PAS, the political ideology of which is to defend and promote Islam and Islamic values. Although passed by the Kelantan legislature, the code cannot be implemented as law, because under the Malaysian constitution crimes and punishments are reserved for federal authority. A constitutional amendment would be required for the code to be implemented. PAS politicians were and are well aware that there has been no such constitutional amendment. Nevertheless, the existence of the code is important as a symbol of PAS's commitment to implementing Islamic values through sharia law. The code also allows PAS to claim it is a 'more Islamic' political party than its opponents.

The genesis of the Indonesian MMI code was a mass meeting in Yogyakarta in August 2000 attended by more than 1,500 Muslims from all over Indonesia (Feillard 2005). Outcomes from the meeting were the decision to establish and actively promote the implementation of sharia in Indonesia because this was God's mandate.[53] It was emphasized that non-Muslims would not be affected by sharia, which would apply only to Muslims (Awwas 2001: 263–70).

In 2002, almost two years after MMI's establishment, its proposal for a sharia code was ready. The code is a close copy or summary of the Kelantan material, except for local Malaysian technicalities[54] and the fact that it ignores the English-derived statute form. Apart from that, the substance is the same. The significance of shared features of the Malaysian and Indonesian material in the two codes lies in the interaction that is occurring between PAS leaders and Indonesian figures. In this case, members of MMI looked to the Malaysian material as a basis for their own code.

Extract 11-19 concerns the definition of *zina* (fornication) in the Kelantan Code Bill. Its provisions are shown side by side with extract 11-20, from the Indonesian MMI code, to illustrate the similarities between them.

Extract 11-19: The Kelantan Code

Sisters in Islam (1995), 'Appendix 1: Kelantan Syariah Criminal Code (II) Bill 1993' [in English], pp. 105–42 in *Hudud in Malaysia: The Issues at Stake*, SIS Forum (Malaysia) Berhad, Kuala Lumpur. Extract: p. 114.

Extract 11-20: The MMI Code

Central Headquarters of the Majelis Mujahidin (2002), 'Proposal for a Criminal Code for the Republic of Indonesia Adjusted to Accord with the Sharia of Islam' [in English], Yogyakarta, 1 July. [Translation of 'Usulan Undang-Undang Hukum Pidana Republik Indonesia Disesuaikan dengan Syari'ah Islam'.]

---

especially the articles of the late Professor Ahmad Ibrahim, whose advice was sought by the drafters of the Kelantan Code.

53 In November 2000 a special pledge was promulgated for MMI members which stated that they would strive to implement sharia in their own lives and those of their families as well as in society, state and nation, and that they would extend the struggle to assist Muslims elsewhere in their efforts to implement sharia (Awwas 2001: frontispiece).

54 For example, it omits references to Malaysian legislation contained in the Malaysian code and specific references to technicalities of the courts.

Extract 11-19: The Kelantan Code

Clause 10

Zina

1. Zina is an offence which consists of sexual intercourse between a man and a woman who are not married to each other and such intercourse does not come within the meaning of 'wati syubhah' as defined in subsection (3).

2. where an offender is validly married and has experienced sexual intercourse in such marriage, such offender is called 'mohsan', but where an offender is not married, or is already married but has not experienced sexual intercourse in such marriage, such offender is called 'ghairu mohsan'.

3. Wati syubhah is a sexual intercourse performed by a man with a woman who is not his wife and such intercourse took place –

    a. in doubtful circumstances in which he thought that with [*sic*] the woman whom he had sexual intercourse was his wife, when in fact she was not; or

    b. in doubtful circumstances in which he believed that his marriage to the woman with whom he had sexual intercourse was valid according to Syariah law, when in fact his marriage to her was invalid.

Punishment for zina

Clause 11

1. Where the offender who commits the offence of zina is a mohsan, such offender shall be punished with the punishment of rejam [rajam], being the punishment of stoning the offender with stones of medium size to death.

Extract 11-20: The MMI Code

Article 15

1. *Zina* is a crime that consists of sexual intercourse between a man and a woman who are not husband and wife and that sexual intercourse does not fall under the definition of '*wati syubhah*' as stated in subsection (3).

2. If the person who commits *zina* has been married and has had sexual intercourse in that marriage, that person who commits *zina* is called '*muhshan*', but if the person who commits it has not yet married or has married but has not had sexual intercourse in that marriage, that person who commits *zina* is called '*ghairu muhshan*'.

3. *Wati Syubhah* is sexual intercourse that is committed by a man with a woman who is not his wife and that sexual intercourse is committed:

    a. in doubtful circumstances where he believes that the woman with whom he is having sexual intercourse is his wife, whereas the woman is not his wife; or

    b. in doubtful circumstances where he believes that the marriage with the woman with whom he is having sexual intercourse is valid according to sharia law, whereas in truth that marriage is not valid according to sharia law.

Article 16

1. If the person who commits *zina* is *muhshan*, that person shall be punished by a *rajam* punishment, namely stoning with stones no larger than a fist until death.

2. Where the offender who commits the offence of zina is a ghairu mohsan such offender shall be punished with the punishment of whipping of one hundred lashes and in addition thereto to one year imprisonment.

2. If the person who commits *zina* is *ghairu muhshan*, that person shall be punished by flogging of one hundred strokes and in addition shall be exiled for one year.

* * * * *

> *Commentary*   The following is another extract from the book *Hudud in Malaysia: The Issues at Stake*, which presents a range of views on the implementation of *hudud* laws. The book was compiled by the Malaysian activist group Sisters in Islam in response to the Kelantan Syariah Criminal Code (II) Bill, passed as an enactment by the Kelantan state government in late 1993 and the subject of heated debate within Malaysia. Included in the book is the position of PAS, the party that promulgated the enactment. The extract sets out the reasons why the Kelantan code and its penalties are important for Malaysian Muslims. It emphasizes that the provisions of the code apply only to Muslims.

Extract 11-21: Parti Islam Se Malaysia (PAS)

Sisters in Islam (1995), 'The PAS View', pp. 51–3 in *Hudud in Malaysia: The Issues at Stake* [in English], SIS Forum (Malaysia) Berhad, Kuala Lumpur. Extract: pp. 51–3.

Proponents of the Kelantan Syariah Criminal Enactment have organised public forums and published several books to explain why Muslims must accept *hudud* laws. They have also reached out to Malaysians of other faiths to quell expected fears. The argument for non-Muslims is based on the simple rationale that Malaysians are by and large law-abiding, family-loving and religious. Because of this, all Malaysians will eventually accept *hudud* because its laws protect people and their property and this can only enhance their peace of mind.

We list here the main reasons offered by PAS to persuade Malaysians to accept *hudud*:–

1. *Hudud* laws are God's laws and this is stated in the *Qur'an*. Muslims must therefore implement and abide by such laws for the betterment of humankind.

> 'Hence, judge between the followers of earlier revelations in accordance with what God has bestowed from on high. And do not follow their errant views; and beware of them, lest they tempt thee away from aught that God has bestowed from on high upon thee. And if they turn away (from his commandments), they know that it is but God's will (thus) to afflict them for some of their sins: for, behold, a great many people are iniquitous indeed. Do they, perchance, desire (to be ruled by) the law of pagan ignorance? But for people who have inner certainty, who could be a better law-giver than God?'
>
> *Sura al-Maidah* (5: 49–50)[55]

---

55   'So [Prophet] judge between them according to what God has sent down. Do not follow their whims, and take good care that they do not tempt you away from any of what God has sent down to you. If they turn away, remember that God intends to punish them for some of the sins they have

2. Muslims have no choice but to accept *hudud*. They cannot pick and choose what they consider reasonable or sensible in Islam and leave out the rest.

> 'Now whenever God and His Apostle have decided a matter, it is not for a believing man or believing woman to claim freedom of choice insofar as they themselves are concerned: for he who (thus) rebels against God and His Apostle has already, most obviously, gone astray.'
>
> *Sura al-Ahzab* (33: 36)[56]

3. Man-made laws have loopholes. Why rely on such laws which are imperfect when God provides us with His laws?

4. Crimes in all forms are becoming more serious. The prisons are overcrowded and a heavy financial burden on the State. Under *hudud*, these problems will be reduced considerably because once an individual is tried, convicted and punished, he or she is released.

Hudud laws are problematic in some countries because individuals abuse the laws.

5. Those who question the laws are not necessarily bad Muslims; they are merely ill-informed. They are influenced by the liberal and immoral West. They are swayed by the belief that everything must be logical. For such people, *hudud* laws should be rejected because the West regards punishments for such laws to be barbaric.

6. Those who reject the laws are apostates.

7. *Hudud* laws are only meant for Muslims.

8. The laws will make everyone safe. In Saudi Arabia, for instance, investors are not fearful of *hudud* laws. Instead they feel safe doing business in that country knowing that criminals will be dealt with severely.

The reason why investors are not coming to Kelantan has nothing to do with *hudud* laws; they are actually prevented from investing in the State by the Federal Government.

9. In time, non-Muslims will see the value of implementing *hudud* laws because they protect the public, prevent crimes and provide just punishments for convicted persons. Under the administration of *hudud*, reform programmes will be made available for offenders.

10. *Hudud* laws should be implemented even though the majority of people do not understand the laws. Take income-tax laws: do most people understand them? If they cannot comprehend the intricacies of income tax laws and yet abide by them, they should be able to do the same for *hudud*.

11.6.2 The Terengganu Bill

> ***Commentary*** The Terengganu (or Trengganu) bill is an elaborated version of the Kelantan code. Like the latter it is not able to be implemented as law because the state legislature has no constitutional power in criminal or public-order matters except to the

---

committed: a great many people are lawbreakers – do they want judgement according to the time of pagan ignorance? Is there any better judge than God for those of firm faith?' (Q5: 49–50, Haleem).
56   Q33: 36 is given in footnote 35.

extent permitted in the Federal Constitution. The bill is in 12 parts with five schedules and covers the same subjects as the Kelantan code. It is more carefully drafted than the Kelantan code, although issues of subsidiary regulations remain unsolved. There is, however, one significant difference between the Kelantan and Terengganu texts. In the latter, each part is prefaced by a citation of the relevant passage in the Qur'an, as shown in the following extract. The inclusion of the Arabic version of the Qur'anic quote is significant because authority for the bill's detailed provisions is thus directly linked to revelation, making it explicit that these laws are based on Qur'anic injunctions.

The following extract on penalties and their application for theft indicates that there are many grounds for exemption from the application of the *hudud* punishment, in this case, amputation.

Extract 11-22: *Syariah Criminal Offence (*Hudud *and* Qisas*)* Terengganu Bill

'Syariah Criminal Offence (*Hudud* and *Qisas*) Terengganu Bill 1423H/2002M' [in English], pp. 291–330 in *Warta Kerajaan Negeri Terengganu* [Terengganu State Government Gazette], Kuala Terengganu. Extract: pp. 305–8.

PART V

SARIQAH [Theft]

Allah SWT[57] said

[verse in Arabic script]

Means:

'As to the thief, male or female, cut off his or her hands: a punishment by way of example from Allah for their crime: and Allah is at [*sic*] exalted in power, full of wisdom.'

(The Holy Quran, Surah Al-Maidah, 5:38)[58]

Sariqah

19. *Sariqah* is of [*sic*] an act of taking or removing dishonestly any movable property from the custody or possession of the owner without his knowledge with the intention to deprive the property from the custody or possession of the owner.

Punishment for *sariqah*

20. Whoever commits *sariqah*, except in the circumstances enumerated in section 21, shall be punished with *hudud* punishment as follows:

(*a*) for the first offence with amputation of his right hand;
(*b*) for the second offence with amputation of part of his left foot; and
(*c*) for the third and subsequent offences with imprisonment for such term as in the opinion of the Court, may [be] likely to lead him to repentance.

---

57 SWT: *Subhanahu wa Ta'ala* (Almighty God).
58 Q5: 38 is given in footnote 27.

When the *hudud* punishment for *sariqah* shall not apply

21. The *hudud* punishment for *sariqah* shall not apply in any of the following circumstances:

(*a*) where the value of the stolen property is less than the *nisab* [the minimum amount Muslims are required to pay as *zakat*];

(*b*) where the offence is not proved by evidence required under the provisions of Part X;

(*c*) where the offender is not a *mukallaf* [Muslim adult of sound mind];

(*d*) where the owner of the stolen property fails to keep his inmovable [*sic*] property in a proper place for it[s] safety or the owner in certain circumstances exposes it to cause [theft];

(*e*) where the offender has not obtained full possession of the stolen property, although its owner have [*sic*] already been deprived of its custody and possession;

(*f*) where the stolen property is of trifling nature and can be found in abundance in the land or is of perishable nature;

(*g*) where the property is of no value according to *Hukum Syarak* [sharia], such as intoxicating drink or instruments used for amusement;

(*h*) where the offence is committed by a creditor in respect of the property of his debtor, who refuses to pay the debt;

Provided that the value of the stolen property shall not exceed the amount of the debt or the value of the stolen property [that] exceeds the amount of the debt does not exceed the *nisab*;

(*i*) where the offence is committed in circumstances of extreme difficulties, such as war, famine, pestilence and natural disaster;

(*j*) where the offence is committed within the family, such as a wife stealing from her husband and *vice versa* or son from his father and *vice versa*;

(*k*) where in the case of an offence being committed by a group of persons, the share of each offender upon dividing the stolen property or the proceeds thereof is less than the *nisab*;

(*l*) where the offender returns the stolen property before the execution of the *hudud* punishment;

(*m*) where the owner of the stolen property denies the theft notwithstanding the confession by the offender;

(*n*) where the offender makes objection accepted by *Hukum Syarak* against the witnesses;

(*o*) where the stolen property is or the circumstances in which the offence is committed are such that according to *Hukum Syarak* there is no *hudud* punishment;

(*p*) where the offence of *sariqah* is proved only by the *iqrar* [statement] of the offender, but he retracts his *iqrar* before the execution of *hudud* punishment;

(*q*) where the offender possesses the stolen property lawfully after the commission of the offence of *sariqah* and before the decision upon the offence of *sariqah* is made;

(*r*) where the offender is allowed to enter the storage place;

(*s*) where the execution of punishment for the amputation of the hand [is] to endanger or threaten the life of the offender;

(*t*) where the left hand of the criminal is non-functionable, mutilated or amputated.

11.6.3   The South Sulawesi Draft Sharia Code

Commentary   The text of the South Sulawesi draft sharia code was prepared in December 2001 by Komite Persiapan Penegakan Syari'at Islam (KPPSI, Committee for the Preparation of Enforcement of Islamic Sharia). KPPSI is a small, self-appointed body claiming some degree of ideological inheritance from earlier Muslim activists, particularly Abdul Qahar Muzakkar, who used armed force to attempt to establish an Islamic state in South Sulawesi in the 1950s and 1960s. KPPSI now sees regional autonomy as the mechanism to achieve the same end.

The purpose of the draft is to outline a method for the 'enforcement' of Islamic sharia in the province of South Sulawesi. The document assumes the existing formal structure of the unitary Republic of Indonesia; the preamble to the draft specifically acknowledges the 1945 Constitution and the laws of the republic on regional government/autonomy (including finance), police, existing judicial systems and the Supreme Court. In short, there is no call for an 'Islamic' state. Instead, as in Aceh, the draft seeks an integration of sharia into existing structures.

The extract below comes from several sections of the draft code. Some sections describe the basis and aims of the code; one lists the implementing agencies in the areas of business and trade.

Extract 11-23: The South Sulawesi Draft Sharia Code

Komite Persiapan Penegakan Syari'at Islam (2001), 'Rancangan Undang-Undang Otonomi Khusus Pemberlakukan Syari'at Islam bagi Propinsi Sulawesi Selatan' [Draft Law for Special Autonomy for the Implementation of Islamic Sharia for the Province of South Sulawesi].[59]

Second Congress for Islamic Community of South Sulawesi

Committee for the Preparation of Enforcement of Islamic Sharia

[...]

Saturday–Monday 14–15 Syawal 1422h/ 29–31 December 2001 AD

The People's Representative Council of the Republic of Indonesia

Draft Law of the Republic of Indonesia No. ...... of 2002

Concerning Special Autonomy for the Implementation of Islamic Sharia for the Province of South Sulawesi [...]

---

59   The English translation for this South Sulawesi draft sharia code is the work of the Asian Law Centre, University of Melbourne, which has kindly given permission for its publication here.

CHAPTER II
Characteristics and Aims

Article 2

(1) The government of the Province of South Sulawesi, characterised by Islamic Sharia, shall be an administration, which is founded on the basis of the Koran and the Sunnah;

(2) The legislative system of the Government of Province of South Sulawesi shall be based on and derived from the Koran and the Sunnah.

Article 3

(1) The legislation of the Province of South Sulawesi shall be based on Qanun[60] or on Regional Laws, the contents of which are in accordance with the principles of Islam, flowing through this Law and a number of other regulations;

(2) The content of the Special Autonomy of the Province of South Sulawesi as derived from regulations, has special characteristics, namely, it lives and breathes Islamic Sharia.

Article 4

The aim of the Government of the Province of South Sulawesi shall be:

a.   To implement Islamic laws in all government and community business;

b.   To carry out government business based on Islamic laws;

c.   To protect the interests of the people and the community with the system outlined in the Koran and the Sunnah. [...]

CHAPTER VI
Special Autonomy for the Implementation of Islamic Sharia [...]

Fifth Section
Economy and Trade

Article 22

(1) The implementation, development and building of the economy and trade in the Province of South Sulawesi shall be organised, based on the values of Islamic Sharia.

(2) Implementation in clause (1) will be further regulated by Qanun.

Article 23

(1) The Council of *Ulama* together with the Executive will form the Body of Supervisors of Economy and Sharia Trade;

(2) The tasks of the body of supervisors of economy and Sharia trade will [include] giving opinions and considerations to legislative [bodies], in particular in the areas of forming Qanun or Decisions of Regents/Mayors, which are related to the fields of the economy and trade.

---

60   Islamic laws or statutes.

Article 24

(1) The Body of Supervisors of Economy and Trade in Article 23 clause (1) shall be formed by the Executive on the agreement of the provincial legislative [bodies] for the body of the supervision of the economy and trade of the Province of South Sulawesi;

(2) The Body of Supervisors of Economy and Trade for the Regencies and Towns shall be formed by the Legislative Body, together with the Executive of the Regencies and Towns.

* * * * *

Commentary The KPPSI's draft code has had a mixed reception in South Sulawesi. There is a view that the close links that the KPPSI has tried to forge with political institutions there – for example, the local government, the administration and the police, governor and mayors – reflect the political motivation of the proponents of the code. In January 2003, Jaringan Islam Liberal (JIL, Liberal Islam Network) organized a workshop in Puncak, West Java, to debate the issues surrounding full implementation of sharia. The following extract is taken from a contribution to the workshop by M. Qasim Mathar, vice-chair of Partai Amanat Nasional (PAN, National Mandate Party) in South Sulawesi.

Extract 11-24: M. Qasim Mathar

M. Qasim Mathar (2003), 'Shari'a: Comparative Perspectives', pp. 237–9 in Burhanuddin (ed.), *Syariat Islam: Pandangan Muslim Liberal* [Sharia: Liberal Islam Views], Jaringan Islam Liberal and the Asia Foundation, Jakarta. [Transcript of comments at a workshop, Puncak, West Java, 10–11 January 2003.] Extract: pp. 238–9.

I have also seen that there is an urge to continue Kahar Muzakkar's struggle,[61] or the DI-TII[62] values. In an implicit way, that spirit lies behind the preamble of the draft. They [that is, the KPPSI drafters] view anything that Kahar Muzakkar struggled for as positive, whereas in the eyes of the majority of ordinary people in South Sulawesi, the rebellion of Kahar Muzakkar not only caused trauma, but what he did went against sharia. This particularly concerns the methods he used.

Next is the claim made on behalf of South Sulawesi society in the two conferences they held. They presented a congress in the name of Kongres Umat Islam Sulawesi Selatan [Congress of the Muslim Community of South Sulawesi]. However, the congress certainly did not represent the Muslim community. They also often claim to have a monopoly on the interpretation of the Qur'an.

Once again, I stress that really their actions smell of politics. They view the people in the DPRD,[63] also the political groupings, politically. This means they do not deal with issues critically; but there is no one at all who dares reject them. Indeed, if

---

61 Abdul Qahar Muzakkar: see commentary to extract 11-23.
62 That is, the radical Islamist movement Darul Islam (DI) and its military wing, Tentara Islam Indonesia (TII, Indonesian Muslim Army).
63 Dewan Perwakilan Rakyat Daerah (the regional parliaments).

we talk about individuals, there are ideas of wanting to reject the wishes of the KPSI [the KPPSI], but in public forums they get scared, because it could result in the loss of votes in the 2004 elections. As I see it, what they understand as sharia Islam is a conception of Islam by a group of Islamic activists not yet in power.

11.7 SHARIA AS ETHNO-NATIONALISM

Commentary Several sharia codes have been drafted not primarily as challenges to secular laws but as symbolic expressions of the Muslim identity of particular communities. The most notable are those of the Muslims of the southern Philippines and the Muslims of Aceh. In 1996 Rasmia Alonto asked Salamat Hashim, the founder and chair of MILF, what the Muslim struggle in the Philippines was actually about. Salamat Hashim replied in a mixture of religious and ethnic-survival terms. Although fighting for a political end (independence), he explained, the form of the struggle was through Islam, which in turn gave the people their special identity. He believed that it was Islam that distinguished the Philippine Muslims from other Filipinos and that the struggle for Islam was the struggle for ethnic survival.

Extract 11-25: Salamat Hashim

Salamat Hashim (2002), 'We Assert Our Legitimate Rights to Self-determination, That Is, Independence' [in English], pp. 40–57 in *Referendum: Peaceful, Civilized, Diplomatic and Democratic Means of Solving the Mindanao Conflict*, Agency for Youth Affairs–MILF, Camp Abubakre As-Siddique, Mindanao. [Transcript of a written interview conducted by Rasmia Alonto in 1996.] Extract: p. 47.

SALAMAT: The Muslim struggle in the Philippines is supposed to be for regaining their independence and to establish a government that will lead to the total Islamization of their way of life in order to be able to do their part in changing the world order with the system designed by the Creator of the universe for mankind and to realize Allah's saying well expressed in the following verses:

> 110. You are the best of peoples
> Evolved for mankind.
> Enjoining what is right,
> Forbidding what is wrong,
> And believing in Allah.
>   *Sura Al-'Imran*[64]

However the struggle has actually been for survival amidst oppression, persecution and genocide and rapidly rose to independence and then declined to autonomy and then gradually developed to take the right direction as explained in the beginning.

* * * * *

---

64 '[Believers], you are the best community singled out for people: you order what is right, forbid what is wrong, and you believe in God. If the People of the Book had also believed, it would have been better for them. For although some of them do believe, most of them are lawbreakers' (Q3: 110, Haleem).

Commentary   The Indonesian central government has granted Aceh autonomy, but not independence. In October 1999, B.J. Habibie, who succeeded Soeharto as president in that year, gave Aceh special regional status (Law No. 44/1999). Among other things, the law allowed the implementation of sharia in social life, but it did not allow the establishment of sharia courts. Then, in August 2001, President Megawati Sukarnoputri signed Law No. 18/2001, which gave Aceh special autonomy status and the authority to establish sharia courts. The Majlis Permusyawaratan Ulama (MPU, Ulama Consultative Council (of Aceh)) became responsible for drafting a Qanun (Islamic law code), later ratified by the Aceh parliament.[65] The Qanun had not been fully drafted in 2004. However, it already consisted of six texts written between 2000 and 2003 and had become the operative law for Muslims in Aceh. The Aceh code represents a special case in that the Indonesian government has recognized it as the official law for Aceh. Of all the recent sharia laws in Southeast Asia, the Aceh code is the only one with this formal status, although its creation and implementation have not been without difficulties (see Hooker and Lindsey, forthcoming).

The Qanun was drafted by scholars trained in both classical Islam and the framework of the Indonesian national state. They were familiar with the national system of religious administration and secular government and drafted the code to include reference to local legislatures (as is the case with the KPPSI code). This approach may be criticized by purists. However, it is pragmatic and presents the MPU as being on the same level as the local parliament with authority to work with it to produce the legislation. Table 11.3 shows the structure of the Aceh Qanun.

The complete Qanun will include sections addressing violence against women in which admissible evidence will include medical reports and DNA testing (Ibrahim 2004). Other sections will cover sharia-inspired financial institutions and the establishment of bodies to improve understanding of religious knowledge. In implementing the Qanun, members of the MPU say they draw on the methods of the Prophet Muhammad, starting at the level of the family and slowly working outwards into society so that human rights are protected and sharia is socialized without violence.

The sections of the Qanun drafted to date focus on public propriety (for example, foreigners and tourists must respect Islamic values in their public behaviour), modesty, education and prayer. In trying to achieve this, the drafters of the Qanun have written provisions that are sensible, workable and, most importantly, not violent. The *hudud* penalty of amputation, for example, is not mentioned in the code.

The courts in Aceh, particularly the religious courts, are oriented towards Jakarta for appointments, promotions and funding. Most importantly, the Mahkamah Agung (Supreme Court) retains control of judicial policy, including policy relating to Islam (see Hooker and Lindsey, forthcoming). Thus the institutions of state (courts, bureaucracy, police) tend to implement the Qanun only sporadically and weakly.

In the following extract, the educative and protective nature of the Qanun is emphasized. The drafters framed the laws in terms of trying to assist individuals to fulfil their religious obligations. A special body, Wilayatul Hisbah[66] (in effect 'sharia police') is given the mandate to 'warn', 'guide' and 'advise' in the hope that those who infringe the Qanun's regulations will conform and not require formal sentencing.

---

65   Details supplied by Dr Tengku H. Muslim Ibrahim, chair of the MPU; see Ibrahim (2004).

66   Wilayatul Hisbah is a term used in classical Islamic texts for those who had the authority to deal with misbehaviour as it occurred. In the contemporary context of Aceh it is understood to refer to those who police Islamic laws.

Table 11.3   The Aceh Qanun

Law No.	Description of Contents	Comment
3/2000	Establishes the MPU.	Increases the political and legal functions of earlier similar bodies. Issues fatwa (*Kumpulan Fatwa*: 2000) and provides guidance and suggestions for policy on law and on government administration based on Islamic principles. Potential for the MPU to have considerable power through direct input into government policy and practice.
43/2001	Refines administration of the MPU.	Addresses bureaucratic issues concerning the MPU.
5/2000	Implementation of Islamic sharia in Aceh (introduction + nine provisions).	The core of Aceh sharia – Islam is central to Aceh and its Muslim population and is the basis of justice, prosperity and moral well-being.
		The sources for the law are the Qur'an, Hadith and the 1945 Constitution.
		Muslims must follow correct doctrine (*aqidah*) according to Sunni schools.
7/2000	The customary laws of Aceh (*adat*) and how they relate to the sharia.	In general terms, *adat* institutions are integrated into government and supported by its agencies.
10/2002	Establishes the Islamic Court (Mahkamah Sharia) for Aceh.	Currently inoperative because it requires the promulgation of the new law (under Presidential Instruction No. 11/2003). Preserves the structure and procedures of the existing religious courts (Pengadilan Agama) and recognizes the overriding jurisdiction of the Supreme Court (Mahkamah Agung). The intention is to widen the jurisdiction of existing Pengadilan Agama from family law and trusts to include criminal and commercial law (see Hooker and Lindsey, forthcoming).
11/2002	Rules for the implementation of sharia in the areas of doctrine (*aqidah*), devotions (*ibadah*) and public expressions (*syi'ar*).	Families are responsible for ensuring family members perform the daily and Friday prayers, and no government or other agencies can obstruct this. All Muslims must observe the fast and wear Islamic dress (not rigidly defined).
	Establishes a special body (Wilayatul Hisbah) that, acting in conjunction with the Aceh police, investigates and prosecutes breaches of the Qanun.	Penalties for breaches of the Qanun are at the discretion of the judge (*ta'zir*). *Hudud* and *qisas* are specifically excluded.
		Ta'zir penalties include fines, imprisonment for up to 2 years and public caning up to 12 strokes.[a]
23/2002	Law for a religious education system based on the Qur'an and Hadith but following also the objectives of the national education system.	The aim is to provide an education for the holistic development of Muslims and to equip them for employment. Curricula must include Islamic studies (Qur'an, Hadith, *aqidah*, *fiqh*, *ibadah*, history of Islam and Muslim societies) as well as secular subjects. Arabic and English are compulsory.

a   Specific guidelines for penalties are to be set by the MPU. The Qanun emphasizes that the purpose of caning is public humiliation and not physical abuse. This is recognized also by laws of the Republic of Singapore which, although a secular state, uses caning as a form of punishment.

Extract: 11-26: The Aceh Qanun

'Penjelasan atas Qanun Provinsi Nanggroe Aceh Darussalam Nomor 11 Tahun 2002 tentang Pelaksanaan Syariat Islam Bidang Aqidah, Ibadah dan Syi'ar Islam' [Elucidation of Qanun of the Province of Nanggroe Aceh Darussalam No. 11 of 2002 Concerning the Implementation of Islamic Sharia in the Fields of *Aqidah*, *Ibadah* and *Syi'ar Islam*].[67]

1. IN GENERAL [...]
In general, Islamic Sharia covers aspects of *aqidah* [faith], *ibadah* [religious observances and rituals], *muamalah* [Islamic laws dealing with issues of daily social life] and *akhlak* [morality]. It is incumbent on every Muslim to be obedient to the entirety of these aspects. Obedience to aspects that govern *aqidah* and *ibadah* are highly dependent on the quality of faith and *taqwa* [piety]. Whereas obedience to aspects of *muamalah* and *akhlak*, aside from being determined by the quality of faith and *taqwa*, are also influenced by the existence of worldly and otherworldly (*ukhrawi*) sanctions for those who contravene them.

In the Islamic legal system there are two kinds of sanctions; namely, sanctions that are otherworldly in nature that will be received in the afterlife, and worldly sanctions that are applied by humans through executive, legislative and judicative power. These two types of sanctions drive the community to obey the provisions of the law. In many ways the enforcement of law demands a role for the state. The law has no meaning if it is not enforced by the state. On the contrary a nation will not be orderly if the law is not enforced.

Legislative efforts to implement Islamic Sharia in the fields of Aqidah, Ibadah (Prayers and the Fast of Ramadhan) as well as *Syiar Islam*[68] are not attempts to regulate the substance of Aqidah and Ibadah. The substantive matters are regulated by the authoritative texts (*nash*) and have been developed by the *ulama* in the various disciplines of the Islamic sciences.

Therefore, the legislative effort to implement Islamic Sharia as regulated by this Qanun is part of an effort to develop, guard, nurture and protect the *aqidah* of Muslims in Nanggroe Aceh Darussalam from various misguided interpretations and/or sects. The only breach of *aqidah* that is punishable in this Qanun is for those persons who spread misguided interpretations and/or sects. Meanwhile the threat of punishment for any person who intentionally leaves the *aqidah* of Islam and/or for anyone who consciously departs from *aqidah* Islam and/or insults or abuses the Religion of Islam shall be regulated in a separate Qanun concerning HUDUD.

This is also the case with the regulation of aspects of *ibadah*, whether of *shalat fardhu* or *shalat Jumat* [prescribed prayers or congregational prayers] or the fast of Ramadhan; it is to encourage, to spur Muslims to perform and increase the quality

---

67 The English translation for this Qanun is the work of the Asian Law Centre, University of Melbourne, which has kindly given permission for its publication here.

68 *Syi'ar Islam* refers to any activity (for example the congregational Friday prayers) that glorifies and celebrates Islam.

of their faith and the quality of their *amal* [good deeds] as well as the intensity of their *ibadah* as a manifestation of their pious devotion that is only for God and no other. This effort also needs to be supported by the conditions and the situation of the implementation of *Sy'iar Islam*, but is still within the sphere of *ibadah* values.

The existence of the criminal sanction of public caning, besides the sanction of imprisonment and/or fines as well as administrative sanctions, is meant as a measure of education and guidance, so that the offender will realize and regret the mistake they committed, and also to escort them to position themselves in Taubat Nasuha [complete and absolute undertaking not to repeat an offence against God's laws]. The carrying out of the punishment of public caning is intended as a preventive and educational measure so that every person will make efforts not to contravene this Qanun in particular and all the provisions of Islamic Sharia in general.

The form of punishment of caning for those who commit a criminal offence is intended as an effort to make offenders realize their error and also to be a warning for the community not to commit criminal offences. The punishment of caning is expected to be more effective because the convicted person feels ashamed and it does not create a risk for their family. The punishment of caning also reduces the expense that must be paid by the government in comparison with the other types of punishment that are currently known in the Criminal Code (KUHP).

The Wilayatul Hisbah as a supervisory institution is granted the role of warning, guiding and advising, so that the cases of contravention of this Qanun that are submitted to the investigators to be followed up and forwarded on to the courts are cases that have been through a process/effort of warning/advice and guidance towards the offender.

* * * * *

Commentary   The author of the following extract is director of the Centre for Pesantren and Democracy Studies and a member of the Central Executive of the women's wing of NU, Muslimat NU. The extract is based on surveys she undertook in Aceh between December 2002 and January 2003 to assess the impact of sharia during the first two years of implementation of the Qanun. She was particularly interested in the reactions of women.

Extract 11-27: Lily Zakiyah Munir

Lily Zakiyah Munir (2003), 'Simbolisasi, Politisasi dan Kontrol terhadap Perempuan di Aceh' [Symbolization, Politicization and Control of Women in Aceh], pp. 127–36 in Burhanuddin (ed.), *Syariat Islam: Pandangan Muslim Liberal* [Sharia: Liberal Islam Views], Jaringan Islam Liberal and the Asia Foundation, Jakarta. Extract: pp. 129–35.

The Pros and Cons of Implementing Islamic Law

It must be acknowledged that the implementation of Islamic law was part of an effort to build up the dignity and status of the Acehnese people which had disappeared as a consequence of protracted horizontal and vertical conflict. This was certainly what the majority of the Acehnese people wanted. However, the government could not properly manage and respond to [the people's] wishes. The situation and circum-stances of Aceh, which was in [a state of] conflict, were certainly not conducive to a fundamental change such as the formalization of Islamic law. There were many who questioned why the desire of the Acehnese people to implement Islamic law in the early days of Independence, or in the 1950s and 1960s, was not heeded. Why then was this gift actually given when Aceh was mired in conflict?

Certainly many people viewed it as a political ploy. If it was really, truly in the interests of Islamic law, why was it not done before when conditions in Aceh were still peaceful and conducive? Almost all informants have mentioned the politi-cal dimensions of this policy of implementing Islamic law. Several comments are quoted below.

'... It's not fair to implement Islamic law in conditions such as these. Perhaps there were certain parties who wanted to exploit the Aceh conflict, so that then the impres-sion outside would be as though Islam in Aceh actually increased violations of basic human rights, couldn't resolve conflicts, etc. ... So with the legitimation of Islamic law there was renewed provocation ...' *(Syarifah Rahmatillah, Director of MISPI)*[69]

'This formalization certainly seems to have political elements, because of pressure to resolve the Aceh problem ...' *(Dra. Raihan Putri, Acehnese women's activist)*

'... This formalization of Islamic law is, well, just the political business of [former governor] Abdullah Puteh. When he didn't know what to do to ease the conflict, Islamic law was implemented so as to tug at the people's heartstrings ... Just look at his wife! Why else would she be distributing free headscarves for women, as though there were no other more important problems? ...' *(Grave-site/tomb custodian)*[70]

'... as part of a political decision in the context of restoring calm to Aceh. It was hoped that, with there being Islamic law, it could act as a calming and stabilizing cure for Aceh ... Thus, executives, legislators and a number or at least several ulema worked together. And that's just at the preliminary stage ... They hoped it would be a cure. Yet in fact it is not the cure, for in Aceh what we need is security. Give us security; give us justice.' *(Dr Yusny Saby, Postgraduate Program Director, Ar-Raniry State Islamic Institute, Banda Aceh)*

There are many more opinions from informants that echo the above extracts. Perhaps somewhat different is the opinion of Dr H. Alyasa Abu Bakar, head of the Aceh State Islamic Law Agency. He spoke at length about historical factors, focusing more on the legal dimensions. For example, he described the various blueprints for legal canons that were being prepared in order to realize a complete (*kaffah*) Islam that encompasses all aspects of life. Also in relation to the Islamic law courts etc., his views, heavily focused on the formal-legal approach, implied great optimism that Islamic law would be implemented in stages. Another informant who was quite optimistic was Dr Tgk. Muslim Ibrahim, MA, chair of the Aceh Ulama Consultative

---

69 MISPI: Mitra Sejati Perempuan Indonesia (True Partnership of Indonesian Women), a non-govern-ment organization.

70 Such a custodian tends the graves of revered people; the graves are often sites of pilgrimage.

Council (MPU) and a member of the drafting team for the sharia Qanun [code]. He acknowledged that the influence of Islamic law on social life was not yet perceptible because although the software did indeed exist in the form of hundreds of codes, it still needed to be formulated in detail.

In a discussion held at Ar-Raniry State Islamic Institute, almost all the participants criticized this policy of formalizing Islamic law, and, interestingly, expressed the following views:

> 'Islamic law in Aceh has existed since the sixteenth century, since [Sultan] Iskandar Muda ... why on earth did the government come up with a new Islamic law policy when Aceh is on Mecca's front doorstep?[71] ... Isn't this an insult from the government?' *(Noviani)*

> 'Islamic law is like the life blood flowing inside the Acehnese people ... When the government legalized Islamic law it was as though the Acehnese people were reborn into Islam, into a new world with a new Islamic law ... I am in less than total agreement with the government's methods, which are far from what is right ... it is as though we have been reborn into Islam, like a newborn baby being welcomed into Islam with the [recitation of the] confession of faith.' *(Nurul)*

11.8   SHARIA AS LOCAL POLITICS

Commentary   Calls for full implementation of sharia at the national level in Southeast Asian nations have not received sufficient support to force governments to move beyond the implementation of personal and family laws for Muslims. In Indonesia, however, there have been some interesting developments at the local and district levels since early 2000. Some local authorities have used the 1999 regional autonomy laws (implemented in early 2000) as the basis for drafting limited sharia regulations for implementation at the local level.[72] This is despite the fact that the regional autonomy laws specifically state that religion remains a state (central government) matter and that districts do not have authority in this area. However, up to the time of writing, the central government has not prevented districts from implementing their own versions of sharia.

The regulations emanating from authorities at the local level give increased power over the public behaviour of Muslim residents in the local area. They can therefore be categorized as expressions of local politics. The increased power is justified on the grounds (stated in their preambles) that traditional local laws and culture (*adat*) are intertwined with sharia and that the norms of *adat* for social stability and well-being are also the norms established in the Qur'an. Thus, the power of local leaders is extended considerably because they feel authorized to intervene in areas of public morality (mas-

---

71   The phrase is *Serambi Mekkah* (Mecca's verandah), an epithet commonly used in Aceh to illustrate the Acehnese people's degree of devotion to Islam.

72   For example, districts in West Java, South Kalimantan, East Java, Gorontalo and West Sumatra have circulated regional government regulations (*peraturan daerah*) that set out rules and penalties with regard to women's public behaviour at night, the observance of the fast, and prohibitions on gambling, alcohol, narcotic substances, pornography and so on (Salim 2003: 222–4).

sage parlours, brothels, cohabitation before marriage and so on) in the name of social stability.

In Indonesia, state-sponsored sharia law covers family law and, more recently, *zakat*. It does not cover issues concerning public morality and it does not refer to *adat*. The new local regulations fill that space. Their titles do not include the word 'sharia',[73] but their drafters and promoters regard them as sharia. They see the regulations as standing as examples of the intention to bring into existence sharia laws that are appropriate for their own purposes, which appear to be as much political as religious.

Extracts 11-28, 11-29 and 11-30 are examples of sharia-inspired local regulations. The first is from the provincial level in West Sumatra, the second is from the district or *kabupaten* level within the province of West Sumatra, and the third is from the provincial level in Gorontalo in northern Sulawesi. Regulation No. 11/2001, issued by the governor of West Sumatra, has been used as the basis for other local regulations in the province of West Sumatra.

The regional regulation in extract 11-28 argues that the social fabric of society and religious and customary norms are undermined by immoral acts. The latter are defined in the regulation as unlawful sexual intercourse (consensual or forced, for payment, or with the same sex); gambling in any form; any form of drink which causes drunkenness or disorientation; narcotics and psychonarcotics; addictive drugs; and publications containing material of a pornographic nature that contravenes religious and *adat* values. The regulation charges individuals and society to report breaches of the regulation to the 'authorities' (the police or local civil officials, including village leaders).

Extract 11-28: Regional Regulation of the Province of West Sumatra

'Peraturan Daerah Propinsi Sumatera Barat Nomor: 11 Tahun 2001 tentang Pencegahan dan Pemberantasan Maksiat' [Regional Regulation of the Province of West Sumatra No. 11 2001 Concerning the Prevention and Elimination of Immorality], Biro Hukum Sekretariat Daerah [Legal Office of the Regional Secretariat], Province of West Sumatra.

Preamble:

a. The Province of West Sumatra is a region having a philosophy of *adat* based on *Syarak*, sharia based on God's Book, and this must be protected and preserved in the norms and values of social life.
b. The translation of the norms mentioned under (a) will be manifested in efforts to prevent and eradicate immorality.
c. Various forms of immorality disrupt social stability and destroy religious norms, *adat* and existing laws.
d. To realize the intentions of (a), (b) and (c) above, the prevention and eradication of immorality needs to be regulated by this regional regulation.

* * * * *

73 And they are presented in the form: District Regulation No. ...... 'Concerning the Prevention and Elimination of Immorality'.

Commentary The provincial-level regional regulation of West Sumatra does not include stipulations about women's dress or seek to restrict the public movement of women at night. At the next administrative level down, however – the district or *kabupaten* level – local government officials have been preparing special regulations of this type for Muslims. In the *kabupaten* of Solok, West Sumatra, for example, at least six local regulations were produced between 2001 and 2004 that included provisions concerning dress codes for women and men, the reading of the Qur'an, local government, good governance and religious donations.[74]

Extract 11-29 sets out dress regulations for local government and office employees. Infringements of dress regulations are dealt with by normal disciplinary bodies. For example, infringements by office workers are dealt with by their superiors and those by schoolchildren by their teachers or parents. Punishments are those normally applied for misdemeanours – reprimands or exclusion, for example. There is no mention of physical punishment.

Extract 11-29: Regional Regulation of the District of Solok

'Peraturan Daerah Kabupaten Solok Nomor 6 Tahun 2002 tentang Berpakaian Muslim dan Muslimah di Kabupaten Solok' [Regional Regulation No. 6 of 2002 Concerning Dress for Muslim Men and Women in the District of Solok], promulgated by the District Head (*Bupati*) of Solok, 11 March 2002.

Section 7

(1) Regulations for dress of Muslim men and women in government and private offices […] are as follows:

A. MALES:
    1) Long trousers
    2) Long/short-sleeved shirt.

B. FEMALES:
    1) Long blouse to cover the hips;
    2) Ankle-length skirt or slacks;
    3) Head covering to conceal hair, ears, neck, nape of neck and breasts.

(2) The aforementioned clothing should not be transparent and not reveal body shape (not be tight).
(3) Stipulations concerning men's and women's clothing are given in more detail in Keputusan Bupati [Bupati's Decree].

* * * * *

Commentary Extract 11-30 is from the regional regulations of Gorontalo in northern Sulawesi. The preamble of the regulation is almost identical with that of the regulation

---

74 The assistance of Yasrul Huda MA in obtaining this material is gratefully acknowledged.

of the province of West Sumatra (see extract 11-28) and covers the same topics. However, the Gorontalo regulation is more detailed and pays greater attention to definitions.
For example, it includes constraints on women's movements after dark and, in contrast
to the regulation from West Sumatra, lists the punishments for infringing the regulation. None of these is a physical punishment and the maximum fine is Rp 5 million or
six months' detention. The Indonesian press has carried reports of local district officials
in other areas using fines and caning against offenders of local sharia codes (see Salim
2003: 223–4).

Extract 11-30: Regional Regulation of the Province of Gorontalo

'Peraturan Daerah Provinsi Gorontalo Nomor 10 Tahun 2003 tentang Pencegahan
Maksiat' [Regional Regulation of the Provincial Government of Gorontalo No. 10
of 2003 Concerning the Prevention of Immorality].

CHAPTER III [...]

Part Three
Prevention of Rape and Sexual Harassment

Section 6

(1) Women are forbidden to go about alone or to be out of their houses without
     being accompanied by a close male relative/husband between midnight and
     4 am, except for reasons that can be defended.
(2) In public places women must wear appropriate and respectable clothing.
(3) It is forbidden to hold beauty contests that present women in tight or minimal
     clothing.

Part Four
Prevention of Pornographic Acts and Pornography

Section 7

(1) Anyone in a public place is forbidden to deliberately expose their bodies or
     behave inappropriately in ways that excite lust.
(2) Owners or managers of internet cafes are forbidden to provide access to those
     wanting access to internet pornography sites.

11.9   SHARIA IN PRACTICE

11.9.1   Fatwa

Commentary   This chapter started with the definition of sharia in its Qur'anic sense:
God's guidance for human beings in all aspects of their lives. The previous extracts and
commentaries show the doctrinal and practical difficulties of interpreting that guidance: what material can be used to assist in interpretation; who is qualified to provide
interpretation; what methods of reasoning are used; what the guiding principles are in

selecting one interpretation over others; who implements; who enforces; and classes of punishments for infringements and disobedience. Contemporary Muslims face many complexities. Some of these are occasioned by the contrast in time and place between the original context of God's revelation of the holy scripture and the demands of modern life. A further factor is the existence of the nation-state and its defining role in legislation and the application of national laws. In all Southeast Asian nations, the state has controlled the forms in which sharia is expressed and implemented but has confined its active implementation to matters of personal and family law.[75] This control has intensified over the past 50 years as a consequence of the increased bureaucratization of 'essential' aspects of sharia such as marriage and divorce procedures. In other, less easily regulated areas of private life, such as inheritance, there is a considerable degree of social avoidance at family and individual level.

One expression of sharia which is outside state control is the fatwa. This is a formal opinion on law and dogma given by a scholar (sometimes a committee of scholars) with the authority to do so. In Indonesia the main bodies issuing fatwa are NU, Muhammadiyah and Persatuan Islam (Persis, Islamic Association), all active from the 1920s, and MUI, established in 1975 by the Indonesian government.[76] Leading Muslim scholars also offer guidance in regular newspaper columns in response to readers' questions. In Malaysia there are active fatwa committees in each state as well as a less active national fatwa committee. In Singapore, fatwa are issued by the MUIS.

A fatwa is not binding but can be immensely influential in guiding the behaviour of Muslims. Fatwa are not precedent and are not necessarily binding over time. For example, in the field of insurance, always a controversial issue for Muslims because gambling is forbidden, the NU has two fatwa, one from 1960 and one from 1992, which directly contradict each other. The 1960 fatwa closely follows the fatwa of an Egyptian scholar[77] first published in 1906. On the grounds that life insurance has no class or category in *fiqh* and that insurance contracts are void as gambling, the practice was declared forbidden (Hooker 2003: 208–9). In 1992, however, the national conference of NU ulema decided otherwise, as outlined in the following extract. The detailed conditions outlined in the fatwa show how carefully the context of modern commercial life has been considered and how much it has shaped the interpretation of *fiqh*.

Extract 11-31: National Conference of NU Ulama

H. Imam Ghazali Said and A. Ma'ruf Asrori (eds) (2005), *Ahkamul Fuqaha, Solusi Problematika Aktual Hukum Islam: Keputusan Muktamar, Munas dan Konbes Nahdlatul Ulama (1926–1999 M)* [Solutions to Actual Problems in Islamic Law: Decisions of the NU National Ulama Conferences, Mid-term Conferences and Congresses, 1926–1999 AD], second revised edition, Lajnah Ta'lif Wan Nasyr (LTN NU), East Java, and Diantama, Surabaya. Extract: pp. 477–8.

---

75 But the situation in Indonesia, for example, is complex. Salim (2003: 229) expresses it as follows: 'The laws on *hajj* services, *zakat* management, and Islamic banking have been enacted in order to facilitate the efficient performance of religious duties for Muslim citizens. No punishment is meted out to those who decline to perform such religious duties'.

76 For further details about Indonesian fatwa, see Hooker (2003).

77 Sheikh Muhammad Bakhit (1854–1935), Mufti of Egypt from 1915 to 1920.

II. Insurance Law

1. Social insurance
Social insurance is permitted with the following conditions:
1.1. Social insurance is not considered to be *akad mu'awadhah* [a commutative contract] but rather *syirkah ta'awuniyah* [gifting the use of something lent which is later returned].
1.2. It is implemented by the government so that any loss is borne by the government and any benefits are returned for the interests of society.

2. Insurance against loss
Insurance against loss is permitted conditionally if the following stipulations are met:
2.1 If the loss insurance takes the form of conditions for objects which become bank collateral.
2.2 If the loss insurance is unavoidable, because of government regulations, such as insurance for goods exported and imported.

3. Life insurance
Life insurance is forbidden except under the following conditions:
3.1 The life insurance incorporates an element of saving.
3.2 When paying the premium, the insured person intends to save (deposit) the benefit with the insurer (the insurance company).
3.3 The insurer intends to keep the savings of the insuree in a manner permitted by sharia law.
3.4 If before the period agreed between the insurer and the insuree as stated in the policy, an unforeseen situation occurs so that the money is required, then the insuree can take or withdraw part of the saved money from the insurer, who has the responsibility to return the amount requested.
3.5 If the insuree is unable to meet the payment of the premiums then:
    3.5.1 The premium becomes a debt which can be paid in instalments from the time when the next premium payment falls due.
    3.5.2 The relationship between the insuree and the insurer does not end.
    3.5.3 The deposited money of the insuree is not forfeited.
    3.5.4 If the insuree dies before the due date then the heirs have the right to take part of the saved money, while the insurer is obliged to return part of the aforesaid money.

4. The delegates [to the congress] support and agree to the establishment of Islamic insurance.

5. Before the goals of Islamic insurance can be achieved, the existing system of insurance should be corrected by eliminating those elements which are forbidden, so that there are no infringements of Islamic teachings. To that end, steps similar to the procedures used with the banking commission should be taken.

11.9.2 Inheritance

Commentary In all societies the transmission of property from one generation to another is always a matter of state concern, especially when it may be taxable. In Muslim societies there is the extra complication of detailed Qur'anic injunctions concerning inheritance (for a listing see Mudzhar 2003: 167). In cases where children and spouses are named as heirs, males receive double the share of females (Q4: 7, 11, 12).[78] At the level of the individual and family, both state and sharia laws are commonly avoided by making bequests before death. The method is gift (*hibah*) by the owner before death to females and, now, the registration of transfer of land. If the property is movable (cash, jewels, shares) the issue of registration does not arise.

Field research in a central Javanese village whose residents were considered to be practising (*santri*) Muslims, many with a *pesantren* education, found that very few considered they understood sharia inheritance laws. In practice customary law was followed. This emphasized the heirs reaching agreement amicably among themselves about how property would be divided. There was also widespread use of *hibah*, as described above (Kamsi 2001: 122–3).

However, the increase in religiosity among many Southeast Asian Muslims (see section 10.1) is reflected in an increasing interest in applying the laws of inheritance as set out in the Qur'an. One example, given in the next extract, indicates the kind of theologically based argumention that is being developed so that the complex sharia laws on inheritance may be applied in contemporary contexts. The author of the extract, Prof. Dr Atho Mudzhar, shows how the principle of '*aul*[79] can be used as the basis for further calculations on the way estates are distributed. He provides examples of cases of '*aul* and comments:

---

78 But, as Professor Mudzhar points out, there are other situations in which males and females may receive equal shares. When parents, brothers and sisters are named as heirs, there are specific situations in which there may be equality of distribution (Mudzhar 2003: 168). The verses cited here are:

'Men shall have a share in what their parents and closest relatives leave, and women shall have a share in what their parents and closest relatives leave, whether the legacy be small or large: this is ordained by God' (Q4: 7, Haleem).

'Concerning your children, God commands you that a son should have the equivalent share of two daughters. If there are only daughters, two or more should share two-thirds of the inheritance, if one, she should have half. Parents inherit a sixth each if the deceased leaves children; if he leaves no children and his parents are his sole heirs, his mother has a third, unless he has brothers, in which case she has a sixth. [In all cases, the distribution comes] after payment of any bequests or debts. You cannot know which of your parents or your children is closer to you in benefit: this is a law from God, and He is all knowing, all wise' (Q4: 11, Haleem).

'You inherit half of what your wives leave, if they have no children; if they have children, you inherit a quarter. [In all cases, the distribution comes] after payment of any bequests or debts. If you have no children, your wives' share is a quarter; if you have children, your wives get an eighth. [In all cases, the distribution comes] after payment of any bequests or debts. If a man or a woman dies leaving no children or parents, but a single brother or sister, he or she should take one-sixth of the inheritance; if there are more siblings, they share one-third between them. [In all cases, the distribution comes] after payment of any bequests or debts, with no harm done to anyone: this is a commandment from God, and He is all knowing and benign to all' (Q4: 12, Haleem).

79 '[A] system of distribution of estate in inheritance in which, because the total of the shares of the heirs as stipulated in the Qur'an exceeds one [...] as indicated by the fact that the denominator is higher than the numerator, the fraction is changed to adjust to the denominator' (Mudzhar 2003: 171).

All the above cases of *'aul* involve the question of how to reconcile Qur'anic injunctions as divine laws with other types of divine law[,] namely the structure of families. All know that the arrangements as to who should die first or who survive whom is solely the authority of Allah, it is a divine law. The cases of *'aul* are evident that at the implementation level a Qur'anic divine law may encounter difficulties with other divine laws, in which case the former should be adjusted to the latter as long as the basic principles are kept (Mudzhar 2003: 172–3).

Mohamad Atho Mudzhar is professor of the sociology of Islamic law at the State Islamic University, Jakarta. He is also head of the Office of Research and Development and Training in the Ministry of Religious Affairs. The extract lists the conclusions he reaches concerning Islamic inheritance law and its application.

Extract 11-32: Mohamad Atho Mudzhar

Mohamad Atho Mudzhar (2003), *Islam and Islamic Law in Indonesia: A Socio-historical Approach* [in English], Office of Religious Research and Development and Training, Ministry of Religious Affairs, Republic of Indonesia, Jakarta. Extract: pp. 174–5.

F. Conclusions

The following conclusions may be drawn from the foregoing discussion, namely:

a. Historically Islamic law of inheritance is neither a full new set of rules imposed on the Muslim communities of the Arabs, nor a mere confirmation of the existing rules of the pre-Islamic Arabs. It is a radical modification of the existing rules, often with some incremental tones, to bring Muslim communities to pay higher respects to women and to be closer to fair and just societies.

b. The incremental tone of the Qur'anic injunctions on the shares of female heirs has not been emphasized, or [has] even [been] neglected in Islamic history. This was worsened by the lingering theories of abrogation on Qur'anic bequest verses, which could have been used as a tool to ensure the absence of discriminatory shares against women or other disadvantaged heirs.

c. The rules of the shares of male heirs as twice as much as that of their female counterparts is not always true[;] in many situations female heirs do get equal shares with those of their male counterparts.

d. In the light of the dynamic spirit of the Qur'anic injunction on inheritance, one may adjust the Qur'anic injunctions, at the implementation level, with all good intentions, to the socio-cultural realities and to the law of nature that might represent God's non-verbal injunctions.

* * * * *

Commentary   Sisters in Islam is a Malaysian non-government organization founded in 1987 by a small group of professional women to support other Muslim women. From the mid-1990s its members have been increasingly active in the media, discussion groups and workshops promoting interpretations of Islam which include respect for and equality of opportunity for women. They have actively supported women's claims in the sharia courts of Malaysia in areas such as divorce, polygamy and inheritance (see chapter 13). In the following extract from one of their memoranda, they list some practical suggestions for improving the position of women under Malaysia's sharia-inspired laws, while still respecting the spirit of the law.

Extract 11-33: Sisters in Islam

Sisters in Islam (2003), 'Violation of Muslim Women's Human Rights: Further Discrimination against Muslim Women under the Selangor Islamic Family Law Bill 2003 through Selective Gender Neutral Provisions' [in English], <http://www.sistersinislam.org.my/memorandums/29052003.htm>, dated 29 May 2003, accessed 13 May 2005.

Introduction

SIS [Sisters in Islam] is especially concerned that Muslim women are being discriminated against under the legal provisions in the Islamic Family Law statutes. SIS is even more concerned that, instead of removing or at least minimising the discriminatory provisions, the new Islamic Family Law Bill, which has now been passed by the Selangor State Legislative Assembly, actually has the effect of increasing discrimination against Muslim women. SIS is troubled by the fact that if the Selangor Islamic Family Law Bill is used as a blueprint for other states to amend their Islamic family laws in the move towards uniformity, it will result in further injustice being done to Muslim women throughout Malaysia. [...]

5. Inheritance
The administration of the syariah laws on inheritance emphasize the provision that male heirs be given a double share under the faraid distribution system,[80] without emphasizing on [*sic*] the rationale for this rule – that the man has the legal responsibility to provide maintenance for the family, and thus every female should always have a man to provide for her needs, be he a father, a brother, a husband or a son. In today's society, however, many women have to earn a living and contribute towards the family needs. Moreover divorced or widowed mothers often have to provide for their children's needs without assistance (or adequate assistance) from the father or male relatives who were traditionally regarded as responsible for the children's maintenance.

There is no mechanism in the present legal system for women to obtain the redress that would reflect on the balance and justice that was originally intended by the syariah.

In pre-Islamic Arabia, women had no inheritance rights and Islam introduced the rule that women should also have the right to inherit property. The concept of men receiving a greater share in inheritance was not a feature that was special to Islamic law. The Distribution Act 1958 for the non-Muslims in this country previously provided that the husband of a deceased woman would receive the whole of her estate,

---

80 Qur'anic stipulations for calculating the proportional distribution of an estate among the heirs.

while the wife of a deceased man would only receive one third of his estate if he had children, or one half if he had no children. However, this discrimination against non-Muslim women has been removed in the 1990s with the amendment to the Distribution Act.

Lack of historical understanding and misconceptions regarding such issues as polygamy as well as men's double share of inheritance, have led members of our society to look upon such provisions as divinely ordained rights conferred upon Muslim men, instead of as divinely ordained limitations upon male rights that had been previously conferred by the patriarchal pre-Islamic society.

Recommendation

Steps should be taken to –

(i)   raise awareness as to the historical circumstances and the rationale for men's double shares;
(ii)   to provide mechanism for women to claim financial support and assistance from male relatives;
(iii) to encourage possible negotiations between male and female heirs for equivalent distributions in light of present day circumstances;
(iv)   besides the faraid system, to consider other concepts in Islamic jurisprudence relating to property and income such as hibah (gift), wasiyah (testamentary disposition), amanah (trust), and waqaf (endowment). […]

11.9.3   Emergency Situations

Commentary   Islam recognizes that in extreme conditions and crises it may be necessary to break sharia laws in order to protect and preserve human life. Defining the contexts in which this extreme behaviour can be allowed and identifying the correct legal principles to support such actions are a matter for legal experts. As indicated in section 11.3, there is always a wide range of opinions by experts in *fiqh* on any matter, and emergency situations are no exception.

The tsunami that devastated coastal areas of northwest Sumatra (Aceh), West Malaysia and Thailand on 26 December 2004 killed tens of thousands of people. In Aceh, most of them were Muslims, for whom sharia requires burial. When it was suggested that for public health reasons cremation should be used, there was unease about whether this would infringe sharia injunctions.

Extract 11-34, from a Malaysian magazine, seeks to determine exactly what constitutes an emergency. It is a useful example of the methodical approach that is a characteristic of Muslims seeking guidance on how to interpret points of law. The writer begins by stating that the massive destruction caused by the tsunami in Aceh in many places left more dead than living. The writer asks whether in such conditions the bodies of Muslims could be cremated (rather than buried) and whether pork could be consumed to sustain the living (in the absence of other food).

The writer of the article approaches these issues firstly by consulting the works of nine scholars of the classical period of Islam for their definition of 'emergency situation' (*dharurah*). He then lists the Qur'anic verses (five separate verses) on which the scholarly definitions are based. He concludes that, based on all these sources, 'emergency' can be understood to be an unavoidable situation in which life is threatened and in which, to prevent loss of life, what is forbidden is permitted. Thus, eating and drinking substances forbidden under normal circumstances is permitted if death would otherwise result. The writer then turns to the specific case at hand (post-tsunami Aceh) and applies to it the principles he has established.

Extract 11-34: Mohd Shawqi al-Yarmouki

Mohd Shawqi al-Yarmouki (2005), 'Saat Apabila "Harus" Atasi "Haram"' [When 'Permissible' Overrides 'Forbidden'], *Milenia Muslim*, 31: 50–1. Extract: p. 51.

Basically, Islamic teachings emphasize that the responsibilities of the living to the dead are to properly look after them, that is, bathing, shrouding, reciting prayers and burying the body. However, in Aceh, because of the tsunami disaster, the situation is rather different because the hundreds of thousands who died outnumbered the survivors, making it very difficult to observe the proper rituals for each of the dead. Therefore, in an emergency situation like this, the bodies may be buried without the normal rituals, to avoid their total neglect and the risk of desecration by wild animals.

On the issue of cremation, there needs to be absolute certainty about whether cremation is essential [and] [w]hether or not unburied bodies that are not cremated endanger the living. Cremation of Muslims is permitted if various authorities, including medical experts, confirm that it needs to be done to avoid an even worse situation. Priority is given to protecting the living over those who have already died. However, if this is not the case, priority should be given to burying the dead.

Based on the reports of health experts, the situation does not yet require cremations. In a report in *Utusan Malaysia* [a newspaper] of Friday, 31 December 2004, the Pan America Health Organization stated that the decaying bodies of tsunami victims did not constitute a source for the spread of disease. [...] Based on this information, clearly the situation in Aceh does not necessitate the cremation of Muslims; rather they should be buried where this can be done.

Similarly, on the issue of eating pork, it is felt that the tsunami in Aceh does not threaten Muslims to the point of eating pork. This is because aid from the whole world, including Malaysia, is pouring into Aceh. At worst, they can 'hold on' and wait for *halal* [permitted] food to arrive. It would be inappropriate to take the easy way out and eat forbidden food while efforts are clearly being made to obtain *halal* food.

* * * * *

Commentary The following extract is from an email posted on the JIL email network in Indonesia. The email was posted by Ulil Abshar-Abdalla, a leading figure in JIL. Of note is the range of sources he cites in his search for guidance on the issue of adherence to sharia laws in emergencies. He starts from the position that the relevant *fiqh* principles should be the principle of the greater public good (*maslahat*) and the essential purposes of sharia (*maqasid al-shari'ah*).

Ulil Abshar-Abdalla wrote his evaluation of the situation in Aceh 11 days after the disaster when thousands of bodies still lay unburied. According to accounts he was receiving from volunteers on the ground, the conditions and the numbers of bodies made the task of burying all of them almost impossible, and there was a real threat that the survivors would be engulfed by a massive outbreak of disease.

Ulil begins by noting the reluctance of all but one Muslim leader to make public statements about the legality of cremation according to sharia.[81] Like the Malaysian commentator Mohd Shawqi al-Yarmouki (extract 11-34) he turns to the classical *fiqh* texts for guidance, but seeks opinions about the permissibility of cremation rather than what constitutes an emergency. He finds nothing in the texts directly concerning cremation. He therefore extrapolates from the closest comparable situation. Unlike the Malaysian commentator, he also draws on Hadith for guidance. His lines of argumentation are clear in the following extract.

Extract 11-35: Ulil Abshar-Abdalla

Ulil Abshar-Abdalla (2005), 'Soal Hukum Membakar Mayat di Aceh' [The Legal Issues Surrounding the Cremation of Bodies in Aceh], email posted on Jaringan Islam Liberal website, <http://groups.yahoo.com/group/islamliberal/>, dated 5 January 2005, accessed 7 January 2005.

My position is that the cremation of corpses in an emergency situation such as the present state in Aceh can be justified through Islamic argument. There are several supporting arguments:

1. As far as I can trace (please correct me if I'm mistaken) in several *fiqh* texts, both classical and modern, there is no specific discussion of cremation or the burning of corpses. What discussion there is ranges from whether a grave may be opened for one reason or another to the interment of more than one body in one grave. Cremation is not touched upon at all.

Although it is not stated explicitly in *fiqh* texts, cremation is clearly forbidden. Firstly, this practice has no precedent in the Sunnah of the Prophet. The Prophet said, *ihfiru, wa ausi'u, wa a'miqu* [Ar.: *'ihfiruu wa 'awsi'uu, wa 'ammiquu*], dig (the grave), widen it and deepen it (Hadith of Hasan, account of Tirmizi). So we are ordered to dig a grave and inter the corpse, not to cremate it or anything else. Second, cremation could be considered as 'showing disrespect to the body' (*intihak hurmat al mayyit* [Ar.: *'intihaaku hurmati 'al-mayyiti*]). This second reason is often cited as a basis to forbid exhumation, as it would show disrespect to the corpse.

2. Islam strongly emphasizes the teaching of 'respect for the deceased'. It is from such teachings that the principle of disrespecting the body is forbidden. We can put forward examples of this. A number of Hadith forbid a person from sitting on top of a grave. One Hadith states: *la tajlisu 'al al quburi wa la tushallu ilaiha* [Ar.: *la tajlisuu*

---

ala 'alqubuuri wala tusalluu `alayhaa]* (do not sit on a grave, and do not pray facing towards it) (Hadith, the account of Muslim from Abi Martsad al Ghanawi). Another Hadith states: *La an yajlisa ahadukum 'ala jamratin, fa takhlashu ila jildihi, khairun lahu min an yajlisa 'ala qabrin* [Ar.: *la'an yajlisa 'ahadukum `alaa jamratin fatakhlusu 'ilaa jildihi, khayrun lahu min 'an yajlisa `alaa qabrin]* (should one of you sit on burning embers, and the ember penetrates to the skin, this is better than had he sat on a grave) (Hadith of the account of al Jama'ah). Another Hadith states: *Kasru 'adzm al mayyiti ka kasri 'adzm al hayyi fi al itsmi* [Ar.: *kasru `azmi 'almayyiti ka kasri `azmi 'alhayyi fi 'al'ithmi] (breaking the bones of a corpse is an equivalent sin to breaking the bones of a living person) (Hadith of Hasan, account of Ibn Majah from Umm Salamah).

2.[82] Nevertheless, in an emergency situation, ulema allow practices that were initially considered to show disrespect to a body, because of an emergency or another need that is legitimate according to sharia. This is evident in a number of opinions of ulema concerning the following matters. In normal circumstances, it is forbidden to exhume a corpse. But this practice is permitted under the following circumstances [...]

[Ulil then gives several examples of grounds for exhuming bodies.]

These examples demonstrate that practices that were initially forbidden to be done to a body, for instance exhumation or operating upon the stomach, are permitted if there is a need that can be justified by sharia. Although not stated explicitly, this permission is clearly based on the jurisprudence rule of *al dlarurat tubih al mahzurat* [Ar.: *'addaruuraatu tubiihu 'almahzuuraati]* (in an emergency, things otherwise forbidden are permissible).

3. There are several rules of jurisprudence that we can use as a guide to consider the legal aspect of cremation. These rules, apart from what I have stated above, are as follows:

a. *Iza dlaqa al amru ittasa* [Ar.: *'idhaa daaqa 'al'amru 'ittasa`]* (if something becomes tight and difficult, then it must be loosened).
b. *La dlarara wa la dlirara* [Ar.: *laa darara wa la diraar]* (danger is not permissible, nor is endangering another person).
c. *Al dlararu yuzal [Ar.: 'addararu yuzaal]* (each danger must be overcome and eliminated).
d. *Yutahammal al dlarar al khas li daf' al dlarar al `am* [Ar.: *yutahammalu 'addararu 'alkhaassu lidaf i 'addarari 'al`ammi]* (a limited danger may be endured to avoid a greater danger).
e. *Al dlarar al asyadd yuzalu bi al dlarar al akhaff* [Ar.: *'addararul 'azyadu yuzaalu biddararil 'akhaffi]* (a more grave danger must be overcome by enduring a lesser danger).

---

82 The original has two sections numbered '2'.

f. *Al dlarar yudfa' bi qadr al imkan* [Ar.: *'addararu yudfa`u biqadril 'imkaan*] (each danger should be overcome through all-out effort).

g. *Al hajah tanzilu manzilat al dlarurah* [Ar.: *'alhaajatu tanzilu manzilata 'addaru-urah*] (an urgent need has the same standing as an emergency situation).

h. *Al masyaqqah tajlib al taisir* [Ar.: *'almashaqqatu tajlibu 'attaysiir*] (a difficulty calls for an easing of the situation).

These eight rules are actually of the same spirit. First, in a pressing or emergency situation, something that under normal circumstances is forbidden becomes permissible. Second, every dangerous situation must be overcome by enduring a lesser danger. [...]

Islam desires an improved situation, *al dinu yusrun* [Ar.: *'addiinu yusrun*] and God does not desire something that is too heavy for mortals to bear: *la yukallifu Allahu nafsan illa wus'aha* [Ar.: *la yukallifu 'allahu nafsan 'illa wus`ahaa*] (God does not demand that someone do something unless he is able); *ma yuridu Allahu li yaj'ala 'alaikum min haraj* [Ar.: *ma yuriidu 'allaahu liyaj`ala `alykum min haraj*] (Allah does not desire difficulty for you); *Yuridu Allahu bikum al yusra wa la yuridu bikum al 'usr* [Ar.: *yuriidu 'allaahu bikum 'alyusra wa la yuriidu bikum 'al`usra*] (God desires facility for you, not difficulty for you).

Based on such considerations, we can justify the 'cleansing' of corpses in the Aceh disaster at present by cremation.

That is my conclusion as far as I understand the main tenets of the teachings of Islam. Hopefully this opinion will be useful input to lighten the burden that the community in Aceh bears at present.

May Aceh recover quickly, and the community there again enjoy a normal life. We pray for those who lost their lives, that their souls be accepted by God, their sins be forgiven, and their good deeds be rewarded many fold.

And God knows the truth, and He is the place of origin and of return.

12 Islam, State and Governance

Greg Fealy

INTRODUCTION

The relationship between Islam and the state has been complex and contentious, both as a matter of doctrine and as historical fact. It is often said that Islam recognizes no separation between 'church' and state, and that politics is an integral element of Islamic life. But as Carl Brown has pointed out, much of Muslim history 'has been characterised by the largely successful attempt to bar government from proclaiming (and then enforcing) religious orthodoxy' (Brown 2000: 3). In effect, regardless of the theory that Islam and the state should be tightly bound together, Muslim communities have usually sought to resist state efforts to determine what is 'correct' Islamic behaviour.

Most aspects of the Islam–state relationship have been subject to intense debate among Muslims. Even matters as basic as whether or not Islam should have a formal role in the state have been disputed. At one end of the spectrum are those sometimes labelled 'secular' Muslims, who argue that there is no explicit Qur'anic or Prophetic requirement for a formal Islamic role in the state. They say that Islamic principles and ethics might guide a nation's political behaviour but that there should be no direct state involvement in religious affairs. Thus, religion is limited to the private sphere and should not enter the public domain. At the other end of the spectrum are those who believe that an 'Islamic state' is central to the Islamic struggle. Islam, they argue, provides a complete system of norms from which politics cannot be quarantined. Pious Muslims must, they say, commit themselves to implementing God's plan for society and the state. According to this view, Islam should permeate both the private and public spheres.

Among those who favour an 'Islamic state', there is much disagreement as to how it is to be defined and constituted. Most 'Islamic state' proponents believe that state implementation of Islamic law (sharia) is essential; consensus is more difficult, however, on the content of Islamic law and how strictly it is to be enforced. Should state responsibility be restricted to the ritual or family law requirements of sharia, or should sharia extend to criminal sanctions as prescribed in the Qur'an (*hudud*)? Should women be obliged to cover their heads and wear 'modest' clothing? Should alcohol and gambling be prohibited? Can a non-Muslim or a woman become head of a majority Muslim state? It is often such practical details of sharia implementation that generate the most heated debate. Beyond these legal issues, there is also contention over the scope of the state's role in facilitating Islamic predication and devotional activities. For example, should the state collect wealth taxes (*zakat*), organize pilgrimages, sponsor mosque construction and the training of preachers, as well as finance and monitor Islamic education?

Within Southeast Asia, there are a number of different forms of state recognition of Islam. Brunei styles itself as a 'Malay Muslim Monarchy'; it is a sultanate and the sultan's power is absolute. Malaysia has Islam as the 'state religion' and since 2001 its government has asserted that the nation is a de facto Islamic state. Indonesia is often described as 'secular', though 'religiously neutral' is a more accurate term as the national doctrine of Pancasila has as its first principle 'Belief in One Almighty God'. In all three nations, there is extensive state involvement in Islamic affairs. The position and aspirations of Muslim minority communities elsewhere in Southeast Asia vary markedly. The Rohingya of Burma seek their own autonomous state within the Union of Myanmar; some sections of the Bangsamoro in the southern Philippines are content with an autonomous Muslim region whereas others seek to create an independent Islamic state; and Muslims in the south of Thailand in general demand greater autonomy and socio-economic equality, but some strive for full independence and a state based on Islam.

Unlike other chapters in this sourcebook, this one is organized by country rather than by theme. The reason is that each country has had specific political circumstances affecting the debate over the formal role that Islam should have within the state. Placing these country items in chronological order allows the reader to follow developments in the public debate.

EXTRACTS AND COMMENTARY

12.1 INDONESIA

Commentary   The 'Islamic state' debate is one of the most divisive issues in Indonesia's political history. In mid-1945, the debate between Islamic leaders and nationalists over whether Indonesia was to be a secular or 'Islamic' state led to deadlock in the committee that was drafting the constitution. Islamic leaders wanted the state to be formally based on Islam. They eventually accepted Sukarno's proposed five principles (Pancasila), the first of which was 'Belief in One Almighty God'. This formulation allowed Muslim groups to argue that Indonesia would be a state based on religion, not a secular state. However, Islamic politicians still sought specific acknowledgement of sharia law, leading to a second impasse. A 'gentlemen's agreement' was arrived at entitled 'The Jakarta Charter'. The charter contained a clause with seven critical words (in Bahasa Indonesia, *dengan kewajiban menjalankan syari'at Islam bagi pemeluk-pemeluknya*) that obliged Muslims to implement Islamic law. This clause was eventually omitted when the constitution was promulgated the day after independence was declared on 17 August 1945. Muslim leaders were bitter at the dropping of the seven words; the struggle to have them reinstated in the constitution became a central part of the Islamist agenda in later years. Islamic parties sought unsuccessfully to insert the seven words into a revised constitution in the late 1950s, and again in the late 1960s. For most of Soeharto's 32-year authoritarian rule, advocacy of the sharia clause in the Jakarta Charter was strongly discouraged. Following his downfall, a number of Islamist parties have several times sought to reinsert the seven words in the constitution, though their proposals have been rejected by large majorities in the Majelis Permusyawaratan Rakyat (MPR, People's Consultative Assembly).

12.1.1   The Jakarta Charter

Commentary   The Jakarta Charter was drafted on 22 June 1945 by a nine-man subcommittee of the Badan Penyeledik Usaha Persiapan Kemerdekaan Indonesia (Investigating Committee for the Preparatory Work for Indonesian Independence). The subcommittee was chaired by Sukarno and contained an equal number of members representing the secular and Islamic positions. In the search for compromise between these two positions, the subcommittee agreed to a wording that acknowledged the status of sharia for Muslims but was vague regarding who was 'obliged' to implement Islamic law: the state or the individual. The charter, minus the seven-word 'sharia clause' (shown in italics in the translation below), became the preamble to the new constitution of the Republic of Indonesia on 18 August 1945.

Extract 12-1: The Jakarta Charter

Piagam Djakarta [The Jakarta Charter], reprinted in Indonesian in Appendix I of B.J. Boland (1982), *The Struggle of Islam in Modern Indonesia*, Martinus Nijhoff, The Hague. Extract: p. 243.

Whereas independence is the right of every nation, therefore colonialism must be eliminated from the world as it is contrary to the character of human nature and justice.

And the struggle of the Indonesian independence movement has now reached a joyful moment, with the Indonesian people safely brought to the portal of an Indonesian state that is free, united, sovereign, just and prosperous.

By the blessings of God Almighty and driven by the noble ideal of a free national life, the Indonesian people hereby declare their independence.

Further, in order to establish a Government of the Independent State of Indonesia that will protect all Indonesian people and the whole of the Indonesian territory, and to advance general welfare, to raise educational standards, and to participate in establishing a world order founded upon freedom, eternal peace and social justice, national independence of the Indonesian people is embodied in the constitution of the state of Indonesia, which takes the form of the Republic of the Indonesian state in which the people are sovereign and which is based upon: Belief in One Almighty God *with the obligation to implement the sharia for adherents of Islam* [emphasis added], a just and civilized humanitarianism, the unity of Indonesia, and a Democracy guided by wisdom arising from consultation and representation, which democracy shall ensure social justice for all Indonesian people.

12.1.2   Zainal Abidin Ahmad

Commentary   Zainal Abidin Ahmad (1911–83) was a Masyumi politician and one of the leading modernist thinkers on the Islamic state issue. Masyumi was the Islamic party formed in 1945 as a united political vehicle for Indonesian Muslims. From 1952, when Nahdlatul Ulama (NU, Revival of the Religious Scholars) split from the party, until 1960, when President Sukarno banned it, Masyumi was largely a modernist party.[1] The following extract is from a book first published by Zainal in 1956 to explain the concepts underlying, and make the case for, an Islamic state in the lead-up to the Konstituante (Constituent Assembly) sessions held in Bandung between December 1956 and June 1959. The Constituent Assembly was an elected body whose purpose was to draft a permanent constitution to replace the 1950 provisional constitution. The assembly became deadlocked on the issue of the insertion of the Jakarta Charter's sharia clause, with the Islamic parties failing to gain the necessary two-thirds majority in a series of ballots in May and June 1959. In July 1959, President Sukarno dissolved the assembly and decreed that Indonesia would revert to the founding 1945 constitution.

Zainal's book was the most detailed and intellectually rigorous of the many publications on the subject of an Islamic state during the mid-1950s, and it soon became a primary reference for Muslim politicians proposing such a state. Zainal went on to become a deputy speaker of both the Constituent Assembly and the Dewan Perwakilan Rakyat (DPR, national parliament). After leaving politics, he served as professor at several academic institutions.

Zainal argues that an Islamic state should be defined not by symbols but by substance and he sets out various criteria for judging if a state is indeed 'Islamic'. Central issues for him are the supremacy of sharia, the upholding of Islamic values and the safeguarding of human rights, including the right to religious freedom. As with many Masyumi leaders of this period, he is critical of the self-declared 'Islamic states' in the Middle East, and sees Pakistan as the model that Indonesia should follow. He also seeks to provide a framework for an 'Islamic' democracy, drawing on scripture, the example of the Prophet and the interpretations of seminal Islamic scholars to support his case.

Extract 12-2: Zainal Abidin Ahmad

Zainal Abidin Ahmad (2001), *[Membangun] Negara Islam* [(Creating) an Islamic State], Pustaka Iqra, Yogyakarta. Extract: pp. 2–31, 65, 118–25, 176–98.

Part I   The Aspiration for an 'Islamic State'

A.   *The Islamic State* [...]

The twentieth century is the century of the rebirth of the desire for an Islamic state. After first being created in the period of the Prophet Muhammad, blessings and peace

---

1   See Chapter 5, Indonesia country overview, for more details about Masyumi.

be upon him, and continued by his Companions, then falling silent and submerged for more than a thousand years, the aspiration for an Islamic State has re-emerged among the world community.

Since the Prophet's era, there has never been a period in which the quest for an Islamic State has caught the attention of humankind as in our present era. [...]

Islamic world awake! [...]

The Islamic State ideal or ideology is not satisfied with 'Islamic' symbols that are displayed by each nation, or with the 'rank' that is borne by their Heads of State. The Islamic State ideology is not a matter of formalism, but a matter of the content and basic principles that are used along with the aspirations supported by that state, in other words, the content, principles and Islamic aspirations that were taught and practised by the Prophet Muhammad, blessings and peace be upon him, and continued by his companions, the Rightly Guided Caliphs, in earlier times.

Because of that, states that call themselves 'Islamic States' (such as Yemen, Saudi Arabia and Egypt) are not yet recognized as conforming with true Islamic ideology, although their Heads of State are Muslim and they promote Islamic movements. This often causes doubt and confused thinking regarding the ideal of an Islamic State. People see the reality of states that call themselves 'Islamic States', with the result that they reject Islamic ideology based on that reality.

Of truly great significance is that the State of Pakistan has pioneered the struggle to create an Islamic ideology. The Pakistan Constitutional Council studied, investigated and explored the foundations, content and form of an Islamic State on an official basis. Drawing on this research, it made its state into the 'Islamic Republic of the State of Pakistan'. It undertook further research in the fields of Islamic law, constitution and the like. This led to the formation of an Islamic State that implements God's law and the teachings of His Prophet. Pakistan's example has been followed by several states and Islamic peoples. [...]

'Daulah Islamiyah', Islamic State. This was not just as taught by the Prophet Muhammad, but was also created during his lifetime. Indeed, there is a special quality in the Islamic faith compared to other religions. Islam does not recognize the teaching of 'separation of religion from the state', but Islam embraces the two – as an expert said: 'a complete civilization'. [pp. 2–3] [...]

B. *The Caliphate and the Abode of Islam* [...]

To describe the ideals pertaining to affairs of state that are alive in Muslim groups across the world, several terms need to be introduced:

1. Caliphate [...]
2. Abode of Islam [...]
3. *Baldatun thayyibatun wa rabbun ghafur* [literally, 'a morally good country that has God's blessings'; the author regards this as the least important term for his treatise] [...]

The term 'caliphate' comes from the Holy Qur'an and the Prophet's Hadith, while the term 'Abode of Islam' emerged from the community. [...] With the term 'caliphate', people's thinking is centred on government leaders as well as political problems. It refers to the form of an Islamic State, that is, a state that is led by a Head of State holding the position of Caliph. With Abode of Islam, the focus of thinking is on the structure of Islamic society, that is, social and economic matters. [p. 6] [...]

The caliphate is a system of governance in accordance with the Islamic teachings brought by the Prophet Muhammad, blessings and peace be upon him. It can be struggled for and established by the Islamic community for people's respective regions and homelands, and can also be created for all Muslims in the world. So it can be national in form for one people, and can also take an international form for all Muslims in the world. [p. 11] [...]

C.   *The Terminology of the 'Caliphate'* [...]

An Islamic State is a state promised by God for the Islamic community, and it has the following characteristics:

1. Sovereignty in the state must be held by the people who have faith in God, as the electors of the caliph, the head of state.
2. Religion must be firmly controlled by the state, both in government and in society.
3. All feelings of fear or anxiety must be completely eliminated, replaced by a sense of true security.
4. Freedom of religion to pay worship to God is upheld in the widest sense. There is no coercion, pressure or persuasion that would remove the sense of freedom and free will. [pp. 21–2] [...]

Part 2   The Basis of an Islamic State

God commands you to hand back your trusts to their rightful owners, and to pass judgement upon men with fairness. Noble is that to which Allah exhorts you. He hears all and observes all.

Believers, obey God and the Apostle and those in authority among you. Should you disagree about anything refer it to God and the Apostle, if you truly believe in God and the Final Day. This will in the end be better and more just. (Q4: 58–9)[2]

The two verses above are the foundation of the establishment of an Islamic State. In the exegetical book *Al-Manar* [The Lighthouse, by the Egyptian Muslim reformer Muhammad Abduh] it is spelled out: 'These two verses are the foundation stones of Islamic State governance'. [...]

Each person who reads the above verses will have no difficulty grasping the fundamentals of the political affairs of state. Without referring to prominent exegetes, we can conclude that the most important political fundamentals in those verses are:

---

2   'God commands you [people] to return things entrusted to you to their rightful owners, and, if you judge between people, to do so with justice: God's instructions to you are excellent, for He hears and sees everything. You who believe, obey God and the Messenger, and those in authority among you. If you are in dispute over any matter, refer it to God and the Messenger, if you truly believe in God and the Last Day: that is better and fairer in the end' (Q4: 58–9, Haleem).

1. The executors of the state are the functionaries holding the noble and holy mandate of the people, which they must fulfil in the best possible way for the people who become their constituents.
2. Officials in judicial institutions have the task of implementing 'justice' in handing down sentences.
3. All the people must elect representatives who will become the 'Uli al-Amri',[3] who are obliged to observe all laws and regulations after the law of God and His Messenger.

Those are the points that are contained in the above verses, which become the basic political principles of an Islamic State. Viewed from the perspective of the *trias politica* system,[4] we find the existence of three main state institutions. The first is the executive, named the 'mandate holder' of the [Islamic] community. The second is judicial institutions, named the 'executors of justice' for all humankind. The third is the legislative institutions, named 'Uli al-Amri', which are the people's representatives in making state laws and regulations that must be obeyed.

Viewed from a juridical standpoint, these verses give us the original source of all law and statutes, that is, laws derived from God and His Messenger, as well as laws created by the Uli al-Amri as the law-making institution (the legislature) that must be upheld by communities of the faithful. Later, if among legislatures (Uli al-Amri) there occurs a conflict of understanding or views, so return to the original source of law, the Law of God and His Messenger. [pp. 30–1] [...]

D. *Sovereignty of the People*

Islam uses the term 'Uli al-Amri' to denote the main foundations of the state, that is, the principle of 'people's sovereignty', which is more popularly known by the name 'democracy'. The command to obey the Uli al-Amri is one level below obeying God and His Messenger. This means there is no command that is higher among fellow humans after the command of God and His Messenger than the command of the Uli al-Amri.

The Uli al-Amri are representatives elected by the people. The principle is sovereignty by the people (democracy). The people have authority and power. [p. 65] [...]

Part 3 The Characteristics of an Islamic State [...]

F. *The Parliamentary State*

VI. What is the difference between Uli al-Amri and the present parliament? [...]
1. The source of all laws and regulations in a parliamentary state is the people. Islam also has the same view, but is even more precise. This is proven in the use of the

---

3 Ar.: *ulw 'al-'amri*; 'those holding authority'. Zainal uses the term to refer both to the people's representatives and to the institution in which they sit, that is, the legislature.

4 *Trias politica* refers to the concept of balance of power within a democracy between three key elements of the state: the executive, the legislature and the judiciary.

term 'Uli al-Amri', which means people's representatives. But there is a virtue in Islam, one that is above the people: determining the legal guidelines and basis of regulations is the law of God and His Messenger, named eternal law (*hukum abadi*). These laws are not numerous, so their character is not to limit or diminish the supreme authority of the people's representatives, but to give clear guidelines and enduring leadership. [pp. 118–19]

G.   *The Republican State* [...]

The *governance of a caliphate* must be created in the form of a *republic*, in which the Uli al-Amri as the people's representatives have supreme authority in the state, [and] in which the head of state is elected according to the people's wishes. This governance can be founded in each nation that has a majority Muslim population and the demonstrated wish to uphold its religious ideology. Governments are caliphal governments in their respective regions. [pp. 124–5] [...]

Part 5   Key Problems in the State [...]

B.   *Creating a Constitution* [...]

Minimum requirements for an Islamic State [...]

To achieve the maximal requirements for an Islamic State is indeed difficult. It is not sufficient to say 'Islam is the official religion of the state', or 'the head of state must be a Muslim', 'the state is based on Islam' or some other formulation. [...] [I]n fact formal features do not fulfil Islamic teachings. Thus it is very important to indicate the minimal form that a state must have to be able to be recognized as an Islamic State. The minimal requirements that a state must have are:

1. Muslim citizens are a majority in the state. This majority also must be realized in the number of people's representatives in the legislatures, from the national to the local.
2. The head of state must be Muslim. Whether this guarantee has to be set out in the constitution or left to practical convention is not the primary issue.
3. The state ideology must be in keeping with Islamic ideology or, at a minimum, not be incompatible with Islamic ideology. The elements of Islamic ideology must be present in the state ideology, although the formulation [may be] called Pancasila [the five principles of the Indonesian state], principal values, or other principles.
4. The laws of the state must not be in conflict with Islamic law. Although the right to determine the law and statutes is the right of the people's representatives, the constitution contains a guarantee that each regulation that is passed is not contrary to Islamic law.
5. The constitution must guarantee that Deliberation and the general bases of democracy are implemented in the form of the state and in the actions of its institutions. Deviation from these foundations means abandoning the character and form of an Islamic State. [pp. 176–7] [...]

Part 6 The Caliph–Head of State

A. *The Position of the Caliph*

The caliph occupies the highest position in an Islamic State. He[5] is the people's representative, who holds leadership of the government to bring about the tranquillity and well-being desired by the people. He is the highest institution in the state; below and beside him are the institutions that carry out the work of government.

As the absolute representative of all the people, he is the Head of State. His position is subject to both substantive and theoretical law, and beneath the Uli al-Amri as the People's Consultative Assembly. He leads and heads the executive, he decides on state legislation together with the people's representatives in the legislature, and beside him are the judicial institutions as the bodies upholding justice. [p. 192] [...]

C. *Requirements for the Head of State*

1. What are the prerequisites for the Head of State?

To achieve a position as high as this, Islamic regulations do not impose conditions that are too strict, provided [the candidate] is able to fulfil his obligations. They do not ask for prerequisites like high learning or broad knowledge, such that the Head of State must be a philosopher, for example. They do not ask for religious knowledge or excessive religious fidelity, for instance that the Head of State must be a great Islamic scholar. [...]

The first and main precondition is that he be a Muslim. This is absolute; it cannot be negotiated and it cannot be swayed by the size of the vote. If this condition is not met, the state cannot be named an 'Islamic State'. [pp. 197–8]

12.1.3 Hamka

Commentary Haji Abdul Malik Karim Amrullah (1908–81), better known simply as Hamka, was one of the most influential Indonesian modernist writers and leaders of the twentieth century. He was active in the modernist mass Islamic organization Muhammadiyah for most of his life and was also drawn to politics. He was a member of Sarekat Islam (SI, Islamic Association), the first genuinely mass-based Islamic-nationalist organization. Formed in 1912, SI suffered a succession of splits from the early 1920s, with one faction forming itself into Partai Sarekat Islam Indonesia (PSII; Indonesian Islamic Union Party). After Masyumi's establishment in 1945, Hamka became a leading figure in the party, though he rejected offers of executive or legislative positions. He wrote prodigiously and with remarkable breadth. His works included scholarly texts on Islamic reform, Sufism and jurisprudence as well as novels, biographies and poetry. Under the Soeharto regime he accepted the position of founding chair of Majelis Ulama Indonesia (MUI, Indonesian Council of Ulama).

The following extract is from Hamka's address to the Constituent Assembly in 1957. The assembly's task was to draft a new constitution to replace the interim 1950

5 In the text, the word *ia* is used, which can mean male or female. It has been translated in the masculine form here because that is almost certainly the way the author intended it.

constitution. Hamka represented Masyumi in the assembly. His speech is notable for its impassioned and eloquent assertion of Islam's centrality to Indonesia's national identity and struggle for independence. He argues that those who reject an Islamic state are victims of the Dutch colonial campaign to de-Islamize the thinking of Indonesians. He repudiates Pancasila as an alternative to Islam and regards the creation of an Indonesian Islamic state as a reassertion of the nation's inherently Islamic character and a means to correct Christian colonial distortions.

Extract 12-3: Hamka

Hamka (2001), 'Islam sebagai Basis Negara' [Islam as the Basis of the State], pp. 97–142 in *Debat Dasar Negara Islam dan Pancasila: Konstituante 1957* [Debate on Islamic and Pancasila-based State: Constituent Assembly 1957], Pustaka Panjimas, Jakarta. Extract: pp. 98–141.

Honourable members, those who defend the Pancasila always talk about 'The Spirit of the Proclamation of 17 August' [the 1945 proclamation of independence]. They say that it is the essence of Pancasila!

We also acknowledge, and have never denied, that the Spirit of the Proclamation of 17 August does exist, but we cannot accept that this spirit is based on the Pancasila! The real spirit of the Proclamation of 17 August was 'the spirit of independence and freedom, the spirit of no longer wanting to be colonized'.

It was that cry for independence that reverberated from Sabang to Merauke! The cry for independence, carried by radio waves to every corner of the motherland, to the mountains, the gorges, the plateaus and the islands. 'Independence: we will not be colonized any longer!' Under the spark of that sentence our unity and agreement emerged of its own accord, whether we were a Muslim or a Christian, a heathen or a shaman, a Balinese Hindu or a Dayak animist.

So in the spirit of independence, the spirit of not wanting to be colonized any more, we each searched for something to base it on, sought a means to give life to it. We wanted to be independent; we did not want to be colonized again! Thus at the start of the Revolution there was a well-known slogan 'Independence or Death!' We knew that the struggle would call for blood, for tears, for lives and for deaths! Because all we had at that moment was the strength of our spirit, whilst our enemy had the strength of their arms.

At that point in time [the 1945–49 revolutionary period] the struggle meant: 'For each one lost, two more will take his place! Better to have the earth as one's pillow than to live as the dead!' Our instinct is to be scared of facing death! But we wanted to make that death worthwhile. Living as a slave is more degrading and worthless than dying fighting for one's aspirations. At that moment there was a tangible need for faith, for belief! So each group sought a basis in its own religious tenets for making that death worthwhile. Each area moved on its own, using its own initiative and its own wisdom! Facing death, to be free! It was long after this that the propaganda for Pancasila began at Amuntai.[6] [...]

---

6 This is a reference to President Sukarno's controversial speech in Amuntai, Kalimantan, in 1953, in which he warned that non-Muslim areas of the country would secede if Indonesia became an Islamic

Muslims, without thinking about whether they were now with Masyumi, PNI, NU, the Socialists, Perti or the Workers' Party,[7] brought to life the spirit of the proclamation of independence on 17 August 1945 through their religious tenets!

People were willing to see the bodies of their sons brought home covered in blood, lifeless, because they spontaneously felt that their sons had died as martyrs! There was no place for fear other than the fear of God!

'God is Most Great!'

Only God is Most Great; all others are insignificant! There is no god but God, there is no other god, no other place of worship, no other source of fear, no other source of mercy, [no other source] of protection but God! When a father receives the news that the son who bears all his hopes has been killed on the battlefield, the first thing he asks is 'Where did the bullet enter – from the front or from behind?' If it entered his back, perhaps he died running to save himself, so his martyrdom is in doubt! But if it entered from the front, it is a sign that he died fighting! One of the seven great sins is fleeing the battle day (*tawalla jaumaz zahf*), turning and running when in combat!

This is what we know; this was the spirit of, or what gave life to, the Proclamation of 17 August – not Pancasila. Truly, Mr Chairman, Pancasila has never been and will never be familiar or popular. You never hear of it! All that has been heard is the cry 'Allahu Akbar' [God is most great]. The fire that burns in the breast to this moment, Mr Chairman, is not Pancasila, but 'Allahu Akbar!'

In fact, it is 'Allahu Akbar!' that is, in essence, in the innermost hearts of most of the defenders of Pancasila who are here today, even to this moment.

If I asked those hearts, asked the defenders of Pancasila, what they felt in their hearts when their beloved sons died and they took them to be buried – was it Pancasila or Allahu Akbar? – surely they would respond: 'Allahu Akbar'.

Only in this way would the heart be satisfied – the heart that never lies!

It is Allahu Akbar that is written in your hearts,[8] which we now ask to be realized. It is Allahu Akbar that holds within it all moral principles [...]. It is Allahu Akbar that becomes your defence when facing great danger! It is Allahu Akbar that becomes your defence when death hangs over your head. It was Allahu Akbar that you were met with when you came out of your mother's womb! [pp. 98–101] [...]

We sometimes smile, Mr Chairman, at endeavours to cover up the truth by lying about history, [endeavours] that are sometimes very obvious to the eye. For instance, in pictures of Prince Diponegoro[9] on horseback, a 'crescent moon' [the symbol of

---

state. The 'Amuntai controversy' had a powerful polarizing effect on the post-1945 debate between nationalists and Islamic parties on the basis of the state. Sukarno's remarks came under strong attack from Muslim leaders, and from this time the Islamic parties spoke out openly against Pancasila as the national ideology. For a good account of this, see Feith (1962: 281–2).

7   PNI: Partai Nasionalis Indonesia (Indonesian Nationalist Party), Perti: Persatuan Tarbiyah Islamiyah (Islamic Education Association). See also the glossary.

8   The 'your' in this case refers to those members of the Constituent Assembly, presumably including Muslim secular nationalists and leftists, who were opposed to the Islamic state proposal.

9   Diponegoro (1785?–1855) is one of the most celebrated figures in Indonesian history. A Javanese prince from the sultanate of Yogyakarta, he led a major rebellion against the Dutch, known as the Java War (1825–30).

Islam] is clearly visible on the horse's saddle [but was then painted out]. So it was a 'Pancasila' painter who deliberately erased that 'crescent moon' from the saddle.

And recently I also saw a painting of Imam Bonjol[10] belonging to the Ministry of Information. In well-known pictures of him, he always has Muslim prayer beads in his hand, so in the Ministry of Information picture the prayer beads have been taken out. Is this also a way to get rid of Islam, replacing it with Pancasila?

That, Mr Chairman, is the mystery of the superficial thinking of the supporters of Pancasila.

Don't they know what the secret of the 'crescent moon' is on the saddle of Prince Amirul Mukminin Abdulhamid Diponegoro? It is a symbol of the conviction that Dutch efforts to take away the faith of the Javanese were totally futile, although they [the Dutch] were victorious in terms of arms.

When the Dutch subjugated Java, they could only take away its material possessions, but they could not take away its faith. [pp. 105–6] [...]

In fact, if Indonesians were conscious of their identity, they would not want those prayer beads removed just because they reject Islam as the basis of the state. Because it is there that the secret of Tuanku Imam Bonjol's strength in opposing the Dutch lay – he who we recognize as being our national champion.

The string of beads is three times 33.

Thirty-three times saying 'Subhanallah', which means God the Most Holy, 33 times saying 'Alhamdulillah', which means All Praise to God, 33 times saying 'Allahu Akbar'! It is only God who is the Greatest. That is the base from which to begin facing all of life's difficulties.

And when they are added up, those 33 times become the 99 names of God, through which the universe is ordered, including our homeland of Indonesia, where we were born and where we fought our struggle and from which we take strength!

They [the secularists] do not want to accept Islam as the foundation of the state, when in fact it is the original background of the largest group in our country, which is deeply rooted and constitutes the Indonesian people's identity. Because they are scared of Islam, people are shameless enough to lie about history, resulting in even the paintings being destroyed.

Perhaps one day in the future, Sentot's turban will be replaced with a *peci* [traditional Muslim rimless felt cap], Kyai Maja's Arab robe will be replaced with a shirt, and Tuanku Nan Renceh Haji's waistcoat will be replaced with a tie.[11]

If we criticize this, it is because it contradicts the real situation. Then we are verbally abused with the accusation 'Hey, you've committed treason!'

Mr Chairman, I invite those of you who defend the Pancasila to return to the truth, to realize that Pancasila has no historical basis in Indonesia.

And we do not fight for Islam as the basis of the state for ourselves.

---

10   Imam Bonjol (1772–1864) was a reformist Islamic leader who became a military commander of Muslim forces against the Dutch during the Padri War (1821–38).

11   All three were Islamic leaders who resisted Dutch colonial rule. Sentot and Kyai Maja were key supporters of Prince Diponegoro in the Java War (1825–30). Abdullah Tuangku Nan Renceh led a rebellion against Dutch forces in Minangkabau, west Sumatra, in 1803.

Not for Masyumi, PSII, NU, Perti, AKUI or PPTI,[12] no; but for all Muslims. Those of you in other parties are also included in this, for our children and grand-children. In the corner of your hearts there is still a glimmer of the light of Faith, which flows in your blood, which was the starting point for the first steps in our fore-bears' struggle in Islam, which got us where we are today. [pp. 107–8] [...]

Pancasila clearly is not capable of being that tenacious defence of spirit; only Islam is. History has proven this. Who knows what the intent was, if there was any danger of the Muslim faithful again being persuaded by the cry 'Allahu Akbar', so that they would be brave enough to challenge their appointed time of death, brave enough to die as martyrs in God's cause (*syahid fi sabilillah*) but after succeeding, this was then denied and it was said that it was the spirit of Pancasila.

You are considerate of the [non-Muslim] minority and restrain yourselves so that they do not become offended, whilst you sacrifice the majority for that. Will this not provoke the animosity of the people, which could be very dangerous and could be handed down through the generations for decades?

The honourable member Karkono[13] negated the strength of Islam because, according to his analysis, most Muslims in Indonesia are Muslims in name only. Most of them still live in the world of animism.

Only their marriages and prayers at ceremonial meals are Muslim; the rest are traditions and indigenous culture, so Islam's influence is only very small.

It is due to this that you, honourable members, cannot accept the foundation of Islam and think that it is Pancasila that is appropriate. Mr Chairman, if we speak with healthy logic, if the basis of Islam is rejected because there are many in the community who still do not understand Islam, when in fact Islam has been grow-ing throughout the Indonesian archipelago for 600 years, surely it is Pancasila that cannot be made the foundation of the state, [and is] 10 times less understood by the majority of our people, because Pancasila was only recently discovered in Indonesia, a dozen years ago, around the time when Japan was about to fall. [pp. 116–17] [...]

My speech is almost over. We have been discussing this for three weeks; ideas have been tested against each other so that they may be combined! I have seen how much you object to accepting Islam as the foundation of the state and also how dif-ficult it is for you to let go of Pancasila. Those of us who fight for the ideal of Islam are not angry with you and do not hate you for your harsh rejection.

What we see in this session is not you, but the consequences of the course of 350 years of history. This society was an Islamic society in the past. The Dutch organized it so that there was a Departemen Onderwijs en Eere Dienst [Department of Educa-tion and Religion]; they ran *Openbare Onderwijs* [public education].

From day one since the Hollands Inlandse School [schools for Indonesians estab-lished by the Dutch], in the public schools you were distanced from the basis of your real heritage of ideas. A thread a day with time becomes a piece of cloth. The Islam

---

12 AKUI: Aksi Kemenangan Umat Islam (Muslim Victory Action); PPTI: Partai Politik Tarikat Islam (Muslim Tarekat Political Party). See also the glossary.

13 Karkono was a PNI member of the Constituent Assembly.

that you studied was the explanation of others. It was the explanation of Snouck Hourgronje[14] and Younbull,[15] whose minds were full of knowledge but whose souls had lost their foundation!

Under the Department [of Education and Religion], Protestant and Catholic missions were promoted. Thus emerged what were called *Bijzondere Onderwijs* [special education], where brains were educated with superior knowledge and souls with Christian teachings. [...]

And both those from the *Openbare Onderwijs* and those from the *Bijzondere Onderwijs* hated Islam with a mindset that had been inculcated in them for many years. [They saw] [r]otten *kiai* [Muslim clerics], country bumpkin *pesantren* students, unfortunate mosque officials – good only for taking care of the body when you died, useful as firewood if there was a revolution, and for reading prayers if there was a ceremonial meal at a reception.

It is only now that we meet and reveal our respective feelings. Now you know that we too are a part of you – we who have been separated for hundreds of years in our feelings, although we have been physically close, with the result that we do not know each other any more because of the thick wall put up between us by others.

Although in this assembly you reject our struggle, we believe that at home you have begun to think; you have long been lost. We have brought things [that were] lost before you again, but there is still something blocking you from taking them. [pp. 140–1] [...]

12.1.4 Nurcholish Madjid

Commentary (by Greg Barton and Greg Fealy) Nurcholish Madjid (1939–2005) was the most influential thinker in Indonesia's reform movement of the 1970s and 1980s. Born in Jombang, East Java, he was unusual in that he had strong traditionalist *and* modernist elements in his family and educational background. His father remained in Masyumi when NU split from the party in 1952, but most of his uncles became NU members. He gained a classical Islamic education in *pesantren* as well as attending the Jakarta State Islamic Institute (IAIN Syarif Hidayatullah Jakarta), eventually gaining his PhD from the University of Chicago in 1984. During the late 1960s, he was regarded as the most promising of emerging modernist leaders. He chaired the influential Islamic student organization known as Himpunan Mahasiswa Islam (HMI, Muslim Tertiary Students Association) from 1966 to 1971 and was nicknamed 'Natsir Muda' (the 'Young Natsir'), such was the expectation that he would succeed the revered former Masyumi leader Mohammad Natsir.

---

14 Christiaan Snouck Hurgronje (1857–1936) was the advisor to the colonial government on Aceh and later an advisor on Islamic and indigenous affairs. He was the chief architect of Dutch policy towards Islam.

15 Hamka is probably referring here to Dr Th. W. Juynboll, the chief architect of Dutch policy towards Islam. He was a professor of Hebrew, Arabic and Islamic institutions at Rijksuniversiteit Utrecht (1917–36) and was the author of several books on Indonesian Islam, including a standard Dutch-language work on jurisprudence.

Two of Nurcholish's most controversial papers were 'The Necessity of Reform of Islamic Thought and the Problem of the Integrity of the *Umat*', which he delivered in January 1970, and 'Reinvigorating Religious Understanding within the Indonesian Muslim Community', which was presented in October 1972. In the 1970 paper, Nurcholish describes what he sees as the dilemma facing Indonesian Muslims: on the one hand, Islam has gone stale intellectually and must strike out in a new direction; on the other hand, pursuing reform could arouse a conservative backlash and endanger the unity of the Islamic community (*umat* or *ummah*; Ar.: *'ummah*). He then sets out the case for reform, beginning with a blunt assessment of what he says is the Muslim community's eschewal of political Islam. He goes on to call for dynamic new thinking, even if that causes disunity among Muslims.

Extract 12-4: Nurcholish Madjid

Nurcholish Madjid (1997), 'Keharusan Pembaruan Pemikiran Islam dan Masalah Integrasi Umat' [The Necessity of Reform of Islamic Thought and the Problem of the Integrity of the *Umat*], pp. 204–14 in Nurcholish Madjid, *Islam, Kemodernan dan Keindonesiaan* [Islam, Modernity and Indonesian-ness], Mizan, Jakarta. Extract: pp. 204–6.

One pleasing fact about Islam in modern-day Indonesia is its rapid development, particularly with regard to the number of (formal) adherents. Regions that previously did not know this faith are now familiar with it, even to the degree that it has become the main religion for residents, along with those religions that already had a presence. And groups of higher social status are now showing greater interest in Islam; if not in their own observances, then at least in their official attitudes. However, one question from our side to which we keep seeking an answer is: to what extent does this development result from a sincere attraction to the ideas of Islam that are put forward by its leaders, both orally and in written form? Or can this quantitative development of Islam be seen as nothing more than a symptom of social adaptation to contemporary political developments in Indonesia, namely the defeat of the communists, which gave an impression of victory for Islam? (And this social adaptation also occurred during the Old Order period [Guided Democracy, 1959–66], because at that time President Sukarno always displayed his interest in Islam, as well as in Marxism, with great passion, notwithstanding how people might judge the motives behind this [interest].)

The answer to the above question may be found in the following question: to what extent were they [Indonesian Muslims] attracted to Islamic parties and organizations? Except for a few, it is clear that they were not attracted to Islamic parties or organizations. Their attitude might be formulated more or less thus: 'Islam yes, Islamic party no!' So if Islamic parties constitute a receptacle of ideas that are going to be fought for on the basis of Islam, then it is obvious that those ideas are now unattractive. In other words, those ideas and Islamic thinking are now becoming fossilized and obsolete, devoid of dynamism. Moreover these Islamic parties have failed to build a positive and sympathetic image; in fact they have an image that is just the opposite. (The reputation of a section of the *umat* with respect to corruption, for example, is mounting as time passes.) [pp. 204–5] [...]

[Nurcholish then refers to the risk that reform will cause tension and disunity within the Islamic community.]

But can that unity exist in a dynamic form and become a dynamic force if it is not based on dynamic ideas? ('There cannot be revolutionary actions without revolutionary theories', said Lenin.) Dynamism is, at any rate, more decisive than maintaining a static state, even though the latter means a greater number of people. The paralysis of the *umat* these days is due, among other things, to the fact that it is closing its eyes tight to its bodily defects. This necessitates the existence of a movement aimed at the renovation of ideas so that the defects may be removed. [...]

[Nurcholish then quotes Andre Beufre in English as follows.]

'Our traditional lines of thought must go overboard, for it is now far more important to be able to look ahead than to have large scale of force whose effectiveness is problematical.' [p. 206] [...]

Commentary　In the latter part of 1972, Nurcholish provoked further controversy regarding his *pembaruan* (reform) concepts with a paper entitled 'Reinvigorating Religious Understanding within the Indonesian Muslim Community'. Part of the paper dealt with the Islamic state issue. Nurcholish saw the campaign for an Indonesian Islamic state as a manifestation of Muslims' self-perceived inferiority and as an outdated part of political Islam's agenda.

Extract 12-5: Nurcholish Madjid

Nurcholish Madjid (1997), 'Menyegarkan Paham Keagamaan di Kalangan Umat Islam Indonesia' [Reinvigorating Religious Understanding within the Indonesian Muslim Community], pp. 239–56 in Nurcholish Madjid, *Islam, Kemodernan dan Keindonesiaan* [Islam, Modernity and Indonesian-ness], Mizan, Jakarta. Extract: pp. 253–5.

The 'Islamic State' Apology

This is an additional discussion, by way of an observation on one of the forms of religious concept within the *umat*. It is necessary to discuss this because of the urgent need to undertake some clarification concerning it.

The idea of the 'Islamic State' has emerged with great force within the Muslim community at certain periods in the past. We are grateful that it does not exist now – at least so it seems outwardly, although remnants of it still linger.

Viewed from the perspective of the history and development of thought, the emergence of the idea of the 'Islamic State' represents, in reality, a kind of apologetic tendency, as indicated in the heading. That apology arose from at least two bases:

The *first* was an apology in relation to modern Western ideologies such as democracy, socialism, communism and others. These ideologies are often totalitarian in character, in the sense that they are comprehensive in scope and cover every sphere of life in detail, particularly the political, social, economic and cultural spheres, and others besides. The apology in relation to modern ideologies gave rise to an ideological–

political understanding of Islam that then led to the ideal of an 'Islamic State', just as there existed democratic states, socialist states, communist states and so forth. This totalitarian ideological–political apperception led to the emergence of apologetic thinking that declared that Islam was not merely a religion, such as Buddhism, Hinduism, Christianity and so on, whose domains of effectiveness are the spiritual, wherein is arranged the relationship between God and man. Islam, it was claimed, is *ad-din* [*din* or faith]. With the word *ad-din* it was hoped and intended that a totalitarian meaning would be conveyed, which would include all aspects of life – political, economic, social, cultural and so on. The apology, it seems, was deemed necessary because in modern life, dominated by Western patterns, the most important aspects of life are the political, economic, social and the rest, rather than the spiritual. It is understandable that this dangerous cultural invasion destroyed the self-esteem of the *umat*, which was backward in precisely those above-mentioned aspects, and brought about a sense of inferiority. Thus the apology was compensation for an inferiority complex. The reason for this was that the *umat* (through its apologists) tried, with apologia which produced an ideological–political appreciation that was totalitarian, to prove that Islam was actually superior to, or at least on a par with, Western civilization, whose modern ideologies embraced the economic, political, social and other domains – precisely those in which the Muslims had failed. As an apology, these ideas had only a brief span of life. After having temporarily satisfied the Muslims and restored their self-respect, the ideas were finally proved to be false. Like a boomerang they struck back at the *umat*. Its condition now is probably more pathetic than at the beginning. Such is the fate of ideas resulting from an apology, whether they have been put down in writing or not. [...] Actually, if a Muslim truly realizes the position of the religious or spiritual aspect of life and is really cognizant and convinced of the superiority of Islam, he will not experience this sense of inferiority. On the contrary, he will have a sense of self-respect when facing anyone. Fortified by a firm conviction in himself and in his religion, he would then become creative in other fields, and with his mind freed from any sense of inferiority, he would readily learn from others who are superior in these fields. Another point is that it can be proved that in the sources of Islamic teaching – particularly the Qur'an – the domain of efficiency in which Islam is most emphatic and most lucid is the spiritual, the domain of religious matters. [...]

> [Nurcholish's objection to the concept of an Islamic state does not stop at its apologetic inspiration, however; another equally significant issue is involved. The modern obsession with the possibility of an Islamic state, he argues, reflects the current unbalanced approach to Islamic jurisprudence (*fiqh*) as much as it does a Muslim inferiority complex.]

Legalism represents the *second* factor that led some sections of the Muslim community to the apologetic concept of an 'Islamic State'. This legalism produced an understanding of Islam that was wholly legalistic, in the form of an Islamic perspective that portrayed Islam as a structure and compendium of law. This legalism is an extension of '*fiqh*-ism'. *Fiqh* is the codification of law resulting from the labours of Muslim savants in the second and third centuries of the Muslim era. The codification was undertaken to fulfil the needs of a legal system that regulated the government and the state, which, at that time, embraced a very large region and a huge populace. This *fiqh*-ism is so dominant in the Muslim community that even reformist movements for the most part still concentrate their objectives in that domain. This legal composition is sometimes also called sharia. The 'Islamic State' is likewise an apology by which the Muslim *umat* hopes to be able to manifest laws and regulations, Islamic sharia, which are superior to other laws. But it is already clear that, despite the renovations of the reformists, *fiqh* has lost its relevance to the present mode of living. Its complete renovation, however, such that it might become suitable for modern life, would require a comprehensive knowledge of modern life in all its aspects, so that it does not become an interest and [matter of the] competency of the Muslim *umat* alone, but of others as well. Its result, then, does not have to be in the form of Islamic law per se, but of law that embraces everybody for the regulation of a life shared by all. [...]

12.1.5 Amien Rais, Mohamad Roem and Nurcholish Madjid

Commentary Nurcholish Madjid's statements on political Islam and the Islamic state issue triggered a debate that would continue throughout the remainder of the Soeharto presidency and into the new millennium. His comments were sharply criticized by older-generation Masyumi and modernist leaders, for whom participation in party politics and support for a state based on Islam had been talismanic. Other younger Muslim leaders, however, came to Nurcholish's defence and took up his ideas. In the Islamic press and in seminars and conferences, both sides put their views, with the 'reformers' often coming under acrimonious attack from their more conservative interlocutors. One such celebrated exchange took place in the most famous of Indonesian Islamic journals, *Panji Masyarakat*, in 1982–83, between Amien Rais, Mohamad Roem and Nurcholish. Amien Rais (1944–) was a young Muhammadiyah activist and intellectual who had recently returned to Indonesia after completing his PhD at the University of Chicago. Mohamad Roem (1908–83) was a former Masyumi leader and deputy prime minister (1956–57) as well as a senior figure in Dewan Dakwah Islamiyah Indonesia (DDII, Indonesian Islamic Propagation Council). Nurcholish was writing from the United States, where he was a PhD candidate, also at the University of Chicago.

In the following extract, Amien's contribution is notable for its unadorned rejection of the Islamic state ideal. The concept is, he argues, not one found in the Qur'an or in Prophetic example. He urges Muslims to concentrate upon what he regards as more substantive issues: sound leadership and acceptance of Pancasila.

Extract 12-6: Amien Rais

Amien Rais (2004), 'Tidak Ada Negara Islam' [There Is No Islamic State], pp. xxii–xxvi in Agus Edi Santoso (ed.), *Tidak Ada Negara Islam: Surat-surat Politik Nurcholish Madjid–Mohamad Roem* [There Is No Islamic State: The Political Letters of Nurcholish Madjid–Mohamad Roem], revised edition, Penerbit Djambatan, Jakarta. Extract: pp. xxii–xxiii.

I don't think that there is an 'Islamic State' in the Qur'an or in the Sunnah. Therefore, there is no command in Islam to adopt an Islamic state. What is more important is that as long as a state runs on an Islamic ethos, implementing social justice and creating an egalitarian society, avoiding the exploitation of man by man or the exploitation of one group by another, according to Islam it is already viewed as a good state. What does it mean if a country uses Islam as the basis for the state if it turns out that it is just an empty formality? Several countries in the Middle East are Islamic states, but is it true that they implement Islamic law as they should? Saudi Arabia, for instance, has no constitution, an oddity for a country in this modern era. Its leaders say that they do not need a constitution because they already have the base of Islamic law. Well, they may say that. But the application of Islamic law there is so narrow and far removed from the idealism of Islam itself. For instance, the principles of the Saudi Arabian monarchy itself are already in conflict with the principles of Islamic doctrine in social and political matters. If we look at the caliphates that replaced the Prophet Muhammad, may blessings and peace be upon him, the system was not an absolute monarchy, but rather a monarchy that used an electoral system. It happened that the Umayyad and Abbasid dynasties that succeeded the sultanate actually diverged from the foundations of Islamic tenets.[16] What about Indonesia? My view is that as long as it [the basis of the state] is not in conflict with Islamic doctrine and all of its principles have been put into practice, that is already really good. But if the Pancasila is an empty formality, where Islam is also an empty formality, naturally we would have to repair that situation together. Islam puts great emphasis on consistency between what is said and what is done.

Indonesian Muslims would be happy if Pancasila, which is wonderful, was truly put into practice consistently. That would mean that sections of Islamic doctrine were being enacted.

> ***Commentary*** Roem replies to Amien's article by arguing that the term 'Islamic state' is less important than realizing a political system in which Islamic values and law are upheld. He contends that although the Qur'an and Hadith may not stipulate an Islamic state, nonetheless, the Prophet at the end of his leadership of the community established a state ordered on Islamic principles and this should be the example followed by modern-day Muslims.

---

16   The first four successors of Muhammad, known as the Rightly Guided Caliphs, ruled for 29 years. Their rule, together with that of Muhammad, is considered by most Muslims to constitute the ideal Islamic age. The Umayyad dynasty ruled from 661 to 750 CE. Its founders were a wealthy clan in Mecca who had opposed Muhammad and there was a rapid expansion of Islam during this dynasty. The Abbasid caliphate ruled from 758 to 1258 CE. The high point of the dynasty during the ninth century was marked by great cultural, scientific and intellectual openness and creativity as well as economic and military might.

After being removed from power, the Umayyads established a rival empire in Spain and, in 929 CE, a rival caliphate. The Islamic culture that flourished in Spain for the next three centuries was dramatically different from the Iranian–Semitic culture that grew up around the Abbasid caliphate.

Extract 12-7: Mohamad Roem

Mohamad Roem (2004), 'Tidak Ada Negara Islam' [There Is No Islamic State], pp. 1–11 in Agus Edi Santoso (ed.), *Tidak Ada Negara Islam: Surat-surat Politik Nurcholish Madjid–Mohamad Roem* [There Is No Islamic State: The Political Letters of Nurcholish Madjid–Mohamad Roem], revised edition, Penerbit Djambatan, Jakarta. Extract: pp. 2–11.

If Dr Amien Rais says, 'There is no Islamic State in the Sunnah', I feel that he is correct. Not only is he correct, but he is also wise, because in Indonesia, it is better if that term is not used, because quite a few people do not like it, and in fact there are those who have an allergic reaction when hearing that term. I am not going to check whether it is true that those words are not there by reading the entire Qur'an and the Sunnah. What I have checked is that in the statutes of Masyumi, the words in that term do not exist.

In that case what exactly does Dr Amien Rais mean? Is it just its name, or more than a name, which is not there? [...]

'What is in a name?', asked that most honoured of British writers, Shakespeare. If people called the rose, which is so fragrant, a rafflesia,[17] it would still smell as sweet.

What on earth is the benefit in forcing oneself (and perhaps others too) to use a term that can cause such strong reactions? That is the wisdom of Dr M. Amien Rais.

So if you are looking for that term in the Sunnah, comprising thousands [of Hadith, or reports of the Prophet's words or deeds], I think it would be totally futile. I think that Dr Amien Rais is right. [pp. 2–3] [...]

> [Roem then refers to Muhammad's period in Medina (622–30), during which time the Prophet developed a political state around the Muslim community. Roem makes repeated reference to a verse in the al-Maeda (Maidah) chapter of the Qur'an (Q5: 3),[18] which he says was revealed to the Prophet after 10 years in Medina. This verse, he comments, marked the 'final inspiration', the completion of what Muhammad had sought to build.]

What picture do we get from the organization and development over those 10 years? The Prophet certainly led the community as a leader. [It was] a community that had twice been to war and ended wars, and he was in charge of all things. It

---

17 The rafflesia plant produces the world's largest flower and is also famous for its highly pungent smell.

18 'You are forbidden to eat carrion; blood; pig's meat; any animal over which any name other than God's has been invoked; anything strangled, victim of a violent blow or a fall, gored or savaged by a beast of prey, unless you still slaughter it [in the correct manner]; or anything sacrificed on idolatrous altars. You are also forbidden to allot shares [of meat] by drawing marked arrows – a heinous practice – the disbelievers have already lost all hope that you will give up your religion. Do not fear them: fear Me. Today I have perfected your religion for you, completed My blessing upon you, and chosen as your religion *islam*: total devotion to God; but if any of you is forced by hunger to eat forbidden food, with no intention of doing wrong, then God is most forgiving and merciful' (Q5: 3, Haleem).

was nothing more and nothing less than that the Prophet grew to become a head of state.

Meanwhile, if we have ever read a Hadith saying that the Prophet then had another title apart from the 'Messenger of God', I myself have never read or heard of it. Did the Prophet give another or a new name after Medina became one with Mecca?[19] I have never read or heard of it, either.

Meanwhile, the community that had been built and organized by the Prophet in Mecca and Medina, did it not constitute a regulated state? I think that the answer is in the affirmative.

So if Dr Amien Rais says that there was no Islamic State, that is indeed true. Meanwhile, I think that what the Prophet created in Yatrib,[20] which was then one with Mecca, was in essence a state, [even though it] was not called an Islamic state by the Prophet himself. Three months after verse 3 of the chapter of al-Maidah was revealed, the Prophet passed on, and he was replaced as head of state by Abu Bakar. The name or title of Caliph of the Muslim faithful was given to Abu Bakar.

To recapitulate: at the end of the Prophet's life, when al-Maidah, verse 3, was revealed, a community had already grown up that was built by and under the leadership of the Prophet himself, that was not given a specific name by the Prophet, but nevertheless had the characteristics of a state, while God had declared its laws perfectly. The one who became leader, who did not use a particular name or title, was the Prophet Muhammad, God's Messenger, a person who was chosen by God Himself. I think that for no more than three months, there was once an Islamic State on earth – not in name (what is in a name?), but rather in substance, in essence.

Since then, I do not think that there has been another state that could equal that state, because whoever its leader was, he could not equal the Prophet. At most, that state could be something to aspire to. [It is a] good aspiration, and humankind is entitled to have it, but it will never be achieved, but rather only be approached as closely as possible.

The Organization of the Islamic Conference, which was established a while ago and occasionally holds summits attended by heads of state [of countries] that for convenience are called Islamic countries, as well as annually holding a conference attended by their foreign ministers, has participants with various types of names. Those who use the name Islamic are in fact a small minority. Among them is the Islamic Republic of Pakistan. The history of this Islamic Republic is interesting. Initially the country was large, consisting of West Pakistan and East Pakistan. The majority of its inhabitants were Muslims. At the time it was the largest Muslim country. [pp. 6–7] [...]

The country that is most well known, and the richest, and the one that is sometimes seen as a model by Muslims throughout the world, is officially called the Kingdom of Saudi Arabia. It is a kingdom, where the head of state is a descendant of the

---

19   Roem's point here appears to be that the Prophet did not call his polity a 'state' but in effect it functioned as an organized state.

20   The pre-Islamic name for Medina.

first king. We should remember that the Prophet was not replaced by his descendants. That is what became of the dispute between the Sunni and Shi'ite groups.[21]

Our beloved country is called the Republic of Indonesia. In my opinion, 'republic' is closer to the Sunnah of the Prophet than 'kingdom'. However, as we can see from the history of Islam, the Prophet did not provide certainty on this matter. [...] Dr Amien Rais has certainly followed in the footsteps of our ancestors, Tjokroaminoto, Agus Salim, Samanhudi, K.H.A. Dahlan[22] and others, who have used simple words, not startling people. H. Samanhudi said that the objective of the Islamic Traders Association was 'Arranging a way of life in line with the teachings of Islam'. According to my memory, those words have not just been reiterated in writing, but said repeatedly. And we certainly could not do anything else but that. If we believe in the teachings of Islam as a truth that can lead us to a life of salvation both on earth and in the hereafter, could we do other than that? In the era of the Islamic Traders Association, our leaders also often said: 'Live in accord with Islam, and there is no need to wait for it to be regulated by state laws, because living as a Muslim surely will not harm others'. [pp. 7–9] [...]

Non-Muslims who say that Islam in Indonesia is characterized by ambiguity, by things that can have various meanings, do not understand that Islam is not just for Arab peoples or Arab nations. It is precisely that ambiguity that gives it its specific characteristics, so that Islam can develop along separate lines in different countries. Islam in Indonesia does not need to be an accurate copy of Islam in Saudi Arabia or Islam anywhere else. What is more, interpretation (*ijtihad*)[23] is an important tenet in the practice of Islam. [pp. 10–11]

> ***Commentary***   Nurcholish responds to the discussion between Amien and Roem by contending that scripture makes clear that God has given humans the reason to determine the precise details of how they organize their communities. As long as Islamic principles can be enacted, a variety of state structures is permissible. In keeping with his advocacy of new thinking, he calls on Muslims to create new conceptions of the state more in keeping with the requirements of contemporary life.

---

21   This is a reference to the historical schism within the Islamic community between the Sunnis and the Shi'ites over who is the rightful successor to the Prophet. Shi'ites believe that the caliph should be a descendant of Muhammad whereas Sunnis favour an elected successor. For Shi'ites, Ali ibn Abi Talib, the fourth caliph and Muhammad's cousin and son-in-law, was the Prophet's appointed successor and he is regarded as the first imam in the sense of being an intermediary between God and humankind. Ali and his descendents are regarded as having superhuman qualities and possessing commanding authority on earth. Sunnis, while acknowledging Ali as the last of the Rightly Guided Caliphs, do not regard him or his descendants as having special spiritual characteristics.

22   All four leaders were prominent figures in early twentieth-century Islamic movements. Umar Said Tjokroaminoto (1882–1934) was the charismatic leader of Sarekat Islam, the first national-level, mass-based Islamic organization (founded in 1912). Samanhudi (1868–1956) was the founder of Sarekat Dagang Islam (Islamic Traders Association), the precursor to Sarekat Islam. Agus Salim (1884–1954) was a modernist Muslim intellectual and another Sarekat Islam leader. Ahmad Dahlan (1868–1923) founded Muhammadiyah in 1912.

23   *Ijtihad* is 'independent reasoning' used to interpret the sources of Islamic law in cases where there is no clear guidance available in the Qur'an or Sunnah.

Extract 12-8: Nurcholish Madjid

Nurcholish Madjid (2004), 'Menyambung Matarantai Pemikiran yang Hilang' [Connecting the Links of Lost Ideas], pp. 12–41 in Agus Edi Santoso (ed.), *Tidak Ada Negara Islam: Surat-surat Politik Nurcholish Madjid–Mohamad Roem* [There Is No Islamic State: The Political Letters of Nurcholish Madjid–Mohamad Roem], revised edition, Penerbit Djambatan, Jakarta. Extract: pp. 28–9.

It is certain that all of the Prophet's deeds (the Sunnah) throughout his life were the embodiment of religion, including the system of human relations he developed in Medina as well as continuations of this. Clearly that was one form of a state. (But it is interesting to note the very controversial opinion of Ibn Taimiyyah[24] that the Prophet was capable of error in his task of conveying divine revelations; outside this task, as is evident in several records in the Qur'an, the Prophet was a human being who, although he was special, could still be wrong.) It is an obligation for all Muslims, and as a logical matter for every follower of a religion or school of thought, to strive as well as they can to manifest in their daily life the tenets that they believe in, including in state and community life. But it is very clear that the formalistic term 'Islamic State' was never used, either by the Prophet himself or by his successors over the centuries. It is also very clear that the term has only emerged among circles of the faithful as a sign of these modern times. If its emergence was studied in relation to the forms of interaction between the faithful and other groups, it would be obvious that the idea, and even more so the formal term, is a historical–sociological variable, not of the essence of Islam itself. [...]

[...] The divine revelations reached the peak of their perfection in the Qur'an, which fulfilled all the needs of humanity for the location of a foundation for their system of living, whilst further developments built on that foundation, namely the edifices of civilization and culture, had to be arranged by human beings themselves, using their reason. That reason, as is frequently mentioned in the Qur'an and its exegesis, is God's mandate for the community of humankind, in order to support their mission as His representatives on earth. In carrying out the mission of developing this world, the rights and obligations of each human are the same, and the manifestation of them clearly demands the formation of a democratic order. In matters pertaining to the state, as is clearly evidenced by Islam's history, Muslims were permitted to work with other groups. (In fact, even the Prophet himself cooperated with the Jews in agriculture at the beginning of the period following the Hijrah,[25] in line with the agreement often referred to now as the 'Medina Constitution'.) [...] So the formal structure of the state order can vary for Muslims, as long as that order provides space for the implementation of the fundamental ideals of Islam.

It is certain that in matters of the state, although conducted openly and in cooperation with non-Muslim groups, a Muslim must have the intention of acting only

---

24 Taqi al-Din Ahmad Ibn Taymiyyah (1263–1328 CE) was a famous Syrian Islamic scholar and jurist. His controversial writings on Prophetic fallibility, Islamic reform and the use of reasoning resulted in his persecution and imprisonment.

25 The withdrawal (*hijrah*) from Mecca to Medina of the Prophet and his followers in 622 CE.

for God, for the sake of His blessings. The use of human reason is the essence of interpretation (*ijtihad*), which actually I have referred to rather inaccurately as secularization. The term 'more evolved *ijtihad*' would of course be safer and seem more original. Pak[26] Roem also stressed the need for the development of *ijtihad* in his writings. I say 'more evolved' because it is clear that the concept of *ijtihad* as it is now known is no longer adequate, and must be expanded so that it becomes more responsive to the real demands of the current era. [...]

12.1.6   Abdurrahman Wahid

Commentary   Abdurrahman Wahid (1939–) is the most influential traditionalist thinker and leader of his generation. He has an impeccable NU pedigree: his grandfather was Hasyim Asy'ari, the organization's co-founder, and his father was Wahid Hasyim, a minister for religious affairs and a deputy chair of NU. Abdurrahman was educated in both the traditional *pesantren* system and state schools in Indonesia and attended the prestigious al-Azhar University in Cairo[27] before graduating in arts from Baghdad University. Fluent in Arabic and English, he read widely in Western and Middle Eastern literature. Upon his return to Indonesia in the early 1970s, Abdurrahman Wahid quickly established a reputation for outspoken advocacy of religious pluralism, human rights and democratization. He became chair of NU in 1984, a position he was to hold for 15 years despite several attempts by the Soeharto regime to remove him from office. In 1998, he became the leading figure in the formation of Partai Kebangkitan Bangsa (PKB, National Awakening Party), which won 13 per cent of the vote in the June 1999 parliamentary elections. He was elected President of Indonesia by the MPR in October 1999, though his period in office was dogged by controversy and political tumult. He was eventually dismissed by the MPR in July 2001. He remains politically active and currently holds the pivotal position of chair of the Majelis Syuro (Consultative Council) of PKB.

Abdurrahman has been a prolific essayist and columnist, writing on topics as diverse as theological revival within Islam, interfaith dialogue, political reform, Javanese culture, cinema and soccer. The following extract is from one of many articles he wrote in opposition to the concept of an Islamic state. His concern here is not only to challenge the claim that there is a coherent Islamic blueprint for such a state but also to assert the compatibility of Islam and secularism. The quotation marks are in the original.

Extract 12-9: Abdurrahman Wahid

Abdurrahman Wahid (1983), 'Islam: Punyakah Konsep Kenegaraan?' [Islam: Does It Have a Concept of the State?], *Tempo*, 26 March: 20. Extract: p. 20.

---

26   A term of respect.

27   Al-Azhar is the most famous Islamic university in the world and many Indonesian Muslim scholars are its graduates. Abdurrahman himself studied at al-Azhar for two years but did not complete his undergraduate studies there. For the influence of al-Azhar on Indonesian Islam, see Abaza (2003); for more on Abdurrahman's career, see Barton (2003).

During the 1940s, in Egypt, Ali Abdel Raziq[28] wrote the book *Al-islam wa qawa'id al-sulthan*, which was then translated into English under the title *Islam and the Bases of Power*. In this book, he rejects the idea that there is a framework for the state in Islam. The Qur'an never mentions an 'Islamic state' (*daulah Islamiyah*), he says. Only a state 'which is good, filled with God's blessings' (*baldatun thayyibatun wa rabbun ghafur*) is mentioned.

That pronouncement, at that time, and in Egypt, invited a strong reaction from the al-Azhar ulema. What were the consequences? He was removed from work 'that was related to Islam and the public interest'. His book was seized, his thoughts were censored, and eventually he was thrown out of the Arab Language Academy.

Why was there such a harsh reaction? Because he accepted the concept of secularism: [that] religion does not have a connection to matters of state. This view was diametrically opposed to the view of the (al-Azhar) community.

But actually, he had put forward argumentation that was quite strong and logical. First, he said, in the Qur'an there is no such doctrine. Second, the behaviour of the Prophet Muhammad himself does not reveal a political character, but rather a moral one. Third, the Prophet never formulated a definitive mechanism for succession [to the position of leader of the Muslim community – that is, the caliph].

If the Prophet had indeed intended to found an 'Islamic state', it is impossible that the problem of leadership succession and handover of authority would not have been formally set out. The Prophet only instructed [his followers] 'to consult on problematic issues'. Matters as important as that [succession] were not instituted concretely; rather [the community leaders] just made do with the dictum that 'their problems should be discussed between them'. Where is there a state with a form such as that?

Indeed, until now, we have not yet heard the final word [on the Islamic state issue]. In Indonesia, we all have the sole political basis of Pancasila. Iran is definitively an Islamic republic. Algeria, an 'Arab socialist' state, has formally declared in its constitution that the official religion is Islam. Although it is not formally an 'Islamic state', Saudi Arabia has declared the Qur'an as its constitution. Very diverse.

There are those who believe that a state has an 'Islamic character' if the essence of Islamic teachings is acknowledged – such as the oneness of God. Islam has an inspirational function: to be the source that encourages the emergence of legislation and state regulations that are humane, though not contrary to Islamic teachings. This is said to be the 'minimalist' view.

In contrast, there is the 'optimalist' wish of people who want Islamic teachings fully implemented, if possible in a literal fashion. A state 'still has to be Islamized' if it is not truly 'totally Islamic'.

However, the strategy that is pursued divides those views internally into two further perspectives: one held by people who want the totality to be achieved in essence, without regarding the formal shape [of the state] as important, and the other

28   Sheikh Ali Abdel-Razik (1888–1966) was a prominent Egyptian reformist thinker of the early to mid twentieth century. A product of al-Azhar and Oxford universities, he wrote extensively on theology and political theory. His *Islam and the Fundamentals of Governance: A Thesis on Caliphate and Government in Islam* (1925) was a highly influential work for 'Muslim secularists'.

by people who demand a formalized form of state as the primary requirement, as was undertaken by Khomeini [in Iran]. For a society like Indonesia's, the answer to the above question must often be sought indirectly: the matter is not discussed openly, but rather through interpretations of the state's sole ideology [Pancasila].

Indeed, it is not easy to discuss the existence or not of the concept of a state. Besides political and other difficulties, there is also a difficulty that is actually technical: there is not yet a shared understanding regarding the terms to be used. Just take, for example, the word 'concept'.

What is meant [by this]? A complete theory of state, thorough and detailed, that is completely different from other theories (just as Marxist economic theories differ from capitalist theories)? If it is that, then clearly it does not yet exist [in Islam]. Or a view on general guidelines on how to regulate the state, in other words, a 'vision relating to the state'? If it is that, then it can be achieved quickly.

There is [another] difficulty resulting from differences about what is meant by 'concept'. For example, is what is intended by 'the Islamic view of the state' only basic values that are the basis for creating a state? Or the formal norms which regulate life within it? Or the institutions which are erected within it? Or a combination of all three?

As long as there is no clarity on these matters, it is in fact futile to put forward the claim that Islam possesses a concept of the state.

12.1.7 Yusril Ihza Mahendra

> *Commentary*   Yusril Ihza Mahendra (1956–) was the founding chair of the Islamist Partai Bulan Bintang (PBB, Crescent Moon and Star Party) and has been a minister in all but one of the four post-Soeharto governments. A professor of law at the University of Indonesia and former Soeharto speechwriter before entering formal politics, Yusril has been a prominent figure in the DDII. His 1993 PhD thesis at Universitas Sains Malaysia compared the politics of Masyumi with Pakistan's Jama'at-i Islami (Ihza Mahendra 1999). PBB has been the most steadfast of Islamist parties in advocating the reinsertion of the seven-word sharia clause of the Jakarta Charter into the constitution. The following is an excerpt from Yusril's foreword to a PBB publication containing speeches of party MPs in the MPR in 2003. He puts the case for amending chapter 29 ('Religion') of the constitution to include the seven words.

Extract 12-10: Yusril Ihza Mahendra

Yusril Ihza Mahendra (2003), 'Sambutan Ketua Umum Partai Bulan Bintang' [Response of the General Chairman of the PBB], pp. vii–viii in Haril M. Andersen, Hamdani, Husni Jum'at, Nasruddin Muharor and Zaun Fathin (eds), *Memperjuang-kan Syariat Islam: Kumpulan Pidato Fraksi Partai Bulan Bintang Pada Sidang Tahunan Majelis Permusyawaratan Rakyat Republik Indonesia Tahun 2000–2002* [Struggling for Sharia Islam: A Collection of Speeches by the PBB Faction in the 2000–2002 Annual MPR Sessions], Fraksi PBB MPR, Jakarta. Extract: pp. vii–viii.

The Jakarta Charter is a constitutional struggle ... the result of a compromise between the desire of Muslims to establish an Islamic state and the wish of nationalists to form a secular state shortly before the proclamation of independence. Unfortunately, however, this formulation was abolished unilaterally by a group of nationalists, without holding an assembly [a meeting of the full committee that had been drafting the constitution] and failing to heed the decision reached through consultation [among the original Jakarta Charter Committee in 1945]. In the end, the proclamation of the Indonesian state took place through the hastily drafted text of an individual. This is why Muslims lack a national juridical foundation when they execute their religious obligations, particularly in court cases (*qada'i*). It is the obligation of the state to uphold these laws among its Muslim citizens. Despite this, Muslims are still able to carry out the teachings of their religion in matters of personal law. [...] To return the seven words of the Jakarta Charter to the 1945 Constitution through an amendment to paragraph 29 would be an effort to reinsert into its body the soul that has until now been drifting around. It is also an effort to provide a constitutional framework for several laws and customs of Muslims, which until now have operated without constitutional backing. For Muslims, it is a legal obligation for each individual to apply sharia Islam and for the state to uphold sharia Islam (*qada'i*). As the state cannot uphold sharia without establishing political parties, it is also a legal obligation for Muslims to establish political parties. The obligation to establish political parties is merely a means for state implementation of sharia Islam. Because of this, Muslims must not act fanatically (*ta'ashub*) towards their political party, as being active in a party is not the goal. The goal is to uphold the sharia, so that the Indonesian state does not prostitute itself to ideologies that are distant from the ideology of the Muslim population as the majority population in Indonesia.

12.1.8   Tate Qamaruddin

> ***Commentary***   In the run-up to the 2004 general and presidential elections, Partai Keadilan Sejahtera (PKS, Prosperity and Justice Party – formerly the Justice Party or PK) was accused by various secular nationalists and non-Muslim groups of having a concealed agenda to restore the Jakarta Charter to the constitution. The party published several responses to the charge, one of which was the following by Tate Qamaruddin, an intellectual and PKS activist. He describes PKS's gradualist approach to the issue of implementing sharia and argues that there are more important matters for Islamic groups to focus on than the status of the Jakarta Charter.

Extract 12-11: Tate Qamaruddin

Tate Qamaruddin (2003), 'Beginilah Partai Keadilan Sejahtera Menegakkan Syari'at Islam: Klarifikasi Fitnah Piagam Jakarta' [Therefore the Prosperity and Justice Party Upholds Islamic Law: A Clarification of the Jakarta Charter Slander], PKS, Jakarta. Extract: pp. 30–1, 45.

The Justice Party is working to apply sharia Islam at all levels of life … Its idealism is contained in one of the principles of its struggle, namely *tadarruj* [proceeding in stages]. The elaboration of *tadarruj* includes performing *da'awi* work [proselytizing] with the following steps:

Firstly, forming a Muslim personality (*takwinusy-syakhshiyyah al-islamiyah*)

Secondly, forming a Muslim or Islamic family (*takwin al-bait al-muslim*)

Thirdly, guiding and improving society (*irsyadul-mujtma' wa ishlahuhu*)

Fourthly, reforming the government to become an Islamic government (*islahul-hukumah*)

Fifthly, restoring the existence of an Islamic caliphate (*I'adatu kayanil-khilafah il-islamiyah*)

Sixthly, becoming a teacher of world civilization (*ustadziyyatul-'alam*) [pp. 30–1]

[…]

Let us not be trapped – consciously or otherwise – into making the Jakarta Charter sacred. Making it sacred […] does not happen through explicit words. Rather it happens in the form of accusing other people of not struggling for sharia Islam merely because they are not championing the insertion of the Jakarta Charter into the Constitution, whereas the accused struggles for sharia Islam through a different method and format from that of the accuser. Such behaviour is akin to saying that the Jakarta Charter is a vision from God that is not subject to further debate and cannot be corrected. Which is the substantial issue: whether we struggle for 'those seven words' contained in the Jakarta Charter, or how society and the state can hold a strong commitment to the overall values of sharia Islam? [p. 45]

12.1.9   Habib Rizieq Syihab

> *Commentary*   The following extract is from a book published in October 2000 as part of the campaign of Front Pembela Islam (FPI, Islamic Defenders' Front) for the re-inclusion of the Jakarta Charter in the constitution. Although entitled a 'dialogue', the question and answer format is entirely the work of FPI's chair and co-founder, Habib Rizieq Syihab (1965–). Habib Rizieq is of mixed Yemeni and Betawi descent and he is a graduate in Islamic law from King Saud University in Riyadh. FPI has gained a high media profile for its attacks on 'places of vice' such as nightclubs, gambling dens and brothels, but it has also been a strong proponent of comprehensive Islamic law implementation. In the following extract, Habib Rizieq argues that inserting the Jakarta Charter in the constitution would not only correct a historical wrong but also provide a strong moral basis for the Indonesian state.

Extract 12-12: Habib Rizieq Syihab

Al-Habib Muhammad Rizieq bin Husein Syihab (2000), 'Dialog Piagam Jakarta' [Dialogue on the Jakarta Charter], pp. 13–39 in *Dialog Piagam Jakarta: Kumpulan Jawaban Al-Habib Muhammad Rizieq bin Husein Syihab Seputar Keraguan Terhadap Penegakan Syari'at Islam di Indonesia* [Dialogue on the Jakarta Charter: A Collection of Answers by Al-Habib Muhammad Rizieq bin Husein Syihab Regarding Doubts Concerning the Enforcement of Islamic Law in Indonesia], Pustaka Ibnu Sidah, Jakarta. Extract: pp. 15–30.

4. Isn't the demand to *'Restore the Jakarta Charter'* at odds with the nationalism of the Indonesian people?

Speaking about the Jakarta Charter and Nationalism, it was precisely Bung Karno [Sukarno], the proclaimer of the Republic of Indonesia who is also the Father of the Indonesian Nationalists, who once stated with breadth of nationalist spirit that **The Jakarta Charter is the result of very hard work between the Islamic and Nationalist Groups and must be upheld**; moreover, without hesitation he signed the Jakarta Charter on 22 June 1945. [p. 15] [...]

> [Habib Rizieq then says that a Japanese officer persuaded Muslim leaders to omit the Jakarta Charter on the grounds that it discriminated against religious minorities.]

6. Isn't that reasoning logical, because in the democratic Republic of Indonesia discriminatory acts are forbidden?

Yes. In this country you cannot undertake any discriminatory action. Justice must be enforced.

Now I would ask in return, where is the discrimination in the sentence *'with the obligation to carry out Islamic law for its adherents'*? Is there any forcing of Islamic law on other religions? Is there any ban on other faiths practising their beliefs and convictions? Are there any minority rights that would be lost?

Clearly the discrimination argument is illogical. [p. 17] [...]

12. Why does the Muslim community have to be forced to uphold Islamic law?

This isn't coercion, but **obligation**. [...]

Let us take an analogy. If a wealthy person builds a big company with his personal capital, then we agree that he has the right to make the rules in that company while not neglecting the rights of his staff, and those rules have to be obeyed by all the company's staff.

Then how about with Almighty God? He created humankind along with all the universe; He facilitated humankind to manage this world; He blessed humankind with all manner of invaluable gifts, such as the five senses, knowledge, livelihood and the like. Doesn't He have the right to make the rules in this Great World which He possesses?! Doesn't He have the right to determine the limits and norms of human life which He created??! And aren't humans obliged to obey the rules of The Creator???!

Now, God's rules are contained in the Islamic law which He has stipulated, and Almighty God is the Element that knows the most about this universe, with the outcome that it is only Almighty God who knows the rules for humans in their lives and livelihoods. That is why God's Law must be enforced on His Earth and humans must obey Him. [...]

14. Doesn't the return of the Jakarta Charter mean that Indonesia will become an Islamic state?

On the contrary, the birth of the Jakarta Charter was the middle path between two desires that were mutually contradictory: first, the desire of the Islamic group to create an **Islamic state**, and second, the desire of the Nationalist group to create a **Secular state**. [pp. 22–4] [...]

16. Suppose the Jakarta Charter smooths the process for creating an Islamic Indonesian state?

There is no problem, if indeed the people and nation want it. What is important is that everything is done through the **constitutional corridor**. [p. 25] [...]

23. Can the Jakarta Charter become the solution to the ideological conflict that is so chronic?

Clearly it can, because it is precisely here that the root of the problem is located. The omission of the Jakarta Charter was a betrayal of democracy and an overturning of the constitution that made many sides disappointed and sick at heart. It is the medicine to restore their rights, which were stolen more than half a century ago. Correct history, uphold the constitution truly and cleanse our democracy of the stain of betrayal! [p. 30]

12.1.10   Muhammad Ismail Yusanto

> *Commentary*   Hizbut Tahrir (HT, Liberation Party) is an international movement founded in Jerusalem in 1953 by the Palestinian Islamic leader Taqiuddin an-Nahbani (1909–77). Its central objective is to re-establish the caliphate. The Turkish government under the leadership of Kemal Atatürk abolished the caliphate, then held by the Ottoman sultan, in 1924. An Indonesian chapter of Hizbut Tahrir was formed in 1982 and quickly acquired a strong following among tertiary students and young intellectuals in Java and Sumatra. Unlike some of its counterparts in several Middle Eastern, Central Asian and European countries, Hizbut Tahrir Indonesia (HTI, Liberation Party of Indonesia) eschews violence and has focused on spreading its message through publications, seminars, preaching and peaceful demonstrations.
>
> Ismail Yusanto (1962–) is a deputy chair of HTI and the public face of the organization in Indonesia. He is an engineering graduate from Gadjah Mada University who has also studied Islamic sciences at the Ulil Albaab Islamic college in Bogor. His paper sets out HTI's case for the restoration of the caliphate.

Extract 12-13: Muhammad Ismail Yusanto

Muhammad Ismail Yusanto (2004), 'Towards the Resumption of an Islamic Way of Life through the Re-establishment of the Caliphate and the Application of Shariah' [in English], paper presented at a conference on 'Islamic Perspectives on State, Governance and Society', Canberra, 30–31 August.

Islam's biggest question as a distinct ideology is how to change a society in accordance with its social vision and will. Such ideological aspirations towards societal change are certainly not unique to Islam, as every ideology struggles with the notion of changing the status quo into an ideal social order [...]. Islamic ideology has derived its thoughts and methods for Islamic social transformation solely from Islamic sources. [...]

The nation's biggest challenge

The Qur'an in Ali Imran, verse 110,[29] states that the Islamic nation is the best of all the nations in the world. However, the reality today has witnessed the complete opposite, where the Muslim nations are far from being the best. Across the Islamic world, with the exception of a few remnants of the joyous and glorious past, regression in educational, cultural, social, economical, political and scientific endeavours has become commonplace.

The fall of the Ottoman Caliphate in 1924 dismembered the vast areas spanning North Africa, the Arabian Peninsula, parts of Europe, Central Asia and South Asia into independent Muslim statelets. Western intellectual invasion ('Westoxication') has challenged a unique Islamic way of thinking by deliberate dissemination of secular ideas. Within a short period of time, the colonials had succeeded in removing Islamic authority, norms and rules from the life of Muslim society. Western intellectual hegemony has further weakened and influenced the minds of the Muslims. The political weakness of the Muslim nations has also contributed to the decline of Islamic thought and effectively crippled the ability to counter Western intellectual domination.

Since the fall of the Ottoman Caliphate, Muslims have faced perpetual problems and conflicts without effective solutions or peaceful resolutions. Chronic Palestinian issues have affected the stability of the international community. Muslim-related issues continue to make headlines – take Chechnya, Dagestan, Kashmir, Pattani (Thailand), Moro (southern Philippines), Afghanistan and Iraq, for example. Fabricated intelligence and faulty accusations of stockpiling weapons of mass destruction and sponsoring terrorism have resulted in the occupation of Iraq and Afghanistan by the US-led coalition forces.

Indonesian Muslims have shared great misery too. Prolonged economic crisis has afflicted millions of Indonesians, who are living below the poverty line; unemployment, lack of education, crime, corruption and malnutrition are rampant. Most importantly, the crisis has affected Muslims, who are the majority of the Indonesian populace.

HT, which adopts *tauhid* [the unity of God] as its ideological underpinning, has scrutinized the crisis and concluded that the primary question that the Muslim nations must address is the absence of an Islamic way of life under the shade of an Islamic

---

29 '[Believers], you are the best community singled out for people: you order what is right, forbid what is wrong, and you believe in God. If the People of the Book had also believed, it would have been better for them. For although some of them do believe, most of them are lawbreakers' (Q3: 110, Haleem).

Caliphate (*Khilafah Islamiyah*) (see *Manhaj Hizbut Tahrir fi al-Taghyir* [Method of Hizbut Tahrir for Change]). In other words, the fall of the Ottoman Caliphate is the mother of all crimes.

The Call (*Dakwah*) for Shariah and the Caliphate
HT has taken the initiative to address the next pertinent question: how to resume the implementation of Islamic norms and rules of Allah in a methodical, comprehensive and organized manner so that they converge towards the primary objective of restoring the dignity that Islam and Muslims deserve [the glory of Islam and the Muslims].

This is where the Call (*Da'wah*) has been placed at a critical juncture. In times of the widespread decline of the Muslim community, the Call, according to Abdul Qadim Zallum[30] (see *Manhaj Hizbut Tahrir fi al-Taghyir*), must proceed by leading, persuading and encouraging the Muslim community at large to resume a comprehensive implementation of Islamic rules and norms in all aspects of life, such as beliefs, rituals, food consumption, dress code and morality, and in a multitude of social interactions, including justice, culture, education, politics, economics and defence, under the unifying leadership of a caliphal state.

The Call must also proceed in a structured and organized manner (*jamaiyyan*). A single person alone, no matter how ingenious, may never achieve the objective of HT as outlined earlier. Moreover, the nature of the Call must be political (*kutlah siyasiy*), since the nature of resuming a comprehensive implementation of Islam under a legal authority is itself political. Any groups who do not concentrate on political movement will not achieve the political objective.

When dealing with an individual, the Call aims to inculcate an Islamic personality (*syakhsiyyah Islamiyyah*), in other words a personality that is shaped by Islam in thought and action. The unique Islamic personality produces an individual whose mental psyche and actions are hardwired with and influenced by an Islamic mindset. In short, the Call promotes a sharia-minded personality, in thought, inclination and action, among Muslim individuals. [...]

HT has emphasized that Unity and Sharia will not be achieved and implemented properly in the absence of a Caliphate. How is it possible to solve the problems of Muslim nations and restore the dignity and honour the *ummah* deserves without a Caliph? How can a Muslim nation that believes in Islam as mercy to mankind stand still in the midst of corruption, economic stagnation, moral decadence, crime and insecurity, teenage brutality and ignorance (*jahilliyya*) in its most vulgar forms? [...]

According to Ibn Katsir,[31] *fitnah* (disorder, treachery) is the sum of deviation (from the creeds) and transgression of the shariah. In other words, Muslims are ordered to struggle to remove deviancy and transgression and to achieve a state whereby

---

30   Abdul Qadeem Zaloom, a Palestinian scholar and founding HT member, replaced an-Nahbani as HT's *amir* upon the latter's death in 1977.
31   Imad al-Din Ismail ibn Umar ibn Katsir (1302–73 CE) was a famous Syrian exegete and historian.

humanity will testify to the Faith. This text and others, in addition to numerous Prophetic traditions, especially during the Medina period, serve as the foundation for the Caliphate's foreign policy: to promote and propagate Islam though *Da'waa* (the Call) and Jihad (military manoeuvres). Clearly, the expansive nature of foreign policy necessitates power and a unified will that can only be achieved under a Caliphate. Moreover, Unity must be the rallying point for Islamic ideology, the system of government and the authority of the Caliph.

In fact, the strategic potential of the *Ummah* is in vain in the absence of a unified leadership. One and a half billion Muslims are floating like foam in the sea, weak and lacking in influence. Natural resources have not been managed effectively and have failed to elevate the standard of living and education of the Muslim masses. Muslim lands continue to be sources of conflict, warfare and instability, including Palestine, Chechnya, Iraq and Afghanistan.

The Arab League, the Organization of the Islamic Conference, Rabithah Alam Islamy[32] and other similar institutions cannot stop the killing machines from taking Muslim casualties daily. Though these organizations are composed of Muslim member states, individual members have vastly different or even opposing interests. Islam serves only as a limited and superficial rallying cry, demonstrated by the failure of Muslim states to deal with the state of Israel, whose territory is only a minute fraction of all Muslim states combined.

The trend of globalization is to move towards unification. In most instances, geographical boundaries are becoming irrelevant and less important. There is no state today that manages to stay by itself in isolation. Economic blocs like AFTA, NAFTA, APEC[33] and so on provide important evidence of this trend. European states are moving towards a unified Europe and are planning beyond economics, for military and political expansion. If the Europeans are marching towards European union, what is stopping an Islamic Caliphate from being born?

12.1.11 Luthfi Assyaukanie

Commentary Luthfi Assyaukanie (1967–) is a prominent young Muslim intellectual and a co-founder of Jaringan Islam Liberal (JIL, Liberal Islamic Network) in Jakarta. Educated in Jordan, Malaysia and Australia, he is a regular columnist in newspapers and magazines and has also edited a book on liberal Islamic thought in Indonesia. In the following article he argues against the restoration of the caliphate, asserting that, historically, this system of political leadership was unstable, disunited and often authoritarian. Moreover, he contends that the concept of a caliphate is anachronistic in the modern world.

---

32   Rabithah Alam Islamy (Muslim World League) was established in Saudi Arabia in 1962 as a forum for discussing Muslim concerns and promoting Islamic interests internationally.
33   The Association of Southeast Asian Nations (ASEAN) Free Trade Area, the North American Free Trade Agreement and Asia-Pacific Economic Cooperation, respectively.

Extract 12-14: Luthfi Assyaukanie

Luthfi Assyaukanie (2004), 'Perlunya Mengubah Sikap Politik Kaum Muslim' [The Need to Change the Political Stance of Muslims], *Media Indonesia*, <http://www. mediaindo.co.id/cetak/berita.asp?id+2004031909372640>, dated 19 March 2004, accessed 23 August 2004.

The caliphate (*khilafah*) is an increasingly unpopular product of classical Islamic thought. The main cause of the unpopularity of this concept is that it can no longer be applied visibly in modern life, where the concept of the nation-state has become the consensus among all modern people. The caliphate, which assumes the presence of an umbrella of political power where a caliph (head of state) has full control over the Muslim states in the world, is an absurd utopian vision. Even in the past when Islamic civilization reached its grandeur, the idea of the caliphate never operated perfectly.

The totalitarian character of the caliphate could only be implemented in a relatively confined geographical area with a relatively homogeneous political community. As a result, in the history of Islam, the concept of the caliphate in its true sense was realized only during the first four decades [after the death of Muhammad], under the governments of Abu Bakar, Umar bin Khattab, Uthman bin Affan and Ali bin Abi Thalib [that is, the four Rightly Guided Caliphs]. Moreover, in Ali's time the institution of the caliphate came under serious threat, culminating in the murder of the caliph and the ascendance of Muawiyah from the Umayyad Clan as Ali's replacement.[34]

In the Umayyad Clan's hands, the institution of the caliphate became a system of authoritarian monarchy. The Umayyad Clan coolly tried to overcome political turmoil. On a certain level it succeeded. But, as the territory of Islam expanded, the Ummayah dynasty could no longer control its domain.

Thus, in the middle of the third century Hijriah [tenth century CE], starting with long and bloody conflicts, the institution of the caliphate, for the first time in the history of Islam, was cleft in two: one under the rule of the Abbasids, who ruled from Baghdad, and the other under the control of the Umayyad Clan ruling from Andalusia. From that moment, the concept of the caliphate, which supposes one political leadership of Islam, became merely a theoretical concept with no reference point in the real world.

The 'caliphate' and totalitarianism

It is surprising that in modern times, some Muslims are trying to revive the concept of a caliphate, which died hundreds of years ago. Surprising because this system has been proven to have failed [...]. Moreover, in the early times of Islam, namely in the time of the four Rightly Guided Caliphs, which is frequently held to be an ideal example, the caliphate system did not operate smoothly. Various conflicts, political tensions and wars marked those times.

---

34   Muawiyah ibn Abi Sufyan (602–80) became the first Umayyad caliph in 661 CE after forcing the son of the assassinated fourth caliph, Ali, to abdicate in his favour.

It is sufficient for us to mention that the last three Rightly Guided Caliphs were all brutally murdered. If the system had really been operating ideally, there should have been a political mechanism that could guarantee the security of the political executive and the calm of the community.

The supporters of the concept of a caliphate frequently hold an idealized notion of this Islamic political system. They imagine that under one Islamic command, Muslims will be directed to conduct their daily activities in accordance with the values and teachings of Islam. Politically, the institution of the caliphate could be exploited to mobilize Muslims in accordance with the desires of the ruler, or caliph. As a result, this model of the caliphate system closely resembles communism or fascism, where all of society must bow down to a totalitarian regime.

Almost all totalitarian systems are established through coercion and violence. Communism is the clearest example in the history of totalitarianism. However, because coercion and violence contravene human nature, this system failed and ended in bankruptcy.

12.2 MALAYSIA

12.2.1 Dato' Wan Zahidi Wan The

Commentary In September 2001, Malaysia's prime minister at the time, Dr Mahathir Mohamad, declared that his country should be regarded as an Islamic state. His statement sparked immediate controversy, drawing fire in particular from liberal Muslims, religious minorities and the Islamist party Parti Islam Se Malaysia (PAS, The Islamic Party of Malaysia). Shortly after Mahathir's speech, the government released a booklet called *Malaysia Is an Islamic State,* setting out its justification for the claim. The booklet was withdrawn from publication several weeks later, though similar accounts can still be found on various government websites. Statements by senior leaders of the ruling party, the United Malays National Organisation (UMNO), are also consistent with the formulations set out in the booklet. Notable in the following extract is the use of classical and contemporary juristic sources in support of the 'Islamic state' claim, and the emphasis on obedience to the government. Dato' Wan Zahidi Wan The was the director-general of the Department of Special Affairs at the time the booklet was published.

Extract 12-15: Wan Zahidi Wan The

Wan Zahidi Wan The (2001), *Malaysia Is an Islamic State* [in English], Department of Special Affairs, Ministry of Information, Malaysia.

INTRODUCTION

To determine whether Malaysia is an Islamic state or not, we need to refer to the opinions of Islamic scholars regarding definition of Islamic states[.] Syaikh Muhammad Abu Zuhirah[35] said as follows:

---

35 Muhammad Abu Zuhrah is a distinguished contemporary al-Azhar historian and jurist.

Islamic States (Darul Islam) are countries which are under the rule of Islamic governments, in the meaning that their strength and defence are in the hands of Muslims.
Countries like these are compelled to be defended by every Muslim.

Muhammad bin Hasan al-Syaibani,[36] a well-known Muslim scholar from the
Hanafi sect[,] defined Islamic state as follows:

Countries which are controlled by Muslims, in which Muslims obtain peace in them.

While according to 'Imam' (leader of prayer in a group) al-Fahistani, who is also a
Muslim scholar of the Hanafi sect:

Islamic countries are countries which state that Islamic governments rule over them.

While Imam Syafi'i[37] said as follows:

[For] [a]ny country that was once an Islamic state, this status will not vanish according
to Islamic 'fiqh' laws, even though Muslims have been defeated in these countries.

This means that Islamic republics which are under communist rule and also other
powers of today are considered as colonised Islamic states and it is the obligation of
Muslims to liberate them when they are able.

Based on the definitions formulated by Muslim scholars and Islamic intellectuals
above, clearly Malaysia is an Islamic state without any doubt and [this] need not be
disputed any more. Malaysia's status as an Islamic state would not be affected, even
though Malaysia is viewed as a secular state in the eyes of modern legislators (the
West).

Such evaluation is made based on man-created laws, but the most important here
is evaluation based on Islamic 'fiqh' laws. Islam does not recognise [the] division of
states [into] 'secular' states and 'religious' states such as [is] understood by Western
legislators. In Islam, the countries in this world are divided into three: (1) Islamic
states (Darul Islam); (2) Kafir States which wage war on Islam (Darul Harb); and
(3) Kafir States which do not wage war on Islam (Darul 'Ahd [Abode of Treaty]).
From the division of states according to Islamic 'fiqh' laws, clearly the last two
[types of] countries are 'kafir' (pagan) states.

Disputing Malaysia's state status would mean placing it [in] one or two types
of 'states of the Kafir' (pagan) people stated above. Apart from it being an office
[offence] in the eyes of Islam itself, [...] it would mean that Muslims are not compelled to defend this country from intrusion of enemies of the state, whereas an
Islamic state – such as [the one described] by Syaikh Muhammad Abu Zuhrah previously – 'is compelled to be defended by every Muslim'. This law is stated clearly
in 'fiqh' holy books[:] that it – whether 'fardhu kifayah' (Muslim's responsibilities)
towards the community) or 'fardhu ain' (religious obligations of the individual Muslim) – depends on the extent of the threats faced by an Islamic state.

---

36 Muhammad bin Hasan al-Shaibani was a prominent student of the famous eighth-century jurist
Abu Hanifa.

37 Muhammad ibn Idris ibn al-Abbas ibn Uthman ibn Shafii (d. circa 819 CE) was a jurist and
theologian and the founder of the Shafi'i school of law which predominates in Southeast Asia.

The fact that Malaysia is an Islamic state actually has also been recognised by some modern legislators who have made a sincere and honest study and evaluation. Yang Ariff Dato' Hashim Yeop A. Sani[38] in his study on the Federal Constitution said:

> Malaysia legally can declare this country as an Islamic state although in reality [it] is a 'secular' state and not all its laws are based on Islamic laws.

Malaysia's position as an Islamic state has been reinforced through a provision in the Federal Constitution which recognises Islam as the official religion of the country. This provision was created through the struggles of UMNO leaders while fighting for the country's independence. Thus, [the] UMNO party has been supported by all levels of the Islamic community, including Muslim scholars, religious prominent figures and Islamic fighters of the country. They have involved themselves whether directly or indirectly in UMNO and also the government in developing, expanding and enhancing Islamic teachings in this country. [...]

CHAPTER TWO: GOVERNMENT'S LEGITIMACY UNDER THE ISLAMIC FIQH LAWS

Before we talk about government's legitimacy according to the views of Islamic fiqh, first of all we will explain the system of appointment of the head of state in an Islamic country. In this respect, al-Mawardi[39] said as follows:

> The appointment of the head of Islamic states occurs through two methods: (1) Through election by leaders of the Islamic community; and (2) Through appointment by the previous government (al-Ahd Territory [region in which there is a covenant between Muslims and non-Muslims]). Both these appointment methods are legitimate with Muslim scholars' consensus.

Such as known, Malaysia's head of state is appointed through the above two methods.

The Yang Dipertuan Agung[40] as the head of state is appointed by the Council of Rulers Meeting[;] the heads of state governments are appointed by the previous King, while the Yang Dipertuan of States are appointed by the Yang Dipertuan Agung. Such as mentioned by al-Mawardi previously, the head of state has the power to appoint the council of ministers. In Malaysia, the Prime Minister who leads the council of ministers is appointed by the Yang Dipertuan Agung from among members of the Dewan Rakyat (House of Representatives) who have obtained the trust of the majority.

On implementation of the 'syura' (consultative) principle, which is one of the basic principles in the Islamic system of government, Syed Al-Syaikh Rasyid Ridha[41] said:

---

38 Tan Sri Hashim Yeop Sani is currently a Supreme Court judge in Kuala Lumpur.

39 Abu al-Hasan al-Mawardi (d. 1058) was one of the most influential of Shafi'i school jurists and is particularly well known for his writings on law and politics.

40 Yang di-Pertuan Agong: the King of Malaysia.

41 Rashid Rida (1865–1935) was a Syrian-born leading Islamic reformer and a powerful figure within the Salafiyya movement.

This syura system is different according to the situation faced by a Muslim and the development of a society because in such matter[s], it is not possible to determine the method of implementation for all places and times.

Syaikh Taha Abd. Al-Baqi al-Surur also said [took] the same view[.] He said:

Syura in Islam is a principle which is general in nature and its method of implementation changes according to developments of the system, civilisation and life of mankind. It can be implemented such as in the beginning era of Islam or such as implemented in this era through the Parliament institution.

While Dr Abdul Hamid Ismail al-Ansari said as follows:

Representative councils such as the Parliament of today can be considered as a 'syura Council' and its members as Syura Council members. The election method implemented in this era is legal in the eyes of Islam.

Regarding election or appointment of non-Muslims as members of parliament and State Assembly (DUN) he viewed the law is ought to [*sic*]. His views are contained in his study to obtain a Ph.D. degree that was submitted to the University of Al-Azhar. His views were not protested by Al-Azhar Muslim scholars who supervised and inspected the thesis.

CHAPTER THREE: MUSLIM'S OBLIGATIONS TO THE GOVERNMENT [...]

[W]e have said briefly the government's obligations to Muslims, thus in this part we will talk about [a] Muslim's obligations to the government. In this respect, Imam Abu Ya'la said the following:

When the government has carried out its responsibilities to Muslims, then it is compulsory to implement two matters to the government: (1) obedience and (2) assisting the government in implementation of its responsibilities.

Even there is evidence from Al-Quran and Hadith which shows it is compulsory to obey the government[;] it is as follows:
Allah s.w.t. [Almighty God] commands:

Oh pious people, be obedient to Allah s.w.t.[,] be obedient to Prophet Muhammad and to 'ulil amri' (people in power) from among you.

Then look **at** Prophet Muhammad's saying, which means:

Anyone who is obedient to me means he is obedient to Allah s.w.t., anyone who betrays me **means** he betrays Allah s.w.t, anyone who is obedient to the government means he is **obedient** to me and anyone who betrays the government means he betrays me.

Prophet Muhammad said:

It is compulsory for every Muslim to obey and submit to the government whether he likes it or not, as long as he is not instructed to commit vices. If he is instructed to commit vices, then do not obey and submit.

Such also is Prophet Muhammad's saying:

You will be ruled by governments after me[;] the good ones will rule you with their goodness and the wicked ones will rule you with their wickedness. Thus you are to listen and obey them for each of their orders which is in line with the truth[;] if they do good then that good is for you and for them but if they commit wickedness then you will obtain good but they will receive consequences from the wickedness they have committed.

Prophet Muhammad said again:

Whoever withdraws his obedience to the government, he will meet Allah s.w.t. without any argument. Anyone [who] dies without obedience to the government, his death will be like death in ignorance.

While in another narrative it is said that Prophet Muhammad said:

Obey your government whatever the situation[;] if [they] rule you with orders which are in line with my teachings then they will be given rewards and you will also be given rewards for obeying them, but if they rule you with orders which are not in line with my teachings then their sins will be borne by them whereas you will be saved from sins.

Prophet Muhammad said:

If you are under governments which ask you to perform prayers, pay tithes and take part in a crusade, then [it] is unlawful for you to scorn them and it is permissible for you to follow them.

[Thus] we quote al-Quran and al-Sunnah 'nas-nas' (authoritative quotations) which compel Muslims to obey an Islamic government ('waliyul amri'). Abu Hurairah interpreted the word 'ulil amri' in verse 59, 'surah' chapter of al-Nisa[42] above as 'the government'.

The principle of obedience to the government is vital in Islam because Muslims' lives and the regulations brought by Islam 'will not be able to be upheld without the existence of a government which is obeyed'. (Therefore obeying the head of state is 'a part of the key fundamentals for Islamic laws which are holy and pure'.)

Departing from this principle too, the behaviour of challenging legitimate government to the extent of leading to a break-up in society which could break up unity and weaken Muslims is an offence which is viewed seriously by religion, such as stated in Prophet Muhammad's sayings:

Anyone who comes to you whereas all of you are united under a government, he wants to commit betrayal and break up your unity, thus he will be killed.

12.2.2 Parti Islam Se Malaysia (PAS)

Commentary In his 2001 'Islamic state' speech, Dr Mahathir challenged the opposition Islamist party, PAS, to show that it also had a coherent concept of how an Islamic

---

42 'You who believe, obey God and the Messenger, and those in authority among you. If you are in dispute over any matter, refer it to God and the Messenger, if you truly believe in God and the Last Day: that is better and fairer in the end' (Q4: 59, Haleem).

state would be realized in Malaysia. This set off a protracted debate within PAS as to how best to respond. Over the next two years, four separate drafts were produced. The early versions, formulated under the guidance of the party's then president, Fadzil Noor, were more pluralistic than the later ones; the final version reprinted below, which emerged after Fadzil Noor's death in 2002, was more Islamist in nature. The following extract sets out the main features of PAS's blueprint for an Islamic state and shows the extent to which the issue had become politicized.

Extract 12-16: *Parti Islam Se Malaysia (PAS)*

Parti Islam Se Malaysia (2004), *The Islamic State Document* [in English], <http://www.parti-pas.org/IslamicStateDocument.php>, dated 8 January 2004, accessed 15 September 2004.

PREFACE BY THE PRESIDENT OF THE ISLAMIC PARTY OF MALAYSIA (PAS)

In the Name of Allah Most Gracious Most Merciful

PRAISE be unto Allah, Lord of the Universe. Peace and Blessings be upon our leader and our Prophet, Muhammad, most honored of all the Prophets[,] and upon his family and his companions, and whoever sincerely follows in their footsteps until the Day of Reckoning.

First and foremost I would like to express my profound gratitude unto the Almighty Allah, for it is only through His grace and permission alone that we are able to publish this monumental document in our struggle, at a time when the entire community is eagerly awaiting its publication. The publication of this document is sufficient evidence to squash allegations made by its enemies that PAS will not establish an Islamic State. It was even alleged that the entire membership of PAS never had the slightest intention of establishing an Islamic State in Malaysia.

Verily the responsibility of establishing an Islamic State is as important as performing the daily obligatory rituals of Islam. This is in fact evident from the principle of an Islamic maxim which states:

> 'If an obligatory act can only be performed with the availability of a specific item, then the procurement of that item is equally obligatory.'

It is with this realization that PAS champions the cause for Islam as a 'Deen wa Daulah' (Way of life and a State) to be established in our beloved country of Malaysia, based on the principles of the Shariah and guided by the dictates of the Almighty Allah:

> 'And We have sent down to you the Book in truth, confirming the Scriptures that came before it, and guarding it in safety. So judge among them by what Allah has revealed, and follow not their vain desires, diverging from the truth that has come to you. To each among you We have prescribed a law and a clear way. If Allah had so willed, He would have made you one nation, but that (He) may test you in what He has given

you; so compete in good deeds. The return of you (all) is to Allah; then He will inform you about that in which you used to differ.'
– Surah al-Maa'idah: 48[43]

As a result of the tireless and continuous efforts from all levels of PAS members, the concept of Islam as a complete way of life has been accepted by the society at large. This confirms the truth in what Allah has said:

'But no, by your Lord, they can have no Faith, until they make you (O Muhammad) judge in all disputes between them, and find in themselves no resistance against your decisions and accept them with full submission.'
– Surah An-Nisa': 65[44]

The aspiration of establishing Islam in the domains of societal and political life has borne fruit when Kelantan and Terengganu are governed by PAS. With this success Islam is being practiced in both governance and administration in these two states within the legal bounds permitted taking into consideration obstacles and limitations that have to be encountered.

With the publication and dissemination of this document, we are hopeful that the Malaysian society will now be able to better appreciate the concept and model of the Islamic State and Government as striven for by PAS since its inception. The document also serves to clarify the concept of a true Islamic state as opposed to a 'pseudo Islamic state'.

Should PAS be mandated to govern Malaysia, God willing, an Islamic state as outlined in this document will be implemented to the best of our ability.

'Towards Victory'

Allahu Akbar!

Dato' Seri Tuan Guru Haji Abdul Hadi Awang
President, Islamic Party of Malaysia (PAS)

THE ISLAMIC STATE DOCUMENT

PREAMBLE

[1.] Islam is both a Belief system and a Deen [faith] – which is a complete and comprehensive way of life, that was revealed by Allah Almighty to the last of the Prophets, Muhammad Ibn Abdullah (may peace be upon him) to be an eternal Guidance and Blessing not only to man but also to the entire Universe. [...]

---

43 'We sent to you [Muhammad] the Scripture with the truth, confirming the Scriptures that came before it, and with final authority over them: so judge between them according to what God has sent down. Do not follow their whims, which deviate from the truth that has come to you. We have assigned a law and a path to each of you. If God had so willed, He would have made you one community, but He wanted to test you through that which He has given you, so race to do good: you will all return to God and He will make clear to you the matters you differed about' (Q5: 48, Haleem).

44 'By your Lord, they will not be true believers until they let you decide between them in all matters of dispute, and find no resistance in their souls to your decisions, accepting them totally' (Q4: 65, Haleem).

2. From the understanding and conviction that Allah is the Creator and Organizer of the whole Universe, springs the belief that Allah is the provider of the guidance and teachings for man to organize the complete system of individual, societal and national life. Islamic political leadership is therefore an important institution necessary for the achievement of human progress.

3. PAS takes full cognizance of the reality and sensitivity of this country's multiethnic, multi-religious and multi-cultural makeup. Hence from its inception, PAS has stated in no uncertain terms, its stance on the status and position of Islam as a comprehensive system of life embracing the entire domain of socio-political life; be it [in] the individual, societal, national and international arenas.

4. The political history of this nation has witnessed that since its inception in 1951, the Islamic Party of Malaysia (PAS) has been committed to and consistent with the observation and practice of parliamentary democracy. PAS has accepted democracy as the best methodology through which it should realize the ambition, vision and mission of its political struggle.

5. As an Islamic political party, PAS advocates the implementation of Islam as a comprehensive way of life, identifying various major guidelines (derived from the vast principles and provisions of the shariah) which are to be implemented in the establishment of an Islamic state.

6. PAS is fully committed in preserving both the interests of the religion (of Islam) and that of the nation and manifests this commitment categorically in the Vision and Mission statements as found in Section 5 (i) and (ii) of the Constitution of the party:

i. To struggle for the establishment of a society and government in this country, that embodies and manifests Islamic values and laws that seek the pleasure of the Almighty

ii. To uphold the sovereignty of the country and the sanctity of the religion of Islam

In Section 7 of the party's Constitution, PAS reasserts that: 'The highest source of authority is the Holy Qur'an, the Prophetic Tradition (Sunnah of ar-Rasul), Consensus (Ijma') of the Ulama' and Analogy (Qiyas) which are clear and evident'.

7. The first Islamic State was established in the multi-racial, multi-cultural and multi-religious society of Medina in the period of the Prophet and the Rightly Guided Caliphates and so shall it need to be established till the end of time.

8. The Constitution of Medina, known as 'Sahifah Medina', has duly stipulated the rights and responsibilities of every citizen in a just manner for the plural society of Medina and those who took abode in the state.

9. The Holy Qur'an and the Sunnah have laid down the broad guiding principles of the Islamic State, which[,] if taken together, primarily lead man to obedience and submission unto Allah. [...]

10. To place the Holy Quran and the Prophetic Tradition (As-Sunnah) as the primary source of legislation in the governance of the state and its judiciary is imperative and mandatory to the Islamic State as evidently emphasized by Allah's commandment in the Quran:

> 'Surely We have sent down to you (O Muhammad) the Book in truth, that you might judge between men by that which Allah has shown you; so be not a pleader for the treacherous.'
> – Surah an-Nisaa': 105[45]

11. The Islamic State based its legislation on the laws of the Almighty Who is Most Gracious and Most Merciful. It is therefore impossible for these laws to be the cause or source of injustice.

12. The Islamic State is an ideal state cherished and longed for by all who love peace and true justice.

13. The true Islamic State is a state which is peaceful and prosperous while receiving the pleasure of Allah the Almighty. When peace is combined with forgiveness from Allah, true peace will result.

14. Muslims are entrusted to say in their prayers:

> 'Truly, my prayer, my worship, my life and my death is only for Allah, Master and Cherisher of the entire Universe.'

The above oath, repeated in the daily prayers of the Muslims, is meaningless unless its true demands are earnestly fulfilled. To fulfil the demands of this oath, it is imperative that a true Islamic state be established.

15. Unless an Islamic State is established, the true import and demands of this oath could not be manifested in its entirety.

16. The Islamic system of government as outlined above is the conviction of a true believer (of Islam) and will lead to the embodiment of Islam in its purest form.

THE CONCEPT (TASAWWUR) OF AN ISLAMIC STATE [...]

The Shariah is the government's main source of guidance for governance in conducting the affairs of the state.

The Muslim citizens of the state would be educated so as to embody the Islamic way of life in its entirety so as to inculcate good moral and spiritual values in the building of the society and the nation. The implementation of Shari'ah further provides the cleansing and purification of society. A virtuous and moral society in turn, entitles itself to further bliss and grace from the Almighty including the solution of problems and overflowing prosperity.

---

45 'We have sent down the Scripture to you [Prophet] with the truth so that you can judge between people in accordance with what God has shown you. Do not be an advocate for those who betray trust' (Q4: 105, Haleem).

The implementation of Shariah, hudud [punishments prescribed in the Qur'an] being a part of it, provides the much required peace and security as crimes would be reduced to its minimum.

> 'And (as for) the male thief and the female thief, cut off their hands as a recompense for that which they committed, a punishment by way of example, from Allah: And Allah is All Powerful, All Wise.'
> – Surah Al-Maaidah: 38[46]

The above stated injunction is from Allah and is mandatory and must be implemented.

Non-Muslim members of the state will continue to enjoy freedom of religious beliefs and rituals and are at liberty to practice their own way of life without any inhibitions or obstructions by the Islamic state. This is as based on the verse of the Quran:

> 'There is no compulsion in religion.'
> – Surah Al-Baqarah: 256[47]

PRIMARY PRINCIPLES AND POLICIES OF THE ISLAMIC GOVERNMENT

1. A State that is based on the Supremacy of Law

The determining characteristic of an Islamic State is its total commitment and will to see that the Shariah is codified into the law of the land and is implemented. Allah is the true Supreme Law-Giver as is consonant with the verse:

> 'The Command is for none but Allah: He has commanded that you worship none but Him: that is the (true) straight religion, but most men know not ...'
> – Surah Yusuf: 40[48]

Allah has ordained the leaders (of Islamic society) to implement what He has revealed and prohibits them from taking recourse to other sources of law. [...]

Only the Muslim members of the state are subjected to the Shari'ah Penal Code (Hudud, Qisas and Ta'zir). The non-Muslim members are given the option of either being subjected to the same penal code or to be subjected to the current penal code of the land.

Allah says in the Holy Quran:

> '(They like to) listen to falsehood, of devouring anything forbidden. So if they come to you, either judge between them or turn away from them. If you turn away from

---

46   'Cut off the hands of thieves, whether they are male or female, as punishment for what they have done – a deterrent from God: God is almighty and wise' (Q5: 38, Haleem).
47   'There is no compulsion in religion: true guidance has become distinct from error, so whoever rejects false gods and believes in God has grasped the firmest hand-hold, one that will never break. God is all hearing and all knowing' (Q2: 256, Haleem).
48   'All those you worship instead of Him are mere names you and your forefathers have invented, names for which God has sent down no authority: all command belongs to God alone, and He orders you to worship none but Him: this is the true faith, though most people do not realize it' (Q12: 40, Haleem).

them, they cannot hurt you in the least. And if you judge, judge in equity between them. For Allah loves those who act justly.'
– Surah al-Ma'idah: 42[49]

If by implementing that which is stated above, PAS is said to be unjust, it is tantamount to saying that Allah is unjust in this injunction. Giving the option to the non-Muslim to choose between Hudud, Qisas and Ta'zir or otherwise is actually divinely-derived and it is not an option provided by PAS. Any contention in this regards, amounts to contesting the Divine Wisdom.

2. Vicegerency – Khilafah [caliphate]

Adam, the first man created by Allah, was designated the position of Vicegerent of Allah on Earth. Vicegerency in this context signifies the position specifically for the guardianship over the religion of Islam and administrating the state according to its teachings. [...]

The meaning of vicegerency implies that man is a representative who will act on behalf of another (in this case, God) and will perform duties in accordance with that position. Hence man[,] and it hereby implies leadership of the nation, must act in full consonance with the dictates of Allah and not according to his whims and fancies. Should he act in contravention to the dictates of the Almighty, he has indeed betrayed the trust and position of vicegerency of God on Earth. [...]

3. 'Taqwa' or God-Fearing

The scholars of Islam define Taqwa or God-Fearing as 'To obey Allah's dictates and to shun what He prohibits'.

'Taqwa' is an important cornerstone of the Islamic State. When this pervades in the nation and its citizenry, the blessing of God descends on society and [taqwa is] simultaneously seen as a natural sentinel against the spread of evil and corruption. [...]

4. Consultation (Shura)

Shura or consultation is one of the primary guiding principles in conducting the affairs of the state. The methodology of consultation has been enjoined by Almighty Allah in the Holy Quran:

'and who (conduct) their affairs by mutual consultation; and who spend out of what we have bestowed on them.'
– Surah asy-Shuraa: 38[50] [...]

Consultation is exercised in all matters pertaining to the administration and solving of problems of the nation, taking into consideration the benefits, advantages and disadvantages. Consultation is conducted only on matters requiring 'ijtihad' or

---

49 'they listen eagerly to lies and consume what is unlawful. If they come to you [Prophet] for judgement, you can either judge between them, or decline – if you decline, they will not harm you in any way, but if you do judge between them, judge justly: God loves the just' (Q5: 42, Haleem).
50 'respond to their Lord and keep up the prayer; conduct their affairs by mutual consultation; give to others out of what We have provided for them' (Q42: 38, Haleem).

concerted opinion. For matters which have injunctions which are 'Qat'i' or clear and undisputable, consultation cannot change that injunction.

The practice of Shura or Consultation would make the House of Representatives a forum wherein the elected representatives can exercise their right to free speech. The members of the House of Senate would subsequently serve the function of check and balance over bills passed by the House of Representatives.

5. Justice and Equality (Al-'Adaalah wal Musaawah)
Al-'Adaalah means justice while al-Musaawah means equality. Both Justice and Equality are other important cornerstones of the governance of an Islamic state. […]

6. Freedom (al-Hurriyah)
Al-Hurriyah or Freedom[,] as an idealism, is cherished by all. The second Caliph of Islam, Omar al-Khattab[,] once said:

> 'Why subjugate and enslave man, while he is born of his mother a free man.'

Before the advent of Islam, slavery was a dominant feature of human society. One of the objectives behind the coming of Islam is to free man of this slavery. The Islamic State guarantees the rights and freedom of the individuals and the citizens of the state. Amongst the rights and freedom protected by Islam are:

a. Freedom of religious beliefs
b. Individual freedom
c. Freedom of speech, political association and assembly
d. Freedom to private ownership
e. Freedom of education (including right to use mother-tongue in education)
f. Freedom of Religion and right to cultural expressions
g. Freedom to engage in business and the search of livelihood.

All the above freedom[s] and the freedom and rights of the citizens especially as enjoined by the Universal Declaration of Human Rights are also protected by the Islamic State. It must not however contravene the provision of Shari'ah. […]

7. Absolute Sovereignty (As-Siyaadah wal-Haakimiyah)
As-Siyaadah wal-Haakimiyah means absolute sovereignty. The Islamic State has an absolute sovereign Who cannot be challenged or interfered with. Absolute sovereignty belongs to Allah Almighty as He is the Creator and hence the Provider and Source of Laws. […]

As-Siyaadah is the characteristic which distinguishes a true Islamic state from a pseudo Islamic state. When as-Siyaadah or Sovereignty is rendered back unto the Rightful Owner i.e. God Almighty, man's position is relegated to the position of a vicegerent i.e. acting on behalf and in accordance to the dictates of the Almighty. To eliminate or debunk the concept of As-Siyaadah is to elevate man to the position of God. Besides, as-Siyaadah provides man the means to always return to and invoke help and solace from the Almighty Allah while he strives for the achievement of those ideals which are seemingly beyond the capability of ordinary men. Through it man becomes a mere servant of Allah seeking His pleasure in this world and in the Hereafter.

12.2.3   Farish A. Noor

> ***Commentary***   Farish Noor (1967–) is one of Malaysia's most prolific and contro-versial young Muslim intellectuals. Trained in political science at the University of Malaya, he has taught at various tertiary institutions in Malaysia and Europe and is currently academic researcher at Zentrum Moderner Orient in Berlin. He has been a long-time campaigner for Islamic pluralism in Malaysia and first rose to prominence as the secretary-general of the International Movement for a Just World (JUST). He has been a sharp critic of both Malaysian government and PAS efforts to Islamize politics and society. The following article is typical of his contributions to public debate on the Islamic state issue. It is a summary of a talk he gave at a public forum on the 'Future of Malaysia and the Islamic State' organized by the Democratic Action Party (DAP), a Chinese-dominated opposition party, at the Malaysian Chinese Assembly Hall in Kuala Lumpur on 19 December 2001.

Extract 12-17: Farish A. Noor

Farish A. Noor, 'No Bated Breaths for Result of Out-Islamising Race' [in English], *Malaysiakini*, <http://www.malaysiakini.com>, dated 22 December 2001, accessed 29 December 2001. [Summary of talk given on 19 December 2001.]

The re-emergence of the thorny issue of the Islamic state in Malaysian politics reads like a local rendition of the theme of the 'Return of the Repressed'. The more we try to avoid the issue, the more it makes its presence felt on the domestic political scene.

Like it or not, we have to address the reality of the Islamic state issue. But what we cannot and should not accept from the outset is the idea that the Islamic state is a *fait accompli*, and that there is no turning back.

These concerns have been raised by a number of political parties, social move-ments, NGOs and political commentators. Other religious groups have also voiced their concern about how the debate over the Islamic state is progressing, demanding that their voices are heard and that they should be given the right to participate in the debate before it goes any further.

In the past few weeks, the Islamic state issue has been debated openly by politi-cal parties like the DAP [Democratic Action Party] and MCA [Malaysian Chinese Association] as well as NGOs like Hakam and Sisters in Islam (SIS) [both prominent liberal NGOs].

That so many groups – none of them linked in any instrumental coalition of any sort – could get so worked up over the question of the Islamic state should come as no surprise to us by now. The Islamic state issue is one that unites as much as it divides, and as soon as it entered the hotly contested terrain of Malaysian politics it managed to redraw the political and ideological boundaries of the nation in no uncertain terms.

Though much has been said and written about the matter already, it is nonetheless useful to question some of the most basic premises upon which the whole debate has been set.

Islamisation and the State

A cursory reading of the mainstream media these days might give one the mistaken impression that the Islamic state issue has been hoisted on the Malaysian populace by one Islamic party in particular – PAS.

Before going any further, we need to dispel this contemporary myth by pointing out that it was the Islamisation race between Umno and PAS that has really brought us to the present impasse.

To 'blame' PAS for bringing the country where it is today would be both unfair and inaccurate: Umno has been just as guilty of playing the Islamisation card and it was the Umno-led government's Islamisation policy which began in the 1980s that really helped to normalise political religion in everyday life, marginalising whatever hopes there might have been for a secular political alternative in the country.

If some senior Umno leaders, bureaucrats and members of the Malay middle-classes are concerned about the tenor and form of political Islam in Malaysia today, they have no-one else to blame but themselves for it was they who helped to create the vast Islamist bureaucratic, institutional, legal and educational system that today has so much power and influence on the Malay-Muslims of the country.

In its effort to out-Islamise PAS, Umno had unwittingly laid down the institutional foundations of an Islamic state long ago thanks to its patronage and support for these institutions.

What is more, the growing conservatism and defensiveness on the part of so many Malay-Muslims can also be accounted for by these institutions that have been at the forefront of the Islamisation race in the country. By projecting an image and understanding of Islam as a religion under threat of subversion and 'contamination' from external threats, they helped to create and foster the ghetto mentality that is prevalent in many quarters of the Malay-Muslim population in Malaysia.

If Umno leaders are worried about the narrow mindset of the demagogues and ideologues of PAS, they should look a little closer at the Islamic educational and bureaucratic institutions they have created under their care and tutelage, and the sort of Islamic education that has been dished out by the ulama and religious teachers in the pay of the state as well.

The net result of this race to out-Islamise each other is the raising of public expectations and the normalisation of wants and aspirations on the part of the Malay-Muslims in the country. [...]

Many Malaysias, many realities

The Islamisation race which began in earnest in the 1980s and 1990s was unique in its apparent disregard for alternative viewpoints and beliefs. Thus it came to pass that the whole Islamisation project has managed to sideline the sensitivities and reservations of the non-Muslims in the country, who happen to make up almost half of the population of Malaysia.

It is ironic to note that in the government's pamphlet 'Malaysia as an Islamic State' (which was subsequently withdrawn) we come across the sentence that reads: 'the reality of Malaysia as an Islamic state is something that can no longer be denied'.

This begs the most obvious question: Which 'reality' is the author/s of the pamphlet talking about? There is no single reality that sums up the complexity of Malaysia's multicultural and multireligious society, and there certainly cannot be a single simple blueprint that serves as the final solution to all its problems.

When talking about the 'reality' of contemporary Malaysian society thus, did the author/s of the pamphlet spare a thought for the countless other 'realities' that may co-exist with his/their own? What of the millions of other Muslim and non-Muslim Malaysians who may well prefer to live in a secular state where all religions are treated with the same degree of respect as their own?

And what of those who prefer to live in a secular state where no religion – Islam or otherwise – would dominate the arena of national politics and serve as the mainframe within which all conduct of politics will be carried out?

The narrow religio-cultural solipsism that is evident in the Islamic state pamphlet serves only to underscore the painful fact that Malaysian society remains as disunited and fragmented as it has ever been, with different ethnic and religious communities living side by side with each other but with precious little contact and understanding in between them. [...]

Islamic or secular loyalty?

Lest it be forgotten, any attempt to introduce an Islamic State in Malaysia will lead to a radical (and irreversible) change to the constitutional framework of the country. The conversion from a secular state to an Islamic state is not simply a matter of semantics.

For the transition also involves the introduction and incorporation of an entirely new moral and political logic, which effectively redesigns and reconstructs the political framework of the country as a whole.

In a secular state, concepts like citizenship, nationality and sovereignty are paramount. But these concepts are framed within a secular framework where one's identity is based on the status of the subject as a private individual rather than [a] member of a faith community.

Conversely, membership [of] a religious state entails a transition to a new ideational framework where some of the most basic political concepts like citizenship, identity and belonging will be altered for good.

Belonging to a religious state where religion X is the dominant religion means that a different understanding of citizenship itself will be introduced, where those who belong to religion X will be the 'natural citizens' of that state and others not.

The Islamists' claim that their model of an Islamic state will give equal treatment and status to all members of the Malaysian public has to be challenged for the contradiction that it is. This is not to say that Islam alone discriminates against non-Muslims. The sad fact is that all religions discriminate as they single out and identify their respective constituencies and the Other.

Political Islam is no different in this respect than the political expression of Christianity, Judaism, Hinduism, Buddhism or any other religion. All religions draw a neat boundary line between their followers and others. For every believer there is always the convenient infidel, heathen or kafir to stand as his/her constitutive other. To claim otherwise would not only be naive – it is also politically Machiavellian and dangerous.

Religious states

In such a religious state, the status and identity of those who do not belong to the dominant faith community will always be hanging in the balance. Are they expected to show the same degree of loyalty and commitment to a state which is built on the name of a religion other than theirs? Would non-Muslims be expected to be loyal to an Islamic state and would they be expected to give the same degree of sacrifice and commitment to uphold the values of a religion that is not their own? [...]

The reality is that the introduction of a religious state in Malaysia will bring about changes that none of us are really prepared for, and what is more these changes can never be reversed once they are installed. Instead, the Malaysian public has been sold tickets for a journey the course of which none of us have anticipated or charted.

The trajectory of Malaysia and Malaysian politics may well be altered for good in the years to come, but as the passive Malaysian public sits by and watches, these decisions are being made on our behalf by self-proclaimed leaders of the religion whom we do not know and did not elect.

Malaysia may well be on the brink of crossing the threshold into the unknown, going where it has never gone before. Oddly enough, the only people who seem ignorant of this fact are we Malaysians ourselves.

12.2.4   Abdullah Badawi

> ***Commentary (by John Funston and Virginia Hooker)***   The history of Islamic civilization is taught widely in Muslim educational institutions but it can also be a subject for political debate. In Malaysia, for example, Prime Minister Abdullah Badawi has launched a program under the rubric 'Islam Hadhari' (Civilizational Islam). The aim of the program is to encourage Malaysia's Muslims to draw on Islamic values to modernize society and the economy so that Malaysia not only is a prosperous and harmonious nation but also has the capacity to meet the challenges of globalization. The concept has been slow to develop because the majority of Malaysians have been puzzled about what the concept actually means, and because its liberal message has sometimes been in conflict with statements by other UMNO leaders and government officials.
>
> In the following extract from one of the prime minister's speeches, it is clear that his Islam Hadhari program raises many points relevant for the individual expression and experience of Islam. It also indicates the degree of guidance which the prime minister claims it is UMNO's duty to provide for all Malaysia's citizens. The translation is the one provided by Prime Minister Dato' Seri Abdullah Haji Ahmad Badawi himself, for an interview with the newspaper *Bernama* on 11 February 2005.

Extract 12-18: Abdullah Badawi

Dato' Seri Abdullah Haji Ahmad Badawi (2004), 'Moving Forward: Towards Excellence' [in English], speech given at the UMNO General Assembly, 23 September 2004, Putra World Trade Center, Kuala Lumpur.

ISLAM HADHARI [...]

17. Islam Hadhari is an approach that emphasises development, consistent with the tenets of Islam and focused on enhancing the quality of life. It aims to achieve this via the mastery of knowledge and the development of the individual and the nation; the implementation of a dynamic economic, trading and financial system; an integrated and balanced development that creates a knowledgeable and pious people who hold to noble values and are honest, trustworthy, and prepared to take on global challenges.

18. Islam Hadhari is not a new religion. It is not a new teaching nor is it a new mazhab (denomination). Islam Hadhari is an effort to bring the Ummah back to basics, back to the fundamentals, as prescribed in the Quran and the Hadith that form the foundation of Islamic civilization. If Islam Hadhari is interpreted sincerely and understood clearly, it will not cause Muslims to deviate from the true path. It is not UMNO's culture to trivialize religion. UMNO has never allowed religion to be used as a political tool. UMNO staunchly opposes the use of Islam as an instrument to manipulate people's beliefs. UMNO has always ensured that Islam and Muslims are protected from such abuse of religion. It was on this basis that UMNO, which was directly involved in formulating the Federal Constitution, inserted Articles that place Islam under the jurisdiction of the Heads of State.

19. As the party that is responsible for ensuring Muslims are able to meet current challenges without deviating from their faith, the doors of ijtihad [interpretation] must remain open, so that interpretations are suited to the developmental needs of the prevailing time and conditions. Policies must be balanced and broad-based development that encompasses the infrastructure and the economy; human resource development via a comprehensive education programme; the inculcation of noble values through spiritual development and assimilation of Islamic values.

20. Islam Hadhari aims to achieve ten main principles:

I.   Faith and piety in Allah
II.   A just and trustworthy government
III.   A free and independent People
IV.   Mastery of knowledge
V.   Balanced and comprehensive economic development
VI.   A good quality of life
VII. Protection of the rights of minority groups and women
VIII. Cultural and moral integrity

IX.   Safeguarding the environment

X.   Strong defenses

21. These principles have been formulated to ensure that the implementation and approach does not cause anxiety among any group in our multiracial and multi-religious country. These principles have been devised to empower Muslims to face the global challenges of today.

22. Islam Hadhari is complete and comprehensive, with an emphasis on the development of the economy and civilization, capable of building Malay competitiveness. The glorious heritage of Islamic civilization in all aspects must be used as a reference and become the source of inspiration for the Malay race to prosper. [...]

12.2.5 Abdul Hadi Awang

Commentary (by Virginia Hooker)   Abdullah Badawi's Islam Hadhari concept provoked a strong reaction from PAS, which regarded it as politically motivated and religiously flawed. The PAS president and former chief minister of Terengganu, Dato' Seri Tuan Guru Haji Abdul Hadi Awang, subsequently produced a book setting out his objections to 'Civilizational Islam'. Hadi Awang (1947–) was raised and educated initially in Terengganu. He completed a bachelor's degree in Medina funded by a scholarship from the Saudi Arabian government. He gained a master's degree in Islamic law from al-Azhar University, Cairo, in 1976.

Hadi Awang begins his book by explaining that the word *hadharah* comes from an Arabic word that means the arrival of people who come to settle permanently in a town and thus move from a nomadic to a settled lifestyle. The great fourteenth-century Muslim scholar Ibn Khaldun used the word in one of his works and explained that the gathering of people in an urban settlement was an instinctive human social process, referred to as *madani* ('civilized') because out of such human groupings come advances in basic technologies and ways of living (Abdul Hadi 2005: 13).

Hadi Awang bases most of his arguments on passages from the Qur'an and Hadith, but also points out where and how the UMNO program is, according to his view, at odds with Islamic principles. The basis of Hadi Awang's argument is that there is only one Islam, so the term 'civilizational Islam' is against basic Islamic teachings. What is essential, he argues, is 'Islamized civilization'. He elaborates this concept and its eight principles in his book.

Extract 12-19: Abdul Hadi Awang

Abdul Hadi Awang (2005), 'Prinsip Hadharah Islamiyyah' [Principles of Islamized Civilization], pp. 86–126 in *Hadharah Islamiyyah bukan Islam Hadhari* [Islamized Civilization not Civilizational Islam], Nufair Street Sdn Bhd, Kuala Lumpur. Extract: pp. 86–126.

The bases and principles of Islamized civilization (*Hadharah Islamiyyah*) require [members of] the Muslim community (*umat Islam*) to become a model for all humankind by implementing Islam in their own lives. They should carry the message of Islam to the whole world. Their role in conveying this message must follow the principles laid down by God in His book and realized by the Messenger of God, blessings and peace be upon him, through his deeds and words. The proof of this truth came through its implementation by the first generation of Pious Ancestors who developed Islamized civilization in the golden age of Islam. Its traces are still evident throughout the world, albeit in a fragmented way. [p. 86]

[The author goes on to list the Islamic principles that must underpin Islamized civilization, elaborating each principle in turn.]

1. Worship of God (*Ibadah*) [...]
2. Islamic government (*Khilafah*) [...]
3. Mandate (to implement God's commands) (*Amanah*) [...]
4. Justice (*Keadilan*) [...]
5. Freedom (*Hurriyyah/Kebebasan*) [...]
6. Completeness [in the sense of Islam as a comprehensive system for organizing human society] (*Syumuliyyah/Lengkap*) [...]
7. Knowledge and wisdom (*Ilmu dan Hikmah/Kebijaksanaan*) [...]
8. Unity (*Wehdah/Kesatuan atau Perpaduan*) [...] [pp. 87–126]

[The thesis of the author is that the UMNO program of Islam Hadhari is misguided, as summarized below.]

Islam Hadhari, the creation of UMNO, only cuts, chops and slices Islam according to its own taste. There are activities they want to link with communal obligation (*fardu kifayah*) purely for the purposes of controlling civil servants, but in their internal politics they forget God. They continue to get soiled with money politics, corruption and fraud. Perhaps they believe that the internal matters of UMNO are beyond the reach of God's laws. They create a culture of immoral activities that ignore God's ways, because after that they can go and perform the *umrah* [pilgrimage]. They believe the *umrah* will automatically take away their sins. Even major sins are considered trivial. Some of them believe sin is a personal matter. Their attitude is as if the government and society have no connection with or responsibility towards God.

The laws of God which must be observed by a government are replaced with man-made laws according to human tastes. Society is engulfed in a most serious crisis of self-righteousness, to the extent that the big issues that concern people do not penetrate their consciences. The big sins are not even challenged, although this should happen in a civilized society. [pp. 90–1]

12.3 BRUNEI DARUSSALAM

12.3.1 Md Zain Haji Serudin

Commentary (by John Funston) The concept of *Melayu Islam Beraja* (Malay Islamic Monarchy) was introduced as the 'state philosophy' of Brunei Darussalam when it 'regained' its independence on 1 January 1984. However, it was only with the publication of Ustaz Md Zain's *Melayu Islam Beraja* 14 years later that an extended elaboration of the concept was set out. According to Ustaz Md Zain, who is minister of religious affairs, the concept embodies the compatibility of Malay nationalism, Islam and a monarchical political system (see also plate 3 in the colour section of this book). The only approved form of Islam is the Sunni branch, named in the document as Ahli Sunah Waljamaah [Ahli Sunnah Wal-Jammah]; in matters of jurisprudence, the Shafi'i school of law is followed (as is the case in most of Southeast Asia). The text also makes clear that non-Muslims are not to proselytize within Muslim communities.

Extract 12-20: Md Zain Haji Serudin

Md Zain Haji Serudin (1998), *Melayu Islam Beraja* [Malay Islamic Monarchy], Dewan Bahasa dan Pustaka Brunei, Kementerian Kebudayaan Belia dan Sukan, Bandar Seri Begawan. Extract: pp. 54, 60–5.

Not Secular

The permanency of Islam as a complete way of life and as the official state religion of the State of Brunei Darussalam implies that the State of Brunei Darussalam is not a secular state because Islam does not provide a place for secularization, whether secularization in the field of politics and the state or secularization in knowledge. Islam does not recognize the separate existence of life in this world and life in the afterworld. [...]

In truth, the philosophy of the Malay Islamic Monarchy is the essence of the identity of the Brunei people and their noble Malay culture, which accepts and experiences Islam as a full and complete way of life, and which fosters a spirit and awareness that Brunei Malays, as the dominant race, have succeeded in shaping the State of Brunei Darussalam and are ready to face the challenges of the future, while sheltering under the system of monarchical rule. [p. 54] [...]

I Islamic Values

The second element in the philosophy of the Malay Islamic Monarchy is the religion of Islam. According to the definition recorded in the working paper of the National Supreme Council of the Malay Islamic Monarchy on Islam, it is:

> The official state religion according to the faith of the Ahli Sunah Waljamaah, of the Syafie [Shafi'i] School[,] which is practised as a way of life that is full, complete and supreme.

This statement not only accepts Islam as the official state religion as written in the constitution of the State of Brunei Darussalam, but also as the way of life of the Malay people of Brunei, that is, the Islamic way, applying the values of Islam in the life of society and also the administration of the Government of Brunei Darussalam, and is a trend in the process of Islamization.

In the effort to strengthen Islam, which is a dominant principle of the Malay Islamic Monarchy, we cannot run away from the question of knowledge that will open the way and provide the light. [pp. 60–1] [...]

II Strengthening Islam

To strengthen Islam in Brunei, six essential factors are observed and implemented:

1 Government officials as representatives of the monarch should protect the endeavours of the State of Brunei Darussalam, the Muslims of Brunei and the religion of Islam.
2 The monarch is the symbol of the unity of the Islamic community in Brunei Darussalam, so the development of Islam in this country will strengthen the position of the monarch.
3 To protect the faith of the Ahli Sunah Waljamaah and distance oneself from and obstruct belief that is contrary to it.
4 To increase explanation about [understanding of] Islam through various channels.
5 To quicken the pace of preaching (*dakwah*), through greater clarity, strength and sharpness.
6 To strengthen the role of Islamic education and Islamic institutions in order to guarantee the purity and effectiveness of Islamic teachings.

To approach these matters [we] wish to present the following points:

1 According to Pehin Datu Seri Maharaja Dato Seri Utama Dr Haji Awang Ismail bin Umar Abdul Aziz,[51] government officials are the representatives of the monarch in guarding the endeavours of the State of Brunei Darussalam, the Muslim people of Brunei and Islam.

Guarding the endeavours of the country, the Muslims and Islam cannot be neglected or taken lightly because neglect or taking things lightly, whether directly or indirectly, will weaken Islam and Muslims in Brunei Darussalam.

If people who are not Muslims are allowed to spread the religion of the infidels using the argument of freedom of religion, then this is wrong from the point of view of the constitution, because the constitution allows people who are not Muslims to practise their religion, not to spread the religion of the infidels to an infidel or to a Muslim.

Islam does not allow a non-Muslim to spread the religion of the infidels to non-Muslims or to Muslims, because the religion of the infidels is wrong and invalid and sinful in the eyes of Islam.

All God's religions which were brought by the prophets before Islam are religions of God that nullify infidels and entreat the worship of God.

With the spread of Islam among the inhabitants of Brunei, this [the process of Islamization] will strengthen the position of Duli Yang Maha Mulia Sultan [the sultan of Brunei] and Yang Di-Pertuan 'Aiiyada Hullahu Taala' [title of the sultan], the symbol of the unity of the Islamic community in the State of Brunei Darussalam, and with a single goal among them, the Brunei community will always be firm and strong. And the presence of various religious beliefs in the State of Brunei Darussalam and of many people who are non-Muslims will

---

51 Currently education minister, and a member of the Bruneian royal family.

weaken the position of the monarch as the symbol of unity and the strength of Islam. [pp. 62–3] [...]

I   Value of the Monarchy

The third element in the philosophy of the Malay Islamic Monarchy is to have a monarch. For Malays, having a monarch provides not only an identity for the Malay race, but also a symbol of the dominance of the Malays in the archipelago. The definition of 'having a monarch', according to the working paper of the National Supreme Council of the Malay Muslim Monarchy, is:

> A monarchy in which the sultan as leader and protector of His Highness's subjects holds the [...] mandate of God in exercising the highest power in governing the country.

The concept of loyalty to the monarch is not limited to loyalty according to Malay culture; in fact Islam calls upon its followers to be loyal to the Ulil Amir [monarch or leader] of a country, as long as the country's leader does not issue orders that are sinful. The authority to rule held by the monarch is also a mandate from God, according to the law of Islam. A monarch who wrongfully uses the authority to rule will be responsible for his actions later on the day of judgement.

The monarchy according to Malay tradition emphasizes a monarchical system that is sovereign and holds a mandate from God. In the context of the Malay Islamic Monarchy the position of the monarch is extremely high and is more clearly depicted in the Puja Sultan [Recitation of Praise of the Sultan] during the Puspa Ceremony [coronation], that is:

> It is the will of God that Your Highness is monarch in this country of Brunei.
>
> It is the will of God that Your Highness is upheld by the subjects of Brunei.
>
> It is the will of God that Your Highness is the leader of the subjects of this country of Brunei.
>
> It is the will of God that Your Highness is the protector of the subjects of this country of Brunei.
>
> It is the will of God that Your Highness is the pillar of this country of Brunei.
>
> It is the will of God that Your Highness is the Yang Di-Pertuan [Leader] of this Country of Brunei.
>
> It is hoped that Your Highness and your descendants will sit forever and peacefully on the throne of the Government of Brunei to rule and lead the subjects of Brunei Darussalam. Amen Ye the Creator of and Power in the Universe.

This recitation of praise is a declaration of praise and loyalty to the sultan who has just been crowned. This recitation of praise is usually recited by the senior minister, the Duli Pengiran Bendahara.

According to P.M. Yusof,[52] as soon as the crown is worn, the Nobat Iskandar [Royal Drum] is sounded seven times, and cannons are fired 21 times each time the Nobat Iskandar is sounded. After that the Pehin Orang Kaya Di-Gadong Seri Lela

---

52   The reference to Yusof carries the following footnote in the original text: 'P.M. Yusof, *Adat*

[senior royal official] with a drawn sword declares his obeisance in front of those assembled, and each time the declaration is made the people who are present bow in obeisance to the sultan, and each time the Nobat Iskandar is sounded the Duli Pengiran Bendahara also recites the recitation of praise to the sultan. [pp. 64–5]

12.4 PHILIPPINES

12.4.1 Salamat Hashim

Commentary (by Kit Collier and Greg Fealy)   Salamat Hashim was the leader of the Moro Islamic Liberation Front (MILF) until his death in 2003. Born in the Maguindanao province of Mindanao in 1942, he went to Cairo's prestigious al-Azhar University in 1959, graduating with a master's degree in 1969. He returned to the Philippines in the early 1970s and became active in politics. He joined Nur Misuari's Moro National Liberation Front (MNLF) shortly afterwards and rose quickly to prominence, his Islamic learning contrasting with the largely secular outlook of Misuari. In 1978, Salamat split from the MNLF in protest at Misuari's acceptance of a peace deal with Manila and formed the MILF, taking with him many of the more Islamically inclined MNLF members. The MILF thereafter became the main source of armed resistance to Philippine government authority.

The following extracts are from transcripts of interviews with Salamat in 1996 and 1999. He explains why Muslim autonomy within the parameters of the Philippine constitution, embraced by the MNLF, is unacceptable to the MILF. The first interview, provided to a member of an influential Moro clan and intended for local consumption, stresses the importance of establishing an Islamic state. This view accords with Salamat's position in *The Bangsamoro Mujahid* (see extract 14-7). However, in the second interview, which was provided to an Australian journalist, Salamat emphasizes themes of freedom, popular sovereignty and economic grievance, dismissing the issue of an Islamic state as a media canard and contradicting his assertion in *The Bangsamoro Mujahid* that the mode of governance is 'beyond the scope of the people's will'.

Salamat's perspective on the Islamic state draws heavily on the ideas of Muslim Brotherhood thinkers such as Hasan al-Banna and Sayyid Qutb. Like al-Banna, Salamat sees the establishment of an Islamic state as 'one of the fundamentals of Islam'. It is the main objective of jihad and the only route to prosperity (*falah*) in this world and the hereafter (Lingga 1995: 39). Echoing Qutb, Salamat holds that Muslims who fail to pledge allegiance to an imam as the head of an Islamic state will die in a condition of ignorance of divine law (*jahilliyah*), and it is thus incumbent on all Muslims to struggle for such a state. This has no definite form, but popular sovereignty is incompatible with the sovereignty of God; elections may be possible depending on the people's level of maturity (Lingga 1995: 35, 54). Salamat not only sees a Bangsamoro Islamic state as a step towards a new caliphate, but appeals for the support of 'Muslim masses everywhere' in achieving such a state.

Istiadat Diraja Brunei [Customs and Traditions in the Bruneian Sultanate], Jawi edition, no publisher, Mac 1958'.

Extract 12-21: Salamat Hashim

Salamat Hashim (2002), 'We Assert Our Legitimate Rights to Self-determination, That Is, Independence' [in English], pp. 40–57 in *Referendum: Peaceful, Civilized, Diplomatic and Democratic Means of Solving the Mindanao Conflict*, Agency for Youth Affairs–MILF, Camp Abubakre As-Siddique, Mindanao. [Transcript of a written interview conducted by Rasmia Alonto in 1996.] Extract: pp. 49, 56–7.

II. DEVELOPMENT [...]

How would you respond to the opinion of some Muslim intellectuals that there is no workable Islamic model of development? That the only workable model of development today, whether it be economic or socio-political, is the liberal-democratic model of the West and Muslims have yet to produce a workable Islamic model of development?

SALAMAT: There is no workable Islamic model for development today because there is no real Islamic State. When a genuine Islamic State exists, [a] workable Islamic model for development will inevitably emerge.

Do you think that the Islamic State may be achieved within your lifetime or at least with your plans, in the next fifty (50) years?

SALAMAT: One can never be sure when is the end of his life here in this world. Perhaps after [a] few seconds or minutes or after [a] few days, months or years. So one cannot be sure of achieving his plan in his lifetime.

But there are indications and good reasons to believe that before the end of the next 50 years, the Islamic State we envision will come into existence, *insha* Allah [God willing]. [p. 49] [...]

III. THE AUTONOMOUS REGION

How disagreeable is the provision for the Autonomous Region in Muslim Mindanao in the 1987 Constitution and why?

SALAMAT: The creation of the so-called Autonomous Region in Muslim Mindanao (ARMM) is part of the counter-insurgency program of the government. The conception behind its formation was not to solve the problem of the Bangsamoro Muslims but to appease and pacify them. As such the provision for the ARMM is in line with that policy.

With reference to the autonomous regions, how has autonomy benefited the Muslims in the Philippines? If at all?

SALAMAT: Since the setting up of the autonomy is meant only to appease and pacify the Muslims, it is not expected to give any benefit to them. In fact it has worsen[ed] the problem[,] particularly this time[,] because it is governed by hand-picked corrupt and morally degenerated people who serve themselves only and have no regard for Islam, the Bangsamoro Muslims and their homeland.

To what extent is Islam implemented in those regions? That is, how far have Islamic principles been translated into institutions?

SALAMAT: People involved in the so-called ARMM have no idea about Islam. Some of them might have learned some Western concept of the religion that made their viewpoint of the faith worst [worse]. Thus we cannot expect them to introduce Islamic institutions to the so-called ARMM. Besides they are not for that purpose. They are there as pawns and tools of the Administration to serve its interest and to counter the struggle of the Bangsamoro Muslims for freedom.

Would you have participated in the drafting of the 1987 Constitution if you were given a chance? What would you have done?

SALAMAT: No, because nothing could be done to solve the Bangsamoro problem in the drafting of the Constitution. Besides[,] Islam, as a complete way of life and system of government, cannot function properly under another Constitution. [pp. 52–3] […]

VIII. THE ISLAMIC STATE

When independence is gained, the first two elements to be eradicated [are] ignorance and poverty. What specific program do you have to achieve this goal?

SALAMAT: Ignorance and poverty are the main causes of human deviation from the right path and the foremost source of all evils. To establish a peaceful, progressive and prosperous society, those two elements must be eradicated. Massive information and education campaign[s] must be launched to fight these two evils. Aside from schools, universities and other learning institutions, mosques and the mass media must be mobilized for this purpose.

With a well-planned information and education campaign and with the use of government facilities, the masses can easily be educated and enlightened. Their perspective and outlook [on] things can be changed [for] the better.

Also a well-planned education and information drive to teach the masses a better way of earning their livings and mobilizing and utilizing available resources around them must be pursued.

This can enlighten and educate them on how to mobilize and utilize the natural resources around them. Allah endowed the world with abundant resources and materials and the main problem [is people's] ignorance to mobilize and utilize these resources and materials. Ignorance will lead [them] to poverty and consequently to deviate from the right path. Therefore it is the responsibility of the state to enlighten [and] teach its people how to mobilize and utilize the resources and materials around [them] and provide them with the necessary facilities.

CONCLUSIONS

What can the Muslim world expect from this part of the Ummah?

SALAMAT: The Muslim world can expect that at least the Muslims in this part of the world will be able to liberate themselves and establish an Islamic State. When the awaited re-emergence of the **Khilafah** (a single Islamic dominion that comprises different Islamic states and governments) [that is, a caliphate] is realized, the Bangsamoro Islamic State will automatically become one of the states comprising the **Khilafah**. [pp. 56–7]

Extract 12-22: Salamat Hashim

Salamat Hashim (2002), 'Referendum: Peaceful and Diplomatic Means of Solving the Mindanao Conflict' [in English], pp. 123–33 in *Referendum: Peaceful, Civilized, Diplomatic and Democratic Means of Solving the Mindanao Conflict*, Agency for Youth Affairs–MILF, Camp Abubakre As-Siddique, Mindanao. [Transcript of an interview conducted by Greg Torode (*South China Morning Post*) and Peter Arford (*The Australian*) on 16 March 1999.] Extract: p. 128.

Chairman Salamat: [...] But we believe that our people can never be satisfied except when they enjoy full freedom.

Full freedom for them to be satisfied that would require living under full Islamic law not the law of the Philippines.

Chairman Salamat: You see people are talking about this Islamic law but this is coming from the media. The media are emphasizing this Islamic state, Islamic law, but as far as the MILF is concerned, we are not after Islamic law. We are after independence, we are after freedom. And when we are free, we will ask our people what type of government they want. If they want a communist government, then we cannot do anything, we have to follow them. If they want a secular government, then we let it be, cannot do anything. We have to follow them. The same thing happens when they want Islamic government, we also have to follow them. What is important is the will of the people. We believe that the problem of our people is that they are not free. They cannot freely express their will.

You see, we have so many natural resources in our area but we cannot freely exploit and develop our natural resources. Just imagine these people who come from Luzon whose activities are considered legal if they utilize the resources of our forests. But if the native inhabitants will try to do the same in utilizing these natural resources, then the government would run after them because they do not have [a] government permit to do it.

12.5   BURMA (MYANMAR)

12.5.1 Rohingya Solidarity Organisation

Commentary (by Curt Lambrecht)   The Rohingya Solidarity Organisation (RSO) was formed in 1982 by Nurul Islam and Mohammad Yunus, the two most prominent contemporary Rohingya dissidents of their generation. Itself a splinter group of the Rohingya Patriotic Front, the RSO has been prone to factionalism and has been officially dissolved and re-formed several times. In 1986, differences between Nurul Islam and Dr Yunus prompted the former to found the Arakan Rohingya Islamic Front (ARIF). In August 1987 the RSO was officially dissolved when its members joined ARIF, though it continued to publish booklets under the RSO banner in 1988. The following extract is from one such booklet. Dr Yunus is credited as supervising the preparation of the text.

The booklet from which the extract is drawn outlines the history and culture of the Rohingya before elaborating in detail the persecution suffered by the 'Muslims of Arakan' (a western state of Burma/Myanmar bordering Bangladesh). It is very much an appeal for justice for the Rohingya as a distinct 'national' ethnic group of Burma, making no reference to, or appeal for, the other persecuted Muslim communities in Burma. The booklet tersely concludes that: 'the Burman regime's policy is not only to finish the Rohingya Muslims from the soil of Arakan and Burma but to erase them from the history of Arakan also' (RSO 1988: i).

The excerpt below echoes the broader discourse of ethnic minorities in Burma during the 1980s. Such people sought zones of ethnic autonomy in Burma rather than outright secession or integration within a multi-ethnic democratic Burmese administrative structure.

Extract 12-23: *Rohingya Solidarity Organisation (RSO)*

Rohingya Solidarity Organisation (1988), *Arakan: People, Country and History* [in English], Publicity and Information Department, Rohingya Solidarity Organisation, Arakan. Extract: p. 30.

ROHINGYA SOLIDARITY ORGANISATION, AND ITS OBJECTIVE, POLICY AND PROGRAMMES

In the chequered history of the Rohingyas many liberation movements appeared and struggled against the tyranny of the Burman chauvinists but failed to achieve their goal. At long last taking lessons from the past history, the Rohingya Solidarity Organisation – the sole Representative of the Rohingya people – has embarked on the field of Jehad-e-fi Sabilillah [jihad in the path of God] with a renewed Islamic vigour and inspiration of the life and movement of our Beloved Holy Prophet (Swallahu Alaihi Wa Sallim) against all forms of tyranny and injustice and has resolved to continue its struggle till a peaceful, just and equitable society is established in Arakan.

Objective, Policy and Programmes

The objective of RSO is to establish a Rohingya Autonomous State because it believes that the inalienable rights of the Rohingyas can only be restored and enforcement of an Islamic Way of Life among the Muslim community can only be achieved through establishing such an autonomous state. The Rohingya Muslims are a peaceful and peace-loving people. History has proved that they never indulged in injustice or tyranny. It has always been the Rohingya who have been victimised by various forces in Arakan. The RSO believes in the peaceful co-existence of different communities irrespective of colour, creed, language, ethnicity and religion. It supports the struggle of the oppressed communities against racism and hegemonism. [...]

The front cover of the December 1989 issue of *Arakan* magazine shows a cruel and well-armed tiger, clearly labelled 'SLORC's Military Tribunal'. SLORC is the State Law and Order Restoration Council set up by the military junta in Burma in 1988. In a mockery of justice, the tiger brings its gavel down on an unarmed Burmese who stands no chance against it. The tiny figures in the foreground trying to resist the might of the tiger are unarmed except for some spears, batons and harvesting sickles. Their nationalist flags and mixed styles of dress indicate that they are Burmese – both non-Muslims and Muslims – who have united to resist the tyranny of the tiger.

12.5.2   Arakan Rohingya Islamic Front (ARIF)

Commentary (by Curt Lambrecht)   The following extract comes from ARIF's monthly newsletter, shortly after the military government had announced that it would not relinquish control to parties democratically elected in 1990, and shortly before some 300,000 Rohingya were to be expelled from Arakan state by the Burmese military. It evinces a moderate political stance that contrasts starkly with the government's vitriolic portrayals of the Rohingya as secessionists and fundamentalist radicals seeking to 'undermine national sovereignty' and to 'disintegrate the union of Burma'.

Extract 12-24: Arakan Rohingya Islamic Front (ARIF)

Arakan Rohingya Islamic Front (1991), 'Why Rohingya Revolution' [in English], *Arakan*, 8(April). Extract: p. 5.

The following are the main causes of the Rohingya Revolution:–

(1)   The genesis of Rohingya revolution is to stop the genocidal massacre, wrongs and injustice perpetuated on the hundreds and thousands of innocent and unarmed men, women and children of the ethnic Rohingyas by the successive Burmese regimes before and after independence on 4 January 1948.

(2)   The present struggle of Rohingyas is to regain their usurped fundamental human rights and freedoms and achieve their natural right to self-determination and self-identification in Arakan. It is also a struggle against racism, chauvinism, growing Burmanization and militarism being practiced by Burma Socialist Programme Party (BSPP) & State Law and Order Restoration Council (SLORC) who have been ruthlessly suppressing democratic and national right[s] of the various ethnic groups of the Union of Burma.

(3)   It has never been the intention of the Rohingya people and their revolution – since its inception in 1948 till today [–] to [secede] Arakan from Burma, but [their intention] has always been to regain and restore their political and national right only through [the] universal concept of democratic struggle. It is only when there is no other recourse left for them to regain their usurped human rights and freedom that they have embarked on armed revolution against [the] government's policies of racial discrimination, genocidal extermination, inhuman oppression, de-Muslimization and expulsion from their hearth and home.

(4)   The revolution is primarily a struggle for the existence with dignity and honour of about 3 million Rohingyas, both at home and abroad, while upholding the principle of peaceful co-existence among all nationalities of Burma. The revolution is also for the repatriation and rehabilitation of about 1.2 million Rohingyas who have been expelled from the country since 1942. [...]

12.5.3   Arakan Rohingya National Organisation (ARNO)

Commentary (by Curt Lambrecht)   Formed in 1998, ARNO was the third short-lived attempt to forge an alliance among the Rohingya political elite. The extract below is typical of earlier and subsequent appeals to the international community (most of which have fallen on deaf ears) calling for intervention in light of the very real suffering that the military government has inflicted upon the Rohingya of Arakan state.

Extract 12-25: Arakan Rohingya National Organisation (ARNO)

Arakan Rohingya National Organisation (1999), 'The Major Problems of the Rohingyas' [in English], in *The Rohingya Problem*, Arakan. Extract: pp. 6–9.

The problems of the Rohingyas are the result of the well-planned conspiracy to rid Arakan of the Muslim population. Their problems are extremely grave and deep-rooted and they are today in sub-human condition. Generally their problems are: […]

(4) **Cultural Problem**: The Rohingyas have had superior culture throughout the history. The influence of their culture had always been great in Arakan and it attracted the Buddhist community of the country in all spheres of national activities. Even the Buddhists (including the kings of Buddhist faith) willingly adopted Muslim names and titles and their women practiced *purda* (veil system). Unfortunately, today the cultural problem becomes one of the most important problems of the Rohingyas in Burma. The concept of Burmanization plays a vital role [in] absorbing various cultures and religions. For the Rohingyas, being Muslims, to retain their cultural identity is more complex and sensitive. Those who are more Burmanized are more acceptable in Burma. The Muslims have to encounter a strong pressure of the Burman culture. Particularly, the Rohingyas have to confront ideological assaults from all directions. Deliberate and persistent attempts have been made to impose the Burman culture and these efforts have become more vigorous on the Rohingyas in recent years under the military regime. Rohingyas are considered [as] practising [a] foreign way of life having no origin in Burma. Burma for the present ruling military SPDC [State Peace and Development Council, the ruling junta] is a Burman nation and their one supreme goal is to bring to life the all-round glory and greatness of their military pride. The nationalist patriots are those who glorify the military. Others are so-called traitors and enemies of the nation. According to them the Rohingyas are to adopt and entertain no ideas but those of glorification of [the] Burman race and culture and Buddhism.

Erasing of Muslim entity: The Muslims or Rohingyas have been told to discard Islamic names and adopt Burman names. They are despised and discriminated against for their belief. Muslim culture, Muslim relics and monuments have been destroyed. Everywhere Muslim and Islamic are razed to the ground. The Muslim names of the places have been changed and are being replaced with names attributed to the Buddhists or Buddhism. Hundreds of mosques have been demolished, including the historic Sandikhan mosque built in 1430 by an Arakan king. Pagodas, monasteries and Buddhist temples, with increased new settlements of settlers of Buddhist faith invited from within and outside the country, have been erected and built, in every nook and cranny of the traditional Rohingya homeland, with the forced labour of the Rohingyas, with a view to changing the demography and ethnic composition of Arakan.

Distortion of Islamic values: Particularly the Muslim students have been brain-washed in schools where anti-Islamic materials are being taught to them. They say that the Muslims have nothing to do in Burma. Their slogan is '*to be a Burmese is to [be] a Buddhist*'. Islam and Islamic culture is always projected in distorted forms through the media. The cultural issues like personal law, status of women in Muslim society, Muslim way of worship and Islamic missionary activities and projection of all these present [a] different picture of Muslims from what actually it is. [In] TV, film, radio, or press, Islam has to be presented in humiliating, derogatory, degrading and distorted forms.

(5) ***Restriction on Freedom of Movement***: The military regime has prohibited [that is, deprived] the Rohingyas of their right to freedom of movement and selection of their places of residence within the state[,] seriously affecting the socio-cultural, economic, educational activities and daily life of Rohingyas. Humiliating movement restrictions faced by Rohingyas today in their homeland are unacceptable to any living creature on earth. The SPDC has seriously restricted [their] travel from one locality to another. No Rohingya can travel without a permit even from one village to another in the same township. Such permit can be obtained by paying bribes to the authority, valid only for 24 hours to a maximum of seven days. Travel to Rangoon, the capital of Burma, has been totally banned for Rohingyas since 1992. Although this practice was only applied to rural Rohingya farmers since the 1960s, it is now also applied to Rohingya businessmen, doctors, engineers, lawyers, students and even the patients who need urgent treatment available only in the capital city.

(6) ***Unresolved Rohingya Refugee Issue***: Since 1942 about 1.5 million Rohing-yas have been expelled or have fled the country for their lives. At present many of them are living in Bangladesh, Pakistan, Saudi Arabia, UAE [United Arab Emirates] and Malaysia. Being unofficial refugees, most of them have no access to work, safe refuge, and basic necessities of life and education for their children. They are still hoping to return to their ancestral homeland of Arakan. Expulsion of Rohingyas from their homeland once in 1978 and another [time] in 1991 caused the Diaspora of nearly 300,000 refugees to Bangladesh and other countries on each occasion. Despite repatriation, the crux of the problem still remains unsolved and persecu-tion against Rohingyas is continuing. There have been new arrivals in scattered and steady numbers along the border, in spite of attempts by Bangladesh authorities to push back or repatriate them. Poor economic condition has not been the only cause of fresh refugee exodus. Forced labour, forced relocation, torture, rape and other atrocities have caused them to flee for their lives. Unfortunately, the role of UNHCR [United Nations High Commissioner for Refugees] does not effectively bring relief to the social, political and spiritual problems of the Rohingyas. [...]

13 Gender and the Family

Sally White

INTRODUCTION

Muslim women in Southeast Asia are generally said to hold a favourable position in society compared to women from many other parts of the Muslim world. Despite regional variation and differentiation according to factors such as class and education, Muslim women in the region are highly visible in the workplace, in the fields, in schools and in the public arena in general. Some of the rights women have they have enjoyed for centuries; others are more recent and result from hard-won struggles. Nevertheless, Muslim women still face many disadvantages vis-à-vis men in contemporary Southeast Asian society. In countries such as Malaysia and Indonesia, prominence is given to gender issues and the inequality women face. In other countries or regions, both men and women are concerned with more basic social issues such as poverty, the defence of the Muslim community, their identity as a Muslim minority, repression by a non-Muslim central government or even civil war, and gender issues do not receive priority.

This chapter is heavily focused on gender discourse in Indonesia and the Malay world for two main reasons. First, it is in these regions that debate on issues of gender is most developed. Second, there are very few sources available for regions that have been the site of conflict for decades, such as Burma, Indochina, southern Thailand and southern Philippines.

In Indonesia and Malaysia in particular, a range of views is evident in debates on gender and the family. In the last decade or so, growing numbers of Muslim women's organizations have emerged campaigning for women's rights. Liberal organizations and individuals, both male and female, are also calling for a gender-sensitive reinterpretation of the sources of Islam, and some sections of mainstream Muslim women's organizations have adopted an agenda that is more pro-women's rights. Global ideas on gender equality have informed a number of international conventions on the rights of women that many countries in Southeast Asia are signatories to, and financial aid has flowed into projects that seek to redress aspects of gender inequality, as well as the more traditional areas of women and children's health, education and economic disadvantage.[1]

On the other hand, there has also been an increase in the number of groups espousing a literal interpretation of the Qur'an, questioning the freedoms given to women in the public sphere, and calling for the implementation of Islamic law (sharia) with strict controls on women's dress and behaviour to curb what is seen as public immorality (Chandrakirana and Chuzaifah 2004). Between these two extremes lie the bulk of Muslims, weighing up what they can reconcile with their faith and what they must reject and, in some cases, what they stand to lose and gain from any changes to women's role in the family and in society. Gender issues can be highly divisive. Debates about whether women should wear Islamic dress, obey their husbands or take on a public role are symbolic of larger issues such as the role of Islam in the modern nation-state, literal versus contextual interpretations of Islamic sources, indigenization versus Arabization, and a fear of Westernization and loss of tradition and identity.

Part of the divisiveness concerning gender issues comes from the importance Muslim societies place on families as the basic building block of the Islamic community (*ummah*), and as the main site of socialization of Muslim values (Eickelman and Piscatori 1996: 80–9). There are also historical roots to this divisiveness; during the colonial period, family law was one of the few areas of law where Muslims had some degree of autonomy, and for minority Muslim communities such as those in Thailand or the Philippines, this continues to be the case today. Issues surrounding Islamic family law became bound up with anti-colonialism, Muslim identity and a resistance to the secularizing tendencies of Western-educated elites. In today's modern nation-states, Islamic family law retains this symbolic importance.

This chapter is divided into four sections. Section 13.1 presents extracts from texts that address the issue of 'women in Islam' in a general sense. Section 13.2 provides examples of texts that attempt to deconstruct the gender ideology provided by the texts in the first section, and demonstrates some of the main techniques and frameworks used to do this. Section 13.3 consists of a series of case studies showing how prevailing notions of gender and women's role in the family have been challenged, and also defended. And section 13.4 examines one attempt to challenge the legal framework enshrining Islamic family law, in the name of gender equity.

EXTRACTS AND COMMENTARY

13.1   GUIDES FOR CREATING THE PIOUS WOMAN AND THE HARMONIOUS FAMILY

Bookshops in Indonesia and Malaysia carry a wide array of texts addressed specifically to women. These are generally prescriptive in character; their aim is to inform women what they must and must not do in order to become pious Muslim

---

1   On financial aid for gender projects, see Burhanudin and Fathurahman (2004: 119–32).

women. The topics covered range from specific requirements of hygiene and dress for women in prayer, women's general appearance and their position in the domestic and public spheres, through to women's relationships with their husbands, parents and neighbours. Sometimes these texts are translations of texts from Pakistan or Middle Eastern countries such as Egypt and Syria. Often they are local products, written generally by (male) ulema. Such texts play an important role in socializing women to conform to what is portrayed as an Islamic model of womanhood, often contrasted with womanhood in the West.

A second means of socializing women is through Islamic education. Islamic schools throughout the region, whether they are traditional boarding schools (*pondok* or *pesantren*) or modern Islamic schools (*madrasah*), as well as study sessions for adult women and classes held in mosques, teach girls and women their duties and obligations as Muslim women.

13.1.1 Definitions of Piety

Commentary Pondok Pesantren Islam Al Mukmin in Ngruki, Solo (Central Java) has gained a certain notoriety with the accusation that its founders, Abu Bakar Ba'asyir and Abdullah Sungkar, were the first two leaders (*amir*) of Jemaah Islamiyah (JI). What is less well known is that it also contains a *pesantren* for girls. A slim textbook aims to socialize girls in 'correct' behaviour according to sharia (Ciciek 2004).The following extract gives a definition of piety for women.

Extract 13-1: Pondok Pesantren Islam Al Mukmin

Pengasuh Pondok (n.d.), 'Ciri-Ciri Wanita Sholihah' [Characteristics of the Pious Woman], pp. 12–17 in *Materi Pelajaran Kewanitaan* [Material for the Education of Women], Pondok Pesantren Islam Al Mukmin, Ngruki, Surakarta. Extract: pp. 12–14.

[A pious woman:]

1. Is obedient and submissive to God.
2. Guards herself when her husband is away. See QS. An Nisa'/4: 34.

[verse in Arabic script]

Means:

Thus pious women are those who are obedient to God and guard themselves behind their husbands' backs because God has guarded them.[2]

---

2 'Husbands should take full care of their wives, with [the bounties] God has given to some more than others and with what they spend out of their own money. Righteous wives are devout and guard what God would have them guard in their husbands' absence. If you fear high-handedness from your wives, remind them [of the teachings of God], then ignore them when you go to bed, then hit them. If they obey you, you have no right to act against them: God is most high and great' (Q4: 34, Haleem).

3. Gives precedence to the rulings of Allah above other rulings. See QS. Al-Ahzab/ 33: 36.

[verse in Arabic script]

Means:

It is improper for believing men and improper for believing women, [if] when God and His Messenger have determined a determination, there will be for them (other choices) concerning their affairs. And whoever betrays God and His Messenger, then truly he or she is misguided, clearly misguided.[3]

The Prophet, blessings and peace be upon him, said:

[verse in Arabic script]

There are no faithful among you until your passions follow what I have laid down. [Hadith]

4. Presents herself as a pious woman.
5. Remains mainly in the home, in accordance with her nature (*fitroh*) and duties.
6. Is not adorned and decorated as women were in the times of pre-Islamic igno-rance (*jahiliyah*).
7. Performs the obligatory prayers (*sholat*).
8. Pays the wealth tax (*zakat*). In accordance with QS. Al-Ahzab/33: 31–33.

[verse in Arabic script]

Means:

Whoever among you all (wives of the prophet) remains obedient to God and His Mes-senger and does pious deeds, certainly We [will] give to them double rewards and We [will] prepare for them noble means of living [wherewithal for living]. Oh wives of the Prophet, you are not like other women, if you are pious then do not be submissive in your speech so that those who have sickness in their hearts become desirous, and utter appropriate utterances.[4]

A woman who is pious or who is often called *Mar'atush sholihah* [a pious woman] is a woman who is truly obedient to God and who carries out all commands as well as observing what is prohibited. She never breaks the rulings of God and always sur-renders her soul and her entire life to serve God alone.

---

3 'When God and His Messenger have decided on a matter that concerns them, it is not fitting for any believing man or woman to claim freedom of choice in that matter: whoever disobeys God and His Messenger is far astray' (Q33: 36, Haleem).
4 'but if any of you is obedient to God and His Messenger and does good deeds, know that We shall give her a double reward and have prepared a generous provision for her. Wives of the Prophet, you are not like any other woman. If you truly fear God, do not speak too softly in case the sick at heart should lust after you, but speak in an appropriate manner; stay at home, and do not flaunt your attractions as they used to in the pagan past; keep up the prayer, give the prescribed alms, and obey God and His Mes-senger. God wishes to keep uncleanness away from you, people of the [Prophet's] House, and make you completely pure' (Q33: 31–3, Haleem).

Obedience means:

1. Surrendering herself to God;
2. Surrendering all the affairs of her life to the law and sharia of God, or in other words: making the Qur'an and the Sunnah the source of law to regulate all aspects of her life;
3. Sacrificing her personal interests to fulfil the holy calling (God);
4. Giving priority to the advice and warnings of God above all others;
5. Protecting herself from all types of strategies and ruses;
6. Implementing the commands of God and His Prophet as well as observing all of His prohibitions.

The attitude of being submissive and obedient towards God will indeed be challenged with trials and obstacles, as well as tests. Because indeed such is woman's *fitroh*. However, the strong faith that exists in a pious woman will make her capable of facing every obstacle.

* * * * *

Commentary   The following Malaysian text was one of five published under the combined title of 'Siri Keluarga Bahagia' [Series on the Happy Family]. The extract is from the book addressed to women as wives. Other books in the series are addressed to men, parents and children, and one is on motherhood.

Extract 13-2: 'Series on the Happy Family'

Harun Ar-Rasyid Hj. Tuskan (2003), 'Kelebihan dan Kemuliaan Wanita' [The Special Nature and Nobility of Women], pp. 1–62 in *Isteri Idaman Yang Menyejukkan Hati Suami* [The Ideal Wife Who Soothes Her Husband], Pustaka Al Shafa, Kuala Lumpur. Extract: pp. 13–15.

C. Women as Noble Beings

If [one's] nature can easily go in the direction of goodness, it can make a woman obedient to the commands of God and easily forgo that which is forbidden by God. Her gentle heart can easily be shaped to love God and the Prophet.

If a woman's heart is fertilized by these two loves, she can become a person who is extremely sensitive to her God. A small misdemeanour committed will feel like a big boulder falling on her head. She will easily be moved to tears because of God. Her heart will easily cry and moan because of the sins she has committed. If these women of faith marry, they will be obedient and loyal wives to their husbands.

There are not many conditions Islam sets on a woman for her to be recognized as pious, and following that to receive the rewards of heaven, which is full of pleasures from Almighty God. She has to fulfil only two conditions, that is:

1. Obedience to God and His Prophet.
2. Obedience to her husband.

1. Obedience to God and the Prophet
What is meant by obedience to Almighty God?

1. To love Almighty God and the Prophet more than anything else.
2. To cover the *aurat*.[5]
3. Not to dress and behave like a heathen (*jahiliah*) woman.
4. Not to travel or be alone with an adult man except one whom she is not permitted to marry.
5. To always assist a man in matters of truth, welfare and obedience to God.
6. To be good to her parents.
7. To always give alms whether in difficult or happy circumstances.
8. Not to be in close proximity to an adult man.
9. To behave well towards her neighbours.

2. Obedience to Her Husband
Obedience to her husband includes, among other things:

1. Carrying out her obligations to her husband.
2. Always pleasing her husband.
3. Safeguarding her honour and her husband's property when he is not at home.
4. Not showing a sour face in front of her husband.
5. Not refusing her husband's request to go to bed.
6. Not going out without the permission of her husband.
7. Not raising her voice against her husband.
8. Not contradicting her husband in matters of truth.
9. Not receiving a guest who is disliked by her husband.
10. Always looking after herself, whether it be physical cleanliness and beauty or the cleanliness of her home.

13.1.2   Differences between Men and Women

> *Commentary*   The concepts of *kodrat* and *fitrah* are at the heart of mainstream understandings of gender difference in Indonesia; in Malay texts the latter term is used more frequently. *Kodrat* (or *kudrat*) is derived from the Arabic *qudrah*, and carries with it connotations of predestination, appropriateness and the ability to do a particular thing (Nasaruddin 1999: 91–2). *Fitrah* (or *fitroh*; Ar.: *fitratun*) means a natural or original characteristic. Underlying both terms is biological essentialism; women's difference is defined by her biology, and on the basis of this difference, she has a role in society that differs from that of men and that is predetermined, immutable and self-evident (White 2004: 149–50).
>
> Gontor Pesantren, founded in East Java in 1926, is one of the oldest and most prestigious *pesantren* in Java. Its alumni include many Indonesian intellectuals and leaders, such as Nurcholish Madjid, Idham Chalid, Hasyim Muzadi, Syafii Maarif, Hidayat Nur

---

5   *Aurat* (Ar.: `awrah*): the parts of the body that must be kept covered in public.

Wahid and Abu Bakar Ba'asyir. In 1990 it opened a separate school for girls, Pesantren Putri Pondok Modern Gontor (Gontor Modern Pesantren for Girls). In 2003 it had almost 3,000 female students, all of whom boarded at the school, and over 300 teachers, most of them female. The *pesantren* prides itself on its all-round approach to girls' education, incorporating many different aspects of what it means to be a pious Muslim woman into the everyday curriculum.[6] Topics covered in these textbooks range from specific religious requirements for women through to housewifely skills such as serviette folding, cooking, sewing and the use of modern kitchen appliances.

Extract 13-3: *Pesantren Putri Pondok Modern Gontor*

Pesantren Putri Pondok Modern Gontor (1997), 'Perbedaan dan Persamaan Laki-Laki dan Wanita' [Differences and Similarities between Men and Women], pp. 10–16 in *Materi Nisaiyah: Kulliyatu-l-Mu'allimat al Islamiyah* [Material for Women: Islamic College for Women Teachers], Book 6, no place. Extract: pp. 11–16.

A. Physical Differences [...]

According to Maududi,[7] 'scientific research in the field of biology has proven the differences between women and men in all matters, from the visible to the invisible, such as form, shape, body type and the structure of the skeleton. Women have their own characteristics, with their body anatomy formed and readied to receive the birth of children and to educate them'.

When a woman approaches adulthood she also begins to menstruate and this influences the function of her body parts. Biological research has shown that during menstruation women's bodies experience the following changes:

1. The physical ability required to control the emotions is reduced so that they become more emotional.
2. Their pulse slows down and blood flow and cell growth decrease.
3. Their desire to be angry increases.
4. Their ability to control hallucinations decreases.
5. The amount of phosphate and chlorophytes in their bodies decreases so that changes occur to the immune system.
6. Their mobility slows down and fat is lost from the hips and other limbs.
7. Breathing becomes more difficult.
8. They become moody and enervated.
9. Their understanding, intelligence and strength of mind decreases. [pp. 11–12] [...]

---

6 For more information on Gontor Modern Pesantren for Girls, see <http://free-cain.tripod.com/gp1. htm> and the article 'Mencetak Wanita Shalihah' [Moulding the Pious Woman], <http://www.republika. co.id/cetak_berita.asp?id=108214&kat_id=105&edisi=Cetak>, dated 26 December 2002, accessed 20 January 2005.

7 Abu al-Ala Mawdudi (1903–79) was an important figure in the Islamic revival on the Indian subcontinent and what became Pakistan from the 1930s onwards.

B. Psychological Differences

1. Women's instincts are stronger than those of men. Therefore the amount of love and affection women give to their children, parents and family is greater than that of men. Women's instincts are more quickly influenced than those of men. The wisdom of this is that feminine instincts accord with their duty to guide and love their children.
2. Women are less consistent in their desires than men. Women have many desires but quickly forget them and form new ones. The wisdom of this is that women have a lifelong duty to maintain their relationship with their husband and follow his orders.
3. Women are less courageous than men. The wisdom of this is of relevance to women's duties in domestic life; that is, in general men give priority to physical strength and bear responsibilities whereas women have the responsibility to obey them. [pp. 13–14] [...]

C. Differences and Similarities in Islam

The similarities between men and women in Islam are as follows:

1. Women are the same as men in that they are both bound by sharia although there are differences in the details of some laws.
2. Women are the same as men in that they are both rewarded and penalized, both in this world and in eschatological matters.
3. Women are the same as men in that they have rights that can be brought before a judge.
4. Women are the same as men in that they can own property and benefit from it.
5. Women are the same as men in that they are free to choose their life partner. Thus, a woman may not be forced to marry a man she does not like.

There are also differences:

1. The sacrifice (*aqiqoh*) for the birth of a son is two goats. For a daughter it is one goat.
2. During prayers for a deceased male, the imam stands level with the head of the corpse; however, for a female, the imam stands in the middle or at the level of the stomach.
3. The urine of a baby girl who is still being breastfed by her mother and is not yet eating solid food should be washed away. For a baby boy it is enough to sprinkle water over it.
4. The share of inheritance between men and women is in a ratio of 2:1.
5. Men may marry up to four wives so long as they treat them all equally. Women, however, may not marry more than one husband.
6. The value of two female witnesses is equal to that of one male witness.
7. Women must cover all of themselves save the face while men must be covered from the navel to the knees.

8. Women are forbidden to shave the hair on their heads while men may do so. As narrated by Ali:

[verse in Arabic script]

'The Prophet of God, on whom be blessings and peace, forbade women to shave their heads' (HR. An-Nasa'i). [Hadith]

9. During congregational prayers men may be the imam for the whole congregation consisting of men and women, or for men or women only.

10. Women are not allowed to be leaders or persons in authority as men are. The Prophet of God, on whom be blessings and peace, said:

[verse in Arabic script]

'No community will prosper (have success) if they entrust their affairs to women' (HR. Bukhori Muslim). [Hadith] [pp. 14–16]

* * * * *

Commentary   *Kodrat* and *fitrah* also form essential elements in the education of girls at Pondok Pesantren Islam Al Mukmin (see also extract 13-1). The contrast drawn here between an Islamic ideal of 'natural' womanhood and purported Western ideals that are said to be 'unnatural' is commonly found in such discussions on womanhood.

Extract 13-4: Pondok Pesantren Islam Al Mukmin

Pengasuh Pondok (n.d.), 'Beberapa Pandangan Masyarakat Tentang Wanita' [Some Views of Society Concerning Women], pp. 5–7 in *Materi Pelajaran Kewanitaan* [Material for the Education of Women], Pondok Pesantren Islam Al Mukmin, Ngruki, Surakarta. Extract: pp. 6–7.

Women are and remain women, who have their own characteristics, personalities, nature and tasks, which are not the same as men's, in accord with their own *kodrat* and *fitroh*.

This strand of philosophy derives from the leadership of Islam – a strand of thinking that is in accord with the original existence of women, all of which is already ordered by regulations decreed by Almighty God.

As for a woman who yearns for freedom and independence, it means she has already freed herself from ties with Almighty God. She has already left Islam, which means that she has also left behind her *fitroh*.

This movement of women demanding the same rights as men, or what we often call the Emancipation of Women, which is currently being promoted, will surely have both positive as well as negative consequences. What is clear is that this movement will damage the woman herself, because she is going against *fitroh*.

This phenomenon of women's struggle sometimes goes so far that many women do what is done by men.

This is very much against what has been determined by Almighty God in His words:

[verse in Arabic script]

Means:

> *Thus when Imron's wife gave birth to their child, she said: O my Lord, truly I have given birth to a girl and God knows best about what she gave birth to. And boy children are not like girl children. Truly I have given her the name Maryam and I [will] protect her and her children in Your (care) from accursed Satan* (QS. Ali Imran/3: 36).[8]

The above verse distinctly and clearly states that come what may, women are not the same as men. Each has tasks that differ according to their *fitroh*. Thus for women who yearn for a happy life, both in this world and in the afterlife, the only path is to surrender and return to their *fitroh*, following the guides and stipulations laid down by Almighty God. [...]

* * * * *

Commentary   This Malaysian text is part of a series called 'Pakej Keluarga Bahagia' [Happy Family Package] consisting of eight books. The following extract comes from the book addressed to men.

Extract 13-5: 'Happy Family Package'

Muhammad Hafizuddin Thani (2003), 'Tanggungjawab Ayah dalam Keluarga' [Responsibilities of the Father in the Family], pp. 41–60 in *Suami Tanggungjawab dan Kepimpinan Rumahtangga* [A Husband's Responsibilities and Household Leadership], Penerbitan Seribu Dinar, Kuala Lumpur. Extract: pp. 56–8.

Male Leadership

God created fundamental differences between men and women. The most basic difference is that He created women as beings with the function of procreation. Women were created to develop their role in accordance with their nature (*kudrat*) as were men. Because of this, Islam differentiates between the function and role of men and of women. However, Islam makes no distinction with respect to religious observances, practices, rewards and punishment. Almighty God said:

> *'And women have rights commensurate with their responsibilities as established. However, husbands are one level higher than their wives'* (Al-Baqarah: 228).[9]

---

8   'but when she gave birth, she said, "My Lord! I have given birth to a girl" – God knows best what she had given birth to: the male is not like the female – "I name her Mary and I commend her and her offspring to Your protection from the rejected Satan"' (Q3: 33, Haleem).

9   'Divorced women must wait for three monthly periods before remarrying, and, if they really believe in God and the Last Day, it is not lawful for them to conceal what God has created in their wombs: their husbands are entitled to take them back during this period provided they wish to put things right. Wives have [rights] similar to their [obligations], according to what is recognized to be fair, and husbands have a degree [of right] over them: [both should remember that] God is almighty and wise' (Q2: 228, Haleem).

Regarding this issue, al-Qurthubi[10] in the book *al-Jaami'li Ahkaamil-Quran* [The Compiler of the Qur'an's Sanctions], Chapter III, states that women have rights that must be given by men, just as is the case with men who possess rights which must be given to them. Almighty God said:

> '*Men are the leaders of women. Because Allah has given more to a section of them (men) over another section (women) and because they (men) have paid maintenance from part of their property ...*' (Al-Nisa': 34).[11]

In connection with this verse, Ibnu Katsir[12] in *Tafsir al-Quranul 'Azhim* [The Explanation of the Great Qur'an] wrote that men are the leaders of women, the older brothers of women, the judges of women, who warn them and correct them when they stray. Almighty God bestowed on men the potential for leadership, such as bravery, strength, completeness and reason. That potential gives them the means to lead and manage their households. By their nature women want to be led by men. Women need protection and the physical and spiritual bravery of men. Such is also the case with children; they need the 'heroic' figure of their father just as they need the gentle and loving figure of their mother. That is why it is essential for a mother to sow feelings of respect and pride in her children towards their father in the process of educating them.

The concept of leadership in this case does not mean using one's authority as one pleases. On the contrary, it is leadership meaning love, protection, education, guidance and humane authority. This leadership does not mean the loss of the feeling of cooperation between husband and wife in overcoming various problems in the home and in caring for the children. The Prophet of God, on whom be blessings and peace, also served and cared for his family at home as an example to his community. Thus, it is not proper for a man to regard housework as unimportant, especially at a time when he is needed by his family. However, involvement of the husband in household chores must not be overdone to the extent that the husband becomes a 'child-carer'.

13.1.3   The Harmonious Family

Commentary   The term *keluarga sakinah* means a family that is 'formed on the basis of a valid marriage, has the blessing of God, and is able to foster feelings of love among

10   Al-Qurthubi (or al-Kurtubi) (d. 1272) was born in Cordova, Spain, at the height of Muslim dominance there. He was a scholar of the Maliki law school (*madhhab*), famous for his commentary on the Qur'an, referred to here.
11   Many Indonesian and Malay texts translate the opening phrase of Q4: 34 as 'Men are the leaders of women'. However, the translation by Shakir refers to men as the 'maintainers' of women and that by Yusuf Ali to men as the 'protectors and maintainers' of women (see <http://www.usc.edu/dept/MSA/quran/>). Haleem translates the opening phrase as 'Husbands should take full care of their wives' (see footnote 2).
12   Ibn Katsir (1302–73 CE), born in Syria, was a follower of the Shafi'i *madhhab*, famous for his Qur'anic exegesis.

family members, so that they have feelings of security, calmness, peace and happiness in attempting to achieve prosperity in this world and the next'.[13]

The concept was first formulated at the 1985 congress of 'Aisyiyah, the women's wing of Muhammadiyah, Indonesia's largest modernist Islamic organization (see also chapter 5). A booklet outlining the subject was published in 1989, after being approved by Muhammadiyah's Majlis Tarjih (Council on Law-making and Development of Islamic Thought).[14] One of 'Aisyiyah's main goals as an organization since this time has been to inculcate in its members the values of *keluarga sakinah*. The focus in the booklet on women's domestic role has been criticized, and the book itself is currently under review by the Tabligh (religious propagation) section of 'Aisyiyah. It remains very influential, however. The concept of *keluarga sakinah* is also understood to be an attempt by Muhammadiyah, through 'Aisyiyah, to work in concert with the government's family planning program, while shifting the focus from limiting the number of children to increasing the prosperity and 'quality' of the family through the use of contraceptive methods (Marcoes-Natsir 2004: 7).

Extract 13-6: *Muhammadiyah and* Keluarga Sakinah

Pimpinan Pusat 'Aisyiyah (1989), 'Hidup Bersuami Istri Fondasi Pembinaan Keluarga Sakinah' [Married Life as the Foundation for the Development of a Happy Family], pp. 11–30 in *Tuntunan menuju Keluarga Sakinah* [Guidance for a Happy Family], Yogyakarta. Extract: pp. 13, 15–22.

The aim of marriage in Islam is to build a household that is peaceful, calm, happy and prosperous, and that is enveloped in love and affection. In other words, a marriage in Islam is aimed at forming a *sakinah* family. This aim will be achieved when the husband, wife, children and other family members all understand and fulfil their own duties, and respect each other's rights. If these rights and duties are not fulfilled, then it is very possible that the aim of marriage will not be achieved. Another possible cause of a failed marriage is if the husband, wife, children or other family members act outside the limits of their authority.

In order to avoid the difficulties and obstacles in the way of forming a *sakinah* family, before entering the married state, the prospective husband and wife should prepare themselves physically, mentally and materially. This includes making sure they have the right level of education and are of the right age and so on. They also need to know the rights and duties of husband and wife and other matters involved in family life according to the teachings of Islam. This can be achieved through education and guidance carried out by existing organizations or educational facilities. [...]

2. The Duties and Rights of Husband and Wife

A very important factor in the formation of a *sakinah* family is the fulfilment of the duties and rights of the husband and wife within family life. A legal relationship is

---

13   Persyarikatan Muhammadiyah, 'Keluarga Sakinah', <www.muhammadiyah.or.id/index.php?option =com_content&task=view&id=248>, accessed 3 June 2005.
14   Majlis Tarjih dan Pengembangan Pemikiran Islam (usually shortened to Majlis Tarjih) was founded in 1927 to consider questions of interpretation on religious issues and deliver rulings on those issues.

created when the marriage contract is formed between husband and wife. As a consequence of this law, each has duties and rights. These are the mutual rights of the husband and wife, the rights of the wife that are the duties of the husband, and the rights of the husband that are the duties of the wife.

a. Rights of Husbands and Wives [...]

b. The Duties of a Husband to His Wife

A husband has the responsibility to lead and protect his family, as stated by God in An-Nisa (4): 34.

[verse in Arabic script]

'Men are the leaders of women [and] because of that, God has favoured some of them (men) above others of them (women) and because they (men) provide some of their wealth to support them [women].'[15]

Because of this superiority, a husband is burdened with the duty to lead and take responsibility for the family he has established. There are also the rights of the wife that become the responsibility of the husband, including providing sufficient means for his wife, for example for her clothing, home, medical treatment and day-to-day needs, according to his capacity. On this matter God stated in Al-Baqarah (2): 233,

[verse in Arabic script]

'And the responsibility of father[s] is to give food and clothing to mothers in a way that is fair.'[16]

In Al-Talaq (65): 5 and 7 it was stated again by God,

[verse in Arabic script]

'Place them (wives) where you reside according to [your] means and don't disturb their (hearts). It should be [that] people with the means give maintenance according to their means. And people of restricted means should give maintenance from the possessions which God has given to them.'[17]

---

15   Q4: 34 is given in footnote 2.

16   'Mothers suckle their children for two whole years, if they wish to complete the term, and clothing and maintenance must be borne by the father in a fair manner. No one should be burdened with more than they can bear: no mother shall be made to suffer harm on account of her child, nor any father on account of his. The same duty is incumbent on the father's heir. If, by mutual consent and consultation, the couple wish to wean [the child], they will not be blamed, nor will there be any blame if you wish to engage a wet nurse, provided you pay as agreed in a fair manner. Be mindful of God, knowing that He sees everything you do' (Q2: 233, Haleem).

17   'This is God's command, which He has sent down to you. God will wipe out the sinful deeds and increase the rewards of anyone who is mindful of Him. House the wives you are divorcing according to your means, in the same way you house yourselves, and do not harass them so as to make their lives difficult' (Q65: 5, Haleem).

'and let the wealthy man spend according to his wealth. But let him whose provision is restricted spend according to what God has given him: God does not burden any person with more than He has given them – after hardship, God will bring ease' (Q65: 7, Haleem).

c. The Rights of a Wife from Her Husband

Good and polite interaction is one of the elements of household happiness. Associating well and politely with one's wife, and being patient about things that one dislikes, is a decree of God set out in An-Nisa (4):19:

[verse in Arabic script]

'*And associate with them properly, later if you do not like them (then be forbearing) because possibly you do not like something although God gave to it much goodness.*'[18]
[...]

Matters that a husband needs to attend to in associating with his wife include:

a. Paying attention to his wife by always guarding her honour and good name, as well as that of the family. If necessary, he can help with his wife's work.
b. Not doing or saying anything that might hurt his wife's feelings. Women, in general, are sensitive and easily hurt.
c. Not giving his wife a task beyond her power.
d. Endeavouring to increase his wife's knowledge, particularly her religious knowledge.
e. Allowing his wife time to visit or maintain relations with her parents, family and neighbours, especially if they are sick.
f. Being patient, calm and generous in dealing with his wife's shortcomings. He should also always give guidance and education to his wife and, most importantly, strengthen her moral character. In addition, the husband must avoid violence and the use of coarse language. [...]
g. Wearing neat and clean clothes in the presence of his wife, because every woman feels happy to see her husband well dressed.

d. The Duties of a Wife to Her Husband [...]

a. A wife must be obedient, loyal and respectful, and be honest and straightforward with her husband in everyday interactions, both in his presence and behind his back. A wife should always be polite, friendly, have an appealing expression on her face and trust completely in her husband.

   She should try to be stylish and attractive, comfort her husband when he is in difficulty, be a calming influence when her husband is uneasy, and raise her husband's hopes when he despairs. On this, God decreed in An-Nisa (4): 34,

[verse in Arabic script]

'*The pious woman is obedient to God and guards herself when her husband is absent.*'[19]

---

18 'You who believe, it is not lawful for you to inherit women against their will, nor should you treat your wives harshly, hoping to take back some of the dowry you gave them, unless they are guilty of something clearly outrageous. Live with them in accordance with what is fair and kind: if you dislike them, it may well be that you dislike something in which God has put much good' (Q4: 19, Haleem).
19 '... Righteous wives are devout and guard what God would have them guard in their husbands' absence. ...' (Q4: 34, Haleem). The full text of the verse is given in footnote 2.

b. A wife has the responsibility for her family, her husband and the safeguarding of their possessions. A wife must have the ability to manage the household and cook well. After all, the household is the consoler of the heart and the refresher of the soul for the husband. On this matter the Prophet of God, blessings and peace be upon him, said,

[verse in Arabic script]

'A woman is the manager of her husband's household and will be asked to take responsibility for it' (HR. Imam Bukhari and Muslim, from Abdullah bin Umar). [Hadith]

c. A wife must have the means to manage the household, dress up and adorn herself for her husband, and care for and educate her children. A wife who has these skills and expertise will make the household a comfortable place of rest, a beautiful place to live in, a delicious restaurant and the main place of education. Islam does not forbid a wife from dressing up and adorning herself, but it should be done only for her husband's benefit. It is extremely improper for a wife to leave her home without her husband dressed in nice clothes and wearing cosmetics and jewellery, while if at home with her husband she only wears everyday clothing.

d. A wife must respect her husband's parents, siblings and family members. She must be very conscious that her husband has a mother and father. It is these two people who have cared for and educated him since he was small, have never counted the cost that had to be expended and have never asked for compensation or return from their child. So it is proper for a husband's father, mother or relatives to expect something from him. Thus, a wife should know that it is not right for her to place her husband in a difficult position should a rift or tension occur between her husband's family and herself. The essence of one of the Hadith of the Prophet is that a child will commit a grave sin if he rebels against his mother (his parents) because of loving and defending his wife. [...]

f. A wife must be prudent, conscientious, and clever at budgeting and using the household money given to her by her husband. This money must be used as carefully and as economically as possible. Of course, this does not mean that she must be stingy towards herself. If there is money left over, it should be put away to face unexpected contingencies.

Household implements should be cared for as well and neatly as possible. A wife must also be conscientious in keeping the home and its furniture clean.

* * * * *

Commentary Nahdlatul Ulama (NU, Revival of the Religious Scholars), Indonesia's largest traditionalist Islamic organization, adopted the term 'Family Welfare' (*Keluarga Maslahah*) after issuing a fatwa in 1969 allowing family planning. An important component of the term is the idea that a smaller family is more likely than a larger one to be prosperous and serve God (Candland and Nurjanah 2004). Hence much of the booklet explaining the term consists of instructions on the use of contraceptive devices. The following extract gives a definition of *Keluarga Maslahah*, and the roles that various family members must play in order for it to be achievable.

Extract 13-7: *Nahdlatul Ulama and* Keluarga Maslahah

Lembaga Kemaslahatan Keluarga Nahdlatul Ulama (1996), *Keluarga Maslahah* [Family Welfare], no place. Extract: pp. 17–18.

Keluarga Maslahah

A *Maslahah* Family is a family that is beneficial and always brings goodness to its surroundings in accordance with the will of Almighty God, the Most Holy and Most High.

The five foundations for welfare that must be safeguarded are:

1. The need to safeguard religion.
2. The need to safeguard the intellect.
3. The need to safeguard life/self and honour.
4. The need to safeguard lineage/descendants.
5. The need to safeguard property.

The Members of a Family and Their Roles

1. The husband: needs and relies on a wife who loves him, knows him, values and respects him, and obeys and is faithful to him, a wife who manages the household conscientiously and treats her husband as the head of the family. A wife is the place to plant the seeds to obtain the descendants he longs for. A mother should also be resolute and wise in caring for and educating her children towards attaining perfection (*insan kamil*) [the perfect human being].
2. The wife: also needs and relies on a husband who loves and cherishes her, understands her femininity and values her humanity. A wife needs the attention and protection of her husband, as the embodiment of the husband's/father's attitude of responsibility for his family. Her natural role is to carry and give birth to children.
3. Children: begin life as babies who are weak human beings and then grow into children, then become teenagers and then finally adults with their own families. This development naturally requires attention, love, affection, nursing, education, good moral guidance, shelter and all kinds of security. Children are the mandate of God and their care will be judged before Him. Children also need to be treated justly by their parents.

13.2 REINTERPRETATIONS OF ISLAMIC TEXTS EMPHASIZING THE EQUALITY OF MEN AND WOMEN

Commentary   The above texts all stress that Islam honours women, that Islam was the first religion to 'liberate' women, giving them rights in many areas of life, such as the right to own property, to inherit and to be regarded as God's creatures. Men and women are held to be equal as religious subjects in the eyes of God, and will be held accountable for their deeds here on Earth. At the same time, these texts present a notion of difference between men and women that is 'God-given' and immutable, said to be grounded in a literal interpretation of the Qur'an and Hadith. On the basis of this difference, women are apportioned different roles in society. The extent of flexibility and freedom given to women by such a worldview varies greatly, and women who follow this tradition of thinking about gender are able to make positive contributions to society and can lead happy and fulfilling lives.

However, in the last decade or two, in countries such as Indonesia and Malaysia, there has been a questioning of how much of what is ascribed to women's *kodrat* is actually 'God-given' and how much is socially created, as well as the extent to which women's role has been circumscribed as a result of her *kodrat*. While not denying women's role in reproduction, and generally not asserting that men and women are 'exactly' the same, Muslims who challenge traditional and mainstream notions of gender place emphasis on looking beyond the literal meaning of texts to the universal values on which they are said to be grounded. These universal values include justice and equality, and are used as a measuring stick against which previously accepted ideas on women, gender and the family are tested.

As elsewhere in the Muslim world, in recent times there has also been a stress on looking at the context of revelation, and situating particular Qur'anic verses or Hadith in time and space. Muslim thinkers such as Fatima Mernissi from Morocco, Ashgar Ali Engineer from India, Leila Ahmad from Egypt, Amina Wadud from the United States (also a member of the Malaysian group Sisters in Islam) and Riffat Hassan from Pakistan argue that patriarchal cultural traditions have influenced the ways in which these views have been interpreted over time. Many of their works have been translated into Indonesian since the beginning of the 1990s and are available in both Malaysia and Indonesia where they are widely cited by gender activists (Abubakar 2002).

The views presented in the extracts in this section do not represent mainstream views in Southeast Asian societies, but they do represent an important minority view that those challenged by it feel obliged to respond to. As a result, gender is a highly contested area in countries like Indonesia and Malaysia today.

The following extract is a good illustration of how universal values are used to inform interpretation of texts on gender. The author, Nasaruddin Umar, of NU background and a professor at Syarif Hidayatullah State Islamic University in Jakarta, is well known in both Indonesia and Malaysia for his work on gender issues in Islam.

Extract 13-8: Nasaruddin Umar

Nasaruddin Umar (2002), 'Pembuka' [Introduction], pp. 1–4 in *Qur'an untuk Perempuan* [The Qur'an for Women], Jaringan Islam Liberal dan Teater Utan Kayu, Jakarta. Extract: pp. 1–4.

The interpretation of the Qur'an is often done on the basis of rejecting gender equality. Works of exegesis have become references in defending the status quo and legalizing the system of patriarchal life, which gives special rights to men and has the tendency to sideline women. Men are viewed as the principal sex, and women as the second sex. Views such as these have settled in nature below the surface of awareness of society and constitute a biased ethos of work between the two types of God's servants.

The primary mission of the Qur'an is to liberate humankind from various forms of anarchy, inequity and injustice. The Qur'an always calls for justice (Q.S. al-Nahl/16:90), security and tranquillity (Q.S. al-Nisa'/4:58), and prioritizes good and the prevention of evil (Q.S. Ali 'Imran/3:104).[20] It is these verses that also bring into being the primary goals of sharia (*maqasid al-syari'ah*).[21]

If there is an interpretation that is not in accord with the principles of justice and human rights, then that interpretation must be reconsidered. Almighty God is Most Just, thus it is not possible that His Holy Book contains anything that is not in accord with these principles.

In Islam there are various controversies connected to gender relations, among others: the origins of the creation of women, and the concepts behind inheritance, witnesses, polygamy, reproductive rights, women's rights to divorce and the public role of women. If we read the verses connected to the said issues quickly, they give the impression that there is bias (injustice) against women. However, if we scrutinize them deeply, using the analytic methods of semantics, semiotics and hermeneutics, and pay attention to the theory of *asbab nuzul* [Ar.: *asbaabun-nuzuuli*; circumstances and context for the revelation (of the Qur'an)], then we can understand that these verses constitute a process of creating justice in a constructive manner in society. All the verses connected to the above issues, for example the origins of women (Q.S. al-Nisa'/4:1), inheritance for women (Q.S. al-Nisa'/4:11), women as witnesses (Q.S. al-Baqarah/2:282), polygamy (Q.S. al-Nisa'/4:3, Q.S. al-Nisa'/4:129), the right of unilateral divorce (Q.S. al-Baqarah/2:231), reproductive rights (Q.S. al-Baqarah/2:223, Q.S. al-Nisa'/4:23), the public role of women (Q.S. al-Ahzab/33:33) and the political rights of women (Q.S. al-Nisa'/4:34),[22] were in fact revealed with

---

20   'God commands justice, doing good, and generosity towards relatives and He forbids what is shameful, blameworthy, and oppressive. He teaches you, so that you may take heed' (Q16: 90, Haleem).

'God commands you [people] to return things entrusted to you to their rightful owners, and, if you judge between people, to do so with justice: God's instructions to you are excellent, for He hears and sees everything' (Q4: 58, Haleem).

'Be a community that calls for what is good, urges what is right, and forbids what is wrong: those who do this are the successful ones' (Q3: 104, Haleem).

21   The primary goals of sharia are discussed further in chapter 11; see also the glossary.

22   'People, be mindful of your Lord, who created you from a single soul, and from it created its mate, and from the pair of them spread countless men and women far and wide; be mindful of God, in whose name you make requests of one another. Beware of severing the ties of kinship: God is always watching over you' (Q4: 1, Haleem).

'Concerning your children, God commands you that a son should have the equivalent share of two daughters. If there are only daughters, two or more should share two-thirds of the inheritance, if one, she should have half. Parents inherit a sixth each if the deceased leaves children; if he leaves no children and his parents are his sole heirs, his mother has a third, unless he has brothers, in which case she has a sixth. [In all cases, the distribution comes] after payment of any bequests or debts. You cannot know which of your parents or your children is closer to you in benefit: this is a law from God, and He is all knowing, all wise' (Q4: 11, Haleem).

'You who believe, when you contract a debt for a stated term, put it down in writing: have a scribe write it down justly between you. No scribe should refuse to write: let him write as God has taught him, let the debtor dictate, and let him fear God, his Lord, and not diminish [the debt] at all. If the debtor is feeble-minded, weak, or unable to dictate, then let his guardian dictate justly. Call in two men

regard to specific cases which happened at the time of the Prophet, blessings and peace be upon him. This means that these verses all have a specific character.

According to Yvonne Yazbeck Haddad,[23] the Qur'an is a source of values which, for the first time in the long history of the human community (*umat*), devised the concept of gender justice. Among the cultures and civilizations that existed at the time of the revelation of the Qur'an, such as the Greek, Roman, Judaic, Persian, Chinese, Indian, Christian and Arabic (pre-Islam) cultures, there was not one that placed women in a more respected or prestigious position than the values introduced by the Qur'an. [In a footnote, the author refers the reader to Haddad (1980: 56).]

However, we also cannot arbitrarily say that every interpretation that is not in accord with contemporary thinking is wrong, because every Qur'anic commentator (*mufassir*) is a 'child of his times'. They also have the right and capacity to understand Qur'anic verses according to the logic and cultural contexts that are in accord

---

as witnesses. If two men are not there, then call one man and two women out of those you approve as witnesses, so that if one of the two women should forget the other can remind her. Let the witnesses not refuse when they are summoned. Do not disdain to write the debt down, be it small or large, along with the time it falls due: this way is more equitable in God's eyes, more reliable as testimony, and more likely to prevent doubts arising between you. But if the merchandise is there and you hand it over, there is no blame on you if you do not write it down. Have witnesses present whenever you trade with one another, and let no harm be done to either scribe or witness, for if you did cause them harm, it would be a crime on your part. Be mindful of God, and He will teach you: He has full knowledge of everything' (Q2: 282, Haleem).

'If you fear that you will not deal fairly with orphan girls, you may marry whichever [other] women seem good to you, two, three, or four. If you fear that you cannot be equitable [to them], then marry only one, or your slave(s): that is more likely to make you avoid bias' (Q4: 3, Haleem).

'You will never be able to treat your wives with equal fairness, however much you may desire to do so, but do not ignore one wife altogether, leaving her suspended [between marriage and divorce]. If you make amends and remain conscious of God, He is most forgiving and merciful' (Q4: 129, Haleem).

'When you divorce women and they have reached their set time, then either keep or release them in a fair manner. Do not hold on to them with intent to harm them and commit aggression: anyone who does this wrongs himself. Do not make a mockery of God's revelations; remember the favour He blessed you with, and the Scripture and wisdom He sent to teach you. Be mindful of God and know that He has full knowledge of everything' (Q2: 231, Haleem).

'"Your women are your fields, so go into your fields whichever way you like, and send [something good] ahead for yourselves. Be mindful of God: remember that you will meet Him." [Prophet], give good news to the believers' (Q2: 223, Haleem).

'You are forbidden to take as wives your mothers, daughters, sisters, paternal and maternal aunts, the daughters of brothers and daughters of sisters, your milk-mothers and milk-sisters, your wives' mothers, the stepdaughters in your care – those born of women with whom you have consummated marriage, if you have not consummated the marriage, then you will not be blamed – wives of your begotten sons, two sisters simultaneously – with the exception of what is past: God is most forgiving and merciful' (Q4: 23, Haleem).

'stay at home, and do not flaunt your attractions as they used to in the pagan past; keep up the prayer, give the prescribed alms, and obey God and His Messenger. God wishes to keep uncleanness away from you, people of the [Prophet's] House, and make you completely pure' (Q33: 33, Haleem).

Q4: 34 is given in footnote 2.

23 Yvonne Haddad is professor of the history of Islam at the Center for Muslim–Christian Understanding at Georgetown University in Washington DC.

with their times. Perhaps what needs to be done is [to think about] how the reinter-pretation of the Qur'an can be considered an ongoing process, which must be done every moment, in line with social changes. How to articulate a number of verses that are judged to be gender-biased in our social environment, by doing research into those verses repeatedly and critically.

* * * * *

Commentary In the following extract, Zainah Anwar of the Malaysian NGO Sisters in Islam demonstrates a contextualist approach to Islamic teachings. Sisters in Islam is the best-known and longest-running organization working on issues of women's rights in Islam in Malaysia. It was formed in 1988 and promotes the reinterpretation of Qur'anic verses on the basis of gender equality. Despite promoting ideas on gender that are not 'mainstream', it has been influential on public policy, and frequently very controversial (Maznah 2002: 231–2; Foley 2004: 61–3).

Extract 13-9: Zainah Anwar

Excerpt from the transcript of an interview with Zainah Anwar conducted by Terry Lane [in English], 'In the National Interest', Radio National, Australian Broadcast-ing Corporation, <http://www.abc.net.au/rn/talks/natint/stories/s915192.htm>, dated 3 August 2003, accessed 6 September 2005.

Terry Lane: To what extent are these sorts of restrictions [on women being wit-nesses] imposed on women based in the Qu'ran, the text of the Qu'ran, and to what extent are they later interpretations. We know for instance that the Qu'ran says that the testimony of one man is equal to that of two women. Now what does that mean, and do you accept that, as a Muslim?

Zainah Anwar: I don't accept that interpretation of the Qu'ranic verse. The prob-lem that we have is that so many of these verses in the Qu'ran are interpreted in isolation, literal interpretation of the verse, because we need to understand that the Qu'ran was revealed within a social historical context. And we need to link that with the objective of the revelation. Now that verse on witnesses, was within a context to ensure that justice is done at a time when women were not so much in public life, when women were not involved in business transactions. In fact it was very much on business transactions, on contracts, witnesses to contracts, and the verse actually says the second woman is to ensure that no mistake is made, the other is to assist that man witness, not one man equals two women. But unfortunately in a very patriarchal society, that verse has been interpreted to mean one male witness equals the two female witnesses. So a lot of the problems that we have today with regard to women's rights in Islam has to do more with interpretations of the Qu'ran, a process that has been dominated by men, within the context of very patriarchal societies. So now of course in the 21st century and the 20th century in the past 30 to 40 years, where within the context of the women's movement, of widespread educa-tion, women are getting educated, women are out there in public life, earning money, being in top positions, all these interpretations, gender-biased interpretations[,] are being questioned. And so this is a challenge that is posed by the women's movement in particular, and human rights movements, to the religious authority. How do you make religion relevant to the lives of women today, who are independent, who are strong, who are opinionated and will not accept an inferior status in life?

Terry Lane: In passing, you referred to the Qu'ran as revealed. Do you mean that literally? Do you mean that this is literally the revealed word of God?

Zainah Anwar: Yes, definitely.

Terry Lane: You say 'Yes, definitely', but if I make a comparison between Islam and Christianity, Christianity only lost its ability to control the lives of women when that very notion of revealed truth was rejected.

Zainah Anwar: Well you see there is a difference between what is revealed by God – and that is the words in the Qu'ran, there are exact verses in the Qu'ran that comes from God, that's revealed from God – and what is human understanding of the word of God. In understanding what is the word of God, there is the human agency, the human intervention. So the minute [you begin] the process of reading the Qu'ran and what you say as a result of reading the Qu'ran, and what you understand as a result of reading the Qu'ran, the process of human agency, of human understanding and human intervention, has come in and interacted with the revealed word. So this is the point we are making, that all these laws that are codified, all these pronounce-ments and fatwahs that are made in the name of God, in the name of Islam, are human understanding of God's word, and because they are human understanding of God's revealed message, therefore it can be challenged, it can be changed, given the context of changing times and circumstances. So we need to make, and this is a big problem that we have as well in the Muslim world, that there is a difference between what is the revealed word and what is human understanding of the revealed word.

* * * * *

Commentary   In Indonesia a number of figures active in NGOs with links to NU, such as Perhimpunan Pengembangan Pesantren dan Masyarakat (P3M, Association for the Development of Pesantren and Society), were among the first to challenge existing ideas concerning gender, around the beginning of the 1990s. They have been joined by figures from other organizations, including the gender section of the Ministry of Reli-gious Affairs, the organizations Rahima and Jaringan Islam Liberal (JIL, Liberal Islam Network) and the gender study centres in Islamic and state universities (Burhanudin and Fathurahman 2004: 113–52). Of the mainstream organizations, the young women's wing of NU, Fatayat NU, and the young women's section of Muhammadiyah, Nasyiatul 'Aisyiyah, have perhaps been the most active on gender issues, although the women's wings of both organizations, Muslimat NU and 'Aisyiyah, have also been involved.

The extract below is from a text by K.H. Husein Muhammad, who runs Pondok Pesantren Darut Tauhid in Cirebon (see also extract 13-24). He has written widely on gender issues, and is a director of both Rahima and the Fahmina Institute in Cirebon, which seek to raise awareness of gender issues in *pesantren*. Other important figures in

Indonesia include Nasaruddin Umar (see extract 13-8), Siti Musdah Mulia (see extracts 13-30 and 13-46), Maria Ulfah Anshor (see extract 13-37), Siti Ruhaini Dzuhayatin, Farha Ciciek, Lies Marcoes-Natsir, Masdar Mas'udi (see extract 13-33) and Sinta Nuri-yah (see section 13.3.6).

Extract 13-10: Husein Muhammad

Husein Muhammad (2001), 'Adakah Keadilan Gender?' [What Is Gender Justice?], pp. 3–13 in *Fiqh Perempuan: Refleksi Kiai atas Wacana Agama dan Gender* [Women's Jurisprudence: Reflections by a Religious Leader on the Discourse of Gender and Religion], Lembaga Kajian Islam dan Sosial, Yogyakarta. Extract: pp. 6–8.

A. Confusion in Understanding the Roots of the Problem

Feminists see that there is confusion or even a mistaken understanding or view of society concerning the essence of social relations that are the basis for the subordination of women and the results that arise from this. In general, people see women as creatures that are weak, while men are strong; women are emotional, men are rational; women are refined (*halus*), men are rough (*kasar*); and so on. These differences are then believed to be determinants of *kodrat*, from the very beginning, or to constitute something God-given. Because of this, they are fixed and cannot be changed. Changing these matters is viewed as going against *kodrat*, or even opposing the stipulations of God. These images of men and women are rooted in the culture of the society. In the view of feminists, characteristics such as those mentioned above simply constitute something that is constructed socially and culturally. In another sense, they are made by humankind itself, not by a decision of God. Social facts show clearly that the said characteristics can be changed, or substituted, or transformed according to time, place and social class. This is what they call gender difference. On this basis, as something that is social and made by humankind, there is the possibility for humankind to change or substitute [these characteristics] in accordance with the context. This concept must be differentiated from the concept of sex. The concept of sex sees differences between men and women purely from the aspect of biology, as in women becoming pregnant, giving birth and breastfeeding, while men have a penis, sperm and an Adam's apple. According to this last-mentioned concept [the concept of sex differences], the differences between men and women are truly *kodrat*, the creation of God, because they are fixed and cannot be changed.

With an understanding such as that, people probably conclude *a priori* that there will be a reversal of roles between men and women [if the concept of *kodrat* is challenged]. 'If that is so, then surely the world will end', they say. However, feminists reject this view. Criticizing the ideology of patriarchy does not mean directly applying the ideology of matriarchy. Actually they simply want to create a pattern of relations between men and women that is just and humane. Mansour Fakih,[24] for

---

24   Dr Mansour Fakih (1953–2004) was the director of the Institute for Social Transformation (INSIST) in Yogyakarta, and was well known for his active involvement in human rights and gender

example, clearly states that gender difference does not actually constitute a problem so long as it does not cause injustice for men or women. However, in fact, differences in gender already create injustice, especially towards women. Gender injustice constitutes a system or social structure in which men or women become victims. Gender injustice manifests itself in the form of marginalization, a process of economic impoverishment, subordination or the view that one does not need to participate in political actions or decisions, stereotyping, discrimination and violence. By understanding the issue of gender difference, it is hoped that views that are more humane and more just will appear. Women have the right of full access to participation in the fields of politics, the economy, society and intellectual life, as well as being valued equally to men. On the other hand, men must also be able, or have the opportunity, to participate fully in the home and in caring for the children.

B. Blocked by Religious Thinking

However, an understanding of gender issues has implications for society that mean it is truly up against extraordinary difficulties, especially when it must confront religious thinking. The more so, when this religious thinking is disseminated by those whom society views as the owners of true authority. Especially if their grip on true authority is held by way of consensus. Even greater difficulties arise when these ways of thinking become religious convictions or are regarded as religion itself.

* * * * *

Commentary   Funding, generally from Western sources, has been given to a number of institutions and organizations in Indonesia to help conduct what are referred to as 'gender sensitivity' training sessions. Pusat Studi Wanita (Women's Study Centres) have been established in many universities. They seek to spread awareness of gender issues among staff and students. Other organizations involved in such training include the young women's wing of NU, Fatayat NU. It has been involved in conducting training sessions for religious leaders (*kiai*) and the female equivalent, *nyai*, in *pesantren*. In the following extract, one of the concepts central to Western feminist thought, the difference between biological sex and socially constructed gender, is addressed in a training module.

Extract 13-11: Fatayat NU

Fatayat NU (1999), 'Modul III: Pengertian Gender' [Module III: Understanding of Gender], pp. 20–30 in *Modul Analisis Gender* [Gender Analysis Module], Pucuk Pimpinan Fatayat NU in cooperation with the Asia Foundation, Jakarta. Extract: pp. 20, 26–9.

---

issues. His book on gender, *Analisis Gender and Transformasi Sosial* [Gender Analysis and Social Transformation] was published in 1994.

WORK SCHEDULE [heading on board]

WIFE

- Clean the house
- Go to the market/do the shopping
- Do the cooking
- Do the washing
- Do the ironing
- Look after the children
- Serve her husband
- Mop the floor
- Etc.

HUSBAND

- Read the paper
- Burn the rubbish
- Fix the leaking roof

Wife: 'Gosh, I've got so much work to do?!'
Husband: 'That's fair, isn't it? The point is, I'm the breadwinner?!' [p. 20]

I. BASIC UNDERSTANDING

- ***GENDER*** is:
  The social difference between men and women, in particular the different behaviours, functions and roles that are determined by the norms of any society.

- ***KODRAT*** is:
  Everything that men and women have that has been determined by **God (The Creator)** and that humankind cannot change or reject. […]

II. THE DIFFERENCE BETWEEN GENDER AND KODRAT

GENDER	*KODRAT*
• Determined by society	• Determined by God
• Changes over time in accordance with developments that influence social norms and values	• Unchanging, universal (does not vary over place or time)
• Differs between societies and cultures	

Wife: 'Ah, is this really a woman's *kodrat*?!' [p. 27]

III. GENDER ROLES

GENDER ROLES are social roles that are determined by sex differences. For example, looking after children and running a household are classified as the role and responsibility of women. It must be understood that these duties constitute women's gender roles, not women's *kodrat*.

IV. GENDERED DIVISION OF LABOUR

A *GENDERED DIVISION OF LABOUR* is a system of dividing work whereby men and women do different types of work. This gendered division of labour is not a problem so long as it does not disadvantage men or women.

V. GENDER ISSUES

GENDER ISSUES are issues that arise because of male and female stereotypes in relation to gender roles and the gendered division of labour.

Gender Issues arise when it becomes clear that there are discriminatory attitudes leading to the different treatment of men and women, for example, relating to pay and salary. Other examples include the different treatment of male and female children in relation to education, upbringing and so on. [pp. 26–9] [...]

13.3   REINTERPRETATIONS ON PARTICULAR ISSUES

Commentary   The previous section looked at general approaches to textual reinterpretation. However, most debate in countries such as Indonesia and Malaysia takes place around particular issues affecting women, the family and gender relations. These debates are informed by the principles described in the texts above, and constitute interesting case studies of how particular individuals or groups seek to apply these principles in practice.

The particular issues chosen have been selected because they are controversial in Southeast Asian Muslim societies, sparking debate within academic and theological circles as well as in the popular press.

Many Muslims in the societies where these discussions take place may not follow the debates in detail, particularly when they take place at a theological level that requires a knowledge of the texts connected to the issue, and of principles of exegesis. Nevertheless, such debates have an impact on public attitudes, often focusing community opinion on a particular moral or philosophical issue.

The issues discussed in this section are not merely theoretical, but rather have become topical because women and men are confronted with concrete social or family problems that require them to reconcile their own behaviour and attitudes with their religious beliefs.

13.3.1   Women's Work Outside the Home and the Concept of *Nafakah*

Commentary   The texts in section 13.1 vary in terms of the emphasis given to women's work. Most of them pay little or no attention to women having a productive role outside the family. Instead, emphasis is placed on a woman's role within the family. Her primary duty is said to be to care for her husband and children.

Nevertheless, large numbers of Muslim women *do* work outside the home, raising the issue of their dual role in the family as a contributor to family income and as the primary carer and housekeeper in the home.

The concept of financial support, or *nafakah*, is central to understanding attitudes towards women's work in Islamic Southeast Asia. It is, as the texts in section 13.1 show, the responsibility of the husband in a Muslim family to provide for his wife and children, in the form of food, housing, clothing and so on. Women may contribute to household income, but it is their right not to do so.

SyariahOnline is a question and answer website run by an Indonesian organization calling itself Pusat Konsultasi Syariah (Centre for Sharia Consultation). Its aim is to increase people's understanding of sharia in Indonesia.[25] Although the centre is not formally affiliated with any political party in Indonesia, most members of the board are said to be actively involved in Partai Keadilan Sejahtera (PKS, Prosperity and Justice Party).[26] The following extract is a good example of the argument that a woman's primary duty is in the home. This response was given in reply to a question from a single woman asking whether it was permissible for her to work outside the home; her parents were insisting that she be independent, but 'other parties say that a woman cannot work outside the home'.

Extract 13-12: SyariahOnline

SyariahOnline, 'Perempuan Yang Bekerja di Luar Rumah' [Women Who Work Outside the Home], <http://syariahonline.com/konsultasi/?act=view&id=3050>, dated 13 October 2003, accessed 16 February 2004.

Answer: […]
Women – as it is usually said – represent half the population. Islam has never been portrayed as ignoring half of the members of its society, freezing or paralysing them, robbing them of their lives, damaging their well-being or not giving them anything at all.

The principal and undisputed task of women is to educate the next generation. God has indeed prepared them both physically and mentally for this noble task, and it may not be forgotten or ignored because of any material or cultural factors whatsoever. There is no one who can substitute for the role of women in this vital duty, and on them depends the future of Muslims. Women make manifest the greatest of riches, that is, human riches (human resources).

May God have mercy on the poet of the River Nile, Hafizh Ibrahim, when he said:

> A mother is the Islamic school, the educational institution. If you prepare her well then you have prepared the basis of the nation.

The activities of women include looking after the household, making her husband happy, and forming a happy, peaceful, loving and affectionate family. This is described by the well-known proverb, 'The service of a woman to her husband is valued as Holy War' (*jihad fi sabilillah*).

* * * * *

Commentary The above extract nevertheless does not claim that women must remain in the home. The following extract from SyariahOnline argues that women do in fact have a right to social engagement. It goes on to recommend certain types of work as

---

25 Details of the organization's structure and goals can be viewed (in Indonesian) at <http://syariah online.com/artikel/?act=view&id=39>, accessed 3 June 2005.

26 Information supplied by Yon Machmudi, currently completing a PhD thesis at the Australian National University on PKS-related movements in Indonesia.

particularly fitted to women's *kodrat*, as well as certain behaviour she must follow outside the home. The answer was given in response to a request for a ruling on whether women should work outside the home, given that this was 'already commonplace'.

Extract 13-13: *SyariahOnline*

SyariahOnline, 'Wanita Bekerja Di Luar Rumah' [Women Working Outside the Home], <http://syariahonline.com/konsultasi/?act=view&id=4067>, dated 18 December 2003, accessed 16 February 2004.

Answer: […]
Basically there are no prohibitions on women working outside the home, as long as the work is not connected with anything forbidden by religion. And, of course, permission from the husband or male guardian is the main prerequisite. A woman who leaves the home without the permission of her husband or guardian is participating in immorality. This means that if a husband or guardian forbids a woman from leaving the house, but she is disobedient and contravenes the rules set for her, then she is being immoral.

Certainly a husband does not have the right to confine or 'imprison' his wife in the home. As a human and member of society, a wife has the right to interact with her environment and also needs to act as a catalyst within society. It is not appropriate, therefore, for a woman always to be behind the walls of her house.

However, if she does leave the house then she must pay attention to some basic matters. These include wearing clothes that properly cover the body, and not creating a scandal by wearing attractive eye make-up to attract the attention of the opposite sex. Also, she must not mix with the opposite sex in the workplace, or associate with a man [in an improper manner], inviting the Devil. She should keep her eyes lowered and not draw the eyes of others to her.

On the issue of the law of employment and women earning a living, basically women do not need to earn a wage by themselves. A woman is also never expected to support her family financially. This is because the person for whom it is obligatory to earn a living is the husband, who is the backbone of the family.

Women should only be employed in areas and types of jobs that are generally appropriate for women. So employment as workmen, truck drivers, car mechanics, hard labourers, petrol station attendants, city bus conductors and so on is not suitable for women. Besides, the presence of women in such areas only reduces the number of employment opportunities for men. The problem is that for men it is obligatory to earn a living, while for women it is not obligatory or even recommended (*sunnah*). If these types of employment are taken away from men and given to women, then many men will be unable to support their wives.

The types of employment that accord with the nature of women are as teachers, educators, nurses, writers, or even doctors specifically for female patients. As well as being appropriate for women, these types of profession are needed by society. The absence of female workers in areas such as these even creates obligations. For example, the profession of women's doctor is obligatory considering that there are greater numbers of women than men. Therefore, Muslim women are required to work as doctors until there are enough of them in that field.

* * * * *

Commentary In Malaysia, the following letter to the editor by Sisters in Islam and a number of other women's organizations, dated 17 March 1999, was published in three major dailies. It argues against the idea that a woman's primary duty is in the home, asserting that in Islam, women have a right to work. The letter was written as a protest against a statement by Nik Aziz Nik Mat, the chief minister (*menteri besar*) of the Malaysian state of Kelantan. An ulema from Parti Islam Se Malaysia (PAS, The Islamic Party of Malaysia), Nik Aziz has often been at the centre of controversies concerning gender issues.[27]

Extract 13-14: Sisters in Islam

Sisters in Islam et al., 'Women and Work in Islam' [in English], letter to the editor, <http://www.sistersinislam.org.my/Letterstoeditors/17031999.htm>, dated 17 March 1999, accessed 22 May 2005.

Datuk Haji Nik Aziz Nik Mat's retrogressive comments on women, work and the family are causing much concern to us in the women's movement.

Nine years after being the Menteri Besar (Chief Minister) of a state which prides itself in once being ruled by a woman and where its women are renowned for their independence, industry and entrepreneurship, we are disappointed that Datuk Nik Aziz's views on women have yet to change to reflect the changing realities and circumstances of women's lives today.

The Menteri Besar of Kelantan asserts that it is man's nature and responsibility to support the family and therefore it is unfair and unnecessary for women to work. Moreover, he considers the home a woman's responsibility and the nurturing of children and housework as naturally women's work.

First, we would like to point out that there is nothing in the Qur'an or in the Hadith which prevents women from working outside the home.

In fact the Qur'an extols the leadership of Bilqis, the Queen of Sheba,[28] for her capacity to fulfil the requirements of the office, for her political skills, the purity of her faith and her independent judgement (Surah an-Naml, 27: 23–44).

If a woman is qualified and the one best suited to fulfil a task, there is no Qur'anic injunction that prohibits her from any undertaking because of her sex.

---

27   Maznah (2002: 237) details the political mileage the government of Malaysia has attempted to make from statements by the chief minister. His supporters allege that his statements are often taken out of context. Interestingly, Nik Aziz threw his support behind the candidature of the head of the women's wing of PAS, Siti Mariah Mahmud, to become one of three vice-presidents of the party in mid-2005 (Zubaidah 2005).

28   The story of Bilqis (or Bilkis, Balkis), the Queen of Sheba, and her conversion to Islam by King Soloman is revealed in chapter 27 of the Qur'an, as noted in the extract. Haleem's translation describing her rule, before her conversion, is as follows: 'I found a woman ruling over the people, who has been given a share of everything – she has a magnificent throne' (Q27: 23, Haleem).

Second, Hadith literature and recorded stories on the life of Prophet Muhammad saw[29] is replete with women leaders, jurists and scholars, and women who participated fully in public life.

Khadija, the first wife of the Prophet, was a successful trader who helped the poor, freed slaves and spread the message of Islam. After her death, the Prophet saw married Aisyah Siddiqa, a formidable young woman who led a Muslim army into battle and taught multitudes of Muslim men and women from throughout the growing world of Islam.

Al-Shifa bint Abdullah was the chief inspector of the Medina market. Umm Waraqa bint Naulal was an imam appointed by the Prophet saw. At the battle of Uhud, women were on the battlefield not only as nurses, but also as fighters.

Third, Datuk Nik Aziz's inclination to deny women the right to work is an unrealistic proposition in today's world.

It is a fallacy to say women do not need work and that men have the primary responsibility to provide for their families. Such statements contradict reality. The basic family structure and economic system in today's society have changed. For most Malaysian families, both parents now have to work in order to provide a decent standard of living for the family.

Many women workers are also single, separated, divorced with small children, or neglected wives of polygamous husbands. It is rare that these women can afford the luxury of staying at home, secure in the comfort that some men in their lives, be it fathers, brothers, ex-husbands or polygamous husbands[,] will be fully responsible for maintaining them. This is just not the reality.

Moreover, the right to work is an inalienable right of women. If this right is denied, it will, as a consequence, deprive women [of] choice in many areas and affect other inter-related rights such as the right to education, the right to mobility, the right to decision making, and to political participation. Women will therefore remain devalued, disadvantaged and disempowered.

Fourth, while women's roles and responsibilities outside the home have changed, working wives still bear almost all the responsibility of unpaid family work, such as child care, housework, and caring for elderly parents.

Women bear the double burden of having to earn a salary to help support the family without any lightening of their responsibilities in the home. The heavy weight of tradition, combined with socialisation, still work powerfully to reinforce the sexual division of labour in the family.

Fifth, to ascribe separate roles to women and men also undermines men's parenting role and denies the social significance of child bearing and rearing.

The role of women in procreation should not be a basis for discrimination. What needs to be emphasised instead is the sharing of responsibility between women and men and society as a whole in the upbringing of children and maintaining a harmonious household.

There is nothing in a man's biological make-up that prevents him from being a nurturer and care giver. The reason why men are not doing more housework and

---

29   Saw; 'blessings and peace be upon him'; see glossary.

child care is because they do not want to. And they are able to enforce their will on women who are conditioned to believe that it is their sole responsibility to preserve the marital relationship and family peace at all cost.

While we agree with Datuk Nik Aziz that it is unfair and oppressive for women to bear the double burden of work and home responsibilities, we disagree with his analysis of this problem and his proposed solutions.

13.3.2 Leadership in the Family

Commentary The concept that the husband is the leader or head of the family is grounded in the interpretation of verse 4: 34 of the Qur'an (see footnote 2). This verse is often seen as tying together the concept of men's leadership and their provision of *nafakah*, thus raising the issue of what happens when the principal source of income is the wife. Others deny that it is only the provision of *nafakah* that gives men leadership of the family; they argue instead that it is men's superior abilities that give them this right not just in the home, but also in the public sphere.

The following extract is from a booklet by Sisters in Islam on the equality of men and women. It gives a reinterpretation of verse 4: 34, based on the term *qawwamuna* (Ar.: *qawwaamuuna*). Here it is said to mean 'have responsibility', whereas the more conventional definition found in Indonesian and Malaysian texts is 'are leaders'.

Extract 13-15: Sisters in Islam

Sisters in Islam (2003), *Are Women and Men Equal before Allah?* [in English], Kuala Lumpur (first published 1991). Extract: pp. 8–10.

5. Verse 4:34 has been commonly cited to subjugate women in the name of Islam. How should this verse be interpreted?

Surat al-Nisa ayat 34 states:

Men are *qawwamuna* over women, (on the basis) of what Allah has [*faddala*][30] preferred some of them over others and (on the basis) of what they spend of their property (for the support of women) ...

This verse has been misinterpreted to mean:

i.   Men have authority over women.
ii. All men are superior to all women.

i. Do men have authority over women?
In the beginning of this verse the Qur'an establishes that men are *qawwamuna* (have responsibility) over women. It does not mean that women are incapable of handling their own affairs, controlling themselves or of being leaders, whether among women, men and women, or even of nations, as has been assumed. Rather, it intends

---

30   *Faddala* (Ar.: *fadlul-lahi*) means to give preference to someone or to set someone before or above someone else.

to establish a responsibility of men for the protection and maintenance of women in a restricted social context. Biologically, only women can bear the future generations of Muslims. The Qur'an creates a harmonious balance in society by establishing a functional responsibility for males to facilitate this biological function of females.

In the Qur'an, responsibility and privileges are linked. Whoever has greater privileges, and other advantages, has greater responsibility and vice versa. The material responsibility of men in the Qur'an, that they are invested with the responsibility of spending for women's support, has corresponding advantages (like a greater portion of inheritance). This verse does not give men inherent superiority. It establishes mutual responsibility in society. Responsibility is not superiority.

ii. Are all men superior to all women?

The Qur'an does not say that 'all men are superior to or better than all women'. Nor even that all men are preferred by Allah *swt* [Almighty God] over all women. Advantages are explicitly specified in the Qur'an. Men have a certain advantage materially, resulting in certain responsibilities (or vice versa). When the Qur'an says that 'some (unspecified gender) are preferred by Allah *swt* over others', it uses general language which corresponds directly with the observable reality in creation: some creatures have some advantages over others – even some humans over others. All men do not always have an advantage over all women, nor all women always over men.

This description of the universal organization in creation is significant in our discussion of the relationship between advantages and responsibilities. Some are more advantaged than some others, thus their responsibility correspondingly increases. Men have an advantage materially, and an increased responsibility: spending 'for the support of women'.

It is important to restrict this verse to the particulars mentioned for two reasons:

a. Only then would it remain consistent with the Qur'anic criterion of evaluation in humankind: 'the most noble of you in the sight of Allah is the one with the most *taqwa* [piety]' (49:13).[31]
b. The resulting arbitrary discrimination creates disharmony between the female and the male.

These two reasons can have negative consequences on the spiritual well being of men. If they are falsely led to believe that they are inherently better than women, without exerting any effort on their part, they might not strive to develop the level of *taqwa* necessary to truly be seen as noble in the sight of Allah *swt*.

* * * * *

Commentary   Ratna Batara Munti, in a booklet on the issue of female-headed households, approaches verse Q4: 34 differently. She examines the context in which the verse was revealed and then examines the current situation in Indonesia where the reality is

---

31 'People, We created you all from a single man and a single woman, and made you into nations and tribes so that you should get to know one another. In God's eyes, the most honoured of you are the ones most aware of Him: God is all knowing, all aware' (Q49: 13, Haleem).

not just that there are many female-headed households due to divorce and widowhood, but also that husband–wife relationships have changed over the years.

Extract 13-16: *Ratna Batara Munti*

Ratna Batara Munti (1999), 'Perempuan sebagai Pemimpin' [Women as Leaders], pp. 34–55 in *Perempuan sebagai Kepala Rumah Tangga* [Women as Heads of the Household], Lembaga Kajian Agama dan Jender, Jakarta. Extract: pp. 48–54.

The context for the revelation of this verse [Q4: 34] was the Arabic milieu, in which violence towards women was a common occurrence. The verse was revealed at the beginning of the formation of the first Muslim society. The practice of violence against women did not immediately disappear, even among the Companions [of the Prophet]. This verse was itself revealed in the context of the beating of Habibah binti Zaid by her husband Sa'ad ibn Rabi'.

> One day Habibah would not follow her husband's wishes, so he slapped her. Habibah's father reported this to the Prophet. In response to the report, the Prophet replied: 'She (Habibah) may pay him back in kind'. Then Habibah and her father went out in order to seek retribution from Sa'ad. But before they had got very far, the Prophet called to them: 'Come back, the angel Gabriel has just come to me'. Then he recited the verse (Q.s. 4: 34), declaring: 'We have one intention about a matter. But God has a different intention. And God's intention is better'.

At that time, women were not treated as they should be, as humans with dignity. Women were subject to various forms of oppression: domestic violence, a lack of inheritance rights, they were possessions just like other property, and most extreme was the practice of burying female children alive. The arrival of Islam brought about reform and raised the status of women. However, changing the pattern of leadership in the family was not a priority at the time. [pp. 48–9] [...]

This concern about causing disruption to the structure of a nascent Muslim society is understandable. In a society in which men had almost limitless authority, it was impossible for women to retaliate against their husbands. Because of this, at the beginning of the verse it is stated that 'Men are the leaders of women because they provide an income and because God has made their portion [of inheritance] above other portions'. With this verse, God intended to stem the Prophet's desire to propose that [women] retaliate against [their] husbands because the context, in which men were the providers for the family, was not appropriate. Clearly, the word 'leaders' (*pemimpin*) in that verse is not a statement that will always be valid, but is closely linked to the social conditions of one particular society. [p. 52] [...]

The reality is that many women now have the same abilities as men, both in terms of knowledge and in terms of leadership skills and various other skills. In sports, for example, there are many women who are professionals in intense sports like bodybuilding, rockclimbing, swimming, boxing, soccer and even weightlifting. The same is also true of the social and political arenas, where we see the emergence of various women figures, either as politicians or company leaders or as leaders of social organizations and institutions. The increasing development of women's abilities and the broadening of their opportunities for work have influenced the elevation of women's bargaining position in relation to men. Because of this it is not surprising that women are in positions of leadership not only outside the household but also within the household, as the census figures indicate.

There has been a profound change in the social position of women from the situation at the beginning of the formation of the Muslim community. Whether we like it or not, this change compels authorities on Muslim law to reinterpret those verses of the Qur'an that speak about women in reference to the situation in the past. This is because the interpretation regarding the superiority of men, which is the justification for their leadership, is no longer consistent with existing facts. This reinterpretation must return to the moral message contained in those verses and to the universal values found in many other verses, namely the values of justice and equality. [pp. 53–4]

* * * * *

Commentary   Yet another approach to the issue of men's leadership in the family is taken by the Indonesian academic Istiadah. After examining various interpretations of the term *qawwamuna*, she argues that even if the term is taken to mean 'leader', this does not imply a relationship between husband and wife of leader and follower.

Extract 13-17: Istiadah

Istiadah (1999), 'Pembagian Kerja dalam Rumah Tangga Menurut Islam' [Division of Chores in the Household According to Islam], pp. 23–56 in *Pembagian Kerja Rumah Tangga dalam Islam* [Sharing of Household Chores in Islam], Lembaga Kajian Agama dan Jender, Jakarta. Extract: pp. 41–4.

The problem is, does *qawwam* [the singular form of *qawwamuna*] mean that the relationship between a husband and wife must be like that between a boss and his subordinates? To answer this question, we will recount the example set by the Prophet, as the most authentic interpreter [of God's word], in his relationship with his wives. Historians have not found examples in the Prophet's family where the [relationship between] husband and wife was like that between a boss and his subordinates, even though [the Prophet] was a person who had great power and authority in determining Islamic law. Historians have instead found the opposite. The Prophet was well known as a very tolerant husband who always treated his wives gently. He was very lenient with his wives, [and] it is this that, according to historians, made the Prophet's wives occasionally seem too forthright with him: some of them were outspoken with him, contradicted him, or angered and upset him all day. [pp. 41–2] [...]

[A Hadith is recounted to support this point.]

This example of the Prophet's behaviour within his family makes it increasingly clear to us that God's messenger, who was commanded to set a good example, never dominated women, or made them servants or slaves, [and] was never harsh, either physically or mentally. [pp. 43–4]

* * * * *

Commentary   The following extract is the result of a three-year project undertaken by the organization Forum Kajian Kitab Kuning (FK3, Forum for the Study of Kitab Kuning). *Kitab kuning* (literally, 'yellow books') are the Arabic texts used in traditionalist *pesantren* throughout Indonesia. The project examined one of the most popular texts used to teach women and girls about their obligations as wives and mothers according to Islam, *Syarh 'Uquud al-Lujjayn fi Bayan Huquq al-Zawjayn* [Commentary on the Joining of the Two Oceans Explaining the Rights of Husbands and Wives] by Sheikh al-Nawawi of Banten (1813–98). It sought to identify where weak or false Hadith, or ones the FK3 team could not find, had been used to support a gender-biased position, and to identify contradictions between Hadith. It was originally published in Arabic, to increase the likelihood that it would be read in *pesantren*.[32] A second book was due out in mid-2005.

Extract 13-18: Forum Kajian Kitab Kuning (FK3)

Forum Kajian Kitab Kuning (2003), 'Kewajiban Istri terhadap Suami' [Duties of a Wife to Her Husband], pp. 43–108 in *Wajah Baru Relasi Suami–Istri: Telaah Kitab 'Uqud al-Lujjayn* [The New Face of Husband–Wife Relations: A Study of the Book *'Uquud al-Lujjayn*], Lembaga Kajian Islam dan Sosial in cooperation with FK3 and the Ford Foundation, Yogyakarta (first published 2001). Extract: pp. 43–6.

God, the Almighty and most worthy of praise, decreed:

[verse in Arabic script]

Men are the leaders of women [and], because of that God has favoured some of them (men) above others of them (women) and because they (men) provide some of their wealth to support them [women]. The pious woman is obedient to God and guards herself when her husband is absent from home, because God guards them. Women whom you fear will be recalcitrant, advise them, and keep away from their bed, and strike them. Then if they obey you, do not seek reasons to make it difficult for them (QS. An-Nisa: 34).[33]

What is meant by men being the leaders of women is that husbands have the authority to educate their wives. God placed men above women because men (husbands) financially support women (wives) in marriage by providing a dowry and household expenses.[34]

Based on this verse (an-Nisa: 34), the majority of jurisprudence (*fiqh*) scholars and exegetes are of the opinion that leadership (*qiwaamah*) positions are limited to men only and are not open to women, because men are superior in managing, thinking, and in physical and mental strength. Women, on the other hand, are usually

---

32   For a sympathetic review of the FK3 book and its aims, see Sukidi (n.d.).
33   Q4: 34 is given in footnote 2.
34   In the framed section, the author is quoting the original text of *'Uquud al-Lujjayn.*

weak and incapable, causing the ulema to consider the superior character of men to be absolute. This point has given rise to the view that leadership by men is God's unchangeable law and does not need to be debated any further. Their opinion is that because men are the leaders, then women are not permitted to take public office, which would make it possible for them to be more powerful than men, even if only as a partner. According to the ulema, this verse clearly demonstrates that only men, and not women, may become *qiwaamah* (leaders), because women are considered incapable of managing household problems, let alone public affairs. Despite discussion of this verse that concludes that the issue of leadership is relevant only to family life, the ulema have used this verse as supporting evidence (*hujjah*) to forbid women from holding public office.

Other ulema are of the opinion that the relationship between men and women in public affairs is a power relationship.

In the Qur'an the leadership position of men is mentioned only in the context of discussion about relations between husband and wife which require one party to lead, and therefore this passage cannot be interpreted to mean leadership in general.

The ulema have different opinions regarding the capability of women to hold public office. The first view is that they should not hold any public office. The second view is that they are permitted to hold public office but may not be Caliph. And the third view is that women may hold public office, but only up to the position of judge.

Apart from all that, we will discover the divine wisdom of God if we carefully examine the use of the phrase 'because Allah has given superiority to some men over some women'. The versions 'because Allah has given superiority to men over women' or 'because it is the superiority of men that defeats women' are not used. Therefore, according to the existing version, the superiority of men is not absolute and not all individual men are superior to all individual women. [pp. 43–5] [...]

From the perspective of current social reality, in our opinion, the superiority of men over women [...] is not entirely correct. For example, many female school and university students have attained higher levels of education and academic achievement than males. This shows that the intellect and cleverness of men does not surpass that of women. Therefore, women are surely capable of becoming scientists, ulema or leaders if they are given the same opportunities as men.

The same argument applies to physical and mental strength; these are relative. [p. 46]

* * * * *

Commentary   The following extract is from a book published in response to the FK3 publication above, defending the text of Nawawi of Banten and its use in *pesantren*, and criticizing the methodology and content of the FK3 publication. It was produced by an organization calling itself Forum Kajian Islam Tradisional (FKIT, Forum for the Study of Traditional Islam), formed by the Pasuruan branch of the NU-affiliated *pesantren* association, Rabithah Ma'ahid Islamiyah (Association of Islamic Pesantren). FKIT consists of a number of young *kiai* from various *pesantren*.[35]

---

35   For more information on FKIT, see <http://www.hidayatullah.com/index.php?option=com_content&task=view&id=1482&Itemid=0>, accessed 18 May 2005.

Extract 13-19: *Forum Kajian Islam Tradisional (FKIT)*

Forum Kajian Islam Tradisional Pasuruan (2004), 'Kewajiban Istri terhadap Suami' [Duties of a Wife to Her Husband], pp. 69–128 in *Menguak Kebatilan dan Kebohongan Sekte FK3 dalam Buku 'Wajah Baru Relasi Suami-Istri, Telaah Kitab 'Uqud al-Lujjayn'* [Revealing the Iniquities and Lying of the Sect FK3 in the Book 'The New Face of Husband–Wife Relations: A Study of the Book *'Uquud al-Lujjayn*'], Rabithah Ma'ahid Islamiyah, Pasuruan District. Extract: pp. 69–72.

> FK3 (page 44). Based on this verse (an-Nisa: 34), the majority of jurisprudence (*fiqh*) scholars and exegetes are of the opinion that leadership (*qiwaamah*) positions are limited to men only and are not open to women, because men are superior in managing, thinking, and in physical and mental strength. Women, on the other hand, are usually weak and incapable, causing the ulema to consider the superior character of men to be absolute. This point has given rise to the view that leadership by men is God's unchangeable law and does not need to be debated any further.

Response.

In the commentary above, FK3 tries to sway the reader to its point of view by using a sophistic argument that falsifies the existence of an opinion. In verse 34 above, which was revealed in connection with the relations between husband and wife, it is stressed that men are the leaders of women. There is no possibility that this verse could have any meaning other than this one, and so there is no scope for anyone to extrapolate from it or have a differing opinion on it. This law is, therefore, the opinion of all ulema. However, FK3 uses a sentence that implies the existence of differing opinions:

> the majority of *fiqh* scholars and exegetes are of the opinion that leadership (*qiwaamah*) positions are limited to men only and are not open to women.

This sentence implies that there has been a divergence of opinion between the 'majority of *fiqh* scholars and exegetes' and 'other minorities'. We ask, who are these minority groups that are brazen enough to have a different opinion on this definitive text? Can FK3 prove the existence of this 'minority' with its different opinions? Undoubtedly they cannot prove this, unless this 'minority' is drawn from among adherents of gender equality as propounded by Jewish and Masonic organizations.

From here the ulema conclude that if in the smallest community, the household, men must lead, then in a larger community like the state, which leads thousands or even millions of households, women should not be given that right. Here we ask FK3, is there a weakness in the conclusion reached by analogy (*qiyas*) here, both rationally (*dalil 'aqli*)[36] as well as traditionally (*dalil naqli*),[37] all the more so given that the version reads '*men are the leaders of women*', and not '*husbands are the leaders of their wives*', so that the implication is more general? If there is no weakness, then this conclusion should be accepted. Also, what is the difference between

---

36 An argument based on reasoning.
37 An argument of principle based on a quotation from the Qur'an or a Hadith.

the implication deduced by FK3 from the story of Queen Bilqis above, as an argument for the capacity of women to lead the public, although this implication is weak as we have discussed, and the implication deduced by the ulema that if in the smallest community women do not have the right to lead, then they certainly do not in larger communities?

Meanwhile, FK3's commentary, 'this point gives rise to the view that leadership by men is God's unchangeable law and does not need to be debated any further', is not a rational argument, but is instead biased, tendentious and aimed at planting hate in the hearts of readers towards the opinions of the majority of ulema. In addition, this commentary gives the impression that the majority argument is found only in verse 34 Surat al-Nisa'. If the work of FK3 were truly rational, then FK3 would have presented all of the majority arguments of the ulema against allowing women to hold public office and discussed them honestly one by one. And FK3 would have had no difficulty in doing so. Are not the majority arguments found in various works, including works possessed by FK3 such as *Fath al-Bari*,[38] *Faidh al-Qadir*[39] and *al-Fiqh al-Islami* by al-Zuhaili?[40] But this is not the place to outline all the arguments on public office.

> FK3 (page 44). Because men are superior in managing, thinking, and in physical and mental strength. Women, on the other hand, are usually weak and incapable, causing the ulema to consider the superior character of men to be absolute.

Response.

FK3's argument, 'causing the ulema to consider the superior character of men to be absolute', is misguided. Firstly, because men have been given their superiority over women by God, and secondly, because the ulema do not deny the possibility of the existence of an individual woman who is superior to men. However, as Ibn Asyur has said, 'the superiority of an individual female is something rare. Therefore, the sharia laws of Islam are valid as a natural majority system, because the creator of the two types is one'. Therefore it is accepted that it is unnecessary to look for further argumentation. [pp. 69–71] [...]

The ulema who are of the opinion that women may not hold public office have been the foremost ulema in every period of time. Self-evident and implicit argumentation based on sharia supports their views.

On the other hand, the opinion that relations between men and women in public affairs is a power relationship does not have strong argumentation, but only sophistic arguments that are weaker than a spider's web. And what is wrong with the above verse being taken as implying by analogy that women are not permitted to hold public office?

It must be explained that although the verse was revealed in the context of husband and wife relations, its scope is wider through argument by analogy, whereby if

---

38 Well-known commentary on the Hadith collection of Bukhari by Ibn Hajar Asqalani (d. circa 1448 CE).

39 Well-known book of jurisprudence by al-Imam al-Munawi (d. circa 1466 CE).

40 Dr al-Zuhaili is a contemporary Syrian scholar of jurisprudence.

in the household women are forbidden from being leaders and must submit to men, this is more so in leading a nation-state that automatically leads thousands or even millions of households. [p. 72]

13.3.3 Women in the Public Sphere

Commentary The issues of women's work and the leadership of the husband in the family are both linked to participation of women in the public sphere. Work takes women away from the domestic sphere, and man's leadership in the family is often presented as the basis for his obligation to represent the family in the public sphere. However, there is widespread acceptance in Southeast Asia of women having a public role. The question is, what type of public role, and to what level of social participation can a woman realistically aspire?

The following fatwa on the position of women in Islam was issued by NU at its mid-term congress in 1997. It clearly lays out its decision that women have a right to a public role while at the same time affirming women's reproductive role as primary. According to some commentators, it sets no limits upon the political heights a woman can reach, but this interpretation has been contested by others who argue it does not allow a woman to hold the highest office in the nation (van Doorn-Harder 2002: 175). The other major Islamic organization in Indonesia, Muhammadiyah, accepted women's public and political role as early as 1972.[41]

Extract 13-20: NU Fatwa on the Position of Women in Islam

'Keputusan Musyawarah Nasional Alim Ulama Nahdlatul Ulama Tahun 1418H/ 1997M, Nomor: ..... 004/Munas/11/1997 tentang Kedudukan Wanita dalam Islam' [Decision of the Nahdlatul Ulama National Ulema Consultation 1418 H/1997 No. ..... 004/11/1997 Concerning the Position of Women in Islam], pp. 55–60 in *Hasil-Hasil Musyarawarah Nasional Alim Ulama & Konferensi Besar Nahdlatul Ulama* [Decisions of the Nahdlatul Ulama National Ulema Consultation & Grand (that is, mid-term) Conference], Jakarta. Extract: pp. 57–60.

Islam gives women the same rights as men to devote themselves to religion, home-land, people and state. [p. 57] […]

[Quotes from the Qur'an and Hadith are presented to support this statement.]

It must be acknowledged that men do indeed have different functions [from those of women] that are caused by *natural and innate (qodrati/fitri) differences*. There are

---

41   See 'Mendudukkan Perempuan Melalui Fikih' [Giving Women a Place through Jurisprudence], <http://www.republika.co.id/mycetak_berita.asp?id=139533>, dated 12 September 2003, accessed 3 June 2005. The decision was made by Majlis Tarjih at the 1972 congress and published as a booklet called 'Adabul Maräh Fil Islam' [Ethics of Women in Islam]. In 2001, it was decided that women could be elected to the Central Board of Muhammadiyah. However, when elections were held at the national conference in July 2005, no women were elected. See 'Gender Issue Overshadows Muhammadiyah Congress', <www.thejakartapost.com>, dated 12 July 2005, accessed 12 July 2005.

also roles in social life for both men and women that are *not predetermined by kodrat* (*non-kodrati*). Each has responsibilities that need to be shouldered and carried out with the support of the other. Such are the words of Almighty God:

> The believers, both men and women, support each other; they order what is right and forbid what is wrong (Sura at-Taubah: 71). [in Arabic script] [Q9: 71, Haleem][42]

The true and natural role of women is the domestic role, of being pregnant, giving birth, breastfeeding, being the primary educator of children and other functions associated with the family that clearly cannot be replaced by men. Almighty God decreed:

> He creates whatever He will – He grants female offspring to whoever He will (Sura Asy-Syura 49). [in Arabic script] [Q42: 49, Haleem][43]

And Islam has set down the rights and duties of women in family life, which must be accepted and followed by both husband and wife.

However, there is also the *public role* of women, where women as members of society and as citizens with state and political rights have demanded that they have a more distinct, transparent and protected social role.

According to the principles of Islam, women are permitted to have *public roles* and are therefore viewed as being capable and having the capacity to hold such public and social roles.

In other words, the position of women in this complex society and nation-state system is wide open, although their quality, capacity, capability and acceptability must be the yardstick. At the same time, the main natural and particular role of women should also not be forgotten.

NU has the responsibility to initiate cultural transformation and promote equality, empowerment and the participation of Indonesian women in the non-predetermined sectors. This in turn will help advance national development in this era of globalization. [pp. 58–60]

* * * * *

> ***Commentary***   The NU fatwa does not directly address the question of whether there are limits on what roles a woman can have in public life. Other groups, however, do set limits, one of which concerns women's ability to function as judges in religious courts. A question on this topic evinced the following answer from SyariahOnline.

Extract 13-21: *SyariahOnline*

SyariahOnline, 'Wanita Jadi Pemimpin?' [Can Women Become Leaders?], <http://syariahonline.com/konsultasi/?act=view&id=1506>, dated 11 June 2003, accessed 21 June 2005.

---

42   The full text of the verse is: 'The believers, both men and women, support each other; they order what is right and forbid what is wrong; they keep up the prayer and pay the prescribed alms; they obey God and His Messenger. God will give His mercy to such people – God is almighty and wise' (Q9: 71, Haleem).

43   'God has control of the heavens and the earth; He creates whatever He will – He grants female offspring to whoever He will' (Q42: 49, Haleem).

Answer:
Women are permitted to hold government office, such as that of queen, president, prime minister and the like, so long as they are not in the highest rank, that is, the Great Authority. For the same reason women may not be judges, as that work generally requires the strength of mind and endurance of a man.

If the position in question is general, of a usual character and does not demand extreme mental endurance, then basically there are no prohibitions against women holding it. This is especially so in all-women communities or groups. However, in a mixed community of men and women, the rules of proper behaviour and association between men and women apply.

In general, positions like this do not contravene the rule of leadership, of men higher than [wo]men. It is not forbidden for a woman to become the superior of men in an organization or company. There is also no prohibition on women who want to become teachers or lecturers of men. [...]

4. Appearing in public
Under normal conditions, it is men who should stand up in front of a public gathering consisting of both men and women. However, under certain circumstances where there is an objective need, determined by either a general or special condition, and there is no one who can do it other than the woman involved, then she may appear in public to deliver predication or give a lesson, providing she abides by Islamic principles.

* * * * *

> *Commentary* In Indonesia, women can be (and are) appointed to the sharia courts to deal with family law matters that come under the jurisdiction of the Marriage Law of 1974 (Noriani 2002: 22–3). In Malaysia, however, women are not eligible to become judges, an issue raised by Sisters in Islam in their 2002 working paper. More recently, in October 2004, the Malaysian magazine *al Islam* featured a discussion of the issue.

Extract 13-22: Noorzila Jamaludin on Mohd. Na'im Mokhtar

Noorzila Jamaludin (2004), 'Hakim Lelaki Pun Emosional' [Even Male Judges Are Emotional], *al Islam*, October: 52–6. Extract: pp. 52–5.

Clear differences in the views of ulema are common in discussion of various issues in Islam, especially if there does not exist a definitive verse [from the Qur'an or Hadith] that forbids or permits something. It is the same with the issue of women as judges. Although the opinion of the majority of ulema is that women are not permitted to be judges, there are also ulema who do permit this.

The Sharia adviser to Bumiputra Commerce Trustee,[44] Mohd. Na'im Mokhtar, discusses this issue based on the various views of the ulema, and explains why, in

---

44   Part of Bumiputra-Commerce Trust Ltd, which is a subsidiary of Bumiputra-Commerce Banking Group, one of the largest banking groups in Malaysia.

his opinion, there is benefit in appointing women judges to the Sharia Court in this country today.

Mohd. Na'im Mokhtar has also served as a Judge of the Lower Sharia Court, Federal Territory, and Petaling, Selangor.

[The rest of the extract quotes Mohd. Na'im Mokhtar.]

'In general, there are three views regarding women judges in discussions among the ulema. The majority of ulema do not permit the appointment of judges from among women. The second view, presented by the ulema of the Hanafi school, does permit women to be appointed to the Islamic judiciary for all except *hudud*[45] and *qisas*[46] cases. Finally, the views of Ibnu Jarir and Ibnu Hazm[47] permit women judges for all cases, including *hudud* and *qisas*.

'The argument used by the majority of ulema in opposing the appointment of women judges is an-Nisa: 34 [Q4: 34], which states that **"Men are the leaders of women, because Allah has given extra to them (men) …"**.[48]

'Interpreting the concept of *fadhalallah* [Ar.: *fadlul-lahi*; giving preference; see footnote 30] in this verse, al-Mawardi[49] is of the opinion that "the extra" that a man possesses relates to intellectual and thinking ability.

'Second, they refer to the Hadith recorded by an-Nasai, Tirmizi and Ahmad, which states that the Prophet said, "There will be no success for any society that surrenders its affairs to women".

'A third argument used by the majority of ulema relies on the analogy between a judge (*qadi*) and a supreme leader (*imamatul uzma*). Since women are not allowed to be appointed caliph, so by analogy they cannot be appointed judges.

'The interpretations used by the majority of ulema consist of several types; first, to close the source of all sin (*sad al-zarai'*), which can be viewed as referring to association between men and women. They say the work of a judge requires the presence of witnesses, and the need to come forward to ask various questions. This can lead to unfounded accusations against the woman.

'Second, the appointment appears to place a woman at the front, when there is a Hadith that says, "turn your back towards the women in the way that they sit behind you during prayer". Using this Hadith as a guide, the ulema state that women must not be appointed as judges because the Prophet asked that women be placed at the back. They use the analogy between the appointment of women judges and this Hadith as if the appointment places women in front of and ahead of men, and that contradicts this Hadith.

'Third, they draw an analogy between prayer and judges. According to them, if women cannot lead prayers, then it is even more the case that they cannot become judges, because the position of a judge is higher than that of an imam during prayer.

---

45   *Hudud* is a category of punishment in sharia law for offences such as adultery, theft and apostasy which have defined penalties.

46   *Qisas* (compensation) is one of the defined penalties for a *hudud* offence.

47   Two famous scholars of medieval classical jurisprudence.

48   Q4: 34 is given in footnote 2.

49   A famous scholar of medieval classical Shafi'i jurisprudence.

'Fourth, transvestites are placed even further back in the prayer row, behind women. They argue that if transvestites, who have the inclination to be women while still having male characteristics, cannot be appointed as judges, then it is even more the case that real women cannot be appointed to hold that position.

'Fifth, women are more emotional and less able to control their emotions than men, and because of this they are not suited to hold a judicial position, which requires a person whose emotions and thoughts are stable.

'Sixth, women experience certain ailments, such as having periods, that do not allow them to hear a case, and this causes the case to be postponed, and injustice to those involved. These ulema believe having periods reduces women's control over the emotions, causing them to get angry easily.

'The last reason why the majority of ulema do not allow the appointment of women judges is that there were no women appointed to the position during the time of the Prophet and his Companions.

'On the other hand, the reasons given by the Hanafi school for permitting the appointment of a woman judge are based on the analogy of a woman giving testimony under oath. Because the Hanafi school does not allow a woman to give testimony under oath in *hudud* and *qisas* cases, women cannot be made judges in these cases but can in other cases.

'Ibnu Jarir and Ibnu Hazm, furthermore, draw an analogy between judges and the institution of fatwa. When issuing a fatwa, it is not a condition that one must be a woman or a man, so the same condition can be used in the appointment of a judge.

'They saw that in the time of the Companions, the person issuing the most fatwa was the wife of the Prophet, Aisyah. Because Aisyah was permitted to issue fatwa, women are permitted to be judges without limitation, including for *hudud* and *qisas* cases. [pp. 52–3] [...]

'With regard to the *sad al-zarai'* argument used by the majority of ulema, this group [those in favour of women's appointment] further argue that if we concentrate too much on that question, we will lose a greater benefit (*maslahah*); that is, the ability and wisdom of women will be sidelined if the principle of *sad al-zarai'* is followed.

'In weighing up the [possibility of] slander, which must be avoided, against the benefits gained from appointing fair-minded women as judges, the greater public benefit comes from appointing female judges.

'Based on these views, it can be concluded that it is essential that women of ability be appointed as judges. A respected contemporary ulema, Dr Yusuf al-Qaradawi,[50] also supports this view. Moreover, nowadays there is general benefit in appointing women as judges.

'Nevertheless, women who are appointed as judges must possess deep knowledge, not be burdened by complex household problems and observe limits in social relations. They must also balance excellence in their careers with the management of their homes, as well as the education of their children.

---

50 See chapter 11 in particular for more information on this influential scholar.

'No matter what, the ability of an individual is the main criterion for appointment to this position. Other criteria also need to be taken into account, for example whether a candidate is married, as this affects the views and confidence of society. The level of society's confidence in a judge is important in safeguarding respect for the Sharia Court.

'But this does not mean that a candidate (man or woman) who is not married cannot be appointed as a judge.

'Differences in opinions and arguments such as this are common in discussions among the ulema. We respect their views, but what is important is that when we wish to practise a certain thing, we look at its suitability for the present age, as long as it is not an issue that falls into the *qati*[51] category.

'This mistaken view of the experts in Islamic jurisprudence (*fuqaha*) has to be seen in the context of a blessing for the Islamic community, especially in the social context of this age. The view of the majority of ulema forbidding women to be judges might have been suitable for their times. But in today's context, other views permitting it are a blessing for us.

'This is what has become an important principle in the way of thinking of various groups in this country. I am inclined to accept the view permitting women to be judges, while at the same time respecting the views of the majority of ulema that forbid it.

'I see this necessity from two angles. First, the achievement of women in education in this country is very good. In local universities, the achievement of female students is better than that of male students, including in the Diploma of Judicial Administration course, which focuses on producing sharia officials for the Sharia Court: judges, registrars, prosecutors, arbitration officers and lawyers.

'In this course, students are taught the tasks of a judge: procedure, protocol and so on. Most of the students in the course are women; sometimes the ratio is 70:30. In examinations, the 10 best students are also women.

'When they leave, those who pass are qualified to be judges, but the 70 per cent who are women students (including the 10 best graduates) are not permitted to become judges, although they can hold other positions. In the end we will lose these clever women who have been trained and have the ability to be judges.

'Besides that, when society looks at the judges of the Sharia Court, who are currently all men, [it sees them] as biased against women. This perception exists and will continue until women are appointed as judges. At least if they were to be appointed, we could prove whether the hypothesis were true or false. Is it true that the question of bias in the Sharia Court is linked with the gender of male judges? So far, the hypothesis is true because we just do not have any other yardstick; women have never been appointed as judges in the Sharia Court.

'If trained women are appointed as judges, at the very least this community perception would be tested. Academics could carry out social research for this purpose.

---

51   The term *qati* or *qat'i* (Ar.: *qat'iyyun*) describes a definitive or categorical principle in the Qur'an or Hadith whose meaning cannot be negotiated or reinterpreted.

Furthermore, in the context of the Sharia Court, the scope of its [the court's] authority involves family cases: men and women.

'In view of this benefit (*maslahah*), we should look at the views of the ulema and the objections presented against the appointment of women as judges. Although there is a view that the position of a sharia judge is critical, and that the appointment of women to hold the position will give rise to problems because of maternity leave and the like, this does not mean that we should explicitly forbid the appointment of women as judges.

'Personally, I am of the opinion that the integrity of the courts rests with the individual judges. When we speak of producing courts of world standard, we look at the individuals in those courts, not just their structure. Most important are the judges, because they are the ones who are seen to carry out justice or otherwise.

'If we appoint judges based on gender without looking at ability, understanding and deep knowledge, then we will be forced to take those who come last in the examination to become judges just because they will not take maternity leave.

'We will be forced to take judges from among those who are less academically qualified, have less understanding and have less intellectual capability. Such judges are not capable of evaluating the facts presented by the parties involved or of determining whether a fact is relevant or not, and then are not able to relate it to the law. This will cause mistakes in making decisions, and thus injustice.

'So this issue is very closely related to the intellectual ability of a judge as an individual. What is the difference between the intellectual ability of a man and a woman? I do not see any difference based on my experience teaching the Diploma of Judicial Administration course. The examination questions given are based on real cases in court, and the best answers come from women students.

'Further, from the point of view of emotions, we have heard cases of judges (males) who show their anger by throwing files, shouting at witnesses or uttering words that are not appropriate for a judge. Does this not involve controlling the emotions?' [pp. 54–5]

* * * * *

Commentary   On 18 March 2005, the American woman Amina Wadud led Friday prayers before a mixed congregation at a place of worship in New York. This act had resonance throughout the Southeast Asian region, but especially in Malaysia because of Wadud's connection to Sisters in Islam, and a previous controversy she had aroused in Malaysia.[52]

The following extract from an article issued by Jabatan Kemajuan Islam Malaysia (Jakim, Malaysian Department of Islamic Development) represents the commonly held position of Muslims in Southeast Asia and, indeed, the Muslim world that a woman

---

52   At an international forum on AIDS and HIV in Kuala Lumpur in 2003, Amina Wadud was accused of attacking Islam and the Quran. 'Amina Wadud, Isu Lama Berulang Kembali' [An Old Issue Returns Again], <http://www.harakahdaily.net/print.php?sid=12276>, dated 24 March 2005, accessed 9 May 2005.

cannot lead prayers before an audience where men are present.[53] Jakim is the central body for the organization and administration of Islamic affairs in Malaysia.

Extract 13-23: Jakim

Ghafani Awang The, 'Suara JAKIM: Agenda Amina Wadud Persenda Hukum Islam' [The Voice of Jakim: Amina Wadud's Agenda in Ridiculing Islamic Law], <http://www.islam.gov.my/portal/lihat.php?jakim=120>, dated 8 March 2005, accessed 9 May 2005.

The main issue in Amina Wadud's latest actions concerns her acting as imam at Friday prayers and giving the sermon, where every row of people praying included both men and women.

Amina Wadud's action in becoming the first Muslim woman in the world to act as imam at Friday prayers and give the sermon has been criticized by ulema throughout the world, including Sheikh Yusuf al-Qardhawi.[54]

According to Sheikh Yusuf al-Qardhawi, experts in Islamic jurisprudence (*fuqaha*) are united in agreement that women are forbidden from being imam at Friday prayers and from reading the sermon. This opinion is based on teachings, and not on the custom of a particular community as has been claimed, [said al-Qardhawi] when giving further reasons to the news agency Islam Online concerning women being forbidden to act as imam for prayers for a male congregation, namely:

- Never in the history of Islam has there been a woman who has become imam at Friday prayers and read the sermon;
- There has not been even one *fuqaha* who has agreed to allow a woman to be imam at Friday prayers and read the sermon;
- Prayer in Islam involves the act of carrying out various movements, both physical and spiritual. It does not consist merely of religious ritual and the non-mixing of men and women. Religious prayer in Islam requires the full attention of the mind, feeling, and giving the heart completely to God.

Islam outlines various rules to ensure that its followers worship God in a manner that is orderly and civilized, in order to achieve complete attentiveness in performing the worship of God.

In line with the greatness of worship, therefore, Islam sets out various guidelines for its performance.

In the rules for performing communal prayer by men and women, the Prophet said: 'The best row for prayer for men is the first row and the worst row [for them] is the last, whereas the best row for women is the row that is right at the back and the worst is the first row' (related by Muslim). [Hadith]

---

53 At the National Congress of Majelis Ulama Indonesia (MUI, Indonesian Council of Ulama) held in July 2005, MUI issued the following fatwa: 'Women are forbidden from leading prayers when men are present in the congregation. Women are only allowed to lead prayers in an all-female assemblage' ('The 11 Fatwas Issued by MUI', <www.thejarkartapost.com>, 11 August 2005).

54 Also spelled al-Qaradawi. See chapter 11 for more information on this influential scholar.

This Hadith is a genuine Hadith. It gives a rule and discipline for communal prayer in the worship of Almighty God.

Islam allows a woman to be the imam for a congregation of women only. Various Hadith related by al-Baihaqi and Darqatani state that Aisyah and Ummu Salamah (the Prophet's wives) were imam for congregations of women only. [...]

In the Hadith related by Bukhari and Muslim, it is furthermore stated that the profoundness and excellence of prayer will determine whether a person goes to heaven or hell. It is clear that prayer is a form of religious worship that is very profound and gives much benefit to the individual who achieves complete absorption in prayer. The high status and reality of prayer in shaping the character of the Islamic community is very clear when God Himself instructed the Prophet to perform the prayers during the Night Journey.[55]

The controversial act of a woman being imam at Friday prayers and reading the sermon very clearly did not take into consideration the high status and profundity of the reality of prayer.

* * * * *

> ***Commentary*** K.H. Husein Muhammad (see also extract 13-10) is known to have supported the position that women can lead prayers before a mixed congregation long before Amina Wadud actually did so. In an interview with Ulil Abshar-Abdalla of JIL, Kiai Husein argues that it is not true that all ulema oppose women leading prayers, and cites a number of prominent followers of the Shafi'i school of law (*madhhab*) to back up this claim. The following extract examines why such views are not well known, and the underlying reasons for defence of the status quo, before Kiai Husein gives his opinion of Wadud's controversial act.

Extract 13-24: Husein Muhammad

Excerpt from an interview with Husein Muhammad conducted by Ulil Abshar-Abdalla, 'KH Husein Muhammad dan Nur Rofi'ah: Perempuan Boleh Mengimami Laki-Laki', [K.H. Husein Muhammad and Nur Rofi'ah: Women May Lead Men in Prayer], Jaringan Islam Liberal, <http://islamlib.com/id/index.php?page=article&id =793>, dated 4 April 2005, accessed 16 May 2005.

Ulil Abshar-Abdalla (UAA): Why then is this view [that women may lead prayers] not very popular among the general public?

K.H. Husein Muhammad (HM): I think we need to question that. Our question is: why does this very long history of Islamic thought hide a lot of other aspects of Islamic thought that are not mainstream? I think that there are many progressive ideas and opinions regarding Islamic law – not just in relation to this issue, but also others – that are not popular and not brought to the fore. That's why I always say that the Islam we have inherited is political Islam; there are always political powers that

---

55 *Israk-Mikraj*, referring to Q42: 1, which has been interpreted to mean that the Prophet Muhammad miraculously ascended to heaven, where he was told to institute the daily prayers.

support particular views and seek to discredit others. In my opinion, the dominant views that have emerged and been supported by those in power in the long-lasting Muslim dynasties clearly show a patriarchal form of discourse.

UAA: So this issue is also closely related to the strength of the grip and domination of the patriarchal culture in Islamic society?

HM: Yes. I am very surprised as to why the patriarchal culture still dominates us. Actually, around the beginning of Islam, religious leaders' views on women were in fact quite progressive. But unfortunately history then turned this around. For many reasons, views on women then became less progressive, and reverted to staunch conservatism. [...]

UAA: What about the common concern that a woman's voice and her position as prayer leader in front of the congregation may cause sexual arousal among men?

HM: I think that the fault lies with our society's construction of sexuality, which is still strongly influenced by a patriarchal bias, and which constantly talks about sexual temptation. In this patriarchal construction of society and sexuality, men are always seen as susceptible to sexual temptation, and women are always seen as tempting men. I think beliefs such as this are over the top, especially if we are talking about the prayer context. And perhaps in other social constructions where these assumptions about temptation no longer exist, this matter would not be considered important. If there were no longer any fantasy or myth surrounding temptation, then there wouldn't be any obstacles to women becoming leaders of prayer services for men. The thing is, the classic Islamic texts refer to this issue too often. And it is always with the basic assumption that women are the source of scandal (*fitnah*).

UAA: If that's so, is it possible that Amina Wadud's attack will be applied in Indonesia?

HM: I think Amina Wadud has been very brave to symbolically oppose the traditions that are entrenched in the construction of Islamic law. So why don't we apply it in Indonesia? In my opinion, we still [need to] look at the context of the situation and the conditions in Indonesia today. If we did put it into practice, wouldn't extraordinary levels of dissension arise? We need to think about that further. What's important is a process of [social] conditioning first. This can be achieved through discourse on *fiqh* or views that allow female prayer leaders.

Steps like this are always important, I think, because, as we know, there was a time when it was difficult for women even to speak in public, because of religious interdiction. In fact, they are still not permitted to read the Qur'an in public. In the past Indonesian women were not allowed to take part in MTQ.[56] But now there is no ban on that here, although in many Middle Eastern countries it is still forbidden and considered taboo.

* * * * *

---

56   *Musabaqah Tilawatil Qur'an*: Contest of Qur'anic Recitation.

Commentary The small but influential Malaysian Muslim women's organization Wanita Pertubuhan Jamaah Islah Malaysia (Wanita JIM, Women of the Malaysian Reform Community) issued the following statement, which was also published on the website of the PAS newspaper, *Harakah Daily*. Wanita JIM, whose membership consists largely of middle-class professional women, expresses disapproval of Amina Wadud's action in this statement. Its reasons, however, differ from those of Jakim (extract 13-23), representing the 'mainstream' or conservative position. The extract is signed by Dr Harlina Halizah Hj Siraj, president of the Central Body of Wanita JIM.

Extract 13-25: *Wanita Pertubuhan Jamaah Islah Malaysia (Wanita JIM)*

Harlina Halizah Siraj, 'The Championing of Muslim Women Needs a Wise Approach' [in English], media statement by Wanita JIM, <http://www.jim.org.my/modules.php ?name=News&file=article&sid=144>, dated 25 March 2005, accessed 9 May 2005.

At the end of last week, the media reported about Amina Wadud acting as Imam and Khatib [speaker, preacher] for Friday Prayers that was attended by a group of men and women in Manhattan, New York. [...]

Wanita JIM has taken the position of rejecting any efforts and actions to introduce something that is an innovation to those pronouncements that have already been established in worship and that have been agreed upon by the majority of ulamas before this. Wanita JIM regards what happened in New York last Friday [as] a bold and extreme move that threatened the balance and harmony of the place of worship that before this day has been a center of activity for the Muslim ummah (community). The ruling that women cannot be the imam in group prayers and are placed in the back rows cannot be seen as an act to reduce the status of women. The truth of the matter is that it is a wise decision that had been practiced since the time of the Prophet PBUH [peace be upon him] to safeguard women.

Wanita JIM is well aware that the ruling that women cannot lead group prayers is not written in black and white in the Quran but the custom of the Prophet has become the guiding principle in establishing accepted practices for the ummah. Wanita JIM is aware that there are differing views among the ulama regarding women imams for jemaah [congregational] prayers that are attended by both men and women. Even so, Wanita JIM adopts the stance that if a woman whose knowledge and depth of understanding [of] the Quran and Hadith should qualify her to lead group prayers attended by men and women, then the best qualified would have been Saidatina Aishah, the prophet's wife r.a. [may God be pleased with her] as the first woman imam and the act of being a woman Imam need not have been started by a woman in metropolitan Manhattan 1400 years after Aishah r.a.

Wanita JIM is of the opinion that these rhetorical efforts only serve to hinder the genuine efforts of a group of sincere Muslims who are striving to improve the lot of Muslim women with a myriad of issues in which Muslim women have been left behind such as health, education, economy and leadership. The action of challenging a religious injunction on an aspect of worship that had been agreed upon for centuries since the dawn of Islam will only succeed in giving cheap publicity that does not in the least help to improve the lot of Muslim women trapped by poverty, culturally demeaning practices against women, and laws that do not reflect the justice that should be an integral part of Muslim law.

* * * * *

Commentary   Another area of public participation for women that has remained controversial is that of participation in politics, that is, standing as candidates in local or national elections or being involved in other political acts, including campaigning and protesting. While women have run as parliamentary candidates throughout the region for many decades, there is residual opposition to this among some Islamist groups.

In the decades leading up to the 1999 elections, the Islamic party PAS had run no women candidates for federal parliament. Prior to the 2004 elections in Malaysia, the women's wing of PAS, Muslimat PAS, published the following piece on its website.

Extract 13-26: Muslimat PAS

Dewan Muslimat PAS Pusat, 'Keperluan Memilih Calon Wanita' [The Need to Vote for Women Candidates], <http://muslimat.parti-pas.org/renungan_read.php?id=15>, dated 15 March 2004, accessed 5 October 2004.

The need to vote for women candidates

- To represent the voice of women, because the number of women continues to increase
- Women better understand the virtues, needs and wishes of women
- The violence that prevails in women's circles [i.e. against women] continues to rise: who should defend them?
- Women's leadership is increasingly needed, the voice of women is increasingly feared
- Women's leadership admits failure to defend women's status
    - women have been made into objects of trade;
    - women have been made into the stuff of advertisements;
    - the protection of women's *aurat* is not attended to;
    - the only thing that is emphasized is development.

THUS.......
IT IS FITTING THAT MUSLIM WOMEN BE GIVEN A CHANCE
WOMEN VERY MUCH NEED TO BE GIVEN RECOGNITION
BECAUSE...

WOMEN ARE MOTHERS
WOMEN ARE WIVES
WOMEN ARE ALSO OUR DAUGHTERS

BECAUSE OF THIS...
THEIR RIGHTS NEED TO BE RESPECTED

THEIR VOICE NEEDS TO BE HEARD
VOTE FOR A WOMAN CANDIDATE

* * * * *

Commentary   The following extract is a fatwa issued by the Sharia Council of PKS, an Islamist party in Indonesia. It was the only party to come close to meeting the voluntary 30 per cent quota for female candidates in the 2004 parliamentary elections.[57] The fatwa is cited on SyariahOnline in answer to a question.

Extract 13-27: Partai Keadilan Sejahtera (PKS)

SyariahOnline, 'Pandangan Fiqih Tentang Caleg Wanita' [Consideration of the *Fiqh* of Women in the Legislature], <http://syariahonline.com/konsultasi/?act=view& id=5368>, dated 28 January 2004, accessed 14 February 2005.

Answer: [...]
Politics is a means to carry out Enjoining of Good Deeds and Forbidding Evil, which God has made one of two principles that bring into being the best community (*umat*). The Islamic *umat* will not achieve virtue, good fortune and nobility anywhere unless every individual Muslim in the *umat* – female or male – wants to implement an Enjoining of Good Deeds and Forbidding Evil.

'You are the best community, born for humankind; [you] enjoin what is right and forbid evil and believe in God ...' (QS. 3:110).[58]

To enjoin good and forbid evil is a joint obligation, with Muslim women participating in this task along with Muslim men. As was declared by Almighty God:

'And the believing men and the believing women, some of them are helpers for others. They enjoin (to do) what is good and forbid what is evil, perform prayers, pay *zakat*, and they obey God and His Messenger' (QS. 9:71).[59]

These duties and obligations apply in the smallest environs, that is, the family, as well as the much broader environs, that is, the nation. The agent can be a person, an individual in society, [but] can also be a community or an institution, because

---

57   PKS met the quota in 65 of 69 electoral districts. However, in terms of seats actually won by women, PKS was only in eighth position. I am grateful to Alan Wall, former director of IFES Indonesia, for providing these figures. The Election Law covering the 2004 elections stated that parties should have at least 30 per cent female legislative candidates but it provided no penalties for not reaching this threshold.

58   '[Believers], you are the best community singled out for people: you order what is right, forbid what is wrong, and you believe in God. If the People of the Book had also believed, it would have been better for them. For although some of them do believe, most of them are lawbreakers' (Q3: 110, Haleem).

59   'The believers, both men and women, support each other; they order what is right and forbid what is wrong; they keep up the prayer and pay the prescribed alms; they obey God and His Messenger. God will give His mercy to such people – God is almighty and wise' (Q9: 71, Haleem).

disobedience of God's word can happen in the environs of the family, society as well as the nation. [...]

[The fatwa then describes the views of both those against women's involvement in parliament and those for it, before making the following judgement.]

Politics is an inseparable part of Islam.

Enjoining good and forbidding evil is a joint responsibility: [for] men and women.

Politics is a means to enjoin good and forbid evil, meaning that the participation of women in the political arena is a necessity.

The participation of women in the world of politics, including by becoming members of the legislature, is permitted on the basis of a real and urgent common good (*maslahat*), provided that the following conditions are fulfilled:

- [She] Receives permission from her husband.
- It doesn't disturb her household duties.
- There is the moral and structural capability to avoid scandal (*fitnah*).
- [She] Must take heed of Islamic regulations when she meets or gathers with men, in matters such as manner of speaking, dress, grooming, association with men without a close relative (*mahram*)[60] being present, or unlimited association.
- The participation of women in parliament is limited by the factor of need, and not limited in terms of specific numbers, whether minimum or maximum. This is in accord with the *fiqh* principle: intent (need) is measured in accordance with the limits of that need (Al Asybah Wan Nadzair).[61]

* * * * *

Commentary   The rise of Megawati Sukarnoputri as a political figure in Indonesia, first as head of Partai Demokrasi Indonesia-Perjuangan (PDI-P, Indonesian Democratic Party of Struggle), then as a front-running presidential candidate in 1999, brought to the fore the issue of whether a woman could become the leader (in this case president) of an Islamic nation (Platzdasch 2000; van Doorn-Harder 2002). Strong positions were taken on both sides of the debate; and there were claims, especially from those who supported the right of a woman to lead a Muslim nation, that the debate was being manipulated for political purposes.

The following extract is part of the conclusion to a book edited by Syafiq Hasyim, a prominent Indonesian commentator on issues of gender. The book contains articles by well-known Muslim public figures that examine the *fiqh* and practice of women as leaders in society, including the permissibility of a woman becoming ruler. Syafiq's conclusion argues against using a commonly cited Hadith to justify disqualifying women from leadership at the highest level.

---

60 *Mahram* literally means 'forbidden'. In Islamic law it describes close male relatives whom a woman may not marry. It is therefore permissible for a woman to be in their company.

61 *Al Asybah Wan Nadzair* [Analogies and Similarities] is the title of a book on jurisprudence.

Extract 13-28: *Syafiq Hasyim*

Syafiq Hasyim (ed.) (n.d.), 'Sebuah Kesimpulan' [A Conclusion], pp. 82–4 in *Kepemimpinan Perempuan dalam Islam* [Women's Leadership in Islam], Jaringan Pendidikan Pemilih untuk Rakyat, no place. Extract: pp. 82–3.

After reading all of the expositions on women's leadership in Islam presented by the authors above, several conclusions are offered as follows. However, the conclusions made here are merely a first step because genuine conclusions are left up to the conscience of each reader.

- The issue of female leadership is still debatable (*khilafiyah*). This means that not one religious proposition has established with certainty that women may not become state leaders. [...]
- There are differing interpretations of Hadith, as well as the Qur'an, on the issue of female leadership. Although the Hadith saying that 'it will be unlucky for a group to surrender its affairs to a woman'[62] is usually used to justify the prohibition on women becoming leaders, there is still a big question mark over it. First, according to Hadith experts, based on its quality this Hadith is included merely in the category of doubtful (*ahad*) Hadith.[63] According to these experts, Hadith in this category do not have a benefit that is definite enough (*qath'iy*)[64] to be used as the basis for making a legal decision. As this Hadith is still in the negotiable (*zhanny*)[65] category, then as Quraish Shihab[66] has made clear, it is possible to reinterpret it or even refute its validity. Second, if examined carefully from a historical viewpoint, that is, for the reasons it came into being, it turns out that this Hadith was a response to the inauguration of a Princess Kisra in Persia, who was considered by the Prophet to be incapable of leading the government. The Prophet's rejection of her was based not on the fact that she was female, but more on her being incapable of holding the reins of government. It is quite possible that if the woman in question had been more capable then the Prophet might not have made this Hadith. Given these two factors, we actually have sufficient reason not to use this Hadith as the means of terminating the right of women to lead. Therefore, from the perspective of Hadith, female leadership is not forbidden at all, and in fact the reverse, as there are still many other Hadith of greater weight and value that support female leadership.

---

62   This Hadith is given in the text as an Arabic transliteration as well as in Indonesian.

63   *Ahad* Hadith are Hadith whose veracity may be true, but they cannot be categorized as absolutely certain because they have not been transmitted by a sufficient number of people. For a brief guide to the classification of Hadith, see <http://www.usc.edu/dept/MSA/fundamentals/hadithsunnah/scienceof hadith/brief1/>.

64   A definition of *qath'iy* (Ar.: *qat`iyyun*) is given in footnote 51.

65   *Zhanny* or *dzanniy* (Ar.: *zanniyyun*) refers to meanings or principles taken from the Qur'an and Hadith that have been reached on the basis of expert argumentation. It therefore implies the use of human powers of deduction to interpret divine meaning.

66   Dr Quraish Shihab is an Indonesian Muslim scholar who has written a number of works on contextual interpretation of the Qur'an. He has held a number of important positions in Indonesia, including minister of religious affairs in the late Soeharto era, and chair of MUI.

13.3.4   Women's Appearance: The Headscarf Debate

Commentary   The issue of women's dress remains controversial in Southeast Asian Muslim societies. Until recent decades, the wearing of the headscarf – called a *jilbab* in Indonesia, a *tudung* in Malaysia and (less commonly) a *hijab* in English-language texts – was not widespread. In Indonesia, the reformist movement promoted the wearing of the *jilbab* for women in the 1920s and 1930s. However, while it was a clearly recognized symbol of piety, it is only since the 1980s that it has become more accepted and popular there. In Malaysia, the move to wear the headscarf began with the Islamic revival in the 1970s.

The following extract shows the importance placed on the wearing of the headscarf in order to cover a woman's *aurat* (those parts of her body that cannot be exposed in public). Many groups of Muslims understand this to be a command of God, and thus intrinsic to notions of personal piety and public propriety.

Extract 13-29: Pesantren Putri Pondok Modern Gontor

Pesantren Putri Pondok Modern Gontor (1997), 'Wanita dan Jilbab' [Women and the *Jilbab*], pp. 28–33 in *Materi Nisaiyah: Kulliyatu-l-Mu'allimat al Islamiyah* [Material for Women: Islamic College for Women Teachers], Book 4, no place. Extract: pp. 28–9, 31–3.

Islam considers women to have special character such that Islam deeply honours and values them. Islam has, therefore, set out some rules for women so that they can live with honour and purity as well as gaining heavenly happiness in the hereafter. These compulsory rules for women include wearing the *jilbab* and averting their gaze. God commanded:

[verse in Arabic script]

'O Prophet! say to your wives, your daughters and the wives of the believers, "They should extend their jilbabs over their entire bodies". This is so that they are more easily identified [as Muslims], and because of this they will not be disturbed ...' (Al-Ahzab 59).[67]

In the Hadith relating the life story of Asma, the daughter of Abu Bakar, the Prophet of God explained that women must cover their whole body save for the face and hands. Almighty God orders women to avert their gaze and forbids them from displaying any jewellery except to their *mahram*, as set out in an-Nuur verse 31; that is, they may only show jewellery to their *mahram*. God commanded:

'... and they may not reveal their ornaments except to their husbands, or their fathers, or the fathers of their husbands, or their sons, or the sons of their husbands, or their brothers, or their brothers' sons, or their sisters' sons, or Muslim women, or the slaves they possess, or the male servants who have no desire (for women), or the children who do not yet understand about the aurat *of women; and they may not strike their feet*

---

67   'Prophet, tell your wives, your daughters, and women believers to make their outer garments hang low over them so as to be recognized and not insulted: God is most forgiving, most merciful' (Q33: 59, Haleem).

so that the ornaments that they hide may be known. And all of you show repentance to God, O believers! so that you will have good fortune' (An-Nuur 31).[68]

Muslim men are responsible for commanding family members and others in their care to wear the *jilbab* and thus guard themselves and their honour. God commands women to wear the *jilbab* and avert their gaze for the purpose of guarding their integrity and purity. Of course, wearing the *jilbab* and averting one's gaze also has other social benefits, even economic ones. [pp. 28–9] [...]

C. REFLECTIONS ON THE *JILBAB*

All of Almighty God's commands contain benefits and goodness for humans and society. God has commanded women to wear the *jilbab* and avert their gaze because of the following spiritual and social benefits:

1. *Wearing the* Jilbab *Signifies Obedience to God*
   Pious Muslim women are those who can follow God's commands and avoid His prohibitions. They will say, 'We hear and obey. We ask for Your forgiveness, O our Lord. To You we return'. Muslim women will feel this whenever they carry out God's orders based on His command:

   '... And whoever obeys God and His Messenger has in fact already achieved a great victory' (al-Ahzab 71).[69]

2. *Wearing the* Jilbab *Signifies Being Accustomed to Adorning Oneself with a Sense of Modesty*
   If a woman loses her sense of modesty or does not guard it, then undoubtedly she has lost her way and become unchaste. The loss of modesty equates with being of little faith, and if a person's sense of modesty increases so too does their faith.

3. *Wearing the* Jilbab *Signifies the Curbing of Sexual Desires*
   Desire always leads humans to evil. The road to heaven is covered with thorns and the road to hell with pleasures. Muslim women who can overcome their instinct to dress up and exhibit themselves, and avert their gaze, will also be able to overcome their desires.

4. *Wearing the* Jilbab *Curbs the Desire to Exhibit Oneself and Display One's Ego*
   A Muslim woman who wears the *jilbab* will be able to concentrate her beauty on her husband, because Islam commands a woman to respect her husband's rights. She will therefore be able to avoid behaviour that harms her husband.

---

68 'And tell believing women that they should lower their gaze, guard their private parts, and not flaunt their charms beyond what [it is acceptable] to reveal; they should let their headscarves fall to cover their necklines and not reveal their charms except to their husbands, their fathers, their husbands' fathers, their sons, their husbands' sons, their brothers' sons, their sisters' sons, their womenfolk, their slaves, such men as attend them who have no sexual desire, or children who are not yet aware of women's nakedness; they should not stamp their feet so as to draw attention to any hidden charms. Believers, all of you, turn to God so that you may prosper' (Q24: 31, Haleem).
69 'and He will put your deeds right for you and forgive you your sins. Whoever obeys God and His Messenger will truly achieve a great triumph' (Q33: 71, Haleem).

5. *Wearing the* Jilbab *Protects Society from Social Disease*
   Adultery, divorce, family breakdown, the spread of crime, the birth of children out
   of wedlock and the consumption of liquor are social diseases caused by women
   not wearing the *jilbab*. Therefore, women who wear the *jilbab* protect society
   from social diseases. Many newspapers and magazines report that criminal activities are caused by women not wearing the *jilbab* and wearing transparent or sug-
   gestive clothing. If young men see these things they become sexually aroused and
   immediately behave in ways prohibited by Islam, including forgetting to study
   and work, thieving, swearing and lying. All this is caused by women who dress
   themselves up and do not wear the *jilbab*.

6. *Wearing the* Jilbab *Protects the Younger Generation from Sexual Freedom*
   Free sex between young men and women is forbidden, and is usually triggered
   by the presence of women not wearing the *jilbab* or dressed improperly. A way
   to avoid this kind of social behaviour is to stay away from women who are not
   wearing the *jilbab*, avoid sources of scandal, fast and pray to Almighty God. [pp.
   31–3]

*   *   *   *   *

> **Commentary**   In Indonesia, among pious or *santri* Muslims, the 'mainstream' view
> is that women are obliged to cover their *aurat* by wearing a headscarf. However, even
> among women who wear the headscarf, there are many who see the issue as one of
> personal choice, and object to any attempts to impose the headscarf on Muslim women.
> The drawing up in recent years of regional sharia regulations that often have as one of
> their first measures the obligation for women to wear the headscarf, has led to oppo-
> sition being voiced by many women activists. In the following extract on the effect
> on women of such regional sharia regulations, the noted 'liberal' Muslim scholar Dr
> Musdah Mulia sets out her fears and objections to such moves. After discussing regula-
> tions that restrict women's movement so as to prevent 'immoral deeds', she goes on to
> discuss the headscarf.

Extract 13-30: Siti Musdah Mulia

Excerpt from an interview with Siti Musdah Mulia conducted by Ulil Abshar-Abdalla,
'Dr Musdah Mulia: Saya Keberatan Kalau Jilbab Dipaksakan' [I Object to the *Jilbab*
Being Imposed], Jaringan Islam Liberal, <http://islamlib.com/id/index.php?page=
article&mode=print&id=176>, dated 23 September 2001, accessed 6 May 2005.

Several regional regulations say that women must wear Islamic dress, meaning the
headscarf (*jilbab*). I don't know where this has come from.

In your opinion, what is the crucial point here?

I think what is crucial is that I agree that Muslim women should wear the headscarf.
But if it is forced, I think it is not Islamic any more, because in my opinion anything
that is imposed is against the essence of Islamic teachings themselves. Religion must

be performed voluntarily, not by force. When there is a regulation, that means that there is force.

If we return to the legal basis of our state, our state is based on law; it is not an Islamic state. If the view is affirmed that Islamic sharia should be applied, I think that the legal basis of our state will need to be debated once more. [...]

I object to the headscarf being imposed on everyone. As a result there would be no freedom for a person to choose, even though in Islam itself there are many opinions regarding the *jilbab*. There are some who say that the *jilbab* is like what I am wearing, and others who say that it must cover everything except the eyes. There are also those who say that Islamic dress only has to cover some parts of the body. If a skirt comes below the knee, this is already in accord with Islamic teachings, because it is considered as covering the essential part.

* * * * *

Commentary In Southeast Asia as elsewhere, wearing the headscarf is not simply an issue of personal piety, but touches on matters of self and communal identity, state control, and minority rights in non-Muslim nations. The decision of the French government in 2004 to ban the wearing of headscarves in state schools as part of its initiative to prohibit the display of conspicuous religious symbols caused great consternation in Southeast Asia. The following letter to the editor from Sisters in Islam, reproduced here in full, gives an outline of these arguments in an international context.

Extract 13-31: Sisters in Islam

Sisters in Islam, 'What's With the Hijab?' [in English], letter to the editor, <http://www.sistersinislam.org.my/Letterstoeditors/120204.htm>, dated 12 February 2004, accessed 17 March 2005.

The West[ern] obsession with the hijab as a symbol of oppression and the Muslim obsession with the hijab as a symbol of piety are both misguided and misplaced.

In banning the wearing of Muslim headscarves and other 'ostentatious' religious symbols in schools, the French Republic has undermined its own fundamental belief in liberty, equality and fraternity. The freedom to teach, practice, worship and observe one's religion in public or in private, alone or in community with others is a fundamental right upheld by the Universal Declaration of Human Rights. This freedom can only be limited by law solely to respect the rights of others and to meet the just requirements of morality, public order and the general welfare in a democratic country.

In limiting this expression of religious freedom, France has not shown how the wearing of visible religious symbols could impinge on the rights of others or could impact adversely on public morality, order or welfare.

Sisters in Islam is opposed to any attempt by any government to legislate on dress – whether it is to force women to cover or uncover their heads. Those protesting the French law as an unjust limitation on freedom of religion must, by the same principle, also protest the state laws of Saudi Arabia and Iran which enforce compulsory hijab in public and the law of Turkey which bans it in public institutions.

What needs to be recognised is the fact that the debate and obsession with a piece of cloth on a woman's head is not so much about faith and piety, but about politics and identity. US President George [W.] Bush justified his war in Afghanistan in the name of liberating the oppressed Afghan women whose encasement under the burqa represents the ultimate symbol of the subjugated Muslim women. But we know today that as Afghanistan crawls towards constitutional democracy, the rights of the Afghan women to a life of equality, justice, freedom and dignity are not the priorities of the Bush administration, nor the United Nations or the interim government in Kabul.

Twenty-five years after the Iranian revolution, women in Iran are defying the religious authorities by displaying as much hair as possible from the front and back of their compulsory headscarves. This widespread display of 'bad' hijab is now beyond state control because the state has lost its legitimacy and moral authority to govern in the name of Islam.

Just as thousands of Muslim women wore the hijab as a symbol of protest against the despotic rule of the Shah of Iran, thousands of women today are defying the hijab ruling to protest against the clerics whose rule has not brought the promised life of justice, freedom and prosperity.

For some Muslims, the hijab is an expression of their faith. For others it is a symbol of their Muslim identity within a dominant non-Muslim environment. Yet, for many others, it is a symbol of resistance against a hegemonic West or an oppressive Government.

For many women from conservative families, the hijab is an empowering garment as it enables them to enter the public space, now regarded as safe and Islamic.

For the West today to view any woman in hijab as a threat to national security or national integration, or a symbol of backwardness, or piety and therefore militancy, is yet again to misunderstand the diversity of meanings, symbols and experiences of the Muslim community.

On the flip side of the same coin are the Muslims who misunderstand the legacy of the Islamic message regarding women as representing the sole pristine meaning of Islam – when this definition of the 'good' Muslim woman gained legitimacy not because it was the only possible interpretation, but because it was the interpretation of the politically dominant, who had the power to declare other readings as 'heretical'.

* * * * *

Commentary   As the above extract indicates, where governments impose restrictions on women or girls wearing the headscarf, the issue quickly becomes a human rights issue that is taken up broadly by the Muslim community. This happened in Indonesia in the 1970s and 1980s, and has been an important issue for Singapore's minority Muslim community since the beginning of 2002, when four young girls were suspended from state primary schools for wearing the *tudung* or *hijab*. The following extract from an interview with Hj Yoyoh Yusroh, a member of the Indonesian parliament for PKS, concerns the banning of the 'long *jilbab*', which covers the shoulders and chest as well as the head and neck, at Sekolah Tinggi Ilmu Statistik (STIS, College for Statistics) in Jakarta. Again, it shows how political the issue of the headscarf for women can become.

Extract 13-32: Yoyoh Yusroh

Excerpt from an interview with Yoyoh Yusroh conducted by Artawijaya, Eman Mulyatman and Heri D. Kurniawan, 'Bila Muslimah Lemah, Siapa Yang Membentengi' [If Muslim Women Are Weak, Who Will Serve as the Fortress?], *Sabili*, 17(10 March 2005): 32–5. Extract: pp. 33–4.

Can you tell us about the outcome of the meeting with the students from STIS?

I see that this is not a standalone issue. It is part of an international conspiracy. It follows on from the ban on wearing the *jilbab* in England and France, and even Germany has introduced a similar policy. Muslim women activists who thought things were safe [had settled down] were also surprised: this was an issue back in 1991, so why has it come up again?[70]

That's what happens with globalization: what takes place in other parts [of the world] can be seen here as well. I thought that with the government agreement on the *jilbab* issue (*SKB tiga menteri*) things had calmed down, but it seems not. There have been flare-ups at several campuses, especially state campuses. [...]

So has the ban on the *jilbab* at STIS taken place because of global pressure or is it just imitative behaviour?

It's just the rules at that particular campus. I mean, it has not come from the government as a result of global pressure. Because it is very much at odds with SBY's[71] statement forbidding women from displaying their midriffs. But God only knows if there is international pressure as a result of the campus incidents. That may be so. Because one strategy for advancing Westernization is through women. If Muslim women's defences are weak, who else will be able to defend Islamic values?

You mean this isn't a standalone issue?

Exactly. We see in Afghanistan, Iran, Turkey, how Kemal Attaturk[72] westernized Turkey. He began by banning the veil.

---

70 After several high-profile court cases in Indonesia in the late 1980s involving schoolgirls who had been forbidden to wear the *jilbab* to state schools, the Directorate General of Primary and Secondary Education issued a decree allowing the wearing of the *jilbab* in state schools (SK No.100/C/Kep/D/1991).

71 SBY: Susilo Bambang Yudhoyono, the president of Indonesia (2004–).

72 Mustafa Kemal Atatürk (1881–1938), founder and first president of the Republic of Turkey.

13.3.5   Reproductive Rights and Abortion

Commentary   The texts in section 13.1 focusing on women's piety and harmony in the family tend to concentrate on women's duties and responsibilities: to God, to their husbands, to their children, to their other relatives. The language of rights for women, while certainly not new in Islamic discourse in Southeast Asia, has been given renewed emphasis in recent years. Reproductive rights are just one of the areas that have been addressed within a framework of rights that all women should enjoy, as Muslims and as citizens.

In the following extract, Masdar Mas'udi of the NGO P3M gives an overview of his understanding of reproductive rights, derived from a woman's biological function of reproduction. His book was one of the first in the region to address such issues.

Extract 13-33: Masdar F. Mas'udi

Masdar F. Mas'udi (1997), 'Islam dan Hak-Hak Reproduksi Perempuan' [Islam and Women's Reproductive Rights], pp. 71–178 in *Islam dan Hak-Hak Reproduksi Perempuan: Dialog Fiqih Pemberdayaan* [Islam and Women's Reproductive Rights: The Dialogue of Empowering Jurisprudence], Mizan, Bandung. Extract: pp. 74–7.

What are women's reproductive rights?

Before we speak in greater detail about the reproductive rights of women, it is best if we understand prior to this that a woman's reproductive rights in Islam are nothing other than rights that must be guaranteed in full because of her reproductive function. These rights are in balance qualitatively with the rights possessed by men (husbands/fathers) as guardians of the function of production (the provision of financial support). In the Qur'an it is said:

[verse in Arabic script]

Women (wives) have rights which are in accordance with their responsibilities or the burdens borne by them, which have to be paid by the man (husband) in a proper manner (QS Al-Baqarah [2]: 228).[73]

And as the guardians of reproduction, women (mothers) possess rights that must be fulfilled by their men (husbands). There are three categories of rights for women/mothers as guardians of the function of reproduction. *First*, the right to guaranteed welfare (*keselamatan*) and health. This right is non-negotiable, remembering the very high risks women face in implementing their reproductive function, beginning with menstruation through to sexual relations, pregnancy, birth and breastfeeding.

Take engaging in sexual relations, for example. It can happen, because the husband has secretly contracted a sexually transmitted disease (STD) like syphilis or HIV, and the affected person either does not know about it or does not want to admit it, that the wife also becomes a victim. Or in implementing family planning, it may not be certain that the contraceptive device used is suitable for the woman's physical

---

73   Q2: 228 is given in footnote 9.

condition or state of health. We know that no contraceptive device, especially the hormonal ones (vaccinations, implants or the pill), is 100 per cent safe. The IUD, if one is not careful or if it is not compatible, can also cause ill effects.

The peak time is when a mother is pregnant, gives birth and breastfeeds. Unconditional health guarantees for mothers are needed at these times, in the form of information on health, nutritious food and other proper provisions for good health.

Second is the right to guaranteed welfare, not just while the vital processes of reproduction (pregnancy, birth and breastfeeding) are taking place, but also at other times, in her position as wife and as the mother of children, as mentioned in the Qur'an:

[verse in Arabic script]

The responsibility is laid on the father's shoulders to provide financial support and protection to the mother of his children, in a way that is fitting (QS Al-Baqarah [2]: 233).[74]

How much financial support should be given to the wife indeed depends on the one hand on need, and on the other hand on the capacity of the husband. What is important is that members of the family are not left without support. If this happens, and the wife is not a willing party to it, then religion opens the door for her to demand justice, including separation or divorce, if the situation truly demands it. [...]

Third is the right to make decisions that are connected to women's (wives') interests, especially those linked to the processes of reproduction. Rights in this third category can be clearly understood from the general explanation in Qur'anic verses about how a decision involving the parties must be made in any situation:

[verse in Arabic script]

Their affairs must be deliberated upon (spoken about and a decision taken) among themselves (QS Al-Syura [42]: 38).[75]

There is no decision involving another person that can be taken unilaterally, including reproductive issues between husband and wife.

* * * * *

Commentary   One area of reproductive rights that remains controversial, despite the existence of successful and, in the case of Indonesia at least, forceful government campaigns, is the use of contraception. One of the reasons for this controversy is a Hadith in which the Prophet is said to have called on Muslims to have more offspring. Other reasons include attitudes among some minority Muslim communities that family planning is a government plot to keep their numbers down, and among certain Muslim radicals that family planning is a Western plot to destroy Muslim communities, which

---

74   The Haleem rendition of the relevant section of the verse is: '... and clothing and maintenance must be borne by the father in a fair manner ...' (Q2: 233). See footnote 16 for the full text of the verse.
75   'respond to their Lord and keep up the prayer; conduct their affairs by mutual consultation; give to others out of what We have provided for them' (Q42: 38, Haleem).

need more Muslims in order to carry out jihad in the name of Islam (Marcoes-Natsir 2004: 4–5).

Although, as the above extract indicates, there is a general acceptance in Indonesia of the permissibility of family planning, there are groups that oppose its use on religious grounds, and others who oppose the way in which the government has forced the issue, without proper consultation with the community and with women themselves (Marcoes-Natsir 2004).

Advice columns found in newspapers and magazines, as well as online or in books, often contain questions about particular methods of contraception. The following extract from the question and answer website SyariahOnline indicates that, for some Muslims, the permissibility of contraception is not clear, and gives an idea of the complexity of the issue.

Extract 13-34: SyariahOnline

SyariahOnline, 'Menggunakan Alat Kontrasepsi dan Menghalangi Kehamilan' [Using Contraceptive Devices and Preventing Pregnancy], <http://syariahonline. com/konsultasi/?act=view&id=6320>, dated 10 March 2004, accessed 16 February 2005.

Question: There are those who say that the use of contraceptive devices is forbidden, but they themselves use other methods to prevent pregnancy such as using a monthly calendar and not having sex during the fertile period. Isn't this the same as family planning? […]

Answer:

> [After declaring that the method of contraception does indeed need to be taken into account in considering the issue, and then presenting a number of fatwa from the Middle East that do not permit the use of family planning except in cases of emergency, the religious scholars give the following decision, setting out both their reasons for accepting family planning and the limitations on this.]

Before the appearance of contraceptive devices at the time of the Prophet, blessings and peace be upon him, there was already one measure to prevent pregnancy by natural means that was used by the Companions and generally known as *'azl* [coitus interruptus], as mentioned in the Hadith: the Prophet, blessings and peace be upon him, said:

Recounted by Jabir: 'We used *'azl* at the time of the Prophet, blessings and peace be upon him, at the time the Qur'an was revealed' (collections of Bukhari and Muslim). [Hadith]

Recounted by Jabir: 'We used *'azl* at the time of the Prophet, blessings and peace be upon him, and the Prophet heard about it, but did not forbid it' (collection of Muslim). [Hadith]

In accordance with this Hadith, measures to prevent pregnancy are permitted through analogy with the law concerning *'azl*. Measures like this include, for example, using a calendar system so that there is no conception during husband–wife relations, using condoms and other things. The use of other contraceptive devices, if they are not dangerous medically, either physically or psychologically, is therefore permitted.

It so happens that the use of contraceptive devices or other means that result in reproductive organs not functioning and in not being able to produce offspring, either by a man or a woman, with or without the other's agreement, with a religious motivation or another motivation, is forbidden (*haram*). And the ulema are agreed that these are forbidden. Examples of forbidden means are vasectomy (cutting the sperm duct) and tubectomy (cutting the fallopian tubes). [...]

The advice from the Prophet, blessings and peace be upon him, to have more offspring does not mean that a Muslim family has to have a child every year. If we are consistent about Islamic teachings, then a Muslim can have one child every three years, because every baby that is born has the right to breastfeed for two years. And similarly a mother has the right to rest.

If understood in the proper way, Islam teaches planning that is mature in managing the family and regulating it well. In this context, family planning is permitted. However, efforts to limit offspring *en masse* at a community level are forbidden – it is forbidden to promote them, to use coercion and to accept them.

* * * * *

Commentary In November 2003, a fatwa on the issue of family planning was discussed by the Assembly of Darul-Iftah[76] of the Philippines and later issued after it had been approved by the Grand Mufti of al-Azhar in Egypt. It was the first fatwa ever issued by the national body of ulema in the Philippines. The fatwa considered the issues surrounding reproductive health in general, accepting that the definition given by the 1994 United Nations International Conference on Population and Development in Cairo was in accord with Islam. Although ulema had previously made pronouncements regarding the permissibility of birth spacing, Muslims have continued to be suspicious of it, fearing that it is a plot by the government to control the number of Muslims. As a result, levels of contraceptive use in the southeren Philippines remain low (Busran-Lao 2000: 225–6).[77]

Extract 13-35: Assembly of Darul-Iftah

Assembly of Darul-Iftah of the Philippines (2003), *Official Ruling (Fatwah) on Reproductive Health and Family Planning* [in English], Case No. 01 dated 22 November 2003, Davao.

---

76 The Assembly of Darul-Iftah is an advisory council of Islamic religious leaders created by the Southern Philippine Council for Peace and Development (SPCPD) to assist it in its duties under the 1976 Tripoli Agreement (a charter for Muslim autonomy in the southern Philippines).

77 The Central Committee of the Moro Islamic Liberation Front (MILF) rejected the fatwa, however, claiming that it would mislead Muslims. The MILF called on Muslims to follow the 'true teachings of Islam' instead ('MILF Rejects Fatwah on Reproductive Health', <www.mindanews.com/2004/04/06nws-fatwah.html>, dated 6 April 2004, accessed 28 June 2005).

The Assembly of Darul-Iftah of the Philippines, after a series of dialogues with respected Ulama in Mindanao[,] has therefore ruled unanimously in agreement with the ruling of Nahdlatul Ulama of Indonesia and other ruling[s] of Islamic Scholars from other Muslim countries on the 27th [day] of Ramadhan 1424 Hijri, corresponding to 22nd of November 2003 in the city of Davao, Philippines[,] the following:

The Assembly upholds Islam as a religion of ease. It supports what God said in the Qur'an: 'And he has not laid upon you in religion any hardship' (22: 78).[78]

The Assembly upholds Islam as a religion of quality. Islam has encouraged its people to increase and populate the earth with the proviso that their quality should not be compromised.

Improved reproductive health condition of the Muslim people benefits the individual Muslims and strengthens the Muslim nation socially, economically, politically and in all other aspects of human life.

A family planning program for the Muslim community in the Philippines should be anchored on the principles of non-coercion, responsible parenthood, and informed choice.

Family planning does not refer to abortion, neither to birth control. It refers to birth or child spacing. It should be a couple's decision.

All methods of contraception are allowed as long as they are safe, legal, in accordance with the Islamic Shariah, and approved by a credible physician[,] preferably a Muslim[,] for the benefit of both the mother and the child.

The permissibility of family planning is for the welfare of the mother and the child and for the couple to raise saleh (goodly) children who are pious, healthy, educated, useful and well-behaved citizens.

The Assembly, therefore, finds that reproductive health and family planning[,] as practiced under valid reasons and recognized necessities, are in accordance with the teachings of Islam.

Blessings and Peace of Allah be to Mohammad (pbuh [peace be upon him]) and his companions.

* * * * *

Commentary   Abortion is generally regarded in Islamic Southeast Asia as forbidden (*haram*), except in special circumstances. However, the high rate of illegal abortions in countries such as Indonesia, and the subsequent risk to life faced by many women, has led to a reassessment of the issue. The following extract is taken from a longer article by the prominent NU ulema K.H. Azis Masyhuri, and sets out the reasons why abortion is forbidden.

---

78   'Strive hard for God as is His due; He has chosen you and placed no hardship in your religion, the faith of your forefather Abraham. God has called you Muslims – both in the past and in this [message] – so that the Messenger can bear witness about you and so that you can bear witness about other people. So keep up the prayer, give the prescribed alms, and seek refuge in God. He is your protector – an excellent protector and an excellent helper' (Q22: 78, Haleem).

Extract 13-36: Fatwa of Nahdlatul Ulama (NU) and Majelis Ulama Indonesia (MUI)

Azis Masyhuri (2002), 'Abortus Menurut Hukum Islam' [Abortion According to Islamic Law], pp. 131–57 in Maria Ulfah Anshor et al. (eds), *Aborsi dalam Perspektif Fiqh Kontemporer* [Abortion from the Perspective of Contemporary Jurisprudence], Balai Penerbit FKUI, Jakarta. Extract: pp. 148–50.

1. Decision of the NU Central Board in Jakarta, 25 September 1969, which said among other things: '… Family planning cannot be carried out by means of abortion'.

2. Decision of the NU Limited Consultative Session concerning the method of family planning in Jakarta, 12–20 July 1979 (where the writer was among those present): 'Abortion is one method of family planning regarded in Islamic law as a criminal act because it eliminates something that has a respected status and is given legal protection (*mukhtaram/ma'sum*). However, it needs to be recorded that among experts in Islamic law (*fuqaha*), the issue is: when does the foetus acquire this legal status? There are opinions (*qaul-qaul*) [by legal scholars] that this status is permitted from the time of conception (*uluq*). And there is also a second opinion that is recorded in the book *I'anah*[79] (IV/130) that is described as an opinion that is stronger (*qual rajih*), which is: this status is acquired after the foetus has reached 120 days (*ba'da nafkhirruh*). With the exception of an emergency situation, when the life of the mother is threatened, for example, the Consultative Session chooses the first opinion in line with the oath of doctors themselves, so that the attitude is one of caution.

3. Decision of the National Consultation of MUI (Indonesian Council of Ulama) in Jakarta, 17–20 October 1983, which among other things states: 'Abortion, including menstrual regulation of any kind, is forbidden by the spirit of Islamic teachings, especially when the foetus already has a soul (at age 4 months in the womb), because the said deed constitutes covert killing, which is forbidden by sharia Islam except to save the mother. Based on this decision, abortion is forbidden. However, under local Islamic law, in emergency situations abortion can be carried out to save the life of the pregnant mother. Thus in Islamic law abortion is strictly forbidden, with some exceptions (emergency situations).

* * * * *

Commentary   Maria Ulfah Anshor, the chair of Fatayat NU, has been heavily involved in promoting discussion of the issue of abortion in Indonesia. She was awarded the Saparinah Sadli Award in August 2004 for her writings on the *fiqh* of abortion, and was one of the editors of the book from which extracts 13-36 and 13-38 are taken. In an interview published on the JIL website, she speaks with Abd Moqsith Ghazali of JIL.

---

79 *I'anah* [Guide] is a four-volume *fiqh* text by the Arab scholar Al-Malibary. It is widely taught in *pesantren* across Indonesia.

While most ulema argue that there is consensus on the issue of abortion, Maria Ulfah Anshor disputes this.

Extract 13-37: Maria Ulfah Anshor

Excerpt from an interview with Maria Ulfah Anshor conducted by Abd Moqsith Ghazali, 'Hukum Fikih Aborsi Tidak Hitam-Putih' [The Jurisprudence of Abortion Is Not Black and White], Jaringan Islam Liberal, <http://islamlib.com/id/index.php?page=article&mode=print&id=734>, dated 13 December 2004, accessed 16 February 2005.

JIL: Now let us elaborate upon what Islamic jurisprudence says about abortion. What did you find in the books of jurisprudence?

MARIA ULFAH ANSHOR: I have tried to conduct research on literature from the four schools of law: Maliki, Hanafi, Shafi'i and Hambali. From this, we have been able to find opinions that are controversial among ulema. Among the followers of the Shafi'i school itself, there are those who permit it and those who forbid it. In other schools, it is the same. This has indeed been a contentious (*khilafiah*) issue since earlier times.

Therefore, I am not choosing which opinion is best and most correct. I just want to emphasize that in jurisprudence, there are these varied views on abortion. Well actually, it is my mission to raise this. The reason: a majority of Muslims in Indonesia say that abortion is forbidden. However, in the law (*fiqh*) books, even in Shafi'i circles which, we should note, are the guide for the majority of Muslims in Indonesia, there are also those who allow it under certain conditions. [...]

* * * * *

Commentary   As extract 13-36 indicates, the question of when life begins is a controversial one. In Indonesia and Malaysia, the mainstream view is that abortion is permitted 'in emergency situations'. However, there are differing views on what constitutes an emergency situation. The two fatwa by NU and MUI in extract 13-36 only take into account situations in which the mother's life is at risk. Other individuals and groups have pushed the boundaries of the definition of an emergency to include a variety of other situations. The following extract is an example of this type of thinking. It is the result of a seminar organized by Fatayat NU on abortion law in Indonesia, held in April 2001. Prominent members of the Islamic community and the women's movement attended, and a drafting team drew up a list of agreed understandings relating to abortion.

Extract 13-38: Seminar on the Jurisprudence of Abortion

Maria Ulfah Anshor et al. (eds) (2002), 'Rumusan Akhir Seminar dan Lokakarya Aborsi dalam Perspektif Fiqh Kontemporer' [Final Formulation of the Seminar and Workshop on Abortion from the Perspective of Contemporary *Fiqh*], pp. 263–4 in *Aborsi dalam Perspektif Fiqh Kontemporer* [Abortion from the Perspective of Contemporary Jurisprudence], Balai Penerbit FKUI, Jakarta. Extract: pp. 263–4.

The drafting team identified three issues, namely: the understanding of life, the understanding of abortion and the law on abortion.

1. Understanding of Life

This issue can be divided into two, biological life and human life. Biological life is when the foetus is aged 0–120 days or before it is ensouled, while what is meant by human life is a foetus that is aged above 120 days (after it is ensouled).

2. Understanding of Abortion

In terms of language, abortion means the induced loss of a child that is not yet fully formed. According to the term, there are two definitions of abortion. The first is the abortion of a child in the womb before it is fully formed during pregnancy, whether the foetus is living or dead. The second understanding is that abortion is the stopping of the process of life after the time of conception.

3. Law on Abortion

The basic law on abortion is that it is prohibited except in cases of emergency. Indicators of an emergency, among others, are:

A. Medical indicators, such as the life of the mother being threatened if an abortion is not performed.
B. Socio-economic indicators, in matters directly connected to the life of a person, where these are very serious.
C. Political indicators, where there is a state authority that gives women no choice but to have an abortion.
D. Psychological indicators, in which women are truly placed in a situation where they are forced to have an abortion, such as in the case of rape.

One note that must be heeded is that only the first indicator applies to a foetus once it is aged 120 days, while socio-economic, political and psychological indicators can be applied before the foetus reaches 120 days (before it is ensouled).

13.3.6 Polygamy

Commentary Polygamy remains a controversial issue in Muslim Southeast Asia. At the National Congress of NU held in Central Java in November 2004, participants were supplied with food by the restaurant Ayam Bakar Wong Solo (Solo BBQ Chicken), whose owner, Puspo Wardoyo, has four wives and promotes the virtues of a polygamous lifestyle whenever he can (see extract 13-42). Led by Sinta Nuriyah, the wife of former Indonesian President Abdurrahman Wahid, women of Muslimat NU staged a boycott of the food and called on others to join them.[80] Sinta Nuriyah declared polygamy to be a form of violence against women, causing suffering to women and children.

---

80 'Sinta Nuriyah Protes Hidangan Muktamar NU' [Sinta Nuriyah Protests against the Food Served at the NU Congress], <http://www.tempointeraktif.com/hg/nasional/2004/11/28/brk,20041128-38,id. html>, dated 28 November 2004, accessed 7 June 2005.

There are a range of positions that Muslims can take on polygamy, from outright abolition, to making it permissible in such a limited range of situations as to make it virtually impossible, to promoting it as a valid and justified form of Islamic marriage and family life.

The following extract from an article by Sukidi, chief editor of the magazine *Amal Hayati*, sets out the anti-polygamy position of Muslim feminists in Indonesia, and reflects arguments used elsewhere in the Muslim world to deny that polygamy is a 'right' of Muslim men. Members of *Amal Hayati*'s editorial council include Sinta Nuriyah, Farha Ciciek and Husein Muhammad.

Extract 13-39: Sukidi

Sukidi (2001), 'Pro Kontra Poligami' [The Pros and Cons of Polygamy], *Amal Hayati*, 2(1): 2–3. Extract: p. 2.

Prominent Muslim feminists like Sinta Nuriyah Rahman, Lies Marcoes-Natsir, Musdah Mulia, Farha Ciciek and Badriyah Fayumi firmly reject polygamy, but tend to look to theological arguments. This is because it is in these theological arguments that Muslim intellectuals who are pro-polygamy base their theological stance on the legality of the practice of polygamy. Muslim feminists who reject polygamy want to use these theological arguments to reconstruct the way we perceive polygamy, which has so far been seen to be 'approved' by Islam.

The pros and cons of polygamy begin with the interpretation of God's word in QS. an-Nisa':3, namely:

> '*And if you fear you will not be able to do justice towards (the rights) of female orphans (if you marry them), then marry (other) women whom you like; two, three or four. But if you fear that you will not be able to behave fairly, then (marry) only one, or the slaves you possess; that is closer to not committing injustice*'.[81]

Briefly the pros and cons are these. Muslim intellectuals who are pro-polygamy, despite their reluctance to be publicly identified, base their practice of polygamy on these words of God. This verse, for intellectuals who are pro-polygamy, is the justification and even the ultimate argument for the permissibility of the practice of polygamy. In particular, part of that verse clearly states: 'then marry women whom you like, two, three, or four …'. In short, this verse is certainly not controversial. It means that polygamy is allowed in Islam. Full stop.

But wait for the response of the feminists who reject polygamy. 'The Qur'an should not be understood in a disconnected or partial way', implores Sinta Nuriyah, suggesting that the verses of the Qur'an should be understood holistically, comprehensively and in their entirety so that contradictions do not arise between one verse and another. This includes understanding polygamy from the point of view of the Qur'an in a holistic way. So QS. an-Nisa':3, which at first gives the impression that polygamy is permissible, must be linked to other verses. Sinta Nuriyah then very fluently quotes QS. an-Nisa':129, namely:

---

81   Q4: 3 is given in footnote 22.

> '*And you will never be able to do justice between [be equally fair to] (your) wives,*
> *even though you may long to do so; because of this, do not incline too much (to the*
> *one you love), so that you leave the others in a state of uncertainty. And if you are*
> *virtuous and guard yourself (from deceit), then truly Allah is All Forgiving and All*
> *Merciful*'.[82]

Sinta Nuriyah's argument with reference to QS. an-Nisa':129 is in fact brilliant.
How could it not be so? So far we have mostly been presented with QS. an-Nisa':3,
which gives the initial impression that polygamy is permissible. But when we are
referred to QS. an-Nisa':129, the extent to which polygamy is in fact not in the spirit
of the teachings of Islam becomes clear and plain. Let us think again about the words
of God in QS. an-Nisa':129, '*And you will never be able to do justice between (your)*
wives, even though you may long to do so ...'. So explicit are these words of God,
that the ideal of Islam is in fact monogamy.

* * * * *

Commentary The following extract is from an article by Hajah Dr Sandar Chit, a
Burmese Muslim and a member of the Islamic Center of Myanmar. She gives the 'moderate' or middle-way position on polygamy, that is, the argument that polygamy is justified, but only in certain restricted situations. Interestingly, the author argues that 'justice'
includes love, as does the previous extract. This is not the position of the majority of
ulema, who argue that justice equates to material things and to conjugal relations.

Extract 13-40: Sandar Chit

Sandar Chit (2003), 'Workshop on the Role and Status of Women in World Religions: Islamic Perspective' [in English], *Engagement*, Judson Research Center Bulletin, 1(December): 47–58. Extract: pp. 53–5.

I would like to touch briefly [on] why and what is the legal status of polygamy in
Islam. The verse which allows polygamy was revealed after the battle of Uhud in
which many Muslims were killed, leaving widows and orphans for whom due care
was incumbent upon the Muslim survivors. The translation of the verse is as follows:

Quran 4: 3

> If you fear that you shall not be able to deal justly with the orphans, marry women of
> your choice, two or three or four; but if you fear that you shall not be able to deal justly
> (with them), then marry only one.[83]

From this verse, a number of facts are evident:

1. That polygamy is neither mandatory, nor encouraged, but merely permitted.
2. That the permission to practice polygamy is not associated with mere satisfaction
   of passion. It is rather associated with compassion toward widows and orphans, a
   matter that is confirmed by the atmosphere in which the verse was revealed.

---

82 Q4: 129 is given in footnote 22.
83 Q4: 3 is given in footnote 22.

3. That even in such a situation, the permission is far more restricted than the normal practice that existed among the Arabs and other people at that time when many married as many as ten or more wives.
4. That dealing justly with one's wives is an obligation. This applies to housing, food, clothing, kind treatment, love etc. for which the husband is fully responsible. If one is not sure of being able to deal justly with them, the Quran says; 'Then (marry) only one' (Quran 4: 3).

This verse, when combined with another verse in the same chapter, shows [the] same discouragement of such plural marriage. The other verse plainly states;

Quran 4: 129

You are never able to be fair and just as between women even if it is your ardent desire.[84]

5. The verse says 'Marry'[,] not kidnap, buy or seduce. What [is] 'Marriage' as understood in Islam? Marriage in Islam is a civil contract, which is not valid unless both contracting parties consent to it. Thus, no wife can be 'forced' or 'given' to a husband who is already married.
    It is thus a free choice of both parties. As to the first wife;

    a. She may be barren or ill and see in polygamy a better solution than divorce.
    b. She may divorce him (unilaterally) if he is married to a second wife provided that the nuptial contract gives her the right of unilateral divorce.
    c. She can go to court and ask for a divorce if there is eviden[ce] of mistreatment or injustice inflicted upon her.

Scholars in the past and at present, Muslims and non-Muslims[,] have consistently pointed out such cases. The following are a few examples, which are tied in with the general approach of Islam to individual and social problems. A man who discovers his wife [is] barren and who at the same time instinctively aspires to have children and heirs. In a situation [such] as this, the man would either have to suffer the deprivation of fatherhood for life or divorce his barren wife and get married to another woman who is not barren.

In many cases, neither solution can be considered as the best alternative. Polygamy would have the advantage of preserving the marital relationship without depriving the man of fathering children of his own. Another situation[,] like a man whose wife becomes chronically ill[,] would have one of [two] possible alternatives: he may suppress his instinctive sexual needs for the rest of his life or divorce his sick wife at the time when she needs his compassion most, and get married to another woman thus legally satisfying his instinctive needs; or he could compromise by keeping his sick wife and secretly have for himself one or more illicit sex partners.

Let us discuss these alternatives from the point of view of the Islamic teaching. The first solution is against human nature. Islam recognizes sex and sexual needs and provides for legitimate means for their satisfaction. The second solution is clearly

---

84   Q4: 129 is given in footnote 22.

less compassionate, especially, where there is love between two parties. Further-more, the Prophet [describes divorce] as the 'Permitted thing which is hated most by Allah' [...] The last solution is plainly against the Islamic teaching, which forbid[s] illicit sexual relations in any form. To sum up, Islam being against immorality, hypo-critical preluge [*sic*] of morality and against divorce unless no better solution is available, provides for a better alternative that is consiste[nt] with human nature and with the preservation of pure and legitimate sex relationships. In situation[s] like this, it is doubtful that any solution would better polygamy, which is after all, an optional solution.

* * * * *

Commentary The following extract is taken from a book written by Harlina Halizah Siraj, the head of the Malaysian women's organization Wanita JIM (see also extract 13-25). It shows the conflicting feelings that many Muslim women have concerning the practice of polygamy: they view it as permitted according to Islam, but nonetheless strongly disapprove of it.

Extract 13-41: Wanita Pertubuhan Jamaah Islah Malaysia (Wanita JIM)

Harlina Halizah Siraj (2001), *Ucapan Dasar PPWN [Perhimpunan Perwakilan Wanita Nasional] 2001: Menerajui Inovasi Pengislahan Keluarga Efektif* [Keynote Address of the Assembly of National Women's Representatives 2001: Providing Leadership for Innovation for Effective Family Reforms], Pertubuhan Jamaah Islah Malaysia, Kuala Lumpur. Extract: pp. 13–14.

In this gender-sensitive context, I was called upon to touch on an issue that is still regarded as sensitive by most of us, brothers and sisters in JIM. Like it or not, I need to give some explanation here to find a common approach among ourselves when-ever this issue is brought forward. When the issue of polygamy is raised, especially when it was mentioned in the proposal for the welfare of single sisters and single mothers which was received during the last PPN[85] in 2000, I found that there were many conflicting opinions among the brothers and sisters. I am worried and con-cerned that sisters might unconsciously hate God's law, for which there is proof and categorical guidance in the Glorious Qur'an, while brothers, on the other hand, will simply consider the flexibility given by God as a benefit, a special right and a 'bonus' for those who are called men.

In fact, the creatures called humans, who are also a type of mammal, are not happy with having just one partner in life. A study in Sweden recently found that the men in that country, on average, have 45 sexual partners throughout their lives, while women were found, on average, to have 30 sexual partners in their lifetimes. What can be concluded here is that it is human nature to be polygamous and polyandrous. It is innate in every man to be inclined to have more than one wife. Nevertheless, a well-rounded Islam limits the number of wives to only four, to ensure that no mal-

---

85 Perhimpunan Perwakilan Nasional (Assembly of National Representatives).

treatment occurs from the aspect of responsibility and accountability. If the Sunnah of the Prophet is used as a strong argument, then men should never forget that the Prophet practised monogamy with Khadijah for nearly 29 years and only practised polygamy in the last six years of his life.

On the other hand, no woman is willing to share her husband and love with another woman. This is a reality that all parties must be aware of. Polygamy, which causes a woman to share with a co-wife, is in truth very bitter and painful. Sensitivity and apprehension towards this issue will surely result in discussion, agreement and fully responsible actions that are more akin to the just Sunnah emphasized by the Prophet, on whom be blessings and peace. I also have to give a firm reminder here that the option of living polygamously is not a popular option among single sisters, as is often stated and suggested with cynicism by many brothers whenever the issue of finding a partner for a single sister is raised. I hope that with this little awareness every one of us will be able to take an attitude that is more just and wise in handling this issue. Remember, let there never be among us those who believe that such a thing could not possibly occur in our own homes! Only God Almighty knows what He has in store for us in the future.

* * * * *

Commentary   As noted above, there are men who promote polygamy. In Indonesia, Puspo Wardoyo is probably the best known of these, in part because of the 'Polygamy Awards' he has organized on a number of occasions.[86] He is a very successful entrepreneur, owning a chain of chicken restaurants, and has four wives. The following magazine extract lays out Puspo Wardoyo's motivations for polygamous marriage. The cover of the magazine is shown in the colour section in this book (see plate 19).

Extract 13-42: Puspo Wardoyo

Puspo Wardoyo (2003), 'Poligami Kebutuhan Bersama' [Polygamy a Common Need], p. 40 in *Kiat Sukses Beristri Banyak: Pengalaman Puspo Wardoyo Bersama 4 Istri* [The Secret to Success with Many Wives: The Experience of Puspo Wardoyo and His 4 Wives], CV Bumi Wacana, Solo. Extract: p. 40.

To be honest, what motivated me to be a polygamist was my understanding of the teachings of Islam. **First**, God has commanded: '*Then marry (other) women whom you like; two, three or four. But If you fear you will not be able to behave fairly, then marry only one*' (QS An-Nisa 4:3).[87]

Second, I am following the example of the Prophet. Because it is in the person of the Prophet that a good model is to be found, as God decreed: 'Certainly there is in the Messenger of God a shining exemplar for those who hope for the mercy of God and the afterlife and recall God's name often' (QS Al Ahzab: 21).[88]

---

86   For more on Puspo Wardoyo, see Nurmila (2005).

87   Q4: 3 is given in footnote 22.

88   'The Messenger of God is an excellent model for those of you who put your hope in God and the Last Day and remember Him often' (Q33: 21, Haleem).

Third, as a human being I also feared that I would fall into adultery if I had only one wife. This is in agreement with the teachings of the Prophet in his Words: 'Of the three groups that are worthy of God's help, one of the last is those who marry to distance themselves from what is forbidden' (HR Tirmidzi from Abu Hurairah). [Hadith]

Fourth, as a leader I felt that I had been given an excess of gifts of spiritual and material wealth from Almighty God Most Holy Most High. Because of this, I also felt that I had greater obligations to fulfil. To demonstrate this in my social life, I must be willing, among other things, to extend my leadership to others, including to other women who need my guidance. Because I am a leader who is able to act justly and am suited for marriage, in order to be more blessed and at the same time follow in the footsteps of the Prophet, then I must be willing to take on the new task or burden of leading other women (after successfully leading [my first] wife to [the life of] a pious woman).

Wives are also asked to be accountable for their leadership as a devout wife (who always supports her husband's faith). If her husband is prepared to lead others, then she is called on not to monopolize her husband's leadership. To demonstrate this in her social life she must be willing to offer her husband's leadership to others, including to other women who need him. In my experience of polygamy, it is in fact the wife or woman who needs polygamy. Because for a woman, polygamy is a means or a method of attaining merit before God. In this way, the motivation for women is that making their husband happy is part of the inner jihad. [...]

[...] A woman will also achieve greater worth if in fact she desires such challenges before she faces them, for example by allowing her husband to undertake the additional duty of marrying again.

* * * * *

Commentary   The following three extracts are from interviews with Puspo's wives, three of whom are university graduates.

Extract 13-43: Puspo Wardoyo's Wives

Excerpts from interviews with three of Puspo Wardoyo's wives, pp. 60, 64–7 and 71–2 in *Kiat Sukses Beristri Banyak: Pengalaman Puspo Wardoyo Bersama 4 Istri* [The Secret to Success with Many Wives: The Experience of Puspo Wardoyo and His 4 Wives], CV Bumi Wacana, Solo, 2003. Extract: pp. 64–7, 71, 60.

'Becoming a Co-wife, Why Be Afraid?' [interview with Anisa Nasution, third wife]

Who proposed to you, did Mr Puspo do it himself?
Oh, no. That's what a marriage partner is; no one can predict it. Only God knows. So one day Mr Puspo's younger brother came to ask me whether I was prepared to become his third wife. Of course I was very surprised, anxious and confused.

My friends and I used to joke about becoming a third wife. But I never dreamed it would happen to me. Even when Rini (his first wife) was sent to convince me, I didn't suspect [it would happen to me]. Rini often invited me to discuss things, and eventually I was able to understand polygamous marriage in Islam. But that didn't mean I accepted his proposal straight away, because I was still worried about what my parents' response would be.

Did your parents know that a married man had proposed to you?
Initially they didn't. Then I plucked up the courage to tell them about the proposal. As I expected, at first my parents were very angry and disappointed. I could understand that, because in my family, where the tradition of Islam has been passed down from generation to generation, no one has had a polygamous marriage. Like all parents, they wanted me to marry a good, single man.

Then yet again I was surprised. Because he is a responsible man, my leader (Mr Puspo) went to meet my parents face to face to propose. But my parents stood their ground and rejected the proposal. [pp. 64–5] […]

[…] In Islam, Muslim women, like Muslim men, are obliged to choose a future husband who has a strong religion and morals – that's the main thing. Smart looks, appearance and wealth are not enough. The Prophet (blessings and peace be upon him) consented to the appeal from a woman who was of marriageable age that she be able to choose her [marriage partner] from among those whom her parents had selected (Hadith).

These two things (religion and morals) will determine the success of a household. If a man who has those characteristics comes along, even if he is already married, shouldn't he be considered as also fulfilling those criteria? So in the end I decided for myself that I would accept Mr Puspo's proposal. My reason was that he had courage and strong morals. [p. 66] […]

What is the reason for the upsurge in extra-marital affairs?
There are many factors which lead people to have affairs outside marriage. One of the reasons is a wife's or even a husband's fear of being open about practising polygamy. Why should we be afraid of polygamy, when it is legal and permitted according to Islam? What we should really fear is adultery, going astray and having an affair. This is what we need to avoid and do away with.

It may be that a person believes in monogamy. But what should be emphasized here is that polygamy is legal and permitted. We should even be proud that [Islam] is the only religion that provides solutions to marital problems, that clearly forbids affairs and adultery. Of course, as the wife of a polygamous husband, I tend towards polygamy rather than monogamy. [p. 67]

'The Sweetness of Polygamy's Beauty' [interview with Intan Ratih Tri Laksmi, fourth wife]

The issue of fairness in polygamy is actually relative. Of course, it depends on the individual's point of view. For my part, I have seen that my husband has consistently tried to be fair to all of his wives. We always need to remember that there is not one human being in this world who can be absolutely fair and perfect, and our husband is the same. I want to emphasize that from a personal view I have seen that my husband has always done his best to act as justly as possible. If something happens that might feel a little unjust, as long as it's not something major, of course we don't need to make an issue out of it. [p. 71]

'Like a Newly Wed' [interview with Rini Purwanti, first wife]

'I think the view that polygamy only benefits men is mistaken. Polygamous men in fact have a heavier burden of responsibility, because they are called on to provide financial support, time, a home and an education for their wives and children', says Rini. The issue [of polygamy], in Rini's view, should thus not be seen simply in terms of its biological benefits. The not insignificant burden of responsibility should also be considered. [...]

Of course, says Rini, not a few people see polygamy as demeaning to the status of women. It is this view that has developed in gender studies and analysis. 'However, what we feel in our family life is in fact the opposite. Polygamy really raises the position of women because their status is clear, they have a husband, financial support and a home. On the other hand, the status of women who only want to marry for money is very low. Let alone a wife who tells her husband he can have any partner or girlfriend he likes as long as he doesn't marry her', says Rini.

This kind of thing is in [Rini's] opinion actually very disparaging and demeaning to women. [p. 60]

* * * * *

Commentary The positive views of polygamy given above appear to represent a minority view. Polygamy appears to be an important contributing factor to divorce in the Malay world (Jones 1994: 231–2, 277–8). The following quotations from women taken from a Sisters in Islam booklet on polygamy paint a very different picture.

Extract 13-44: Sisters in Islam

Sisters in Islam (2002), *Islam and Polygamy* [in English], Kuala Lumpur. Extract: p. 1.

'I did not even know that he had married another woman. He just came home one day and said he had married another, as though he was telling me he had got his bonus. Do I not matter? What about this baby I am breastfeeding, does she not matter?'
– interview with 28-year-old woman, mother of two children

'Whenever we have a disagreement, he often says to me, 'Remember your place, I can always marry another, and then you'll know [the consequences]. You can agree or you can be without a husband – the choice is yours'. What kind of a choice is this?'
– interview with 35-year-old woman

'When I tell him that I don't believe Islam allows men to ill-treat women in this way (polygamy), he says that I am challenging the word of God, that I will become a murtad [apostate] if I question this law. So, even though in my heart I feel this is wrong, I don't say it anymore – he might just divorce me on the grounds that I am a non-believer! Who will support me and my kids then?'
– interview with 40-year-old woman, mother of four, two still school-going

'I do not understand, Your Honour. If he considers himself someone who has pity, then why does he not pity our kids?'
– 39-year-old mother of five whose husband applied for permission for a polygamous marriage in the Islamic Court of the Federal Territory, in January 2001 edition of *Mingguan Wanita* [Women's Weekly]

13.4   LEGAL CHALLENGES TO PREVAILING ISLAMIC LAW

Commentary   As discussed in chapter 11, in Indonesia the Kompilasi Hukum Islam (KHI, Compilation of Islamic Law) forms the basis for decisions made in religious courts on issues of marriage, inheritance and gifts for pious purposes. In October 2004, a working group from the Ministry of Religious Affairs headed by Siti Musdah Mulia – Pokja Pengarusutamaan Gender (Gender Mainstreaming Team) – came up with a revised version of the KHI, called the Counter Legal Draft KHI (CLD KHI). The revised draft, funded by the Asia Foundation, caused great controversy. It was launched by the minister of religious affairs at the time, Said Agil Husin al Munawar, but he withdrew the draft from discussion just two weeks later because of the controversy it had aroused. The shelving of the CLD KHI was confirmed by the new minister, Muhammad Maftuh Basyuni, later that month. However, women's groups have not given up hope that the draft will at the very least be made available again for public discussion.

In Malaysia, a similar project to draw up a revised law on marriage began in 2005. Foreign donors have provided funds to Sisters in Islam to develop its own alternative family law bill.

13.4.1   The CLD KHI

Commentary   The following table appeared on the website of the Indonesian online magazine, *Jurnal Perempuan* [Women's Journal]. Attributed to the Gender Mainstreaming Team, Ministry of Religious Affairs, Republic of Indonesia, it outlines the main reforms the CLD KHI would introduce.

Extract 13-45: Gender Mainstreaming Team

Eko Bambang S., 'Istri Punya Hak Menceraikan dan Hak Merujuk Suami' [A Wife Has the Right to Divorce and Reconcile with Her Husband], *Jurnal Perempuan*, <http://www.jurnalperempuan.com/yjp.jpo/?act=berita%7C-180%7CX>, dated 4 October 2004, accessed 7 October 2004.

Table of Changes to Critical Issues in the
Counter Legal Draft to the Compilation of Islamic Law

No.	Critical Issue	KHI Presidential Instruction No. 1/1991	Counter Legal Draft to the KHI
1	Understanding of marriage	Implementing it constitutes a religious obligation to Almighty God	Is not a religious obligation, but normal human social relations
2	Guardian of the bride (*wali nikah*) [representative of the bride, acting as her legal guardian]	Is one of the required pillars of marriage	Is not a required pillar of marriage; a woman may marry without one
3	Registration	Is not included as a pillar of marriage; is only an administrative obligation	Is a pillar of marriage, because a marriage is not valid without registration
4	Minimum age for marriage	16 years for the prospective wife and 19 years for the prospective husband	21 years, with no differentiation between prospective wife or husband
5	Marriage payment from groom to bride (*mahar*)	Obligatory for prospective husband to give it to the prospective wife	Obligatory to be given to or received by the prospective husband or wife, or both, in accordance with local custom (*adat*)
6	Interfaith marriage	Completely prohibited	Can occur within limits to achieve the goals of marriage
7	Polygamy/polyandry	Can occur under certain conditions	Prohibited (*haram li ghairihi*)
8	Wife's right to divorce and reconciliation (*rujuk*)	A wife does not have the right to divorce or reconcile with her husband	A wife has the right to divorce and to reconcile with her husband (equal to the husband's rights)
9	Prescribed waiting period after divorce (*'iddah*)	*'Iddah* is only for the wife, not for the husband	*'Iddah* is imposed on husband and wife
10	Prescribed mourning period for a widow (*ihdad*)	*Ihdad* is only for the wife, not for the husband	*Ihdad* is imposed on the husband and wife after [the death of] their partner
11	Provision of financial support (*nafkah*)	Is the husband's obligation	Is the joint obligation of the husband and wife; reproduction by the wife is equivalent to the provision of *nafkah*
12	Marriage contracts for a pre-defined period	Not regulated	Regulated; marriage is dissolved upon the ending of an agreement made at the time of marriage

13	Marital disobedience (*nusyuz*)	It is only possible for a wife to commit *nusyuz* vis-à-vis her husband	*Nusyuz* can be committed by a husband or a wife vis-à-vis their partner
14	Rights and obligations	The rights and obligations of husband and wife are not the same, but are biased	The rights and obligations of husband and wife are the same
15	Inheritance involving different religions	Different religions are an obstruction (*mani'*) to inheriting	Different religions are not an obstruction (*mani'*) to inheriting
16	Share of sons and daughters [in inheritance]	Share of sons and daughters is 2:1	Share of sons and daughters is 1:1 or 2:2
17	Gifts for pious purposes (*wakaf*), different religions	People of a different religion are forbidden from giving and receiving *wakaf*	People of a different religion are permitted to give and receive *wakaf*

Source: Gender Mainstreaming Team, Ministry of Religious Affairs, Republic of Indonesia, 2004.

* * * * *

Commentary   The following extract is taken from an interview with Dr Siti Musdah Mulia, chief researcher at the Ministry of Religious Affairs, who led the project to revise the KHI.

Extract 13-46: Siti Musdah Mulia

Excerpt from an interview with Siti Musdah Mulia conducted by Muninggar Sri Saraswati, 'Islamic Law Revision Promotes "Common Sense among Muslims"' [in English], *Jakarta Post*, <http://www.thejakartapost.com/yesterdaydetail.asp?fileid=20041009.B05>, dated 9 October 2004, accessed 11 October 2004.

Some say your team's draft revision is a revolution in Islamic law.

I don't think so. For example, the ban against polygamy is not new to Muslim societies. It came into effect in Tunisia in 1959 and then Turkey. […]

What has been the public response so far?

We have held a series of discussions and the opposition is unbelievable on two issues: interfaith marriage and polygamy. Most of the participants could accept other articles in the draft. Some of them told me that if articles on interfaith marriage and polygamy were approved, they would prefer to be atheists.

What is the actual danger of interfaith marriage? Corruption is more dangerous than interfaith marriage, as the former harms the nation. Actually, Islam provides many opinions on interfaith marriage. I just cannot understand why it must be banned. You can not agree [that is, you can disagree] with interfaith marriage, but you cannot order others to follow your belief.

Polygamy causes various social excesses, particularly at the expense of the abandoned wives and children whose status in society is affected. Actually, we believe

Islam is monogamous. Polygamy is for prophets and those who are on the same level as prophets, not for common human beings like us. People might boast they can uphold fairness in practicing polygamy, but why are 90 percent of polygamous marriages not registered with the state? They must hide their status.

Therefore, our draft says that an Islamic marriage is not legal without registering it with the state. [...]

Some people have accused your team of not having convincing arguments to back up some of the articles in the draft?

They may say that, but we studied thousands of books and *fiqih* [legal prescriptions] over two years. We do not make a textual analysis only as a textbook does not talk; it's humans who talk. My team consists of seven men and three women. We are not paid for this work.

* * * * *

> **Commentary**   As noted above, there was a great deal of opposition to the CLD KHI. Although the draft was widely welcomed by women activists, not all women welcomed it. Below is an extract from an interview with Prof. Dr Hj Huzaemah Tahido Yanggo, who, together with Prof. Dr Nabilah Lubis and Prof. Dr Zakiah Darajat, has published a book objecting to the draft. The interview appeared in the newspaper *Republika* on 18 February 2005.

Extract 13-47: Huzaemah Tahido Yanggo

Excerpt from an interview with Huzaemah Tahido Yanggo conducted by Yusuf Assidiq, 'Hukum Islam Sangat Demokratis' [Islamic Law Is Very Democratic], *Republika*, <http:www.republika.co.id/cetak_berita.asp?id=187997&kat_id=105&edisi= Cetak>, dated 18 February 2005, accessed 2 May 2005.

What initially motivated you to write the book *Kontrovesi Revisi KHI* [Controversial Revisions to the KHI]?

When I saw that the Counter Legal Draft KHI prepared by the Gender Mainstreaming Team of the Ministry of Religious Affairs was upsetting society. This is understandable, keeping in mind that the contents of the draft, in my opinion, are in opposition to the Qur'an, as well as the Sunnah and other sources of Islamic law that are authoritative (*mu'tabarrah*). [...]

What are in fact the concerns in the Islamic community?

In the view of the drafters of the counter KHI, the CLD KHI constitutes a renewal of Islamic law. This is a basic issue about which we must be on our guard. Because in fact, what has been formulated is just a deviation from and transformation of original Islamic law. Actually, if they were to study Islam more deeply, particularly issues of Islamic law, they would find that Islamic law is very democratic, as well as attentive to the question of justice. The Qur'an and the Hadith, for example, teach about the issues of democracy and justice, but unfortunately there are still many people who do not understand these [teachings]. In essence, those who formulated the CLD KHI have changed the understanding of Qur'anic texts according to their own understanding based on the primary goals of sharia (*maqasid as-syari'ah*), that is, by enshrining values as well as principles of social justice in it, benefit to the community of humankind, universal compassion and local wisdom. However, what they do not realize is that what has been formulated is already outside the bounds of a renewal of Islamic law, as well as damaging Islamic teachings themselves.

With regard to developments over time, how in fact do the Qur'an and Hadith see this issue?

The Qur'an is like a set of instructions for humankind, and the Sunnah constitutes an interpretation or clarification of the purpose of the Qur'an. Thus it can be said that the Qur'an and Sunnah are a guide for the community of humankind. So long as humanity upholds both of them, then it will surely never go astray. Indeed, there are exceptions. Regarding texts that have negotiable meanings (*dzanny al dilallah*), [we] are able to implement a new interpretation by way of reason (*ijtihad*) which has been determined and is already well known in the world of Islam. The determiners and maintainers of benefit for the greater good are God and His Messenger by way of divine revelation, not humanity whose logic is extremely limited. Because what is considered good according to reason is not necessarily good according to the Qur'an and Sunnah.

Women's issues take up most of the draft KHI. How do you see this?

As in the matter of the analysis of the book *Islam Menggugat Poligami* [Islam Challenges Polygamy],[89] what is needed is an overhaul of the Marriage Law (UUP) No. 1/1974. But if this is done the disadvantages will outweigh the benefits, because there is a strong possibility that matters that have already achieved national consensus may all be changed, and this [the new law] would be difficult to implement. However, there is a way it could be overhauled. That is by way of the KHI, because the KHI constitutes a simplification of the UUP and its status in law is based on a Presidential Instruction (Inpres). It is not a law yet. In fact, in 2003 the Ministry of Religious Affairs drafted a Law Concerning the Application of Religious Justice, the contents of which are an overhaul of the KHI, and it has already been submitted to parliament. However, in the formulation I have seen, not all of what has been proposed by women, even if it is not in opposition to Islamic sharia, has been accommodated.

Because of this, the team has devised a CLD KHI which stands in opposition to sharia Islam.

---

89 The reference here is to a book by Siti Musdah Mulia (Musdah Mulia 2004), who led the project to revise the KHI (see extract 13-46).

14 Jihad

Greg Fealy

INTRODUCTION

Jihad is a major element in Islamic belief. Its literal meanings are 'to endeavour', 'to strive' or 'to struggle', and 'to fight'. The Qur'an commands Muslims to struggle in the path of God (Ar.: *jihaadun fii sabiilil-laahi*) following the example of the Prophet Muhammad and his Companions. Jihad can take a wide variety of forms. It can mean the personal struggle to make oneself a better Muslim through prayer and fasting, and by acquiring a deeper knowledge of the faith. It can mean a broader exertion to improve society through charitable works, religious teaching, political activity, economic initiative and social leadership. It can also mean fighting against injustice, ignorance and oppression through preaching and writing. Finally, it can mean armed struggle or holy war, particularly against enemies of the faith. Indeed, jihad is the only legal form of warfare permitted in Islam.

The contrast between the different types of jihad is captured in Prophetic tradition. Muhammad is said to have returned from battle and told his followers: 'We return from the lesser jihad [Ar.: *jihaadun 'asgharun*] to the greater jihad [Ar.: *jihaadun 'akbarun*]'. The greater jihad is the more challenging because it entails struggling against one's own personal desires, such as greed, lust and vanity.

How contemporary Muslims view the non-violent and violent conceptions of jihad depends in part on context and perception. Most Muslims follow an irenic approach to jihad, one in which the focus is on personal piety and community service. A minority, however, believe that their community faces a hostile environment, and is under grave threat from external forces ranging from global capitalism and Western cultural imperialism to local authoritarian government and anti-Islamic military crusades. According to some who are of this latter view, the only valid response is to wage armed jihad, including terrorist attacks.

Traditionally, Islamic jurists have imposed strict requirements on the waging of violent jihad. Holy war may only be declared by a duly constituted state authority, and the launch of hostilities is forbidden until the 'enemy' has refused calls to convert to Islam or negotiate peace. Once war is joined, non-combatants are immune from attack, as also are women, children, the sick and the elderly, provided they have not fought against Muslim forces. Since the 1970s, however, a new stream of jihadist thinking has emerged which allows for aggression towards those not involved in anti-Islamic conflict and which also uses excommunication (Ar.: *takfiirun*) to deem fellow Muslims apostate who can then be killed. Internationally, such groups as al-Qaeda, Gama'a Islamiyah and Laskar-i-Tayyiba have used such interpretations to justify the killing of non-combatants and Muslims.

In Southeast Asia, violent jihadist groups constitute a tiny minority of the Islamic community. Historically the Darul Islam movement[1] in Indonesia has been one of the largest and most enduring jihadist organizations, but in recent decades other groups such as Jemaah Islamiyah (JI), the Moro Islamic Liberation Front (MILF) and the Abu Sayyaf Group have adopted armed jihadist, including terrorist, methods.

EXTRACTS AND COMMENTARY

14.1   GENERAL EXPLANATION OF JIHAD

Commentary   The concept of jihad and its method of implementation have been subject to multiple interpretations. There is little dispute among Islamic scholars regarding the meaning of Qur'anic references to the spiritual aspects of jihad and also the requirement for physical defence of the Muslim community. Before presenting extracts containing more contentious views of jihad, this opening section sets out two mainstream interpretations of the concept and its realization.

14.1.1   Didin Hafidhuddin

Commentary   Dr Didin Hafidhuddin is a prominent Islamic scholar who is in high demand as a speaker and writer on religious matters (see colour plate 17). A lecturer at Institut Pertanian Bogor (IPB, Bogor Agricultural Institute) and former rector of the Ibn Khaldun University in Bogor, Didin first gained a high public profile in the 1999 elections when he was nominated for the Indonesian presidency by Partai Keadilan (PK, Justice Party). In recent years he has written extensively on issues such as Islamic banking, wealth taxes and Muslim responses to contemporary social problems. In this extract, he discusses the diverse meanings and interpretations of jihad.

Extract 14-1: Didin Hafidhuddin

Didin Hafidhuddin (2004), 'Memakai Jihad Secara Kaffah' [Using Jihad in a Complete Way], pp. 93–7 in Hasyim Muzadi, Didin Hafidhuddin and Ahmad Syafii

---

1   The Darul Islam movement arose in the late 1940s in West Java. In 1949 it declared the establishment of an independent Islamic State of Indonesia, headed by Darul Islam's leader, S.M. Kartosoewirjo. The movement waged a violent campaign against republican forces in several provinces throughout the 1950s and was defeated only in 1962, when Kartosoewirjo was captured, tried for sedition and executed.

Maarif (eds), *Refleksi Tiga Kiai* [Reflections of Three *Kiai*], Penerbit Republika, Jakarta. Extract: pp. 93–7.

In an etymological (linguistic) sense, jihad means being devoted to carrying out the commands of Almighty God and applying His teachings at the core of real life. '*And people who strive for Us (seek [our] blessings) truly We will show them our ways. And truly God will really be with those who do good*' (QS 29:69).[2]

In another verse, Almighty God also emphasizes that jihad is always associated with faith and relocation (QS 2:218 and QS 8:72).[3] This indicates that the struggle to establish God's religion will only be realized if it is founded on faith and the desire to relocate oneself, that is, the yearning and attempt to leave behind imperfect deeds heavy with the qualities of sins against Almighty God.

Jihad must be reflected in all of life's activities. Starting from the struggle to control lusts, such as struggling to address lazy, greedy, stingy, deceitful, corrupt, jealous and spiteful tendencies, and other evils. Lest we be controlled and guided by our lusts. [p. 93]

Whatever happens, it is lust that shall determine man's level of nobility. Man's level of nobility shall be lower than that of animals, even the lowliest of animals, if lust succeeds in enslaving man's behaviour. Man shall achieve the highest level of nobility in comparison to God's other creatures when his lust is subjugated to the teachings of God and His Prophet.

So burdensome is this struggle against lust that God's Prophet, blessings and peace be upon him, told his apostles after the battle of Badar[4] had ended that Muslims had just concluded a small (*ashghar*) struggle, namely the battle of Badar, in pursuit of a greater (*akbar*) struggle. What God's Prophet meant was the struggle against lust. At the apocalypse, Almighty God shall call all those souls subjugated and obedient to him with a name most beautiful, namely *nafsul muthmainnah* [peaceful souls] as recorded in QS 89:27–30.[5]

Jihad must also be carried out with absolute patience and fortitude. This will cause us to be ever consistent in performing all manner of good deeds. Almighty God dearly loves those who are always consistent in performing good works, even though in the eyes of men the deeds done may be considered insignificant and lowly.

---

2 'But We shall be sure to guide to Our ways those who strive hard for Our cause: God is with those who do good' (Q29: 69, Haleem).

3 'But those who have believed, migrated, and striven for God's cause, it is they who can look forward to God's mercy: God is most forgiving and merciful' (Q2: 218, Haleem).

'Those who believed and emigrated [to Medina] and struggled for God's cause with their possessions and persons, and those who gave refuge and help, are all allies of one another. As for those who believed but did not emigrate, you are not responsible for their protection until they have done so. But if they seek help from you against persecution, it is your duty to assist them, except against people with whom you have a treaty: God sees all that you do' (Q8: 72, Haleem).

4 The battle of Badr was fought in 624 by the Prophet and his followers against a much larger Meccan army. The victory of the Muslim forces was seen as demonstrating divine guidance.

5 '[But] you, soul at peace: return to your Lord well pleased and well pleasing; go in among My servants; and into My Garden' (Q89: 27–30, Haleem).

A woman in the time of the Prophet was sent to heaven by God due to the consistency of her actions, even though to some the woman's deeds seemed very simple. Every day the woman cleaned the mosque of all dirt and contaminants, so that the purity of the mosque was always maintained. People could perform worship in the mosque in safety without having to be afraid of contamination. Most evident is the recompense that God gives for all man's deeds, be they only so big as a tiny seed (QS 99:7–8).[6] [p. 94]

Jihad can also be performed with wealth (*amwaal*). Namely with alms, charitable contributions, donations, sacrificing wealth to build educational facilities, economic infrastructure, health facilities and such-like intended to develop the reserves of the faithful. This is emphasized in QS 8:60.[7] In this verse, God emphasizes that Muslims should always make numerous preparations (read: not acting randomly) to face each and every evil conspiracy perpetrated by enemies of God. These preparations must be complete in nature and encompass all lines of defence and all aspects of the lives of believers.

It is time for Islam to carry out jihad in a planned and organized fashion, and not just rely on emotion. It is organized struggle (jihad) that will cause God's enemies to quake. One aspect of jihad that is also very important is battle (*qitaal*). Battle is called for in Islam to defend oneself from tyrannical deeds, from torture, and to defend and disseminate Islamic teachings, as reflected in the Qur'an (QS 22:38–39).[8] Almighty God shall also bring victory to Muslims in their battles, measured not by sheer numbers, but by the strength of Muslims' allegiance to His teachings as reflected in their attitudes and behaviour. [p. 95]

History has shown how Muslim forces in the battle of Badar were able to subdue the forces of the Quraisy unbelievers despite the small number of their troops and their improvised weaponry (QS 3:123).[9] Or what about the story of Thalut [David], who was considered inferior and weak, being able to face and defeat Jalut [Goliath], who was considered all-powerful and a superpower, by the grace of God (QS 2:249).[10] When followers of Islam felt arrogant at the battle of Hunain, because their numbers were quite plentiful, what occurred was a situation of disarray.

---

6 'whoever has done an atom's-weight of good will see it, but whoever has done an atom's-weight of evil will see that' (Q99: 7–8, Haleem).

7 'Prepare whatever forces you [believers] can muster, including warhorses, to frighten off God's enemies and yours, and warn others unknown to you but known to God. Whatever you give in God's cause will be repaid to you in full, and you will not be wronged' (Q8: 60, Haleem).

8 'Those who have been attacked are permitted to take up arms because they have been wronged – God has the power to help them – those who have been driven unjustly from their homes only for saying, "Our Lord is God". If God did not repel some people by means of others, many monasteries, churches, synagogues, and mosques, where God's name is much invoked, would have been destroyed. God is sure to help those who help His cause – God is strong and mighty' (Q22: 38–9, Haleem).

9 'God helped you at Badr when you were very weak. Be mindful of God, so that you may be grateful' (Q3: 123, Haleem).

10 'When Talut set out with his forces, he said to them, "God will test you with a river. Anyone who drinks from it will not belong with me, but anyone who refrains from tasting it will belong with me; if he scoops up just one handful [he will be excused]". But they all drank [deep] from it, except for a few. When he crossed it with those who had kept faith, they said, "We have no strength today against

God then lent aid to His obedient and faithful flock and brought disaster and destruction upon the unbelievers (QS 9:25–26).[11] Another verse (QS 3:146)[12] also described just how great the trials faced by the Prophets and their followers were in waging war on the infidel, but because of their extraordinary patience, all obstacles (battles) could be surmounted.

In fighting against an enemy, Islam stipulates several regulations, among them being: (a) [one must have] a true purpose for God alone; (b) one is not permitted to hope for the coming of an enemy, but should an enemy be encountered, one must stand firm (*al-hadits*); (c) one is not permitted to kill the elderly, women, children and civilians (QS 2:190[13] and several Hadith); and (d) one must have abundant patience, a united front and strong weaponry (QS 8:60).[14]

Islam's teachings on jihad are truly beautiful and noble. God has even likened faith and undertaking jihad in His path to a deal that will save His flock from fearful torment, and God shall purchase with heaven all the wealth and souls of His flock who join the noble struggle (QS 61:10–13).[15] Verily this victory is most imminent. Yet this victory will never be achieved without struggle. Struggle will not succeed without sacrifice. And jihad, both with wealth (*amwaal*) and with soul (*anfus*), is the truest form of sacrifice. *And God alone knows the truth.* [pp. 96–7]

14.1.2 Azyumardi Azra

Commentary Professor Azyumardi Azra is the rector of the State Islamic University Syarif Hidayatullah in Jakarta. He is one of Indonesia's leading historians and a prominent commentator on a wide range of Islamic issues. In recent years, he has been a vocal critic of militant Muslim groups, particularly those that resort to violence in pursuing their goals. He has also been at pains to assert what he sees as the essentially

---

Goliath and his warriors". But those who knew that they were going to meet their Lord said, "How often a small force has defeated a large army with God's permission! God is with those who are steadfast".' (Q2: 249, Haleem).

11 'God has helped you [believers] on many battlefields, even on the day of the Battle of Hunayn. You were well pleased with your large numbers, but they were of no use to you: the earth seemed to close in on you despite its spaciousness, and you turned tail and fled. Then God sent His calm down to His Messenger and the believers, and He sent down invisible forces. He punished the disbelievers – this is what the disbelievers deserve' (Q9: 25–6, Haleem).

12 'Many prophets have fought, with large bands of godly men alongside them who, in the face of their sufferings for God's cause, did not lose heart or weaken or surrender – God loves those who are steadfast' (Q3: 146, Haleem).

13 'Fight in God's cause against those who fight you, but do not overstep the limits: God does not love those who overstep the limits' (Q2: 190, Haleem).

14 Q8: 60 is given in footnote 7.

15 'You who believe, shall I show you a bargain that will save you from painful punishment? Have faith in God and His Messenger and struggle for His cause with your possessions and your persons – that is better for you, if only you knew – and He will forgive your sins, admit you into Gardens graced with flowing streams, into pleasant dwellings in the Gardens of Eternity. That is the supreme triumph. And He will give you something else that will really please you: His help and an imminent breakthrough. [Prophet], give the faithful the good news' (Q61: 10–13, Haleem).

tolerant nature of Indonesian Islam, especially given the tendency among sections of the Western media to portray Southeast Asian Muslims as 'radical' or narrowly 'conservative'. In the following extract, he argues that violent or extremist jihad is contrary to Islamic norms. Words in quotes are given in English in the text.

Extract 14-2: Azyumardi Azra

Azyumardi Azra (2004), 'Epilog: Islam, Globalisasi Kekerasan, dan Tantangan Demokrasi' [Epilogue: Islam, the Globalization of Violence, and the Challenge of Democracy], pp. 119–27 in Rudhy Suharto, Wihaji PWH and Chamad Hojin (eds), *Terorisme, Perang Global, Masa Depan Demokrasi* [Terrorism, Global War, the Future of Democracy], Matapena, Depok. Extract: pp. 121–4.

Islam and Terrorism

Prominent figures and religious communities have agreed to condemn all forms of violence, including wars and terrorism attacks. As was mentioned at the start of this article, terrorists and terrorism have become the new icon of violence. For some groups, 'terrorism' is a very difficult moral issue, making it hard to define. The general, popular definition of 'terrorism' put forward by some experts is 'any violent political action that does not have moral and legal justification, [notwithstanding] whether that violence is committed by a revolutionary group or a government/state[']. But there are differing opinions among various groups of experts and governments regarding what is 'justifiable' and 'unjustifiable' political violence, depending on who is assessing this. 'Unjustifiable' political violence for some people or groups may be very 'justifiable' for another group.

Terrorism as political violence is totally at odds with human ethics. Because the negative consequences are very great and far-reaching, it is clear that terrorism is contrary not only to human values but also to religious teachings. Islam – as a religion of compassion, [which is] hospitable and peaceful for all groups – teaches a human ethic that strongly stresses universal humanity (*al-ukhuwwah al-insâniyyah*). Islam urges its community of believers to struggle to create peace, justice and respect. But that struggle must not be undertaken by means of violence, terrorism and war. Each struggle for justice, peace and harmony must start from the premise that justice and peace are universal values which have to be upheld and defended by humankind.

Islam recommends and provides the justification for Muslims to struggle, to wage war (*harb*) and to use violence (*qitâl*) against oppressors, enemies of Islam, and outside forces who are hostile towards and do not want to live peacefully with Islam or Muslims (see Q.S. al-Baqarah 2: 190–1, 216–17; al-'Anfâl 8: 59–60; al-Tawbah 9: 36, 38; al-Hajj 22: 39–40; al-'Ahzâb 33: 60–2; Hujarât 49: 9–10).[16] These verses of the Qur'an refer to groups, not to individuals. Muslims are seen as one group (*ummat*),

---

16   Q2: 190 is given in footnote 13.

'Fight in God's cause against those who fight you, but do not overstep the limits: God does not love those who overstep the limits. Kill them wherever you encounter them, and drive them out from where they drove you out, for persecution is more serious than killing. Do not fight them at the Sacred Mosque

not individual Muslims. Likewise, the enemies of Muslims and Islam are referred to as a 'group', not as individuals. Thus, according to Islam, violent actions towards individuals are invalid and immoral. Included in this understanding is the 'sweeping' of individuals who are assumed to be 'representatives' of Islam's enemies.[17]

It is obligatory for Muslims to uphold what is good and resist evil (*amar al-ma`rûf wan nahy al-munkar*). There are many ways to carry out this obligation. But it is clear according to Islamic teachings that the use of violence – even more so terror and war – are criminal acts. In fact, using violence to uphold virtue and eliminate evil constitutes a form of injustice and tyranny (*zhulm*).

Quite a few Qur'anic verses describe individuals and groups that are oppressed by society and those in power (Q.S. al-A`râf 7: 123–6; Yûnus 10: 108–9; Ibrâhîm

---

unless they fight you there. If they do fight you, kill them – this is what such disbelievers deserve' (Q2: 191, Haleem).

'"Fighting is ordained for you, though you dislike it. You may dislike something although it is good for you, or like something although it is bad for you: God knows and you do not." They ask you [Prophet] about fighting in the prohibited month. Say, "Fighting in that month is a great offence, but to bar others from God's path, to disbelieve in Him, prevent access to the Sacred Mosque, and expel its people, are still greater offences in God's eyes: persecution is worse than killing". They will not stop fighting you [believers] until they make you revoke your faith, if they can. If any of you revoke your faith and die as disbelievers, your deeds will come to nothing in this world and the Hereafter, and you will be inhabitants of the Fire, there to remain' (Q2: 216–17, Haleem).

'The disbelievers should not think they have won – they cannot escape. Prepare whatever forces you [believers] can muster, including warhorses, to frighten off God's enemies and yours, and warn others unknown to you but known to God. Whatever you give in God's cause will be repaid to you in full, and you will not be wronged' (Q8: 59–60).

'God decrees that there are twelve months – ordained in God's Book on the Day when He created the heavens and earth – four months of which are sacred: this is the correct calculation. Do not wrong your souls in these months – though you may fight the idolaters at any time, if they first fight you – remember that God is with those who are mindful of Him' (Q9: 36, Haleem).

'Believers, why, when it is said to you, "Go and fight in God's way", do you dig your heels into the earth? Do you prefer this world to the life to come? How small the enjoyment of this world is, compared with the life to come!' (Q9: 38, Haleem).

'Those who have been attacked are permitted to take up arms because they have been wronged – God has the power to help them – those who have been driven unjustly from their homes only for saying, "Our Lord is God". If God did not repel some people by means of others, many monasteries, churches, synagogues, and mosques, where God's name is much invoked, would have been destroyed. God is sure to help those who help His cause – God is strong and mighty' (Q22: 39–40, Haleem).

'If the hypocrites, the sick at heart, and those who spread lies in the city do not desist, We shall rouse you [Prophet] against them, and then they will only be your neighbours in this city for a short while. They will be rejected wherever they are found, and then seized and killed. This has been God's practice with those who went before. You will find no change in God's practices' (Q33: 60–2).

'If two groups of the believers fight, you [believers] should try to reconcile them; if one of them is [clearly] oppressing the other, fight the oppressors until they submit to God's command, then make a just and even-handed reconciliation between the two of them: God loves those who are even-handed. The believers are brothers, so make peace between your two brothers and be mindful of God, so that you may be given mercy' (Q49: 9–10, Haleem).

17 'Sweeping' in this context refers to raids undertaken by militant Islamic groups to drive Westerners, particularly Americans, from a city or region. Although it is often threatened, there have been few instances where Islamic groups have succeeded in 'sweeping' Westerners from a city.

14: 12; al-Ahqâf 46: 35).[18] In such situations, believers are advised to continue to hold firm to their faith and to remain always on the right path, and at the same time to face with fortitude the oppression, injustice and violence that they suffer. In cases like this, the Qur'an does not recommend the use of counter-attack or war. On the contrary, the Qur'an continues to enjoin striving for peace as much as possible before undertaking self-defence that might involve the use of force.

In that last [mentioned] context, the Qur'an does urge Muslims to wage war as a last resort (jihad) against those enemies of Islam and Muslims who do not want peace (Q.S. al-Baqarah 2: 190–3, 216–17; al-Tawbah 9: 41; al-Hajj 22: 39–40; al-Mumtahinah 60: 1–3).[19] But it is important to state that these Qur'anic verses speak about oppressed people who are driven from their homeland, and the Qur'an tells them to organize themselves to defend themselves in order to gain their freedom from oppression and to attain respect/dignity for themselves and their religion (*izzu al-Islâm wa al-Muslimîn*). Thus we find two aspects in these verses, internal and external. Internally, the Qur'an asks those who are oppressed to be steadfast in their struggle, to defend their lives and belief. Externally, when a society defends and sus-

---

18 'but Pharaoh said, "How dare you believe in Him before I have given you permission? This is a plot you have hatched to drive the people out of this city! Soon you will see: I will cut off your alternate hands and feet and then crucify you all!" They said, "And so we shall return to our Lord. Your only grievance against us is that we believed in the signs of our Lord when they came to us. Our Lord, pour steadfastness upon us and let us die in devotion to You".' (Q7: 123–6, Haleem).

'Say, "People, the Truth has come to you from your Lord. Whoever follows the right path follows it for his own good, and whoever strays does so to his own loss: I am not your guardian". [Prophet], follow what is being revealed to you, and be steadfast until God gives His judgement, for He is the Best of Judges' (Q10: 108–9, Haleem).

'"why should we not put our trust in God when it is He who has guided us to this way we follow? We shall certainly bear steadfastly whatever harm you do to us. Let anyone who trusts, trust in God."' (Q14: 12, Haleem).

'Be steadfast [Muhammad], like those messengers of firm resolve. Do not seek to hasten the punishment for the disbelievers: on the Day they see what they had been warned about, it will seem to them that they lingered no more than a single hour of a single day [in this life]. This is a warning. Shall any be destroyed except the defiant?' (Q46: 35, Haleem).

19 Q2: 190 is given in footnote 13 and Q2: 191 in footnote 16.

'but if they stop, then God is most forgiving and merciful. Fight them until there is no more persecution, and [your] worship is devoted to God. If they cease hostilities, there can be no [further] hostility, except towards aggressors' (Q192–3, Haleem).

Q2: 216–17 are given in footnote 16.

'So go out, no matter whether you are lightly or heavily armed, and struggle in God's way with your possessions and your persons: this is better for you, if you only knew' (Q9: 41, Haleem).

Q22: 39–40 are given in footnote 16.

'You who believe, do not take My enemies and yours as your allies, showing them friendship when they have rejected the truth you have received, and have driven you and the Messenger out simply because you believe in God, your Lord – not if you truly emigrated in order to strive for My cause and seek My good pleasure. You secretly show them friendship – I know all you conceal and all you reveal – but any of you who do this are straying from the right path. If they gain the upper hand over you, they will revert to being your enemies and stretch out their hands and tongues to harm you; it is their dearest wish that you may renounce your faith. Neither your kinsfolk nor your children will be any use to you on the Day of Resurrection: He will separate you out. God sees everything you do' (Q60: 1–3).

tains itself or another social group from outside aggression, then in truth all of that is a struggle for justice and peace.

'Jihad' with the meaning 'war', therefore, is an action to defend oneself (*defensif*), not [an] aggressive [action]. Jihad according to Islamic concepts is *bellum justum* (just war) and *bellum pium* (pious war), and war for peace and harmony. Jihad with the meaning of war is often associated or even identified by the West with 'terror' and 'terrorism'. The extent to which jihad can be changed to become 'terror' and 'terrorism' has to be viewed against the moral justification for those actions of jihad, as well as whether or not it is in accord with other aspects of Islamic teachings.

Jihad can also have a very broad meaning. Simply, jihad is divided into two: *jihâd akbar*, that is, jihad to resist those uncontrollable desires in each and every Muslim; and *jihâd asghar*, that is, war to oppose the enemies of Islam and Muslims. Jihad can also carry the meaning 'every earnest effort that is undertaken to do good (*fi sabîlillâh*) and that is intended as an act of devotion to Almighty God'. And a person who dies performing such an act of devotion can be called a *syahîd* ('martyr'), in the same manner as those who perish in jihad defending themselves from the enemies of Muslims and Islam.

In all these perspectives, it must be acknowledged, Muslim individuals and groups that carry out political violence can be found to have some elements of moral justification. Acts of political violence (terrorism) that are performed by Palestinian fighters and groups to oppose the terrorism ('state terrorism') of the Israeli Zionist state, for example, are morally justified by the oppression they have suffered over a long time. The Palestinian people have had their rights to obtain justice and peace taken away by Israel, which is supported almost without 'reserve' [reservation] by the United States and many other Western nations. But it is also hard to deny that there are Palestinian fighters and groups – and also people who have Muslim names who attacked the WTC [World Trade Center] in New York and the Pentagon – who have no moral justification whatsoever for attacking and killing civilians who have absolutely no connection with the problems of injustice and oppression.

Although there is an element of moral justification in the struggle undertaken by Muslim groups like the PLO [Palestine Liberation Organization], the Palestinian fighters should continue to strive for a livelihood and the development of other methods (peaceful) to oppose oppression and injustice. This is important because the struggle to fight injustice and oppression which is undertaken by those Muslim groups has already been stigmatized as 'Muslim terrorism' or even 'Islamic terrorism' that serves to damage and destroy the image of Islam as a religion of peace and tranquillity (Islam, *salâm* [peace]).

14.2 SALAFI JIHADISM

Commentary In recent years, jihad has come to be regarded in the West as synonymous with 'holy war' and terrorism, although, as is apparent from the foregoing, this is a far narrower conception of the term than most Muslims have. Indeed, many Muslims object to jihad being viewed exclusively as an aggressive act, even more so if the term is closely associated with terrorist attacks. Within the Muslim community and some scholarly circles, a preferred term for 'Islamic terrorists' is 'Salafi jihadists'. There are several reasons for preferring the latter. First, it avoids the problematic issue of defining terrorism. Second, 'Salafi jihadism' is a more specific term derived from a doctrinal understanding widely held among those Muslims engaged in violent jihad. Although such people may not describe themselves as 'Salafi jihadists', they do see themselves proudly as both *salafi* and jihadist. Thus, 'Salafi jihadism' is a less loaded descriptor for those who see the use of violence as a primary form of jihad. The term 'Salafi jihadism' is explained further in the terminology section of chapter 1 (Box 1.1).

The contemporary *salafi* movement is diverse and fragmented but it has several common features. It is socially conservative, strongly anti-Western, usually apolitical and intolerant of political subversion. Most salafists pursue their religious objectives through non-violent activities such as teaching, preaching, and intellectual pursuits such as carrying out research and publishing.

A small minority of salafists are jihadist, in that they believe that violent jihad is the only way to achieve their goals. This Salafi jihadist movement rose to prominence with the war of the *mujahidin* (those who fight a holy war) against Soviet forces in Afghanistan in the late 1970s and 1980s. Commonly, Salafi jihadists believe that Islam's foes in the West are engaged in a relentless campaign to destroy the faith (see also chapter 15). They regard it as obligatory for Muslims to join in the war to defend Islam. For an example of Salafi jihadist imagery, see plate 16 in the colour section of this book.

The following extracts present a variety of Salafi jihadist perspectives on the need to combat Islam's enemies, including through the use of 'terror' attacks. These texts also make apparent a strong pan-Islamist perspective on the part of their authors. Two of the extracts – those of Imam Samudra and particularly Mukhlas – are quoted at length. The reasons for this are three-fold. First, they reveal a great deal about the Salafi jihadist ideology and psychology. Second, they are not widely available to a Western audience and, in the case of the Mukhlas text, have been sighted by very few Southeast Asians. And third, the harmful impact of terrorism on Southeast Asian security and on the image of the region's Muslims requires that considerable attention be given to explaining the motivations of terrorists, even though they constitute only a tiny minority of Southeast Asia's Muslim community. The space devoted to Salafi jihadist documents should not, therefore, be taken as an indicator of the popularity of such views.

14.2.1   General Struggle Guidelines of Jemaah Islamiyah

Commentary   JI was founded in Malaysia on 1 January 1993 by the Indonesian religious scholar Abdullah Sungkar, according to an 'official statement' issued in 2003.[20] Over the next decade it would grow to become Southeast Asia's most lethal terrorist organization. Since 2000 it has been responsible for a string of terrorist attacks, the largest being the Bali bombings of 12 October 2002, which killed 202 people and left over 300 others seriously injured. JI is also the region's only genuinely transnational terrorist group, with active cells, at least until recently, in the Philippines, Singapore, Malaysia

---

20   Mu'nim Mulia, Ustadz (probably a pseudonym), 'Pernyataan Resmi al-Jamaah al-Islamiyyah' [Official Statement of Jemaah Islamiyah], 6 October 2003. This statement was circulated within JI circles and several JI sources claim that it is genuine.

and Australia. It has operational ties with the MILF and the Abu Sayyaf Group in the Philippines and has at times had close, though not necessarily subordinate, relations with al-Qaeda.[21]

The status of the General Struggle Guidelines of JI – the *Pedoman Umum Perjuangan Al-Jama'ah Al-Islamiyyah*, or PUPJI as the document is commonly known – has been the subject of some dispute, particularly in Indonesia, though most analysts in regional and Western governments, and terrorism scholars, regard the document as authentic. According to the Indonesian police and the interrogation transcripts of Aly Ghufron Nurhasyim (alias Mukhlas), a senior JI figure, the first volume of the PUPJI was approved by JI leaders in December 1995 and the second volume containing the organization's constitution and structural arrangements (*Nidhom Asasi*) was approved in mid-1996. The document was widely used in JI training and as a guide for leadership deliberations until at least 2001 when, according to one JI member, most copies were destroyed for fear they would fall into police hands. Police discovered a copy during a raid on a JI command post in December 2002 (Neighbour 2004: 134; Nasir 2005: 102–3).

The aim of the document was to set out the ideological foundations, basic structures and operational methods of JI. Undoubtedly JI instructors would have elaborated on the document during training sessions, and senior members were expected to have a thorough understanding of its content and rationale.

The PUPJI is difficult reading. The style is dry, formal and often inexplicit as to detail, befitting its 'general guidelines' title. In line with its function as a manual, it is carefully structured and organized into chapters, sections and subsections. Descriptions of aims and functions are given in sparse and direct language.

When describing the aims of its programs, the compilers of the PUPJI support each point with at least one specific Qur'anic reference and repeatedly emphasize that it is the Prophet's example that is being followed.

Among other things, the PUPJI prescribes that JI:

- is a covert, highly centralized and, at least in theory, tightly structured organization;
- is based on *salafi* principles, that is, a desire to emulate strictly the norms and example of the first three generations of Muslims;
- has as its ultimate aim the re-establishment of a global caliphate, though this is to be preceded by a local Islamic state; and
- places great emphasis on both predication (*dakwah*) and armed jihad.

Of particular interest is the process described in the PUPJI for achieving an Islamic state and caliphate. This is to be attained gradually, by establishing through preaching and education 'safe Islamic bases' in which observance of Islamic law is high and the 'secular' Indonesian state has little or no influence. Such bases become the beachheads for a broader program of converting the Islamic community to JI's creed and then creating an Islamic state in which sharia can be implemented comprehensively. Armed jihad facilitates this program by destabilizing and destroying infidel governments.[22]

---

21 For the most authoritative and detailed accounts of JI, see ICG (2002a, 2002b, 2003, 2004, 2005a). For more general accounts, see Jones (2003, 2005); Sidney Jones is also the main author of the ICG reports. Other useful accounts can be found in Abuza (2003), Barton (2004), Neighbour (2004), Bubalo and Fealy (2005) and Nasir (2005).

22 For a discussion of the PUPJI, see Nasir (2005: 102–25); Abegebriel, Abeveiro and SR-Ins Team (2004: 830–94), including an extract from the PUPJI on pp. 873–93; Neighbour (2004: 133–5, 320); and ICG (2003: 11).

Extract 14-3: General Struggle Guidelines of Jemaah Islamiyah

Majlis Qiyadah Markaziyah Al-Jama'ah Al-Islamiyyah [Central Leadership Council of Jemaah Islamiyah] (1996), *Pedoman Umum Perjuangan Al-Jama'ah Al-Islami-yyah* [General Struggle Guidelines of Jemaah Islamiyah], 30 May. Extract: pp. 3–18, appendices.

[…] Al-Jama'ah Al-Islamiyah [that is, Jemaah Islamiyah], a community of Muslims that was born and stands with other true Muslim communities in the arena of preaching and jihad in the path of God, with an eye to ensuring it abides by the straight path of Islamic principles, has compiled these General Struggle Guidelines.

The General Struggle Guidelines are an outline that can give a general picture of the community's actions, which fuse fundamental values with precise, oriented and focused operational steps. [p. 3] […]

PRINCIPLE ONE
OUR SOLE OBJECTIVE IS TO SEEK GOD'S BLESSINGS ACCORDING TO THE MEANS GOD AND HIS PROPHET HAVE LAID DOWN.

PRINCIPLE TWO
OUR CREED IS THAT OF THOSE WHO FOLLOW THE TRADITIONS OF THE PROPHET AND COMMUNITY USING THE APPROACH OF THE PIOUS ANCESTORS (*Ahli Sunnah wal Jama'ah 'ala minhajis salafish shalih*).

PRINCIPLE THREE
OUR UNDERSTANDING OF ISLAM IS A COMPREHENSIVE ONE IN LINE WITH THE UNDERSTANDING OF THE PIOUS ANCESTORS.

PRINCIPLE FOUR
THE OBJECTIVE OF OUR STRUGGLE IS TO HAVE MANKIND SUBMIT TO GOD ALONE BY RESTORING THE CALIPHATE ON EARTH.

PRINCIPLE FIVE
OUR PATH IS THE PATH OF FAITH, WITHDRAWAL (*hijrah*)[23] AND JIHAD IN THE PATH OF GOD.

PRINCIPLE SIX
OUR MEANS ARE:
1. KNOWLEDGE AND PIETY.
2. CONVICTION AND RESIGNATION TO GOD'S WILL.
3. GRATITUDE TO GOD AND PATIENCE.
4. AN ASCETIC LIFE AND THE GIVING OF PRIORITY TO THE HEREAFTER.
5. LOVE OF JIHAD IN THE PATH OF GOD AND LOVE OF A MARTYR'S DEATH.

---

23 Literally, 'flight', but it can also have the meaning of seeking refuge or withdrawing from danger.

PRINCIPLE SEVEN
OUR LOYALTY IS TO GOD, HIS PROPHET AND PEOPLE OF FAITH.

PRINCIPLE EIGHT
OUR ENEMY IS SATAN IN THE FORM OF SPIRITS
AND IN THE FORM OF HUMAN BEINGS.

PRINCIPLE NINE
THE BONDS LINKING OUR COMMUNITY ARE BASED ON OUR COMMON
PURPOSE, DOCTRINE AND UNDERSTANDING OF RELIGION.

PRINCIPLE TEN
WE PRACTISE ISLAM IN A PURE AND TOTAL WAY ADVANCING FROM A
COMMUNITY TO A STATE BASED ON ISLAM TO A CALIPHATE. [pp. 5–6]

METHOD OF THE MOVEMENT TO ESTABLISH THE FAITH

I. Interpretation:
The method of the movement to establish the faith contains the guiding principles for systematic steps essential to upholding the faith.

II. Function:
The method of the movement to establish the faith is realized in the Ten Principles. They function as a principal guide for the Operational Methodology.

III. Stages: [...]
A. Preparation for Establishing an Islamic State
1. Creation of a Community
   a. Establishment of rightly guided and pious leadership.
   b. Establishment of a solid leadership base.
   c. Implementation of a secret organization.
   d. Building faith and loyalty.
   e. Commanding good and forbidding evil.
   f. Moral supervision.

2. Development of Strength
   a. Education.
   b. Preaching.
   c. Developing a safe haven.
   d. Developing jihad.
   e. Developing military mobilization.
   f. Developing safe leadership bases.
   g. Developing territory.
   h. Human resource development and training.
   i. Finance.
   j. Intelligence.
   k. Collaboration with and coordination of other communities.

3. **Use of Strength**
    a. Issuing warnings and reminders.
    b. Armed jihad.
B. **Establishment of an Islamic State**
    1. **Establishing a State**
        a. Bureaucracy.
        b. Military mobilization and recruitment.
        c. Jihad.
        d. Governance.
        e. Finance.
        f. Developing an Islamic society.
        g. Education.
    2. **Strengthening the Islamic State**
    3. **Coordination and Collaboration with Other Islamic States**

C. **Establishment of a Caliphate** [p. 7] [...]

BASIC ORGANIZATIONAL STRUCTURE (*Nidhom Asasi*) [p. 13] [...]

CHAPTER I
NAME, CHARACTERISTICS AND PLACE

Article 1
This community is called the 'Islamic Community' (*al-Jama'ah al-Islamiyah*).

Article 2
1. This community is a community of Muslims (*Jama'atun minal-Muslimin*).
2. This community is transnational in nature.

Article 3
The community's centre of administration is at a location that fulfils our requirements.

CHAPTER II
BASIS, AIMS AND COURSE OF STRUGGLE

Article 4
1. The community is based on the Qur'an and Sunnah in accordance with the under-
    standing of the Pious Ancestors.
2. The aim of this community is to create an Islamic State as the basis for re-estab-
    lishing a Caliphate in the way of the Prophet.

Article 5
To achieve these aims, the community will undertake: predication, education, commanding good and forbidding evil, withdrawal and war in the path of God.

CHAPTER III
ORGANIZATION

Article 6

1. The community is led by a Commander (*Amir*).
2. In undertaking his tasks, the Commander is assisted by Leadership Councils (Majelis-Majelis Qiyadah), an Advisory Council (Majelis Syuro), a Legal Rulings Council (Majelis Fatwa) and a Council for Upholding Religious Morality (Majelis Hisbah).
3. The Leadership Councils consist of the Central Leadership Council (Majelis Qiyadah Markaziyah), Regional Leaders Council (Majelis Qiyadah Manthiqiyah) and District Leaders' Council (Majelis Qiyadah Wakalah).

CHAPTER IV
ADMINISTRATION

Article 7

The Commander is elected and installed by the Advisory Council.

Article 8

1. The Commander takes oaths [of allegiance] from members.
2. The Commander appoints and dismisses members of the Advisory Council, members of the Central Leadership Council, members of the Legal Rulings Council and members of the Council for Upholding Religious Morality.
3. The Commander convenes deliberations of the central councils.
4. The Commander levies routine and incidental fees on members.
5. The Commander issues sanctions and re-educates community members who breach community regulations.
6. The Commander undertakes contact with outside groups who are seen as bringing benefit to the community.

Article 9

1. The Commander leads the administration of the community.
2. The Commander in leading community administration consults with the Advisory Council, Leadership Councils, Islamic Law Council and/or Council for Upholding Religious Morality.
3. The Commander gives training to members to understand and carry out Islam's teachings.
4. The Commander defends and protects members and is mindful of their welfare.
5. The Commander implements Islamic law where it may be applied.
6. The Commander appoints temporary officials if he has difficulty carrying out his duties.

Article 10

The term of a Commander is terminated by:
a. Death.

b. And/or infirmity.
c. And/or by being dismissed by the Advisory Council after being proven to have clearly behaved in a godless way.
d. After being proven to have been externally pressured to the point of being weak in managing the community in accordance with Islamic law. [pp. 14–15] [...]

CHAPTER X
MEMBERSHIP

Article 30

An individual is eligible to be a member of the community if he or she fulfils the following conditions:
a. Is a Muslim, upholding the principles of the Pious Ancestors in matters of faith, and practising devotions free of innovations and superstitions.
b. Understands the teachings of God and His Prophet regarding the community.
c. Understands and accepts the Ten Principles of the method of the movement to establish the faith.
d. Takes the oath of allegiance from the Commander of the community directly or by letter or through the person he appoints.
e. Has reached puberty [and is therefore of age].
f. Has gone through the selection process [p. 18] [...]

EDUCATION [...]

IV. AIM OF EDUCATION
To create a generation that is attached to God and that is able to build an Islamic State in the context of realizing devotion only to Almighty God in their lives, both as individuals and as a community. [Appendices: p. 21] [...]

BUILDING UP SAFE BASES

I. MEANING
   1. Meaning of Safe Bases
   Meaning of safe bases is a base that is safe from the enemy's power.
   2. Meaning of Safe Bases
     a. Creating safe bases is part of building up an area in which the community can take refuge for training.
     b. Building safe bases covers all efforts, activities and actions aimed at creating this safe zone free from the enemy.

II. FUNCTION OF SAFE BASES
   1. As a solid headquarters, geographically, demographically, politically and militarily.
   2. As an area to which Muslims can come to seek refuge.
   3. As a base from which preachers and holy war fighters can go forth. [...]

IV. CRITERIA FOR A SAFE BASE

1. Geography:
   a. The location of the territory is advantageous for defence.
   b. The condition of the ground is good for defence.
   c. There is a source of logistics.
2. Demography:
   a. The majority of residents have already welcomed the call of the preaching and are ready for self-sacrifice.
   b. The authorities are unable to fully control the Islamic community.
   c. The leadership group is under the control of the 'followers of the movement' (*abnaul harokah*).
   d. The followers of the movement are ready and able to provide protection.
3. Politics:
   a. The formal as well as informal leadership of society is dominated by the followers of the movement.
   b. [Who are] able to neutralize the enemy's political pressure.
   c. There is outside recognition through cooperation as well as diplomatic means. [Appendices: p. 30] [...]

ARMED JIHAD

I. DEFINITION

Definition of Armed Jihad:

1. The meaning of armed jihad is *Qital* [War].
2. *Qital* is to embark on war in the path of God in order to combat the enemies of God and His Prophet, including infidel rulers, polytheists, apostates, atheists, the Islamically corrupt and their lackeys. [...] [Appendices: p. 37]

III. FUNCTIONS:

1. To defeat the power of the sinful rulers (*toghut*)[24] (who are a source of calumny) who always thwart preaching in the way of the Prophet (Al-Anfal: 39).[25]
2. To fight tyranny and establish the truth so as to prevent the spread of destruction on the face of the earth (Al-Baqoroh: 251; Al-Hajj: 39–40).[26]

---

24 Toghut was the name of a goddess in pre-Islamic Mecca but in the Qur'an is used variously to denote false deities and evil. In contemporary jihadist literature *toghut* usually refers to leaders who are enemies of Islam.

25 '[Believers], fight them until there is no more persecution, and [your] worship is devoted to God alone: if they desist, then God sees all that they do' (Q8: 39, Haleem).

26 'and so with God's permission they defeated them. David killed Goliath, and God gave him sovereignty and wisdom and taught him what He pleased. If God did not drive some back by means of others the earth would be completely corrupt, but God is bountiful to all' (Q2: 251, Haleem).

Q22: 39–40 is given in footnote 16.

3. To protect the existence and honour of all Muslims and assist the oppressed (Annisa: 75).[27]
4. To humiliate God's enemies and cause them to tremble, and to prevent them from doing evil (Attaubah: 29, Al-Anfal: 60, Annisa: 84).[28]
5. To distinguish and separate the believers from the infidels/hypocrites and to pave the way for a martyr's death (Ali-Imron: 140–142).[29]
6. To test the faith (Muhammad: 4).[30]
7. To strengthen power on the face of the earth with the objective of upholding God's law, which means justice and living under God's protection. [...]

V. TARGET:

1. To establish an Islamic Caliphate based on the way of the Prophet.
2. The method of the movement to establish the faith is armed jihad which aims to restore the Islamic State. [Appendices: pp. 39–40]

14.2.2   International Martyrs' Battalion

Commentary   Shortly after the Bali bombings of 12 October 2002, a statement appeared on a website called Istimata ('prepared to die', martyrs) claiming responsibility for the attack and setting out the reasons for it. Imam Samudra, a central figure in the bombings (see extract 14-5), was probably responsible for establishing the website and determining its content. Draft copies of the statement, or 'Istimata Declaration' as it is sometimes called, were found on his laptop computer when it was seized by police (*Kompas*, 8 July 2003). He also tipped off the Indonesian media to the site's existence, telling a journalist that 'this website contains the hope of my struggle' (*Kompas*, 5 December 2002). The site comprised almost identical statements in Indonesian and

---

27   'Why should you not fight in God's cause and for those oppressed men, women, and children who cry out, "Lord, rescue us from this town whose people are oppressors! By Your grace, give us a protector and helper!"?' (Q4: 75, Haleem).

28   'Fight those of the People of the Book who do not [truly] believe in God and the Last Day, who do not forbid what God and His Messenger have forbidden, who do not obey the rule of justice until they pay the tax and agree to submit' (Q9: 29, Haleem).

Q8: 60 is given in footnote 7.

'So [Prophet] fight in God's way. You are accountable only for yourself. Urge the believers on. God may well curb the power of the disbelievers, for He is stronger in might and more terrible in punishment' (Q4: 84, Haleem).

29   'if you have suffered a blow, they too have suffered one like it. We deal out such days among people in turn, for God to find out who truly believes, for Him to choose martyrs from among you – God does not love evildoers – for Him to cleanse those who believe and for Him to destroy the disbelievers. Did you think you would enter the Garden without God first proving which of you would struggle for His cause and remain steadfast?' (Q3: 140–2, Haleem).

30   'When you meet the disbelievers in battle, strike them in the neck, and once they are defeated, bind any captives firmly – later you can release them by grace or by ransom – until the toils of war have ended. That [is the way]. God could have defeated them Himself if He had willed, but His purpose is to test some of you by means of others. He will not let the deeds of those who are killed for His cause come to nothing' (Q47: 4, Haleem).

English. No mention is made of JI in the statement (perhaps not surprising given JI's clandestine nature), and the only group named is the 'International Martyrs' Battalion'.

The declaration is important, too, for what it reveals about the jihadist logic of JI. It paints a picture of global Islam under siege from non-Muslim forces. Like many al-Qaeda statements, it lists numerous places in the world where Muslims, including non-combatants such as women and children, are being killed and oppressed. The perceived existence of an anti-Islamic pogrom is essential to the 'reciprocity' argument used to validate extreme jihad. The 'indiscriminate' use of violence by Islam's enemies becomes the justification for the Bali bombers responding in kind. Also significant is the 'international' nature of the statement's closing demands. Withdrawal of Western forces from Saudi Arabia and Afghanistan and the closure of the US detention complex at Guantanamo Bay are common demands of jihadist groups in the Middle East, Africa and Central Asia.

Extract 14-4: *International Martyrs' Battalion*

International Istimata Battalion (2002), 'Statement' [in English], <http://www.istimata.com/nyata/htm>, accessed 12 December 2002.

STATEMENT

Let it be known that every single drop of Muslim blood, be it from any nationality or from whatever place, will be remembered and accounted for. Thousands of Muslims have perished, notably in Palestine, Afghanistan, Iraq, Kashmir, Gudjarat and in various places in the Asian continent. Elsewhere in Europe, Muslims were mercilessly prosecuted [persecuted] in Bosnia and Kosovo. While in Africa, Muslims were brutally killed in Sudan. The heinous crime and international conspiracy of the Christians also extends to the Philipine [*sic*] and Indonesia. This has resulted in the 'Muslim Cleansing' in Moro [southern Philippines], Poso, Ambon [Indonesia] and the surrounding areas. It is clearly evident that the Crusade is continuing and will not stop.

The attack on the Islamic State of Afghanistan by the International Christian community and its allies (Allied Force), under the Bush (may the Curse of Allah be upon him) leadership, will not be forgotten. Bush himself acknowledged that the so-called war of 'Undefinite Justice' [*sic*] is really a Crusade. Every blow will be repaid. Blood will be redeemed by blood. A life for a life.

'International Justice', Democratic Values and the efforts as well as the rulings of the United Nations are just empty promises. The Muslim community has never benefited nor received any justice from the *Toghut* [infidel rulers; see footnote 24].

'… and fight the unbelievers as a single entity, as they fight you (Muslims) in total …' (At-taubah: 36).[31]

---

31 Q9: 36 is given in footnote 16.

One Muslim to another Muslim is like a single body. If one part is in pain, then the other part will also feel the pain.

To all you Christian unbelievers (*kafir*)! If you define this act [the Bali bombings] on your civilians as heinous and cruel, your [you] yourself have committed crimes which are more heinous. What about the 600 thousand babies in Iraq and half a million children in Afghanistan including their mothers who are treated as combatants. They are assumed to be at fault and consequently should bear the brunt of thousands of your bombs???!!!!.

Where is your rationality and your conscience???!!!.

The cries of babies and the screams of the Muslimah [Muslim women] as well as the diplomatic efforts of a small number of Muslims has never succeeded in stopping your brutality and it will never succeed.

Well, here we are the Muslimin [Muslims]!!!

Well, here we are, as blood relatives of those who have died as a result of your aggression.

Well, here we are, the muslimin!!!

Our hearts are in pain and we will harnest [*sic*] the pain of the death of our brothers and sisters. We will never let your cruelty on our brothers go unpunished. You will bear the consequences of your actions wherever you are......

We are responsible for the incident in Legian St. Kuta, Bali at Saturday Night, October, 12, 02, also near U.S. General Consulate building in Jalan Hayam Wuruk 188, Denpasar, Bali at the same night.

Our demands are as follows:

1. You will not feel safe from our attacks as long as the Jews and the Christians remain in Masjidil Haram, Masjidil Nabawi and Masjidil Aqsa.[32]
2. People from your countries will experience death, wherever they are, as long as the Allied Force (International Christians and their friends: America, England, Germany, Australia, France, Canada, Netherland, Italy, Japan, China, India, Sweden and others) do not leave Afghanistan.
3. The civilians of your countries will receive the above treatment, as long as our brothers, who you classify as terrorists, remain as prisoners and are tortured in prisons, especially at Guantanamo.
4. With special reference to Indonesian citizens working at BIN (National Intelligence Agency)[33] under the armpits of CIA. If you are a Muslim, seek forgiveness from Allah. Find another job that does not contribute to the sufferings and cause harm to the Muslimin. If you persists in helping the American unbelievers, spy upon the Muslims and spread lies in the Muslim community, we will have no

---

32   The Grand Mosque in Mecca, the Mosque of the Prophet Muhammad in Medina and al-Aqsa Mosque on Temple Mount in Jerusalem; they date from the founding years of Islam and are the holiest of sites for Muslims.

33   Badan Intelijen Negara (BIN, National Intelligence Agency) is Indonesia's main civilian intelligence service.

hesitation in treating you in the same manner as your kafir masters, the American colonials and world terrorist.

Kuta, Oct-12-02
Katibatul Maut Al-Alamiyah
(International Istimata Battalion)

14.2.3 Imam Samudra

Commentary Imam Samudra (alias Abdul Aziz) was a senior JI figure and also the field leader of the Bali bombing team. Born in Serang, Banten, in 1970, Samudra was drawn into Darul Islam circles through his contact with local religious scholars and from there was recruited to go to Afghanistan to fight against the Soviet occupation. After JI was formed in 1993, he joined that organization and became a leading recruiter in the West Java–Banten region. He was arrested in November 2002 and later convicted of terrorism for his role in organizing and carrying out the Bali bombings. He was sentenced to death by firing squad and is currently on death row.

While in jail awaiting trial, Samudra wrote extensively, producing a lengthy diary. This became the basis of his *I Fight Terrorists*, which was published in 2004. Part autobiography, part manifesto and part practical guide to jihad, this work is now in its third printing and has sold over 12,000 copies.

The following extracts reveal a good deal about the thinking of those involved in JI attacks. Samudra's writings set out the view commonly held in jihadist circles that the Islamic world is under mortal threat from the non-Muslim world, especially Jews and Christians. Much space is devoted to the plight of Muslims across the globe, and Samudra seeks to convince readers that violent jihad is the only means of response for pious Muslims. He lauds religious scholars (*ulama* or ulema) who have fought on the battlefield and dismisses Islamic scholars who regard non-violent jihad as more virtuous than militant forms. He then mounts a defence of the Bali bombing chiefly on the grounds of pay-back for the non-Muslim 'slaughter of Muslims'. Note that the 'bomb' bullet points are in the original.

Extract 14-5: Imam Samudra

Imam Samudra (2004), *Aku Melawan Teroris* [I Fight Terrorists], Jazera, Solo. Extract: pp. 67–70, 93–118.

A ruling (fatwa) on death from the frontline [chapter title]

There's no need to be tricked by the title. I really am a troublesome demon who reeks of death. But don't misconstrue this; it doesn't mean that I'm an anarchist or paranoid. I'm just normal, you know.

I've said before that in the matter of jihad, before I implemented it, at controversial points I would adhere to the fatwa of holy-war religious scholars (*ulama mujahid*), namely ulema who have fought on the battlefield of jihad themselves.

It's just like with a patient: if the sickness they're suffering from is in a general category, then they'll go to a general practitioner. But if their disease has reached a certain stage, for instance with obstetrics, naturally they would go to an obstetrician for treatment. Someone with a toothache will go to a dentist. And so on. Theoretically, a general practitioner could understand obstetrics or dentistry, but in practice it would obviously be otherwise.

We can carry this logic over into the context of jihad. How could those ulema who have never fought a jihad or been on the battlefield possibly understand the issues and complexities of jihad?

The *ulama mujahid*, whose clothes have been covered with the dust of jihad, whose sweat has mingled with the smell of ammunition and shells, whose ears are used to the whizzing of bullets, whose hearts have at times palpitated when meeting and fighting with enemy combatants, who have seen pools of blood everywhere, who have been wounded as the Messenger of God was when his teeth were broken by an enemy spear during [the battle of] Uhud,[34] of course they better understand, more fully comprehend and are more suited to responding to the problems of the Muslim faithful, especially with regard to jihad.

In Islam, those on the jihad battlefield, who guard the defensive bastions and who stand on alert at the frontline, are usually called 'people of the frontier' (*ahluts-tsughur*).[35] And the ulema who are in those places are referred to as 'ulema of the frontier' (*ulama ahluts-tsughur*).

Ulema of the frontier are closer to God, are more often reminded of death and are closer to gaining God's guidance. How could this not be so? They are always facing the enemy, facing bullets and bombs, which theoretically could cause wounds and death. Situations like these will automatically guide them to repeat constantly the confession of faith as a form of worship of God, leading them to be more prepared to face death, and distancing them from worldly things like rank, popularity, wealth and so on. [...]

There is no ulema of the frontier who has never taken up arms and fought a jihad against the infidels. [pp. 67–9] [...]

There were the greats like Shalahuddin Al Ayyubi, Umar Mukhtar and others. Following that there were renowned jihadists like Sheikh Asy-Syahid Dr. Abdullah Azzam (who died a martyr in 1987 in Pakistan), Sheikh Aiman Azh-Zhawahiri, Sheikh Sulaiman Abu Ghaits, Sheikh Mullah Omar and Sheikh Usamah bin Ladin. They were all on the frontline of the jihad in Afghanistan. [...]

The International Jewish and Christian media have given them appalling labels. They have been called terrorists, hard-line Islam, extremists, radicals and so on, in an effort to create erroneous public opinion throughout the world. Israel and America have created the image that they, the people of the frontier, are a race of cruel and

---

34   The battle of Uhud took place in 625 CE on the outskirts of Medina between the Muslim forces led by the Prophet Muhammad and the Meccans. Although the Meccans were ultimately driven off, Muhammad was injured in battle and the Muslims suffered heavy losses.

35   *Tsughur* literally means 'gap' or 'space' and historically has referred to vulnerable parts of the borders of Muslim states where battles often occurred with non-Muslim enemies. Thus, in this context, the *ahluts-tsughur* are those who fight to protect the Islamic community from its foes.

sadistic monsters. In fact, in essence it is they themselves who are cruel and sadistic. They are Draculas spawned by Monsters.

Draculas crying dracula!! Monsters crying monster!!! [p. 70] [...]

The situation is that Muslims have been lulled to sleep on so many issues, suffering from a syndrome of lack of confidence due to the jargon of 'Muslims are terrorists' from the fangs of the Draculas spawned by Monsters, and that Muslims in general have chosen to remain silent or don't care, as long as the appetites of their 'stomachs' and 'below the stomach' are not disrupted. When the ulema are also increasingly busily submerged in their collections of holy books and the echo of loudspeakers, they no longer care about the despoiling, vilifying and colonization of Mecca and their holy lands. It was preordained by God that a group of holy war fighters would be born who were truly aware and understood what they had to do.

- In 1993 the first attack on the WTC [World Trade Center] took place, carried out by Ramzi Yusuf. Praise be to God.
- Four years after that (1997) the attacks on the US army headquarters in Khabar, Riyadh and Dhahran, Saudi Arabia, took place.
- In 2000 there was another martyr's attack (martyr's bombing operation) against the USS Cole, an American warship in the Yemen Sea.
- On 11 September 2001 there was another attack that greatly humiliated and hurt the Draculas spawned by Monsters. The WTC and the Pentagon, as the economic and military centres of America and its gang, were broken through and totally collapsed. Sheikh Usamah bin Ladin claimed coordination of the attack and prayed for those involved in this truly fantastic jihad operation – that they would hopefully become martyrs.
- On 12 October 2002, praise be to God, there was the next attack on Uncle SAM (*stupid and moron* [*sic*, original words in English]) and his gang in Bali, a piece of land in Indonesia, where the majority is Muslim.

And God willing, in the future there will be other jihad operations even better and more fantastic in all regards. All of this will add to the long list of Muslim resistance to the colonizing nations and their cronies. [pp. 93–4] [...]

The Meaning of Jihad

[Imam Samudra commences this section by describing the three 'meanings' of jihad: (1) an 'etymological' definition which is 'effort' or 'trying seriously' to achieve something; (2) a terminological meaning of 'struggling' to uphold God's law; and (3) the legal meaning of waging war against those infidels who attack Islam. This extract begins with the third meaning.]

- In terms of sharia, jihad means fighting the infidels who wage war on Islam and Muslims. This understanding is better known as 'jihad in the path of God'. As far as I remember, these three definitions above have the consensus of the Pious Ancestors who came before, in particular from the four schools of Islamic legal thought (Shafi'i, Hambali, Maliki and Hanafi). So there are no differences of opinion on the issue of the definition of jihad.

Those who wish to study this matter in more depth can read a book entitled *Al-Jihadu Sabiluna* [Jihad Is Our Path] by Sheikh Abdul Baqi Ramdhun. Also *Kitabul Jihad* [Book of Jihad] by Sheikh Ibnul Mubarak, or *Fi At-Tarbiyah al-Jihadiyah wal-Bina* [Education and Guidance in Jihad] by Sheikh Asy-Syahid Dr. Abdullah Azzam. Or they can also read other books related to jihad written by competent ulema actively involved in the world of jihad. [...]

The Bali Bombing = Jihad in the Path of God

Based on intention or the planned targets, it is clear that the Bali bombings were jihad in the path of God, because the main targets were colonizing peoples like America and its allies. This is even clearer with the large-scale massacres of Muslims in Afghanistan in the month of Ramadan in 2001, which were witnessed by almost all of humankind in every corner of the globe. The colonizing nations who massacred the weak and innocent babies are what are referred to as polytheists (infidels), who should be fought against as God decreed. [Q9: 36 is quoted here; see footnote 16.] [pp. 108–9] [...]

Truly, all of the crimes and tyranny of the colonizers cannot just be ignored. Muslims must rise up and oppose them with all their might and in every way. Islamic law decrees that resistance is through jihad.

So, the Bali bombings were one form of response carried out by a few Muslims who were aware of and understood the meaning of defence and of the dignity of Muslims. The Bali bombing was part of the resistance aimed at the colonizer, America, and its allies. The Bali bombing was a jihad which had to be carried out, even if it was only by a few Muslims. [p. 114] [...]

- **Attacking Civilians in the Colonizing Nations as a Fair and Just Act**

Nevertheless, what has happened is that the colonizing nations have continued, are continuing and will continue to massacre the civilians of Muslim nations. However, America and its allies have exceeded the bounds. God is the most Holy, God is the most Righteous! God does not permit His servants to remain in a state of anxiety and degradation. God does not permit His servants to be played foul by the infidels. War will be met with war, blood with blood, lives with lives, and transgressions with the same.

> *Whoever exceeds the boundaries against you, then answer their attacks in the same way that they have done to you ...* (Al-Baqarah: 194).[36]

So waging war on civilians (if indeed they really are civilians) from the colonizing nations is an appropriate act for the sake of balance and justice. Blood for blood, lives for lives, and ... civilians for civilians! That is balance. [Q16: 126 is quoted here.[37]] [p. 116] [...]

---

36 'A sacred month for a sacred month: violation of sanctity [calls for] fair retribution. So if anyone commits aggression against you, attack him as he attacked you, but be mindful of God, and know that He is with those who are mindful of Him' (Q2: 194, Haleem).

37 'If you [people] have to respond to an attack, make your response proportionate, but it is best to stand fast' (Q16: 126, Haleem).

War is indeed cruel, war is horrifying, war is painful, and war is terrifying. But nevertheless, ... permitting the brutality of the colonizing nations towards Muslim peoples is more brutal. Allowing that horror, that fear and that pain to continue to afflict Muslims as a result of the brutality of the blood-sucking monsters is even more cruel. [p. 118]

14.2.4 Mukhlas

Commentary Aly Ghufron bin Nurhasyim (better known as Mukhlas) is a senior JI leader whose many writings and interviews have provided a rich insight into the mindset of Indonesian Salafi jihadists, that is, those who seek to emulate the first three generations of Muslim leaders and who regard violent jihad as essential to defending the faith. Born in Tenggulan, East Java, in 1960, Mukhlas graduated from the Al Mukmin *pesantren* (Islamic boarding school) in Ngruki, Central Java, in 1982. He became a protégé of Abu Bakar Ba'asyir and Abdullah Sungkar, the founders of Al Mukmin, following them into exile in Malaysia in the mid-1980s before joining the *mujahadin* in Afghanistan to fight against the Soviet forces. He was reportedly the head of JI's Mantiqi I (the region command covering Singapore and Malaysia) and played a key role in the Bali bombings of October 2002. Mukhlas was arrested in December 2002 and sentenced to death by a Bali court in October 2003. At the time of writing he was awaiting execution by firing squad, having had his appeal rejected by the Supreme Court.

Like Imam Samudra, Mukhlas wrote prolifically while in jail, producing, by his own account, four books (*Jakarta Post*, 5 January 2004). The longest of these unpublished manuscripts was 'The Bali Bomb Jihad: A Defence', dated March 2003. As the title suggests, Mukhlas's primary concern was to provide a religious and moral justification for the Bali bombings. In the manuscript he quotes extensively from the Qur'an, from the life of the Prophet Muhammad and from famous Islamic scholars in order to find Islamic sanction for his actions, and he offers a detailed account of how and why the Bali bombings were perpetrated. Page numbers in the extract follow those given in the handwritten manuscript.

Extract 14-6: Mukhlas

Aly Ghufron bin Nurhasyim (Mukhlas) (2003), 'Jihad Bom Bali: Sebuah Pembelaan. Operasi Peledakan Bom Legian dan Renon. 12 Oktober 2002' [The Bali Bomb Jihad: A Defence. Operation Legian and Renon Bomb Explosions. 12 October 2002], Bali District Police Jail, Denpasar, 25 March. Extract: pp. 35–7, 40–1, 50, 95–130.

A. According to Islamic law
According to sharia law Almighty God commands the faithful to become terrorists, as His decree (Al Anfal (8): 60) says:

> And <u>prepare to face them with whatever force you can</u> and <u>horses tethered for war</u> (which are part of those preparations), so that you make the <u>enemies of God your enemies and others whom you do not know of</u>, yet God knows of, TREMBLE. Whatsoever you expend in <u>God's path</u> will surely be repaid sufficiently to you and you will not be wronged.[38] [...]

---

38   Q8: 60 is given in footnote 7.

2 Target of preparations

In the verse above it is clearly indicated that the target of preparations is: YOU FRIGHTENING THE ENEMIES OF GOD AND YOUR ENEMIES AND OTHER ENEMIES WHOM YOU DO NOT KNOW OF, BUT GOD KNOWS OF.

Explanation:

'You frighten' is a translation of the word *turhibuun*, derived from the word *rahiba-yarhabu*, which means to be afraid, to tremble or to panic (Malay). Then the first letter of the Arabic alphabet (*alif*) is added to it so that it becomes *arhaba-yurhibu*, which means: to repeatedly frighten ... to terrify ... to create panic. Those who frighten, who terrify or who create panic are referred to as *murhib* (the verbal noun from the word *arhaba*) or they can also be called *irhaabii* [...] Which means: those who frighten, terrify or create panic in the community. They are referred to as *irhaa-biyuun* [the plural of *irhaabii*], which means people who are frightening, terrifying or causing panic.

This is why the word *irhaabii* is popular with Arabs to refer to a terrorist.

So it is clear that it is those who are pious who follow the command to prepare [and be ready].

This verse then talks about their preparations. They can make the enemy tremble, repeatedly frighten them or terrorize them. So the most appropriate words to refer to them – and 'God is All-knowing' – are *irhaabii* or *murhibuun*. The translation into Indonesian or English is *teroris*/terrorist, and their behaviour is referred to as *irhaabii* or terror. The conclusion is that the pious were commanded by Almighty God to become *irhaabii* or terrorists, namely those who can make the enemies of Almighty God and their enemies, as well as enemies they are not aware of but of whom Almighty God knows, tremble, be afraid and be overwhelmed by fear. [pp. 35–7] [...]

So they [Western countries] began to think seriously about at least two major issues which they perceived of as being dangerous, namely:

1 An Islamic State implemented by the *mujahidin* as the fruit of their jihad to date.
2 The phenomenon of thousands of Muslim youths returning to their respective countries after graduating victoriously from the programs of the Afghanistan Jihad University with all sorts of expertise and skills: from firing pistols to shooting Stinger missiles, from riding horses to driving tanks and piloting helicopters, from throwing grenades to firing rockets, from making one-gram bombs to making bombs weighing tonnes, and so on.

The moment of the humiliating defeat of the Russian army arrived. Then not long after it was followed by the fall of their puppet government, which at the time was headed by President Najibadlis.[39]

This situation is increasingly terrifying and frightening for the West, especially America and its lackeys. What would be most appalling for them is the establishment

---

39   That is, President Najibullah, the last Marxist president of Afghanistan (1987–92).

of a true Islamic State as was created by the Messenger of God, may blessings and peace be upon him, and his Companions, may God's blessings be upon them.

So they [Western countries] began to redouble their schemes, working hard day and night without pause to cause chaos and set the *mujahidin*, especially their leaders, against each other through various activities and devious programs. The essence of their objective is: to foil the establishment of a true Islamic State.

Because they understand and truly realize that a true Islamic State would imperil their position and in fact the whole world as they see it. So they set up fake Islamic states in order to misrepresent them to the international community and to Muslims in particular.

Why are they so phobic about a true Islamic State? To analyse this matter in detail would require an entire book, but in essence it is more or less because of the following:

1 An Islamic State is the embryo for establishing an Islamic Caliphate once more on earth, and the adoption of an Islamic Caliphate is a sign of the imminent fall of the power of the West and its allies.
2 A true Islamic State in line with sharia is tasked with and obliged to carry out or conduct *jihad hujumi* (a Jihad for the expansion of territory) at least once a year.
3 With the implementation of a true Islamic State, the curtain of doubt that has covered the eyes of the international community, and Muslims in particular, would be revealed and pulled back. Because, to date, all the news and information they have been receiving about an Islamic State has been terrifying and cruel, because all the pictures in their minds have only been about hands being cut off, stoning to death, jihad and so on. The wonder and beauty, as well as the greatness, of perfect Islamic edifices has never been imagined.

    Besides our own ignorance, this situation is caused by the influence of Western propaganda, which is always denigrating the Islamic State through various kinds of mass media.

    It has already been explained that Islam, naturally, cannot be understood partially. All of its parts are beautiful and great, including its laws of death by stoning, cutting off of hands and jihad. But what needs to be underscored is that this beauty will not be realized unless it is manifested in an Islamic edifice or system, in other words, in an Islamic State. [pp. 40–1] [...]

[...] It is clear that, from the beginning, the enemies of Islam, especially America, have not been happy about the creation of a government like this [that is, the Taliban government in Afghanistan] because in the future it would be dangerous for them and their allies, in fact for the whole world.

In light of this, they are always thinking about finding the right ways and pretexts and opportunities to destroy this dangerous administration without sacrificing their influence in the international political arena.

What should happen is what happened next: suddenly there was that awe-inspiring attack that completely crushed the WTC building to smithereens and turned the Pentagon upside down. This attack made America reel and made its leaders dazed and confused, as though these incidents were just a nightmare. It was hard [for them] to accept the reality [of what happened] because never before had they, or even their intelligence experts, imagined it. In their minds, the most they had predicted were the usual attacks, like those on their embassies, their ships, their personnel and their interests.

These events also made them feel endlessly frustrated, even more humiliated than the humiliation felt by the Russian army after it left Afghanistan in defeat. How could a country that is called a superpower, that has such sophisticated detection instrumentation, not be humiliated when five of its planes were hijacked all at once without it being detected? How could it not be humiliated when a giant bird in the form of a transportation plane (not a combat fighter) came slowly and as big as that, but was still not detected at the Pentagon, a symbol of the greatness of American power where they said even a fly could be detected. That's how it is when Almighty God desires, such things happen so that human beings do not become arrogant and proud of the tiny achievements they have made. [p. 50] [...]

[Mukhlas then discusses in considerable detail the bombings of the Sari Club and Paddy's Bar in Denpasar on 12 October 2002. He sets out the reasons for choosing these nightclubs over the many others in the Balinese capital and then provides a closely argued justification for the attacks, particularly the deaths and injuries to women, non-combatant foreign men and Muslims.]

C. Aim of the Bali Bomb operation

After we know of, understand and witness such terrible attacks from the enemies of Islam upon Muslims, both physical and non-physical, military and non-military, what must we do? Should we bind ourselves only to the methodology of Habil [Abel], the first son of the Prophet Adam, namely that even if we are attacked, if we die we shall die as martyrs? Or should we just implement assiduously a program of education and elevation on the basis that if all Muslims are pious the situation will change of its own accord, that at the moment Muslims are being slaughtered left and right because of their own faults and [we should] let them be slaughtered as it is a warning and punishment from Almighty God, that the important thing is to 'look after yourself'. Does this verse not instruct us to order that which is good and prevent that which is evil (see Al Maidah (5): 105)?[40]

Or is it enough for us to just run proselytizing (*dakwah*) programs, including organizing seminars and discussions? Then we could send the results to the enemies of Islam so that they cease their attacks, both military and non-military.

Or is it enough for us to gather together as many Muslims as possible and then invite these Muslims to demonstrate at all of their embassies, their consulates and so forth? [...]

To us, and our view is based on the axioms of the Qur'an and Sunnah and the facts on the ground, the enemies of Islam, from past times to the present day, including the

---

40   'You who believe, you are responsible for your own souls; if anyone else goes astray it will not harm you so long as you follow the guidance; you will all return to God, and He will make you realize what you have done' (Q5: 105, Haleem).

Jews, America and their lackeys, do not understand the language of diplomacy. They only understand the language of force; they will not understand except through the language of <u>force</u>. [p. 95] […]

There are truly very many facts on the ground, among others, for example, why during the period of the Afghanistan jihad did the leaders of America unabashedly praise the *mujahidin* and their leaders? – because they possessed <u>force</u>.

Another example is that the WTC and Pentagon events made them afraid and apoplectic (a disease arising out of overwhelming fear). […]

So we conclude that the enemies of Islam (America and its allies) will not understand spoken or written language, but only the language of force.

Because of that, we communicate with them through bomb explosions so that they hear and pay attention.

The aims of a bomb explosion are as follows:

1   To terrorize, frighten and make tremble the enemies of Islam and Muslims. […] Fear is one type of God's armies.

Only its role is of great importance in determining victory or defeat in battle and war. The Prophet, blessings and peace be upon him, aided by Almighty God and by fear, was made victorious facing his enemies, whereby Almighty God threw fear into the hearts of his enemies. […]

Hopefully God Almighty will put fear into the hearts of the enemies of Islam and Muslims through the Bali Bomb explosions. If they are haunted by fear, God willing at least their evil plans and programs, both military and non-military, will be hampered, or thank God if we can cause their conspiracy and their networks throughout the world, particularly in Indonesia, to fail and break up.

2   To reject the viciousness and brutality of the enemies of Islam (the Jews, America and their allies) […]

Almighty God has made it law that resistance against force in Islam shall be called jihad. He has done this so that there will not be a group of mortals on this earth who act arbitrarily towards other groups because they feel that no other group dares oppose them. [pp. 96–7]

As a result, we attempted to resist them with what strength we had in the form of a bomb. Hopefully, through this bomb explosion, Almighty God will repel the attacks of the enemies of both Islam and Muslims and hold back their brutality.

3   To avenge their brutal attacks on Muslims […]

As has been stated previously, the enemies of Islam and Muslims, particularly the Jews, America and their allies, have acted brutally, slaughtering, murdering, obstructing and wounding Muslims everywhere.

The whole world witnessed their brutality in Afghanistan, where merely to kill innocent civilians thousands of bombs were dropped, with each bomb weighing a tonne; try to imagine one tonne of standard explosive material, TNT and so forth, being dropped from the sky above. Compare this with the explosion in Legian

(Sari Club). The explosive at SC weighed about one tonne too, although we must remember it was not standard explosive material, but even a bomb like that could cause such destruction. The terrific power of one tonne of TNT dropped from the sky above is unimaginable, and it wasn't just once, but hundreds or thousands of times. Where is there greater brutality than that?

Such a brutal attack cannot be allowed to pass just like that; it must be responded to. [p. 98] [...]

D. Tourists as a target

It should be known that our intention in exploding a bomb in Bali was not to wreck the beauty and image of Bali, although it turned out that the explosion did have some influence on that. And we did not feel hate or resentment towards Bali on account of the majority of its inhabitants being non-Muslim.

And it should also be understood, so that any evaluation of the operation is not mistaken, that we exploded the bomb at the Sari Club and Puddi's Pub [*sic*] not because they were places of immorality, with entertainment, music, dancing and *joget* [erotic dancing], drunkenness, free relations between men and women and so on, because if our target had been places of vice we need not have gone all the way to Bali and exhausted ourselves doing so, because these days there are places of immorality everywhere – nightclubs, drunkenness, fornication, dancing, gambling and so on.

So why did we choose Bali as our target? Because, as everyone knows, Bali is the area most often visited by foreign tourists, particularly from Western and other countries, which, note well, are the countries that ally themselves with America and participate directly in the coalition army led by it in the crusade to destroy the Islamic government of Afghanistan and slaughter Muslims there. These countries include: America, England, India, Australia, France, Germany, Canada, Japan, China, Israel and so forth.

E. The SARI CLUB as the main target

We made the Sari Club our main target after conducting a survey for about a month, during which we obtained solid data that this entertainment venue was especially for whities.

Indonesians were not allowed to enter the venue, including security officers; the only Indonesians who could enter were people who had a connection to the SC, such as its employees and its owner; we didn't find this regulation in any other club, although it may be in place in many others. [pp. 99–100] [...]

F. The reason for making tourists from countries allied with the Jews and Americans the target

Perhaps some people would say that they [the victims] were innocent people who did not oppose us, so why target them?

To determine and evaluate whether or not they were innocent, and whether or not they opposed us, requires data, but we are people of faith and Almighty God has provided us with guidance on how we should act towards infidels:

a It is not forbidden for us to act well or justly towards them, if they do not wage war on us because of our religion and drive us out of our country.

b On the other hand, it is forbidden to act well or justly towards infidels who wage war and drive us out, and it is even forbidden to be their friend.

Can we be certain whether the tourists from those countries were from infidel group (a) or infidel group (b)? Of course we cannot, as we do not have clear data, but what is clear and beyond doubt is that the governments of the countries the tourists came from do wage war on Islam and Muslims, as they have shown in Afghanistan and other places, and these are just the clearly evident examples, not hidden acts including non-military attacks.

Thus, we think that at the very least we must be wary (*hazar*) of them (4: 71, 102),[41] and that it is not permissible to think positively about infidels, because positive thoughts are for believers, not for infidels, let alone infidels whose position is not yet clear (49: 12).[42]

Now we return to the jihad of retribution.

We desired to respond to the brutality of the leaders and armies of those countries that had murdered and slaughtered our women and our children, but at the time we did not have the capacity to attack and kill them. [pp. 100–1] [...]

• Should our actions be considered an excessive deed because in the operation Muslims and other people who did not know they would be killed were forced to be included as targets?

  We say that if you have acknowledged that our acts were part of jihad, then hasn't every jihad operation throughout history always run the risk of sacrificing innocent civilians? [...]

• During the Badar War [see footnote 4], circumstances forced some Muslims to be struck by the Muslim army's arrows because the polytheists made them a human shield (An Nisa (4): 97).[43]

---

41 'You who believe, be on your guard. March [to battle] in small groups or as one body' (Q4: 71, Haleem).

'When you [Prophet] are with the believers, leading them in prayer, let a group of them stand up in prayer with you, taking their weapons with them, and when they have finished their prostration, let them take up their positions at the back. Then let the other group, who have not yet prayed, pray with you, also on their guard and armed with their weapons: the disbelievers would dearly like you to be heedless of your weapons and baggage, in order for them to take you in a single assault. You will not be blamed if you lay aside your arms when you are overtaken by heavy rain or illness, but be on your guard. Indeed, God has prepared a humiliating punishment for the disbelievers' (Q4: 102, Haleem).

42 'Believers, do not indulge many of your suspicions – some suspicions are sinful – and do not spy on one another or speak ill of people behind their backs: would any of you like to eat the flesh of your dead brother? No, you would hate it. So be mindful of God: God is ever relenting, most merciful' (Q49: 12, Haleem).

43 'When the angels take the souls of those who have wronged themselves, they ask them, "What circumstances were you in?" They reply, "We were oppressed in this land", and the angels say, "But was God's earth not spacious enough for you to migrate to some other place?" These people will have Hell as their refuge, an evil destination' (Q4: 97, Haleem).

- The Prophet of God, blessings and peace be upon him, and his Companions, may God bless them, once directed their catapults at the people of Taif, who were hiding in their forts together with women and children and even some Muslims.
- And there have been many other events similar to the one described above during battles experienced by the Companions, may God bless them, the second and third generation of followers and their followers.
- In jihad jurisprudence, *mujahidin* are permitted to direct their weapons at their enemies even if their enemies have women and innocent children with them and moreover have Muslim captives there, on the condition that the aim is to destroy the enemy and not to kill the Muslim captives, women and children. [pp. 105–6] [...]

[Mukhlas then discusses whether the Bali bombers sinned in killing (1) women and children as well as other non-combatants and (2) fellow Muslims in the attack. He concludes his discussion with the following points.]

Did the Bali Bomb operation violate these prohibitions?

- We say no, we can't be included in the category of those who broke those prohibitions. Some of the reasons are as follows:

a The prohibition has an exception, namely Illa Bil Khafi [literally, 'exception because of fear'], which means: an attack can be carried out as long as there is a sound reason for it. It is justified by sharia, on matters such as the Qishas [Ar.: *qisaasun*; 'retribution', a life for a life], the killing of apostates, the stoning of fornicators who are married and so forth, including jihad.

b To kill an infidel in connection with jihad is a most excellent act. The Prophet, blessings and peace be upon him, said: the infidel and his killer (the *mujahid*) will not be together in hell.
Explanation: Because the unbeliever who was killed will be in hell while his killer (the believer/*mujahid*) will be in heaven.

c Almighty God orders that infidels involved in causing dissension or opposing Muslims must be killed (Al-Baqarah (2): 191).[44]

d There were Muslim men and women who died along with the targets, but we did not intend to kill them so our error cannot be categorized as having violated the prohibition, as has been explained above. [p. 107]

[In the closing section of his text Mukhlas discusses the validity of suicide bombing according to Islamic law, and he quotes various scholars in support of the practice. He also lists the rewards that will befall someone martyred in this way. This is followed by a rare account of the preparation of the two suicide bombers involved in the Bali attack. He places particular emphasis on a dream by one of the suicide bombers, which he took as a sign of divine endorsement of the planned attack.]

---

44   Q2: 191 is given in footnote 16.

A. Martyrdom/suicide bomb operation

In the Bali bomb incident, two young men donated themselves (*mewakafkan dirinya*)[45] to die as martyrs. The two youths came and met with me two or three days before the explosion and said they were prepared to die as martyrs, and asked me to give them beneficial advice.

Before I gave them advice, I first asked them whether they were truly ready to conduct a martyrdom/suicide bomb operation, or whether someone was forcing them to. They both answered that they were ready and that no one was forcing them. We have long aspired to die as martyrs [they said].

Then I gave the proper advice:

First: Concerning sincerity, I felt it important to remind them of this as it is one of the two conditions for good deeds to be accepted. At the time, if I remember correctly, in my advice to them I mentioned a Hadith of the Prophet, blessings and peace be upon him, in which there is a man who wages war because he is brave, another who fights because of booty, another because of nationalism and another because he wants to show his position, and a Companion, may God bless him, asked the Prophet, blessings and peace be upon him, which of them was in the path of God? The Prophet, blessings and peace be upon him, answered: Whomsoever wages war to uphold the Word of God most High, then he is in the path of God. Because of this, in conducting the operation you must be truly sincere in solely seeking the blessings of Almighty God, seeking His reward and upholding His religion. Let not your motives be even a little mixed with seeking public approbation, such as wanting to be called a martyr, brave and so forth, that's more or less what I told them about sincerity. [...]

Second: Concerning the excellence of martyrdom in the path of God, I read them several verses and Hadith, among others Q.S. Muhammad (47): 4, 5, 6.

> He will not let the deeds of those who are killed for His cause come to nothing. He will guide them and put them into a good state; He will admit them into the Garden He has already made known to them. [Q47: 4–6, Haleem] [...]

Meaning: The Prophet, blessings and peace be upon him, said: Six or seven matters apply to those who are martyred for Almighty God:

1 Their sins will be forgiven at their death.
2 They will be shown their position in heaven.
3 They will be safe from the tortures of the grave.
4 They will be safe from the terrifying day of judgement.
5 They will be adorned with faith and matched with 72 heavenly angels.
6 And upon their heads will be placed a crown of glory, just one of whose rubies is better than any that is on the earth.

---

45 This use of the term *wakaf* (Ar.: *waqfun*) to refer to donating one's life as a religious endowment is highly unusual. Normally *wakaf* entails the donation of property or money to be used for the benefit of fellow Muslims.

7   They will be granted the right of intercession for 70 of their relatives. [pp. 110–11]
    [...]

[Mukhlas then refers to a Kuwaiti publication he has read which sets out the opinions
of noted Middle Eastern ulema, including 'Sheikh Mohd. Sholeh al-Utsaimin, Sheikh
al-Bani and Sheikh Bin Baz', regarding the legality of suicide bombing.]

I conclude from their opinion, but God alone knows the truth, that:

1   Not one of the sheikhs was of the opinion that the law that applies to a suicide
    bomb is the same as that for a normal suicide, meaning killing oneself because
    one has lost hope or because of satanic desires.
2   They were of the opinion that a suicide bombing could not be perpetrated without
    sound calculations of the benefits for Muslims and the harm to their enemies,
    because if the ratio is only 1 to 1, or 2 to 3, then Sheikh Utsaimin considered
    suicide bombing not to be permitted.
3   This means that the law may be applied if it brings benefits for the *mujahidin* or
    Muslims. [p. 117] [...]

Dr Yusuf Al Qurdhowi [Qaradawi], who is renowned as a moderate ulema whose
opinions are sometimes off the mark, may God Almighty grant guidance to him,
thinks that suicide bombings are permissible, but for the moment only in Palestine.

Conclusion:
1   A suicide operation using one's own weapons or those of another is permissible
    if it conveys significant benefits to Muslims and causes significant harm to the
    enemies of Islam.
2   It is experts in jihad issues who determine whether or not an operation conveys
    benefits for Islam, and whether it causes harm to the enemy. [p. 118] [...]

Returning to the two Brothers who conducted the martyrdom operation:
After I had finished giving them my advice, I asked them: 'Did either of you have
a dream?' Why did I ask about dreaming? Because I feel that the dreams of a pious,
faithful person, all the more so a *mujahid*, are very important even though they cannot be used as a reason or argument. But at a minimum they have meaning behind
them.

In one of the Hadith narrated by Imam Bukhari, it is stated that among the dreams
of the faithful at the end of time there will be almost none that are falsehoods. There
are three types of dream:

1   From Almighty God.
2   From oneself.
3   From Satan. [...]

•   One of them answered, I had a dream, Teacher! Please tell me about your dream
    [I said]. Then he told of his dream as follows:

After he developed the intention and signed up to conduct a martyrdom bomb
operation, one night he performed the recommended prayer and then slept. In his
sleep he dreamt that he was flying towards Mecca, and upon arrival there he clearly

saw the shape and colour of the Ka'bah[46] from the air, and so he desired to go down and look upon the Ka'bah from close up, and to go and circumambulate the Ka'bah and pray there.

But as he was going to land, there was a voice from the sky indicating that he was forbidden to land there and he was ordered to continue his flight to Afghanistan. He followed the instruction and flew towards Afghanistan. When he arrived there, upon landing he was embraced by Sheikh Usamah bin Laden (may God guard him), and he touched cheeks with him, and they asked about each other's news. Then Sheikh Usamah asked, 'Do you want to conduct a suicide bomb operation?', and he answered 'Yes, God Willing'.

The sheikh directed him to bathe before doing so, and instructed him to go towards the back, namely towards the river, so he went to the river and saw a beautiful river with clear water where many *mujahidin* were bathing.

He then bathed thoroughly and put on new clothes, then he woke up and exclaimed in surprise: God Most High (*Subhanallah*).

After I had heard his dream I said to him, 'Glad news my brother [...] God willing glad news, your dream, God willing, is a True Dream'. [pp. 119–20] [...]

Such is the discussion of the Bali Bomb Jihad that I can present. I hope that with this simple book I can help the Indonesian nation and other nations, particularly Muslims, to understand our holy and noble mission in this operation. [p. 130]

14.3 REGIONALIST JIHAD

Commentary In the preceding section, Salafi jihadists have depicted their struggle in strongly pan-Islamist terms. They have an acute awareness of events elsewhere in the Islamic world and place the perceived hostility towards Muslims in a global context. While there is a sense of the local imperatives of jihad, their struggle has a broader, transnational objective. In a number of areas within Southeast Asia, such as the southern Philippines and southern Thailand, jihadist movements have a more powerful local sentiment. While aware of jihadist activity in other parts of the Muslim world, these movements place primary emphasis on defending their 'homeland' and their communities against the depredations of the state and the non-Muslim majority. Accordingly, their rhetoric borrows elements from the global Salafi jihadist discourse but remains steadfastly local in its preoccupations. Drawing on local oral and literary traditions, the language in these texts is often passionate and vivid, reflecting a deep sense of grievance.

14.3.1 Salamat Hashim

Commentary The late leader of the MILF, Salamat Hashim, wrote and spoke extensively on jihad issues as they relate to the independence struggle of Muslim com-

---

46 The Ka'bah is the cube-shaped 'House of God' in Mecca towards which all Muslims face when praying and around which they circumambulate as part of the pilgrimage. It is shown in the colour section of this book (see plate 12).

munities in the southern Philippines. His education at the famous Islamic university, al-Azhar, in Cairo gave him a detailed knowledge of Islamic law and history, which he drew on when shaping the MILF's thinking on jihad. In the following extract, Salamat describes how jihad has become central to the MILF's struggle against oppression by the Philippine government and to its demand for independence, although he also connects this to the global fight against Islam's enemies. The term 'Bangsamoro' is the common self-descriptor used by Muslims in the southern Philippines.

Extract 14-7: Salamat Hashim

Salamat Hashim (1985), *The Bangsamoro Mujahid* [in English], Bangsamoro Publications, Mindanao. Extract: pp. 5–6, 14–15, 18–19.

Some personalities in the revolution, owing to their insufficient knowledge of the real essence of Jihad, advocate the idea to the effect that the sole and singular objective of our struggle is simply to liberate our homeland giving no importance to the system of government that shall be established when victory is achieved. In accordance with such view, the people at large possess the prerogative to select any system of government responsive to their worldly needs. Whether it be a duplication of the present system of Western-oriented government or the materialistic system of the communists is supposedly within the province of the people's mandate. Here lies the fundamental point of distinction. For in Islamic revolutions (Jihad in the Way of Allah), the system of government which shall be established is pre-determined by Qur'anic principles and the traditions of Prophet Muhammad (peace be upon him). Hence, the matter of selecting a system of government for the community is completely beyond the scope of the people's will and prerogatives.

The former case clearly illustrates a revolutionary line akin to the communist or western orientation. From the Islamic viewpoint, this is totally unacceptable since it is a clear departure from the true objectives of Jihad [pp. 5–6] [...]

If a Muslim community is the object of aggression, persecution or oppression, each and every able-bodied Muslim in that community must respond to the call for Jihad. In fact, in the light of present day realities obtaining in the Bangsamoro homeland, Jihad remains to be the only criterion in examining the validity, and degree of a Muslim's faith.

Indeed, in this crucial stage in the history of the Bangsamoro Muslims, any individual Bangsamoro who deviates from our Jihad and who deliberately refuses to involve his wealth and life in furtherance of our just cause is a munafiq (hypocrite) in accordance with Islamic point of view, hence, all his prayers, fasting and haj are of no avail.

Liberty and freedom are among the most indispensable facets in the life of a Muslim both as an individual and as [a] member of the community. [The] Islamic system of belief, worship, behaviour, character and conduct, customs and traditions could not be made to bend and harmonize with un-Islamic philosophy. Once liberty and freedom of the Muslims are threatened, all other aspects of their lives become less important. The defense and preservation of religious freedom and liberty occupy the highest order of priority in their existence for it is the atmosphere of freedom which guarantees for them a truly Islamic way of life. [pp. 14–15] [...]

(b) *The Cause We are Fighting For:* Earlier we mentioned that a true Bangsamoro mujahid must have in his fingertips the cause and the fundamental principles and philosophy of Islam. With similar zeal, he must study the history of the Bangsamoro people. He must consider it his bounden duty to teach his children and all members of his family about the history of our country and forebears. We must inculcate into the minds of our children the notion that Islam was the earliest religion established in the Islands, now called the Philippines, and the first political institution, civilization and culture in the area. We must take pride in the historical fact that the Bangsamoro Muslims were an independent people having their system of government and indigenous set of laws long before the rest of the inhabitants in the Philippines had a taste of [a] systematized form of government and social life. This independence, however, was lost due to subsequent plots and machinations of foreign invaders and colonial powers such as the Spaniards and the Americans supported by Filipino collaborators. [pp. 18–19]

14.3.2   Fatwa Council of the Moro Youth Union

Commentary (by Kit Collier)   The following fatwa issued by Sheikh Datu Ramzie Uzman Al-Buluani, head of the Fatwa Council, Moro Youth Union, was carried on the English-language website of the MILF-linked Moro Information Agency and reiterates Salamat Hashim's position that in the circumstances of the southern Philippines, jihad is the responsibility of 'each and every' Muslim. It follows an established precedent in spelling out three conditions under which jihad becomes an individual obligation (*fardhu a'yn*; Ar.: *fardu 'aynin*) rather than a collective duty (*fardhu kifaya*; Ar.: *fardu kifaayatin*) not binding on individuals. The conditions listed by the Moro Youth Union are similar to those upheld by the late Saudi Grand Mufti Bin Baz, appearing more specific than the injunction of the influential Egyptian Islamist Sayyid Qutb (b. 1906, executed 1966) to permanent personal jihad (Roy 2002: 41–2, 254).

The fatwa cites the authority of prominent Qatari Sheikh al-Qaradawi, and relies heavily on verses from Qur'anic chapters 8 and 9, which are especially popular among Moro *mujahidin*. The same chapters were stressed by Abu Sayyaf founder Abdulrajak Janjalani in his own ruling around 1990 that jihad is *fardhu a'yn* (Tan 2003b: 98; Wadi 1998: 40). The author also draws imaginatively on Hadith to seek the widest possible support – through prayer, the wealth tax (Ar.: *zakaah*), and home front and propaganda efforts – from those unable to take up arms, reflecting the influence of left-wing 'sectoral' mobilization techniques in the Philippines.

Extract 14-8: Fatwa Council of the Moro Youth Union

Ramzie Uzman Al-Buluani (2004), 'The Shariah Ruling on the Status of Jihad in the Bangsamoro Homeland' [in English], Fatwa Council of the Moro Youth Union, <http://www.moroinfo.com/fatawa1.html>, accessed 31 July 2004.

Dear Brothers and Sisters in Islam,

Assalamo alaikom Warahmatullahi Wabarakatuho [Peace be upon you and God's mercy and His Blessings]

In the light of the current events in our homeland, we, in the Fatwa Council of Moro Youth Union[,] feel obliged to release this sort of Islamic verdict (Fatawa Islam iyyah), whereby we reaffirm and reiterate the Islamic and Shariah ruling on the status of Jihad in the Moro homeland.

We hope that this humble work will help awaken the Bangsamoro people to fulfill their tasks and obligations towards the current Jihad in our Homeland. [...]

SHARIAH RULING ON JIHAD

There are two types of Shariah rulings on Jihad: (a) Fardhu Kifaya (Collective Obligation), and (b) Fardhu A'yn (Individual Obligation).

(a) **Fardhu Kifaya**: In the normal situation, where there is no threat from the enemies, the ruling regarding Jihad is Fard Kifaya, which means if some individuals in the community perform it, the rest are no longer liable for it.

On the other hand, if no individual performs it, the entire community will be held liable. According to Imam Ibn Rushd: The Jurists agreed unanimously that Jihad is a collective obligation (Fard Kifaya), except for 'Abd Allah Ibn Al-Hasan who said it is voluntary.

The majority of the Jurists adopted this view base[d] on the saying of Almighty Allah in Surah Al-Taubah, which, reads as:

> '*And the believers should not all go out to fight. Of every troop of them, a party only should go forth, that they (who are left behind) may gain sound knowledge in religion, and that they may warn their folk when they return, so that they may beware.*' (Al-Taubah: 122)[47]

Such is the Shariah ruling on Jihad where the situation is normal.

(b) **Fardhu A'yn**: The Muslim Jurists have also unanimously agreed that there are certain circumstances under which the ruling on Jihad becomes an individual obligation (Fardhu A'yn) the same as the ruling on Prayer (Salat), Fasting (Siyam) and [wealth tax] (Zakah) [Ar.: *salaah*, *sawmun* and *zakaah*]. The Jurists identified those circumstances as follows:

1- When a Muslim Attend the battlefield

When a Muslim Join[s] the battlefield, at that time they are oblige[d] to fight the enemies. This is evidenced by the saying of Almighty Allah, [which] reads as:

---

47 'Yet it is not right for all the believers to go out [to battle] together: out of each community, a group should go out to study the religion, so that they can teach their people when they return and so that they can guard themselves against evil' (Q9: 122, Haleem).

'O ye who believe! When ye meet an army, hold firm and think of Allah much, that ye may be successful.' (Al-Anfal: 45)[48]

2- When the Muslim ruler commands someone to fight

If The Muslim ruler commands someone to fight it will be incumbent upon him to obey the order, as Ibn 'Abbas, may Allah be pleased with him, reported that the Prophet, peace and blessings be upon him, said:

'There is no migration after the conquest (of Makkah [Mecca]); but let there be a Jihad and good intention, and if you are called (by the Muslim ruler) to fight, then go forth immediately.' (Reported by Al-Bukhari) [Hadith]

And Allah, Exalted be He, says:

'O ye who believe! What aileth you that when it is said unto you: Go forth in the way of Allah, ye are bowed down to the ground with heaviness. Take ye pleasure in the life of the world rather than in the Hereafter? The comfort of the life of the world is but little in the Hereafter.' (At-Tawbah: 38)[49]

3- When the enemies commit a gross injustice against the Muslims

If the enemies commit a gross injustice against the Muslims by either attacking or occupying Muslim land or country, or by inflicting some harm to Muslims personality or dignity, Jihad becomes an individual obligation (Fardhu A'yn) to all Muslims living in that country and upon all Muslims living in the neighboring Countries till the enemies are driven out from the occupied Muslim land.

THE MORO SITUATIONS RELEVANT TO FARDHU A'YN JIHAD

If we examine the past and the current situation of the Bangsamoro Muslims in our homeland, we could easily establish the relevance of the Moro situation to the circumstances under which, according to the classical and contemporary Jurists and Ulamas, the Jihad is Fard Ayn and obligatory to all Muslims living in the occupied land to take part in the Jihad to liberate the Muslims land from the hands of the infidels.

And it is also obligatory to all Muslims living in the neighboring countries to provide them necessary support and assistance.

There are several facts, which justify constituting Fardhu A'yn Jihad based on the interpretations of the Qur'anic verses and the Prophetic traditions made by different classical and contemporary Muslim jurists and scholars.

Firstly, the Bangsamoro Homeland was illegally occupied and annexed by the Philippine Government to its territory. This is a solid ground to constitute a Fardhu A'yn Jihad in our Homeland till our land is liberated.

Secondly, the Bangsamoro people are being subjected to all kinds of aggression, discrimination, [and] ethnic cleansing by the Philippine Government.

---

48   'Believers, when you meet a force in battle, stand firm and keep God firmly in mind, so that you may prosper' (Q8: 45, Haleem).
49   Q9: 38 is given in footnote 16.

Some evidences are the emergence of the bloodthirsty Christian vigilantes (ILAGA),[50] who massacred several thousands of Muslims in our Homeland.

Recently, in Pikit North Cotabato, the Philippine Colonial Government has attacked the Bangsamoro Muslims, using ground forces supported by heavy artillery and aerial bombardment, while they are preparing to offer congregational prayer marking the world-wide celebration of the Islamic holy day of 'Eidul-Adha [Feast of the Sacrifice].

These few mentioned brutalities of the Colonial Government have clearly rationalized the Fardhu A'yn Jihad, which obliges every one of us, male and female, professionals, business men, farmers and Muslims in every sector to join the Jihad in the way of Allah and fight according to their respective abilities and capabilities.

Many evidences from the Holy Qur'an and Sunnah proved this. Among those are:

1- Allah says:

'And fight in the way of Allah those who fight you, but transgress not the limits. Truly Allah likes not the transgressor.' (Al-Baqarah: 190)[51]

2- Allah says:

'Whoever transgress the prohibition against you, you transgress likewise against them.' (Al-Baqarah: 194)[52]

3- Allah says:

'And what is wrong with you that you fight not in the cause of Allah, and for those weak, ill-treated and oppressed among men, women, and children, whose cry is: "Our lord! Rescue us from this town whose people are oppressors; and raise for us from you one who will protect, and raise for us from you one who will help".' (Al-Nisa: 75)[53]

4- Allah says:

'If they withdraw not from you, nor offer you peace, nor restrain their hands, take hold of them and kill them wherever you find them.' (Al-nisa: 91)[54]

5- Allah says:

'And fight the Mushrikin (disbelievers in the ones of Allah) collectively as they fight against you collectively).' (Al-Taubah: 36)[55] [...]

---

50   The Ilaga were a feared, military-backed, anti-Moro vigilante group active in Mindanao during the late 1970s and the 1980s.

51   Q2: 190 is given in footnote 13.

52   Q2: 194 is given in footnote 36.

53   Q4: 75 is given in footnote 27.

54   'You will find others who wish to be safe from you, and from their own people, but whenever they are back in a situation where they are tempted [to fight you], they succumb to it. So if they neither withdraw, nor offer you peace, nor restrain themselves from fighting you, seize and kill them wherever you encounter them: We give you clear authority against such people' (Q4: 91, Haleem).

55   Q9: 36 is given in footnote 16.

These are the evidences from the Holy Qur'an, definitely requiring the Muslims to wage Jihad against those who betrayed them and commit gross injustice by occupying their lands.

Taken together all these evidences, all the Muslim Jurists from different schools of thought unanimously agreed that in such a situation where the Muslim lands is occupied by the enemies, the Jihad is Fardhu A'yn to all Muslims living in that area.

In such circumstance, a Muslim should come out and takes part in the fighting even without the permission from his parents, and a woman should come out and fight even if without permission from her husband. [...]

CONTEMPORARY MUSLIM SCHOLARS ON JIHAD AGAINST OPPRESSORS:

The contemporary Muslim Scholars have agreed that the present aggression and oppression being done against the Muslims in some Muslim minority countries substantiate a Fard A'yn Jihad, thus, requiring all Muslims in that respective area to defend themselves, their religion, and lands by fighting in the way of Allah. We shall mention here some of their Statements:

According to Sheikh Nasiruddin Al-Albanie: 'Jihad is of two types. The first one is Fard Ayn, which is a Jihad against the enemies who attack and occupied the Muslim land and Country, like in Palestine'.

According to Al-Sheikh Yousuf Al-Qaradawi: 'Those who fight in the defense of their lands, honor, and religion against a tyrannical oppressive force, which does not fear Allah nor have mercy on any creature[,] are fighting in the best kinds of Jihad. And there is a scholarly consensus (Ijma`) that whoever fights in defense of his religion, land and household, and is killed in that fighting is considered a Martyr (Shahid)'. [...]

The classical and contemporary Muslim jurists and scholars[,] therefore, have unanimously agreed on the obligatory [nature] of Jihad under such circumstances. This has further strengthened our belief that Jihad nowadays in our Homeland is Fard Ayn.

Al-Sheikh Yousuf Qaradawi asserts that: This is the best kind of Jihad and those who get killed in this Jihad will be considered as Martyr (Shahid). [...]

THE VIOLATION OF THE SIGNED PEACE AGREEMENT BY THE GRP IS A VALID GROUND TO DECLARE JIHAD AGAINST THEM:

Among the solid ground to declare Jihad against the present Philippine Government is the latest blatant violation of the letter and spirit of the GRP-MILF [Government of the Republic of the Philippines–Moro Islamic Liberation Front] Peace Agreements.

The Philippine Government has breached the peace agreement by launching a massive military attack against the MILF and the Bangsamoro Muslims preparing to offer congregational prayers marking the world-wide celebration of the Islamic Holy Day of Eidul-Adha in Pikit North Cotabato. Islam has a very clear and strict rule regarding the breaking of an agreement. It forbids the Muslims to behave treacherously towards the other party.

In case the breaking of a treaty or agreement becomes necessary due to the non-observance of the other party thereof, the Muslims are enjoined to inform openly the other party so that both may be set on [an] equal footing.

This principle is ordained by the verse in the Holy Qur-an [which] reads as:

'If you fear treachery from any people throw back to them on equal terms (that there will be no more covenants between you and them). Certainly Allah likes not the treacherous.' (Al-Anfal: 58)[56]

There is, however, an exception to this principle. The Islamic Law allows the Muslims to attack the other party, if the later [latter] violates openly the treaty and take some specific inimical actions against them.

In such a clear case, the Muslims are granted a right to take a military action against such a treacherous party without giving any ultimatum. Allah Almighty Says:

'But if they violate their oaths after their covenant, and attack your religion then fight the leader of [the] disbeliever. For sure their oaths are nothing to them – so that they may stop evil actions.' (Al-Taubah: 12).[57]

And Allah Says:

'How (can there [be] such a covenant with them) that when you are over powered by them, they regard not the ties, either of kinship or of covenant with you? With (good words from) their mouths they please you, but their hearts are averse to you, and most of them are Fasiqu'n.' (Al-Taubah: 8)[58]

This verse revealed the reason why there can be no peace agreements with these people. The reason is that they are evil-doers because they have no sense of moral responsibility nor do they hesitate to break the moral limits. […]

Therefore, the declaration of an all out Jihad by Im'amul Mujahideen Al-Sheikh Salamat Hashim against the GRP, as a response to GRP military attack[,] is legitimate and justifiable. […]

WORKABLE MEANS TO PARTICIPATE IN OUR JIHAD

Hence, we have established that Jihad nowadays is Fard A'yn to all the Bangsamoro people till our land is completely liberated from the hands of infidels.

However, it is permissible that not all the Bangsamoro people will personally take part in the firing line.

Therefore, there are recommended workable ways and means to help and participate in our Jihad in the way of Allah. They are the following:

---

56 'And if you learn of treachery on the part of any people, throw their treaty back at them, for God does not love the treacherous' (Q8: 58, Haleem).
57 'But if they break their oath after having made an agreement with you, if they revile your religion, then fight the leaders of disbelief – oaths mean nothing to them – so that they may stop' (Q9: 12, Haleem).
58 '[What sort of a treaty could there be] when, if they were to get the upper hand over you, they would not respect any tie with you, of kinship or of treaty? They flatter you with their tongues, but their hearts are against you and most of them are transgressors' (Q9: 8, Haleem).

Firstly, we should make Du`aa [invocatory prayers] for our Mujahideen brothers fighting in the front line and recite Du`aa Al-Qunut [supplicatory prayers seeking guidance or protection] in our prayer.

Secondly, any Moro civilians, businessmen, farmers who could not take part in the frontline for valid reasons should help to provide the needs of the Mujahideen going to battle ground, [and] take care [of] their families by helping them to provide their needs during their absence.

Those who help the Mujahideen in this manner will have the same reward to which the Mujahideen is entitled as the Prophet Mohammad Peace be Upon Him said:

> *'He who equips a Ghazi (Fighter) in the way of Allah is as if he has taken part in the fighting itself; and he who looks after the dependants of a Gazi in his absence is as if he has taken part in the fighting itself.'* (Al-Bukhari and Muslim) [Hadith]

Thirdly, the Bangsamoro living and working in the overseas, should pay their Zakah, and may collect charity among themselves and from their wealthy Arab employers and send it through the assigned trustworthy channel to the Mujahideen in the Homeland.

Fourthly, the Bangsamoro Professionals, writers and University level students, should explain through media and any other possible means the oppression happening to the Bangsamoro people. Similarly, they should refute by writing articles, publications etc. the black propagandas being waged against the Bangsamoro struggle.

Fifthly, We have to check our own intentions for our struggle in the cause of Allah, and be warned of the Prophetic Hadith in which the Prophet, peace and blessings be upon him, states:

> *'Whoever dies without having striven for the cause of Allah or having had the intention of doing so, has died following one of the branches of hypocrisy.'* (Reported by Muslim) [Hadith] [...]

14.3.3 Assulook Ismulyameena

Commentary   The provenance and status of the following document, 'Carrying Out Jihad in Pattani', is not straightforward. The introduction states that the pen name of the author is 'Assulook Ismulyameena' and that the text was written in Malaysia in mid-2002. According to the Thai government, the document was found on at least one of the Muslim victims of a battle with Thai security forces at the historic Krue Se Mosque in Pattani, southern Thailand, on 28 April 2004. (This mosque is pictured in the colour section of this book; see plate 5.) Government spokesmen stated that 'Ismail Jaafar, alias Poh Su, a 55-year-old Kelantan native', and Abdul Wahab, an Islamic teacher from Yala province in southern Thailand, were the co-authors (*The Nation*, 18 September 2004). Ismail reportedly has had a long history of activism in southern Thailand and was subsequently arrested and then released without charge by the Malaysian police. Though some of the details regarding the document's origins are in dispute, there can be little doubt that the text has been circulating among disaffected Muslim communities in southern Thailand (ICG 2005b: 23, 26; 'The (Un)making of a Militant: He Thought He Was Invincible, but He Almost Died at Krue Sae', *New Straits Times Online*, 12

September 2005). It has a place in this sourcebook because it offers a rare view of jihadist thinking among Thai Muslims and their sympathizers in the northern states of peninsular Malaysia. The original document is in Malay written using the Arabic script (Jawi script), but this English translation is based on a Thai-language version of the original Malay. The influence of the Thai translation is evident in the transliteration of terms derived from Arabic.

The document is in the form of a training manual and sets out teachings and prayers for each day of a week-long course. It has several features. There is a strong sense of grievance at what is seen as the trampling of Malay-Muslim rights in southern Thailand, and the author refers repeatedly to the abuse and repression suffered by Muslims and the loss of wealth and opportunities under Thai rule. There is also a powerful sanguinary imagery, with frequent reference to blood sacrifice in order to redeem the honour and independence of the Pattani people. The tone is both passionate and hortatory.

Extract 14-9: Assulook Ismulyameena

Assulook Ismulyameena (pseudonym) (2002), 'Berjihad di Pattani' [Carrying Out Jihad in Pattani], Kelantan, August, 20 pages. Extract: pp. 2–14.[59]

In the name of God who is very merciful and kind:

Day 1 […]
The author of this book will eventually die. … But what he has written will remain forever because of its distribution by preachers who have stood up for the continuation of this plan and are its representatives, much like army generals. Use this book under the name 'Martyr Warrior, Imam Syahid, Light of Jihad'. Martyr Warriors will arise in the land of Pattani by the light of *jihad pishabillilloh* [Ar.: *jihaadun fii sabiilil-laahi*; jihad in the path of God with death leading to martyrdom], and be taken up by younger generations with pride and inspiration.

Martyr Warrior will speak this sentence with his own voice: 'May peace be with all of you'. Hope that this sentence will receive responses from the general public, gentlemen, ladies, the wealthy and the poor, adults and children, the healthy and the unhealthy. This has been spoken especially for all young Pattani fighters and for the souls whose blood is filled with belief and loyalty. Wake up oh my brothers who are still sleeping. Wake up oh my brothers who are still ignorant. Oh my brothers who are still forgetting. Oh my brothers who still don't know, do know that Prophet Muhammad (blessings and peace be upon him) is one of the great generals of the Martyr army. He led the army to attack and at the same time recited a verse in the Qur'an saying 'Almighty God' and invited all humans to believe in Almighty God and His Prophets.

For all believers … the Prophet Muhammad (blessings and peace be upon him) has invited us to strengthen God's religion and conquer back the land of Mecca. The

59   This is an edited version of a translation supplied by the International Crisis Group (ICG). We are grateful to Francesca Lawe-Davies from the ICG for making available to us both Thai and English translations of this document. We would also like to thank John Funston and Chintana Sandilands at the Faculty of Asian Studies, Australian National University, for checking and revising the translation.

Prophet Muhammad (blessings and peace be upon him) is our great general, and will be in front of us at every moment. [...]

Our great general has encouraged and invited us to set up an army to fight to bring back the power of Islam that was once destroyed by peoples of other religions. The Prophet has invited us to unite in the establishment of an army to conquer back the city of Mecca from those of other religions. Therefore, do these actions bring us down or lead us to devastation as accused? No. Oh my brothers ... but these actions were the command from our God and His advocates. [...]

Oh all Martyr Warriors ... It is a pity that we are sitting still, not knowing anything, and still having fun watching and hearing our children being suppressed under the power of the possessor. The wealth that by right belongs to us has been robbed and the wealth of our country has been taken away. Our freedom has been limited; our culture and religion have been suppressed. Where has our responsibility for the safety of our children and peoples gone? Reflect on it, oh all Martyr Warriors. Actually our parents and brothers who have died and those who died as warriors for our nation in the past, they have left us with a warrior's blood. On this day let us call for, invite and encourage those who possess this blood to emerge and resurrect with us, even though it may cause so much pain and bring tears. Succession of a warrior's blood will occur. At the same time we pray for the souls of the Martyr Warriors by yelling in all corners of the battlefield: 'There is no god but God and Muhammad is the Messenger of God. We are your advocates. Almighty God. Almighty God. Almighty God'. [pp. 2–3] [...]

Day 2
[...] On this honourable and precious second [day] ... the author has stood up with strength, inviting and requesting all Martyr Warriors to stand up in collaboration to strengthen the power of the union, to fight and conquer back our beloved Pattani country, to recover our pride, to strengthen our religion that has been trampled on. We shall collaborate to protect our children, wives, possessions and the wealth of the country with our lives. Therefore, God has promised us heaven. [...]

Thank you God. ... The answers and explanations that the Prophet has given are all true. And it serves as evidence that everything that is in the possession of each individual is by right that person's proper possessions, whether it is land, objects, houses, money, children and wives, country, culture, or even the most important thing of all, which is the right to believe in a religion. Therefore, let us turn our heads together and cooperate to protect these things, even though we may lose our lives.

Once again the author calls for and gives encouragement to all of you. Oh fellow countrymen, I ask you to join the Martyrs' army. Step onto the battlefield ... and I will support you with spirit. And I will call on, invite and provoke the warrior's blood that has been passed on from our ancestors, to [make us] stand up and fight. Where have all the warrior's spirit, blood and heart gone? Look how much our senior citizens are tortured, all the way to our children and wives. Who else is there to be responsible and to protect them?

All Martyr Warriors please be reminded of how important we are. Though we may lose our lives, this death is considered the death of a warrior for the nation. Oh my brothers, please know that the death of all the Martyr Warriors does not mean that they are dead. Instead, they are still living beside God. They are only resting for a while, by God's command. God has arranged for them an honourable holiday place. God has given them great fortunes. [...] Oh my brothers! ... Are you afraid that you would die so? Don't think like that! ... Know and accept that death will happen to all of you at the selected time, no matter where you are hiding. [...]

Now ... Let all of us come and fight until God blesses us with victory, making His and our enemies surrender. That is, the victory of Martyrs, or victory because we are able to defeat His and our enemies. Understand that the lives of all Muslims who believe in God and the Prophets have inherited the Martyr's blood, a blood-line left by our ancestors who have sacrificed through jihad. And the blood that fell from the bodies of these warriors, their cries, tears and blood that has stained the ground red, a red colour that will cover all the land. And the colour will radiate into the sky, making it appear red in the morning and evening, east and west. This is a sign that Pattani has been shattered, and therefore brings all the warriors out to fight in the ways of God (Jihad). The voice of both male and female warriors will be heard everywhere, as a signal that they are facing and attacking the enemy. 'Almighty God, Almighty God, Almighty God.' With this sound, weak lives and souls will be awakened and strengthened. The sound shows rage, and at the same time shows that you are following jihad. It also gives encouragement and invites others to join in. [...] Come, and join the fight ... Go out to fight – all of you who inherit the warrior's blood-line. Go out and absorb the values of the warriors; let every part of your bodies absorb this belief. Let us look and let us listen ... all the parents and small children who have the courage, pray that God will select all of you as leaders ... or as people who will rescue their destiny. Therefore, make yourselves ready and do not show any weakness. End your fears absolutely ... God will stay with us forever ... [...]

I have stated before, haven't I ... that God is on our side. ... Consider, look and listen ... He himself has forewarned us not to forget all the equipment needed in a battle. Bring and use anything you can find to frighten the enemy. You may use this to destroy and kill unorthodox people who are your enemy. Therefore, we have been selected and praised by God, to prepare to face our enemies. Oh all my brothers, always remember that as Islamic people who have faith in God and the Prophets, do not be proud and rely only on modern weapons. We must hope for help from God. Only He has the most efficient and powerful weapons. Also, know that no matter how many men there are in the army, He can still stop them and chase them away. And even though we only have a small army, with help from God, we absolutely can win. [pp. 4–6] [...]

Day 3
[...] Fellow Martyr Warriors, the protection of our rights is necessary ... Even though those things are objects, children, wives, fathers, mothers, other Islamic people or people of the same nationality. Above all we must protect the purity of our Islamic religion from being stepped on by any party wanting to destroy the meaning and the following of Islamic teachings. [...]

My fellow warriors! Even though it may seem difficult for us believers to distinguish between friends and traitors, finally we have found that God has suggested a way that is not difficult at all. He has explained clearly to believers that … when a person takes the side of an unorthodox person as his leader, maybe it is because he wants something in return, or wants to devastate our honourable Islamic religion. Therefore, it is obvious that people who belong to the same group as unorthodox people are the most dangerous of God's and of our enemies. This is because they are among the group of un-Islamic people. [p. 7] […]

Day 4
[…] In the hostility that may occur during war in the future, you must be careful! We must not use our aggression in ways such as killing children and women or destroying houses, valuables and agricultural sites, because God does not favour such behaviour. And if anyone in your group has been selected as leader of the army, do not be rigid to the people under you. Forgive them if they have made mistakes, because if you are too harsh with them, they may not work or they may escape [desert] from the army. Isn't it actually God that made your heart gentle? […]

Fellow gentlemen and ladies! … Know that on every battlefield there must be loss of life, especially in battles which are responses to God and the Prophet. Such wars release us from being suppressed by the infidels and their allies, who are not feeling comfortable because of the existence of such strong believers in God (Islam). That makes them feel uncomfortable and restrains them from doing things the way they want to. Our struggle is a fight to liberate our beloved home country, which has been conquered by royalties [*sic*] of the infidels and their allies. For this reason, we need every believer to make sacrifices in all aspects. So hurry and give us as much support as you can. Also, read and listen to what God has to say about giving the necessary support. […]

Oh all young male and female Martyrs, please know that all the advocates of Prophet Muhammad (blessings and peace be upon him) have in the past sacrificed their lives to act as a shield to protect the Prophet from the enemy's weapons. They were willing to sacrifice their lives according to God's path, to make the Prophet safe from the enemy's weapons. They died in the way of the Martyrs, and the Prophet was able to stay alive to continue his mission. This mission was to bring all humans into the ways that God permits. At the same time the whole world still needs to follow the Prophet's teachings in order to protect humans from ignorance in leading their lives. These are the things that the Prophet has done as a role model (Sunnah) that we have heard and seen from the news from all regions. Some fellow Muslims are ready to be suicide soldiers. They are not people who bring themselves to devastation, but [rather] people who are answering God's desires on the battlefield. Do you all accept that the advocates of Prophet Muhammad (blessings and peace be upon him) have in the past led themselves to downfall and dishonour? Therefore, it is not necessary that we receive the information that the infidels and traitors present. It is already clear that they are the enemies of God and the Prophet. [pp. 9–11] […]

Day 6

[…] Oh all young Martyr Warriors! This is not the time for us to stand still and watch … And by watching in all corners of the world you will see infidels chasing and killing Muslims. The infidels have allied together all over the world to exterminate our fellow Muslims. This may be why it is not the time for us to cry, as we are not able to watch or listen to our children and wives being tortured and banished from our homeland by the infidels. We cannot tolerate seeing our possessions and rights taken away, and our children made into slaves. [pp. 13–14]

14.4   MODERATE AND LIBERAL INTERPRETATIONS OF JIHAD

Commentary   The views of jihad expounded above, particularly those of the Salafi jihadists, have been strongly contested by mainstream and liberal Muslim leaders and scholars. They argue that extreme forms of jihad are based on both a misunderstanding of scripture and a distorted perception of the modern world and the nature of the threat to Islam. They assert not only that the use of mass-casualty violence is unjustified, but also that it is counterproductive because it distracts Muslims from more important matters such as striving for equality, justice and prosperity. They also argue that violent jihad further stigmatizes Islam in the eyes of non-Muslims.

14.4.1   Masdar F. Mas'udi

Commentary   Masdar Mas'udi (1954–) is one of the leading intellectuals and reform-minded activists in Nahdlatul Ulama (NU, Revival of the Religious Scholars), Indonesia's largest traditionalist Islamic organization. He heads the prominent Jakarta non-government organization Perhimpunan Pengembangan Pesantren dan Masyarakat (P3M, Association for the Development of Pesantren and Society) and has written extensively on matters as diverse as gender equality in Islam, women's reproductive rights, Islam's role in the state, new theological trends, pluralism and social development. He has also served in senior roles within NU, including a period as acting chair in 2004. The following extract challenges the militant and sectarian interpretations of jihad and advocates a conceptualization of jihad which is charitable and peaceable.

Extract 14-10: Masdar F. Mas'udi

Masdar F. Mas'udi (2004), 'Islam, Perdamaian dan Kekerasan: Kontekstualisasi Maka Jihad' [Islam, Peace and Violence: Contextualization of the Meaning of Jihad], pp. 71–84 in ASEAN Youth and Student Network (ed.), *Gerakan Radikal Islam di Indonesia dalam Sorotan* [Radical Islamic Movements in Indonesia under the Spotlight], AYS-NET, Jakarta. Extract: pp. 71–84.

The position of jihad in the entirety of the construct of Islam is very important. As such, some in the Islamic community have suggested that a sixth pillar of Islam, namely jihad, be added. We also once heard suggestions that social justice be added to the pillars of faith as in the reform era. If we discuss religion then we cannot stray from that because religion is a doctrine.

In the Qur'an, the word jihad is mentioned repeatedly in no less than 38 forms. Among the verses some state that in Islam, only two things are required for a guarantee of salvation: faith and jihad [...] Not just one verse, but several, stress that faith and jihad are the path to salvation.

On account of this, it is understandable that the term or concept of jihad has become vital, popular and important in Islam. Perhaps if we use other verses to try to describe the two paths to salvation, faith and pious charity, where there is perhaps an equivalence between jihad and pious charity, then, more or less, faith is personal whereas jihad is overtly public, faith is latent, hidden within, and jihad is its actualization.

As such, jihad obtains an extremely broad meaning, as all actualization of faith as religious commitment is jihad. A person wanting to pray needs to perform jihad in the sense of a jihad of self-restraint (*jihadun nafs*), which is a great jihad (*jihad akbar*). But in reality, a great jihad is defeated by a small jihad (*jihad asghar*). If a great jihad is the jihad of self-restraint, then outward jihad is its manifestation. That [the jihad of self-restraint] is what is more popular, and to call a person a *mujahid* hardly has the connotation of someone skilled at self-restraint, but rather [has the connotation of] a courageous person able to conquer their enemy, where the enemy is concrete and visible. Although self-restraint is a great jihad, a *mujahid* is rarely connected with the ability to restrain oneself internally. The process of jihad is the actualization of faith, meaning that personal faith is made public.

It is this process that made jihad start to be popular, as the Islamic community began to come into contact with other groups, other groups not always meaning groups of a different religion. Even within other circles in the Islamic community, whose interpretation differs, sometimes the word jihad is used to mean upholding an interpretation and school of law (*madzhab*),[60] for example, jihad in the sense of wiping out superstition. This [kind of] jihad is surely related to and directed at fellow Muslims, because it is fellow Muslims holding different interpretations who – according to their accusers of course – practise superstition or innovation. This is the case even though all parties have agreed that 'directed at other people' refers to people who are not part of the Islamic community. This is what verses in the Qur'an that point to the target of jihad often refer to, namely facing infidels. So there is a personification of the target of jihad. While the jihad of self-restraint means resisting personal urges that are impulses that emanate from oneself, it is clear that the physical target of outward jihad in many verses is the infidel. [pp. 71–3] [...]

Ambiguity of the Concept of an Infidel [...]

Jihad against infidels was not a problem in the age of the Prophet, because he, through his capacity for divine revelation, was able to define certain persons or groups as infi-

---

60 This reference to *madzhab* encompasses not just the specific legal codes set out in each of the four classical schools of law, but also the methodology that Islamic scholars within each school use in responding to new jurisprudential issues.

dels and hypocrites. We believe that the Prophet was able to define certain persons as infidels, believers, hyprocrites and so on. Their behaviour in taking up arms against the Prophet also made this very clear. But in our present society, things are no longer so black and white. Is every person of a different conviction an infidel, and can every person who does not share our religion be treated as an infidel and a target of jihad? [...]

As such, it is God who needs to ascertain whether or not one is a *mujahid*. One cannot enter heaven as one wishes just because one says 'I believe in God'; one must endure a trial. This is what has become a heated debate. [pp. 74–5] [...]

Even if the difference of opinion, mainly among Sunnis, cannot be resolved, there is no need for us to call each other infidels. Al-Ghazali[61] has said that as long as a person believes in the truth of the confession of faith (*syahadat* [Ar.: *shahaadah*]), then we may not call that person an unbeliever. So the key is in the confession of faith, which is somewhat more fluid and not so rigid merely on account of differences in legal opinion (*furu'* [Ar.: *furuu`un*]). *Furu'* of faith need not make a person an unbeliever. As I have said above, jihad is waged if its target has been defined successfully and the target is an infidel. The question is, who knows whether or not a person is an unbeliever? Defined in terms of jurisprudence, there are two types of unbeliever: an unbeliever who is hostile (*kafir harbi*); and an unbeliever who agrees to live peacefully (*kafir mustamin/zimmi*). [p. 77] [...]

Contextualization of the Meaning of Jihad

[...] As a result, the target of jihad no longer needs to be defined person by person. This gives us the opportunity to interpret the target of jihad not as a person or group but as something impersonal. To use a sociological term, a system/structure that is infidel/unjust or discriminatory is the newest target of jihad and is far more strategic than targets of a person-by-person nature.

As such, if we still use jihad as a core concept of our religion, then it retains its relevance because jihad becomes hard work to truly uphold what is right. It is just that its target must be redefined not as a person, because we are weak in defining the faith that is in each of our hearts, but rather as a group whose definition must be taken further and re-evaluated with an impersonal meaning. As a result, jihad now means how to uphold a more just system and order of political and social life by breaking down systems and structures that are unbelieving, unjust and discriminatory.

Because of this, the method of jihad is politics, meaning discussing/engaging in discourse, changing policy and supervising the maintenance of policy. This is the form of jihad that is relevant for us in the context of the state and the nation. We cannot be shackled from the outset in defining whether a person is a friend or a foe. Everyone in our united nation of Indonesia is our brother/friend and we have a common target of jihad, namely a system or structure that is unbelieving, unjust and discriminatory. [pp. 78–9] [...]

Actually, Islam is humble towards the cultural heritage and civilization of others; this is what we need to get under our belts so that we do not become small-minded.

---

61   Abu Hamid al-Ghazali was a famous twelfth-century theologian and philosopher.

Try to imagine if we rejected everything that comes from the West – we would not be able to do anything; for instance, using electricity has a cultural heritage whether we like it or not. So there needs to be openness. [p. 80] [...]

So do not interpret it [jihad] to mean that Jews and Christians will continue to hate you and wage war on you; that is a very long way from its meaning. It means that there are Jews and Christians who are not at ease, because you have not yet entered or will not enter their religion.

This stance that Christians and Jews will not accept Muslims (*walantartlo*)[62] is common to all people, including Muslims who will not rest until Christians become Muslims. [...] All groups are proud of their own group; if you are proud of your own group but not of others that is the same thing, but that verse [Q2: 120] is not an order or an injunction for us to hate people or cause the destruction of others. The meaning of the verse has been overly twisted if it becomes provocative, as it refers to a common psychological fact. How should we face people who are different? I think we should be mature and take the stance that it was God who created different people and different religions.

We need not aspire to be God and judge difference in this world. The time for this will come and it will be God who judges. [p. 82] [...]

Islam is not well understood as a religion of charity, as the emphasis has always been more on faith. [...]

In this context we are not talking about colours or symbols, but [saying that] the service/morality [aspect] of Islam has been underemphasized; the emphasis has been more on doctrine, faith and symbols as identity. In this life there is always competition, and I think defeating the enemy with jihad means resisting our own stupidity and laziness. [...]

I think it is more important to translate Islam as service (*amali*) and define the enemies frequently found within us, namely stupidity, laziness and so on. We do not need to be too outward looking, continually looking for faults and weaknesses in other people. [pp. 83–4]

14.4.2   Faqihuddin Abdul Kodir

Commentary   Faqihuddin Abdul Kodir (1971–) is an academic and liberal activist. He is a graduate in Islamic law from Damascus University, Syria (1996), and gained his master's degree in Islamic jurisprudence from the International Islamic University, Kuala Lumpur (1999). A lecturer at the Sekolah Tinggi Agama Islam Negeri (STAIN, State Islamic College) in Cirebon and secretary-general of the Fahmina Institute (a non-government organization), he has written and edited several books on gender, sexuality and social justice issues and is also a regular contributor to Jaringan Islam Liberal

---

62   *Walantartlo* is a reference to a verse stating that Jews and Christians will always want to convert Muslims to their faiths: 'The Jews and the Christians will never be pleased with you unless you follow their ways. Say, "God's guidance is the only true guidance". If you were to follow their desires after the knowledge that has come to you, you would find no one to protect you from God or help you' (Q2: 120, Haleem).

(JIL, Liberal Islam Network). In the extract below, Faqihuddin surveys the changing interpretations of jihad, with particular attention to the role of women. He examines the etymology and shifting historical meanings of jihad and argues for a return to the 'original' understanding of the term as focusing on ritual and proselytization rather than war. Moreover, he contends that women should not be excluded from war, particularly in defence of the Islamic community.

Extract 14-11: Faqihuddin Abdul Kodir

Faqihuddin Abdul Kodir (2002), 'Saatnya Perempuan Pegang Kendali Perjuangan' [It's Time Women Held the Reins of Struggle], *Swara Rahima*, 4(2): pp. 9–15. Extract: pp. 9–12, 14–15.

> When the world makes plurality of life an inevitability, dialogue becomes the primary medium for championing ideas, concepts and thoughts, and also religious truths. All forms of physical violence become illegitimate, and are in fact opposed. Thus jihad in the sense of warfare has ceased to be relevant for present conditions. It is time jihad was restored to its original meaning, of commitment to campaigning for brotherhood, peace and justice, which surely constitutes the main teaching of Islam. In this regard, women – who are always symbolic of peace – are most entitled to take the reins (jihad) and add colour to the struggle for justice and peace. [Abstract]
>
> In many religious rituals (read: worship) of a public nature, women are frequently not fully involved. Jihad – in the conventional religious view – is one of the public forms of worship that place women on an unequal footing with men. Hence jihad for women, by any definition, revolves only around the bed, the kitchen and the well, or – even when it refers to war – women's jihad extends only to providing services, nursing and entertainment. This constitutes a domestication of women through religious teachings, which is certainly not consistent with the spirit of equality and justice of Islam. [Sidebar]

The redefinition of jihad thus constitutes a necessity, even an inevitability. Particularly in its relationship to the role of women and contemporary conditions, which have so reduced the meaning of jihad that it can only be understood in the sense of war or physical violence. Jihad in the sense of war must be understood as a historical fact of the contact between the faithful of the past with other religious groups of their time. Even in classical readings, jihad was originally not interpreted as warfare or physical violence, such that reinterpretation – besides being necessary and inevitable – may also find its roots in early texts such as the Qur'an and Hadith.

Classical Jihad: In Search of the Authentic Meaning

Jihad is defined by Muhammad bin Abu Bakr al-Razi (d. 666H/1268AD) in the dictionary *Mukhtar al-Shihah* [Compilation from the al-Shihah (Dictionary)] as being identical to the words *mujahadah* [fighting, battle], *ijtihad* [independent judgement] and *tajahud* [engaging in war], namely expending all one's capabilities (*badzl al-wus'*). In the investigations of Ibn Manzur (630–711H/1232–1311AD) into all derivations of the word jihad in verses of Arabic poetry, its meanings also revolved only around the signifier *al-juhd*, namely expending energy, effort, capabilities and strength, and the word *al-jahd*, namely commitment, or something difficult and tiring. Among them was the word *jahad* for 'land that is difficult to prepare for cultivation'. Even intercourse (intimate relations) can be classified as jihad, because it requires commitment and exertion that is quite tiring (Ibn Manzhur, *Lisan al-'Arab* [Arabic Language (Dictionary)], Ch. 3, pp. 133–5). This means, in early language, the word jihad knew only connotations of energy, capability, commitment, strength and something of difficulty, and knew no other meaning. [p. 9]

The word jihad was already familiar before the Qur'an was handed down. The Qur'an then made use of it, including in the first verses that were handed down. It is a serious error to say that the obligation to undertake jihad only began when the Prophet Muhammad was in Medina. The call to jihad had already been handed down during the Mecca period, and in fact in the Qur'an there is a verse that uses the word jihad in the phrase *jihadan kabiran* [great jihad or total jihad], a phrase not encountered in other verses. In the chapter of al-Furqan, verse 52, the Prophet Muhammad, blessings and peace be upon him, was commanded to wage total jihad (*jihadan kabiran*) against unbelievers with the Qur'an, not with swords or violence. Perhaps here it is necessary to cite the said verse:

> '*And truly We have made it rain on humankind on and off so that they take lessons (from it); but the majority of humankind resist and reject (the gift); And if We [had so] wished, truly We [would] send to every country someone to give warning (a messenger); so don't you (O Muhammad) follow the unbelievers, and **strive** against them **with the Qur'an** with **great striving**.*'[63]

Another verse about jihad handed down in Mecca was in the chapter of al-Nahl. In verse 110 it was mentioned that the people who relocated to avoid violence then undertook jihad and exercised patience in order to win forgiveness and love from Almighty God.[64] Meanwhile verse 69 of the chapter of al-'Ankabut, which was also handed down in Mecca, explains that people who wage jihad in the way of God will be guided by Him.[65]

Jihad in these Mecca verses[66] certainly cannot be interpreted as physical violence or war against enemies and opponents, let alone friends, because the Mecca period

---

63 'many times We have repeated this to people so that they might take heed, but most persist in their ingratitude – had it been Our will, We would have sent a warner to every town – so do not give in to the disbelievers: strive hard against them with this Qur'an' (Q25: 50–2, Haleem).

64 'But your Lord will be most forgiving and most merciful to those who leave their homes after persecution, then strive and remain steadfast' (Q16: 110, Haleem).

65 Q29: 69 is given in footnote 2.

66 Analysis of the circumstances, time and place of the revelation of the Qur'an to the Prophet Muhammad is a vital part of Qur'anic interpretation. The analyses show basic differences between the verses revealed when the Prophet was living in Mecca and those received when he was forced to flee Mecca and move with his followers to Medina. The Mecca verses establish the basic doctrinal beliefs of Islam. It was in Medina that the first society based on Islamic principles was established, and the verses revealed in this context offer guidance on relations between individuals, governance and relations with non-believers, including the just reasons for waging war. The Haleem translation of the Qur'an indi-

was a period of total resignation, patience and commitment for 13 years to campaign for the teachings of Islam, without violence. The Mecca period was a period of formation, placement, introduction and linking with various communities, which required quite intense dialogue.

During this period, jihad constituted a commitment to convey the message of truth and justice with utmost preparedness to bear all risks. For Dr Muhammad Sa'id Ramadhan al-Buthi,[67] jihad in this sense is the most fundamental principle of Islamic proselytization. We certainly cannot say that the Prophet, blessings and peace be upon him, did not wage jihad war in Mecca because he was afraid or lacking in courage before the unbelievers. Rather it was due entirely to commandments and principles. The meaning of jihad in the sense of proselytization without violence is a principle, such that the underlying meaning of jihad in no way refers to violence or warfare, but more to a sense of astuteness and dedication in conveying the truth (al-Buthy, *al-Jihad fi al-Islam; Kaifa Nafhamuhu wa Numarisuhu* [Jihad in Islam: How We Understand and Practice It], 1996, Dar al-Fikr, Damascus – Syria, pp. 12–22).
[...]

The Qur'an itself cites special terms for physical battle, namely *al-qital* [battle] and *al-muharabah* or *al-hirabah* [both meaning 'war'], which most assuredly have their own specifications and stipulations. The Qur'an surely has a meaning of its own when it differentiates between jihad and *qital* (physical battle). Jihad cannot be considered the same as *qital*, because the Qur'an itself did not class them as being the same. This means that jihad is not identical to physical battle or *qital*. The term jihad should be returned to its original meaning of the Mecca period. That is, all sincere efforts to campaign for the values of truth and justice. Several classical Muslim clerics were also aware of this, such that when talking about the concept of war in Islam they tended to choose the term *al-sayr* [attack] or *al-ghazawat* [war] or *al-ma'rakah* [battlefield] rather than the expression jihad. [p. 10]

The Qur'an's pronouncement of the non-violent jihad of Mecca as *jihadan kabiran* is a reinforcement that jihad is not physical violence, but the fully dedicated submission of all energy and strength to advocating the values of righteousness. Similarly, in various Hadith texts, jihad is not understood just as physical combat. This means that the Prophet himself, blessings and peace be upon him, defined jihad in a variety of ways, such that he created texts that were susceptible to multiple meanings. Among them were that the best jihad is that which brings truth to authoritarian power and to the taming of lust; that the smallest (*ashgar*) jihad are battles, whereas the greatest (*akbar*) jihad is the taming of lust; and also that the best jihad of all is the pilgrimage to Mecca. [...]

At one point Aisyah [the Prophet's third wife], may God be well pleased with her, asked about jihad for women, and was answered by the Prophet, blessings and peace be upon him; 'Your jihad is to make the pilgrimage' (Ibn Hajar al-'Asqallani, *Fath al-Bari* [The Victory of the Creator], Ch. 6, p. 168). This means, the pilgrimage

---

cates at the start of each chapter (*sura*) whether the chapter is from the Mecca or the Medina period (see Haleem 2004: xviii).

67   An academic in the Sharia Faculty of the University of Damascus, Syria.

constitutes a jihad. Also in this vein was the declaration by the Prophet, blessings and peace be upon him, to a woman who came asking about jihad, that the running of a household has the same value as jihad (see *Ta'liq wa Takhrij 'ala Syarh 'Uqud al-Lujain'* [Explanatory Remarks and Hadith Research on 'A Commentary on the Joining of the Two Oceans'], pp. 43–5).[68] This must be understood as an opening of the term jihad to many interpretations, not as a demarcation of women's jihad, let alone a prohibition or a domestication of women's roles. Because conclusions of demarcation and prohibition would ignore the many female disciples reported to be female warriors alongside the Prophet, blessings and peace be upon him. We might mention, for example, Nusaibah bint Ka'ab, may God be well pleased with her, Umm 'Athiyyah, may God be well pleased with her, Al-Rabi' bint al-Mu'awwidz, may God be well pleased with her, Umm Sulaim, may God be well pleased with her, and several other women.

Certainly in the discipline of Islamic jurisprudence (*fiqh*) – which views Islam from a legal perspective – jihad is often interpreted as warfare. Clerics of *fiqh* are often swept along by this interpretation, such that the original meaning of jihad is increasingly lost. We might mention, for example, Imam al-Thabari (224–310H/839–923AD) who wrote the law book *al-Jihad* [Jihad], and also Ibn Rushd (520–595H/1126–1198AD) in his tome *Bidayat al-Mujtahid* [Introduction for a Muslim Legal Specialist]. But it must also be emphasized that Ibn Rushd himself stated that there are eight types of jihad in Islam: [including] jihad of the heart, jihad of the tongue, jihad by the hands and jihad by the sword. This means, for Ibn Rushd, that the jihad of warfare is only one possible meaning, not the totality of its meaning. [p. 11] [...]

In the 'jihad of warfare', women are not treated the same as men. In terms of the obligation to wage war, for example, women are equated with small children, the infirm, cripples, amputees, the blind, the paralysed and the elderly. Just like them, women are not obliged to wage war because they are considered weak, or not possessed of the qualifications necessary to fight in a war. Women are weak creatures who must be defended, not strong creatures who can defend. There are even some who state that women, because of their weakness, are forbidden to join in fighting a war (see Al-Syirbini, *Mughni al-Muhtaj* [Satisfying a Seeker (of Legal Knowledge)], Ch. 4, p. 216).

In the view of Dr Wahbah al-Zuahili, a quite famous *fiqh* writer, women are forbidden from going to war because they are bound by obligations of 'service' to their husbands, like servants who have obligations of service to their masters. This means that women may be permitted to go to war if they receive their husband's blessing, except in a situation of emergency where enemies storm into Muslim areas, in which case everyone has an obligation to wage war, including women (*Al-Fiqh al-Islami wa Adillatuhu* [Islamic Jurisprudence and Its Argumentation], Ch. 6, pp. 418–19).

For the same reason (namely weakness), female enemies must also be protected, cannot be killed, and when war ceases automatically become slaves and servants to Muslims, for reasons of protection. They are unlike men, who are surrendered to a

---

68   The book entitled *'Uquud al-Lujjayn*, by al-Nawawi (1813–98) of Banten, is described further in chapter 13.

government decision between being executed, freed, detained, exchanged or made servants. Women are faced with only one choice, namely a most certainly humiliating slavery – albeit in the interests of protection – whereas men face more than one choice.

The concept of a 'jihad of warfare' in *fiqh* cannot be separated from the past history of the Muslim faithful. In fact, if traced back before Islam, the *kabilah-kabilah* [Kabyle tribes] of North Arabia also had moral-laden conditions of warfare which were later touted as Islamic morals. The concept of a 'jihad of warfare' also developed simultaneously with the expansions undertaken by the caliphs, from the time of the Rightly Guided Caliphs [that is, the first four caliphs, 632–61 CE]. It goes without saying that this concept has enjoyed the full support of every ruler in the history of Islam. *Firstly* because this concept facilitates mobilization of the masses for formation into the ruler's forces to combat enemies (the infidels), as they are guaranteed blessings from Almighty God and if they should fall will go straight to heaven. Secondly, it will add to the ruler's legitimacy in the eyes of the community. When Muslim territories are fragmented, the accommodation of a 'jihad of warfare' against unbelievers and the ability to subdue them will increase the people's legitimation of and sympathy for Islamic rulers who wage a 'jihad of warfare', as opposed to other rulers. Furthermore we cannot deny the historical fact that there have been many purification movements in Islam that have accommodated a 'jihad of warfare' against enemies, both Muslim and non-Muslim.

This means that a politicization of the 'jihad of warfare' has most definitely occurred, such that it is very difficult indeed to differentiate between the original concept, which was apolitical, and the political concept derived from it. In the background of this politicization is of course a variety of matters loaded with worldly values, fleeting and not touching upon the teachings of Islam. This does not preclude the possibility that the prohibition against women waging a 'jihad of warfare' is also based on political considerations, or at the very least politics dominated by men. This all makes the reinterpretation of the meaning of jihad and the involvement of women in jihad inevitable. Despite the fact that the Qur'an firmly states that a *jihadan kabiran* is a jihad which is non-violent. [p. 12] [...]

As was stated by Abu Bakr al-Razi (d. 666H [1268 CE]), jihad is a total surrender of all strength, energy, finances and thoughts to realize the most substantial Islamic values such as justice, equality and welfare for all, without discrimination based on race, ethnicity, skin colour or even religion and belief.

Women's Jihad
There are many things that must be straightened out in terms of matters relating to women and religious interpretation. These include jihad and women, so that the definition of jihad is more in keeping with the spirit borne by the Qur'an and more relevant to the realities of life. The *fiqh* perspective that women are weak and hence need not – or even are forbidden to – wage war has now lost its rationale. Weakness and strength are not directly linked to gender, but to training, diet and will. Women are strong too, and can even be stronger than men. Past history also shows women's capacity to wage war, to mention, for example, Nusaibah bin Ka'ab, may God be well

pleased with her, who unsheathed her sword to foil enemies who were going to slay the Prophet, blessings and peace be upon him, at the Battle of Uhud when the male disciples were beaten into retreat. When the Khandaq War was raging and the post of Medina was handed over to Hasan bin Tsabit, when enemies stole into Medina, Hasan stood quaking before them and the one to step forward to oppose them – and in fact kill them – was the female disciple Shafiyyah. Queen Syajaratuddur in Egypt was also a war hero who received the sceptre of leadership after she succeeded in leading military forces against the invading Mongols. More than a little recent history also documents the capability and heroism of women in fighting wars.

The argument of 'bondage to obligations of service', such that women are not permitted to wage war without the blessing of their husbands, must also be reconsidered. Nowadays war has become a profession, associated with expertise and abilities that may be embraced by men or women. This profession is associated more with the relations between a state and its citizens than with the relations between husbands and wives. Not to mention that the totality of 'a wife's service to her husband' has been challenged by many parties, including from within *fiqh* circles. According to the analysis of the Forum for the Study of Kitab Kuning (FK3)[69] of Ciganjur, most of the Hadith that have become references for the 'obligation of service' are weak (*dha'if*), and in fact many are false (*maudha'*).

There are also Hadith that talk about 'women's jihad'. As emphasized at the beginning of this essay, these texts put forward a definition of jihad which means it is not understood only as war. Or they open the text of the term jihad to many definitions in keeping with demand and developments. These Hadith texts must also be understood as demonstrating the Prophet's appreciation of household work, in order that it not be considered lowly and be performed only by women. Household work is also valued highly by Almighty God, such that whosoever wishes to obtain high status may perform it, male or female. [p. 14] [...]

If the obligation to wage jihad is interpreted communally (*fardh kifayah*), as most clerics state, it is aimed at the capacity, readiness and ability of the faithful, not at one gender to the exclusion of the other. Women and men are the same before regulations and laws, including in matters of involvement in state defence. Women have the absolute right to be involved in state defence according to their ability and desire. In fact, the state is obliged to conduct civil defence training for every citizen so that they can protect themselves and defend their country (*Al-Mar'ah wa al-'Amal al-Siyasi* [Women and Political Action], IIIT: 1995, Herndon, Virginia, USA). [...]

Nowadays, women are the greatest victims of inequality and authoritarianism. Thus they may become the focus of a contemporary interpretation of jihad to jumpstart the struggle to realize justice for all.

The struggle for women's justice is of course not solely for women, but for a just life for all, for peace for all and welfare for all, men and women. Jihad is the struggle for true peace, while the substance of religion is peace. And women are possessed

---

69   This is a reference to Forum Kajian Kitab Kuning (FK3, Forum for the Study of Kitab Kuning), a group of religious scholars and activists who produced a gender-based reinterpretation of jurisprudential texts commonly used in *pesantren* (see extract 13-18).

of the symbols of peace. Jihad, religion and women are a unit. Religion exists for justice, peace and love. Women are its ties, guardians and engineers, while jihad is its instrument. Thus it is time for women to take control of the leadership to wage a jihad of justice and create for humankind true peace and a life full of love. [p. 15]

15 Interactions: Global and Local Islam; Muslims and Non-Muslims

Greg Fealy and Virginia Hooker

INTRODUCTION

Landon (1949) described Southeast Asia as 'a cross-roads of religion', referring to the ways in which, for two millennia, a succession of major religions had spread through the region and adapted to pre-existing beliefs. The result has been a series of rich, highly protean religious cultures that have suffused the region's political and social life. The history of Islam in Southeast Asia is one of complex interactions with other faiths and with Muslim communities in other parts of the world. This chapter is concerned with the contemporary interactions that have helped shape the character of Islam in the region. Such relations have frequently been a source of debate and tension within Southeast Asian Muslim communities because they raise two pivotal normative issues. First, how inclusive or exclusive should Muslims be towards people of other faiths? Is Islam properly a tolerant and pluralistic religion or should it be wary and defensive in its engagement with non-Muslims, regarding the faith as a complete and totalistic system? Second, should the content of regional Islam closely follow an 'orthodox' Middle Eastern form or should it contain distinctive local religious and cultural traditions? In effect, what are the limits to diversity within Islam and what are the most authoritative sources of correct practice and thought?

To begin with the second issue, Southeast Asian Muslims have commonly been receptive to new ideas and practices from the Middle East (and, to a lesser extent, other parts of the Islamic world such as South and Central Asia), but have applied these in a selective and often specifically local way. This indigenizing process has varied markedly over time and place in the region. At the syncretic end of this spectrum, many Muslims regard a blending of Islamic and pre-existing religious practices as not only permissible but also desirable. They argue that 'localized' Islam has greater spiritual and cultural richness for the region's Muslims and they see 'Arabization' of the faith as incompatible with and dangerous to social traditions and dynamics. At the other end of the Islamic spectrum are those who seek to strictly apply norms and ritual devotions from the Middle East, arguing that 'indigenous' Islam is tainted by non-Islamic elements and that more 'pure' forms of practice are needed.

Relations with the non-Muslim world have been even more ambivalent. While the great majority of Southeast Asian Muslims live peacefully with non-Muslim communities, there is nonetheless a long history of localized religious tensions and occasional violent conflict. In Indonesia and the Philippines, this has mainly taken the form of Muslim–Christian violence; in Thailand and Burma, conflict has predominantly been between Muslims and Buddhists. Furthermore, in contemporary Muslim communities, there is a widespread perception that Islam is being undermined by global non-Muslim forces. In its more extreme forms, this is cast as a conspiracy, usually by Christians and Jews, to subjugate and destroy Islam and the Muslim community, the *ummah* (Ar.: *'ummah*). Relations with Christians and Jews have aroused ambivalence among Muslims since the early days of Islam. On the one hand, they are regarded as 'People of the Book' (Ar.: *ahlul-kitaabi*), that is, those who possess scriptures previously revealed by God. According to the Qur'an, Jews and Christians have a special legal standing within Islamic communities, known as *dhimmi* (Ar. *dhimmiyyun*; 'non-Muslims protected by law'), and their rights to practise religion and be defended against attack are, at least in theory, guaranteed.[1] On the other hand, some Qur'anic verses and Hadith also warn about the consequences of trusting non-Muslims and indeed often condemn non-Muslims in strong terms. Attitudes towards the Christian West have been especially fraught since the spread of European colonialism across most of the Islamic world from the sixteenth to early twentieth centuries. In recent decades, sharp differences have emerged among Southeast Asian Muslims as to appropriate relations with the West.

While there are many divisions among Muslim groups, the concept of the *ummah* as an encompassing community of all who follow Islam (as distinct from non-Muslims) is a powerful and emotionally laden one. This is most vividly illustrated during the performance of the pilgrimage to Mecca (see plate 12 in the colour section of this book). In Mecca all Muslims, whatever their origins or status, acknowledge the global unity of 'Muslimhood' and the bonds between those of the same faith. It is this sense of 'Muslimhood' that may be used by Muslim leaders to call on the faithful to defend their religion against any kind of threat, physical or intellectual.

The extracts in this chapter follow others in the sourcebook in presenting a broad spectrum of views on attitudes to the interactions between Muslim communities, and between Muslims and non-Muslims. A reading of the extracts suggests at least one general hypothesis based on the position of Muslims in their national populations. The extracts indicate that where Muslims are a majority of the population, they have the opportunity to reflect on the forms their expression of Islam may take. It is in such contexts that debates about indigenization can take place with a sense of confidence about developing ways in which local communities can be differentiated from the Islamic heartlands of the Middle East. The corollary of this 'confidence' is the

---

1 *Dhimmi* are, however, subject to various restrictions and imposts, including a requirement to pay tax on their income and land. Apart from Christians and Jews, *dhimmi* groups may include Zoroastrians, Sabeans and Hindus.

danger of fragmentation within the national *ummah* as various Muslim communities develop their own 'style' of Islam. This can attract the criticism of fellow Muslims and be labelled as 'deviant'. There is evidence of this in Indonesia.

Where Muslims are a minority of the national population, on the other hand, there seems to be less concern with conscious attempts to develop localized expressions of Islam. Rather, attention is focused more on strengthening Islamic identity through contact with Muslim communities in other nations, especially the heartlands of Islam, and with other Muslim minorities.

But regardless of the exact nature of the relationships between regional and global Islamic communities and Muslim and non-Muslim communities, their very interaction has played a powerful role in shaping the diversity of, and giving definition to, contemporary Southeast Asian Islam.

This chapter is divided into two parts. The first presents a range of views on the relationship between the local and international Muslim communities. The second covers a range of issues to do with encounters between Muslims and non-Muslims. This second part is divided into three sections: perceived non-Muslim threats to Islam (15.2.1), pluralism and tolerance (15.2.2) and reactions to the 'war on terror' (15.2.3).

EXTRACTS AND COMMENTARY

15.1   GLOBAL VERSUS LOCAL INTERACTIONS

Anwar Ibrahim

Commentary   Dato' Seri Anwar bin Datuk Ibrahim Abdul Rahman (1947–) is one of the most controversial figures in contemporary Malaysian politics. Educated in Malay studies at the University of Malaya, Anwar Ibrahim (as he is better known) founded the influential youth organization Angkatan Belia Islam Malaysia (ABIM, Malaysian Islamic Youth Organisation) in 1971. He was arrested in 1974 for leading student demonstrations against rural poverty and spent almost two years in detention without trial under Malaysia's Internal Security Act. Much to the surprise of many of his colleagues, he was recruited to the United Malays National Organisation (UMNO) by Prime Minister Mahathir in 1982 and entered cabinet the following year, eventually becoming deputy prime minister in 1993. His close relations with Mahathir soured during the mid-1990s and he was sacked from cabinet in 1998. Shortly afterwards he was tried and found guilty of sexual misconduct and corruption, though many observers questioned the fairness of his trial. He spent six years in jail before his conviction was overturned on appeal in 2004. Since his release he has kept a high profile as a commentator on political and religious affairs, but has yet to declare if he intends to return to formal politics.

In the following extract, Anwar reflects on the nature of Southeast Asian Islam, particularly in comparison with Islamic cultures in the Middle East and South Asia. He expounds the view that Southeast Asian Muslims are less burdened by historical legacies and have been better able to rise to the challenges of a rapidly modernizing world. In his view, moderation, the special characteristic of Islam in Southeast Asia, has resulted in a beneficial pragmatism in relations between Muslims and non-Muslims.

Extract 15-1: Anwar Ibrahim

Anwar Ibrahim (1996), 'Islam in Southeast Asia' [in English], pp. 111–25 in *The Asian Renaissance*, Times Books International, Singapore. Extract: pp. 111–15, 122–3.

[…] Islam came to Southeast Asia borne on the seas by sufis and merchants rather than overland by soldiers brandishing swords. Conversion was by choice, not coercion, beginning with the urban ruling class and the trading community. Historical accounts in the Malay and Javanese annals (*Sejarah Melayu* and *Babad Tanah Djawi*) record the interchangeability of roles between sufi mystics, preachers and traders in the course of the propagation of the religion. […]

This peaceful and gradual Islamization has moulded the Southeast Asian Muslim psyche into one which is cosmopolitan, open-minded, tolerant and amenable to cultural diversity. Of course, their outlook is also fashioned by the strong presence of people of other faiths who reciprocate Muslim tolerance. Unlike non-Muslims in the West, their perception of Islam is not distorted by the prism of the Crusades. The suggestion by Orientalist scholars that this mutual tolerance is because, in Southeast Asia, Islam is merely a 'thin veneer'[2] having no profound impact on the beliefs and practices of Muslims, has been largely debunked, although a superficial study of the *abangan* [nominal or non-devout Muslim] trait among the Javanese would render some truth to the argument. Nevertheless, as a prominent Muslim scholar, Professor Syed Muhammad Naquib al-Attas,[3] asserts, Islam transformed the 'essential character and world view of the Malay–Javanese civilization' to one which is essentially 'modern' – from a perspective based on magic, myth and superstition to that which is scientific and rational, in conformity with the spirit of the Quran.

Almost without exception, Muslim nations have experienced colonialism. Many have not quite fully recovered from its traumatic after-effects, as manifested in extreme attitudes towards the West. There are those who blame the West and invoke the Western bogey for every conceivable failing of their own. And while antipathy towards the West may have been justified in the immediate post-colonial years, there is no reasonable excuse for the persistence of such an attitude. At the other extreme are the culturally dispossessed elite classes, who remain spellbound and enchanted with the West. While Southeast Asian Muslims are not altogether immune to these internal tensions, they have neither allowed them to paralyse nation-building nor to poison their relations with the rest of the world. Instead of nursing bitterness about

---

2 This is a reference to van Leur's influential *Indonesian Trade and Society: Essays in Asian Social and Economic History* (van Leur 1955).

3 Born in 1931 in Indonesia but regarded as one of Malaysia's foremost intellectuals, al-Attas is the founder and director of the International Institute of Islamic Thought and Civilization in Kuala Lumpur. His contributions to Islamic philosophy have been recognized with honorary positions at a number of universities and academies outside Malaysia.

the past, they choose the path of magnanimity, which reflects the essential Malay character. [...]

By being moderate and pragmatic, Southeast Asian Muslims are neither compromising the teaching and ideals of Islam nor pandering to the whims and fancies of the times. On the contrary, such an approach is necessary to realize the societal ideals of Islam such as justice, equitable distribution of wealth, fundamental rights and liberties. This approach is sanctioned in a saying of the Prophet of Islam, to the effect that 'the best way to conduct your affairs is to choose the middle path'. [Hadith]

This principle of *aswatuhâ* [Ar.: *'awsaṭuhaa*] – the middle path – which corresponds to the Confucian *chun yung* and the golden mean of Aristotelian ethics, reinforces the moderate elements in the Southeast Asian Muslim character and shapes the understanding and practice of Islam. This moderation leads to a pragmatic approach in social, economic and political life. [...]

Moderation and pragmatism warrant that extreme emotions be kept under tight rein. Whilst recognizing the legitimate rights of victims of oppression and persecution to use whatever means available to liberate themselves, the head must rule the heart, and passion must give way to sobriety. For if it were otherwise, it will be a sure-fire formula for violence and destruction. Reason and common sense must prevail in order for us to view things in the proper perspective and set our priorities right.

A major predicament of Muslims is the failure to come to terms with present-day realities. It should be recognized that the causes of general confusion and malaise of the Muslims are rooted in history. Islamic civilization, after all, is only just 'recovering' after a long period of decline. With the fall in 1492 of the Muslim kingdom of Granada to the *reconquista* of Ferdinand of Aragon and Isabella of Castille, Islamic civilization was severed from Europe, where it had established itself during the preceding eight centuries as an integral part of that continent. The Islamic world took its own course of development, quite oblivious to the gigantic enterprise of the Renaissance and the Enlightenment, and degenerated into complacency. [pp. 111–15] [...]

The Southeast Asian region has been often cited as a case where Muslims have come to terms with modernity. Their less illustrious history could be the explanation. Throughout history, Southeast Asian Islam has remained on the margins, even as the number of its adherents swells to surpass that of the Arabs, Turks and Persians. But this lack of historic greatness is a boon. The Arabs, Turks or Persians are weighed down by the millstone of greatness. On the other hand, the Malays are less haunted by the ghost of the past, more attentive to present realities, and have greater awareness of their many shades and nuances. No doubt, the arrival of Islam in the Malay world about seven centuries ago had ushered in a new period. Yet, the most successful Malay-Muslim kingdom before the advent of European colonialism, the Malaccan maritime kingdom, a city which Tomé Pires[4] described in his *Suma Oriental* as '... made for merchandise, fitter than any other in the world ... to which trade and commerce between the different nations for a thousand leagues must come ... in (which)

---

4 Tomé Pires was a Portuguese apothecary and traveller who lived in Malacca between 1512 and 1515, after its defeat by the Portuguese. He later published an account of his experiences (see Cortesao 1944).

very often 84 languages have been found spoken, every one distinct', rose and fell within barely a century. Intellectual and philosophical creativity in the Malay world reached its height only in the seventeenth century in Aceh, in the works of Hamzah Fansuri[5] and Nuruddin al-Raniri.[6] Towards the turn of the last century, there was the figure of Raja Ali Haji,[7] who had tremendous influence in subjects ranging from theology and history to language. None of these figures, however, could be ranked with the great scholars and interpreters of Islam from among the Arabs and Persians.

The culture of tolerance is the hallmark of Southeast Asian Islam. When a band of Muslim fanatics went around desecrating Hindu temples in Malaysia 20 years ago, the chorus of Muslim condemnation was unequivocal. The full force of the law was brought to bear upon the perpetrators. Such violent outbursts are the work of deviants who have no place in any society which professes to uphold the moral teaching of any religion. Thus, extremism in all its forms must be wholly repudiated. [...] A plural, multi-religious society is living perpetually on the brink of catastrophe. Relations between Muslims and non-Muslims must be governed by moral and ethical considerations. [pp. 122–3] [...]

Abdurrahman Wahid

> *Commentary*   Abdurrahman Wahid was one of the most influential Muslim thinkers in Indonesia from the 1970s to 1990s (for a brief biography, see section 12.1.6). One of the topics on which he wrote and spoke extensively was that of the nature of the relationship between Indonesian and Middle Eastern Islam. Abdurrahman was fluent in Arabic and well acquainted with the Middle East. He was educated in both Egypt and Iraq – he graduated from Baghdad University with a bachelor of arts – and visited the region frequently. Despite this, he was critical of Indonesian Muslims who modelled themselves on their Middle Eastern counterparts and he argued strongly for fostering Islamic practices that were compatible with local cultures and political circumstances. He urged Muslims to celebrate diversity within their faith and not regard the Middle East as the

---

5   Hamzah Fansuri was a Muslim intellectual and mystic whose exact dates of birth and death are unknown. Born in Barus on Sumatra's west coast some time in the sixteenth century, he probably died before the beginning of the seventeenth century. His writings are among the earliest to survive from that period and he was the first to use the Malay language for theological debate. His concept of Islam and his esoteric mystical poetry were very influential in the development of Islamic scholarship in seventeenth-century Aceh.

6   A prolific scholar born in Gujerat, India, Nuruddin al-Raniri was active at the royal court of Aceh in the mid-seventeenth century. After settling in Aceh to teach under royal patronage, he strongly criticized the metaphysical concepts of Hamzah Fansuri. Several of Nuruddin's works are still set texts in Southeast Asian religious schools.

7   Raja Ali Haji was a member of the Malay-Bugis aristocracy in the nineteenth-century sultanate of Riau-Lingga, one of the surviving offshoots of the fifteenth-century Malay sultanate of Malacca. He was instrumental in bringing leading scholars of Islam to teach in Riau-Lingga (south of Singapore). At his urging, his relatives, the rulers of the sultanate, became patrons of Islam and fostered Islamic scholarship; they continued to do so after his death in the early 1870s. Raja Ali Haji wrote texts on good governance (following Islamic principles), the first grammar of Arabic for Malay speakers, and an epic history of the Malayo-Indonesian world from the late seventeenth to mid-nineteenth centuries.

benchmark for 'proper' Islamic behaviour and thinking. The extract below is based on an interview he gave to Abdul Mun'im Saleh, a journalist and intellectual affiliated with Nahdlatul Ulama (NU, Revival of the Religious Scholars). In it, Abdurrahman explains that throughout history Islam has been adapted by the cultures that have embraced it and claims that this has not corrupted the essential elements of Islam.

Extract 15-2: Abdurrahman Wahid

Abdurrahman Wahid (1989), 'Pribumisasi Islam' [Indigenizing Islam], pp. 81–96 in Muntaha Azhari and Abdul Mun'im Saleh (eds), *Islam Indonesia Menatap Masa Depan* [Indonesian Islam Looks to the Future], Perhimpunan Pengembangan Pesantren dan Masyarakat, Jakarta. Extract: pp. 82–3.

The danger of the process of Arabization or the process of identifying oneself with Middle Eastern cultures is that it takes us away from our own cultural roots. More than that, it is not certain that Arabization is appropriate for our needs. Indigenization is not an attempt to avoid resistance from the forces of local culture but rather [to avoid] the disappearance of that culture. The essence of the indigenization of Islam is necessity, not the avoidance of the polarization of religion and culture, because indeed such polarization is unavoidable.

A starting point for the attempt to reconcile [religion and culture] is to ask that revelation be understood by evaluating the contextual factors, including an awareness of law and a sense of justice. In this process, the assimilation of Islam with culture cannot happen, because assimilation means the loss of original characteristics. Islam must retain its Islamic characteristics. The Qur'an must remain in Arabic, particularly in the prayers, because these things constitute the norms [of Islam]. Translations of the Qur'an are intended only to facilitate understanding, not to replace the Qur'an itself.

The indigenization of Islam is not 'Javanization' or syncretism, because the indigenization of Islam only takes local needs into account in formulating religious laws, without changing the laws themselves. It is also not an attempt to abandon [Islamic] norms through culture. Rather, it is so that those norms can accommodate cultural needs using opportunities provided by variations in the understanding of *nash* [Ar.: *nassun*; legal principles or argumentation], and providing a role for *Ushul Fiqh* [Ar.: *'usuulul fiqhi*; the principles of jurisprudence] and *Qaidah Fiqh* [the rules of jurisprudence]. Syncretism, on the other hand, is an attempt to combine theology or an ancient belief system about the supernatural with Islam through an aspect of its eschatology, which becomes a form of pantheism. This kind of syncretism is exemplified in the ancient temples of 1,000 gods in India, Iran and the Middle East. Each colonizer introduced new gods to be worshipped along with the old gods. In a final step even humans can be deified (as in Confucianism) and also angels. Angels can be approached to intervene with the god's powers, so that they become more powerful than the god itself.

Indigenization of Islam is part of the history of Islam, both in its place of origin and elsewhere, including Indonesia. The two histories form a great river that flows on to be joined by other tributaries that make the river even bigger. The linking with

a new tributary means the injection of new water that changes the colour of the existing water. At later stages, the flow of the river may even be affected by filthy industrial effluent. Even so, it remains the same river with the same water. The purpose of
this example is [to show] that the process of the struggle with historical reality does
not change Islam; it only changes the manifestations of Islamic religious life. [...]

Mahathir Mohamad

> *Commentary*   Dr Mahathir Mohamad (1925–) was prime minister of Malaysia from
> 1981 to 2003 and president of the ruling Malay nationalist party, UMNO, for the same
> period. His policies of affirmative action for Malays and his later 'Vision 2020' for all
> Malaysians were combined with bold economic policies to transform Malaysia from
> an agriculturally based to a high-technology society. He leaves a legacy of massive
> buildings and a 'multi-media supercorridor', but also memories of active use of the
> Internal Security Act to incarcerate a number of Malaysian activists and religious lead-
> ers without trial. His sacking and public humiliation of his deputy, Anwar Ibrahim,
> in 1998 polarized Malaysian society and led to a sharp drop in UMNO's vote in the
> 1999 general election. He has become an international spokesperson for what he sees
> as the plight of Islam in the contemporary world. In this extract from a lengthy speech
> to the Organization of Islamic Conference (OIC) (see also extract 15-7), he criticizes
> the global *ummah* for its divisions and its failure to unite and confront the 'enemies'
> of Islam. The OIC is a peak international forum for Muslim political leaders. It was
> formed in 1969 to support the cause of Palestinians and promote greater international
> solidarity among Muslims.

Extract 15-3: Mahathir Mohamad

Mahathir Mohamad (2003), 'Speech by the Prime Minister of Malaysia, the Hon. Dr
Mahathir bin Mohamad, at the Opening of the Tenth Session of the Islamic Summit
Conference at Putrajaya, Malaysia, on October 16, 2003' [in English], <www.oic-oci.
org/Al-Mootamar/sep2000/Sept2000-58-59.pdf>, accessed 12 December 2003. [As
of 24 February 2006 available at <http://www.al-huda.com/Article_4of27.htm>.]

7. The whole world is looking at us. Certainly 1.3 billion Muslims, one-sixth of the
world's population[,] are placing their hopes in us, in this meeting, even though they
may be cynical about our will and capacity to even decide to restore the honour of
Islam and the Muslims, much less to free their brothers and sisters from the oppression and humiliation from which they suffer today.

8. I will not enumerate the instances of our humiliation and oppression, nor will I
once again condemn our detractors and oppressors. It would be an exercise in futility
because they are not going to change their attitudes just because we condemn them.
If we are to recover our dignity and that of Islam, our religion, it is we who must
decide, it is we who must act.

9. To begin with, the Governments of all the Muslim countries can close ranks and
have a common stand if not on all issues, at least on some major ones, such as on

Palestine. We are all Muslims. We are all oppressed. We are all being humiliated. But we who have been raised by Allah above our fellow Muslims to rule our countries have never really tried to act in concert in order to exhibit at our level the brotherhood and unity that Islam enjoins upon us.

10. But not only are our Governments divided, the Muslim ummah is also divided, and divided again and again. Over the last 1400 years the interpreters of Islam, the learned ones, the ulamas[,] have interpreted and reinterpreted the single Islamic religion brought by Prophet Muhammad S.A.W, so differently that now we have a thousand religions which are often so much at odds with one another that we often fight and kill each other.

11. From being a single ummah we have allowed ourselves to be divided into numerous sects, mazhabs [schools of law] and tarikats [Sufi groups], each more concerned with claiming to be the true Islam than [with] our oneness as the Islamic ummah. We fail to notice that our detractors and enemies do not care whether we are true Muslims or not. To them we are all Muslims, followers of a religion and a Prophet whom they declare promotes terrorism, and we are all their sworn enemies. They will attack and kill us, invade our lands, bring down our Governments whether we are Sunnis or Syiahs, Alawait [Alawite] or Druze[8] or whatever. And we aid and abet them by attacking and weakening each other, and sometimes by doing their bidding, acting as their proxies to attack fellow Muslims. We try to bring down our Governments through violence, succeeding to weaken and impoverish our countries.

12. We ignore entirely and we continue to ignore the Islamic injunction to unite and to be brothers to each other, we the Governments of the Islamic countries and the ummah.

13. But this is not all that we ignore about the teachings of Islam. We are enjoined to Read, Iqraq[,][9] i.e. to acquire knowledge. The early Muslims took this to mean translating and studying the works of the Greeks and other scholars before Islam. And these Muslim scholars added to the body of knowledge through their own studies.

14. The early Muslims produced great mathematicians and scientists, scholars, physicians and astronomers etc. and they excelled in all the fields of knowledge of their times, besides studying and practising their own religion of Islam. As a result the Muslims were able to develop and extract wealth from their lands and through their world trade, able to strengthen their defences, protect their people and give them the Islamic way of life, Addin,[10] as prescribed by Islam. At the time the Europeans of

---

8 The Alawite and Druze are Middle East-based religious sects whose origins lie in Shi'a Islam. The Alawite are found mainly in northern Syria; the Druze live mainly in Lebanon, Israel, Syria and Jordan. While the Druze see themselves as Muslims, most Muslims regard them as outside the faith.

9 The Arabic word for 'read' or 'study' and the word that is associated with the revelation of the Qur'an to Muhammad as described in chapter 96 of the Qur'an.

10 That is, *din* or *deen*. The term is often given the short-hand translation of 'faith' or 'religion' but is more accurately described as a 'religious way of life' in which Muslims live in obedience to God and are prepared to account for their actions (and be rewarded for pious behaviour) on the Day of Judgement. It is an all-encompassing concept that includes deeds, thoughts and character.

the Middle Ages were still superstitious and backward, the enlightened Muslims had already built a great Muslim civilisation, respected and powerful, more than able to compete with the rest of the world and able to protect the ummah from foreign aggression. The Europeans had to kneel at the feet of Muslim scholars in order to access their own scholastic heritage.

Patani United Liberation Organization (PULO)

> *Commentary* The Patani United Liberation Organization (PULO) was founded in 1968 by Tengku Bira Kotanila (also known as Kabir Abdul Rahman), an ethnic-Malay Thai Muslim. In its early days it attracted strong support from younger Muslims in southern Thailand frustrated with their political and socio-economic deprivation. Although committed to the establishment of an independent Islamic state, PULO is essentially ethno-nationalist in motivation. At its height in the early 1980s, it enjoyed generous funding from Middle Eastern sources and claimed to have more than 20,000 fighters. Splits developed within PULO in the mid-1980s and the organization's insurgency activities and influence waned during the 1990s. In the following extract, PULO makes the case for the three southern states of Thailand – Narathiwat, Pattani and Yala – to be regarded as part of Malaysia and the wider *ummah*, not Thailand. This exemplifies the attraction of linkage with the wider *ummah* for a minority group that perceives its position in its 'homeland' as threatened and oppressed.

Extract 15-4: Patani United Liberation Organization (PULO)

Patani United Liberation Organization (no date), 'Frequently Asked Questions', translation from the Thai, <http://www.pulo.org/index2.htm>, accessed 15 November 2004. [This website is no longer available.]

How can Patani Raya regain its independence? Who will support them? Nobody wants to support separatist movements, do they?

Siam helped East Timor to fight for its independence. Why didn't Siam take sides with Indonesia who is its ally in ASEAN?

Patani and Kelantan are part of the same territory. They have a close relationship with the Aceh people in Sumatra as well as the Trengganu, Kedah, and Perlis people [in Malaysia]. Malays in these areas feel very close to each other as they are regularly in contact with each other and often intermarry. Hundreds of thousands of Patani people have migrated to Malaysia and many have had great success in Malaysia. There are also a large number who have become members of the Royal Family. For example, the grandmother and grandfather of the King of Malaysia, who is the Sultan of Perlis, are from Janah, Songkhla. The Queen is also a member of the Patani Royal Family. For them, Patani is an ancestral homeland and has great importance for the ethnic history of the Malayan people.

If you ask a Malaysian which book they feel the proudest about and which is the most beautiful (*suay*) book in the National Museum of Malaysia[,] [t]he answer will be *Sejarah Patani* [History of Patani]. When Malaya was about to gain its independence from the United Kingdom, the proposed name of the country was Lankasuka, which was the former name of Patani. This indicates the close relationship between Malaya and Patani. Thousands of PULO members are Malaysian. The founder of the BRN [Barisan Revolusi Nasional, National Revolutionary Front] movement, Abdul Karim, is also Malaysian. Also, the leader of Mujahideen Patani is Malaysian. There are more than 280,000 Malaya-Patani people who have Malaysian nationality and a Thai ID card.

Salamat Hashim

> ***Commentary***　　Salamat Hashim (1942–2003), the founder of the Moro Islamic Liberation Front (MILF), had the highest profile in the international Muslim community of any Filipino Islamic leader. He had a good knowledge of the Middle East and many high-level contacts there, due in part to his postgraduate education at al-Azhar University in Egypt during the late 1950s. Section 12.4.1 provides further details about his life.
>
> 　Salamat Hashim fostered links with both mainstream and jihadist organizations elsewhere in Southeast Asia. For example, the MILF has shared training, and occasionally operational tasks, with Jemaah Islamiyah (JI). In the following extract an appeal is made for all Muslims (the *ummah*) to rise up against the oppression inflicted on some communities of Muslims, in Europe, the Middle East, Kashmir and the southern Philippines. Salamat Hashim warns that non-Muslims (*kufr*; Ar.: *kufrun*) are attacking Muslims because they fear the growing power of Islam. He invokes a strong sense of the brotherhood of Islam that knows no boundaries.

Extract 15-5: Salamat Hashim

Salamat Hashim (2001), 'On MILF vis-a-vis Bosnia and Chechnya', pp. 139–42 in *The Bangsamoro People's Struggle against Oppression and Colonialism* [in English], Agency for Youth Affairs–MILF, Darussalam, Camp Abubakre As-Siddique, Mindanao. Extract: pp. 140–1.

Greetings of *salaam* to the struggling Muslim nation of the Bangsamoro and to the oppressed peoples of the world whose destiny and salvation lies in and with Islam.

　At this critical instance when the newly-independent Muslim Republic of Chechnya in the Caucasus and the Central European Muslim Republic of Bosnia-i-Hercegovina are confronting the formidable might of Russian imperialists and the Serbian fascists respectively, I ask and appeal to our Muslim brethren in the Bangsamoro homeland to join the Muslims of the world in fervently praying for the fraternal Muslim peoples of Chechnya and Bosnia-i-Hercegovina that they will be able to surmount the present difficulties and hardships imposed upon them by the satanic forces of *kufr* and global arrogance and that they may emerge victorious for the glory of Allah, His Prophet (s.a.w.) in Islam.

　Our Holy Prophet Muhammad (s.a.w.) said that all Muslims form one inseparable body; what hurts one part hurts all the others. Chechnya and Bosnia-i-Hercegovina,

like the Bangsamoro people and homeland, are parts of that one body of Islam that is
the Ummah al-Islamiyyah. As such, the untold sufferings of Muslim peoples of these
countries hurt us as much as they do to the Muslims in all other parts of the globe.
In like manner, their victory is our victory for this would mean the triumph of *haqq*
[truth] over *baatil* [falsehood] and *imaan* [faith] over *kufr* [unbelief], in short, the
triumph of Islam, our *deen* [religious way of life; see footnote 10].

The noble Jihad of the Muslim peoples of Chechnya and Bosnia-Hercegovina,
though it is waged in the very heartland of Europe, echoes the Jihad of our oppressed
people here in the Bangsamoro as well as those of our similarly oppressed Muslim
brothers in the Zionist-occupied Palestine, Lebanon, Kashmir and other countries.
For this Jihad, which is now taking place in almost all parts of the Ummah, demonstrates in all clarity and removes all remaining doubts that the global powers of *kufr*
declared war on Islam, the Muslims and the oppressed peoples in order to perpetuate
the present unjust world order of *jahiliyyah*[11] whereby the strong could go on terror-
izing the weak, the oppressors could continue their enslavement of the oppressed and
the exploiters could maintain their predatory stranglehold over the exploited.

As far as this goes, the arrogant powers of the *kufr* know that Islam is militantly
opposed to and will always militantly oppose, as in the time of the beloved Messenger of Allah (s.a.w.) fourteen centuries ago, this unjust world order of *jahiliyyah*
which they – the *kuffar* [infidels] – have imposed on the peoples of this planet. They
are fully aware that the cries of 'Allahu Akbar' [God is the greatest], from the tiny
villages of Africa to the modern cities of Europe, and from the countryside of Asia
to the industrial centers of the American continent, can now be heard emanating not
only from the minarets of *masajid* [mosques] but from the hearts of the masses who
have hearkened to the liberating message of *Tawhid* [the doctrine of the unity of
God]. With this development, the global powers of *kufr* know that the days of their
illegitimate and oppressive governments and decadent societies are numbered as the
power of Islam grows in strength in the very hearts and minds of the peoples of the
world. Thus, [this is] the reason behind the war against Islam.

Arakan Rohingya Islamic Front (ARIF)

> *Commentary*   The Arakan Rohingya Islamic Front (ARIF) was formed in 1987 as a
> breakaway group from the Rohingya Solidarity Organisation. One element of ARIF's
> campaign for Rohingya rights was to mount in international Islamic forums the case
> for external support for an autonomous Rohingya state within Burma (Myanmar). The
> following extract is taken from ARIF's appeal to the 18th Session of the Islamic Con-
> ference of Foreign Ministers (ICFM), held in Riyadh in March 1989. The ICFM is
> organized under the aegis of the OIC. In essence, ARIF argues that if Muslim minori-

---

11 *Jahiliyyah* (Ar.: *jaahiliyyah*; also spelled *jahilliah* and *jahiliyah* in this chapter) comes from an
Arabic word meaning 'to be ignorant'. In the history of Islam, it refers specifically to the inhabitants
of Arabia and their culture before the revelation of Islam and its spread by the Prophet Muhammad. In
current usage, it is often used to refer disapprovingly to non-Muslims and their culture.

ties such as the Rohingya are not protected from non-Muslim depredations by the OIC (symbolizing the global *ummah*), then Muslim majority communities will be under greater threat.

Extract 15-6: *Arakan Rohingya Islamic Front (ARIF)*

Arakan Rohingya Islamic Front (1989), 'ARIF Appeals to the 18th Session of ICFM' [in English], *Arakan*, June. Extract: pp. 13–16.

(4) The Rohingyas are made culturally degenerated, politically liquidated and economically crippled. They have been invariably made targets of genocide, oppression and repression, massacre, murder and secret killing, rape and loot, drive and expulsion through armed operations, campaign of terror, dragnet arrest and detention, imprisonment and deportation, apartheid and chauvinism, vandalism and valification [*sic*] of landed and waqf [religious] properties, religious sacrilages [*sic*], destruction of Mosques, Madrassahs [Islamic schools], houses and villages, settlements of Buddhists on Muslims' land, humiliating restriction on movement and in seeking education and forced labour, restriction on Dawah [proselytization] activities, etc.

(5) The Rohingya Muslims are deprived of employment, trade and commerce. Prejudical [*sic*] and racist laws and extreme poverty have conspired to force them to die in starvation or become servitors to the Buddhists.

(6) No development works are undertaken in Muslim areas. The government has no intention to develop the economy of Arakan. Her rich natural resources remain unexplored and manpower unharnessed. Arakan was once called the granary of rice, but it has now become difficult for the Rohingyas to eke out two square meals a day.

(7) Distortion and corruption of Muslim history and distruction [*sic*] of Muslim relics have been going on. They are obliterating the Muslim character of Arakan. The name of Arakan is now changed to 'Rahkine Pray' and the provincial capital Akyab to 'Sittwe' which are attributed to the Buddhists only and are unknown in the history.

The government totally jackboot our fundamental human rights and freedoms. Many appeals and representation[s] have been made to redress our grievances, but all were turned down. Instead, the only response we receive from the government is genocidal action, oppression, suppression and extermination. To profess Islam is as if a crime and the popular slogan in the country is 'to be a Burmese is to be a Buddhist'. As there is no other recourse left, we in our selfdefence, embark on Jihad to achieve our right to Self-Determination.

As stated above, the Rohingya Muslims have been balancing [on] a knife's edge between life and death. Good sense does not prevail in the mind of the present military dictator General Saw Maung. Amassed armed forces, who take the law in their own hands, have been deployed in the Muslim areas which we can not let go unchallenged.

We are professing Jihad [and] gearing up guerilla activities against the enemies with poor resources amidst various handicaps. Inspite of these, our Mujahideen and the Rohingya people have annihilated the enemies in the recent guerilla operations.

Request:

(1) To recognize and grant Observer Status to Arakan Rohingya Islamic Front (ARIF) professing Jihad in Arakan;
(2) To include the problems of the Rohingya Muslims in the agenda of the 18th Islamic Conference of Foreign Ministers (ICFM) for an efficacious solution of the Rohingya problems;
(3) To extend allout support including the modest support of the Islamic Solidarity Fund (ISF) to the Arakan Rohingya Islamic Front;
(4) To repatriate the unofficial Rohingya refugees and extend to them facilities for socio-economic pursuits, including job opportunity by the respective OIC member-states where they have been taking refuge till a congenial atmosphere is created in Arakan for their safe return;
(5) To pressurize the government of Burma to immediate by [immediately] withdraw all black laws and armed forces from Rohingya Muslim areas in Arakan.

As we accept OIC as a Champion for the protection of the Muslim minorities in non-Muslim countries, we seek allout support and hearing from ICFM through OIC.

In conclusion, if Muslim minorities are allowed to disappear, Muslim majorities would sooner or later follow suit. Supporting Muslim minorities is, therefore, not a matter of mere suggestion for a Muslim; it is an Islamic duty and a necessity for the survival of the entire Muslim Ummah.

15.2   MUSLIMS AND NON-MUSLIMS

Commentary   The extracts in this section reflect a variety of perspectives on attitudes towards non-Muslims and whether contact and communication with them is permissible. The views expressed range from criticism of the activities of Christian missionaries and tirades against Jews and Christians to the need for harmony with non-Muslims, support for interfaith dialogue and discussion of the concept of pluralism. In this section, we can see clearly the divisions between those who understand Islam as a religion of universal principles, one that is inclusive and tolerant of all faiths, and those who reject that concept and argue for the exclusive nature of Islam.

15.2.1   Perceived Non-Muslim Threats to Islam

Mahathir Mohamad

Commentary   A recurring theme in much of the contemporary Islamic literature in Southeast Asia, as in many other parts of the Muslim world, is that Islam and the Muslim community are under attack from non-Muslims, especially Jews and Christians. The nature of the perceived 'attack' can take various forms, from overt military and diplomatic offensives to economic exploitation or subtle and insidious cultural and spiritual corruption of Islamic values. This sense of threat is presented most stridently in Islamist texts, but is present in more muted terms in mainstream discourse as well.

Like extract 15-3, the passage below is from Dr Mahathir Mohamad's speech to the OIC in October 2003. Here he pursues the themes of the oppression of Muslims and the success of the Jews, themes that appear also in some other extracts in this section. The anti-Semitic comments in the speech aroused widespread criticism, but also received considerable support from a range of Muslim groups. In the speech Mahathir describes the achievements of Islam, especially during the medieval period. He then outlines the reasons (as he sees it) for the decline of Islamic civilization and urges Muslims to again rise to world prominence. In particular, he criticizes the lack of solidarity and common purpose within the international Islamic community and bemoans the failure of many Muslim societies to embrace modernity and exploit new sciences and technology as a means of gaining greater prosperity and independence from non-Muslim nations. Though not stated explicitly, it is clear that he regards Malaysia as a model for modern Islamic development.

Extract 15-7: Mahathir Mohamad

Mahathir Mohamad (2003), 'Speech by the Prime Minister of Malaysia, the Hon. Dr Mahathir bin Mohamad, at the Opening of the Tenth Session of the Islamic Summit Conference at Putrajaya, Malaysia, on October 16, 2003' [in English], <www.oic-oci. org/Al-Mootamar/sep2000/Sept2000-58-59.pdf>, accessed 12 December 2003. [As of 24 February 2006 available at <http://www.al-huda.com/Article_4of27.htm>.]

15. The Muslims were lead [led] by great leaders like Abdul Rahman III, Al-Mansur, Salah El Din Al Ayubi[12] and others who took to the battlefields at the head of their forces to protect Muslim land and the ummah.

16. But halfway through the building of the great Islamic civilization came new interpreters of Islam who taught that acquisition of knowledge by Muslims meant only the study of Islamic theology. The study of science, medicine etc. was discouraged.

17. Intellectually the Muslims began to regress. With intellectual regression the great Muslim civilisation began to falter and wither. But for the emergence of the Ottoman warriors, Muslim civilisation would have disappeared with the fall of Granada in 1492.

---

12   Abdul Rahman III (r. 921–61) was the *amir* of the Umayyad caliphate in Cordoba. There are several notable Islamic leaders who bore the name al-Mansur, but Mahathir may well have had in mind the Abbasid caliph of that name (r. 754–75) who oversaw the rapid military, economic and cultural expansion of the empire. Salah al-Din (Saladin) (d. 1193) commanded the Muslim forces during the third period of the Crusades (1180s–90s). He defeated the Christian crusader forces in several battles but made peace through a truce with Richard the Lionheart at Acre in 1192. He was also the founder of the Ayyubid dynasty, which reunited Egypt, Syria and Mesopotamia.

18. The early successes of the Ottomans were not accompanied by an intellectual renaissance. Instead they became more and more preoccupied with minor issues such as whether tight trousers and peak caps were Islamic, whether printing machines should be allowed or electricity used to light mosques. The Industrial Revolution was totally missed by the Muslims. And the regression continued until the British and French instigated rebellion against Turkish rule [and] brought about the downfall of the Ottomans, the last Muslim world power[,] and replaced it with European colonies and not independent states as promised. It was only after World War II that these colonies became independent.

19. Apart from the new nation-states we also accepted the western democratic system. This also divided us because of the political parties and groups that we form, some of which claim Islam for themselves, reject the Islam of other parties and refuse to accept the results of the practice of democracy if they fail to gain power for themselves. They resort to violence, thus destabilising and weakening Muslim countries.

20. With all these developments over the centuries the ummah and the Muslim civilisation became so weak that at one time there was not a single Muslim country which was not colonised or hegemonised by the Europeans. But regaining independence did not help to strengthen the Muslims. Their states were weak and badly administered, constantly in a state of turmoil. The Europeans could do what they liked with Muslim territories. It is not surprising that they should excise Muslim land to create the state of Israel to solve their Jewish problem. Divided, the Muslims could do nothing effective to stop the Balfour and Zionist transgression.

21. Some would have us believe that, despite all these, our life is better than that of our detractors. Some believe that poverty is Islamic, sufferings and being oppressed are Islamic. This world is not for us. Ours are the joys of heaven in the afterlife. All that we have to do is to perform certain rituals, wear certain garments and put up a certain appearance. Our weakness, our backwardness and our inability to help our brothers and sisters who are being oppressed are part of the Will of Allah, the sufferings that we must endure before enjoying heaven in the hereafter. We must accept this fate that befalls us. We need not do anything. We can do nothing against the Will of Allah.

22. But is it true that it is the Will of Allah and that we can and should do nothing? Allah has said in Surah Ar-Ra'd verse 11[13] that He will not change the fate of a community until the community has tried to change its fate itself.

23. The early Muslims were as oppressed as we are presently. But after their sincere and determined efforts to help themselves in accordance with the teachings of Islam,

---

13   'each person has guardian angels before him and behind, watching over him by God's command. God does not change the condition of a people [for the worse] unless they change what is in themselves, but if He wills harm on a people, no one can ward it off – apart from Him, they have no protector' (Q13: 11, Haleem).

Allah had helped them to defeat their enemies and to create a great and powerful Muslim civilisation. But what effort have we made especially with the resources that He has endowed us with.

24. We are now 1.3 billion strong. We have the biggest oil reserve in the world. We have great wealth. We are not as ignorant as the Jahilliah[14] who embraced Islam. We are familiar with the workings of the world's economy and finances. We control 57 out of the 180 countries in the world. Our votes can make or break international organisations. Yet we seem more helpless than the small number of Jahilliah converts who accepted the Prophet as their leader. Why? Is it because of Allah's will or is it because we have interpreted our religion wrongly, or failed to abide by the correct teachings of our religion, or done the wrong things?

25. We are enjoined by our religion to prepare for the defence of the ummah. Unfortunately we stress not defence but the weapons of the time of the Prophet. Those weapons and horses cannot help to defend us any more. We need guns and rockets, bombs and warplanes, tanks and warships for our defence. But because we discouraged the learning of science and mathematics etc. as giving no merit for the akhirat [hereafter], today we have no capacity to produce our own weapons for our defence. We have to buy our weapons from our detractors and enemies. This is what comes from the superficial interpretation of the Quran, stressing not the substance of the Prophet's sunnah and the Quran's injunctions but rather the form, the manner and the means used in the 1st Century of the Hijrah [Islamic calendar]. And it is the same with the other teachings of Islam. We are more concerned with the forms rather than the substance of the words of Allah and adhering only to the literal interpretation of the traditions of the Prophet.

26. We may want to recreate the first century of the Hijrah, the way of life in those times, in order to practise what we think to be the true Islamic way of life. But we will not be allowed to do so. Our detractors and enemies will take advantage of the resulting backwardness and weakness in order to dominate us. Islam is not just for the 7th Century A.D. Islam is for all times. And times have changed. Whether we like it or not we have to change, not by changing our religion but by applying its teachings in the context of a world that is radically different from that of the first century of the Hijrah. Islam is not wrong but the interpretations by our scholars, who are not prophets even though they may be very learned[,] can be wrong. We have a need to go back to the fundamental teachings of Islam to find out whether we are indeed believing in and practising the Islam that the Prophet preached. It cannot be that we are all practising the correct and true Islam when our beliefs are so different from one another.

27. Today we, the whole Muslim ummah[,] are treated with contempt and dishonour. Our religion is denigrated. Our holy places desecrated. Our countries are occupied. Our people starved and killed.

---

14   Peoples of pre-Islamic Arabia; see footnote 11.

28. None of our countries are truly independent. We are under pressure to conform to our oppressors' wishes about how we should behave, how we should govern our lands, how we should think even.

29. Today if they want to raid our country, kill our people, destroy our villages and towns, there is nothing substantial that we can do. Is it Islam which has caused all these? Or is it that we have failed to do our duty according to our religion?

30. Our only reaction is to become more and more angry. Angry people cannot think properly. And so we find some of our people reacting irrationally. They launch their own attacks, killing just about anybody including fellow Muslims to vent their anger and frustration. Their Governments can do nothing to stop them. The enemy retaliates and puts more pressure on the Governments. And the Governments have no choice but to give in, to accept the directions of the enemy, literally to give up their independence of action.

31. With this their people and the ummah become angrier and turn against their own Governments. Every attempt at a peaceful solution is sabotaged by more indiscriminate attacks calculated to anger the enemy and prevent any peaceful settlement. But the attacks solve nothing. The Muslims simply get more oppressed.

32. There is a feeling of hopelessness among the Muslim countries and their people. They feel that they can do nothing right. They believe that things can only get worse. The Muslims will forever be oppressed and dominated by the Europeans and the Jews. They will forever be poor, backward and weak. Some believe, as I have said, this is the Will of Allah, that the proper state of the Muslims is to be poor and oppressed in this world.

33. But is it true that we should do and can do nothing for ourselves? Is it true that 1.3 billion people can exert no power to save themselves from the humiliation and oppression inflicted upon them by a much smaller enemy? Can they only lash back blindly in anger? Is there no other way than to ask our young people to blow themselves up and kill people and invite the massacre of more of our own people?

34. It cannot be that there is no other way. 1.3 billion Muslims cannot be defeated by a few million Jews. There must be a way. And we can only find a way if we stop to think, to assess our weaknesses and our strength, to plan, to strategise and then to counter attack. As Muslims we must seek guidance from the Al-Quran and the Sunnah of the Prophet. Surely the 23 years' struggle of the Prophet can provide us with some guidance as to what we can and should do.

35. We know he and his early followers were oppressed by the Qhuraish [the most powerful tribe in Mecca at the time of the Prophet]. Did he launch retaliatory strikes? No. He was prepared to make strategic retreats. He sent his early followers to a Christian country and he himself later migrated to Madinah [Medina]. There he gathered followers, built up his defence capability and ensured the security of his people. At Hudaibiyah he was prepared to accept an unfair treaty, against the wishes of his companions and followers. During the peace that followed he consolidated his strength and eventually he was able to enter Mecca and claim it for Islam. Even then

he did not seek revenge. And the peoples of Mecca accepted Islam and many became his most powerful supporters, defending the Muslims against all their enemies.

36. That briefly is the story of the struggle of the Prophet. We talk so much about following the sunnah of the Prophet. We quote the instances and the traditions profusely. But we actually ignore all of them.

37. If we use the faculty to think that Allah has given us then we should know that we are acting irrationally. We fight without any objective, without any goal other than to hurt the enemy because they hurt us. Naively we expect them to surrender. We sacrifice lives unnecessarily, achieving nothing other than to attract more massive retaliation and humiliation.

38. It is surely time that we pause to think. But will this be wasting time? For well over half a century we have fought over Palestine. What have we achieved? Nothing. We are worse off than before. If we had paused to think then we could have devised a plan, a strategy that can win us final victory. Pausing and thinking calmly is not a waste of time. We have a need to make a strategic retreat and to calmly assess our situation.

39. We are actually very strong. 1.3 billion people cannot be simply wiped out. The Europeans killed 6 million Jews out of 12 million. But today the Jews rule this world by proxy. They get others to fight and die for them.

40. We may not be able to do that. We may not be able to unite all the 1.3 billion Muslims. We may not be able to get all the Muslim Governments to act in concert. But even if we can get a third of the ummah and a third of the Muslim states to act together, we can already do something. Remember that the Prophet did not have many followers when he went to Madinah. But he united the Ansars and the Muhajirins[15] and eventually he became strong enough to defend Islam.

41. Apart from the partial unity that we need, we must take stock of our assets. I have already mentioned our numbers and our oil wealth. In today's world we wield a lot of political, economic and financial clout, enough to make up for our weakness in military terms.

42. We also know that not all non-Muslims are against us. Some are well disposed towards us. Some even see our enemies as their enemies. Even among the Jews there are many who do not approve of what the Israelis are doing.

43. We must not antagonise everyone. We must win their hearts and minds. We must win them to our side not by begging for help from them but by the honourable way that we struggle to help ourselves. We must not strengthen the enemy by pushing everyone into their camps through irresponsible and unIslamic acts. Remember Salah El Din and the way he fought against the so called Crusaders, King Richard of

---

15   The Ansar (literally, 'helpers') were those Medinans who accepted Muhammad as Prophet when he came to the city in 622 CE; the Muhajirin ('emigrants') were those who had accompanied the Prophet on his *hijrah* (withdrawal) from Mecca.

England in particular. Remember the considerateness of the Prophet to the enemies of Islam. We must do the same. It is winning the struggle that is important, not angry retaliation, not revenge.

44. We must build up our strength in every field, not just in armed might. Our countries must be stable and well administered, must be economically and financially strong, industrially competent and technologically advanced. This will take time, but it can be done and it will be time well spent. We are enjoined by our religion to be patient. Innallahamaasabirin.[16] Obviously there is virtue in being patient. [...]

50. I am aware that all these ideas will not be popular. Those who are angry would want to reject it out of hand. They would even want to silence anyone who makes or supports this line of action. They would want to send more young men and women to make the supreme sacrifice. But where will all these lead to? Certainly not victory. Over the past 50 years of fighting in Palestine we have not achieved any result. We have in fact worsened our situation.

51. The enemy will probably welcome these proposals and we will conclude that the promoters are working for the enemy. But think. We are up against a people who think. They survived 2000 years of pogroms not by hitting back, but by thinking. They invented and successfully promoted Socialism, Communism, human rights and democracy so that persecuting them would appear to be wrong, so they may enjoy equal rights with others. With these they have now gained control of the most powerful countries and they, this tiny community, have become a world power. We cannot fight them through brawn alone. We must use our brains also.

52. Of late because of their power and their apparent success they have become arrogant. And arrogant people, like angry people[,] will make mistakes, will forget to think.

53. They are already beginning to make mistakes. And they will make more mistakes. There may be windows of opportunity for us now and in the future. We must seize these opportunities.

54. But to do so we must get our acts right. Rhetoric is good. It helps us to expose the wrongs perpetrated against us, perhaps win us some sympathy and support. It may strengthen our spirit, our will and resolve, to face the enemy.

55. We can and we should pray to Allah S.W.T. for in the end it is He who will determine whether we succeed or fail. We need His blessings and His help in our endeavours,

56. But it is how we act and what we do which will determine whether He would help us and give us victory or not. He has already said so in the Quran. Again [see] Surah Ar-Ra'd verse 11.[17]

---

16   Ar.: *'innal-laha ma`as-saabiriina*; God is with those who are patient.
17   Q13: 11 is given in footnote 13.

57. As I said at the beginning, the whole world is looking at us, the whole Muslim ummah is placing their hopes in this conference of the leaders of Islamic nations. They expect us not just to vent our frustrations and anger, through words and gestures; not just to pray for Allah's blessings. They expect us to do something, to act. We cannot say we cannot do anything, we the leaders of the Muslim nations. We cannot say we cannot unite even when faced with the destruction of our religion and the ummah.

Mohammad Natsir

Commentary Mohammad Natsir (1908–93) was the leading modernist thinker and politician of his time. Educated in the Dutch secondary and tertiary systems, he became active during the 1930s in Persatuan Islam (Persis, Islamic Association), a modernist organization of puritanical orientation. In 1945 he was a founding member of the Masyumi party, rising to the chairmanship four years later. He became prime minister in 1950 in the short-lived first cabinet of the unitary Indonesian Republic. During the mid to late 1950s, Natsir was an outspoken critic of President Sukarno's attempts to dismantle parliamentary democracy. In 1957 he joined the PRRI/Permesta regional rebellion.[18] He was arrested shortly after his surrender in 1961 and spent five years in jail. Soeharto's New Order regime (1966–98) refused to allow Natsir and other former Masyumi leaders a role in politics. Denied political space, he focused on preaching and educational activities, founding Dewan Dakwah Islamiyah Indonesia (DDII, Indonesian Islamic Propagation Council) in 1967 as his main organizational vehicle.

In the following two extracts, Natsir expresses concern at what he sees as the conversion to Christianity of many Muslims from the mid-1960s. This so-called Christianization issue was a powerful grievance within modernist circles throughout the Soeharto period. In the first extract Natsir refers to Christian missionary activity among Muslim communities; in the second he appeals to Christian leaders to take action to prevent conversions. Failure to reach agreement on the Christianization issue became an enduring source of bitterness for modernist Muslims, particularly those associated with DDII.

Extract 15-8: Mohammad Natsir

M. Natsir (1980), 'Kode Toleransi Beragama 1967' [The Code of Religious Tolerance 1967], pp. 207–10 in *Islam dan Kristen di Indonesia* [Islam and Christianity in Indonesia], Media Dakwah, Jakarta. Extract: pp. 207–9.

The activities of Protestant and Catholic missionaries in Indonesia seem to have increased after the [attempted] Communist coup of 30 September 1965. The families of Communists in detention and poor Muslims are their primary targets. Scores

---

18 Pemerintah Revolusioner Republik Indonesia (PRRI, Revolutionary Government of the Republic of Indonesia) and Piagam Perjuangan Semesta Alam (Permesta, Universal Struggle Charter) were linked rebellions in Sumatra and Sulawesi, respectively, during the late 1950s.

of thousands of people have been forced to convert to Christianity as a result of the blandishments and sweet talk of these missionaries.

There are various kinds of missionary organizations, and their methods of operating and their activities are at odds with Pancasila (Freedom of Religious Association).[19]

In 1967, the missions began building churches and Christian schools in Muslim areas in a way that seriously offended Muslims.

Christian churches and schools sprang up 'like mushrooms after rain' all over Indonesia.

As a result unfortunate incidents occurred: the destruction of a church at Meulaboh in Aceh (June 1967), the destruction of a church in Ujung Pandang (Macassar) (October 1967) and the destruction of the Protestant School at Palmerah, Slipi, in Jakarta.

These incidents occurred because the demands of Muslim groups made to the relevant authorities and to the government (including that the establishment of Christian churches and schools require the permission of the local government concerned) did not receive a positive response. [p. 207] [...]

Under Pancasila there is freedom to join any of the following religions: Islam, Christianity, Protestantism, Roman Catholicism and Balinese Hinduism. This does not mean that converting Muslims to Christianity is in accord with Pancasila. If there is to be competition to spread the various religions, let it be done among Indonesians who do not yet have a religion.

The Pancasila platform urges mutual respect among religious groups. If a Muslim is converted to Christianity, this conflicts with that principle.

If, as in Meulaboh, there is a society that has almost never met Christians, and an imposing church is built, a question arises about whether there is still mutual respect as intended by Pancasila.

The dominance or power in the form of material wealth on the part of the Christians, which is used to convert those Muslims who are vulnerable and poor in material possessions, offends Muslims. That sort of freedom goes too far, just as the destruction of churches goes too far. And if things continue on in this vein, it will mean the end of Pancasila as a platform or shared pulpit.

The destruction of churches has certainly offended Christians. But the problem should not be viewed symptomatically, by just attending to the visible symptoms. It is like someone suffering from malaria, with a fever, and giving them a cold compress: it will not take away the malaria.

---

19 Pancasila has five 'principles': belief in the one supreme God; just and civilized humanity; national unity; democracy led by wisdom and prudence through consultation and representation; and social justice. These principles are set out in the Preamble of the 1945 Constitution of the Republic of Indonesia and form the basis of the Indonesian state. Natsir had previously been a strong critic of Pancasila but his reference to it in this context reflects the New Order's insistence that 'Pancasila values' be upheld. In effect Natsir is arguing that 'Christianization' is contrary to the regime's own interpretation and application of Pancasila. He seems to interpret the first principle in a very free sense, as meaning 'One God but not necessarily one religion'.

You have to seek the real cause of the disease, because fever is only one of the symptoms of a person with malaria.

Islam has a positive code on religious tolerance that should not be feared by those of other faiths.

But when Christians who are ahead in material and intellectual terms convert Muslims to Christianity, this is certainly going too far. One example of this material advantage is distributing rice to poor and disadvantaged Muslims in the Yogyakarta region, and then urging those who take the rice to convert to Christianity.

In Islam, Muslims who convert to Christianity are hypocrites (*munafik*). And realize this: if people like that embrace Christianity they are hypocritical Christians too, because they converted just for rice. [pp. 208–9]

> **Commentary**   The second Natsir extract is drawn from a 1968 Idul Fitri sermon. The sermon was delivered shortly after a series of meetings between Muslim and Christian leaders to discuss issues related to preaching outside one's own religious community. Muslim leaders sought assurances from Christian leaders that missionary activity would not occur among Muslim communities. The tone of Natsir's speech indicates his disappointment at the response of the Christian leaders.

Extract 15-9: Mohammad Natsir

M. Natsir (1980), 'Baiklah Kita Berpahit-Pahit! 1968, Khutbah 'Idul-Fithri Tahun 1387, di lapangan Proyek Senen Raya Jakarta' [All Right, We Should Face Up to Difficulties! 1968, Idul Fitri Sermon 1387, at the car park of Senen Raya Project, Jakarta], pp. 215–28 in *Islam dan Kristen di Indonesia* [Islam and Christianity in Indonesia], Media Dakwah, Jakarta. [Reprinted from *Harian Abadi*, 5 May 1969.] Extract: pp. 225–8.

ALL RIGHT, WE SHOULD FACE UP TO DIFFICULTIES!

These events are some illustrations of the implementation of the commands God gave to our Esteemed Muhammad, may blessings and peace be upon him and ourselves as his followers. Therefore, to convey [this message] to our fellow citizens and People of the Book [Jews and Christians; see introduction]:

> *'Say! I have faith in whatever scripture God has revealed and I have been commanded to act justly to all [my] Brothers. God is our Lord and the Lord of [my] Brothers. To us our good deeds and to our Brothers their good deeds. There is no (religious) dissension amongst us. God brings us all together. And to Him also we shall return.'*
>
> *(Asy Syura 15)*[20]

---

20   'So [Prophet] call people to that faith and follow the straight path as you have been commanded. Do not go by what they desire, but say, "I believe in whatever Scripture God has sent down. I am commanded to bring justice between you. God is our Lord and your Lord – to us our deeds and to you yours, so let there be no argument between us and you – God will gather us together, and to Him we shall return".' (Q42: 15, Haleem).

God's Prophet and we as His *ummah* are commanded to appeal to all fellow human beings of God's family who are People of the Book:

'Oh People of the Book!

Let us return to the just words (a point of contact) between us both, which is that we worship only God. And let us not have any other gods but Him, and let not some of us become followers of gods other than God .... And when they turn away, say to them:

Bear witness that we (are) Muslims!'

(Ali Imran: 64)[21]

That is our appeal, honestly and sincerely. But if our Brothers reject our appeal to find common ground in this meeting, no matter. We will still be able to live peacefully side by side and in accord. We have only one request:

'ISYHADUU BI ANNAA MUSLIMUN!'
[Ar.: *'ishhaduu bi-'annaa muslimuuna*]

'Witness (and acknowledge) that we are Muslims.' That is, we are people who already have a faith. The Islamic faith. We are people who already have an identity, namely Islam. Do not question our identity. Do not let us cause trouble for each other in this matter of religion. [...] Let us mutually respect each other's identity. So that we can continue to be good friends and companions in God's realm, a family that is united.

We the Islamic *ummah* do not *a priori* regard as enemies people who are not Muslims. But clearly, too, Almighty God forbids us from being friendly with people who cause trouble for our religion, the Islamic religion. In fact, we may even be seen as despotic if we do this.

'There is no other way for those who attack you in matters of religion and drive you from your villages, and assist the persecutors to expel you; God forbids you to make friends of them; and whosoever makes friends of them then they are the oppressors.'
(Al-Mumtahinah 9)[22]

That is Almighty God's warning to our Islamic *Ummah*.

We sincerely hope that our Brother countrymen who are Christian *will not* have [the same] intention as certain Jewish and Christian groups who are pointed out in the Qur'an:

'... And the Jews and Christians will not like you, unless you follow their religion.'
(Al-Baqarah 120)[23]

---

21   'Say, "People of the Book, let us arrive at a statement that is common to us all: we worship God alone, we ascribe no partner to Him, and none of us takes others beside God as lords". If they turn away, say, "Witness our devotion to Him".' (Q3: 64, Haleem).

22   'But God forbids you to take as allies those who have fought against you for your faith, driven you out of your homes, and helped others to drive you out: any of you who take them as allies will truly be wrongdoers' (Q60: 9, Haleem).

23   'The Jews and the Christians will never be pleased with you unless you follow their ways. Say, "God's guidance is the only true guidance". If you were to follow their desires after the knowledge that has come to you, you would find no one to protect you from God or help you' (Q2: 120, Haleem).

Let us hope that it *will not* be like that. Because if it is like that, then it will sever our ties of brotherhood, and will also cut the ties of happiness and sorrow that have woven us all together.

I hope that in the future we *do not take different paths!* With all the sad consequences that this would entail.

Occasionally between Brother and Brother *it is all right for us to speak out.* That is, we should not just look on and sit on our hands.

Because if there is something that we cherish more than anything else it is our *religion* and our *faith.* That is what we want to bequeath to our children and grandchildren. This is what Almighty God obliges us to guard and protect, so that it is safe and sound, and becomes our religion purely because of God.

We can be friends together.

If not, we will be all alone.

In keeping with God's command, which says:

> *'There is only one thing I entrust to you. That is that you uphold the religion of God, in twos and singly (sincerely), then reflect on it.'*
>
> *(Saba: 46)*[24] [...]

May Almighty God allow us to find in our homeland a group like the one described in God's words as the group that is closest to us, the Islamic *Ummah,* namely:

> *'You will surely meet a group of people most close in loving friendship with the believers. That is those who say: Truly we are of the ummah of the Christians.'*
>
> *(Al-Maidah: 82)*

> *'That is, it is because there are priests and monks among them, and because they are not arrogant.'*
>
> *(Al-Maidah 82)*[25]

Hopefully that is their character.

May it not be that we cannot sit together, except when they have been able to convert Muslims to Christianity. [...]

Hamka

Commentary Natsir urged respectful relations between Muslims and Christians but other leaders saw danger in extensive contact between Muslim and 'Western' society. The respected Indonesian scholar Hamka went further and depicted Western influence as sinister and a conspiracy to undermine Islam. Hamka, the popular name of Dr Haji Abdul Malik Karim Amrullah (1908–81), was a very influential figure who wrote pro-

---

24 'Say [Prophet], "I advise you to do one thing only: stand before God, in pairs or singly, and think: there is no sign of madness in your companion [the Prophet] – he is only warning you before severe suffering arrives".' (Q34: 46, Haleem).

25 'You [Prophet] are sure to find that the most hostile to the believers are the Jews and those who associate other deities with God; you are sure to find that the closest in affection towards the believers are those who say, "We are Christians", for there are among them people devoted to learning and ascetics. These people are not given to arrogance' (Q5: 82, Haleem).

lifically, including an exegesis of the Qur'an for Indonesians. In the late 1970s he was the chair of Majelis Ulama Indonesia (MUI, Council of Indonesian Ulama). In the following extract, written for the well-regarded Islamic magazine *Panji Masyarakat* [Banner of the Community], he blames a range of 'bad' influences on Indonesian culture on 'the West', describing them as a deliberate attempt to destroy Islam. He describes various movements and people deemed hostile to Islam, including Zionism, evangelism, missionaries and orientalists. In just two paragraphs, negative desriptions of 'Western culture' and Zionism, Christian missionaries and Christian scholars, are combined and blamed for undermining and threatening Islam. These sentiments are developed further in some of the other extracts below.

Extract 15-10: Hamka

Hamka (2002), 'Pokok Pegangan Hidup Kita' [Our Basic Principles for Living], pp. 146–50 in Yousran Rusydi (ed.), *Dari Hati ke Hati: Tentang Agama, Sosial-Budaya, Politik* [Heart to Heart on Religion, Society, Politics], Penerbit Pustaka Panjimas, Jakarta. Extract: p. 150.

At present we are witnessing the spread of free association between men and women, partner swapping and free sex outside of marriage, as is done in Western countries. The penetration of Western culture into Islamic countries is inevitably intended to destroy the basic principles of Islam that regulate matters of descent. This intention is supported among other things by the publication of pornographic books and pictures as well as films. Muslims are strictly forbidden to gamble; because of this casinos have been established. It is strongly forbidden to drink alcoholic beverages, so advertisements for alcohol have been introduced. And should there be an ulema who is able to pronounce beer permissible to Muslims, he will receive praise for being a 'progressive' ulema.

   Zionism, evangelism, and missionaries and orientalists, though they all come from varying disciplines, have but one aim, namely to strip away the three basic principles from the hearts of the young generation of Muslims, specifically belief in the Oneness of God; not differentiating between all of God's messengers and the last of their kind, Muhammad; and living not just for the here and now. There is also the continuation of life [the hereafter]!

Ahmad Sumargono

Commentary   Ahmad Sumargono (1943–) is a leading conservative Muslim activist and politician. An economics graduate from the University of Indonesia, he first achieved national prominence as the executive chair of Komite Indonesia untuk Solidaritas Dunia Islam (KISDI, Indonesian Committee for World Islamic Solidarity), an organization affiliated with the Islamic proselytization organization DDII. KISDI was formed in 1986 to promote the cause of overseas Muslim communities in conflict areas such as Palestine, Bosnia, Kashmir and Chechnya. After Soeharto's resignation in 1998, Sumargono became a founding member of Partai Bulan Bintang (PBB, Crescent Moon and Star Party) and was elected to the national parliament in 1999. An ardent preacher, he is best known for his speeches attacking Western policies towards Indonesia, in particular perceived Christian and Jewish undermining of Islam. The following extract is from a speech delivered in Jakarta on 5 April 1998, at the height of the financial crisis in Indonesia. It refers to the International Monetary Fund (IMF) 'bailout' in which the Soeharto government agreed to a range of reforms in return for access to a multi-billion dollar financial aid package intended to stabilize the economy. The extract is typical of a number of Sumargono's sermons during the late 1990s in accusing international agencies of acting to undermine Indonesian sovereignty and prosperity and of seeking to subjugate the Islamic community.

Extract 15-11: Ahmad Sumargono

Ahmad Sumargono (1999), 'Jangan Korbankan Kehormatan Kita, demi 3 Miliar USD' [Don't Sacrifice Our Honour for US$3 Billion], pp. 116–20 in *Saya Seorang Fundamentalis: Refleksi Ideologis H. Ahmad Sumargono* [I am a Fundamentalist: Ideological Reflections of H. Ahmad Sumargono], Global Cita Press, Jakarta. Extract: p. 118.

Returning to the IMF, okay, we can say that we respect the decision of the RI [Republic of Indonesia] government to accept 'IMF pressure'. Perhaps the funds that we need from the IMF are truly vital to rescue our economy, which has been on the verge of disaster. We certainly find it difficult to reject the presence of the IMF because we are not able to reject the IMF – as Malaysia has done. Because we are weak. Okay, we admit our weakness, so that we let our dignity be trampled on by foreign peoples, and we are sure that behind them are the Jews.

However, what we need to evaluate is this: 'why have we become weak' so that we become the plaything of other peoples – as depicted by the Messenger of God, blessings and peace be upon him, that we are froth. So many in number, but weak. Imagine, even Singapore can offer to help us with [the promise of] US$10 billion in aid. That insignificant country meddles in the appointment of the vice president.[26]

Brothers, we are weak because our mentality is indeed weak. We are of poor quality. We have not developed and strengthened our identity as a Muslim people. It's as if we are embarrassed to be Muslims. To announce to the world that we are a Muslim people. To build the Islamic identity of every citizen who is a Muslim. We must believe that it is only the power of Islam that is capable of confronting the international imperialists, who are currently commanded by Jewish and Christian forces. God's command: *'He is God. He it is who has sent His Messenger, bringing guidance and the true religion to be victorious over other religions. Even though the polytheists detest it' (QS. As Shaf: 9).*[27]

---

26   This is probably a reference to adverse Singaporean comment on the successful nomination of B.J. Habibie as vice-president in March 1998.
27   'it is He who sent His Messenger with guidance and the religion of truth to show that it is above all [other] religions, even though the idolaters hate it' (Q61: 9, Haleem).

Irwan Prayitno

Commentary   One of the new phenomena to emerge within Indonesian Islam during
the 1980s and 1990s was a movement known as Gerakan Tarbiyah (Education Movement). It drew its inspiration primarily from Egypt's Muslim Brotherhood and reflected
a deep disillusionment among younger Muslims about existing Islamic parties and
organizations in Indonesia. It placed emphasis on personal piety, high academic and
professional achievement, community service and the gradual Islamization of society
through predication and education. In its early days the Tarbiyah movement was primarily religious and social, and steadfastly avoided political activity. But as the New Order
regime began to falter in 1997 and early 1998, Tarbiyah activists assumed a leading
role in the student protests that led ultimately to Soeharto's resignation in May 1998.
Shortly after this, sections of the Tarbiyah movement formed Partai Keadilan (PK, Justice Party) as their primary political vehicle.

A key ideological concept in both Muslim Brotherhood and Tarbiyah circles is that
of *ghazwul fikri* [Ar.: *'al-ghazwul-fikriyyu*] or the 'war of ideas'. This concept holds
that there is a fundamental dichotomy in the world between that which is Islamic and
that which is non-Islamic or *jahiliyyah* (see footnote 11). Moreover, the non-Islamic
sphere is engaged in a war of ideas with the Islamic community that must be resisted
if Muslims are to create a strong and pious community. Among the many Western concepts that have penetrated and 'contaminated' the thinking of Muslims are the so-called
'isms' such as materialism, communism, orientalism and capitalism. Tarbiyah activists
believe that Islam is a complete and self-sufficient system and that undue encroachment
of infidel thinking or practices represents an inherent threat to the faith.

Irwan Prayitno (1963–) is a leading figure in the Tarbiyah movement and PK, which
was renamed Partai Keadilan Sejahtera (PKS, Prosperity and Justice Party) in 2003. A
psychology graduate of the University of Indonesia, he gained his doctorate in management studies from Universiti Putra Malaysia before returning to Indonesia to join the
newly formed PK in 1998. He was elected to parliament in 1999 and again in 2004,
representing his home province of West Sumatra. He has featured prominently in PK/
PKS training programs, including preparing two large volumes of material for Tarbiyah
activists and the party cadre. The following extract is representative of the extensive
literature within Tarbiyah and PKS circles on *ghazwul fikri*.

Extract 15-12: Irwan Prayitno

Irwan Prayitno (2003), 'Al Ghazw al-Fikri' [War of Ideas], pp. 3–4 in *Kepribadian
Dai* [The Character of Preachers], Pustaka Tarbiatuna, Bekasi. Extract: pp. 3–4.

In general, the Islamic community is not aware of the dangers of the war of ideas
(*al-ghazw al-fikri*). This phenomenon is proved by the number of Muslims who, consciously or otherwise, adhere to the thoughts, behaviour and lifestyle of the infidels
(the West). Muslims' unawareness of this danger has caused them to lose their [sense
of] identity and self-confidence as Muslims. Moreover, pride in pagan (*jahiliyah*)
behaviour has been turned into a culture. [...]

The infidels, who suffered successive defeats at the hands of Islam during the
crusades, have since looked for an alternative way of destroying the Islamic community. They will never be willing to stop and will never stop attacking until the Islamic

community follows their religion. The strategy they have chosen to destroy Islam is *al-ghazw al-fikri*. *Al-ghazw al-fikri* is an ideological, cultural, mental and conceptual attack waged continually in a systematic, organized and well-planned fashion. The result is the emergence of a change in the personality, lifestyle and behaviour of the Muslim community.

The aim of *al-ghazw al-fikri* is to make Muslims give up their religion. These efforts started before the fall of the Islamic caliphate, and began with the severing of ties between Islamic countries under the Islamic caliphate, causing the emergence of nationalist groups and national ideologies. The separation of religion and state, orientalism, Christianization and the women's emancipation movement are also *al-ghazw al-fikri* activities that have shown their results among a proportion of the Islamic community who have become ignorant of their religion (*jahiliyah*). In general, the perpetrators of *al-ghazw al-fikri* are Jews, Christians, Zoroastrians, Polytheists, Hypocrites (*Munafikin*), Atheists and infidels. Their method of attacking the Islamic community and making it forget its genuine identity is through propaganda, education, instruction, books, the print media, clubs, sport, foundations, institutions, entertainment, films and music.

The danger of *al-ghazw al-fikri* can deceive the Islamic community and tend to turn them into infidels, loving them, obeying them, following their way of life, adopting similar behaviour, until they give their loyalty to these infidels. They will receive damnation and torment from God, as God has removed Himself from them. The life of Muslims who fall into the trap of *al-ghazw al-fikri* changes to become a life of ignorance (*jahiliyah*) [...]

In general, *jahiliyah* is the system, concept and deeds of individual life that rest in the darkness beyond the light of Islam.

> **Commentary** Another element of PKS's *ghazwul fikri* discourse is trenchant anti-Semitism (see also plate 15 in the colour section of this book). PKS writers draw heavily on anti-Zionist literature from the Middle East to propagate conspiracy theories with wide currency in the Islamic world regarding Jewish control of international finance and politics. The extract below is a typical example of this discourse.

Extract 15-13: Irwan Prayitno

Irwan Prayitno (2003), 'Yahudi sebagai Hizbus Syaithan Menguasai Dunia' [Jews as the Party of Satan Dominating the World], pp. 111–16 in *Kepribadian Dai* [The Character of Preachers], Pustaka Tarbiatuna, Bekasi. Extract: pp. 111–12.

1. The Jews' Obsession with Dominating the World

The Jews aspire to control the world by conquering every system owned by each nation or state. Whatever method the Jews may employ through their Zionist movement, their aim is always to control the world. At present, the world's political, economic, legal and social systems, wherever they have developed, are controlled by Jews. This urge to control the world is founded on a conviction that God has appointed Jews as the leaders of nations and the heirs of the earth and all that is legitimate in it. Islam holds the same conviction, called a caliphate, namely that a faithful and pious organ has been given a mandate to develop and tend the earth and all that is in it. This conviction on the part of Muslims will motivate Jews to wage war on Islam, because Islam has the potential to defeat the Jews. [...]

The Jews work hard to wage war on the Muslim community, so that Muslims will follow them, as mentioned in the Qur'an, Al Baqarah, verse 120: '*The Jews and Christians will not be pleased with you until you follow their religion. Say: "Surely God's guidance is true". And surely if you follow their desires after knowledge has come to you, then God will no longer be your protector and helper*'.[28] [p. 111] [...]

To achieve this obsession they have employed all means. The Jews are widely known to have orchestrated various secret movements. They have also been behind many catastrophes throughout history. There are indications that the September 11 tragedy was a Jewish conspiracy to corner Islam, so that Israel could justify attacks on Palestinians using terrorism as a reason. [...] Islam does not have a history of attacking innocent civilians. [...]

The history of the Jews is full of evil, such as cruel slavery, arrogance, extreme patriotism, blind fanaticism to their bloodline, material greed, a usurious economic system, and other evil behaviour such as being suck-ups, slippery, cruel, hypocritical, with rotten intentions, stubborn, seizing other people's possessions by illegitimate means and obstructing humans from the path of Islam. [...]

This behaviour is the behaviour of the devil. They have systematically planned their crimes in coordination, as a community, nation, state and agency. [...] The actions of the United States in attacking Islamic states are also the result of the strong Jewish lobby in the United States. The Jews control world or foreign politics through the hand of the United States or other world bodies like the United Nations. An effective way to conquer the world, which they follow, is by economic means. History also shows that the Jews defeat other people through their economic strength, namely through a system of bank interest and control of assets using unjust and dishonest trade practices. [pp. 112–13]

Luthfi Assyaukanie

> ***Commentary*** A sharply contrasting view of *ghazwul fikri* and the influence of Western thinking comes from Luthfi Assyaukanie of Indonesia's Jaringan Islam Liberal (JIL, Liberal Islam Network). (Further information about him is given in section 12.1.11.) He argues that ideas from within the Muslim world have proven more harmful than those from the West.

Extract 15-14: Luthfi Assyaukanie

Luthfi Assyaukanie, 'A Battle of Thoughts' [in English], Jaringan Islam Liberal, <http://islamlib.com/en/page.php?page=article&id=692>, dated 3 September 2005, accessed 10 January 2006.

---

28   Q2: 120 is given in footnote 23.

The term 'ghazwul fikri' is very popular in Islamic circles. This term originated from the Arabic language and literally means 'battle of thought' though who used it for the first time is not known. The works of Sayyid Qutb, Muhammad Qutb, Said Hawwa,[29] and the ideologists of the Muslim Brethren often used this term with a 'crusader's' spirit.

The users of this term believe that Western thought tends to attack and to have a negative impact on Muslim thought. Those thoughts may poison and keep Muslims away from Islam. 'Therefore', as Muhammad Qutb said, the 'battle of thought is far more dangerous than physical war'. They also believe in the existence of 'influence theory' wherein a Muslim will be influenced and trapped in the nets of Zionism and crusaders whenever they study the Westerner's and particularly the orientalist's work in detail.

I think, 'ghazwul fikri', 'influence theory', must be observed critically. Since every thought – whatever and wherever its source – is a form of 'battle' and has influence upon anyone engaged in it.

The Muslims who have observed and engaged with Western thought have never been destructive. On the contrary, they are reformists whose names are recorded honourably in the history of Islamic modern thought. Take[,] for example, Rif'at Tahtawi, Muhammad Abduh, Al-Kawakibi, Taha Hussein, Muhammad Iqbal, Fazlur Rahman, Syed Hussein Nasr, Hassan Hanafi, and Nurcholish Madjid.[30] They are all reformists who have contributed a lot to the development of Islamic thought.

On the contrary, people who read the works of the advocates of 'ghazwul fikri' and influence theory, have become engaged in destruction and violence. Take for example Osama ben Laden and the 19 terrorists who exploded the WTC on ninth [*sic*] of September 2001[,] all of whom were familiar with the books of Sayyid Qutb. In an interview far before the 9/11, Osama admitted that *Fi Dhilal al-Qur'an* [In the Shade of the Qur'an] by Sayyid Qutb was the most influential book he had ever read.

The most important *ghazwul fikri* for the Muslim now is to fight against the simplistic and foolish thoughts which frequently require them to hate and taunt their 'enemy' while the true enemy is themselves.

---

29   Sayyid Qutb (1906–66) was an influential Egyptian Islamist. Muhammad Qutb (1915–) is an Islamic scholar and the brother of Sayyid Qutb. Said Hawwa is a Syrian Islamic scholar and prominent Muslim Brother ideologist.

30   Rifaa al-Tahtawi (1801–73), an Egyptian scholar and journalist, was one of the pioneers of the Islamic reform movement. Muhammad Abduh (1849–1905) was a leader of the Egyptian Salafiyya movement. Abd al-Rahman al-Kawabiki (d. 1902), also known as al-Sayyid al-Furati, was a Syrian Islamic revivalist. Taha Hussein (or Husayn) (d. 1971) was an internationally famous Egyptian novelist whose writings criticized the backwardness of traditional Islamic thinking. Muhammad Iqbal (1876–1938) was a Punjabi intellectual who urged that Islamic thinking be reformed and that science and technology be used to improve the conditions of human existence. Fazlur Rahman (1919–88) was a Pakistani philosopher and liberal scholar who wrote extensively on Islam and modernity. Syed Hussein Nasr (1933–) is a prominent contemporary Iranian traditionalist scholar and theologian. Hassan Hanafi (1935–) is an Egyptian reformist thinker and academic. Nurcholish Madjid (1939–2005) was an Indonesian intellectual who urged the liberal and contextual interpretation of Islam.

It is the time for Muslims to think positively, openly, critically, and to dare to take their own position without being ruled over by authoritarian thought in the name of religion.

The most important *ghazwul fikri* for the Muslim now is to fight against the racist, intolerant, and hateful thoughts held towards others. Some of those thoughts are the inheritance of the past, and the rest are their own conceptions derived from an anti-Western and anti-Orientalist schizophrenia.

Abu Bakar Ba'asyir

> *Commentary*   Abu Bakar Ba'asyir (1938–) is a leading conservative Islamic scholar and preacher who has been widely accused, but found not guilty, of being the leader of JI and having direct involvement in its terrorist activities. Of Yemeni extraction, he was educated at Gontor Pesantren and at al-Irsyad University in Solo. He became active in Gerakan Pemuda Islam Indonesia (GPII, Indonesian Islamic Youth Movement) in the early 1960s and in 1972 established, with Abdullah Sungkar, the Al Mukmin Pesantren in Ngruki, Central Java. In 1982, both Ba'asyir and Sungkar were tried and found guilty of subversion and jailed for nine years. Upon early release in 1985, they fled to Malaysia to escape further charges. During the 1980s both men were active in Darul Islam, but fell out with the organization's leaders in the early 1990s. This led Sungkar, in January 1993, to establish JI. After Sungkar died in 1999, Ba'asyir is believed to have replaced him as JI's emir (commander). In 2000, Ba'asyir oversaw the formation of a new organization, Majelis Mujahidin Indonesia (MMI, Council of Indonesian Mujahideen), whose primary aim was to champion the enactment of sharia in Indonesia. He now serves as MMI's emir. Ba'asyir was arrested in 2002 and later convicted and jailed for using counterfeit documents and for immigration offences and conspiracy.[31]
>
> The extract below, from a sermon delivered to students at Ba'asyir's *pesantren* in late 2002, raises themes common to many of his public statements. He regards the comprehensive implementation of sharia as essential to living a fully Islamic life but warns that Islam's enemies are bent upon preventing this. He speaks with particular fervour about the threat posed by Christians and Jews. The translation is an edited version of the sermon from a filmed recording of the speech. In this translation, the terms 'Allah' and 'God' are used interchangeably.

Extract 15-15: Abu Bakar Ba'asyir

Abu Bakar Ba'asyir, 'Abu Bakar Bas'yir [*sic*] Sermon' [in English], edited translation from 'Four Corners' (television current affairs program), Australian Broadcasting Commission, <http://www.abc.net.au/4corners/stories/s711753.htm>, dated 28 October 2002, accessed 12 January 2005.

Allah has divided humanity into two segments, namely the followers of Allah and those who follow Satan. The party of God, and the party of Satan. [...] And God's

---

31   The biographical information is drawn from Awwas (2003: 31–49), ICG (2002b: 6–17) and Nasir (2005: 116, 305–6).

group are those who follow Islam, those who are prepared to follow his laws and struggle for the implementation of Sharia, that is [Hisbullah].[32] Meanwhile what is meant by Satan's group is humanity which opposes Allah's law, humanity which wishes to bring pressure to bear upon Allah's law, and wishes to throw obstacles in the path of the implementation of Allah's law. Hisbullah has character and enthusiasm to defend Sharia law. For Hisbullah Sharia law is more important than life itself. Sharia is priceless as compared to life itself. Life without Sharia is nothing. There is no worth to life, even more so wealth. Everything that is in the world, if it does not have Sharia, means nothing – it has no worth. Accordingly, for Hisbullah one must be prepared to forfeit one's life for Sharia. Not only material possessions, family or happiness[;] one must be prepared to sacrifice life itself in the name of Sharia. […]

The second quality of Hisbullah is: to those people they tolerate differences of opinion, they help each other, they love their families and they're [their] Muslim brothers and sisters as much as they love themselves. If their Muslim brother or sister falls upon hard times, they too will feel their pain. Accordingly they work hard to help their Muslim brothers or sisters who have fallen upon hard times to overcome their difficulties. They do not embrace non-believers[;] they do not request the assistance of non-believers, even if the non-believers have more material wealth, weapons, power than they do. They will still consider themselves to be better, to be bestowed with more grace, than the non-believers. Don't be humble[;] you are great if you follow Allah's laws. Do not ever request assistance from non-believers, particularly in the implementation of Sharia[;] be clear in rejecting non-believers. There should be no tolerance towards the principles of non-believers. But clearly Hisbullah would rather free themselves of life than be lost in the world of non-believers. […]

[Ba'asyir then directs his comments to non-Muslims.]

[…] We would rather die than follow that which you worship. We do not want to cooperate. This is the workings of religion. We reject all of your beliefs, we reject all of your ideologies, we reject all of your teachings that are associated with social issues, economics or beliefs. Between you and us there will forever be a ravine of hate and we will be enemies until you follow Allah's law. This is Hisbullah in the context of dealing with non-believers. However, although Hisbullah enshrines this type of character, this is felt by non-believers as harsh, [as] even Allah himself acknowledges. Mohammed will be stern with non-believers, and what is meant by stern here does not mean to pursue or hurt non-believers[;] what is meant is sternness in the sense of self confidence and the desire to not compromise even in a small way with respect to our faith as opposed to that of the non-believers. This is the character of Hisbullah. Brothers and sisters, Hisbullah in this sense does not mean we cannot make peace with non-believers[.] Hisbullah can live side by side with non-believers. We can live peacefully with non-believers, we can live [with] and help non-believers in the matters of the world, on the proviso that those non-believers do not disturb the workings of Sharia law, as long as those non-believers do not place obstacles before

---

32　The more common spelling of this term in Indonesia and Malaysia is Hizbullah (the party of God). The square brackets are in the original.

the implementation of Sharia law and its proponents. Then Hisbullah are prepared to live side by side with non-believers, to be peaceful, to help each other in the matters of the world, on the condition that the non-believers are not allowed to disturb Sharia law, the implementation of it nor its proponents. This is the nature of Hisbullah. Hence the natural progression for Hisbullah, for Allah's party, is Jihad. The struggle to defend the law of God, the implementation of Sharia because Hisbullah believe that this life has no meaning without Sharia. [...]

Brothers and sisters, why is this character called Jihad? Because the character of followers of Satan is always opposing Allah. Allah in heaven wills that non-believers grow to internalise the light of Allah and Allah will perfect that light, even though non-believers may be angry. Therefore the meaning of this verse[33] underlines that the character of non-believers is such that they always work hard to oppose Islam. There is no non-believer who allows the development of Islam, who will allow Islam to be free[;] non-believers must work hard to threaten Islam and the laws thereof. This is the character of non-believers. Non-believers will always expend their wealth to impede the way of God, to impede the law of Islam. Non-believers will expend not insignificant sums to destroy Islam. This is the character of non-believers.

Brothers and sisters, there are even non-believers who[,] in their efforts to attack Islam to extinguish the light of Islam, [...] use two methods. The first one is [that] they embark upon a war of thought. The basic premises of Islam are changed so that Muslims themselves do not understand their own faith. Many Muslims do not comprehend their religion because its precepts have been interfered with by non-believers. Jihad on one hand is understood to be a war against one's own desires. On the other hand Jihad is described as evil and violence, murder. So Muslims then wrongfully interpret the meaning of Jihad, to the point where there are Muslims who are afraid of Jihad. If Muslims are afraid of Jihad, then they will be weak. Worship is interpreted as only prayer, so it is limited by prayer. And so forth in other instances. They endeavour with all their might so that Muslims will wish to compromise their worship [and] law and fraternise with non-believers. This is the target of non-believers. So that accordingly Muslims become soft and Muslims are soft because they allow themselves to compromise in the realm of Islam. Do not accept the invitation of non-believers who wish for you to become soft and what is meant by soft here is the desire to compromise with non-believers, the desire to adapt to non-believers, their clothing, their culture, if there is a need to drink alcohol, then to do so in the desire to compromise with them. This is what is meant by soft and this is the method of non-believers in their endeavour to attack Islamic thought. [...]

If non-believers have the weapons capacity, the funding, then they will go to war against Islam. In the Koran Allah has said they will always wage war against you, they will always attack you as long as they have the capacity. Brothers and sisters Muslims [*sic*], we now can feel the efforts of non-believers to threaten Islam. Jews and America are waging a war on Muslims in order that there are many participants, and those who do not wish to participate are attacked and those who wish to are given funding. Then in the process of waging war against Islam they use

---

33 Details of the verse are not given in the translation on the ABC's website.

that which is mentioned in the Koran as values, they create a war wherein it is not clearly stated it is a war against Islam but they use a smokescreen which is currently being described as 'terrorists'. The non-believers of America and the non-believers of Israel are currently developing the issue of terrorism, however what they mean by terrorism[,] according to the definition of America, are all of the followers of Islam. All followers of Islam in this world are terrorists. Then they create Islamic organisations which are directed by terrorist organisations, such as Al Qaeda. Then in the case of Jemmah Islamiaah it is international terrorists, then people are sent in and[,] once in, they are terrorists. This is the intent of non-believers in their framework to attack in their quest to destroy the vision of Muslims[;] this is what is currently going on including in our own country.

15.2.2 Pluralism and Tolerance

Commentary Many Southeast Asian Muslims believe that non-Muslims often treat Muslims unjustly, both globally and domestically. Nonetheless there is a strong tradition of religious tolerance and pluralism in Islam. The diversity of faith communities in the region is centuries old, and constructive interaction between them has developed over time. This occurs more readily in countries where Muslims are in the majority. Easy relations seem to be more difficult in nations with minority Muslim populations (such as Thailand and the Philippines), where interaction is more limited and usually triggered by the need to bring peace after conflict. In Burma, there is little evidence of systematic interaction.

The great majority of Muslims in Southeast Asia nevertheless live harmoniously in communities that are, more often than not, religiously and ethnically diverse. Muslim leaders, intellectuals and activists expend considerable effort in upholding and celebrating what is seen as Islam's inherently tolerant nature. In this section, a range of extracts sets out the richness of this aspect of Islamic discourse in the region.

Chandra Muzaffar

Commentary Dr Chandra Muzaffar (1947–) is one of Malaysia's leading activists and a board member of many international human rights bodies. In 1977 he founded Aliran, a movement to monitor threats to civil society and the environment in Malaysia, and was its president until 1991. He is the director of the International Movement for a Just World (JUST), an international citizens organization working for the creation of a world guided by a spiritual and moral vision for right living. In 1987 he and a number of other moral activists were detained for two months under Malaysia's Internal Security Act, a move that attracted international criticism of the Malaysian government. Chandra is a major contributor to debates about Islam in the modern world. In the following extract he chooses tolerance as his theme, placing it in the wider frame of Islamic history as well as in the more particular context of multi-religious life in Malaysia. As explained in chapter 6, all Malays in Malaysia are Muslims. They make up about 60 per cent of the total population, the other 40 per cent being predominantly Chinese (Buddhists and Christians) and Indians (Hindus, Sikhs and a small number of Muslims).

Extract 15-16: Chandra Muzaffar

Chandra Muzaffar (1996), 'Tolerance in the Malaysian Political Scene' [in English], pp. 121–48 in Syed Othman Alhabshi and Nik Mustapha Nik Hassan (eds), *Islam and Tolerance*, Institute of Islamic Understanding Malaysia, Kuala Lumpur. [First published 1994.] Extract: pp. 146–8.

As non-Malays and non-Muslims understand their accommodation through an internal view of history, they should also be made aware of the role of Islam in casting the Malay value-system in a more inclusive, less exclusive mould, so much so that acceptance of the other has since become part and parcel of Malay political culture. More than that, the non-Muslim communities as a whole should develop a more profound, a more balanced outlook on Islam and Muslims. They should get rid of the biases, the prejudices, the hostilities and the antagonisms that a lot of them harbour against the religion. As Islam becomes more and more important in the life of the nation in the future, these negative attitudes towards the religion could emerge as a formidable barrier to inter-ethnic harmony. In this connection, one cannot help but observe with a tinge of sadness that since Merdeka [Independence, 1957] hardly any non-Muslim scholar, theologian, journalist, politician or social activist has made it his mission to reduce the negative perceptions of Islam within the non-Muslim communities in the country. And yet in the West which, in a sense, is the source of so much of the pejorative thinking on Islam there are a number of outstanding personalities in public life today who are willing to correct the unjust, unfair portrayals of the religion.

This brings us to the role of Malays and Muslims themselves *vis-a-vis* Islam and the accommodation of the non-Malay, non-Muslim population. While accommodation of the others, as we have shown, has been extraordinary, the Malay-Muslim community no doubt realises that there are elements in the relationship between the Malays and Muslims, on the one hand, and the non-Malays and non-Muslims, on the other, which do not blend with Islamic values and principles. Applying an indigenous–non-indigenous dichototomy to public policies related to social justice is unacceptable to Islam. If the central concern is justice – helping the needy or rewarding the deserving – ethnic affiliations or communal considerations should not be allowed to cloud our judgement.[34] By incorporating genuine, universal Islamic values and principles into public policies which impact upon non-Muslims in education, commerce and industry, it is quite conceivable that they will begin to appreciate the religion's commitment to justice and fairness. After all it was Islam's passion for justice and fairness manifested in the total repudiation of any form of racial, ethnic or even religious discrimination which attracted millions of non-Muslims to the faith in the first few centuries of its history. Within the Malaysian context the emergence of justice as a sacred principle of both policy and practice will certainly contribute to the integration and accommodation of the non-Muslim population.

---

34   At this point, a footnote in the original reads: 'I have elaborated on this in my "Malaysia Bumiputraism and Islam", *Readings on Islam in Southeast Asia*', Ahmad Ibrahim, Sharon Siddique and Yasmin Hussain (eds.) (Institute of Southeast Asian Studies, Singapore, 1986)'.

What is required is more than the application of the Islamic concept of universal justice. The Malay-Muslim leadership of Malaysia has one of those rare opportunities in history to establish a society which embodies the spirit of universalism contained in the Holy Qur'an in all its manifestations. As we have observed, the translation of Qur'anic universalism in its totality into social reality is something which has alluded [eluded] the Muslim world for so long. A delicately balanced multi-ethnic, multi-religious society like ours compels the Muslim to develop creative ways of integrating its diverse communities guided by Qur'anic universalism.

Novriantoni

> ***Commentary*** The pamphlets written under the banner *Buletin al-Tasamuh* [Bulletin of Tolerance] were distributed during Friday services at over 300 mosques in and around Jakarta between July 2001 and early 2004. They were the concept of Lingkar Studi-Aksi untuk Demokrasi Indonesia (LS-ADI, Study-Action Circle for Indonesian Democracy), an activist and advocacy group that is part of NU's Program Pendidikan Agama dan Demokrasi (Program for Education in Religion and Democracy).[35] Because it is obligatory for Muslims to attend the Friday noon prayers, there is potentially a vast audience for such pamphlets. The pamphlets aimed to counter the more conservative and militant literature that was widely available in Indonesian mosques and prayer rooms, putting forward a more pluralist interpretation of Muslim scripture. Like less liberal material, the tone of the pamphlets was direct and constructed to persuade through argumentation. The material in the pamphlets was also presented in a way that would catch the attention of those attending prayers and sermons.
>
> The author of this extract, Novriantoni, is a young Muslim intellectual who graduated from al-Azhar University in Cairo and obtained a master's degree in sociology from the University of Indonesia. He is also a member of JIL.

Extract 15-17: Novriantoni

Novriantoni (2002), 'Solidaritas untuk Palestina' [Solidarity for Palestine], *Buletin Al-Tasamuh*, 12(26 April), Lingkar Studi-Aksi untuk Demokrasi Indonesia, Jakarta. Extract: pp. 2–4.

The demonstrations by the Indonesian Islamic community (*ummah*) that break out when the Palestine–Israel conflict becomes heated are [a sign of its] solidarity. In various ways the Indonesian Islamic *ummah* displays its solidarity with the struggle of the Palestinian people. Very often, that solidarity is marked by rising anger against Israel. It is not rare for that anger to take the form of sharp criticism of America, which until now has been trusted and seen by the Arab world, even the international world, as the 'mediator in the conflict'. For many Muslims, America is the 'suspect'

---

35 Information supplied by Lisa Noor Humaidah, former editor of *Buletin Al-Tasamuh*, and Anick H. Tohari, program coordinator of LS-ADI.

that has abetted Israeli atrocities. Sentence has already been passed on Israel as the guilty party.

The religious doctrine of Islam advocates the promotion of solidarity. This is based on the following Hadith: 'Those who do not involve themselves with the affairs of the Islamic *ummah* are indeed not from their group'. From such Hadith – and there are many others, like the one that compares the Islamic *ummah* to a single living organic system (or *matsal al-jasad*)[36] in which there is mutual empathy if one of its parts is suffering – the Islamic *ummah* has a strong motivation to be involved in, defend and struggle for the common destiny. This manifestation of mutual involvement, interest, care and sometimes defence has an etymological meaning (linguistically) from the Arabic word *al-tadlâmun* [Ar.: *at-tadaamunu*], or solidarity.

However, doctrine also states that solidarity is not limited to and for the Islamic *ummah*. It also demands that the Islamic *ummah* show solidarity with other *ummah* [other religious communities] in the context of defending universal virtues: virtues that are acknowledged by all. Detention, rape, oppression and injustice endured by any human being, no matter where, are also included in the call for solidarity which should be heeded by the Islamic *ummah*. Certainly we hear often that the Qur'an advocates helping one another in matters concerning virtue and piety (*al-birr wa al-taqwa* [Ar.: *'al-birru wat-taqwaa*]), (and conversely) it condemns scheming to do evil and [create] enmity (*al itsm wa al-'udwan* [Ar.: *al-'ithmu wal-'udwaanu*]). Other verses in the Qur'an advocate that we not be incited to behave unjustly because of hatred for another [ethnic] group (*walâ yajrimannakum syana'ânu qaum 'alâ 'an lâ ta'dilû* [Ar.: *walaa yajrimannakum shana'aanu qawmin 'alaa 'al-laa ta'diluu*]). [...]

It is understandable that the Indonesian Islamic *ummah*'s defence of and bias towards Palestine exists. They feel that their brothers and sisters are still enshackled by colonialism and that their rights are being belittled. Yet sadly, that solidarity is still dominated by the flaring up of emotions and anger that is often out of control. Also, solidarity for Palestine is often coloured by religious symbols that give the impression of conflict motivated by religion. On this last point, inaccurate assessments are made about the facts of the conflict. As a result misguided expressions of solidarity are made.

> [The author of the extract then says that there are various grounds to challenge the claim that the Palestine–Israel conflict is a religious conflict, that is, Islam versus the Jews and Christians. These reasons include the exodus of the Jews out of Europe as a solution to Europe's problems with the Jews, a fact that the author says has nothing to do with religion. He points out that Zionism is a secular ideology that is quite separate from religion. Despite this, he continues, some Indonesian groups of Muslims use religious symbols to fuel mass protests, and employ verses from the scriptures to arouse the emotions of the masses. He warns that to fight jihad on behalf of Palestine without assessing the geopolitical and actual conditions in the area indicates that the feeling of solidarity is not well thought through.]

---

36   Ar.: *muttasilul jasadi*; a more common Arabic term for this is *'al-jasadul-waahidu*.

Alwi Shihab

Commentary A respected writer on contemporary Islam and interfaith dialogue, Alwi Abdurrahman Shihab (1946–) has doctorates from Ain Shams University in Egypt (1990) and Temple University in the United States (1996). He has held various positions at Hartford Seminary, Connecticut, including as visiting professor in Islamic law and deputy director of the Macdonald Center for the Study of Islam and Christian–Muslim Relations. He has served as Indonesia's foreign minister (1999–2001) and more recently as coordinating minister of social affairs (2004–05). He has also been the chair of Partai Kebangkitan Bangsa (PKB, National Awakening Party), the fourth largest party at the 1999 and 2004 elections.

This extract forms the conclusion to an article on Muslim–Christian relations. In it Alwi Shihab writes that, despite fourteen centuries of contact, hostility rather than amity has been the dominant mode of interaction. He outlines practical steps that can be taken to improve the relationship.

Extract 15-18: Alwi Shihab

Alwi Shihab (1999), 'Hubungan Islam dan Kristen Memasuki Abad 21' [Christian and Muslim Relations on the Eve of the 21st Century], pp. 317–42 in Komaruddin Hidayat and Ahmad Gaus (eds), *Passing Over: Melintasi Batas Agama* [Passing Over: Going beyond the Boundaries of Religion], Gramedia Pustaka Utama Bekerjasama dengan Yayasan Wakaf Paramadina, Jakarta. Extract: pp. 337–40.

Conclusion: The Need for Ethical Dialogue

Because Muslims and Christians have previously lived together as neighbours, greater efforts are needed to build mutual trust. Only at this level can we, as a faith community that has a shared fate and the same humanitarian responsibilities, build a community that is caring. To achieve this, several urgent problems of our times must be solved.

First, one of our failures as members of religious societies in both communities is the tendency to make it possible for religion to be manipulated by religious leaders. It is the moral responsibility of religious leaders to safeguard their religion from misuse and exploitation for narrow political interests. An illustration that is fairly indicative of the phenomenon in the Islamic world is the two Islamic conferences on the [first] Gulf War, one organized by Saudi Arabia and the other by Iraq. Each was motivated by a spirit based on the Qur'an and Hadith, yet they arrived at conflicting conclusions.

Second, what happens more often is that excellent theories and ideas are ignored and are not effective at a practical level. Although Vatican Council II began its declaration on Islam by saying that 'Christians should respect Muslims', the Catholic Church began an ambitious program that went against that position. Thirty years have passed and that noble aim has not been realized within the general community. It is therefore crucial that more strenuous efforts be made so that the spirit of Vatican Council II can truly be felt by people in the street.

Third, in almost every case, both communities are not prepared to engage in self-criticism about their mutual existence, but tend to be defensive when facing an approaching conflict and unpleasant reality. To bring such a difficult situation to an end, it would make good sense to establish a committee or representative group that is prepared to act as a mediator in the context of improving mutual understanding. This may be utopian, but it is crucial in a situation in which both communities are increasingly challenged by the same global problems.

Fourth, any process of dialogue supposes an equal relationship in which both communities accept and respect each other on agreed terms. In the context of Muslim–Christian dialogue this equality must be seen as desirable. There are [only a] few Muslims who know a great deal about Christianity and who can engage in dialogue with equal knowledge. This is a gap that must be bridged by Muslims so that dialogue may guide individual members of both communities. Moreover, it is very saddening that Christian missionary activists are dominated at this time by evangelicals who cannot accept the reality of religious pluralism. Similarly, the majority of active Muslim proselytizers are those who feel that the only religion that is acceptable in the sight of God is Islam; they do not understand it to mean human religious feeling and total surrender to God. In the light of this reality, conflict is bound to occur. What is happening here is that many people do not value dialogue, because they see inter-religious dialogue as no more than an inter-religious tea party at which everyone tries to behave as well as possible without being prepared to touch on significant religious issues.

Fifth, undeniably one of the greatest obstacles to building Christian–Muslim relations is ideas about proselytizing. Both Islam and Christianity are committed to this. Muslims are obliged to invite humanity to enter Islam, and likewise Christianity must spread the faith to humanity to enter the way of salvation through Christ. All issues rest on how both communities implement their mission precisely and with respect for human nobility while avoiding open or covert manipulation.

Therefore it is very urgent that both communities work together to conduct their missions based on common ethical principles or a code of conduct whose implementation is agreed jointly. Ideally, proselytizing or missionary work should change in a qualitative sense from the old paradigm of the invitation [to enter Islam] or the baptism of Christians, to bringing people to surrender to God. In other words, missionary work and proselytizing should take the form of a mutual exchange of views and not [be conversion by] force.

Finally, noting the reality that Islam now constitutes a part of actual society in north America and Europe, just as Christianity constitutes a part of actual society in India, Pakistan and Indonesia, it is important that those of us who are thinking hard about the future free ourselves from the tendency to think in terms of a dichotomy between 'Middle Eastern Islamic civilization' on the one hand and 'Western Christian civilization' on the other. There is now only one world in which Muslims and Christians live together everywhere.

It is therefore essential for both communities to realize that they are close to each other, in the face of the challenges of moral degeneration, cynicism and unbelief that are manifest in our social, political and cultural environment. When both communities can lift themselves above the old history of hostility and step out towards an acknowledgement of commonly held concerns, this will open the way for the Muslim and Christian *ummah* to enter the new century.

M. Istijar

> ***Commentary*** The celebration of Christmas in Indonesia has long been a controversial subject among Islamic scholars. At least since the 1960s, ulema have debated whether Muslims should acknowledge Christmas through such acts as wishing Christian acquaintances 'Merry Christmas', exchanging gifts or attending Christmas-related events. MUI, for example, has repeatedly warned Muslims against involvement in Christmas-related activites. There have also been attacks on churches at Christmas time, the most notorious being the coordinated bombings of more than 30 churches across Indonesia on 24 December 2000, resulting in the deaths of 19 people.
>
> The following extract from a *Buletin al-Tasamuh* article by M. Istijar is based on interviews with several prominent Muslim leaders about the permissibility of wishing Christians a happy Christmas. Istijar is a young journalist with the Jakarta daily newspaper *Harian Warta Kota* [News of the City Daily]. Whereas extract 15-18 by Alwi Shihab discusses the principles of interaction between Christians and Muslims, this extract deals with the actual practice of interfaith relations, presenting views for and against.

Extract 15-19: M. Istijar

M. Istijar (2002), 'Mengucapkan Selamat Natal: Implementasi Rahmatan li al-'alamin' [Saying Happy Christmas: Implementing Compassion for all Humankind], *Buletin al-Tasamuh*, 27(27 December), Lingkar Studi-Aksi untuk Demokrasi Indonesia, Jakarta. Extract: pp. 2–4.

The debate about the question of whether the Muslim community may or may not say happy Christmas to those who celebrate it is always coming up. It is as though the issue remains the subject of a never-ending debate. So far, the issue has focused on two views. The *first* states that to express greetings marking a religious celebration like Christmas is permissible. This view is put forward by Komaruddin Hidayat, professor at the State Islamic University of Syarif Hidayatullah Jakarta. Komaruddin says that expressing greetings to mark a day of [religious] celebration is valid. Saying happy Christmas is basically a form of people-to-people relations, *habluminannas* [Ar.: *hablun minan-naasi*]. This is the same as when we celebrate a birthday, begin a new [stage of] life and so on. Christmas is a very special day, like the celebration of Idul Fitri by the Muslim community. Thus it is permissible, in order that the ties of brotherhood between humans may be strengthened. […]. The ulema of al-Azhar [university] in Egypt and Imam Khomeini in Iran often issued greetings to mark the holy days of other faiths.

The *second* view states that expressing greetings to celebrate Christmas is not permissible. Hidayat Nur Wahid, president of the Justice Party [PK], says that the Islamic community is not permitted to say happy Christmas. Because if we say happy

Christmas to Christians it is as if we are acknowledging that Jesus Christ – translated into Arabic as the Prophet Isa the Messiah, son of Mary – was born on 25 December. Christmas is not only a celebration of a birth as we celebrate Maulid Nabi, the birthday of the Prophet Muhammad, blessings and peace be upon him, but also an obligatory act of devotion performed by the Christian community. According to him [Hidayat Nur Wahid], when we say happy Christmas we are also acknowledging Christian teachings. This does not mean that the Muslim community is intolerant, that it does not respect different religions, but rather that this is stated in sharia law.

Hidayat Nur Wahid agrees with the fatwa issued in 1981 by the Indonesian Council of Ulama (MUI) chaired by K.H. M. Sukry Ghozali, which forbade the Muslim community from joining in celebrations, including saying happy Christmas to those who celebrate it.

In contrast to the two leaders above, Hasyim Muzadi[37] (chair of the Central Board of NU) is of the opinion that the Islamic community should respect Christmas celebrations by those who celebrate it. This respect is a form of social interaction, or people-to-people relations. The aim of this is to nurture and strengthen ties of goodwill between different religions. The fatwa issued by MUI in 1981 was really to strengthen and revitalize the Muslim community.

The 1981 MUI fatwa also mentions that participating in Christmas celebrations with those who celebrate it indicates that we are of the same faith as them. Komaruddin Hidayat is of the opinion that there are two choices that can be made. *First*, if we are convinced that our faith does not change when we offer Christmas greetings or form a Christmas committee or join celebrations in church, and if we stay convinced, then we may do it.

But if we feel that what we do may shake our faith and our belief in our religion, then it is best if we do not do it, but this should be conveyed politely. Joining in should not be interpreted as believing.

Differing interpretations about the date of the birth of Jesus Christ or Isa the Messiah constitute the basis for differing ways of worship between the Muslim and Christian communities. Isa the Messiah or Jesus Christ is a prophet in the Qur'an (Qur'an 3: 45–47).[38] Actually Christians know that 25 December is just an approximation of the birthdate of Jesus Christ. Just as the birth date of the Prophet Muhammad is also an approximation, only closer, because at that time there was no calendar, added Komaruddin Hidayat.

The ulema also agree that there are many things that can be done by the Muslim community to strengthen mutual goodwill, such as joint social-service activities and voluntary activities to clean up the roads or neighbourhood. In every aspect of life

---

37   In addition to his role as chair of NU since 1999, Hasyim Muzadi (1944–) is a prominent advocate of interfaith dialogue and 'moderate' Islamic doctrines.

38   'The angels said, "Mary, God gives you news of a Word from Him, whose name will be the Messiah, Jesus, son of Mary, who will be held in honour in this world and the next, who will be one of those brought near to God. He will speak to people in his infancy and in his adulthood. He will be one of the righteous". She said, "My Lord, how can I have a son when no man has touched me?" [The angel] said, "This is how God creates what He will: when He has ordained something, He only says, 'Be', and it is"' (Q3: 45–7, Haleem).

we can help one another, visit friends of different religions. Such behaviour nurtures harmony and religious reconciliation.

Nurcholish Madjid

> ***Commentary*** In the four years following Soeharto's resignation in 1998, Indonesia experienced a wave of sectarian violence. The most severe conflicts occurred in Ambon (Maluku), Western and Central Kalimantan, and Poso (Central Sulawesi), where thousands died in brutal Muslim–Christian violence, but a number of other areas were also subject to violence on a lesser scale. In addition, the number of attacks on places of worship, most commonly churches but also mosques and Hindu temples, rose dramatically. At the height of this violence, Nurcholish Madjid wrote the following appeal for religious tolerance in which he sets out what he sees as the inherently pluralist nature of Islam.

Extract 15-20: Nurcholish Madjid

Nurcholish Madjid (2001), 'Pendahuluan: Etika Beragama dari Perbedaan menuju Persamaan' [Introduction: Religious Ethics from Difference to Similarity], pp. 1–8 in Nur Ahmad (ed.), *Pluralitas Agama: Kerukunan dalam Keragaman* [Religious Plurality: Harmony in Diversity], Penerbit Buku Kompas, Jakarta. Extract: pp. 1–6.

> '*Do not quarrel with followers of (other) scriptures except in the best way (for example, good manners, tolerance) [and] unless there are those of them who are unjust. And say, "We believe in teachings (scriptures) revealed to us and revealed to you. My God and your God are one, and we (all) submit to Him".*' (QS *al-Ankabut*/29:46)[39]

This is being written at a time when our nation is confronting major problems that have yet to be completely resolved. These weigh heavily on our minds. One of those major problems is the fact that we have recently been unfortunate enough to witness a troubling of the atmosphere of interfaith relations in our homeland, to the extent that many lives, as well as respect and property, have been lost. Indonesians are rightly proud – and respected by others – as being a people who possess a very high level of religious tolerance and harmony. However, the intensity of the recent conflict in our society, which is thought to have involved religious adherents in a level of atrocity that is difficult to comprehend, makes it reasonable to pose the question, 'Is there some way to bring together the faiths in this country so that they (the religious communities) do not have to destroy each other?' […]

The words of God quoted at the start of this piece clearly prohibit the Islamic community from creating conflict with adherents of other scriptures, unless it is done in the best possible way, including ensuring politeness and tolerance, except towards those who act unjustly. The Islamic community is, moreover, commanded to stress

---

39   '[Believers], argue only in the best way with the People of the Book, except with those of them who act unjustly. Say, "We believe in what was revealed to us and in what was revealed to you; our God and your God are one [and the same]; we are devoted to Him".' (Q29: 46, Haleem).

always that all of us, the followers of different scriptures, together worship the One Almighty God, and together surrender ourselves unto Him.

In fact, even if we think that we know for certain that other people are praying to an object that is not the One Almighty God, we are still forbidden from behaving improperly towards those people. According to the Qur'an, such an attitude will cause them to attack us and act equally disrespectfully towards the One Almighty God, as a consequence of this ill-informed hostility. Even towards those who carry out such attacks and behave impropery, we must still preserve good worldly social relations. The words [of the Qur'an] apply here: '*For you, your religion; for me, my religion*' (QS *al-Kafirun*/109:6).[40]

This quotation is not a question of lack of concern for other faiths, let alone a loss of hope; rather it is driven by an awareness that religion cannot be coerced, and that each person, regardless of their faith, must be respected as a fellow creature of the One Almighty God. […]

One God, Different Paths
The basic view is that the One Almighty God has determined the idiom, means, method and path for each group of human beings, so that it is wrong if there is mutual repudiation between fellow humans or coercion by one to make others follow their idiom, means, method or path. Instead, human beings should start out from their respective positions, then compete with each other to achieve the greatest good. God commanded:

> '*And We (God) reveal to you (Muhammad) the scripture (the Qur'an) as support for the truth of the scriptures that preceded it and to support this scripture. So implement law (wise teachings) among them in accordance with what has been revealed by God and do not follow the desires of those who are distant from the truth that has come to you. To everyone among you (all humankind) we show the path to the truth and the way to implement it. If God had so wished, He would certainly have made you all (all human beings) a single group. But ([He] made various ones) so that He could test you all according to the things (ways and methods) that have been bestowed on you. So compete to do good. And God alone is the place of return. Later He will explain to you the things that you disagree on.*' (QS *al-Maidah*/5:48).[41]

Such is the teaching regarding relations and social intercourse based on the view that each religion strives for the truth through its own means and path. So it is hoped that religious people will wholeheartedly understand and carry out that religious command without any sense of being incited or intimidated, let alone repudiated. Because of that, a religious attitude that is inclusive (open) to each individual religious community is a pressing necessity that we need to constantly seek to realize peacefully in this plural republic.

---

40 'you have your religion and I have mine' (Q109: 6, Haleem).
41 'We sent to you [Muhammad] the Scripture with the truth, confirming the Scriptures that came before it, and with final authority over them: so judge between them according to what God has sent down. Do not follow their whims, which deviate from the truth that has come to you. We have assigned a law and a path to each of you. If God had so willed, He would have made you one community, but He wanted to test you through that which He has given you, so race to do good: you will all return to God and He will make clear to you the matters you differed about' (Q5: 48, Haleem).

That each religious adherent is expected to carry out his or her religious teachings seriously, in keeping with the teachings of the prophets, is, according to the Islamic perspective, valid. *'Truly'*, said God, *'We (God) have revealed the Torah, in which is the guidance and the light, and in that book the prophets who submitted to God implemented laws for those who followed Judaism, also the Rabbis and ulema who followed the Book of God that they upheld and who bore witness to that book'* (QS al-Maidah/5:44).[42]

So this command of God shows very firmly that even Jews, if they carry out their faith properly as taught by the prophets who submitted their fate to God (*pasrah*), will also be regarded as being among the people who have *submitted to their fate* (*muslim*). Therefore, the continuation of this verse warns Jews who do not practise their faith in accordance with God's law that it is precisely they who will be classed as infidels (rejecting the truth), because they are not people who submit to fate. *'Do not fear fellow humans'*, God urged, *'and do not fear Me, and do not sell My words cheaply. Whosoever does not carry out the law revealed by God is an infidel (rejects the truth)'*. Detailed laws were revealed to the Jews as well, such as that an eye must be paid for with an eye, a nose with a nose, and an ear with an ear. They must do all this; if they do not, they will be classed as unjust (QS al-Maidah/5:45).[43]

As we know, the Torah was revealed to the Jews by God through the Prophet Moses, peace be with him, and the other prophets who directly followed him. Then God sent Jesus the Messiah with the Gospels (the Glad News). The followers of Jesus Christ referred to the Gospels as the 'New Testament', to accompany the Torah which they called the 'Old Testament'. The Jews did not acknowledge Jesus the Messiah or his Gospels, and rejected the idea of having both an Old Testament and a New Testament; the Qu'ran, however, acknowledges the authority of both. The Qur'an insists that the Gospels that God revealed to the Prophet Jesus the Messiah affirmed the truth of the Torah, containing guidance and illumination as well as advice for pious people. They [the Jews] must acknowledge that fact; if not, they will be classed once again as godless people (inclined to evil) (QS al-Maidah/5:46–7).[44]

A command of God to all followers of scripture everywhere declares that if they are truly people of faith and piety, God will forgive them all their sins and send them the eternal joys of heaven. Later, another command to Jews and Christians – which

---

42 'We revealed the Torah with guidance and light, and the prophets, who had submitted to God, [and] the rabbis and the scholars all judged according to it for the Jews in accordance with that part of God's Scripture which they were entrusted to preserve, and to which they were witnesses. So [Children of Israel] do not fear people, fear Me; do not barter away My messages for a small price; those who do not judge according to what God has sent down are rejecting [God's teachings]' (Q5: 44, Haleem).

43 'In the Torah We prescribed for them a life for a life, an eye for an eye, a nose for a nose, an ear for an ear, a tooth for a tooth, an equal wound for a wound: if anyone forgoes this out of charity, it will serve as atonement for his bad deeds. Those who do not judge according to what God has revealed are doing grave wrong' (Q5: 45, Haleem).

44 'We sent Jesus, son of Mary, in their footsteps, to confirm the Torah that had been sent before him: We gave him the Gospel with guidance, light, and confirmation of the Torah already revealed – a guide and lesson for those who take heed of God. So let the followers of the Gospel judge according to what God has sent down in it. Those who do not judge according to what God has revealed are lawbreakers' (Q5: 46–7, Haleem).

directly or indirectly shows a recognition of the existence of their religion and teachings – promises abundant prosperity from above (the sky) and from beneath their feet (the earth) if they truly uphold the teachings of the Torah and the Gospels along with the teachings that God has revealed to them (QS *al-Maidah*/5:66).[45]

Meanwhile Muslims, who in this country are the largest religious community, are taught to believe in the Torah and the Gospels in addition to the Book of Psalms, which was revealed by God to the Prophet David, peace be upon him, as well as other holy books. In this matter, we can conclude from God's confirmation to the Prophet Muhammad, may God's blessings and peace be upon him, that he had to believe in any holy book that was revealed to humankind by God. This attitude is expressed in the combination of basic guides to relations with those religions that existed at that time, that is, the religions based on the holy texts revealed by Almighty God to those who lived at the same time as the Prophet, may God's blessings and peace be upon him (QS *an-Nahl*/16:26).[46]

We should foster the attitude to truth that he [the Prophet] provides to develop our plural society and nation. Regardless of differing religious means, methods or paths to God, the God we want to approach is nonetheless the same God, the One Almighty God. God to whom all hands extend to gain His protection. God from whom all the lowly seek His glory, and yearn for His ease for all their difficulties. That is the God of all humankind, without exception.

Zainah Anwar

> ***Commentary*** Marriage between individuals of different faiths is a complex issue for Muslims. The Qur'an does not permit marriage between Muslims and non-Muslims[47] and a Muslim woman may only marry a Muslim man.[48] The Qur'an does permit Muslim men to marry women 'of the Book', that is, Jews or Christians.[49]

---

45 'If they had upheld the Torah and the Gospel and what was sent down to them from their Lord, they would have been given abundance from above and from below: some of them are on the right course, but many of them do evil' (Q5: 66, Haleem).

46 'Those who went before them also schemed, but God attacked the very foundations of what they built. The roof fell down on them: punishment came on them from unimagined directions' (Q16: 26, Haleem).

47 'Do not marry idolatresses until they believe: a believing slave woman is certainly better than an idolatress, even though she may please you. And do not give your women in marriage to idolaters until they believe: a believing slave is certainly better than an idolater, even though he may please you. Such people call [you] to the Fire, while God calls [you] to the Garden and forgiveness by His leave. He makes His messages clear to people, so that they may bear them in mind' (Q2: 221, Haleem).

48 'You who believe, test the believing women when they come to you as emigrants – God knows best about their faith – and if you are sure of their belief, do not send them back to the disbelievers: they are not lawful wives for them, nor are the disbelievers their lawful husbands. Give the disbelievers whatever dowries they have paid – if you choose to marry them, there is no blame on you once you have payed their dowries – and do not yourselves hold on to marriage ties with disbelieving women. Ask for repayment of the dowries you have paid, and let the disbelievers do the same. This is God's judgement: He judges between you, God is all knowing and wise' (Q60: 10, Haleem).

49 'Today all good things have been made lawful for you. The food of the People of the Book is lawful for you as your food is lawful for them. So are chaste, believing, women as well as chaste women

In Malaysia and Indonesia, laws regulating inter-religious marriage have been enacted. In 1973, the New Order government in Indonesia introduced a Marriage Bill that among other things aimed to restrict polygamy and permit inter-religious marriage. This met with widespread protest from Muslims who believed that the bill was an attempt to secularize laws for Muslims. It was also believed that the bill facilitated Christianization, because Muslims would have to abandon their faith to marry Christians. The level of protest forced the New Order government to amend the bill in 1974 but the status of inter-religious marriage remains unclear. In Indonesia, non-Muslims (and only non-Muslims) may marry at the civil registry.

In Malaysia, the situation is clear: Muslims can only marry Muslims, with implications that are set out in the extract that follows. Zainah Anwar is executive director and one of the founding members of the Malaysian non-government organization Sisters in Islam. It was founded in 1987 to act as an advocate for women's rights within an Islamic framework and to work for equality, justice and democracy for all Malaysian Muslims, especially women.

Extract 15-21: Zainah Anwar

'Feminist Islam', excerpt from the transcript of an interview with Zainah Anwar conducted by Terry Lane [in English], 'In the National Interest', Radio National, Australian Broadcasting Corporation, <http://www.abc.net.au/rn/talks/natint/stories/s915192.htm>, dated August 2003, accessed 20 September 2004.

Zainah Anwar: [...] Now you have other groups, you have other women's groups, human rights groups, individual scholars, intellectuals, who are now engaging in this debate, if not at least you know coming to our – we have monthly study sessions at our office, and people of other faiths, men, are coming to the study sessions.

Terry Lane: Of other faiths?

Zainah Anwar: Yes, you know, Christians, Hindus, who are interested in knowing Islam better, in understanding Islam better so that they can speak out and claim their right as a citizen of Malaysia to engage in this debate: What Islam? Whose Islam is the right Islam? Because for them, even though the Islamic parties say that these religious laws, Islamic laws, will not govern the lives of many Muslims, of course they will be affected, if they are to live in an Islamic State.

Terry Lane: I'm thinking[,] particularly in a situation where a Muslim is married to a non-Muslim, the tensions must be terrific.

Zainah Anwar: Well actually a Muslim cannot marry a non-Muslim. In Malaysia the non-Muslim has to convert to Islam, and when you have an Islamic party that wants to introduce the death penalty for apostasy for those who leave Islam and the breakdown of the divorce rate among Muslims is very high, are you going to – that Chinese woman who converts to Islam in order to marry a Muslim and upon divorce,

---

of the people who were given the Scripture before you, as long as you have given them their dowries and married them, not taking them as lovers or secret mistresses. The deeds of anyone who rejects faith will come to nothing and in the Hereafter he will be one of the losers' (Q5: 5, Haleem).

she wants to leave the religion to go back to her family and her support system, are you going to send her to death because she wants to leave the religion? So these are the kinds of debate.

Terry Lane: And is that a serious threat?

Zainah Anwar: Well, it is in the law, it is in the Hudud law of Kelantan and Terengganu [even though] these laws cannot be implemented.[50]

Terry Lane: So it's really only federal control stopping these laws being implemented by a couple of States?

Zainah Anwar: Yes, that's right. If they want to challenge the constitution they can still go ahead and implement that law, but that would lead to a constitutional crisis and the federal government will have to take action. But yes, these laws are already on the statute books of two states in Malaysia, but they just don't have the power to implement these laws. So the concern is, what if the Islamic party were to win power at the federal level, and control the federal government, and the impact that this will have on everyone, not just Muslims, but also on non-Muslims, even though they say that 'Don't worry, these laws will not affect you'. Of course it will affect you.

Terry Lane: Is it a serious possibility?

Zainah Anwar: No, I don't think so, I don't think they can win absolute control …

Terry Lane: Because as I understand it, the two states which have PAS governments are in fact the states where the other racial groups, the Chinese and Indians, have a small representation in those states, so these are predominantly Malay states.

Zainah Anwar: Yes over 90% Malay Muslim in these states, and they are the more traditional states of Malaysia.

Hidayat Nur Wahid

> ***Commentary*** The preceding section includes two extracts (15-12 and 15-13) representing some of the more sectarian aspects of PKS's internal discourse. PKS regards itself as religiously tolerant, however, and it has a good record of accommodating and cooperating with non-Muslim and non-Islamist groups. More than 30 of its legislative candidates in the 2004 general election were non-Muslim and the party chose non-Muslim running mates in several key local elections in 2005.
>
> The following extract gives an indication of the diversity and complexity of views within PKS on interfaith issues. H.M. Hidayat Nur Wahid (1940–) is the best known of the party's current leaders and intellectuals. He is a former PK/PKS president (2000–04); since 2004 he has been the chair of Indonesia's supreme decision-making body, the Majelis Permusyawaratan Rakyat (MPR, People's Consultative Assembly). After

---

50   The Malaysian states of Kelantan and Terengganu have drafted sharia law bills that include penalties for apostasy. However, because the ninth schedule of the federal constitution does not allow criminal law to be legislated by the states, the Kelantan and Terengganu bills cannot be implemented.

studying at the famous Gontor Pesantren in East Java and the State Islamic Institute Sunan Kalijaga in Yogyakarta, he continued his education in Saudi Arabia, gaining his PhD from the Islamic University in Medina in 1992. Before entering practical politics, he worked as an academic at various institutions, including the State Islamic University Syarif Hidayatullah Jakarta. In the article from which the extract is drawn, Hidayat examines the thinking of classical Islamic scholars on the matter of interfaith relations and concludes that Islam should be regarded as tolerant of other religions but not pluralistic.

Extract 15-22: Hidayat Nur Wahid

Hidayat Nur Wahid (2004), 'Islam dan Pluralisme Agama: Perspektif Pemikiran Islam Klasik' [Islam and Religious Pluralism: The Perspective of Classical Islamic Thought], pp. 41–63 in *Mengelola Masa Transisi: Menuju Masyarakat Madani* [Managing the Transition Period: Towards Civil Society], Penerbit Fikri, Jakarta. Extract: pp. 59–63.

[The article begins with a detailed survey of classical opinions on religious pluralism. Hidayat states that the Qur'an makes it clear that the only 'claim of truth' that Muslims recognize is that of Islam, and that the Qur'an also rejects the 'claim of salvation' put forward by Jews and Christians (pp. 42–3). He also writes that adherents of each religion are convinced that their faith possesses the ultimate truth, but that this should be upheld in a mutually respectful manner (pp. 52–3).]

Islam and Religious Tolerance

Based on the references of classical Islamic thinkers to the Qur'an and the Sunnah, as well as to the behaviour of the Rightly Guided Caliphs, even though classical Islamic thinkers reject religious teachings other than Islam and do not recognize the concept of religious pluralism, they place great importance on religious tolerance, on living in harmony, on mutual respect and cooperation to develop civilization and social life. There are several intellectual bases for why, without the pluralism factor, Islamic thinkers were convinced of the need for religious tolerance as well as its realization. Among them are:

1. Islamic ideology teaches respect for human beings. As was stressed by God in His command:

[verse in Arabic script]

'*We have honoured the children of Adam.*' (QS. Al-Isra: 70)[51]

2. Many verses in the Qur'an state that the obligation of the Prophet, blessings and peace be upon him, is only to inform, not to coerce. God decreed:

[verse in Arabic script]

---

51 'We have honoured the children of Adam and carried them by land and sea. We have provided good sustenance for them and favoured them specially above many of those We have created' (Q17: 70, Haleem).

'So, give warning to them; indeed you are the admonisher but not the one who controls them.' (QS. Al-Ghasyiyah: 21–23)[52]

The Qur'an also stresses religious freedom unambiguously, because that is indeed the truth of Islam itself.

3. There are verses in the Qur'an that mention that, besides the existence of an obligation to preach using Qur'anic means, there are religious differences that are also part of God's will, which indeed gives the freedom to choose (QS. Al-Kahfi: 28 and Yunus: 89).[53]

4. There are verses in the Qur'an that instruct us to be just to everyone, including non-Muslims. The Qur'an also commands us to be of noble character, even towards polytheists (QS. al-Maidah: 8).[54]

5. There are various testaments of the Prophet, blessings and peace be upon him, regarding the Ahlu Dzimmah,[55] as well as the good example that he practised in his relations with the People of the Book, even with polytheists. He emphasized this in the statement:

[quotation in Arabic script]

'Certainly they have rights like the rights of Muslims, and [they] also have responsibilities like the responsibilities of Muslims.'

Providing a good example of tolerance was then undertaken by the Rightly Guided Caliphs [...]. Because of that, in addition to practising the principle of tolerance towards the Ahlu Dzimmah, the classical Islamic thinkers – especially the jurisprudents – often defended the interests of the People of the Book and the Ahlu Dzimmah. [pp. 59–60] [...].

[Hidayat then offers historical cases of three Islamic scholars – Abu Yusuf al-Qadhi, Ibnu Hazm and Ibnu Taimiyah – who exemplified this principle of tolerance.]

In this kind of tolerant thinking, even non-Muslim groups who live within Islamic society have a number of rights in common with those of Muslims, such as the right to work, the right to [free] speech, the right to learn, the right to govern and the right

---

52 'So [Prophet] warn them: your only task is to give warning, you are not there to control them. As for those who turn away and disbelieve, God will inflict the greatest torment upon them. They will finally come before Us' (Q88: 21–3, Haleem).

53 'Be steadfast along with those who pray to their Lord morning and evening, seeking His approval, and do not let your eyes turn away from them out of desire for the attractions of this worldly life: do not yield to those whose hearts We have made heedless of Our Qur'an, those who follow their own low desires, those whose ways are unbridled' (Q18: 28, Haleem).

   'God said, "Your prayers are answered, so stay on the right course, and do not follow the path of those who do not know".' (Q10: 89, Haleem).

54 'You who believe, be steadfast in your devotion to God and bear witness impartially: do not let hatred of others lead you away from justice, but adhere to justice, for that is closer to awareness of God. Be mindful of God: God is well aware of all that you do' (Q5: 8, Haleem).

55 The Ahlu Dzimmah (Ar.: *ahludh-dhimmati*), or *dhimmi*, are the non-Muslim minorities protected by Islamic law (see introduction to this chapter).

to property, even possessions that are prohibited by Islam but allowed by their own religious laws. They also have places of worship in keeping with their own religious teachings. [p. 62] [...]

Thus we can conclude that classical Islamic thinking was utterly convinced that there is an absolute truth, namely Islam, that guarantees salvation both in this world and in the hereafter. Because of this, it does not acknowledge the principle of pluralism. However, at the same time, and drawing on the same ideological understanding, it places great importance on tolerance of other religions. On that basis, it very much accepts the reality of religious pluralism and the diversity of religious communities. Together with non-Muslims, the Islamic community builds on the teachings and civilization that are able to spread Islamic values as compassion for all humankind (*rahmatan lil al-alamin*). [p. 63]

Majelis Ulama Indonesia (MUI)

> ***Commentary*** MUI is a government-sponsored peak forum of ulema representing all of the major Islamic groups in Indonesia. It was established by the Soeharto regime in 1975 and operates under the aegis of the Department of Religious Affairs. According to to its website, its purpose is to 'bring together ulema, lay Muslim leaders and intellectuals and unite the movement and actions of the Islamic community'. MUI's decisions are not binding on the Islamic community but are intended as a guide. Historically, its role has often been controversial. During the Soeharto period it was frequently accused of being a compliant tool of the regime; since the late 1990s, its critics have alleged that it has become a bastion of conservative thinking – a charge MUI leaders deny. One of MUI's most controversial recent decisions was to advise Muslims that pluralism, liberalism and secularism were prohibited according to Islamic law. Although condemned by some liberal and mainstream groups, the MUI's 'anti-pluralism' fatwa has also been defended by a wide range of Muslim leaders and organizations. Partai Persatuan Pembangunan (PPP, United Development Party), for example, decided in early 2006 to issue a fatwa on pluralism, liberalism and secularism similar to that of MUI.

Extract 15-23: Majelis Ulama Indonesia (MUI)

Majelis Ulama Indonesia, 'Pluralisme, Liberalisme, Sekularisme Agama' [Pluralism, Liberalism, Religious Secularism], Keputusan Fatwa Majelis Ulama Indonesia, Nomor 7/Munas VII/II/MUI/2005 [Council of Indonesian Ulama, Fatwa Decision No. 7/National Consultation VII/II/MUI/2005], <http://www.majelisulama.com/mui_in/fatwa.php?id=137&PHPSESSID=b4cc4408734c8bbc4b7fe52499e675de>, dated 26–29 July 2005, accessed 12 December 2005.

CONSIDERING:

a. That recently the concepts of religious pluralism, liberalism and secularism along with other similar kinds of concepts have been proliferating within society;

b. That the proliferation of the concepts of religious pluralism, liberalism and secularism in society has given rise to concern, leading a section of society to ask MUI to issue a Fatwa regarding this problem;

c. That because of this, MUI sees the need to issue a Fatwa regarding the concepts of religious pluralism, liberalism and secularism as a guide for the Islamic community. [...]

TAKING NOTE OF: The Opinion of the Session of Commission C on Fatwa of the MUI National Consultation VII 2005.

Placing Our Trust in Almighty God. [...]

DETERMINES: FATWA REGARDING RELIGIOUS PLURALISM ACCORDING TO ISLAM

First: General Stipulation

In this Fatwa, what is meant by

1. Religious pluralism is a concept that teaches that all religions are the same and therefore the truth of each religion is relative; because of that, each religious adherent may not claim that it is only their faith that is right while other faiths are wrong. Pluralism also teaches that all religious adherents will enter and live side by side in heaven.

2. Religious plurality is a reality in that in the nation or in certain regions there exist adherents of various religions who live side by side.

3. Liberalism is understanding authoritative religious texts (the Qur'an and Sunnah) through the use of free reasoning and only accepting religious doctrines that are entirely in keeping with this reasoning.

4. Secularism is separating worldly affairs from religion [which is] only to be used for ordering personal relations with God, while relations between fellow human beings are ordered only on the basis of social contracts.

Second: Legal Stipulation

1. Religious Pluralism, Secularism and Liberalism as defined in the first section are concepts that are contrary to the teachings of Islam.

2. It is prohibited for the Islamic community to follow the concepts of Religious Pluralism, Secularism and Liberalism.

3. On issues of belief and ritual, the Islamic community is obliged to have an exclusive attitude, meaning that it is prohibited to mix the belief and ritual of the Islamic community with the belief and ritual of adherents of other religions.

4. For those in the Muslim community who live with other religious adherents (religious plurality), in social matters that are unrelated to belief and ritual the Islamic community can have an inclusive attitude, meaning that they can continue to socialize with adherents of other religions as long as it is not mutually harmful.

15.2.3   Responses to the 'War on Terror'

Commentary   The attacks of 11 September 2001 on the World Trade Center (WTC) in New York and the Pentagon in Washington DC had a far-reaching impact on the attitudes and policies of major Western nations towards the Muslim world. A key element of this was the Bush administration's declared 'war on terror'. This campaign took a variety of forms, most obviously the conducting of military, intelligence and police operations against terrorist groups, but also including generously funded programs in the Muslim world to promote 'moderate' and tolerant manifestations of Islam. These direct and indirect anti-terrorism measures have drawn differing reactions in Southeast Asia. Many commentators are critical of 'the West', but others are critical of their own groups for not doing more to condemn violence in the name of Islam and to understand the root causes of terrorism.

Irfan Awwas

Commentary   Irfan Suryahardi Awwas (1960–) is a prominent campaigner for the comprehensive implementation of sharia in Indonesia. A student of Gontor Pesantren, he was jailed for thirteen years during the New Order period for distributing 'seditious' material. In 2000, he played a major role in the establishment of the MMI and became chair of its executive. (Plate 13 in the colour section of this book shows him delivering the opening address at an MMI congress in 2003.) He is active as a writer and publisher, and his Wihdah Press has become the main publisher of MMI-related literature. Irfan is a staunch critic of the 'war on terror', seeing it as an instrument in a broader campaign by the West to enervate Islam.

Extract 15-24: Irfan Awwas

Irfan Awwas (2003), 'Pengantar Penerbit' [Publisher's Introduction], pp. v–xiii in H. Luthfi Bashari, *Musuh Besar Ummat Islam: Zionisme, Sekularisme, Jaringan Islam Liberal, Salibisme, Atheisme, Sinkretisme, Oportunisme* [The Islamic Community's Big Enemies: Zionism, Secularism, the Liberal Islam Network, Crusaders, Atheism, Syncretism, Opportunism], Wihdah Press, Yogyakarta. Extract: pp. vi–ix.

The firestorms of anger, hatred and fear of Islam have combined, motivating the US to act not only as the world's police force but also as a butcher that slaughters small states on the basis of unproven accusations. Since the beginning of the twenty-first century America has been the biggest contributor to disorder in the world. The scorched earth campaign in Afghanistan, the attack on Iraq and support for Israel to slaughter the Palestinians are just some examples of this. The US has positioned itself as a dangerous threat to world peace by continuously carrying out political terrorism. As well as using military strength, the US has used democracy and human rights as tools to maintain and carry out its imperialistic penetration, a political system that is aimed at colonizing other states and gaining worldly power and wealth.

On the first anniversary of the attacks on the Pentagon and the WTC building, the US arbitrarily listed the names of international terrorists who then became the targets of revenge operations. It had earlier issued a list of countries which were categorized as an axis of evil: Iran, Iraq, Libya, Sudan and a number of others. In preparation for launching a military attack on Iraq, America even moved the base of its military operations to Qatar. Its reason [for the attack on Iraq] was that Iraq had ignored the resolution of the UN Security Council prohibiting the production of weapons of mass destruction, despite the fact that scores of states around the world have developed chemical, biological and nuclear weapons, including the US and Israel. As well as the accusations above, Saddam Husein's regime was suspected of harbouring Usamah Bin Ladin in the Land of the Thousand and One Nights [Iraq]. However, according to Tariq Aziz, Prime Minister of Iraq, the real reason was that America and Britain wanted to get control of Iraq's oil and redraw the map of the country by destroying the Saddam Husein regime and then replacing it with an American puppet regime.

The closure of the US embassy in Jakarta and in other Asian countries in a way that was *over acting* [in English in original] is clearly part of these terror politics aimed at destroying Indonesia's image. The US wants to show the international world that 'Al-Qaidah cells exist in Indonesia and therefore that the US embassy in Jakarta and the consulate general in Surabaya are at risk of terrorist attacks', explained Ralph L. Boyce, the US Ambassador in Jakarta.

The United States' ambition to eliminate terrorism and its use of anti-humanitarian democracy have revealed its true nature as an imperialist nation. They slaughter human beings and slander many people. They carry out terrifying thought attacks by hurling charges and accusations at the Muslim community. They want to destroy the image of Islam, pervert its teachings, and lead astray and frighten Muslims. The accusations of terrorism directed at Islamic leaders who fight for the implementation of sharia law are clearly meant to repress the struggle to build Islamic supremacy. Every power that opposes US global interests is labelled terrorist, and in this way the US feels that it has the legitimacy to wage war on them and slaughter thousands of human souls. This is considered valid and legal.

Faithfulness to Islam is considered to be the biggest threat to imperialist domination. This is the basis of their attack on the concept of 'Returning to Islam', which they carry out with weapons and money. In every corner of the Islamic world they are busy distancing Muslims from Islam using their evil propaganda. They present Islam as stunted and terrifying by manufacturing false thinking out of Islamic concepts, with the result that there is a huge difference between the real Islam and what they perceive as Islam.

They say that Islam is a reactionary religion that opposes ideas of reform to develop a world civilization in tune with the modern era. Or that Islam is a personal religion only and is not concerned with issues of politics and governance. They have popularized this misguided version of Islam to hide the true teachings of Islam. Their purpose is clear, to prevent Muslims from advancing and creating a proper government that guarantees happiness and provides a proper life for them as human beings.

The false understandings of Islam that have been propagandized so shamefully have unfortunately also influenced and stimulated key figures in Muslim circles. By offering financial largesse, America has snared the participation of certain leaders lured by the power of the West. A section of the educated and elite leaders of Islamic mass social organizations have swallowed the propaganda uncritically, and there are even some who have been willing to become America's stooges and agents of imperialism.

What happened next? The roles that should be played by the infidels have now been replaced by their Muslim agents, which in the West's terminology are called a *proxy force* [in English in original] (intermediaries). The unbelievers, the People of the Book, now feel represented by these proxy force agents, so they do not need to deplete their energy by publishing their despicable propaganda but just supply funds and infidel ideas that are then developed and packaged by their in-country agents. The broadcast of *Different Colours of Islam* on RCTI and SCTV some time ago and the condom advertisements on TPI and Lativi,[56] both the subject of legal appeals by the Mujahideen Council [MMI], are examples of this. They [the TV programs] were actually funded by foreign organizations such as the Asia Foundation and the Ford Foundation, which is a social organization funded by Jews.

Ismail Lutfi Japakiya

> **Commentary** Dr Ismail Lutfi Japakiya is a prominent southern Thai Muslim scholar and leader who trained in Saudi Arabia. The Islamic college he established, Yala Islamic College, is one of the best funded and equipped schools in the 'deep south'. In recent years Lutfi has supported government efforts to repudiate jihadist teachings in Thailand. He was appointed to the National Reconciliation Commission advising the government on ways to reduce the violence in Thailand's southern provinces. The following is a brief extract on the increased 'Islamophobia' after the terrorist attacks on the World Trade Center in New York.

Extract 15-25: Ismail Lutfi Japakiya

Ismail Lutfi Japakiya (2004), *Islam: Sasana Haeng Santiphap* [Islam: A Peaceful Religion], translated from the Arabic into Thai by Chufam Usman, Soon Borigarn Sangkhom, Wittaylai Islam Yala, Pattani [Centre for Social Service, Yala Islamic College, Pattani]. Extract: p. 8.

Since the destruction on September 11 (2001), the world still carries on with the consequences. This unacceptable event for everyone has now become the biggest excuse by the enemies of Allah to light the fire of extended war and suppress Islamic organizations, including all levels of Islamic educational institutes. No exception is made even for strict Muslims who fear God and who are committed to peace. They are accused of being terrorists. It is considered necessary to keep an eye on them

---

56   RCTI, SCTV, TPI and Lativi are all television stations. The *Different Colours of Islam* program was partly funded by US sources.

– they are a danger to the international community and must be destroyed. (Please Allah help us.)

At this time a new word has arisen in the international community, namely 'Islamophobia'. It means fear of Islam. Several methods are used by the West to spread this. Sometimes by exaggerating things; sometimes by twisting the truth and inventing stories.

Abu Ridho

> *Commentary*   Abu Ridho is the pen name of Abdi Sumaithi (1949–), a Muslim intel-
> lectual and leading figure in PK/PKS. Raised in a traditionalist NU family, he rose to
> prominence in the modernist-dominated DDII as a writer, translator and activist. He
> studied Arabic culture at the State Islamic Institute Sunan Kalijaga in Yogyakarta in
> the early 1970s, then undertook a master's degree at Imam Ibn Saud University in
> Riyadh, graduating in 1978. An ardent admirer of the Muslim Brotherhood, he became
> a leading promoter in Indonesia of the organization's thought and practices. He was a
> founding member of PK and entered parliament in 2004; he is currently chair of the
> PKS parliamentary faction. In the following two extracts, he expresses a view widely
> held in Islamist circles that the 'real' terrorists in the world are the United States and
> the Zionists.

Extract 15-26: Abu Ridho

Abu Ridho (2001), *Siapakah Teroris Sesungguhnya* [Who Are the Real Terrorists], Seri Tarbiatuna AR-04, Pustaka Tarbiatuna, Jakarta. Extract: pp. 14–15.

At the moment, the question arises: 'Is it possible for a government to be "terror-ist"?' The United States, at least, would answer 'Yes', although it is not impossible that the state that is currently displaying its imperial muscles, both as a government as well as individually and in groups, has become the champion of world terrorists. This country [...] thinks that there exist in this world terrorist governments that must be treated as transnational criminals. As a result, using standards that it has created itself in keeping with its political, economic and imperial interests, Wash-ington has a list of countries that it says are supporters of international terrorism. [...] Certainly [there are] countries that have been classified by the United States as terrorist states or supporters of terrorists not purely because they have in the past undertaken acts that can be classed as terror or because they have been assessed as harbouring 'terrorists'. Rather, what is more important, according to the American and Zionist view at least, is that those countries do not want to bow to the imperial wishes of the United States. America sees majority Muslim countries in particular as countries that support terrorism when all that they are doing is trying to uphold Islam. For America, a country's upholding of Islam is viewed as a threat to the West. Because of that, any country that strives to implement Islam in its political system, in the view of America, can validly be stamped a 'terrorist' state or a country that protects 'terrorists'.

Extract 15-27: Abu Ridho

Abu Ridho (2001), *Jihad atau 'Terorisme'?* [Holy War or 'Terrorism'?], Seri Tarbiat-una AR-03, Pustaka Tarbiatuna. Extract: pp. 28–9.

Louis IX, the French king, [...] is often mentioned as being one of the first people to call for increased attacks on Islam and Muslim groups, not only conventional attacks through physical war but also cultural assaults. He was very aware that the secret spirit of jihad and the bravery of Islam's soldiers in war were located primarily in Islam's jihad teachings as part of the teachings of Islam itself. In his memoirs, which later became the reference for launching various types of attacks on Islam and Muslims, he noted: 'After going down a long path, now all is very clear for us; the destruction of the Muslim community through conventional warfare is impossible, because they possess a clear system based on the concept of jihad in the path of God (*jihad fi sabilillah*). With that system, they will never be defeated. Because of that, the West must follow another path (not the military path), namely the ideological path of undermining the roots of this system and emptying it of its strength, commitment and valour. The aim is no other than to destroy the basic concepts of Islam'.

Suripto

> *Commentary*   Suripto (1936–) is best known in Indonesia as a commentator on security and intelligence matters. A lawyer by training, he is a former chief of staff at Badan Koordinasi Intelijen Negara (Bakin, State Intelligence Coordinating Agency) (1967–70) and a former secretary-general of the Department of Forestry and Planta-tions (1999–2001). In 2004 he was elected to the national parliament, representing the PKS. In recent years he has gained a high profile as a terrorism analyst. A common theme of his commentaries is that terrorist attacks in Indonesia and other regions of Southeast Asia are part of a conspiracy by Western intelligence agencies to subjugate Islam and force Muslim nations to follow the policy dictates of the United States and other Western nations. The extract below was written shortly after the October 2002 Bali bombings.

Extract 15-28: Suripto

Suripto, S.H. (2003), 'Kata Pengantar' [Foreword], pp. ix–xv in Dedi Junaedi, *Kon-spirasi di Balik Bom Bali: Skenario Membungkam Gerakan Islam* [The Conspiracy behind the Bali Bomb: A Scenario to Silence the Islamic Movement], Bina Wawasan Press, Jakarta. Extract: pp. x–xiv.

As a terrorism analyst, I have striven to analyse the Bali Bomb case using a deductive approach. Taking this deductive analytical approach as a starting point, the bombing incident in Legian, Kuta, Bali, on 12 October 2002 can be presumed to have involved a foreign–international conspiracy. A day after that incident (13 October 2002), John Howard, the Australian Prime Minister, accused al-Qaeda of being the perpetrator. Then, on the same day (as the explanation from the Australian Prime Minister), the

US President, George Walker Bush, said via a CNN TV broadcast that the pattern of the bombing in Bali was similar to the pattern of bombings carried out by Middle Eastern terrorists. Moreover, early on 13 October 2002, Israel's Institute for Counter-Terrorism (ICT) boldly stated that Islamic militants linked to al-Qaeda were definitely behind that sensational attack.

Furthermore, Yael Shahar (an ICT researcher) accused Abubakar Ba'asyir of being the prime suspect. Similarly, in the English press, in *The Guardian* on 15 October 2002, Dr Rohan Gunaratna (the author of the book *Inside Al Qaeda: Global Network of Terror*) drew the conclusion that Indonesia could easily become a terrorist base. In like vein, Singapore's Senior Minister and former Prime Minister Lee Kuan Yew, [...] long before the Bali Bomb incident, had [...] alleged that [Ba'asyir] was a Muslim terrorist leader and the head of Jemaah Islamiah in Southeast Asia. In May 2002, Lee had also said that there were al-Qaeda sleeper cells in Indonesia. This allegation reached a peak with a report in *Time* magazine (17 September 2002) quoting CIA documents. It stated that Umar al-Faruq had admitted that al-Qaeda had twice tried to kill President Megawati Soekarnoputeri. Al-Qaeda was said to have long held ties with radical Islamic groups in Indonesia.

From these statements, both before the Bali Bomb explosion and several days after that event, we gained the impression that a *black propaganda* [in English in original] effort aimed at Indonesia was being launched systematically by foreign countries. It should be understood that *black propaganda* is the preparation and dissemination of false reports that are arranged in such an amazing way that ordinary people will believe those falsehoods to be the truth. Processing news and information in this way is part of the work of intelligence operations.

So the claims and accusations of George Walker Bush, John Howard, Lee Kuan Yew, Rohan Gunaratna, Yael Shahar, *Time* magazine and Israel's Institute for Counter-Terrorism are probably based on reports and information supplied by the intelligence agencies. [...]

If that is the case, what is the background, objective and target of the black propaganda? As is known, initially some Indonesian officials denied the accusation that Indonesia was a terrorism base, even though, before the Bali Bomb incident, bomb explosions had occurred repeatedly in many places. Undoubtedly foreign countries were irritated by these denials because they felt that their black propaganda was not working.

But once the Bali Bomb event happened, especially the horrifying bomb explosion at the Sari Club, the black propaganda that had systemically been carried out until then began to get traction. This means that they [foreign countries] now have strong argumentation and grounds for accusing Indonesia of being a terrorist base in Southeast Asia. At the same time, it is as if they have gained evidence to allege that radical groups like Majelis Mujahidin Indonesia, Front Pembela Islam, Forum [Komunikasi] Ahli Sunnah Wal Jamaah or Laskar Jihad are terrorists.[57] [...]

---

57   That is, MMI, FPI (Islamic Defenders Front), the Ahli Sunnah Wal-Jammah Communication Forum and the Holy War Fighters. All have been accused of having 'links' to terrorist groups such as JI and al-Qaeda (see, for example, Abuza 2003), accusations that they emphatically deny.

In the case of the Bali Bomb, the question now is: who was the architect or instigator of the Bali Bomb explosion? In other words, who was the brains, the intellectual actor or the sponsor of the bombing in Bali? As I have said repeatedly, both in speeches as well as in the print and electronic media, the bomb explosion in Bali was undertaken by professional terrorists of international calibre, not amateurish local terrorists.

Now, based on a deductive analytical process and descriptions of the contents and residue obtained from the bomb that exploded at the Sari Club, there are indications that this was a C-4 type bomb or maybe a type of micro-nuclear SADM [special atomic demolition munition]. And the terrorists who have the potential and capacity to plan as well as carry out such a horrifying bombing presumably [...] are those groups or institutions that are referred to as state terrorism. Well, the ones who are well-known as experts in undertaking state terrorism on an international scale are the CIA (America), Mossad (Israel) and MI-6 (Britain). History already points to evidence of how these intelligence agencies have planned and carried out terror in various countries, such as the CIA in Southeast Asia, Central Asia, Central America and Latin America, Mossad in Africa and the Middle East, [and] MI-6 in the Middle East and Asia (especially in former colonial states). These three world-class intelligence agencies usually work together in their operations. But they can also operate individually. [...]

So the tragic event of 12 October 2002 may have been an operation drafted by intelligence agencies like the CIA, Mossad and MI-6, while its implementation may have been carried out by a group of people in Indonesia who had long been infiltrated and taken advantage of by those intelligence agents.

Anwar Ibrahim

Commentary While most Muslim commentators in Southeast Asia have been critical of the 'war on terror', a number of prominent Islamic leaders have expressed support for the counter-terrorism campaign and called on Muslims to look at what is wrong within their own societies rather than accuse the non-Muslim West of hostility and aggression. One example of this viewpoint is given by the following article, reproduced here in full, by former Malaysian Deputy Prime Minister Anwar Ibrahim (see commentary to extract 15-1 for biographical details). He wrote this piece while in jail for sodomy and corruption offences, convictions that were later overturned on appeal. He argues that the lack of political and social rights in many Muslim nations has contributed to the rise of Islamic terrorism, and warns the West against strengthening cooperation with authoritarian regimes in the name of fighting extremism.

Extract 15-29: Anwar Ibrahim

Anwar Ibrahim, 'Who Hijacked Islam? Repressive Muslim Regimes Are Partly to Blame for Osama bin Laden' [in English], *Time Asia*, <http://www.time.com/time/asia/news/magazine/0,9754,178470,00.html>, dated 8 October 2001, accessed 16 January 2006.

'Let not your hatred of others cause you to act unjustly against them.'
– The Koran[58]

Never in Islam's history have the actions of so few of its followers caused the religion and its community of believers to be such an abomination in the eyes of others. Millions of Muslims who fled to North America and Europe to escape poverty and persecution at home have become the objects of hatred and are now profiled as potential terrorists. The nascent democratic movements in Muslim countries will regress for a few decades as ruling autocrats use their participation in the global war against terrorism to terrorize their critics and dissenters.

This is what Mohamed Atta[59] and his fellow terrorists and sponsors have done to Islam and its community worldwide by their murder of innocents at the World Trade Center and the Pentagon. The attacks must be condemned, and the condemnation must be without reservation. The foremost religious authorities are outraged and have issued statements denouncing the monstrous murders. All efforts to punish the perpetrators must be supported.

One is therefore perturbed by the confusion among Muslims who responded to the attack with a misplaced diatribe against the U.S. In Malaysia, the government-controlled media have been deployed to stir up anti-American sentiments, while members of the political Elite use a different language for international diplomacy. Certainly there are legitimate grievances against the U.S. and good reason for despondency over the fate of the Palestinians, who now face an even more arrogant Israel. But this is not the time for sermonizing or moralizing over U.S. foreign policy. Had we Malaysians been the victims of such a tragedy, we would find such hectoring tasteless and repulsive.

One wonders how, in the 21st century, the Muslim world could have produced an Osama bin Laden. In the centuries when Islam forged civilizations, men of wealth created pious foundations supporting universities and hospitals, and princes competed with one another to patronize scientists, philosophers and men of letters. The greatest of scientists and philosophers of the medieval age, ibn Sina, was a product of that system. But bin Laden uses his personal fortune to sponsor terror and murder, not learning or creativity, and to wreak destruction rather than promote creation.

Bin Laden and his protégés are the children of desperation; they come from countries where political struggle through peaceful means is futile. In many Muslim countries, political dissent is simply illegal. Yet, year by year, the size of the educated class and the number of young professionals continue to increase. These people need space to express their political and social concerns. But state control is total, leaving no room for civil society to grow.

The need for Muslim societies to address their internal social and political development has become more urgent than ever. Economic development alone is clearly insufficient: it creates its own tensions in the social and political spheres, which must be addressed. A proper orientation must be developed for Muslim engagement with

---

58   Q5: 8 is given in footnote 54.
59   Mohammad Atta was one of the key planners of and participants in the 11 September 2001 attacks on the World Trade Center and the Pentagon.

the world at large. Participation in the global processes must not be the monopoly of the government.

It is the sense of alienation and the perception that the world is against them that nurture bitterness among those who resort to terrorism. Confusion and anger against the global order and its only superpower have been brought about by the failure of the Muslim world to address two crucial issues: Afghanistan's descent into chaos and anarchy as a result of the Soviet invasion and the subsequent rise of the Taliban, and the suffering inflicted on the Muslim masses in Iraq by its dictator as well as by sanctions imposed on that long-suffering nation.

For ethical reasons, Muslims will support the global initiative against terrorism. But there is a growing perception that autocrats of all types will seize the opportunity to prop up their regimes and deal a severe blow to democratic movements. Russian President Vladimir Putin will use it to defend atrocities in Chechnya, Israel to defend its intransigence and Malaysia its detentions without trial.

Necessity will prompt the U.S. to seek the collaboration of the governments of Muslim countries. This is understandable. But they do not hold all the answers to terrorism. The growth of democracy, political participation and civil society is the final answer. By softening its endorsement of the struggle for democracy and the protection of human rights, the U.S. will inadvertently strengthen dictatorial regimes, thus replicating past associations with Marcos, Suharto and the Shah of Iran.

For more than 100 years, the Muslim world has had to grapple with the problem of modernity. Of greatest urgency is the effort to inculcate an intellectual and political orientation that promotes democracy and openness. Intellectuals and politicians must have the courage to condemn fanaticism in all its forms. But they must, in the same breath, equally condemn the tyrants and oppressive regimes that dash every hope of peaceful change.

Abd A'la

Commentary Following international acts of Islamist terrorism and violence against adherents of other faiths, some Muslim groups in Southeast Asia have begun to seek the reasons behind acts of violence committed in the name of Islam. They have begun their own 'war against terror' through the promotion of active acceptance of pluralism and condemnation of brute force and violence as solutions to difference and inequality.

Acts of terror and sectarian violence are not new in Indonesia despite the Pancasila principle of belief in the one supreme God which provides the ideological basis for religious pluralism. In an effort to identify the reasons for acts of terror, a number of NGOs and government bodies have been examining the apparent passivity of the Muslim community in responding to the challenges that hard-line interpretations of Islam pose for 'ordinary' Muslims. Just one example is a seminar organized by the Central Board of Fatayat NU (the young women's section of NU), with funding from the Ford Foundation. After the seminar, young NU activists were invited to expand the theme of pluralism and inclusivism into a collection of essays for publication. One of the invited authors was Abd A'la, a lecturer at State Islamic Institute Sunan Ampel in Surabaya and a member of the National Board of the International Center for Islam and Pluralism in

Jakarta. In his chapter, Abd A'la takes a wide-ranging view of the topic. He begins by stating that despite predictions that the death of religion is imminent, the opposite has in fact occurred, and religiosity has increased. With that increase in religiosity has come an escalation of evil and violence, in the face of which religion (Islam) has remained silent or has even been used as the trigger for evil.

Abd A'la refers to the historical roots of pluralism in Islam from the time of the Prophet Muhammad and his Companions. He recognizes that not all Muslims accepted an inclusive approach to Islam, pointing to the Kharajite movement of the late seventh century, which was exclusivist, intolerant of other Muslims and openly hostile to non-Muslims. He asserts that the neo-revivalist (fundamentalist) groups of the nineteenth century developed in reaction to modernity and that a sense of cultural and religious insecurity drove such groups to take a highly defensive and sectarian position. The extract presented here gives Abd A'la's views on how violence and fundamentalism can be countered. In developing his arguments he draws on an eclectic array of contemporary writers on these issues, including Karen Armstrong, Kate Zebiri, Charles Kimball, Bassam Tibi and Fazlur Rahman, as well as Indonesian translations of writings by Khaled Abou El Fadl, John L. Esposito, Martin van Bruinessen, Andrée Feillard and the Iranian intellectual Abdul Karim Soroush. These names, which are just a sample of the sources cited by Abd A'la, provide an indication of the breadth of reading undertaken by some of Southeast Asia's younger generation of Muslims. The extract also indicates the steps these progressive Muslims believe must be taken if violence in the name of religion is to be prevented.

Extract 15-30: Abd A'la

Abd A'la (2005), 'Pluralisme dan Islam Indonesia ke Depan: Ketakberdayaan Umat dan Politisasi Agama sebagai Tantangan' [Pluralism and Indonesian Islam in the Future: The Impotence of the Muslim Community and the Challenge of Politicized Religion], pp. 135–45 in Sururin (ed.), *Nilai-Nilai Pluralisme dalam Islam: Bingkai Gagasan yang Berserak* [Pluralism in Islam: Framing Scattered Concepts], Bandung, Nuansa. Extract: pp. 142–3.

THE FUTURE OF ISLAM AND THE ISLAMIC COMMUNITY IN INDONESIA

If Muhammadiyah and Nahdlatul Ulama can be taken as representative of the Indonesian Muslim community, then the Islam that will develop in Indonesia will have a face that is tolerant, friendly, civil, even pluralist. Besides assuming such a religious form with strong historical roots, both organizations will continue to be committed to efforts to develop humanistic and illuminating religiosity at various levels, both culturally and structurally.

Even so, the existence of fundamentalism (or radicalism or whatever it is called) must not be ignored. The national and international socio-political situation is one of the determining factors in the emergence and spread of this movement. Socio-political conditions that are not conducive [to pluralism], such as repressive states and an unjust international [world] order, will strengthen the existence of fundamentalist movements.

Linked with this, substantial democracy needs to be developed and rolled out at the local and global levels. Through the development of democracy, the government will be expected to take part in collective policies and at the same time respect human rights.[60] Along with this, the external politics of all nations – especially first-world nations – must foster policies that reflect the values just mentioned so that justice and true equality will pervade world affairs.

Linked with that, the development of civil society is something that must be achieved. Without a society that is civilized and self-sufficient, it is very difficult to develop states that are truly democratic. Indeed, what happens is the emergence of states – with all their apparatuses – oriented towards issues of power: to achieve, defend or preserve power, 'whether or not in the name of democracy'.

In its turn, a strong civil society can be expected to extricate society from the backwardness that has trapped it for so long. Backwardness – economic and educational – is a reality experienced by the majority of Muslims in Indonesia at the grassroots level, making them totally powerless. They are easily made the objects of particular interest groups and tools for divisive politics, so that they become victims and scapegoats. Indeed, such conditions provide a real opportunity for them to use religion as a political vehicle to oppose their long-term political exploitation.

In responding to this situation, socio-religious organizations like NU and Muhammadiyah that are the real embryos of civil society in Indonesia need to become proactive in developing such a society. Political practice that at present continues to reflect socio-religious institutions needs to be directed to become a transforming political force that can illuminate society and the nation in general. At the same time, these two major pillars of the Indonesian Islamic community must be more creative, intense and systematic in strengthening the economy and the education of the masses at the grassroots level.

Success in creating conducive conditions [for pluralism] such as those mentioned above constitutes a success for the pluralist Islamic community in fashioning a safe, tranquil and bright future. Similarly, failure to manage this issue would be the beginning of a gloomy future. And that may give rise to all kinds of possibilities, out of all of which violence in the name of religion – explicitly or implicitly – has a strong chance of becoming the dominant phenomenon.

---

60 Here the author provides a footnote referring to Soroush (2002: 184).

Copyright Permissions

Chapter 10

Material reprinted from Saharom Abd Aziz, 'Pengangguran Pelajar Lulusan Agama: Apa Penyelesaiannya?' [Unemployed Religious Studies Students: Is There a Solution?], in *Majalah i*, March 2005, p. 21, by permission of Saharom Bin Abd, the Editor, *Majalah i*; material reprinted from Azyumardi Azra, 'Kebangkitan Sekolah Elite Muslim: Pola Baru "Santrinisasi"' [The Rise of Elite Muslim Schools: A New Pattern of '*Santri*-ization'], in *Pendidikan Islam: Tradisi dan Modernisasi Menuju Milenium Baru* [Islamic Education: Tradition and Modernization Approaching the New Millennium], PT Logos Wacana Ilmu, Jakarta, 1999, pp. 69, 79–80, by permission of PT Logos Wacana Ilmu; material reprinted from Jamal Mohamed U Soe Thien, 'Transcending Rituals: Gearing to Develop Values', in *The Muslim Reader* (Nazry Bahrawi, ed.), 23(1), 2005, pp. 9–10, and material reprinted from Hamka, 'Introducing Tasawwuf' [excerpt from Hamka's Tasauf Moderen, originally published 1939, English translation by Nazri Abdullah], in *The Muslim Reader* (Nazry Bahrawi, ed.), 22(2), 2004, p. 9, by permission of Darul Arqam Singapore; material reprinted from Oman Fathurrahman, '"Menjadi Islam" melalui Seni' ['Becoming Islamic' through Art], in *Buletin al-Tasamuh*, 23, 27 September 2003, pp. 2–4, by permission of Oman Fathurrahman; material reprinted from Margaretha Andi Agus, 'Hijrah Usai Umroh' [Change after the *Umroh*], in *Noor*, 7 December 2004, p. 62, and material reprinted from Leli Nurrohmah, 'Menilik Pendidikan bagi Perempuan' [Looking at Education for Women], in *Noor*, March 2005, p. 103, by permission of *Noor* magazine; material reprinted from Ulil Abshar-Abdalla, '"Over-Moralisasi" dalam Soal Inul: Tentang Tempat Agama dalam Ruang Publik' ['Over-moralization' in the Inul Case: The Place of Religion in the Public Sphere], in FX Rudy Gunawan (ed.), *Mengebor Kemunafikan: Inul, Seks, dan Kekuasaan* [Drilling Hypocrisy: Inul, Sex and Power], Kawan Pustaka and Galang Press, Depok and Yogyakarta, 2003, pp. 143–7, by permission of Galang Press; material reprinted from Anharudin, 'Kesaksian Seorang Anak Petani Muslim' [Testimony of a Farmer's Son], p. 209, and material reprinted from Yudi Latif, 'Dari Islam Sejarah, Memburu Islam Ideal (Mi'raj Tangisan Seorang Kurban Sejarah)' [From Historical Islam, Chasing Ideal Islam (The Tearful Journey of a Victim of History)], pp. 233 and 239–40, and material reprinted from Tb. Furqon Sofhani, 'Antara Serang dan Bandung: Sebuah Pencarian Gagasan' [Between Serang and Bandung: A Search for Ideas], pp. 134–5, and material reprinted from Saiful Muzani, 'Transformasi Ilmu dan Masyarakat: Obsesi Seorang Anak Desa' [The Transformation of Knowledge and Society: A Village Child's Obsession], pp. 158–9, in Ihsan Ali-Fauzi and Haidar Bagir (eds), *Mencari Islam: Kumpulan Otobiografi Intelektual Kaum Muda Muslim Indonesia Angkatan 80-an* [Seeking Islam: Intellectual Autobiographies of Young Indonesian Muslims of the Generation of the 80s], Penerbit Mizan, Bandung, 1990, by permission of Penerbit Mizan; material reprinted from Hamka, 'Pokok Pegangan Hidup Kita' [Our Basic Principles for Living], in

Islam Bidang Aqidah, Ibadah dan Syi'ar Islam' [Elucidation of Qanun of the Province of Nanggroe Aceh Darussalam No. 11 of 2002 Concerning the Implementation of Islamic Sharia in the Fields of *Aqidah, Ibadah* and *Syi'ar Islam*], by permission of Professor Tim Lindsey, Asian Law Centre, University of Melbourne; material reprinted from Anwar Ibrahim (1996), 'Islam in Southeast Asia', in *The Asian Renaissance*, Times Books International, Singapore and Kuala Lumpur, p. 119, by permission of Time Inc.

Chapter 12

Material reprinted from Muhammad Ismail Yusanto, 'Toward the Resumption of an Islamic Way of Life through the Re-establishment of the Caliphate and the Application of Shariah', paper presented at a conference on 'Islamic Perspectives on State, Governance and Society', Canberra, 30–31 August 2004, by permission of Muhammad Ismail Yusanto; material reprinted from Arakan Rohingya Independence Front, 'Why Rohingya Revolution', in *Arakan*, 8, April 1991, by permission of Mr Nurul Islam; material reprinted from Nurcholish Madjid, 'Keharusan Pembaruan Pemikiran Islam dan Masalah Integrasi Umat' [The Necessity of Reform of Islamic Thought and the Problem of the Integrity of the Umat] and 'Menyegarkan Paham Keagamaan di Kalangan Umat Islam Indonesia' [Reinvigorating Religious Understanding within the Indonesian Muslim Community], in Muhammad Kamal Hassan (ed.), *Muslim Intellectual Responses to 'New Order' Modernization in Indonesia*, Dewan Bahasa Dan Pustaka Kementarian Pelajaran Malaysia, Kuala Lumpur, 1980, pp. 188–233, by permission of Dewan Bahasa Dan Pustaka; material reprinted from Hamka, 'Islam Sebagai Basis Negara' [Islam as the Basis of the State], in *Debat Dasar Negara Islam dan Pancasila: Konstituante 1957* [Debate on Islamic and Pancasila-based State: Constituent Assembly 1957], Pustaka Panjimas, Jakarta, 2001, pp. 97–142, by permission of Pustaka Panjimas; material reprinted from Dato' Wan Zahidi Wan The, 'Malaysia Adalah Sebuah Negera Islam', Department of Special Affairs, Ministry of Information, Malaysia, 2001, by permission of the Department of Special Affairs, Ministry of Information, Malaysia.

Chapter 13

Material reprinted from Azis Masyhuri, 'Abortus Menurut Hukum Islam' [Abortion According to Islamic Law], pp. 148–50, and Maria Ulfah Anshor, 'Rumusan Akhir Seminar dan Lokakarya Aborsi dalam Perspektif Fiqh Kontemporer', pp. 263–4, in Maria Ulfah Anshor et al. (eds), *Aborsi dalam Perspektif Fiqh Kontemporer* [Abortion from the Perspective of Contemporary Jurisprudence], Balai Penerbit FKUI, Jakarta, 2002, by permission of Balai Penerbit; material reprinted from Ghafani Awang Teh, 'Suara JAKIM: Agenda Amina Wadud Persenda Hukum Islam' [The Voice of Jakim: Amina Wadud's Agenda in Ridiculing Islamic Law], http://www.islam.gov.my/portal/lihat.php?jakim=120, dated 8 May 2005, by permission of Jabatan Kernajuan Islam Malaysia; material reprinted from Noorzila Jamaludin, 'Hakim Lelaki Pun Emosional' [Even Male Judges Are Emotional], in *Al Islam*, October 2004, pp. 52–5, by permission of Pengarang Majalah Al Islam; material reprinted from Muninggar Sri Saraswati, 'Islamic Law Revision Promotes "Common Sense among Muslims"', http://thejakartapost.com/yesterdaydetail.asp?fileid=20041009.B05, dated 9 October 2004, by permission of the *Jakarta Post*; material reprinted from Sisters in Islam et al., 'Women and Work in Islam', http://www.sistersinislam.org.my/Letterstoeditors/17031999.htm, dated 17 March 1999, and material reprinted from Sisters in Islam, 'What's With the Hijab?', http://www.sistersinislam.org.my/Letterstoeditors/120204.htm, dated 12 February 2004, and material reprinted from Sisters in Islam, *Are Women and Men Equal before Allah*, Kuala

reprinted from Husein Muhammad, 'Adakah Keadilan Gender?' [What Is Gender Justice?], in *Fiqh Perempuan: Refleksi Kiai atas Wacana Agama dan Gender* [Women's Jurisprudence: Reflections by a Religious Leader on the Discourse of Gender and Religion], Lembaga Kajian Islam dan Sosial, Yogyakarta, pp. 6–8, by permission of Lembaga Kajian Islam dan Sosial, Yogyakarta.

Chapter 14

Material reprinted from Salamat Hashim, *The Bangsamoro Mujahid*, Bangsamoro Publications, Mindanao, 1985, pp. 5–6, 14–15, 18–19, by permission of Mohager Iqbal, chairman and chief information officer, Moro Islamic Liberation Front; material from Dr Mohammad Yunus, *Arakan: People, Country and History*, Publicity and Information Department, Rohingya Solidarity Organisation, Arakan, 1988, p. 31, by permission of Mr Nurul Islam; material reprinted from Faqihuddin Abdul Kodir, 'Saatnya Perempuan Pegang Kendali Perjuangan' [It's Time Women Held the Reins of Struggle], in *Swara Rahima*, 4(2), February 2002, pp. 9–15, by permission of *Swara Rahima*.

Chapter 15

Material reprinted from M. Istijar, 'Mengucapkan Selamat Natal: Implementasi Rahmatan li al-'alamin' [Saying Happy Christmas: Implementing Compassion for all Humankind], in *Buletin Al-Tasamuh*, 27, 27 December 2002, pp. 2–4, and material reprinted from Novriantoni, 'Solidaritas untuk Palestina' [Solidarity for Palestine], in *Buletin Al-Tasamuh*, 12, 26 April 2002, pp. 2–4, Lingkar Studi Aksi untuk Demokrasi Indonesia, Jakarta, by permission Mr Anick HT; material reprinted from Nurcholish Madjid, 'Etika Beragama dari Perbedaan menuju Persamaan' [Introduction: Religious Ethics from Difference to Similarity], in Nur Achmad (ed.), *Pluralitas Agama: Kerukunan dalam Keragaman* [Religious Plurality: Harmony in Diversity], Penerbit Buku Kompas, Jakarta, 2001, pp. 1–8, by permission of PT Kompas Media Nusantara; material reprinted from Chandra Muzaffar, 'Tolerance in the Malaysian Political Scene', Syed Othman Alhabshi and Nik Mustapha Nik Hassan (eds), *Islam and Tolerance*, Institute of Islamic Understanding, Kuala Lumpur, 1994 (reprinted 1996), pp. 139–40, 141, 146–8, by permission of the Institute of Islamic Understanding Malaysia; material reprinted from 'Feminist Islam', transcript of an interview with Zainah Anwar, 'In the National Interest', ABC Radio National, <http://www.abc.net.au/rn/talks/natint/stories/s915192.htm>, dated August 2003, by permission of the Australian Broadcasting Commission and ABC online, ©2003; material reprinted from Luthfi Assyaukanie, 'A Battle of Thoughts', http://islamlib.com/en/page.php?page=article&id=692, dated 3 September 2005, by permission of Luthfi Assyaukanie; material reprinted from Ahmad Sumargono, 'Jangan Korbankan Kehormatan Kita Demi 3 Miliar USD' [Don't Sacrifice Our Honour for US$3 Billion], in Ahmad Sumargono, *Saya Seorang Fundamentalis: Refleksi Ideologis H. Ahmad Sumargono* [I am a Fundamentalist: Ideological Reflections of H. Ahmad Sumargono], Global Cita Press, Jakarta, 1999, p. 118, by permission of Global Cita Press; material reprinted from Suripto, S.H., 'Kata Pengantar' [Foreword], in Dedi Junaedi, *Konspirasi di Balik Bom Bali: Skenario Membungkam Gerakan Islam* [The Conspiracy behind the Bali Bomb: A Scenario to Silence the Islamic Movement], Bina Wawasan Press, Jakarta, 2003, pp. x–xiv, by permission of Suripto S.H; material reprinted from Abd A'la, 'Pluralisme dan Islam Indonesia ke Depan: Ketakberdayaan Umat dan Politisasi Agama sebagai Tantangan' [Pluralism and Indonesian Islam in the Future: The Impotence of the Muslim Community and the Challenge of Politicized Religion], in Sururin (ed.), *Nilai-nilai Pluralisme dalam*

Islam: Bingkai Gagasan Yang Berserak [Pluralism in Islam: Framing Scattered Concepts], Bandung, Nuansa, 2005, pp. 142–3, by permission of Penerbit Nuansa; material reprinted from Abu Bakar Ba'asyir, 'Abu Bakar Bas'yir Sermon' (no date), edited translation from 'Four Corners', Australian Broadcasting Commission, <http://www.abc.net.au/4corners/stories/s711753.htm> dated 28 October 2002, by permission of the Australian Broadcasting Commission and ABC online, ©2005; material reprinted from Anwar Ibrahim (1996), 'Islam in Southeast Asia', in *The Asian Renaissance*, Times Books International, Singapore and Kuala Lumpur, pp. 111–15, 122–3, by permission of Time Inc.

Maps

Maps of Southeast Asia, Burma (Myanmar), Cambodia and Vietnam, Indonesia, Malaysia, southern Philippines and southern Thailand reprinted by permission of Coombs Cartographic Services, Research School of Pacific and Asian Studies, College of Asia and the Pacific, Australian National University.

Photos

Photos by Gerhard Jörén, Stu Smucker, Karl Malakunas, Ryan Anson, Alex Baluyut, Mark Fallander and Kemal Jufri by permission of Onasia.com; photos by Steve Raymer by permission of Getty Images; photo by Reza by permission of National Geographic/Getty Images; photo of building in Sulu by permission of Kit Collier, ANU; photos of 'The Burning of Jolo' and Rameer Tawasil by permission of Bobby Timonera; photo of 'Berdzikir bersama Inul' and the artist by permission of K.H. A. Mustofa Bisri and family; photo of Mangkunegaran Mosque by permission of M. Ichsan, Yayasan Binar.

References

Abaza, Mona (2003), 'Indonesian Azharites', *Sojourn*, 18(1): 139–53.

Abdul Hadi Awang (2005), *Hadharah Islamiyyah bukan Islam Hadhari* [Islamized Civilization not Civilizational Islam], Nufair Street Sdn Bhd, Kuala Lumpur.

Abegebriel, A. Maftuh, A. Yani Abeveiro and SR-Ins Team (2004), *Negara Tuhan: The Thematic Encyclopaedia* [God's State: The Thematic Encyclopaedia], SR-Ins Publishing, Yogyakarta.

Abubakar, Irfan (2002), 'Islam and Gender Books Published in Indonesia (1990–2003)', *Jurnal Kultur*, 2(2): 131–48.

Abuza, Zachary (2003), *Militant Islam in Southeast Asia: Crucible of Terror*, Lynne Rienner, Boulder CO.

Adamec, Ludwig W. (2001), *Historical Dictionary of Islam*, Scarecrow Press, Lanham MD and London.

Ahmad Fauzi Abdul Hamid (2004), 'State Monopoly of Religious Orthodoxy: The Case of the Banning of Darul Arqam in Malaysia', paper presented to the 13th Colloquium of the Malaysia Society of Australia entitled 'Globalisation, Islam and Identity in Malaysia and Singapore', Australian National University, Canberra, 26–27 November.

Ahmad Hussein Syed (2000), 'Muslim Politics and the Discourse on Democracy', pp. 74–107 in Francis Loh Kok Wah and Khoo Boo Teik (eds), *Democracy in Malaysia: Discourses and Practices*, Curzon Press/Nordic Institute of Asian Studies, Richmond.

Albritton, Robert (2000), 'Studying Political Diversity among Muslims of Southern Thailand', pp. 377–87 in Isma-ae Alee et al. (eds), *Islamic Studies in ASEAN*, College of Islamic Studies, Prince of Songkla University, Pattani.

Ali, Z. (1991), 'Notes on the Islamic Art of Champa', pp. 123–44 in *Le Campa et le Monde Malais*, Actes de la Conférence Internationale sur le Campa et le Monde Malais, Publications du Centre d'Histoire et Civilisations de la Péninsule Indochinoise, Paris.

al-Qardlawy [al-Qaradawi], Yusuf (1987), *Ijtihad dalam Syari'at Islam: Beberapa Pandangan Analitis tentang Ijtihad Kontemporer* [Ijtihad in Islamic Law: Some Analytical Views on Contemporary Ijtihad], translation by Dr H. Achmad Syathori, PT Bulan Bintang, Jakarta.

Amnesty International (1992), 'Union of Myanmar (Burma): Human Rights Violations against Muslims in the Rakhine (Arakan) State', London, May.

Amnesty International (2004), 'Cambodia: Jemaah Islamiyah Suspects Must All Be Brought to Trial Now', press release, 6 September, <http://news.amnesty.org/index/ENGASA 236092004>, accessed 23 May 2005.

Andaya, Barbara Watson and Yoneo Ishii (1999), 'Religious Developments in Southeast Asia, c. 1500–1800', pp. 164–227 in Nicholas Tarling (ed.), *The Cambridge History of Southeast Asia*, Volume 1, Part 2, Cambridge University Press, Cambridge.

Anwar, Colin and Supalak Karnjonkundi (2004), *Fai Tai: Krai Jut?* [Fires in the South: Who Is Responsible?], Indochina Publishing, Bangkok.

Arasaratnam, Sinnappah (1989), *Islamic Merchant Communities of the Indian Subcontinent in Southeast Asia*, sixth Sri Lanka Endowment Fund lecture delivered at the University of Malaya on 11 October 1989, Kuala Lumpur.

Ariff, Mohamed (1991), 'Introduction', in Mohamed Ariff (ed.), *The Islamic Voluntary Sector in Southeast Asia*, Institute of Southeast Asian Studies, Singapore.

Asia Foundation and ARMM (Department of Education, Autonomous Region in Muslim Mindanao) (2004), *Survey and Directory of Madaris Institutions in the Philippines*, June.

Awwas, Irfan Suryahardi (ed.) (2001), *Risalah Kongres Mujahidin I dan Penegakan Syari'ah Islam* [Proceedings of the First Mujahidin Congress and the Enforcement of Sharia], Wihdah Press, Yogyakarta.

Awwas, Irfan Suryahardi (2003), *Dakwah dan Jihad Abubakar Ba'asyir* [Predication and Jihad of Abubakar Ba'asyir], Wihdah Press, Yogyakarta.

Azra, Azyumardi (2004), *The Origins of Islamic Reformism in Southeast Asia: Networks of Malay–Indonesian and Middle Eastern 'Ulama' in the Seventeenth and Eighteenth Centuries*, Allen & Unwin, Sydney, and University of Hawai'i Press, Honolulu.

Ball, Desmond (2004), *The Boys in Black*, White Lotus, Bangkok.

Barton, Greg (1995), 'Neo-modernism: A Vital Synthesis of Traditionalism and Modernism in Indonesian Islam', *Studia Islamika*, 2(3): 1–75.

Barton, Greg (2003), *Abdurrahman Wahid: Indonesian President, Muslim Democrat*, University of New South Wales Press, Sydney.

Barton, Greg (2004), *Indonesia's Struggle: Jemaah Islamiyah and the Soul of Islam*, University of NSW Press, Sydney.

Baswedan, Anies Rasyid (2004), 'Political Islam in Indonesia: Present and Future Trends', *Asian Survey*, 44(5): 669–90.

BEAM (Philippines–Australia Basic Education for Assistance in Mindanao) (2004), *Madrasah Education in ARMM: A Survey Outcome Conducted by BEAM-HOME Task Force*, March.

Benda, Harry J. (1958), *The Crescent and the Rising Sun: Indonesian Islam under the Japanese Occupation 1942–1945*, W. van Hoeve, The Hague.

Boland, B.J. (1971), *The Struggle for Islam in Modern Indonesia*, Martinus Nijhoff, The Hague.

Braighlinn, G. (1992), *Ideological Innovation under Monarchy: Aspects of Legitimation Activity in Contemporary Brunei*, VU University Press, Amsterdam.

Brown, L. Carl (2000), *Religion and State: The Muslim Approach to Politics*, Columbia University Press, New York.

Buat, Musib M. (1976), 'Survey of Muslim Adat (Customary) Law and the Role of the Agama Courts', pp. 110–62 in *Studies on Muslim Laws (Shariah) and Customary Laws (Adat)*, Department of Public Information, Manila.

Bubalo, Anthony and Greg Fealy (2005), 'Joining the Caravan? The Middle East, Islamism and Indonesia', Lowy Paper No. 5, The Lowy Institute for International Policy, Sydney.

Burhanudin, Jajat and Oman Fathurahman (eds) (2004), 'Tentang Perempuan Islam: Wacana dan Gerakan' [Concerning Muslim Women: Discourse and Movement], Penerbit Gramedia Pustaka Utama in cooperation with Pusat Pengkajian Islam dan Masyarakat (PPIM), UIN Syarif Hidayatullah, Jakarta.

Busran-Lao, Yasmin (2000), 'An Analysis on Gender, Reproductive Health and Women's Rights in the Autonomous Region in Muslim Mindanao (ARMM)', pp. 223–35 in Sisters in Islam (ed.), *Islam, Reproductive Health and Women's Rights*, Kuala Lumpur.

Candland, Christopher and Siti Nurjanah (2004), 'Women's Empowerment through Islamic Organisations: The Role of the Indonesia's Nahdlatul Ulama in Transforming the Government's Birth Control Program into a Family Welfare Program', Case Study for World Faiths Development Dialogue Workshop, New Dehli, 9–11 February, <http://www.wfdd.org.uk/programmes/case_studies/>.

Chaiwat Satha-Anand (2004), 'Praying in the Rain: The Politics of Engaged Muslims in Anti-war Protest in Thai Society', *Global Change, Peace & Security*, 16(2): 151–67.

Chakravarti, Nalini Ranjan (1971), *The Indian Minority in Burma: The Rise and Decline of an Immigrant Community*, Oxford University Press for the Institute of Race Relations, London and New York.

Chanda, N. (1986), *Brother Enemy*, Collier Books, New York.

Chandra Muzaffar (1987), *Islamic Resurgence in Malaysia*, Penerbit Fajar Bakti, Petaling Jaya.

Chandra Muzaffar (2005), 'Beyond the RITE Path: The "Values" Approach to Islam', *Muslim Reader*, 23(1): 3–8.

Chandrakirana, Kamala and Yuniyanti Chuzaifah (2004), 'The Battle Over a "New" Indonesia: Religious Extremism, Democratization and Women's Agency in a Plural Society', *International Centre for Islam and Pluralism (ICIP) Journal*, 1(2): 1–26, <http://www.icipglobal.org>.

Che Man, W.K. (1990a), 'The Thai Government and Islamic Institutions in the Four Southern Muslim Provinces of Thailand', *Sojourn*, 5(2): 255–82.

Che Man, W.K. (1990b), *Muslim Separatism: The Moros of Southern Philippines and the Malays of Southern Thailand*, Oxford University Press, Singapore.

Che Man, W.K. (1991), 'The Administration of Islamic Institutions in Non-Muslim States: The Case of Singapore and Thailand', Teaching and Research Exchange Fellowships Report No. 10, Institute of Southeast Asian Studies, Singapore.

CIA (Central Intelligence Agency) (2005), 'The World Factbook 2005', <http://www.cia.gov/cia/publications/factbook/>.

Ciciek, Farha (2004), 'Shariah for Women's Power?! (A Story of Women's Struggle at al Mukmin Ngruki)', paper presented to a conference on Islamic Perspectives on the State, Society and Governance in Southeast Asia, Canberra, 30–31 August.

Collins, W. (1996), 'The Chams of Cambodia', Centre for Advanced Studies Research Report, Phnom Penh, <http://www.cascambodia.org/chams.htm>, accessed 5 October 2004.

Cortesao, A. (translator) (1944), *The Suma Oriental of Tomé Pires*, Hakluyt Society, London.

Crispin, S.W. (2003), 'Targets of a New Anti-terror War', *Far Eastern Economic Review*, 10 July, <http://www.feer.com/>, accessed 23 May 2005.

Daungyewa Utarasint (2005), 'Wadah: The Muslim Faction in Thai Political Party', paper presented to the Ninth International Conference on Thai Studies, Northern Illinois University, DeKalb IL, 3–6 April.

Day, A. (1983), 'Islam and Literature in South-east Asia: Some Pre-modern, Mainly Javanese Perspectives', in M.B. Hooker (ed.), *Islam in South-east Asia*, E.J. Brill, Leiden.

de Féo, Agnès (2005), 'Le Royaume Bouddhique Face au Renouveau Islamique' [The Buddhist Kingdom Facing Islamic Revival], *Les Cahiers de l'Orient*, 78: 99–114.

Department of Statistics Malaysia (2000), 'Population and Housing Census 2000: Press Statement', <http://www.statistics.gov.my/English/frameset_pressdemo.php>, accessed 18 February 2005.

Dovert, S. and R. Madinier (2003), 'Communauté *Cham* et Missionaries Fondamentalistes au Cambodge', pp. 69–80 in S. Dovert and R. Madinier (eds), *Les Musulmans d'Asie du Sud-est Face au Vertige de la Radicalisation*, Les Indes Savants, Paris.

Effendy, Bahtiar (2004), *Islam and the State in Indonesia*, Institute of South East Asian Studies, Singapore.

Eickelman, Dale F. and James Piscatori (1996), *Muslim Politics*, Princeton University Press, Princeton NJ.

Eliraz, Giora (2004), *Islam in Indonesia: Modernism, Radicalism and the Middle East Dimension*, Sussex Academic Press, Brighton/Oregon.

Farish Noor (2002), *The Other Malaysia: Writings on Malaysia's Subaltern History*, Silverfishbooks, Kuala Lumpur.

Farish Noor (2003), 'The Localization of Islamist Discourse in the *Tafsir* of Tuan Guru Nik Aziz Nik Mat, *Murshid'ul Am* of PAS', pp. 195–235 in Virginia Hooker and Norani Othman (eds), *Malaysia: Islam, Society and Politics*, Institute of Southeast Asian Studies, Singapore.

Fassi Fehri, A. (1993), *Issues in the Structure of Arabic Clauses and Words,* Kluwer Academic Publishers, Dordrecht, Boston, London.

Fathurahman, Oman (2003), 'Reinforcing Neo-Sufism in the Malay–Indonesian World: Shattariyyah Order in West Sumatra', *Studia Islamika*, 10(3): 29–94.

Fealy, Greg (2001), 'Islamic Politics: A Rising or Declining Force?', pp. 119–36 in Damien Kingsbury and Arief Budiman (eds), *Indonesia: The Uncertain Transition*, Crawford House, Adelaide.

Fealy, Greg (2003), 'Divided Majority: The Limits of Indonesian Political Islam', pp. 150–68 in Shahram Akbarzadeh and Abdullah Saeed (eds), *Islam and Political Legitimacy*, RoutledgeCurzon, London and New York.

Fealy, Greg (2004), 'Islamic Radicalism in Indonesia: The Faltering Revival?', pp. 104–21 in Daljit Singh and Chin Kin Wah (eds), *Southeast Asian Affairs 2004*, Institute of Southeast Asian Studies, Singapore.

Feillard, Andrée (2005), 'Les Moudjahiddines d'Indonésie Réunis en Congrès à Solo' [Indonesian Mujahideens in Congress in Solo], *Les Cahiers de l'Orient*, 78: 27–40.

Feith, Herbert (1962), *The Decline of Constitutional Democracy in Indonesia*, Cornell University Press, Ithaca, New York.

Foley, Rebecca (2004), 'Muslim Women's Challenges to Islamic Law: The Case of Malaysia', *International Feminist Journal of Politics*, 6(1): 53–84.

Fraser, Thomas M. (1960), *Rusembilan: A Malay Fishing Village in Southern Thailand*, Cornell University Press, Ithaca NY.

Funston, John (1981), 'Malaysia', pp. 165–89 in Mohammed Ayood (ed.), *The Politics of Islamic Reassertion*, Croom Helm, London.

Funston, John (2005), 'The Malay Electorate in 2004: Reversing the 1999 Result?' pp. 132-156, in Saw Swee-Hock and K. Kesavapany (eds) *Malaysia: Recent Trends and Challenges*, ISEAS, Singapore.

Funston, John (2006), 'Terrorism in Thailand: How Serious Is It?', pp. 92–106 in Cavan Hogue (ed.), *Thailand's Economic Recovery*, Institute of Southeast Asian Studies, Singapore.

Geertz, Clifford (1976), *The Religion of Java*, University of Chicago Press, Chicago and London.

Gowing, Peter Gordon (1979), *Muslim Filipinos: Heritage and Horizon*, New Day Publishers, Quezon City.

Gräf, Bettina (2005), 'In Search of a Global Islamic Authority', *ISIM Review*, Spring: 47.

Haddad, Yvonne Yazbeck (1980), *Contemporary Islam and the Challenge of History*, State University of New York, New York.

Haleem, M.A.S. Abdel (2004), *The Qur'an: A New Translation*, Oxford University Press, Oxford.

Harahap, M. Yahya (1992), 'Informasi Materi Kompilasi Hukum Islam: Mempositifkan Abstraksi Hukum Islam [Background to the Compilation of Islamic Law: Positivizing Abstract Islamic Law]', *Mimbar Hukum*, 5(3): 21–63.

Hefner, Robert (2000), *Civil Islam: Muslims and Democratization in Indonesia*, Princeton University Press, Princeton.

Hernowo and M. Deden Ridwan (eds) (2002), *Aa Gym dan Fenomena Daarut Tauhid: Memperbaiki Diri Lewat Manajemen Qalbu* [Aa Gym and the Phenomenon of Daarut Tauhid: Self-improvement through Heart Management], 8th printing, Mizan, Penerbit Hikmah and Pesantren Virtual Daarut Tauhid, Bandung.

Hickey, G.C. (1982), *Free in the Forest: Ethnohistory of the Vietnamese Central Highlands 1954–1976*, Yale University Press, New Haven and London.

Hisyam, Muhamad (2001), *Caught between Three Fires: The Javanese Pangulu under the Dutch Colonial Administration 1882–1942*, Seri INIS XXXVII, INIS, Jakarta.

Hooker, M.B. (1983), 'Introduction: The Translation of Islam into Southeast Asia', pp. 1–22 in M.B. Hooker (ed.), *Islam in South-east Asia*, E.J. Brill, Leiden.

Hooker, M.B. (1984), *Islamic Law in South-east Asia*, Oxford University Press, Singapore.

Hooker, M.B. (1986), 'The Law Texts of Muslim South-east Asia', pp. 347–434 in M.B. Hooker (ed.), *Laws of South-east Asia.*, Vol. I, Butterworth, Singapore.

Hooker, M.B. (1999), 'Qadi Jurisdiction in Contemporary Malaysia and Singapore', pp. 57–75 in Wu Min Aung (ed.), *Public Law in Contemporary Malaysia*, Longman, Kuala Lumpur.

Hooker, M.B. (2003), *Indonesian Islam: Social Change through Contemporary Fatawa*, Allen & Unwin, Sydney, and University of Hawai'i Press, Honolulu.

Hooker, M.B. and T.C Lindsey (2002), 'Public Faces of Syariah in Contemporary Indonesia: Towards a National *Mazhab*?', *Australian Journal of Asian Law*, 4(3): 259–94.

Hooker, M.B and T.C. Lindsey (forthcoming), *Syari'ah in Southeast Asia: Volume 1: Indonesia: The New State Mazhab.*

Horikoshi Hiroko (1975), 'The Dar'ul Islam Movement in West Java (1948–62): An Experience of Historical Process', *Indonesia*, 20: 59–76.

Horton, A.V.M. (2001), 'Negara Brunei Darussalam: Economic Gloom and the APEC Summit', pp. 95–109 in Daljit Singh and Anthony Smith (eds), *Southeast Asian Affairs 2001*, Institute of Southeast Asian Studies, Singapore.

Howell, Julia Day (2001), 'Sufism and the Indonesian Islamic Revival', *Journal of Asian Studies*, 60(3): 701–29.

Human Rights Watch (2002), 'Burma: Rape, Forced Labor and Religious Persecution in Northern Arakan', New York.

Hunt, L. (2004), 'Cambodia: Cham Offensive', *Far Eastern Economic Review*, 29 July, <http://www.feer.com/>, accessed 23 May 2005.

Ibrahim, Muslim (2004), 'Penerapan Syari'at Islam di Aceh' [The Application of Shariah in Aceh], paper presented to the conference, 'Islamic Perspectives on the State, Society, and Governance in Southeast Asia', Canberra, 30–31 August.

ICG (International Crisis Group) (2002a), 'Indonesia Backgrounder: How the Jemaah Islamiyah Terrorist Network Operates', Asia Report No. 43, Jakarta/Brussels, 11 December, <http://www.crisisgroup.org/home/index.cfm?l=1&id=1397>.

ICG (International Crisis Group) (2002b), 'Al-Qaeda in Southeast Asia: The Case of the "Ngruki Network" in Indonesia', Asia Briefing No. 20, Jakarta/Brussels, 8 August (corrected 10 January 2003), <http://www.crisisgroup.org/home/index.cfm?l=1&id=1765>.

ICG (International Crisis Group) (2003), 'Jemaah Islamiyah in Southeast Asia: Damaged but Still Dangerous', Report No. 63, Jakarta/Brussels, 26 August, <http://www.crisisgroup. org/home/index.cfm?l=1&id=1452>.

ICG (International Crisis Group) (2004), 'Indonesia Backgrounder: Jihad in Central Sulawesi', Asia Report No. 74, Jakarta/Brussels, 3 February, <http://www.crisisgroup.org/ home/index.cfm?id=2500&l=1>.

ICG (International Crisis Group) (2005a), 'Recycling Militants in Indonesia: Darul Islam and the Australian Embassy Bombing', Asia Report No. 92, 22 February <http://www.crisis group.org/home/index.cfm?id=3280&l=1>.

ICG (International Crisis Group) (2005b), 'Southern Thailand: Insurgency, Not Jihad', Asia Report No. 98, 18 May, <http://www.crisisgroup.org/home/index.cfm?id=3436&l=1>.

Ihza Mahendra, Yusril (1999), *Modernisme dan Fundamentalisme dalam Politik Islam: Perbandingan Partai Masyumi (Indonesia) dan Partai Jama'at-i-Islami (Pakistan)* [Modernism and Fundamentalism in Islamic Politics: A Comparison of the Masyumi Party (Indonesia) and the Jama'at-i-Islami Party (Pakistan)], Paramadina, Jakarta.

Iik Arifin Mansurnoor (1996), 'Socio-religious Changes in Brunei after the Pacific War', *Islamic Studies*, 35(1): 45–70.

Iik Arifin Mansurnoor (2002), 'Islam in Brunei Darussalam and Global Islam: An Analysis of Their Interaction', pp. 71–98 in Johan Meuleman (ed.), *Islam in the Era of Globalization: Muslim Attitudes towards Modernity and Identity*, Routledge Curzon, London.

Iik Arifin Mansurnoor (2005), 'L'Islam à Brunei Entre Renaissance et Radicalisme' [Negotiating Islamic Revivalism and Religious Radicalism], *Les Cahiers de l'Orient*, 78: 47–60.

Imtiyaz Yusuf (1998), 'Islam and Democracy in Thailand: Reforming the Office of *Chularajamontri/Shaikh al-Islam*', *Journal of Islamic Studies*, 9(2): 277–98.

Ismail, Rose (ed.) (1995), *Hudud in Malaysia: The Issues at Stake*, SIS Forum (Malaysia) Berhad,Vinlin Press, Kuala Lumpur.

Ismail Yusanto (2003), 'Selamatkan Indonesia Dengan Syariat Islam', pp. 137–71 in Burhanuddin (ed.), *Syariat Islam Pandangan Muslim Liberal*, Jaringan Islam Liberal and the Asia Foundation, Sembrani Aksara Nusantara, Jakarta.

Jakim (Jabatan Kemajuan Islam Malaysia) (2003), *JAKIM 35 Tahun*, Jakim, Office of the Prime Minister, Kuala Lumpur, <www.islam.gov.my/jakim35tahun/>, accessed 21 February 2005.

Jamasali, Jasmin (2005), Contribution to a workshop on Contemporary Southeast Asian Islam: Perspectives on State, Governance and Society Workshop, Bogor, 27 February – 1 March 2005.

Jamhari (2002), 'Javanese Islam: The Flow of Creed', *Studia Islamika*, 9(2): 1–46.

Jilani Ahmed (1999), *The Rohingyas of Arakan: Their Quest for Justice*, Dhaka.

Jomo, K.S. and Ahmad Shabery Cheek (1992), 'Malaysia's Islamic Movements', pp. 79–106 in J.S. Kahn and Francis Loh Kok Wah (eds), *Fragmented Vision: Culture and Politics in Contemporary Malaysia*, Allen & Unwin, Sydney.

Jones, Gavin W. (1994), *Marriage and Divorce in Islamic South-east Asia*, Oxford University Press, Kuala Lumpur and New York.

Jones, Sidney (2003), 'Jemaah Islamiyah: A Short History', *Kultur*, 3(1): 105–14.

Jones, Sidney (2005), 'The Changing Nature of Jemaah Islamiyah', *Australian Journal of International Affairs*, 59(2): 169–78.

Kahn, Joel (2003), 'Islam, Modernity, and the Popular in Malaysia', pp. 147–68 in Virginia Hooker and Norani Othman (eds), *Malaysia: Islam, Society and Politics*, Institute of Southeast Asian Studies, Singapore.

Kamsi (2001), 'Kewarisan Benda Tetap pada Masyarakat Santri (Studi Kasus Desa Maguwoharjo Depok Sleman)' [Property Inheritance in a *Santri* Community (Case Study of Maguwoharjo Village, Depok Sleman)], *Jurnal Ilmu Syari'ah Asy-Syir'ah*, 35(2):101–24.

Kelana and Lai Choy (eds) (1998), *Kamus Perwira: Bahasa Melayu/Bahasa Inggeris* [The Valiant Dictionary: Malay/English], Penerbitan Daya Sdn. Bhd., Selangor.

Kennedy, Charles (1988), 'Islamization in Pakistan', *Asian Survey*, 28(3): 307–16.

Kershaw, Roger (2001), 'Malay, Monarchical, Micro-state', pp. 1–35 in John Funston (ed.), *Government and Politics in Southeast Asia*, Institute of Southeast Asian Studies/Zed Books, Singapore.

Kershaw, Roger (2003), 'Partners in Realism: Britain and Brunei amid Recent Turbulence', *Asian Affairs*, 34(1): 46–53.

Kiernan, B. (1985), 'Orphans of Genocide: The Cham Muslims of Kampuchea under Pol Pot', *Bulletin of Concerned Asian Scholars*, 20(4): 2–33.

Khin Yi, Daw (1988), *The Dobama Movement in Burma (1930–1938),* Southeast Asia Program, Cornell University, Ithaca NY.

Kumar, Ann and John McGlynn (1996), *Illuminations: The Writing Traditions of Indonesia*, Lontar Foundation, Jakarta, and Weatherhill Inc., New York and Tokyo.

Landon, Kenneth Perry (1949), *Southeast Asia: Cross-roads of Religion*, University of Chicago Press, Chicago IL.

Layish, Aharon (2004), 'The Transformation of Sharia from Jurists' Law to Statutory Law in the Contemporary Muslim World', *Die Welt des Islams*, 44(1): 85–113.

Le, Hong Hoa Ansari (2002), 'Vietnamese Muslims', Ho Chi Minh City, <http://geocities.com/vietmuslim/vnmuslims.html>, accessed 5 October 2004.

Leider, Jacques (2005), 'L'Islam Birman en Danger de Radicalisation' [Burmese Islam in Danger of Radicalism], *Les Cahiers de l'Orient*, 78: 125–38.

Liew, Chin-Tong (2004), 'Articulating an Islamic State in Multiethnic Malaysia: The Case of PAS', Bachelor of Asian Studies Honours thesis, Faculty of Asian Studies, Australian National University, Canberra.

Lingga, Abhoud Syed Mansur (1995), 'The Political Thought of Salamat Hashim', MA thesis, University of the Philippines.

Lintner, B. (2002a), 'Bangladesh: Breeding Ground for Muslim Terror', *Asia Times*, 21 September.

Lintner, B. (2002b), 'Religious Extremism and Nationalism in Bangladesh', paper presented at an international workshop on Religion and Security in South Asia, Asia Pacific Center for Security Studies, Honolulu, 19–22 August.

Loos, Tamara (2004–05), 'Siam's Subjects: Muslims, Laws, and Colonialism in Southern Thailand', *Southeast Asia Program Bulletin*, Cornell University, Winter–Spring, pp. 6–11.

Majul, Cesar Adib (1999), *Muslims in the Philippines*, third edition, University of the Philippines Press, Quezon City (first published 1973).

Mansouri, F. (2004), *Essential Arabic Phrase Book*, Periplus Essential Phrase Books.

Mansouri, F. (2005), 'Agreement Morphology in Arabic as a Second Language: Typological Features and Their Processing Implications', pp. 117–53 in Manfred Pienemann (ed.), *Cross-linguistic Aspects of Processability Theory*, John Benjamins, Amsterdam.

Marcoes-Natsir, Lies (2004), 'The Brittleness of a Woman's Womb in Shari'ah', *International Centre for Islam and Pluralism (ICIP) Journal*, 1(1): 1–5, <http://www.icipglobal.org>.

Masud, Khalid (1977), *Islamic Legal Philosophy: A Study of Abu Ishaq Al-Shathibi's Life and Thought*, Islamic Research Institute, Islamabad.

Matheson, Virginia and M.B. Hooker (1988), 'Jawi Literature in Patani: The Maintenance of an Islamic Tradition', *Journal of the Malaysian Branch of the Royal Asiatic Society*, 61(1): 1–86.

Maznah Mohamad (2002), 'At the Centre and the Periphery: The Contributions of Women's Movements to Democratization', pp. 216–40 in Francis Loh Kok Wah and Khoo Boo Teik (eds), *Democracy in Malaysia: Discourses and Practices*, Curzon, Richmond, Surrey.

McKenna, Thomas M. (1998), *Muslim Rulers and Rebels: Everyday Politics and Armed Separatism in the Southern Philippines*, University of California Press, Berkeley CA.

McVey, Ruth (1989), 'Identity and Rebellion among Southern Thai Muslims', pp. 33–52 in A. Forbes (ed.), *The Muslims of Thailand, Volume 2: Politics of the Malay-speaking South*, Center for Southeast Asian Studies, Gaya.

Md Zain bin Haji Serudin, Haji (1998), *Melayu Islam Beraja: Suatu Pendekatan*, Dewan Bahasa dan Pustaka, Bandar Seri Begawan.

Milner, A.C. (1983), 'Islam and the Muslim State', pp. 23–49 in M.B. Hooker (ed.), *Islam in South-east Asia*, E.J. Brill, Leiden.

Milner, Anthony (2002), *The Invention of Politics in Colonial Malaya*, Cambridge University Press, Cambridge.

Min Naing, Wa Khae Ma Maung (2003), 'Myanmar Naing Ngan Hnint Islam Tha Thana' [Myanmar and Islamic Religion], Summer Islamic Course, Volume 2, Islamic Centre of Myanmar, Rangoon, April.

Ministry of Home Affairs (2003), *White Paper: The Jemaah Islamiyah Arrests and The Threat of Terrorism*, Republic of Singapore, Singapore.

Moeslim Abdurrahman (1997), *Islam Transformatif* [Transforming Islam], Pustaka Firdaus, Jakarta (first published July 1995).

Mohamad Yusop bin Awang Damit (2002), 'Negara Brunei Darussalam: Light at the End of the Tunnel', pp. 81–91 in Daljit Singh and Anthony Smith (eds), *Southeast Asian Affairs 2002*, Institute of Southeast Asian Studies, Singapore.

Mohamad Yusop bin Awang Damit (2004), 'Brunei', pp. 7–9 in Russell Heng and Dennis Chew (eds), *Regional Outlook: Southeast Asia 2004–2005*, Institute of Southeast Asian Studies, Singapore.

Mudzhar, Mohamad Atho (2003), *Islam and Islamic Law in Indonesia: A Socio-historical Approach*, Office of Religious Research and Development and Training, Ministry of Religious Affairs, Republic of Indonesia, Jakarta.

Musdah Mulia, Siti (2004), *Islam Menggugat Poligami* [Islam Challenges Polygamy], PT Gramedia Pustaka Utama, Jakarta.

Nakamura Rie (1999), 'Cham in Vietnam: Dynamics of Ethnicity', PhD thesis, University of Washington, Washington DC.

Nakamura Rie (2000), 'The Coming of Islam to Champa', *Journal of the Malaysian Branch of the Royal Asiatic Society*, 73(1): 55–66.

Nasaruddin Umar (1999), *Kodrat Perempuan dalam Islam* [Women's Essential Nature in Islam], Lembaga Kajian Agama dan Jender, Jakarta.

Nasharudin Mat Isa (2001), 'The Islamic Party of Malaysia (PAS): Ideology, Policy, Struggle and Vision towards the New Millennium', Islamic Party of Malaysia, Kuala Lumpur.

Nasir Abas (2005), *Membongkar Jamaah Islamiyah: Pengakuan Mantan Anggota JI* [Uncovering Jemaah Islamiyah: The Confessions of a Former JI Member], Grafindo Khanazah Ilmu, Jakarta.

Nasution, Harun (chief editor) et al. (1992), *Ensiklopedi Islam Indonesia* [Encyclopedia of Indonesian Islam], Penerbit Djambatan, no place given.

Nawrahta (1995), *Destiny of the Nation,* News and Periodicals Enterprise, Rangoon.

Neighbour, Sally (2004), *In the Shadow of Swords: On the Trail of Terrorism from Afghanistan to Australia*, HarperCollins, Sydney.

Ner, M. (1941), 'Les Musulmans de l'Indochine Française, *Bulletin de l'Études Française d'Extrême Orient*, 41: 151–200.

Nidhi Aeusrivongse (2004), 'Understanding the Situation in the South as a "Millenarian Revolt"', *Sinlapa Watthanatham*, 25(8), June, pp. 110–24. Translated in *Kyoto Review of Southeast Asia*, review essay, March 2005, <http://kyotoreview.cseas.kyoto-u.ac.jp/issue/issue5/index.html>, accessed 15 May 2005.

Nishii Ryoko (2003), 'Religious Subject and the Body at Death: Dynamics of Muslim–Buddhist Relations in a Southern Thai Village', paper presented to the annual conference of the Asian Studies Association of America, New York, 27–30 March.

Noer, Deliar (1973), *The Modernist Movement in Indonesia, 1900–1942*, Oxford University Press, Singapore.

Noriani Nik Badli Shah, Nik (2002), *Women as Judges*, SIS Working Paper Series, Sisters in Islam, Kuala Lumpur, July.

Nurmila, Nina (2005), 'Polygamy and Chickens', *Inside Indonesia*, 83: 19–20.

Omar Farouk Bajunid (1988), 'The Muslims of Thailand: A Survey', pp. 1–30 in A. Forbes (ed.), *The Muslims of Thailand, Volume 1: Historical and Cultural Studies*, Center for Southeast Asian Studies, Gaya.

Osborne, M. (2004), 'The "Khmer Islam" Community in Cambodia and Its Foreign Patrons', *Issues Brief*, Lowy Institute for International Policy, Sydney, November, <http://www.lowyinstitute.org/Publication.asp?pid=191>.

OUP (Oxford University Press) (1999), *Australian Oxford English Dictionary*, South Melbourne.

OUP (Oxford University Press) (2006), 'Oxford English Dictionary Online', <http://dictionary.oed.com/>.

Panda, Ali B. (1993), 'Maranaw Ulama Political Leadership in Marawi City: An Alternative to Traditional Politics', PhD dissertation, Asian Studies, University of the Philippines, Quezon City.

Pergas (Singapore Islamic Scholars and Religious Teachers Association) (2004), *Moderation in Islam in the Context of Muslim Community in Singapore*, Singapore.

Platzdasch, Bernhard (2000), 'Islamic Reaction to a Female President', pp. 336–49 in Chris Manning and Peter van Diermen (eds), *Indonesia in Transition: Social Aspects of Reformasi and Crisis*, Institute of Southeast Asian Studies, Singapore.

Ravaisse, P. (1922), 'Deux Inscriptions Coufiques du Campa', *Journal Asiatique*, 11(20): 247–89.

Republic of the Philippines (2004), *Report on the Implementation of the 1996 Final Peace Agreement between the Government of the Republic of the Philippines (GRP) and the Moro National Liberation Front (MNLF)*, Office of the Presidential Adviser on the Peace Process, Manila.

Ricklefs, M.C. (1998), *The Seen and Unseen Worlds in Java, 1726–1749: History, Literature and Islam in the Court of Pakubuwana II*, Allen & Unwin, Sydney.

Ricklefs, M.C. (2006), *Mystic Synthesis in Java: A History of Islamisation from the Fourteenth to the Early Nineteenth Centuries,* Eastbridge, White Plains, New York.

Riza, Achmad Kemal (2004), 'Continuity and Change in Islamic Law in Indonesia: The Case of Nahdlatul Ulama *Bahtsul Masail* in East Java', Master of Arts (Asian Studies) thesis, Faculty of Asian Studies, Australian National University, Canberra.

Roff, W.R. (ed.) (1974), *Kelantan: Religion, Society and Politics in a Malay State*, Oxford University Press, Kuala Lumpur.

Roff, W.R. (2003), 'Social Science Approaches to Understanding Religious Practice: The Special Case of the Hajj', pp. 37–54 in Virginia Hooker and Norani Othman (eds), *Malaysia: Islam, Society and Politics*, Institute of Southeast Asian Studies, Singapore.

RPF (Rohingya Patriotic Front) (1976), *Rohingya's Outcry and Demands*, Arakan.

Roy, Olivier (2002), *Globalised Islam: The Search for a New Ummah*, Hurst, London.

RSO (Rohingya Solidarity Organisation) (1988), *Arakan: People, Country and History*, Publicity and Information Department, Rohingya Solidarity Organisation, Arakan.

Saleeby, Najeeb M. (1905), *Studies in Moro History, Law and Religion*, Department of the Interior Ethnological Survey Publications, Vol. 4, No. 1, Bureau of Public Printing, Manila.

Saleeby, Najeeb M. (1908), *The History of Sulu*, Department of the Interior Ethnological Survey Publications, Vol. 4, No. 2, Bureau of Public Printing, Manila.

Saliha Hassan (2003), 'Islamic Non-governmental Organisations', pp. 97–114 in M.L. Weiss and Saliha Hassan (eds), *Social Movements in Malaysia: From Moral Communities to NGOs*, RoutledgeCurzon, London.

Salim, Arskal (2003), 'Shari'a in Indonesia's Current Transition: An Update', pp. 213–34 in Arskal Salim and Azyumardi Azra (eds), *Shari'a and Politics in Modern Indonesia*, Institute of Southeast Asian Studies, Singapore.

Salim, Arskal and Azyumardi Azra (2003), 'The State and Shari'a in the Perspective of Indonesian Legal Politics', pp. 1–17 in Arskal Salim and Azyumardi Azra (eds), *Shari'a and Politics in Modern Indonesia*, Institute of Southeast Asian Studies, Singapore.

Sandar Chit (2003), 'Workshop on the Role and Status of Women in World Religions: Islamic Perspective', *Judson Research Center Bulletin*, 1: 47–58.

Scott, William Henry (1989), *Filipinos in China before 1500*, China Studies Program, De La Salle University, Manila.

Scupin, Raymond (1980), 'The Politics of Islamic Reformism in Thailand', *Asian Survey*, 20(12): 1,223–35.

Scupin, Raymond (1995), 'Historical, Ethnographic, and Contemporary Political Analyses of the Muslims of Kampuchea and Vietnam', *Sojourn*, 10(2): 301–28.

Scupin, Raymond (1998), 'Muslim Accommodation in Thai Society', *Journal of Islamic Studies*, 9(2): 229–58.

Selth, A. (2003), *Burma's Muslims: Terrorists or Terrorised?* Strategic and Defence Studies Centre, Australian National University, Canberra.

Selth, A. (2004), 'Burma's Muslims and the War on Terror', *Studies in Conflict and Terrorism*, 27:107–26.

Smith, M.J. (1991), *Burma: Insurgency and the Politics of Ethnicity*, Zed Books, London.

Snouck Hurgronje, C. (1931), *Mekka in the Latter Part of the 19th Century: Daily Life, Customs and Learning of the Moslems of the East-Indian Archipelago*, Brill, Leyden. [Translation by J.H. Monahan.]

Solamo-Antonio, Isabelita (2003), *The Shari'a Courts in the Philippines: Women, Men and Muslim Personal Laws*, Pilipina Legal Resources Inc., Davao City.

Soroush, Abdul Karim (2002), *Menggugat Otentisitas dan Tradisi Agama* [Contesting Religious Authenticity and Tradition], Mizan, Bandung.

Stevens, A.M. and A.E. Schmidgall-Tellings (eds) (2004), *A Comprehensive Indonesian–English Dictionary*, Ohio University Press, Athens OH.

Sukidi Mulyadi (n.d.), 'Dekonstruksi Ketidakadilan Jender: Perspektif Feminis Muslim' [Deconstructing Gender Injustice: The Muslim Feminist Perspective], <www.scripps.ohiou.edu/news/cmdd/buku2.htm>, accessed 18 May 2005.

Sulaiman, M.M.M. (2003), 'Ulama in Myanmar' [in Burmese], unpublished paper presented at the conference, Nadwah 'Ulama Nusantara II Sumbangan Ulama dan Tokoh Agama Borneo [Nadwah Ulama of (Malay) Archipelago II: The Contribution of Ulama and Religious Leaders of Borneo], Kuching, 14–16 June.

Surin Pitsuwan (1985), *Islam and Malay Nationalism: A Case Study of the Malay-Muslims of Southern Thailand*, Thai Khadi Research Institute, Thammasat University, Bangkok.

Suryadinata, Leo, Evi Nurvidya Arifin and Aris Ananta (eds) (2003), *Indonesia's Population: Ethnicity and Religion in a Changing Political Landscape,* Institute of Southeast Asian Studies, Singapore.

Tan, Samuel K. (2003a), *Filipino Muslim Perceptions of Their History and Culture as Seen through Indigenous Sources*, University of the Philippines Press, Manila.

Tan, Samuel K. (2003b), *Internationalization of the Bangsamoro Struggle*, second edition, University of the Philippines, Quezon City.

Trankell, I.B. (2003), 'Songs of Our Spirits: Possession and Historical Imagination among the Cham in Cambodia', *Asian Ethnicity*, 4(1): 31–46.

U Khin Maung Sein (1987), *Islamic Laws* [in Burmese], 2nd edition, Yangon.

US State Department (2001), 'International Religious Freedom Report', <http://www.state.gov/g/drl/rls/irf/2001/index.cfm?docid=5577>, accessed 29 March 2005.

US State Department (2004), 'International Religious Freedom Report 2004', 15 September, <http://www.state.gov/g/drl/rls/irf/2004/index.htm>.

van Bruinessen, Martin (1990), '*Kitab Kuning*: Books in Arabic Script Used in the *Pesantren* Milieu', *Bijdragen tot de Taal-, Land- en Volkenkunde*, 146(2&3): 226–69.

van Bruinessen, Martin (1996a), 'Traditions for the Future: The Reconstruction of Traditionalist Discourse within NU', pp. 163–89 in Greg Barton and Greg Fealy (eds), *Traditional Islam, Nahdlatul Ulama and Modernity*, Monash Asia Institute, Clayton.

van Bruinessen, Martin (1996b), 'Islamic State or State Islam? Fifty Years of State–Islam Relations in Indonesia', pp. 19–34 in Ingrid Wessel (ed.), *Indonesien am Ende des 20 Jahrhunderts*, Abera-Verlag, Hamburg.

van Dijk, C. (1981), *Rebellion under the Banner of Islam: The Darul Islam Rebellion in Indonesia*, Martinus Nijhoff, The Hague.

van Doorn-Harder, Nelly (2002), 'The Indonesian Islamic Debate on a Woman President', *Sojourn*, 17(2): 164–90.

van Leur, J.C. (1955), *Indonesian Trade and Society: Essays in Asian Social and Economic History*, W. van Hoeve, The Hague.

Vickery, M. (1986), *Kampuchea*, Francis Pinter, London.

Wadi, Julkipli M. (1998), 'Philippine Political Islam and the Emerging Fundamentalist Strand', *UP-CIDS Chronicle*, 3(1): 33–42.

Warren, James Francis (2002), *Iranun and Balangingi: Globalization, Maritime Raiding and the Birth of Ethnicity*, New Day Publishers, Manila.

Wehr, Hans (1966), *A Dictionary of Modern Written Arabic* (edited by J. Milton Cowan), Otto Harrassowitz, Wiesbaden.

White, Sally Jane (2004), 'Reformist Islam, Gender and Marriage in Late Colonial Dutch East Indies, 1900–1942', PhD thesis, Research School of Pacific and Asian Studies, Australian National University, Canberra.

World Bank (2003), *Social Assessment of Conflict-affected Areas in Mindanao*, Manila.

Yegar, M. (1966), 'The Panthay (Chinese Muslims) of Burma and Yunnan', *Journal of Southeast Asian History*, 7: 73–85.

Yegar, M. (1972), *The Muslims of Burma: A Study of a Minority Group*, Otto Harrassowitz, Wiesbaden.

Yegar, M. (2002), *Between Integration and Secession: The Muslim Communities of the Southern Philippines, Southern Thailand, and Western Burma/Myanmar,* Lexington Books, Lanham MD.

Yunus, M. (1994), *A History of Arakan: Past and Present*, Magenta Color, no place given.

Yunus, M. (1995), 'A Memorandum on the Genocide of the Rohingya Muslims of Arakan in Burma', unpublished manuscript.

Zainah Anwar (1987), *Islamic Revivalism in Malaysia*, Pelanduk Publications, Petaling Jaya.

Zein, Kurniawan and Sarifuddin HA (2001), *Syariah Islam Yes, Syariah Islam No*, Paramadina, Jakarta.

Zubaidah Abu Bakar (2005), 'Winds of Change for Women of PAS', <www.harakahdaily.net/print.php?sid=13095>, dated May 2002, accessed 9 May 2005.

Index

Printed in the United States
78447LV00001B/25-32

9 789812 303684